W9-APU-106

sixth edition

# The St. Martin's Handbook

sixth edition

# The St. Martin's Handbook

**Andrea A. Lunsford**
Stanford University

A section for multilingual writers with

Paul Kei Matsuda
Arizona State University

Christine M. Tardy
DePaul University

A section on academic and professional writing with

Lisa Ede
Oregon State University

Bedford / St. Martin's
Boston ♦ New York

**For Bedford/St. Martin's**

*Senior Developmental Editor:* Carolyn Lengel
*Senior Production Editor:* Michael Weber
*Senior Production Supervisor:* Dennis J. Conroy
*Marketing Manager:* John Swanson
*Art Director:* Lucy Krikorian
*Text Design:* Anne Carter
*Copy Editor:* Wendy Polhemus-Annibell
*Photo Research:* Martha Friedman
*Cover Design:* Donna L. Dennison
*Composition:* Monotype, LLC
*Printing and Binding:* R.R. Donnelley & Sons Company

*President:* Joan E. Feinberg
*Editorial Director:* Denise B. Wydra
*Editor in Chief:* Karen S. Henry
*Director of Development:* Erica Appel
*Director of Marketing:* Karen Melton Soeltz
*Director of Editing, Design, and Production:* Marcia Cohen
*Managing Editor:* Shuli Traub

Library of Congress Control Number: 2009927041



Manufactured in the United States of America.

5 4 3 2 1 0

f e d c b a

*For information, write:* Bedford/St. Martin's, 75 Arlington Street, Boston, MA 02116 (617-399-4000)

ISBN-10: 0-312-66483-4 (hardcover; with 2009 MLA & 2010 APA updates)
ISBN-13: 978-0-312-66483-1

ISBN-10: 0-312-44317-X (paperback)
ISBN-13: 978-0-312-44317-7

**Acknowledgments**

**African Economic Research Consortium.** "International migration: Friend or foe of African economic development?" Excerpt from press release, Friday, May 27, 2005, posted on *African Economic Research Consortium* homepage. www.aercafrica.org.

**American Heritage Dictionary of the English Language, Fourth Edition.** "Letter." Copyright © 2006 by Houghton Mifflin Company. Reproduced by permission from *The American Heritage Dictionary of the English Language Fourth Edition.*

**Article. A131086129.** From www.web6infotrac.galecroup.com. Copyright © The Gale Group. Reprinted by permission of The Gale Group.

Acknowledgments and copyrights are continued at the back of the book on pages 939–942, which constitute an extension of the copyright page.

# Preface

For years now, I have been saying, "These are exciting times for writers and teachers of writing." Sometimes I wonder just how much more excitement we can take! Writing teachers today find themselves working with a whole new range of media while still attending to the demands of teaching students to write and document traditional print texts. Vocabulary is changing before our very eyes, as are spelling, punctuation, and mechanics. Audiences on the Web call for new thinking about how to craft messages for worldwide audiences and how to work with others across long distances. In a time of such challenging possibilities, taking a rhetorical perspective is particularly important. Why? Because a rhetorical perspective rejects either/or, right/wrong, black/white approaches to writing in favor of asking what choices will be most appropriate, effective, and ethical in a given writing situation.

*The St. Martin's Handbook* has always taken such a perspective, and the numerous changes to the sixth edition reflect this tradition. Throughout, this book invites student writers to take each choice they make as an opportunity for critical engagement with ideas, audiences, and texts. As I've incorporated new material, I've been careful not to lose sight of the mission of any handbook: to be an accessible reference to students and instructors alike.

## Research for *The St. Martin's Handbook*

From the beginning, *The St. Martin's Handbook* has been informed by research on student writing. The late Robert J. Connors and I first began work on *The St. Martin's Handbook* in 1983, when we realized that most college handbooks were based on research into student writing conducted almost fifty years earlier. Our own historical studies had convinced us that student writing and what teachers think of as "good" writing change over time, so we began by gathering a nationwide sample of more than 21,000 marked student essays and carefully analyzing a stratified sample to identify the twenty surface errors most characteristic of contemporary student writing. (You can find articles detailing this research study in *From Theory to Practice: A Selection of Essays* by Andrea A. Lunsford, available free from Bedford/St. Martin's.)

Our analysis of these student essays revealed the twenty errors that most troubled students and teachers in the 1980s (spelling was by far the most prevalent error then) as well as the organizational and other global issues of greatest concern to teachers. Our findings on the twenty most common errors led to sections in *The St. Martin's Handbook* that attempt to put error in its place, presenting the conventions of writing as rhetorical choices a writer must make rather than as a series of rules that writers must obey.

Every subsequent edition of *The St. Martin's Handbook* has been informed by research, from a national survey of student writers on how they are using technology to a series of intensive interviews with students and focus group sessions with first-year writing instructors. In preparing for the sixth edition of this text, I've had an opportunity to look back over twenty-plus years of research, all of which has emphasized my original historical understanding that writing conventions and notions of correctness can and do change. With this long view in mind, in 2004 I began to plan for a new research study, one that would replicate the study Bob Connors and I did some twenty years ago.

When Karen Lunsford and I undertook this study, we quickly found that more than student writing had changed in the last twenty years. What had been a fairly simple process of canvassing teachers and program directors twenty years ago had by 2004 turned into a nightmarish thicket of institutional review board regulations. The impediments led to a smaller sample of student writing, but with perseverance we were able to elicit well over 2,000 marked student essays and, from them, to select a stratified sample of roughly 900 essays that represented a strong national sample.

The results of our analysis of these essays inform this new edition and demonstrate the dramatic changes that have taken place in the last twenty years. As expected, all but a tiny number of these essays were word processed, but the changes run much deeper than this change in technology. Our study shows that writing assignments, which were dominated by personal narrative essays twenty years ago, have shifted to argument and research-based argument today. As a result, the errors that plague student writers have shifted as well, and today errors associated with citation practices rank high on the list of most frequent errors. The *Handbook*'s coverage of research and documentation has been updated and made more visual with these student challenges in mind. In addition, spelling — twenty years ago the number one error by some 300 percent — now is much less problematic, thanks in large part to spell checkers. Intriguingly, however, the new number one error — wrong word — may be related to students' placing too much confidence in spell checkers and allowing them to replace misspelled words with incorrect ones (such as *defiantly* for *definitely*).

Finally, this reading of a large national sample of student essays brings some good news for students and teachers of writing. First, students today are writing much more than they were twenty years ago (the average length in 1985 was 411 words; today, the average length is 1051, more than double). More important, they are tackling increasingly complex topics; they are also using more complicated structures that result, sometimes, in what might be called "faulty sentence structure" but that, on closer look, often reveal attempts to stretch syntactic muscles in new ways or to create a kind of special effect in writing.

So today, well over twenty years after I began working on *The St. Martin's Handbook*, I am optimistic about students and student writing. As always, this book seeks to serve students as a ready reference that will help them make appropriate grammatical and rhetorical choices. Beyond this immediate goal, though, I hope to guide students in understanding and experiencing for themselves the multiple ways in which truly good writing always means more than just following the rules. Truly good writing, I believe, means applying those rules in specific rhetorical situations for specific purposes and with specific audiences in ways that will bring readers and writers, teachers and students, to spirited conversation as well as to mutual understanding and respect.

## Features of *The St. Martin's Handbook*

**A FOCUS ON GOOD WRITING, NOT JUST CORRECTNESS.** To write rhetorically effective texts, students must understand how to follow conventions that depend on their audience, situation, and discipline.

**DETAILED COVERAGE OF CRITICAL THINKING AND ARGUMENT.** Research conducted for this edition reveals that assignments in first-year writing classes today call primarily for argument. *The St. Martin's Handbook* provides the information student writers need to respond most effectively to their contemporary writing assignments, including practical advice for analyzing and composing verbal and visual arguments *and* two complete student essays.

**UP-TO-DATE ADVICE ON RESEARCH AND DOCUMENTATION.** With the once-clear distinction between print and electronic sources growing increasingly blurred, *The St. Martin's Handbook* includes completely revised and updated coverage of library, Internet, and field research, along with chapters on working with sources and avoiding plagiarism and full coverage of MLA, APA, *Chicago*, and CSE styles.

**ESSENTIAL HELP FOR WRITING IN THE DISCIPLINES.** Student writers will find strategies for understanding discipline-specific assignments, vocabulary, style, and use of evidence, along with complete student writing assignments by real students: research papers in MLA, APA, *Chicago*, and CSE styles; first-year writing assignments in the humanities, social sciences, and natural sciences; and business documents.

**THOROUGH ATTENTION TO WRITING IN ANY MEDIUM.** With advice on netiquette, document design, online texts, and oral and multimedia presentations — and real-life student samples including poster and PowerPoint presentations, print and electronic portfolio cover letters, and email — *The St. Martin's Handbook* shows students how writing in electronic and multimedia environments does (and doesn't) differ from writing for traditional print genres.

**UNIQUE COVERAGE OF LANGUAGE.** Practical advice helps students communicate effectively across languages and cultures — and shows how to use varieties of language both wisely and well. Extra help for multilingual writers appears in five chapters and in boxed tips throughout the book.

**A USER-FRIENDLY INDEX.** Entries include everyday words (such as *that* or *which*) as well as grammatical terms (such as *relative pronoun*), so students can find information even if they don't know grammatical terminology.

## New to This Edition

### *Handbook* coverage based on new research into student writing patterns

As noted above, to update *The St. Martin's Handbook*'s 1986 research into student writers' twenty most common errors, Karen Lunsford and I completed a new study of writing from first-year composition courses nationwide. New coverage in the sixth edition addresses the issues we found.

### More help with research and documentation

- With the results of the study showing new kinds of common problems related to documentation, the sixth edition of the *Handbook* includes step-by-step, visual advice on evaluating sources and on documenting print and online sources in all four documentation styles.

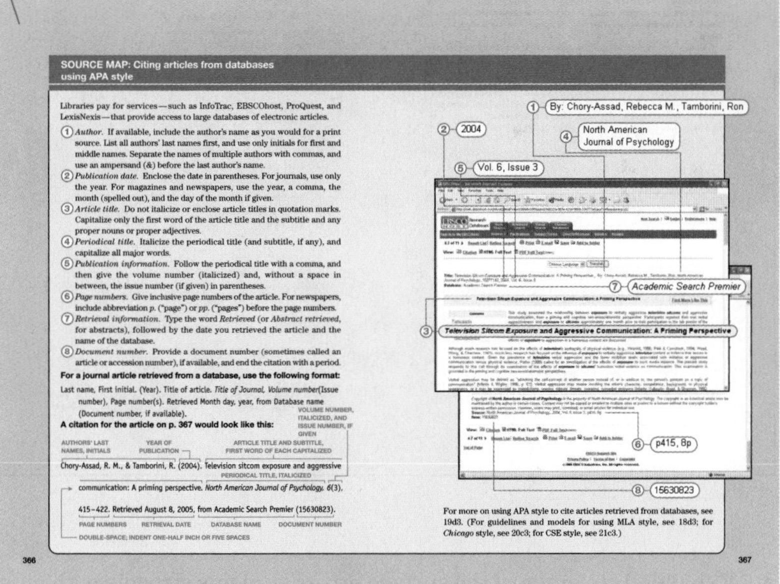

SOURCE MAP: Citing articles from databases using APA style

Libraries pay for services—such as InfoTrac, EBSCOhost, ProQuest, and LexisNexis—that provide access to large databases of electronic articles.

① *Author.* If available, include the author's name as you would for a print source. List all authors' last names first, and use only initials for first and middle names. Separate the names of multiple authors with commas, and use an ampersand (&) before the last author's name.

② *Publication date.* Enclose the date in parentheses. For journals, use only the year. For magazines and newspapers, use the year, a comma, the month (spelled out), and the day of the month if given.

③ *Article title.* Do not italicize or enclose article titles in quotation marks. Capitalize only the first word of the article title and the subtitle and any proper nouns or proper adjectives.

④ *Periodical title.* Italicize the periodical title (and subtitle, if any), and capitalize all major words.

⑤ *Publication information.* Follow the periodical title with a comma, and then give the volume number (italicized) and, without a space in between, the issue number (if given) in parentheses.

⑥ *Page numbers.* Give inclusive page numbers of the article. For newspapers, include abbreviation *p.* ("page") or *pp.* ("pages") before the page numbers.

⑦ *Retrieval information.* Type the word *Retrieved* (or *Abstract retrieved,* for abstracts), followed by the date you retrieved the article and the name of the database.

⑧ *Document number.* Provide a document number (sometimes called an article or accession number), if available, and end the citation with a period.

**For a journal article retrieved from a database, use the following format:**

Last name, First initial. (Year). Title of article. *Title of Journal, Volume number*(Issue number), Page number(s). Retrieved Month day, year, from Database name (Document number, if available).

**A citation for the article on p. 367 would look like this:**



Chory-Assad, R. M., & Tamborini, R. (2004). Television sitcom exposure and aggressive communication: A priming perspective. *North American Journal of Psychology, 6*(3), 415–422. Retrieved August 8, 2005, from Academic Search Premier (15630823).



For more on using APA style to cite articles retrieved from databases, see 19d3. (For guidelines and models for using MLA style, see 18d3; for *Chicago* style, see 20c3; for CSE style, see 21c3.)

366 367

- Thoroughly revised coverage of research includes up-to-the-minute advice on using databases and the other electronic sources that today's students turn to first.

## *A new Top Twenty*

- The Top Twenty lists the problems that occur most often in student writing today. Students can find editing their papers an overwhelming task; the Top Twenty helps them set priorities. A quick-reference section on the orange pages at the front of the book offers a brief look at each common problem and cross-references to more detailed information elsewhere in *The St. Martin's Handbook.*

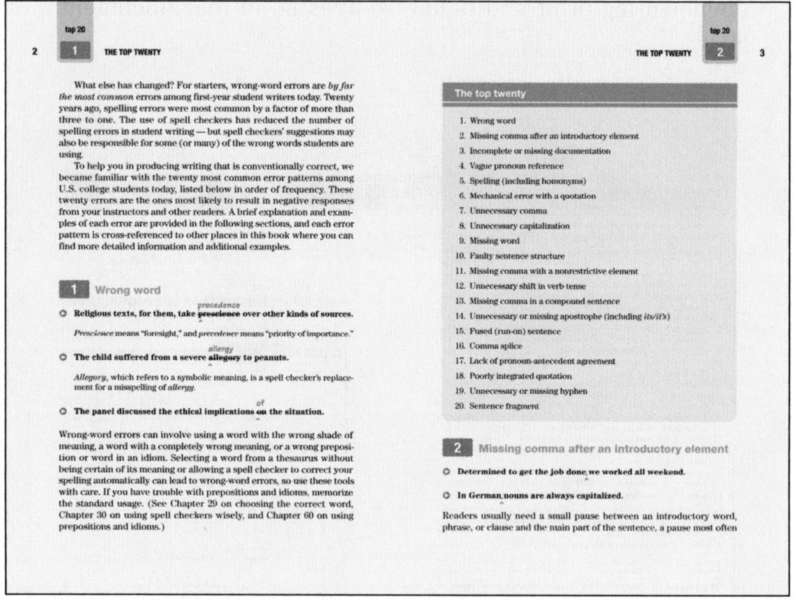

2 top 20 1 THE TOP TWENTY

What else has changed? For starters, wrong-word errors are *by far the most common* errors among first-year student writers today. Twenty years ago, spelling errors were most common by a factor of more than three to one. The use of spell checkers has reduced the number of spelling errors in student writing — but spell checkers' suggestions may also be responsible for some (or many) of the wrong words students are using.

To help you in producing writing that is conventionally correct, we became familiar with the twenty most common error patterns among U.S. college students today, listed below in order of frequency. These twenty errors are the ones most likely to result in negative responses from your instructors and other readers. A brief explanation and examples of each error are provided in the following sections, and each error pattern is cross-referenced to other places in this book where you can find more detailed information and additional examples.

**1 Wrong word**

- **Religious texts, for them, take ~~prescience~~ precedence over other kinds of sources.**

  *Prescience* means "foresight," and *precedence* means "priority of importance."

- **The child suffered from a severe ~~allegory~~ allergy to peanuts.**

  *Allegory*, which refers to a symbolic meaning, is a spell checker's replacement for a misspelling of *allergy*.

- **The panel discussed the ethical implications ~~on~~ of the situation.**

Wrong-word errors can involve using a word with the wrong shade of meaning, a word with a completely wrong meaning, or a wrong preposition or word in an idiom. Selecting a word from a thesaurus without being certain of its meaning or allowing a spell checker to correct your spelling automatically can lead to wrong-word errors, so use these tools with care. If you have trouble with prepositions and idioms, memorize the standard usage. (See Chapter 29 on choosing the correct word, Chapter 30 on using spell checkers wisely, and Chapter 60 on using prepositions and idioms.)

top 20 THE TOP TWENTY 2 3

**The top twenty**

1. Wrong word
2. Missing comma after an introductory element
3. Incomplete or missing documentation
4. Vague pronoun reference
5. Spelling (including homonyms)
6. Mechanical error with a quotation
7. Unnecessary comma
8. Unnecessary capitalization
9. Missing word
10. Faulty sentence structure
11. Missing comma with a nonrestrictive element
12. Unnecessary shift in verb tense
13. Missing comma in a compound sentence
14. Unnecessary or missing apostrophe (including *its/it's*)
15. Fused (run-on) sentence
16. Comma splice
17. Lack of pronoun-antecedent agreement
18. Poorly integrated quotation
19. Unnecessary or missing hyphen
20. Sentence fragment

**2 Missing comma after an introductory element**

- **Determined to get the job done, we worked all weekend.**
- **In German, nouns are always capitalized.**

Readers usually need a small pause between an introductory word, phrase, or clause and the main part of the sentence, a pause most often

- Expanded coverage of the surface errors students struggle with most helps students understand and avoid common mistakes.

### *More attention to visual literacy*

- **A NEW CHAPTER ON THINKING VISUALLY.** Chapter 4 encourages students to consider the visual impact of their work through every step of the writing process.

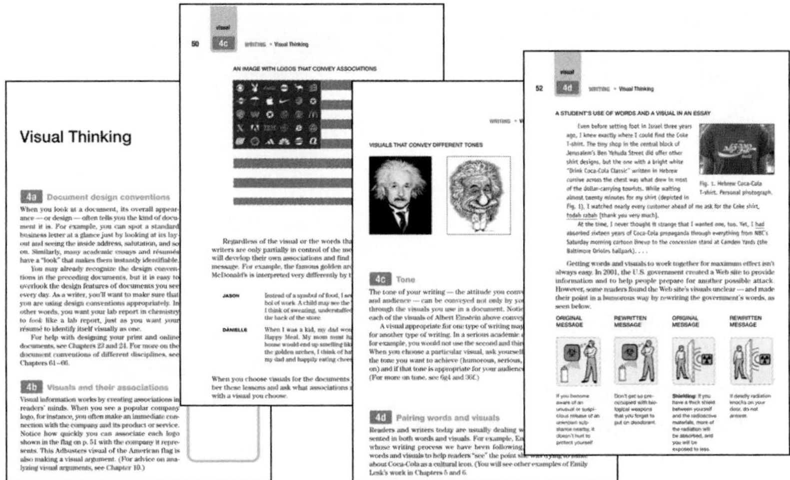


- **MORE VISUAL EXPLANATIONS OF ACADEMIC CONCEPTS.** Research strategies, design analysis, peer review, and other important ideas and skills are explained visually throughout *The St. Martin's Handbook.*

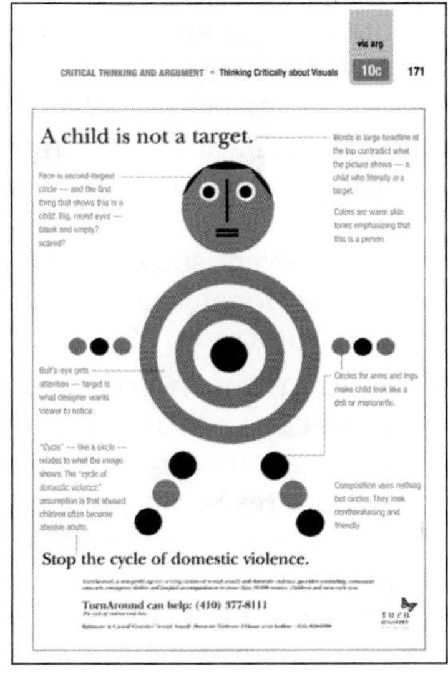

## *New advice on academic writing — with help for every college writer*

- **A NEW INTRODUCTORY CHAPTER ON EXPECTATIONS FOR COLLEGE WRITERS.** Chapter 1 shows students the ropes of college writing, giving them the information they need to master academic conventions, including the conventions for responding effectively to instructors' written comments.

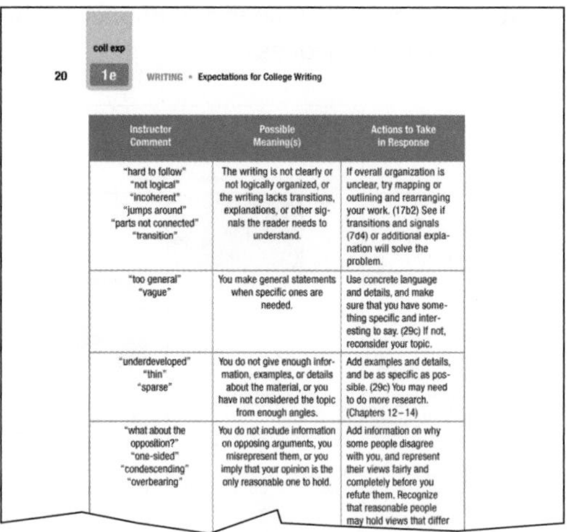

20 coll exp 1e WRITING • Expectations for College Writing

| Instructor Comment | Possible Meaning(s) | Actions to Take in Response |
|---|---|---|
| "hard to follow" "not logical" "incoherent" "jumps around" "parts not connected" "transition" | The writing is not clearly or not logically organized, or the writing lacks transitions, explanations, or other signals the reader needs to understand. | If overall organization is unclear, try mapping or outlining and rearranging your work. (17b2) See if transitions and signals (7d4) or additional explanation will solve the problem. |
| "too general" "vague" | You make general statements when specific ones are needed. | Use concrete language and details, and make sure that you have something specific and interesting to say. (29c) If not, reconsider your topic. |
| "underdeveloped" "thin" "sparse" | You do not give enough information, examples, or details about the material, or you have not considered the topic from enough angles. | Add examples and details, and be as specific as possible. (29c) You may need to do more research. (Chapters 12–14) |
| "what about the opposition?" "one-sided" "condescending" "overbearing" | You do not include information on opposing arguments, you misrepresent them, or you imply that your opinion is the only reasonable one to hold. | Add information on why some people disagree with you, and represent their views fairly and completely before you refute them. Recognize that reasonable people may hold views that differ |

- **NEW "TALKING THE TALK" BOXES.** Answers to real student questions clarify common misconceptions about academic work — from how to distinguish between collaborating and cheating to when to use the first person.

- **UNIQUE COVERAGE OF PEER REVIEW.** With a focus on peer review as a key part of the writing process, *The St. Martin's Handbook* helps students benefit from comments, and offer useful comments, during every stage of the writing process, for any kind of project — including a research project.

496 multimed 25d PRINT, ELECTRONIC, AND OTHER MEDIA • Oral and Multimedia Presentations



and speaking directly to the reader to make an emphatic point. The repetition throughout *Persepolis* makes it look and feel more like a children's book.

[slide 4] In addition to simplification through repetition, there's a second simplifying process, that of filtering. *Persepolis* is filled with violent elements. One good example is the torture and execution of guerilla fighter Ahmadi. Marjane recounts, "In the end he was cut to pieces." The dismemberment is one of the most violent images that we see in the book. However, Satrapi's representation filters the horror. [point to illustration] This figure doesn't seem real — it looks neatly sectioned and hollow, like a doll. We see the image presented as a child might imagine it.

So, let me conclude by answering why Satrapi's visual voice is so effective. Remember, she is connecting to the world of childhood through comics. Her story seems very grim and adult — too grim for children. But it is a child's story, or rather the story of a character standing on the threshhold of the adult world. So the graphic novel is an ideal way to reveal both the conflicting aspects of the child's voice and the balance between these aspects. For the author to explain the child Marjane's particular, slightly uncomfortable vantage point, the in-between genre of the graphic novel is a perfect fit.

[slide 5] Thanks! Are there any questions?

- **MORE THAN THIRTY-FIVE REAL, COMPLETE STUDENT WRITING SAMPLES.** Twenty models of arguments, research projects, presentations, disciplinary writing, portfolios, and presentations appear in the book — with many more on the Web site.

### *New, more inclusive coverage for multilingual writers*

Two new contributors, leading second-language experts Paul Kei Matsuda (University of New Hampshire) and Christine M. Tardy (DePaul University), address the wide-ranging needs of today's multilingual students — whether international students, recent immigrants, or Generation 1.5 student who have grown up in the United States.

- **A NEW CHAPTER ON STRATEGIES FOR ADAPTING TO UNFAMILIAR GENRES AND CONTEXTS.** Creative tips, both visual and textual, help multilingual students tackle academic writing in any discipline.

acad

FOR MULTILINGUAL WRITERS • Writing in U.S. Academic Contexts 56d 787

| Original Abstract from a Social Science Paper | Inappropriate Borrowing of Ideas and Sentences |
|---|---|
| Using the interpersonal communications research of J. K. Brilhart and G. J. Galanes, and W. Wilmot and J. Hocker, along with T. Hartman's personality assessment, I observed and analyzed the leadership roles and group dynamics of my project collaborators in a communications course. Based on results of the Hartman personality assessment, I predicted that a single leader would emerge. However, complementary individual strengths and gender differences encouraged a distributed leadership style, in which the group experienced little confrontation and conflict. Conflict, because it was handled positively, was crucial to the group's progress. | Using the interpersonal communications research of J. K. Brilhart and G. J. Galanes, and W. Wilmot and J. Hocker, along with T. Hartman's personality assessment, I observed and analyzed the leadership roles and group dynamics of my peers in a communications course. Based on findings of the Hartman personality assessment, I predicted that one leader of the group would appear. However, complementary individual strengths and differences in gender resulted in a distributed leadership style, in which there was little confrontation and conflict. Because it was handled positively, conflict was crucial to the group's progress. |

copy the whole sentence or sentence structure verbatim, however, or your borrowed sentences may seem plagiarized (Chapter 16 and 18c).

The first example on the previous page illustrates effective borrowing. The student writer borrows phrases that are commonly used in academic writing in the social sciences to perform particular functions. Notice how the student also modifies these phrases to suit his or her needs.

The next example above illustrates poor borrowing practices. The student plagiarizes both ideas and whole sentences from the original text.

**56d** Strategies for learning from search engines

To multilingual writers, Internet search engines such as Google offer more than a tool for finding information. They also provide a useful way of developing vocabulary or checking sentence structure and word usage. A number of common strategies can help. For example, you can include a wildcard in a keyword search to find all the forms of a word; a wildcard search using *reciproc** will yield *reciprocate, reciprocating, reciprocated,*

- **PRACTICAL TIPS FOR SUCCESS IN U.S. COLLEGE WORK.** Advice appears in a unique section and in boxed tips throughout the book. See a complete list of "For Multilingual Writers" boxes on p. I-30.

## A Wide Array of Ancillaries

*Bedford/St. Martin's Research Pack*

**WITH CLOTHBOUND BOOK:**

ISBN-10: 0-312-46226-3
ISBN-13: 978-0-312-46226-0

**WITH PAPERBOUND BOOK:**

ISBN-10: 0-312-46227-1
ISBN-13: 978-0-312-46227-7

### *Print resources*

*Instructor's Notes,* Sixth Edition

**ANDREA A. LUNSFORD AND ALYSSA O'BRIEN**

ISBN-10: 0-312-43115-5
ISBN-13: 978-0-312-43115-0

*The St. Martin's Pocket Guide to Research and Documentation,* Fourth Edition

**ANDREA A. LUNSFORD AND MARCIA MUTH**

ISBN-10: 0-312-44225-4
ISBN-13: 978-0-312-44225-5

*The St. Martin's Workbook,* Fifth Edition

**LEX RUNCIMAN**

ISBN-10: 0-312-43119-8
ISBN-13: 978-0-312-43119-8

*From Theory to Practice: A Selection of Essays,* Third Edition

**ANDREA A. LUNSFORD**

ISBN-10: 0-312-56729-4
ISBN-13: 978-0-312-56729-3

*The St. Martin's Guide to Teaching Writing,* Sixth Edition

**CHERYL GLENN AND MELISSA GOLDTHWAITE**

ISBN-10: 0-312-45133-4
ISBN-13: 978-0-312-45133-2

*The St. Martin's Sourcebook for Writing Tutors,* Third Edition

**CHRISTINA MURPHY AND STEVE SHERWOOD**

ISBN-10: 0-312-44226-2
ISBN-13: 978-0-312-44226-2

*Assigning, Responding, Evaluating,* Fourth Edition

**EDWARD M. WHITE**

ISBN-10: 0-312-43930-X
ISBN-13: 978-0-312-43930-9

## *New media resources*

*The St. Martin's Handbook* Book Companion Site
bedfordstmartins.com/smhandbook

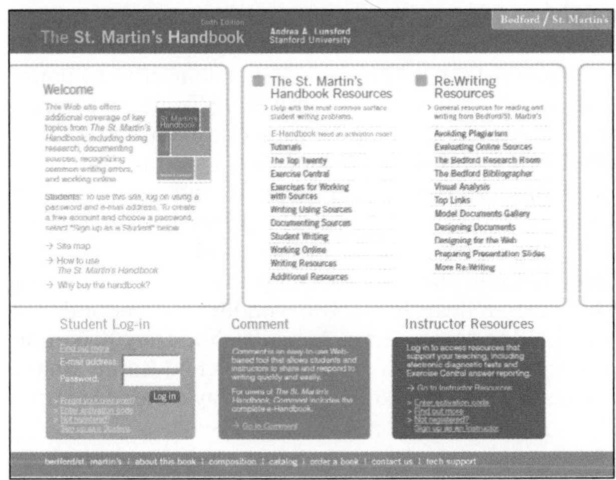

*Online e-Handbook* free when packaged with a new book

*Comment* with *The St. Martin's Handbook*
ISBN-10: 0-312-45138-5; ISBN-13: 978-0-312-45138-7

Content for Course Management Systems including Blackboard, WebCT, and Angel

Exercise Central to Go for Handbooks by Andrea A. Lunsford CD
ISBN-10: 0-312-43114-7; ISBN-13: 978-0-312-43114-3

Re:Writing bedfordstmartins.com/rewriting

Exercise Central bedfordstmartins.com/exercisecentral

## Acknowledgments

*The St. Martin's Handbook* remains a collaborative effort in the best and richest sense of the word. For this edition, I am enormously indebted to Carolyn Lengel, whose meticulous care, tough-minded editing, great good humor, and sheer hard work are everywhere apparent. Also invaluable have been the contributions of Kristin Bowen, a friend, colleague, and terrific editor. I am also deeply indebted to friend and colleague Nick Carbone, whose extensive and detailed review of all material relating to online writing and research have been, simply, the *sine qua non*. As always, Nancy Perry, Denise Wydra, Joan Feinberg, and Erica Appel have provided support, encouragement, and good advice, and my former editor Marilyn Moller continues to provide support and friendship. Michael Weber has managed the entire book from manuscript to bound book with skill and grace — and together with Shuli Traub and Dennis Conroy has made an enormously complex project run smoothly. Judy Voss and Wendy Polhemus-Anibel, the *Handbook's* multitalented copyeditors, edited and reorganized the text efficiently and sensibly. Mara Weible has deftly managed the many new media projects related to this book and kept them all on track. In matters large and small, Stephanie Butler has provided valuable assistance; I am particularly grateful for her perspective on library research. For the wonderful cover and interior design, I am indebted to Anne Carter, Anna Palchik, Lucy Krikorian, and Donna Dennison. I am fortunate indeed to have had Karen Melton Soeltz and John Swanson as my marketing team; in my experience, they set the standard. And, as always, I am grateful to the entire Bedford/ St. Martin's sales force; they are the very best.

## Contributors

For this edition, I owe special thanks to Paul Kei Matsuda and Christine Tardy, who wrote helpful and innovative new materials for multilingual writers that appear throughout the book; they have also updated and revised materials created for a previous edition by Franklin Horowitz of Teachers College of Columbia University. My friend and constant collaborator Lisa Ede has offered not only her ongoing support and sharp wit but also advice and counsel on the section on academic and professional writing, for which I am particularly grateful. Special thanks also go to colleague Lex Runciman for his contributions to the *Workbook*, to Christina Murphy and Steve Sherwood for their excellent new edition of the *Sourcebook for Writing Tutors*, to Alyssa O'Brien for her brilliant work on the *Instructor's Notes*, to Mike Hennessy for his work on the preface to the *Instructor's Notes* and on the tutorial in the *Handbook*, and to Melissa Goldthwaite for a thorough-going and theoretically smart revision of *The St. Martin's Guide to Teaching Writing*. In addition, I am grateful to Melissa Graham Meeks for her careful work on peer review and her always sound advice on electronic media and to Katherine Frank, Tessa Joseph, Donna Light-Donovan, Michelle McSweeney, and Deb Person for their contributions to the book and to its companion Web site. Brenda Brueggemann and Marian Lupo brought their wealth of knowledge of disabilities studies to revisions of the Considering Disabilities boxes throughout the book. I appreciate their generosity and friendship.

As always, I am extremely fortunate to have had the contributions of very fine student writers, whose work appears throughout this text or on its companion Web site: Michelle Abbott, Carina Abernathy, Milena Ateyea, Julie Baird, Jennifer Bernal, Valerie Bredin, Taurean Brown, Tessa Cabello, Ben Canning, Leah Clendening, David Craig, Kelly Darr, Allyson Goldberg, Tara Gupta, Dana Hornbeak, Ajani Husbands, Bory Kea, James Kung, Nastassia Lopez, Heather Mackintosh-Sims, Merlla McLaughlin, Jenny Ming, Laura Montgomery, Elva Negrete, Katie Paarlberg, Shannan Palma, Teal Pfeifer, Amrit K. Rao, Heather Ricker, Amanda Rinder, Dawn Rodney, Rudy Rubio, Melissa Schraeder, Bonnie

Sillay, Jessica Thrower, and Dennis Tyler. I am especially grateful to Emily Lesk, whose imaginative and carefully researched essay appears in Chapter 6.

### Editorial advisers

I am deeply thankful for innumerable helpful comments and suggestions from the members of *The St. Martin's Handbook* editorial advisory board:

Nora Bacon, University of Nebraska at Omaha
Rick Cole, Boston University
Judith M. Davis, Hampton University
Christy Desmet, University of Georgia
Judith G. Gardner, University of Texas at San Antonio
Sara Jameson, Oregon State University
Michael A. Keller, South Dakota State University
Winnie M. Kenney, Southwestern Illinois College
Heidi Aronson Kolk, Washington University, St. Louis
Carole P. Lane, University of Arkansas, Fayetteville
Stephen M. Levin, Columbus State University
Annie S. Perkins, Norfolk State University
Anne E. Raines, University of Arkansas, Fayetteville
Eileen B. Seifert, DePaul University

### Reviewers

For *The St. Martin's Handbook*, we have been blessed with a group of very special reviewers whose incisive comments, queries, criticisms, and suggestions have improved this book immeasurably:

Julie Bergan Abraham, South Dakota State University; Leonard Adame, Butte College; Susan P. Allen, Greenville Technical College; Jeanne Allison, Southwestern Illinois College; Linda S. Anderson, Washington University in St. Louis; Chris Baesler-Ridge, Southern Connecticut State University; Andrea Beaudin, Southern Connecticut State University; Clare Blatchley, Southern Connecticut State University; Sandy Buelow, South Dakota State University; William Burns, Fairfield University; Yuet Sim D. Chiang, University of California, Berkeley; Karen Lentz Clark, University of Arkansas, Fayetteville; Rick Cole, Boston University; Genevieve Coogan, Houston Community College-Northwest; Avon Crismore, Indiana University-Purdue University; Beth Daniell, Kennesaw State University; Scott Downing, DePaul University; Clark Draney, College of Southern Idaho; Anne M. Farmer, Allen County Community

College; Laurie Ferrell, South Dakota State University; Lori Feyh, Missouri State University; Katherine Frank, Colorado State University-Pueblo; Judith G. Gardner, University of Texas at San Antonio; Karen Gardiner, University of Alabama; Elizabeth L. Harris, University of Houston-Downtown; Brian Hayes, DePaul University; Gwen K. Horsley, South Dakota State University; Catherine E. Howard, University of Houston-Downtown; Nancy Hull, Calvin College; Kate Johnson, Community College of Philadelphia; Connie Kendall, University of Kentucky; Winnie M. Kenney, Southwestern Illinois College; Pam Kingsbury, University of North Alabama; Lewis S. Klatt, Calvin College; Marsha Kruger, University of Nebraska at Omaha; Carole P. Lane, University of Arkansas-Fayetteville; Mary Elizabeth Lang, Southern Connecticut State University; John Levine, University of California, Berkeley; Lori Lovell, Valdosta State University; Debra Matier, College of Southern Idaho; Paul Kei Matsuda, Arizona State University; Susan McKinnis, Allen County Community College; Melissa Graham Meeks, University of North Carolina at Chapel Hill; H. Collin Messer, Calvin College; Rebecca M. Mills, Hillsborough Community College; Jette Morache, College of Southern Idaho; Samantha A. Morgan-Curtis, Tennessee State University; Chandra Tyler Mountain, Dillard University; Marguerite Newcomb, University of Texas at San Antonio; Michelle Orr, Washington University in St. Louis; Matthew Parfitt, Boston University; Chere L. Peguesse, Valdosta State University; Jerald Ross, Southwestern Illinois College; Roy Ruane, Houston Community College-Southwest; Carolyn E. Rubin-Trimble, University of Houston-Downtown; John Schaffer, Blinn College; Eileen B. Seifert, DePaul University; Marti Singer, Georgia State University; Jennifer Sloggie, Christopher Newport University; Trixie G. Smith, Middle Tennessee State University; Maggie Sokolik, University of California, Berkeley; Linda Strahan, University of California, Riverside; John W. Taylor, South Dakota State University; Deborah Coxwell Teague, Florida State University; Edee Tenser, The College of New Rochelle; Bill D. Toth, Western New Mexico University; Martha A. Townsend, University of Missouri; Peter C. Townsend, Miami Dade College; David V. Urban, Calvin College; Joan Wedes, University of Houston-Downtown; Deanna M. White, University of Texas at San Antonio; Malcolm Williams, University of Houston-Downtown; Michelle Winn, University of California, Berkeley; and Jewel Sophia Younge, DePaul University.

### Research study participants

For this edition, I am grateful to the more than 2,000 students who allowed us to study their writing. Most special thanks go to Karen Lunsford of the University of California, Santa Barbara, and to her outstanding graduate student team, Alison Brown, Elizabeth Freudenthal, James Ford, and Paul Rogers; and to Stephanie Butler, Keith Paine, Linda Winters, and Suzanne M. Wise in New York for their work in collecting and managing the student writing. In addition, my heartfelt thanks to those writing teachers and WPAs who helped satisfy IRB requirements across the country and who submitted sets of marked student essays; this book would not have been possible without their most valuable assistance.

Finally, I wish to offer very special thanks to the extraordinary community of teacher-researchers at the Breadloaf School of English, whose responses to this text have helped to shape and refine its goals.

I could go on and on in praise of the support and help I have received, for I am fortunate to be part of a unique scholarly community, one characterized by compassion as well as passionate commitment to students and to learning. I remain grateful to be among you.

Andrea A. Lunsford

# A Note to Students

The main goal of *The St. Martin's Handbook* is to help you become a competent and compelling writer — both throughout and beyond your college years.

This text encourages you to carefully analyze your own prose. Most chapters not only provide explanations and opportunities for practice but also ask you to apply the principles presented directly to your own writing. If you follow these directions, they will guide you in becoming a systematic self-critic — and a more effective writer. As your writing improves, so will your reading, your thinking, and your research.

I hope that this book will prove to be a useful reference. But in the long run, a book can be only a guide. You are the one who will put such guidance into practice as you work to become a precise, powerful, and persuasive writer. Why not get started on achieving that goal right now?

*Andrea A. Lunsford*

## How to Use *The St. Martin's Handbook*

This book has been designed to be as easy as possible to use. Depending on what information or advice you're looking for, you may want to consult any or all of the following:

- **TABLES OF CONTENTS.** If you know what general topic you're looking for (such as using commas), the **Brief Contents** on the inside front cover will lead you to the chapter where you'll find that topic. If you're looking for a specific kind of information within a general topic (such as using commas in a series), the detailed **Contents** on the inside back cover or the even more detailed **Contents** following this introduction can lead you to this information.
- **INDEX.** The index covers everything in the book. It's especially useful for finding specific words you need help with (such as *that* or *which*) but don't know the exact technical term for (*relative pronouns*).

- **THE TOP TWENTY.** On pp. 1–12 you will find explanations and examples of the top twenty problems in the writing of U.S. college students today, with references to pages in the book where you can find additional information about avoiding and editing these problems.
- **DOCUMENTATION GUIDELINES.** For information on documenting sources, see the chapters on MLA (Chapter 18), APA (Chapter 19), *Chicago* (Chapter 20), and CSE (Chapter 21) styles.
- **REVISION SYMBOLS.** If your instructor uses revision symbols to mark up your drafts, consult the list of symbols at the back of the book and its cross-references to sections where you'll find more help.
- **GLOSSARIES.** The **Glossary of Terms** (p. 921) defines grammatical and writing-related terms; the **Glossary of Usage** (p. 931) gives help with troublesome words (such as *accept* and *except*).

## Navigating Pages

1. **GUIDES AT THE TOP OF EVERY PAGE.** Headers tell you the title of the part and chapter, the chapter number and section letter, and the page number. An abbreviated title on the tab allows quick flipping.
2. **BOXED TIPS THROUGHOUT THE BOOK.** Directories for boxes appear on pp. I-30–31.
   - *"Talking the talk"* **boxes** help you understand academic language and concepts.
   - *"For multilingual writers"* **boxes** offer advice for those who speak, understand, or write languages in addition to English.
   - *"Considering disabilities"* **boxes** help you make your work accessible to readers with disabilities and point out strategies and resources for writers with disabilities.
3. **HAND-EDITED EXAMPLES.** Many examples are hand-edited in blue, allowing you to see the error and its revision at a glance. Pointers and boldface type make examples easy to spot.
4. **CROSS-REFERENCES.** Cross-references to the Book Companion Site appear in every chapter to direct you to online resources — from a tutorial on avoiding plagiarism to additional grammar exercises, model student writing, and more. Cross-references to other parts of the book appear in parentheses throughout.
5. **GUIDELINE AND SUMMARY BOXES.** Green boxes appear in most chapters to help you check your drafts with a critial eye and revise or edit as need be.

 1

## FOR MULTILINGUAL WRITERS: English capitalization

Capitalization systems vary considerably among languages, and some languages (Arabic, Chinese, Hindi, and Hebrew, for example) do not use capital letters at all. English may be the only language to capitalize the first-person singular pronoun (*I*), but Dutch and German capitalize some forms of the second-person pronoun (*you*). German capitalizes all nouns; English used to capitalize more nouns than it does now (see, for instance, the Declaration of Independence). 2

## 52e Unnecessary capitalization

Do not capitalize a compass direction unless the word designates a specific geographic region.

- **Voters in the South and much of the West tend to favor socially conservative candidates.**

- **John Muir headed ~~West,~~ west, motivated by the need to explore.** 3

Do not capitalize a word indicating a family relationship unless the word is used as part of the name or as a substitute for the name.

- **I could always tell when Mother was annoyed with Aunt Rose.**

**bedfordstmartins.com/smhandbook** For more exercises on using capitalization, go to Exercise Central and click on **Capitalization**. 4

### Editing for capitalization 5

- Capitalize the first word of each sentence. If you quote a poem, follow its original capitalization. (52a)
- Check to make sure you have appropriately capitalized proper nouns and proper adjectives. (52b)
- Review where you have used titles of people or of works to be sure you have capitalized them correctly. (52b and c)
- Double-check the capitalization of geographic directions (*north* or *North*?), family relationships (*dad* or *Dad*?), and seasons of the year (*winter*, not *Winter*). (52e)
- In email, check to see that you have capitalized words as you would in print and have followed other email conventions. (52f)

## A Tutorial on Using *The St. Martin's Handbook*, Sixth Edition

For this book to serve you well, you need to get to know it — to know what's inside and how to find it. The following tutorial is designed to help you familiarize yourself with *The St. Martin's Handbook*; the answers appear on pp. xxvi–xxvii. You can also find an interactive tutorial that walks you through responding to an assignment and revising a draft at **bedfordstmartins.com/smhandbook/tutorials**.

### GETTING STARTED WITH *THE ST. MARTIN'S HANDBOOK*

1. Where will you find advice on revising a rough draft of an essay?
2. Where will you find quick information on identifying and fixing sentence fragments?
3. Where will you find guidelines on documenting electronic sources, such as information found on a Web site?
4. Where will you find advice for multilingual writers?

### PLANNING AND DRAFTING

5. Where in the *Handbook* can you find general guidelines on planning and drafting an essay?
6. Where can you find information about how to make and support the thesis of an argument?
7. You need to give an oral presentation, and you want to see an example of a script to accompany PowerPoint slides. Where would you find such information in the *Handbook*?
8. You want to include a photograph in the writing assignment you are working on, but you are not sure whether the one you have chosen fits with what you are saying. Where will you find advice about how visuals and words work together?

### DOING RESEARCH

9. You have a topic but don't know where to begin your research. How can the *Handbook* help you narrow down your options?
10. You've found Web sites related to your topic, but you aren't sure how reliable they are. Where can you find help in evaluating them?
11. You have forgotten to write down the name of the author of an essay that includes a quotation you want to use in your final project. Can you omit the author's name? Where can you find the answer in the *Handbook*?
12. Your instructor has asked you to use MLA style. How do you document information obtained from a DVD source?

## EDITING

13. As you edit a final draft, you stop at the following sentence: *Winning may be the name of the game but it isn't a name I care for very much*. Should you put a comma before *but*? How and where do you find this answer?
14. You speak several languages, and you still confuse the English prepositions *in* and *on*. Where in the *Handbook* can you find help?
15. Your instructor has written *ref* next to this sentence: *Transmitting video signals by satellite is a way of overcoming the problem of scarce airwaves and limiting how they are used*. Where do you look in the *Handbook* for help responding to your instructor's comment?
16. You have spell-checked your document. Do you still need to proofread it? What information does the *Handbook* provide?

## MEETING YOUR INSTRUCTORS' EXPECTATIONS

17. You have gotten a draft of your paper back from your instructor with the comment *underdeveloped*. How can the *Handbook* help you find out what you need to do to revise?
18. You have been asked to read a newspaper article and write a one-page response. Where would you go for information on how to meet this assignment?
19. You turned in a revised draft, but your instructor says you have only corrected minor errors. Where can you find information on doing thorough revisions?
20. You have been asked to look at a classmate's electronic draft and make suggestions. How can you find out more about reviewing the work of your peers?

## WRITING IN ANY DISCIPLINE

21. You have a take-home exam in political science. You've never before written a political science paper, so you're not sure how to proceed. Do political science papers follow any set format? Where in the *Handbook* can you look for help?
22. You need to write a lab report for your chemistry class. Is there a model in the *Handbook*?
23. For a literature course, you're writing an essay interpreting a poem by Emily Dickinson. Where can you find help in the *Handbook*?
24. You need to submit an electronic portfolio for your writing class. Where in the *Handbook* can you find information about what to include and how to present the work?

## *Answers to the tutorial*

1. Chapter 6.
2. Chapter 39, on sentence fragments.
3. Chapter 18 covers documenting sources, including electronic sources, in MLA style; Chapters 19–21 cover documenting sources in APA, *Chicago*, and CSE styles, respectively.
4. Part 11 includes five chapters (Chapters 56–60) that cover language issues of special interest to students who speak languages in addition to English. Page I-30 has a directory to all the materials in the *Handbook* for multilingual writers.
5. Chapter 5 offers guidelines on exploring, planning, and drafting.
6. Looking up *arguments* in the index leads you to section 9e on the elements that make up an argument and to Chapter 11, which explains how to construct an effective argument.
7. Looking in the directory of student writing points you toward the sample PowerPoint presentation slides and script in 25d. (Other sample student presentations appear on the book's Web site at **bedfordstmartins.com /smhandbook** under **Student Writing**.)
8. Looking up *visuals* in the index leads to the entry "how words work together with visuals," a reference to section 4d. You could also find this information by flipping through Chapter 4 on visual elements.
9. Chapter 13, "Conducting Research," includes section 13b, "Using the library to get started."
10. Skimming the table of contents leads you to Chapter 14, on evaluating sources, and in particular to 14c, on evaluating usefulness and credibility, and to 14d, on reading sources critically.
11. Consulting the index under *citations*, *documentation*, or *acknowledging sources* takes you to Chapter 16, "Acknowledging Sources and Avoiding Plagiarism," where you will find that you must include all of the necessary elements of a citation. "The Top Twenty," on the orange pages before Chapter 1, points out that incomplete documentation is one of the three most common problems in student writing today. You can also look up *note-taking* to get pointers from Chapter 14, "Evaluating Sources and Taking Notes," that will help you avoid the mistake in the future.
12. The table of contents leads you to Chapter 18, which provides a full discussion of MLA documentation conventions. It also lists a directory to MLA style, which leads you to section 18c3 on documenting electronic sources.
13. Looking up *but* in the index leads to 46b, which explains that a comma usually precedes a coordinating conjunction such as *but* when it joins two independent clauses in a compound sentence. You could also get to this section by turning directly to Chapter 46, on using commas, and looking for examples of how to use commas in similar sentences. Looking at "The Top Twenty," on orange pages before Chapter 1, will show you that omitting a comma in a compound sentence is one of the most common errors students make.
14. The table of contents tells you that Chapter 60 covers prepositions; 60a includes a set of strategies for using prepositions idiomatically, including several examples of sentences using *in* and *on*.

15. A list of revision symbols appears on p. I-32 of the *Handbook*. Consulting this list tells you that *ref* refers to "unclear pronoun reference" and that this subject is discussed in Chapter 34.
16. Looking up *proofreading* in the index will take you to an entry on spell checkers and proofreading. The information in section 30e points out that spell checkers miss many kinds of mistakes — there is no substitute for careful proofreading!
17. Looking up *instructor comments* in the index or skimming the table of contents will lead you to section 1e, a chart on learning from instructor comments.
18. The index includes an entry for *reading* that will take you to Chapter 2, "Reading, Writing, and Research." Section 2c1 includes guidelines for critical reading and a sample reading with annotations. Skimming the table of contents will also lead you to section 1c, on expectations instructors have about the reading you do in college.
19. In the index, you'll find an entry for *reviewing drafts* that directs you to a "Talking the Talk" box in Chapter 6. A directory to all the book's "Talking the Talk" boxes, which answer frequently asked questions about academic work, appears on p. I-31.
20. Looking under *peer review* in the index, or scanning the table of contents, will lead you to section 6b, a detailed look at how to act as a peer reviewer — and how to react when your work is under review.
21. Part 12 covers academic and professional writing in general, and Chapter 63 covers social science subjects. Chapter 66 offers tips on take-home exams.
22. Consulting the index under *chemistry*, you see that Chapter 64, on writing for the natural and applied sciences, contains a chemistry lab report.
23. Chapter 62, on writing for the humanities, provides guidelines for close readings of literature and a student paper comparing two poems by e.e. cummings. (On the book's Web site, you can also find a glossary of literary terms at **bedfordstmartins.com/smhandbook** under **Writing Resources**.)
24. Looking up *portfolio* in the index or skimming the table of contents will take you to sections 66e, on planning a portfolio, and 66f, on assembling it. In 66h, you will see an example of a student's portfolio homepage.

# Contents

PART 6

# Sentence Grammar 565

sixth edition

# The St. Martin's Handbook

# The Top Twenty: A Quick Guide to Troubleshooting Your Writing

Although many people think of correctness as absolute, based on unchanging rules, instructors and students know better. We know that there are rules, but they change with time. "Is it okay to use *I* in essays for this class?" asks one student. "My high school teacher wouldn't let us." In the past, use of first person was discouraged by instructors, sometimes even banned. But today, most fields accept such usage in moderation. Such examples show that rules clearly exist but that they are always shifting and that they thus need our ongoing attention.

The conventions involving surface errors — grammar, punctuation, word choice, and other small-scale matters — are a case in point. Surface errors don't always disturb readers. Whether your instructor marks an error in any particular assignment will depend on his or her judgment about how serious and distracting it is and what you should be giving priority to at the time. In addition, not all surface errors are consistently viewed as errors: some of the patterns identified in the research for this book are considered errors by some instructors but as stylistic options by others.

Shifting standards do not mean that there is no such thing as correctness in writing — only that *correctness always depends on some context*. Correctness is not so much a question of absolute right or wrong as of the way the choices a writer makes are perceived by readers. As writers, we all want to be considered competent and careful. We know that our readers judge us by our control of the conventions we have agreed to use, even if the conventions change from time to time.

Research for this book reveals a number of changes that have occurred over the past twenty-plus years. First, the kind of writing students are doing in their first-year composition classes has shifted from a primary focus on personal narrative to research essays and arguments. As a result, students are writing longer essays than they did twenty years ago and working much more often with sources, both print and nonprint. Thus it's no surprise that students today are struggling with the conventions for using and citing sources, a problem that did not show up in most earlier studies of student writing.

What else has changed? For starters, wrong-word errors are *by far the most common* errors among first-year student writers today. Twenty years ago, spelling errors were most common by a factor of more than three to one. The use of spell checkers has reduced the number of spelling errors in student writing — but spell checkers' suggestions may also be responsible for some (or many) of the wrong words students are using.

To help you in producing writing that is conventionally correct, you should become familiar with the twenty most common error patterns among U.S. college students today, listed on the next page in order of frequency. These twenty errors are the ones most likely to result in negative responses from your instructors and other readers. A brief explanation and examples of each error are provided in the following sections, and each error pattern is cross-referenced to other places in this book where you can find more detailed information and additional examples.

## 1 Wrong word

- **Religious texts, for them, take ~~prescience~~ precedence over other kinds of sources.**

  *Prescience* means "foresight," and *precedence* means "priority of importance."

- **The child suffered from a severe ~~allegory~~ allergy to peanuts.**

  *Allegory*, which refers to a symbolic meaning, is a spell checker's replacement for a misspelling of *allergy*.

- **The panel discussed the ethical implications ~~on~~ of the situation.**

Wrong-word errors can involve using a word with the wrong shade of meaning, a word with a completely wrong meaning, or a wrong preposition or word in an idiom. Selecting a word from a thesaurus without being certain of its meaning or allowing a spell checker to correct your spelling automatically can lead to wrong-word errors, so use these tools with care. If you have trouble with prepositions and idioms, memorize the standard usage. (See Chapter 29 on choosing the correct word, Chapter 30 on using spell checkers wisely, and Chapter 60 on using prepositions and idioms.)

## The top twenty

1. Wrong word
2. Missing comma after an introductory element
3. Incomplete or missing documentation
4. Vague pronoun reference
5. Spelling (including homonyms)
6. Mechanical error with a quotation
7. Unnecessary comma
8. Unnecessary or missing capitalization
9. Missing word
10. Faulty sentence structure
11. Missing comma with a nonrestrictive element
12. Unnecessary shift in verb tense
13. Missing comma in a compound sentence
14. Unnecessary or missing apostrophe (including *its/it's*)
15. Fused (run-on) sentence
16. Comma splice
17. Lack of pronoun-antecedent agreement
18. Poorly integrated quotation
19. Unnecessary or missing hyphen
20. Sentence fragment

## 2 Missing comma after an introductory element

- **Determined to get the job done, we worked all weekend.**

- **In German, nouns are always capitalized.**

Readers usually need a small pause between an introductory word, phrase, or clause and the main part of the sentence, a pause most often signaled by a comma. Try to get into the habit of using a comma after every introductory element. When the introductory element is very short, you don't always need a comma after it. But you're never wrong if you do use a comma. (See 46a.)

## 3 Incomplete or missing documentation

- **Satrapi says, "When we're afraid, we lose all sense of analysis and reflection.**~~.~~**"** ^(263).

  The writer is citing a print source using MLA style and needs to include the page number where the quotation appears.

- **According to one source, James Joyce wrote two of the five best novels of all time**~~.~~ ^(Modern Library 100 Best).

  The writer must identify the source. Because the *Modern Library 100 Best* is an online source, no page number is needed.

Be sure to cite each source as you refer to it in the text, and carefully follow the guidelines of the documentation style you are using to include all the information required (see Chapters 18–21). Omitting documentation can result in charges of plagiarism (see Chapter 16).

## 4 Vague pronoun reference

**POSSIBLE REFERENCE TO MORE THAN ONE WORD**

- **Transmitting radio signals by satellite is a way of overcoming the problem of scarce airwaves and limiting how ~~they~~** ^the airwaves **are used.**

  Does *they* refer to the signals or the airwaves? The editing clarifies what is being limited.

**REFERENCE IMPLIED BUT NOT STATED**

- **The company prohibited smoking, ~~which~~** ^a policy **many employees resented.**

  What does *which* refer to? The editing clarifies what employees resented.

A pronoun — a word such as *she, yourself, her, it, this, who*, or *which* — should refer clearly to the word or words it replaces (called the *antecedent*) elsewhere in the sentence or in a previous sentence. If more than one word could be the antecedent, or if no specific antecedent is present in the sentence, edit to make the meaning clear. (See 34f.)

## 5 Spelling (including homonyms)

- **No one came forward to ~~bare~~ *bear* witness to the crime.**
- **Ronald ~~Regan~~ *Reagan* won the election in a landslide.**
- **~~Every where~~ *Everywhere* we went, we saw crowds of tourists.**
- **The wolves stayed ~~untill~~ *until* the pups were able to leave the den.**

The most common kinds of misspellings today are those that spell checkers cannot identify. The categories that spell checkers are most likely to miss include homonyms (words that sound alike but have different meanings); compound words incorrectly spelled as two separate words; and proper nouns, particularly names. Proofread carefully for errors that a spell checker cannot catch — and be sure to run the spell checker to catch other kinds of spelling mistakes. (See 30e.)

## 6 Mechanical error with a quotation

- **"I grew up the victim of a disconcerting confusion~~"~~,**" **Rodriguez says (249).**

  The comma should be placed *inside* the quotation marks.

- **Captain Renault (Claude Rains) says that he is** " **shocked — shocked! to find gambling going on in here" (*Casablanca*).**

  Both the beginning and the end of the quotation (from the film *Casablanca*) should be marked with quotation marks.

Follow conventions when using quotation marks with commas (46h), semicolons (47d), question marks (48b), and other punctuation (50e). Always use quotation marks in pairs, and follow the guidelines of your documentation style for block quotations and poetry (50a). Use quotation marks to mark titles of short works (50b), but use italics for titles of long works (54a).

## 7 Unnecessary comma

**BEFORE CONJUNCTIONS IN COMPOUND CONSTRUCTIONS THAT ARE NOT COMPOUND SENTENCES**

- **This conclusion applies to the United States/ and to the rest of the world.**

No comma is needed before *and* because it is joining two phrases that modify the same verb, *applies*.

**WITH RESTRICTIVE ELEMENTS**

- **Many parents/ of gifted children/ do not want them to skip a grade.**

No comma is needed to set off the restrictive phrase *of gifted children*; it is necessary to indicate which parents the sentence is talking about.

Do not use commas to set off restrictive elements — those necessary to the meaning of the words they modify. Do not use a comma before a coordinating conjunction (*and*, *but*, *for*, *nor*, *or*, *so*, *yet*) when the conjunction is not joining two parts of a compound sentence. Do not use a comma before the first or after the last item in a series, and do not use a comma between a subject and verb, between a verb and its object or complement, or between a preposition and its object. (See 46j.)

## 8 Unnecessary or missing capitalization

- **Some ~~Traditional~~ traditional Chinese ~~Medicines~~ medicines containing ~~Ephedra~~ ephedra remain legal.**

Capitalize proper nouns and proper adjectives, the first words of sentences, and important words in titles, along with certain words indicating directions and family relationships. Do not capitalize most other words, and proofread to make sure your word processor has not automatically added unnecessary capitalization (after an abbreviation ending with a period, for example). When in doubt, check a dictionary. (See Chapter 52.)

## 9 Missing word

- **The site foreman discriminated ^[against] women and promoted men with less experience.**

- **Christopher's behavior becomes ^[so] bizarre that his family asks for help.**

Be careful not to omit little words, including prepositions (60a), parts of two-part verbs (60b), and correlative conjunctions (31b7). Proofread carefully for any other omitted words, and be particularly careful not to omit words from quotations.

## 10 Faulty sentence structure

- **~~The information which high~~ ^[High] school athletes are presented with ~~mainly includes~~ information on what credits ^[they] need~~ed~~ to graduate, ~~and thinking about the college~~ which ~~athletes are trying~~ ^[colleges to try] to play for, and ^[how to] apply.**

- **People who use marijuana can build up a tolerance for it ~~will~~ ^[and] want a stronger drug.**

When a sentence starts out with one kind of structure and then changes to another kind, it confuses readers. If readers have trouble following the meaning of your sentence, read the sentence aloud and make sure that it contains a subject and a verb (31c). Look for mixed structures (41a), subjects and predicates that do not make sense together (41b), and comparisons with unclear meanings (41e). When you join elements (such as subjects or verb phrases) with a coordinating conjunction — *and, but, for, nor, or, so,* or *yet* — make sure that the elements have parallel structures (37b).

## 11 Missing comma with a nonrestrictive element

- **Marina, who was the president of the club, was first to speak.**

  The reader does not need the clause *who was the president of the club* to know the basic meaning of the sentence: Marina was first to speak.

A nonrestrictive element — one that is not essential to the basic meaning of the sentence — could be removed, and the sentence would still make sense. Use commas to set off any nonrestrictive parts of a sentence. (See 46c.)

## 12 Unnecessary shift in verb tense

- **A few countries produce almost all of the world's illegal drugs, but addiction ~~affected~~ affects many countries.**

- **Priya was watching the great blue heron. Then she ~~slips~~ slipped and ~~falls~~ fell into the swamp.**

Verb tenses tell readers when actions take place: saying *Ron went to school* indicates a past action whereas saying *he will go* indicates a future action. Verbs that shift from one tense to another with no clear reason can confuse readers. (See 36a.)

## 13 Missing comma in a compound sentence

- **The words "I do" may sound simple, but they mean a life commitment.**

- **Meredith waited for Samir, and her sister grew impatient.**

  Without the comma, a reader may think at first that Meredith waited for Samir and her sister.

A compound sentence consists of two or more parts that could each stand alone as a sentence. When the parts are joined by a coordinating conjunction — *and, but, so, yet, or, nor,* or *for* — use a comma before the conjunction to indicate a pause between the two thoughts. In very short sentences, the comma is optional if the sentence can be easily understood without it. Including the comma, however, will never be wrong. (See 46b.)

## 14 Unnecessary or missing apostrophe (including *its/it's*)

- **Overambitious parents can be very harmful to a ~~childs~~ child's well-being.**
- **Pedro Martinez is one of the ~~Met's~~ Mets' most electrifying pitchers.**
- **The car is lying on ~~it's~~ its side in the ditch. ~~Its~~ It's a white 2004 Passat.**
- **She passed the front runner, and the race was ~~her's.~~ hers.**

To make a noun possessive, add either an apostrophe and an *-s* (*Ed's book*) or an apostrophe alone (*the boys' gym*). Do *not* use an apostrophe with the possessive pronouns *ours, yours, hers, its,* and *theirs*. Use *its* to mean *belonging to it*; use *it's* only when you mean *it is* or *it has*. (See Chapter 49.)

## 15 Fused (run-on) sentence

- **The current was swift. ~~he~~ He could not swim to shore.**
- **Klee's paintings seem simple, but they are very sophisticated.**
- **~~She~~ Although she doubted the value of meditation, she decided to try it once.**

A fused sentence (also called a run-on sentence) is created when clauses that could each stand alone as a sentence are joined with no punctuation or words to link them. Fused sentences must either be divided into separate sentences or joined by adding words, punctuation, or both. (See Chapter 38.)

## 16 Comma splice

- **Westward migration had passed Wyoming by, even the discovery of gold in nearby Montana failed to attract settlers.** [correction: comma → ;]

- **I was strongly drawn to her, she had special qualities.** [insert: for]

- **We hated the meat loaf, the cafeteria served it every Friday.** [correction: comma → that; "it" struck out]

A comma splice occurs when only a comma separates clauses that could each stand alone as a sentence. To correct a comma splice, you can insert a semicolon or period, connect the clauses clearly with a word such as *and* or *because*, or restructure the sentence. (See Chapter 38.)

## 17 Lack of pronoun-antecedent agreement

- **Each of the puppies thrived in ~~their~~ new home.** [insert: its]

Many indefinite pronouns, such as *everyone* and *each*, are always singular.

- **Either Nirupa or Selena will be asked to give ~~their~~ speech to the graduates.** [insert: her]

When antecedents are joined by *or* or *nor*, the pronoun must agree with the closer antecedent.

- **The team frequently changed ~~its~~ positions to get varied experience.** [insert: their]

A collective noun can be either singular or plural, depending on whether the people are seen as a single unit or as multiple individuals.

- **Every student must provide his own uniform.** [insert: or her]

With a singular antecedent that can refer to either a man or a woman, you can use *his or her*, *he or she*, and so on. You can also rewrite the sentence to make the antecedent and pronoun plural or to eliminate the pronoun altogether.

Pronouns must agree with their antecedents in gender (for example, using *he* or *him* to replace *Abraham Lincoln* and *she* or *her* to replace *Queen Elizabeth*) and in number. (See 34f.)

## 18 Poorly integrated quotation

showed how color affects taste:

- **A 1970s study of what makes food appetizing "Once it became apparent that the steak was actually blue and the fries were green, some people became ill" (Schlosser 565).**

According to Lars Eighner,

- **"Dumpster diving has serious drawbacks as a way of life" (~~Eighner~~ 383). Finding edible food is especially tricky.**

Quotations should fit smoothly into the surrounding sentence structure. They should be linked clearly to the writing around them (usually with a signal phrase) rather than dropped abruptly into the writing. (See 15b.)

## 19 Unnecessary or missing hyphen

- **This paper looks at fictional and real-life examples.**

  A compound adjective modifying a following noun may require a hyphen.

- **Some of the soldiers were only eleven/years/old.**

  A complement that follows the noun it modifies should not be hyphenated.

- **The buyers want to fix/up the house and resell it.**

  A two-word verb should not be hyphenated.

A compound adjective that appears before a noun often needs a hyphen (55a). However, be careful not to hyphenate two-word verbs or word groups that serve as subject complements (55d).

## 20 Sentence fragment

**NO SUBJECT**

**Marie Antoinette spent huge sums of money on herself and her favorites. ~~And~~** *Her extravagance* **helped bring on the French Revolution.**

**NO COMPLETE VERB**

**The old aluminum boat** *was* **sitting on its trailer.**

*Sitting* cannot function alone as the verb of the sentence. The auxiliary verb *was* makes it a complete verb.

**BEGINNING WITH A SUBORDINATING WORD**

**We returned to the drugstore, ~~Where~~** *where* **we waited for our buddies.**

A sentence fragment is part of a sentence that is written and punctuated as if it were a complete sentence. A fragment may lack a subject, a complete verb, or both. Fragments may also begin with a subordinating word (such as *because*) that makes the fragment depend on another sentence for its meaning. Reading your draft out loud, backwards, sentence by sentence, will help you spot sentence fragments easily. (See Chapter 39.)

# Part 1

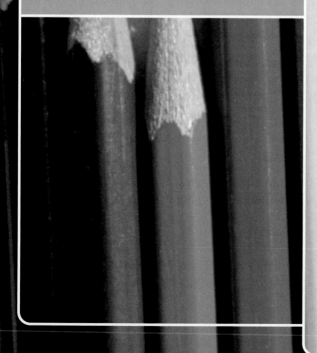

# THE ART AND CRAFT OF WRITING

# 1 Expectations for College Writing

You may expect certain things from college such as help in securing a first job or a position in a new field. But in the unpredictable working world, learning specific skills you need to get a particular job may be less useful than learning a wide variety of skills that will serve you well in any position you hold. The skills a college education can help you develop — such as critical reading and writing — will help you succeed both in college and in life. So in addition to knowing what you expect from college, you need to understand what your college instructors will expect of you. Making your expectations for your college education match up with what your instructors expect will be one of your most significant challenges in college.

## 1a Preparing to meet expectations

A generation ago, many college students counted on holding one job throughout their careers and expected college to prepare them for that single job. Today's students, however, are likely to hold a number of positions — and each new position will call for new learning. That's why looking at your college years as simply a step you have to take on the way toward your first job is a big mistake. College must do much more than simply prepare you for that first work experience, and you may need to adjust your expectations of what college should do *for* you in order to understand what your instructors will expect *from* you. Your instructors — and your future colleagues and supervisors — will expect you to demonstrate your ability to think critically, to consider ethical issues, to find as well as solve problems, to do effective research, and to work productively with people of widely different backgrounds. In each of these endeavors, writing will be of crucial importance, since writing is closely tied to thinking, to collaboration, and to communication.

So writing is going to be a key part of your life from now on. Whether you are doing college assignments, keeping others informed on the job, or acting as a concerned consumer or citizen, your success will depend on the ability to communicate clearly and competently in writing.

But if you are like most students, you may not have written anything much longer than five pages before coming to college. Perhaps you have done

**TALKING THE TALK: Conventions**

"Aren't conventions really just rules with another name?" Not entirely. Conventions — agreed-on language practices of grammar, punctuation, and style — convey a kind of shorthand information from writer to reader. In college writing, you will generally want to follow the conventions of standard academic English unless you have a good reason to do otherwise. But unlike hard-and-fast rules, conventions are flexible; a convention appropriate for one time or situation may be inappropriate for another. You may also choose to ignore conventions at times to achieve a particular effect. (You might, for example, write a sentence fragment rather than a full sentence, such as the *Not entirely* at the beginning of this box.) As you become more experienced and confident in your writing, you will develop a sense of which conventions to apply in different writing situations.

only minimal research. Your college classes will demand much more from you as a writer; meeting these demands will help prepare you for all the writing you will need to do in the future. You can begin the process of learning by considering what your instructors expect you to be able to do. Of course, expectations about academic writing vary considerably from field to field — but becoming familiar with widespread conventions will prepare you well for most academic situations. To become an effective college writer, consider some of the expectations your instructors hold about writers, readers, and texts.

## 1b Expectations about college writers

### *Establishing authority*

In the United States, most instructors expect student writers to begin to establish their own authority — to become constructive critics who can analyze and interpret the work of others and can eventually create new knowledge based on their own thinking and on what others have said. But what does establishing your authority mean in practice?

- Assume that your opinions count (as long as they are informed rather than tossed out with little thought) and that your audience expects you to present them in a well-reasoned manner. In class discussion, for example, you can build authority by stating an opinion clearly and then backing it up with evidence.

- Draw conclusions based on what you have read, and offer those conclusions in a clear and straightforward way.
- Build your authority by citing the works of others, both from the reading you have done for class and from good points your instructor and other classmates have made.

### *Being direct*

Your instructors will most often expect you to get to your main point quickly and to be direct throughout an essay or other project. Good academic writing prepares readers for what is coming next, provides definitions, and includes topic sentences. (See 26f for a description of the organization that instructors often prefer in student essays.) To achieve directness in your writing, try the following strategies:

- State your main point early and clearly; don't leave anything to the reader's imagination.
- Avoid overqualifying your statements. Instead of writing *I think the facts reveal*, come right out and say *The facts reveal*.
- Avoid digressions. If you use an anecdote or example from personal experience, be sure it relates directly to your main point.
- Make sure to use examples and concrete details to help support your main point.
- Make your transitions from point to point obvious and clear. The first sentence of a new paragraph should reach back to the paragraph before and then look forward to what is to come.
- If your essay or project is longer than four or five pages, you may also want to use brief summary statements between sections, but be careful to avoid unnecessary repetition.

## 1c Expectations about college readers

Your instructors expect you to be an actively engaged reader — to respond to class readings and to offer informed opinions on what the readings say. Keep in mind that instructors are not asking you to be negative or combative; rather, they want to know that you are engaged with the text and with the class. Here are some expectations many college instructors have about what good reading requires you to do:

- Carefully note the name of the author and the date and place of publication; these items can give you clues to the writer's purpose and audience.
- Understand the overall content of a piece, and be able to summarize it in your own words.
- Formulate informed and critical questions about the text, and bring these questions up in class.
- Understand each sentence, and make direct connections between sentences and paragraphs. Keep track of repeated themes or images, and figure out how they contribute to the entire piece.
- Note the author's attitude toward and assumptions about the subject. Then you can speculate on how the attitude and assumptions may have affected the author's thinking.
- Distinguish between the author's stance and how the author reports on the stances of others. Keep an eye open for the key phrases an author uses to signal an opposing argument: *while some have argued that, in the past,* and so on.
- Go beyond content to notice organizational patterns, use of sources, and choice of words.

## 1d Expectations about college texts

Your instructors hold different expectations for the various kinds of written work you produce in college, especially as conventions vary from discipline to discipline. But some general guidelines apply (see p. 18).

Beyond such guidelines, instructors hold additional expectations about organization, sentence structure, paragraph structure, idea development, use of evidence, and formatting for the kinds of texts you will produce in college. Research for this book confirms that readers depend on writers to organize and present their material — using sections, paragraphs, sentences, arguments, details, and source citations — in ways that aid understanding. Here are some things your writing needs

## U. S. academic style

- Consider your purpose and audience carefully, making sure that your topic is appropriate to both. (Chapter 3)
- State your claim or thesis explicitly, and support it with examples, statistics, anecdotes, and authorities of various kinds. (Chapters 9–11)
- Carefully document all of your sources. (Chapters 18–21)
- Make explicit links between ideas. (7d and e)
- Consistently use the appropriate level of formality. (Chapters 28 and 29)
- Use conventional academic formats, such as research projects, literary analyses, and position papers. (Chapters 11–21, and 62–65)
- Use conventional grammar, spelling, punctuation, and mechanics. (Chapters 31–55)
- Use an easy-to-read type size and typeface, conventional margins, and double spacing. (Chapter 23)

to do to help establish your credibility and to help readers understand your point:

- Follow logical organizational patterns, and provide clear signals that will help readers follow the overall thread of what you are trying to say (5e3 and 7d).
- Guide readers through your writing by using effective and varied sentences that link together smoothly (Chapters 42–45).
- Develop paragraphs logically and completely, and make it easy for readers to understand how and why you are going from one paragraph to the next (7c1 and e).
- Use ample supporting evidence — good reasons, examples, or other details — to illustrate or support a clear, specific point. Choose evidence that helps readers understand your point and offers proof that what you are saying is sensible and worthy of attention (9e).
- Design and format the project appropriately for the audience and purpose you have in mind (Chapter 23).

## 1e Learning from instructor comments

Even the most experienced and best writers make mistakes — and any piece of writing can benefit from revision. Instructor comments on any work that you have done can help you identify mistakes, particularly ones that you make repeatedly, and can point you toward larger issues that prevent your writing from being as effective as it could be. Whether or not you will have an opportunity to revise a particular piece of writing, you should look closely at the comments from your instructor.

In responding to student writing, however, instructors sometimes use phrases or comments that are a kind of shorthand — comments that are perfectly clear to the instructor but may be less clear to the students reading them. The instructor comments in the following chart, culled from over a thousand first-year student essays, are among those that you may find most puzzling. Alongside each comment you'll find information intended to make the comment clearer to you — and to allow you to revise as your instructor recommends. If your paper includes a puzzling comment that is not listed here, be sure to ask your instructor what the comment means and how you can fix the problem.

| Instructor Comment | Possible Meaning(s) | Actions to Take in Response |
|---|---|---|
| "thesis not clear" | The main point of your writing is hard to find or hard to understand. | Make sure that you have a main point, and state it directly. (6c) The rest of the paper will need to support the main point, too — this problem cannot be corrected by adding a sentence or two. |
| "trying to do too much" "covers too much ground" | Your main point is very broad. | Focus your main point more narrowly so that you can say everything that you need to in a project of the assigned length. (5b) You may need to cut back on some material and then expand what remains. |

*(continued on p. 20)*

(continued from p. 19)

| Instructor Comment | Possible Meaning(s) | Actions to Take in Response |
|---|---|---|
| "hard to follow"<br>"not logical"<br>"incoherent"<br>"jumps around"<br>"parts not connected"<br>"transition" | The writing is not clearly or not logically organized, or the writing lacks transitions, explanations, or other signals the reader needs to understand. | If overall organization is unclear, try mapping or outlining and rearranging your work. (17b2) See if transitions and signals (7d4) or additional explanation will solve the problem. |
| "too general"<br>"vague" | You make general statements when specific ones are needed. | Use concrete language and details, and make sure that you have something specific and interesting to say. (29c) If not, reconsider your topic. |
| "underdeveloped"<br>"thin"<br>"sparse" | You do not give enough information, examples, or details about the material, or you have not considered the topic from enough angles. | Add examples and details, and be as specific as possible. (29c) You may need to do more research. (Chapters 12–14) |
| "what about the opposition?"<br>"one-sided"<br>"condescending"<br>"overbearing" | You do not include information on opposing arguments, you misrepresent the opposition, or you imply that your opinion is the only reasonable one to hold. | Add information on why some people disagree with you, and represent their views fairly and completely before you refute them. Recognize that reasonable people may hold views that differ from yours. (11e3) |
| "repetitive"<br>"you've already said this" | You repeat arguments or reuse evidence, or you have a tendency to overuse certain words or phrases in your writing. | Revise any parts of your writing that repeat an argument, point, word, or phrase; avoid using the same evidence over and over. |

| Instructor Comment | Possible Meaning(s) | Actions to Take in Response |
|---|---|---|
| "awk"<br>"awkward" | You have chosen an inappropriate word, or your sentence is confusing. | Ask a peer or your instructor for suggestions about revising awkward sentences. (Chapters 36–41) |
| "syntax"<br>"awkward syntax"<br>"convoluted" | Your sentence may be too long, or the parts of the sentence may not be clearly related. | Read the sentence aloud to identify the problem; revise or replace the sentence. (Chapters 36–41) |
| "unclear" | Your reader does not understand your point. | Find another way to explain what you mean; add any background information or an example that your audience may need to follow your reasoning. |
| "tone too conversational"<br>"not an academic voice"<br>"too informal"<br>"colloquial"<br>"slang" | You use slang or colloquial terms inappropriately, or you do not show enough respect for your readers. | Look for overly informal words and phrasing you can revise. Consider your audience, and revise material that addresses or refers to that group too familiarly or informally. (Chapter 29) |
| "pompous"<br>"stilted"<br>"stiff" | You use inappropriately stuffy, strange, or showy language. | Make sure you understand the connotations of the words you use, and revise any that contribute to a pompous, excessively old-fashioned, or peculiar tone. (29b) |
| "set up quotation"<br>"integrate quotation" | You use a quotation that does not fit into the sentence around it, you have not introduced the quotation, or you neglect to explain the significance of the quotation. | Read the sentence containing the quotation aloud; revise it if it does not make sense as a sentence. Introduce every quotation with information about the source. Explain each quotation's importance to your work. (Chapter 15) |

*(continued on p. 22)*

(continued from p. 21)

| Instructor Comment | Possible Meaning(s) | Actions to Take in Response |
|---|---|---|
| "your words?" "source?" "cite" | You use someone else's words or ideas without citing the source. | Mark all quotations clearly. Cite paraphrases and summaries of others' ideas. Give credit for help from others, and remember that you are responsible for your own work. (Chapter 16) |
| "doc" | You omit all or part of the source information required by the documentation style you are using, or you make punctuation or other errors in your in-text citations. | Check the citations to be sure that you include all of the required information, that you punctuate correctly, and that you omit information not required by the documentation style. (Chapters 18–21) |

## THINKING CRITICALLY ABOUT YOUR EXPECTATIONS FOR COLLEGE WRITING

How do you define good college writing? Make a list of the characteristics you come up with. Then make a list of what you think your instructors' expectations are for good college writing, and note how they may differ from yours. What might account for the differences — and the similarities — in the two lists? Do you need to alter your ideas about good college writing to meet your instructors' expectations? Why, or why not?

# Reading, Writing, and Research

# 2

More than two thousand years ago, a Roman writer named Quintilian set out a plan for education, beginning with birth and ending only with old age and death. Surprisingly enough, Quintilian's recipe for a lifelong education has never been more relevant than it is today. Some of your biggest challenges as a student will be learning how to learn; how to communicate what you have learned across vast distances, to larger and increasingly diverse sets of audiences; and how to do so using a wide range of media and genres. Along the way, you will probably be doing more — and more different kinds of — writing than ever before, in addition to using the other communicative arts of reading, speaking, listening, and doing research.

## 2a Writing today

Chances are that you think of writing as putting words on paper or onscreen, and until recently such a definition would have served fairly well. But not today. Writing in this century often includes much more than words; visual images, graphics, and sound can create and carry an important part of the message. Perhaps most important, writing often contains many voices, as, with increasing ease, we bring ideas from the Web and other sources into what we write.

Writing today is often collaborative as well. For example, you may work with a team to produce an illustrated report, on the basis of which members of the team make a key presentation; you and a colleague may carry out an experiment, discuss and write up the results, and present your findings; or you and others in your group may divide up the work for a class project for a business course and then pool your efforts in meeting the assignment.

Perhaps most notably, today's expanded sense of writing challenges us to think very carefully about what the writing is for (its purpose) and whom it can and will reach (its audience). Electronic writing, in particular, may reach a much larger audience than the writer anticipated — and this expanded reach can have unintended consequences, both good and bad. For example, if a humorous Web log receives favorable mention on a high-traffic Web site, the blog's writer may find that the stories she has written to amuse her friends and relatives also attract the attention of thousands of strangers who respond enthusiastically to her work. But if that same blog reveals secrets about her workplace, she could just as easily end up explaining herself to a very unamused employer. Writers can no longer assume that they write only to a specified audience or that they can easily control the dissemination of their messages. We now live not only in a city, a state, and a country but also in the world — and we write to speakers of many languages, to members of many cultures, to believers of many creeds.

If it is true that "no man [or woman!] is an island," then it is equally true that no piece of writing is an island, isolated and alone. Instead, all writing is connected to a web of other writings and words that it may be extending, responding to, or challenging. Today, when an email message can literally circle the world in seconds, it's important to remember this principle: all writing exists within a broad and rich context in which any writer says or writes something to others for a purpose. In short, as a writer today, you need to remember several key points:

- Writing, one of the world's oldest technologies, uses an expansive array of tools, from pencil and pen to software programs and video-streaming capacities.
- Writing is visual as well as verbal; design elements are key to the success of many documents.
- Writing is often collaborative — from planning and designing to producing the final product.
- Writing is increasingly multilingual, as writers bring in other languages and as improvements in technology allow for faster and easier global communication.
- Writing has the potential to reach massive audiences in a very, very short time.
- Writing today is primarily public; once on the Web, it takes on a life of its own. As a result, writers need to consider their own — and others' — privacy.

Chapters 2–8 show you how closely related writing is to reading, speaking, listening, and researching. All of these arts of communication interweave in the act of writing.

## 2b Writing processes

The writing process may have been presented to you as a linear march from plan to outline to draft to final copy. But most writers will confirm that writing rarely, if ever, proceeds in such a neat, orderly way. Rather, the writing process is a collection of activities that often overlap and sometimes even occur simultaneously. As a result, this process is often described not as linear but as recursive, meaning that its goals or stages are constantly flowing into and influencing one another, without any clear break between them. At a given moment, for example, a writer may be deciding how to organize a paragraph. A moment later, that same writer may be using the knowledge gained from that decision to help her revise the wording of a sentence. And while working on the sentence, she might think of a new point to add to the paragraph, which then might encourage her to rethink the paragraph's overall organization.

There is no single correct writing process. In fact, there are as many different writing processes as there are writers — more, if you consider that individual writers vary their writing processes each time they sit down to write! Even though the various parts of the writing process overlap, recur, and result in different processes altogether, looking at the parts one by one can still be useful.

- *Exploring.* During this stage, you consider your rhetorical situation — the context in which your writing occurs, the purpose of the writing, and the audience you are addressing (Chapter 3). Exploring also calls for a preliminary investigation of your topic: brainstorming, reading, browsing resources, checking out graphics or images you may need, or talking to friends and classmates about your ideas (5a).
- *Narrowing a topic and researching.* Writing worth reading often starts with a question or puzzle or idea that calls for thinking about what you already know (5a), narrowing a topic (5b), coming up with a working thesis (5c), and gathering information (5d).
- *Organizing and designing.* Sometimes an organizational plan (5f) will occur to you at an early stage, helping to shape your thesis and direct your research. More often, though, a plan will grow out of the thesis or your search for information. You should also think carefully about how to design a piece of writing (Chapter 23). Use your plan for organization and design as a guide as you produce a first draft.

- *Drafting.* Even if you have thoroughly explored your topic, you will almost certainly discover more about it while drafting. Sometimes these new insights will cause you to turn back and revisit your plan, research, approach, audience, or purpose. Drafting, then, is not just putting ideas down on paper. More often than not, it involves coming up with new ideas. Remember that the goal of drafting is not a final copy or even a version good enough to show someone else. Smooth sentences and ideal wording can come later. In your first draft, just write until you run out of ideas to explore (5g).
- *Reviewing.* Reviewing calls for you or another reader to look at your draft with a critical eye to reassess the main ideas, organization, paragraph structure, sentence variety, word choice, attitudes toward topic and audience, and the thoroughness with which the topic is developed. In addition to analyzing the draft yourself, you should get responses from other people, such as friends, classmates, tutors, or your instructor (6a).
- *Revising.* Revising involves reworking your draft on the basis of the review. It also means polishing to achieve memorable prose. It may mean writing new sentences, moving paragraphs, eliminating sections, doing additional research for information or images, or even choosing a new topic and starting over (6b–h).
- *Editing, formatting, and proofreading.* Editing involves making what you have written ready to meet those traditional conventions of written form usually called "correctness." Sentence structure, spelling, mechanics, punctuation — all should ordinarily meet conventional standards. Editing may sometimes lead you to reconsider an idea, a paragraph, a transition, an organizational pattern, or a format — and you could wind up planning or drafting once again. When all editing and formatting are finished and you have a final text, spell-check and proofread it to catch and correct any typographical errors (6i and j).

### EXERCISE 2.1

One of the best ways to improve your writing process is to analyze it from time to time in a writing log. In a computer file or notebook, answer the following questions about your writing:

- How do you typically go about preparing for a writing assignment?
- When and where do your best ideas often come to you?
- Where do you usually write? Are you usually alone and in a quiet place, or is there music, conversation, or other sound in the background?

- What materials do you use? What do you find most and least helpful about your materials?
- What audience do most assignments ask you to address? How much thought do you typically give to your audience?
- What strategies do you typically use to explore a topic?
- How do you usually write a first draft? Do you finish in one sitting, or do you prefer to work in sections?
- How do you typically revise, and what do you pay most attention to as you revise?
- If you get stuck while writing, what do you usually do to get moving again?
- What is most effective about your writing and your writing process?
- What about your writing and your writing process worries you? What specific steps can you take to address these worries?
- What is your favorite part of your writing process — and why?

You can also use the log to jot down your thoughts about a writing project while you are working on it and after you have completed it. Studying your notes on your writing process will help you identify patterns of strength and weakness in your writing and allow you to see how your writing process changes over time and for different writing assignments or situations.

## 2c Reading processes

All readers build worlds in their minds made of words and images. Think of a time when you were reading and suddenly realized that you were not absorbing content but just looking at a jumble of marks on a page or a screen. Only when you went back and concentrated on the meanings of those words and images were you really reading.

### 1 Critical reading

Reading critically means asking questions about what you are reading — questions about the meaning of the text and how that meaning is presented or about the author and his or her purpose for writing, for example. A critical reader does not simply accept what the author says but analyzes why the text is convincing (or not convincing). Writer Anatole Broyard once cautioned readers about the perils of "just walking through" a text. A good reader, he suggested, doesn't just walk but "stomps around" in a text — highlighting passages, scribbling in the margins, jotting questions and comments. The guidelines and example that follow can guide you toward stomping around in your own reading.

## Guidelines for critical reading

*Preview the text to consider preliminary questions.*

- What does the title tell you?
- What do you already know about the subject? What opinions do you have? What do you hope to learn?
- What information can you find about the author and his or her purpose, expertise, and possible biases?
- What can you learn from considering when, where, and how the text was published?
- What effects do visuals, subdivisions, and headings have?
- What do you expect the main point of the text to be?

*Read and annotate the text.*

- What key terms and ideas do you identify?
- What statements do you agree with? disagree with?
- What sources does the text cite?
- What do you find confusing or unclear? What do you need to look up?

*Summarize what you have read, and jot down ideas and questions.*

*Analyze the text.*

- What are the main points? Do they match your expectations?
- What evidence does the text provide? How are examples used? What other evidence or counter-evidence occurs to you?
- Are the sources trustworthy?
- How do the words and visuals work together?
- What are the author's underlying assumptions?
- Was the author's purpose accomplished?
- What is intriguing, puzzling, or irritating about the text?
- What would you like to know more about?

*Reread the text, and check your understanding.*

### *Preview and annotation*

The article "Many Women at Elite Colleges Set Career Path to Motherhood," by Louise Story, appeared on pp. A1 and A18 of the *New York Times* on September 20, 2005. The first portion of the article appears on pp. 30–31, with a student's preview notes and annotations.

**bedfordstmartins.com/smhandbook** To read the article in its entirety, click on **Writing/Resources.**

### *Summary*

Here is how the same student summarized Louise Story's article "Many Women at Elite Colleges Set Career Path to Motherhood" (pp. 30–31).

> A group of women at Ivy League schools told a reporter who surveyed and interviewed them that they planned to stop working or cut back on work when they had children. The reporter suggests that the women's responses are evidence of a trend and of "changing attitudes."

### *Analysis*

Here are some of the student's notes for an analysis of Louise Story's *New York Times* article, part of which appears on pp. 30–31. Because the student felt that the article — and her response to it — raised many unanswered questions, she decided to research responses to the article as well as information about how the writer came up with the data cited.

> The evidence for a trend seems pretty skimpy. The reporter interviews several students who indicate that they plan to stop working or work part-time when they have children. The reporter says "many" students feel this way. But according to the numbers the reporter provides, she talked to just 138 people out of an unknown number of responses to an email survey. The reporter doesn't provide any information about what previous generations of women at Ivy League schools felt about working or staying home with their children either, so there's no way to identify this point of view as a change in college women's attitudes — even though the reporter uses the phrase "changing attitudes" twice.

**bedfordstmartins.com/smhandbook** For background and responses to this article, click on **Writing Resources.**

Title suggests the author's conclusion (typical of newspaper headlines). Is this a new trend? Why is it important enough to be on the front page?

Who is Cynthia Liu? a typical female Yale student? How can I tell?

# Many Women at Elite Colleges Set Career Path to Motherhood

By LOUISE STORY

Who is Louise Story? Google her name to see if her article generated any response.

Cynthia Liu is precisely the kind of high achiever Yale wants: smart (1510 SAT), disciplined (4.0 grade point average), competitive (finalist in Texas oratory competition), musical (pianist), athletic (runner) and altruistic (hospital volunteer). And at the start of her sophomore year at Yale, Ms. Liu is full of ambition, planning to go to law school.

So will she join the long tradition of famous Ivy League graduates? Not likely. By the time she is 30, this accomplished 19-year-old expects to be a stay-at-home mom.

Main point, as expected from the title. But she's only one example — how many are like her?

"My mother's always told me you can't be the best career woman and the best mother at the same time," Ms. Liu said matter-of-factly. "You always have to choose one over the other."

At Yale and other top colleges, women are being groomed to take their place in an ever more diverse professional elite. It is almost taken for granted that, just as they make up half the students at these institutions, they will move into leadership roles on an equal basis with their male classmates.

Generalizations about how women are "groomed" — but no evidence.

There is just one problem with this scenario: many of these women say that is not what they want.

How many is "many"? The same word appears in the title.

Many women at the nation's most elite colleges say they have already decided that they will put aside their careers in favor of raising children. Though some of these students are not planning to have children and some hope to have a family and work full time, many others, like Ms. Liu, say they will happily play a traditional female role, with motherhood their main commitment.

Is "many" more than "some"? Who did the writer talk to? Whose stories did she focus on (besides Cynthia Liu's)? Whose did she leave out — and why?

Much attention has been focused on career women who leave the work force to rear children. What seems to be changing is that while many women in college two or three decades ago expected to have full-time careers, their daughters, while still in college, say they have already decided to suspend or end their careers when they have children.

Who says? Where are the sources for these claims?

"At the height of the women's movement and shortly thereafter, women were much more firm in their expectation that they could somehow combine full-time work with child rearing," said Cynthia E. Russett, a professor of American history who has taught at Yale since 1967. "The women today are, in effect, turning realistic."

Expert source — her quotation underscores the main point. Do other experts disagree?

Is it realistic to expect to be able to raise a family without working?

Dr. Russett is among more than a dozen faculty

members and administrators at the most exclusive institutions who have been on campus for decades and who said in interviews that they had noticed the changing attitude.

Many students say staying home is not a shocking idea among their friends. Shannon Flynn, an 18-year-old from Guilford, Conn., who is a freshman at Harvard, says many of her girlfriends do not want to work full time.

"Many" — that word is here a lot. Here's another student example, but, again, just one person.

"Most probably do feel like me, maybe even tending toward wanting to not work at all," said Ms. Flynn, who plans to work part time after having children, though she is torn because she has worked so hard in school.

"Men really aren't put in that position," she said.

Wonder why nobody is asking why expectations are different for men?

Uzezi Abugo, a freshman at the University of Pennsylvania who hopes to become a lawyer, says she, too, wants to be home with her children at least until they are in school.

Another student says the same thing. Total of three so far.

"I've seen the difference between kids who did have their mother stay at home and kids who didn't, and it's kind of like an obvious difference when you look at it," said Ms. Abugo, whose mother, a nurse, stayed home until Ms. Abugo was in first grade.

While the changing attitudes are difficult to quantify, the shift emerges repeatedly in interviews with Ivy League students, including 138 freshman and senior females at Yale who replied to e-mail questions sent to members of two residential colleges over the last school year.

Author conducted interviews and an email survey. The sample seems pretty small, though, and comes from a single school.

The interviews found that 85 of the students, or roughly 60 percent, said that when they had children, they planned to cut back on work or stop working entirely. About half of those women said they planned to work part time, and about half wanted to stop work for at least a few years.

Interview results. What about the survey results? How many were sent out, and how many were completed? The author doesn't say.

Two of the women interviewed said they expected their husbands to stay home with the children while they pursued their careers. Two others said either they or their husbands would stay home, depending on whose career was furthest along.

85 + 2 + 2 = 89, and she interviewed 138. What about the others?

The women said that pursuing a rigorous college education was worth the time and money because it would help position them to work in meaningful part-time jobs when their children are young or to attain good jobs when their children leave home. . . .

I wonder if they're paying for college themselves!

**bedfordstmartins.com/smhandbook** For the rest of this article, click on **Writing Resources.**

### 2 Reading as a writer

Since reading is closely related to writing, one good way to improve your writing is by paying close attention to what you read, taking tips from writers you especially admire. What makes the writing effective for you as a reader? Try to identify qualities that you can imitate in your own writing.

### 3 Reading online

Writers today do a lot of reading online — and while some online reading is similar to reading print texts, there are some important differences. Eye-tracking studies conducted by the Poynter Institute found that print news readers' eyes go first to photos and graphics. But readers of online news turn first to news briefs and captions. Research shows that online readers commonly skim a text; they are also likely to want to control the text rather than be guided by it, choosing to leap back and forth or to find their own paths.

Many Web sites — and especially news sites — offer you the opportunity to click on a button for a print-friendly, or text-only, version of the story. Use this option if your interest in reading the article is primarily with the text rather than the visuals.

#### EXERCISE 2.2

Following the guidelines in 2c, read one of the assigned essays from your course text or the student essay in Chapter 9 or 11 of this book. Summarize the reading briefly, and note any thoughts you have about your critical reading process (in your writing log, if you keep one).

#### CONSIDERING DISABILITIES: Screen readers

Keep in mind that many people who are blind or vision impaired use screen readers, software programs that scan text and read it aloud. These programs cannot access "styled" texts well. These texts include those saved as HTML and those with fancy fonts, colored fonts, and very large fonts.

When forwarding emails it is best to remove any beginning-of-line carats (>) since these are often read — each and every one — as "greater than" by a screen-reading program. Always give a brief and descriptive subject line in an email; blind and vision-impaired users who might be reading your mail with a screen-reading program benefit greatly from such pointed information.

## 2d Doing research

The reading and writing you do in college are part of what we broadly think of as research. In fact, much of the work you do in college may turn an informal search into various kinds of more formal research. An idea that comes to you over pizza, for example, may lead you to conduct a survey that in turn becomes an important piece of evidence in a research project for your sociology class.

Many of your writing assignments will require extensive or formal research. Even if you know the topic very well, your research will be an important tool for establishing credibility with your audience and thus gaining their confidence in you as a writer. (For more on research, see Chapters 12–17.)

## 2e Talking and listening

For a number of reasons, the arts of language — reading, writing, speaking, and listening — are often treated separately in school. As text has taken on more and more importance in our society, reading and writing have come to take precedence over talking and listening in most formal education.

However, it may be both impractical and unwise to draw strict boundaries among these arts. After all, writers are always readers of their own texts. Speakers, too, create texts that can be "read" and analyzed, both visually and verbally. When we are part of the audience for a comedian onstage or on television, we appear to be listening, but we are also reading the presentation, taking note of facial expressions, gestures, and other body language. And if we go on to analyze and discuss the comic's performance, then we are creating additional information — another text.

### 1 Talking to learn

In your college work, you will do plenty of talking and listening, and those activities will add immeasurably to the quality of your thinking and learning. Plan to talk over your work with others, to engage in collaborative learning, and to speak purposefully in all your classes. This kind of talking can help you in all of the following areas:

- making points you can use later
- explaining your ideas to others and getting immediate feedback

- testing out ideas to see how others, including your instructor, will respond
- working out problems with writing and other assignments
- putting what you learn into your own words
- warming up for writing or reading assignments

### 2 Listening to learn

The flip side of talking is listening, an art that is of tremendous importance to success in personal relationships as well as in college. You can maximize the value of listening if you use these tips:

- Really listen — consistently and attentively. Practicing this kind of concentration will yield surprisingly quick results.
- Try to listen purposefully. Concentrate on the big points and on what you most need to know.
- Ask questions that will yield answers worth listening to, that will help you get the information you need.
- Take notes. Try to repeat information in your own words.

## 2f Taking notes

In much college work, good note-taking is a kind of survival skill, and learning how to take notes most effectively will add to your success as a critical reader, writer, and listener. Here are some guidelines to help you review your own note-taking processes:

- *Know your purpose.* Are you taking down a quotation to use in an essay? recording key words and phrases during a lecture to study for an exam? recording the major points in a reading assignment? Knowing the reason for your note-taking can help you decide exactly what you should write down.
- *Consider how you think best.* Does it help you to write notes as you listen to a lesson or lecture? Or does the act of writing distract you so that you lose track of what you are reading or hearing? Decide whether you should take notes while reading and listening — or whether it is more effective for you to listen or read first and then take notes soon afterward.

## CONSIDERING DISABILITIES: Note-taking

Remember that we learn in a very wide range of ways and that note-taking may be more difficult for some students than for others. Especially for dense or hard-to-understand material, consider working with classmates to share and compare notes. Doing so will give all of you new perspectives on the material covered in class. Reading and writing software can also assist users with various literacy needs, providing assistance in reading, transcribing, and memorizing notes as well as in creating study guides from notes or course material.

- If you are taking notes while reading or attending a lecture, *look for the major points, and note their relationships to one another*. When you want to recall information from a reading or a lecture, a series of random jottings is usually less helpful than a series of clearly related points.
- *Label your notes* so that you can remember where they came from. If you are taking notes in class, simply head the paper or electronic document with the course title and date. If you are taking notes from a print source, note the book's or the article's author, title, and place and date of publication. If you are taking notes from an online document, print a copy, and write down the URL as well as the date and time of your access. (For more on taking notes for research, see 12g and Chapter 14.)

## THINKING CRITICALLY ABOUT READING AND WRITING

To think critically about your own writing, try approaching it as a reader. Choose a piece of writing that you completed for an earlier class and that you have not recently read. Using the guidelines for critical reading on p. 28, preview, read, and analyze the writing as objectively as you can. What impression does it make on you as a reader? What questions does it leave you with? Write a one-page report analyzing your piece of writing from a critical reader's point of view.

# 3 Rhetorical Situations

What do a magazine article on stem-cell research, a letter to Visa about an error on your bill, an email to your sister, a comment on a blog about global warming, and an engineering report on ways to strengthen the New Orleans levees all have in common? To write successfully, the writers of all of these texts must analyze their particular rhetorical situation and then respond to it in appropriate ways.

## 3a Your rhetorical situation

As a writer or speaker, you must think about the topic or message you want to get across, your relationship to the audience you are writing for, and the context you are writing in. Context includes your values and beliefs and those of your audience; your background knowledge and that of the audience; your time and space limitations; your purpose; the medium and genre you are working in; your style and level of language; and a variety of other factors. Taken together, these factors constitute the rhetorical situation.

## 3b Deciding to write

Because elements of the rhetorical situation, like purpose and audience, are such important considerations in effective writing, you should start thinking about them at an early stage, as soon as you make the decision to write. In a general sense, of course, this decision is often made for you. Your editor sets a deadline for a newspaper story; your professor announces that a research project is due next month; your employer asks for a full report on a complex issue before the next management meeting. But even in such situations, consciously deciding to write is important. Experienced writers report that making up their minds to begin a writing task represents a big step toward getting the job done.

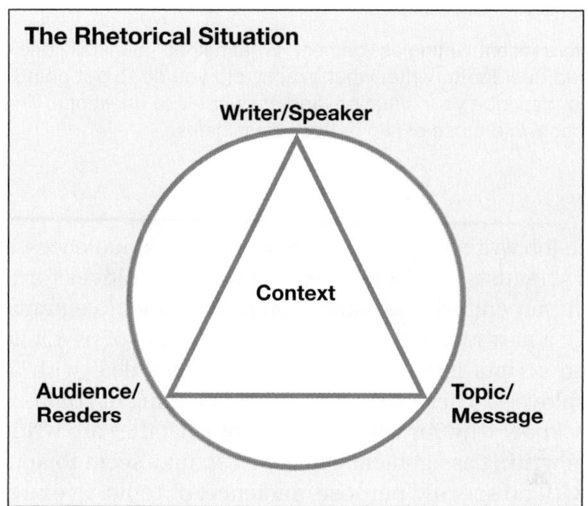


## 3c The topic or problem

When a topic is left open, many writers put off getting started because they can't think of or decide on a topic. Experienced writers say that the best way to choose a topic is literally to let the topic choose you. The subjects that compel you — that puzzle, confuse, irritate, or in some way pose a problem for you — are likely to engage your interests and hence evoke your best writing. You can begin to identify a topic or problem by thinking through the following questions:

- What topics do you wish you knew more about?
- What topics are most likely to get you fired up?
- What about one of these topics is most confusing to you? most exciting? most irritating? most tantalizing?
- What person or group might this topic raise problems for?

Remember that regardless of the topic you choose, it must be manageable. To limit your topic to a manageable size, make the topic as explicit as possible (rather than "The war in Afghanistan," for example, narrow it to "The use of special forces in the Kabul area"). For help with limiting a topic, see 12c.

### EXERCISE 3.1

Think back to a recent writing assignment. What helped you finally decide to write? Once you had decided to write, what exactly did you do to get going? In a paragraph or two, describe your situation, and answer these questions. Then compare your description with those of two or three classmates.

## 3d The assignment

Most on-the-job writing addresses specific purposes, audiences, and topics: a group of scientists produces a report on food additives for the federal government; an editorial assistant composes a memo summarizing the problems in a new manuscript for an editor; a team of psychologists prepares video scripts intended to help companies deal with alcoholism among employees. These writers all have one thing in common: specific goals. They know why, for whom, and about what they are writing.

College writing assignments, in contrast, may seem to appear out of the blue, with no specific purpose, audience, or topic. In extreme cases, they may be only one word long, as in a theater examination that consisted of the single word *Tragedy!* At the opposite extreme come assignments in the form of fully developed, very specific cases (often favored in business and engineering courses).

In between the one-word exam and the fully developed case, you may get assignments that specify purpose but not audience — to write an essay arguing for or against censorship on the Internet, for example. Or you may be given an organizational pattern to use — to compare and contrast two of the novels you have read in a course — but no specific topic. Because comprehending an assignment accurately and fully is crucial to your success in responding to it, you should always make every effort to do so.

### *Emily Lesk's assignment*

In this and the next several chapters, we will follow the writing process of Emily Lesk as she developed an essay for her first-year English course at Stanford University. Her class was given the following assignment:

> Explore the ways in which one or more media (television, print advertising, and so on) have affected an aspect of American identity, and discuss the implications of your findings for you and your readers.

Emily saw that the assignment was broad enough to allow her to focus on something that interested her, and she knew that the key word *explore* invited her to examine — and analyze — an aspect of American identity that was of special interest to her. Her instructor said to assume that she and members of the class would be the primary audience for this essay. Emily knew her classmates and instructor, and she felt comfortable having them as the primary audience: she knew what their expectations were and how to meet those expectations. But Emily also hoped to post her essay on the class Web site, thus reaching a wider audience — in fact, her essay might be read by anyone with access to the Internet. With this broad and largely unknown audience in mind, Emily determined to be as clear as possible and to take nothing for granted in terms of explaining her point of view and supporting her thesis.

## Analyzing an assignment

- What exactly does the assignment ask you to do? Look for such words as *analyze, classify, compare, contrast, describe, discuss, define, explain*, and *survey*. Remember that these words may differ in meaning among disciplines — *analyze* might mean one thing in literature, another in biology.
- What knowledge or information do you need? Do you need to do any research? (5a7 and 5d)
- Do you need to find illustrations or other visuals? What purpose will they serve? (Chapter 4)
- How can you limit — or broaden — the topic or assignment to make it more interesting? Do you have interest in or knowledge about any particular aspect of the topic? Be sure to check with your instructor if you wish to redefine the assignment. (5b)
- What problem(s) does the topic suggest to you? How might the problem(s) give you an interesting angle on the topic? (3c)
- What are the assignment's specific requirements? Consider genre, length, format, organization, and deadline — all of which will help you know the scope expected. Your instructor is not likely to expect extensive library research for a paper due in twenty-four hours, for example. If no length is designated, ask for guidelines. (3d)
- What is your purpose? Do you need to demonstrate knowledge of certain material? Do you mainly need to show your ability to express certain ideas clearly? (3e)
- Who is the audience for this writing? Does the task imply that you will assume a particular readership besides your instructor? (3h)

### EXERCISE 3.2

The following assignment was given to an introductory business class: "Discuss in an essay the contributions of the Apple and Microsoft companies to the personal computing industry." What would you need to know about the assignment in order to respond successfully? Using the questions in the box on p. 39, analyze this assignment.

## 3e Purposes

Writing college essays, reports, and other assignments almost always involves multiple purposes. On one level, you are writing to establish your credibility with your instructor, to demonstrate that you are a careful thinker and an effective writer. On another level, though, you are writing to achieve goals of your own, to say as clearly and forcefully as possible what you think about a topic.

For example, if you are writing an essay about free speech on campus, your purposes might be to inform your readers, to persuade them to support or oppose speech codes, or even to clarify in your own mind the issues related to free speech on college campuses. If you are writing a profile of your eccentric grandfather, you might be trying to amuse your readers and to pay tribute to someone who has been important to you.

In ancient Rome, the great orator Cicero noted that a good speech generally fulfills one of three major purposes: to delight, to teach, or to move. Today, our purposes when we communicate with one another remain pretty much the same: we seek to *entertain* (delight), to *inform or explain* (teach), and to *persuade or convince* (move).

Most of the writing you do in college will address one or some of these purposes, and it is thus important for you to be able to recognize the overriding purpose of any piece of writing. If, for example, a history professor asks you to explain the events that led up to the 1964 Civil Rights Act (primary purpose: to explain) and you write an impassioned argument on the need for the act (primary purpose: to persuade), you have misunderstood the purpose of the assignment.

For most college writing, you should consider purpose in terms of the assignment, the instructor's expectations, and your own goals.

### *Emily Lesk's purposes*

As she considered the assignment (see p. 38), Emily Lesk saw that her primary purpose was to explain the significance and implications of her topic to herself and her readers, but she recognized some other purposes as well.

### Analyzing your purposes

- What is the primary purpose of the assignment — to entertain? to explain? to persuade? some other purpose? What does this purpose suggest about the best ways to achieve it? If you are unclear about the primary purpose, talk with your instructor. Are there any secondary purposes to keep in mind?
- What are the instructor's purposes in giving this assignment — to make sure you have read certain materials? to determine your understanding? to evaluate your thinking and writing? How can you fulfill these expectations?
- What are your goals in carrying out this assignment — to meet expectations? to learn? to communicate your ideas? How can you achieve these goals?

Because this essay was assigned early in the term, she wanted to get off to a good start; thus, one of her purposes was to write as well as she could to demonstrate her ability to her classmates and instructor. In addition, she decided that she wanted to find out something new about herself and to use this knowledge to get her readers to think about themselves.

## 3f Language

Although most of your college writing will be done in standard academic English, some of it may demand that you use specialized occupational or professional varieties of English — those characteristic of medicine, say, or computer science or law or music. Similarly, you may wish to use regional or ethnic varieties of English to catch the sound of someone's spoken words. You may even need to use words from a language other than English — in quoting someone, perhaps, or in using certain technical terms. In considering your use of language, think about what languages and varieties of English will be most appropriate for reaching your audience and accomplishing your purposes (see Chapter 28).

### EXERCISE 3.3

Consider a writing assignment you are currently working on. What are its purposes in terms of the assignment, the instructor, and you, the writer?

### FOR MULTILINGUAL WRITERS: Bringing in other languages

If you are familiar with languages other than English, you may want or need to include words, phrases, or whole passages in another language. When you do so, consider whether your readers will understand that language and whether you need to provide a translation, as in this example from John (Fire) Lame Deer's "Talking to the Owls and Butterflies":

> Listen to the air. You can hear it, feel it, smell it, taste it. *Woniya waken* — the holy air — which renews all by its breath. *Woniya, woniya waken* — spirit, life, breath, renewal — it means all that.

In this instance, translation is necessary because the phrase Lame Deer is discussing has multiple meanings in English. (See 28e for details about how to provide translations in your text.)

## 3g Rhetorical stance

"Where do you stand on that?" is a question often asked, particularly of those running for office or occupying positions of authority. But writers must ask the question of themselves as well. Understanding where you stand on your topic — your rhetorical stance — has several advantages: it will help you examine where your opinions come from and thus help you address the topic fully; it will help you see how your stance might differ from the stances held by members of your audience; and it will help you establish your credibility with that audience. This part of your rhetorical stance — your *ethos* or credibility — helps determine how well your message will be received. To be credible, you will need to do your homework on your subject, present your information fairly and honestly, and be respectful of your audience.

A student writing a proposal for increased services for people with disabilities, for instance, knew that having a brother with Down syndrome gave her an intense interest that her audience might not have in this topic. She would need to work hard, then, to get her audience to understand — and share — her stance.

### Examining your rhetorical stance

- What is your overall attitude toward the topic? How strong are your opinions?
- What social, political, religious, personal, or other influences have contributed to your attitude?
- How much do you know about the topic? What questions do you have about it?
- What interests you most about the topic? Why?
- What interests you least about it? Why?
- What seems important — or unimportant — about the topic?
- What preconceptions, if any, do you have about it?
- What do you expect to conclude about the topic?

## 3h Audience

Skilled writers consider their audiences carefully. In fact, one of the characteristic traits of a mature writer is the ability to write for a variety of audiences, using language, style, and evidence appropriate to particular readers. The key word here is *appropriate*: just as a funeral director would hardly greet a bereaved family with "Hi, there! What can I do for you?" neither would you be likely to sprinkle jokes through an analysis of child abuse written for a PTA. Such behavior would be wildly inappropriate given the nature of your audience.

Although an instructor may serve as the primary audience for much of your college writing, you may sometimes find yourself writing for others: lab reports addressed to your class, business proposals addressed to a hypothetical manager, or information searches posted to an online audience that is potentially so vast that making any solid assumptions about its members is impossible. Every writer can benefit from thinking carefully about who the audience is, what the audience already knows or thinks, and what the audience needs and expects to find out.

### *Emily Lesk's audience*

In addition to her instructor, Emily Lesk's audience included the members of her writing class and her potential online readers. Emily saw that her classmates were mostly her age, that they came from diverse ethnic backgrounds, and that they came from many areas of the country. Her online readers could be almost anyone.

## 1 Addressing specific audiences

Thinking systematically about your audience can help you make decisions about a writing assignment. For example, it can help you decide

### Analyzing your audience

- What person or group do you most want to reach? Is this audience already sympathetic to your views?
- How much do you know about your audience? In what ways may its members differ from you? from one another? Consider education, geographic region, age, gender, occupation, social class, ethnic and cultural heritage, politics, religion, marital status, sexual orientation, disabilities, and so on. (Chapter 27)
- What assumptions can you make about your audience members? What might they value — brevity, originality, conformity, honesty, security, adventure, wit, seriousness, thrift, generosity? What goals and aspirations do they have? Remember that writing today can reach countless readers, so you need to take special care to examine how — and if — distant readers will understand references, allusions, and so on.
- What languages and varieties of English do your audience members know and use? What special language, if any, will they expect you to use? (Chapter 28)
- What stance do your audience members have toward your topic? What are they likely to know about it? What preconceived views might they have?
- What is your relationship to the audience?
- What is your attitude toward the audience?
- What attitudes will audience members expect you to hold? What attitudes might disturb or offend them?
- What kind(s) of response(s) do you want to evoke?

what sort of organizational plan to follow, what information to include or exclude, and even what specific words to use. If you are writing an article for a journal for nurses about a drug that prevents patients from developing infections from intravenous feeding tubes, you will not need to give much information about how such tubes work or to define many terms. But if you are writing about the same topic in a pamphlet for patients, you will have to give a great deal of background information and define (or avoid) technical terms.

#### EXERCISE 3.4

Describe one of your courses to three audiences: your best friend, your parents, and a group of high school students attending an open house at your college. Then describe the differences in content, organization, and wording that the differences in audience led you to make.

### 2 Appealing to your whole audience

All writers need to pay very careful attention to the ways in which their writing can either invite readers to participate as part of the audience or leave them out. Look at the following sentence:

> As every schoolchild knows, the world is losing its rain forests at the rate of one acre per second.

The writer here gives a clear message about who is — and who is not — part of the audience: if you don't know this fact or have reason to suspect it is not true, you are not invited to participate.

There are various ways you, as a writer, can help make readers feel they are part of your audience. Be especially careful with the pronouns you use, the assumptions you make, and the kinds of support you offer for your ideas.

#### *Using appropriate pronouns*

The pronouns you use can include or exclude readers. When bell hooks says "The most powerful resource any of us can have as we study and teach in university settings is full understanding and appreciation of the richness, beauty, and primacy of our familial and community backgrounds," she uses "us" and "we" to connect with her audience — those who "study and teach in university settings." Using "us" and "we" to speak directly to your audience, however, can sometimes be dangerous: those who do not see themselves as fitting into the "we" group can feel

## CONSIDERING DISABILITIES: Your whole audience

Remember that considering your whole audience means thinking about members with varying abilities and special needs. If you are writing to veterans in a VA hospital or to a senior citizens' group, for example, you can be sure that most audience members will be living with some form of disability. But it's very likely that any audience will include members with disabilities — from anorexia to dyslexia, multiple sclerosis, or attention deficit disorder — and that there may be significant differences within disabilities. Approximately 54 million Americans were living with a disability in the year 2000 — an average of 1 in 5 Americans! All writers need to think carefully about how their words reach out and connect with such very diverse audiences.

left out — and they may resent it. So, in thinking about your audience, remember to take special care with the pronouns you use to refer to your readers.

### *Avoiding unfounded assumptions*

Be careful about any assumptions you make about your readers and their views, especially in the use of language that may unintentionally exclude readers you want to include. Use words like *naturally* and *of course* carefully, for what seems natural to you — that English should be the official U.S. language, for instance, or that smoking should be outlawed — may not seem at all natural to some members of your audience. The best advice about any audience you wish to address is to take nothing about them for granted.

### *Offering appropriate evidence*

The evidence you offer in support of your arguments can help draw in your readers. A student writing about services for people with disabilities might ask readers who have no personal experience with the topic to imagine themselves in a wheelchair, trying to enter a building with steps but no ramp. Inviting them to be part of her audience would help them accept her ideas. On the other hand, inappropriate evidence can leave readers out. Complex statistical evidence might well appeal to public-policy planners but may bore or even irritate ordinary citizens. (For more on building common ground with readers, see Chapter 27.)

## 3i Online rhetorical situations

Although the contexts for online communication are changing rapidly, you should remember certain facts. First, online contexts offer many new ways to get information and join conversations. Today, anyone can review books on Amazon.com or contribute to any number of wikis. To write effectively in such contexts, you will need to sharpen your critical-thinking skills to distinguish what is reliable, accurate, and useful to you and others.

Second, online contexts are primarily public. What may seem like private email conversations are routinely archived and accessible to a variety of other people. Therefore, you will need to consider whether you are willing to have what you are putting online become public knowledge (22b).

Third, online messages travel. Just as you may clip a paragraph out of a message and send it on to a friend, so your online messages may be forwarded to others, downloaded, and disseminated. As a result, you have to consider how such traveling may affect the messages you send — and keep careful track of what you may be moving from one context to another. In the same way, think carefully before you forward someone else's messages: do you have the writer's permission to do so?

Finally, online writing is faster than other forms of written communication, so people expect to be able to process and respond to messages quickly. Thus even lengthy messages may need to be clearer and more concise online than offline. (For more information about writing effectively online, see Chapters 22 and 24.)

**bedfordstmartins.com/smhandbook** For more information about netiquette, click on **Writing Online.**

### THINKING CRITICALLY ABOUT RHETORICAL SITUATIONS

**Reading with an Eye for Purpose and Audience**

Advertisements provide good examples of writing that is tailored carefully for specific audiences. Find two ads for the same product that appeal to different audiences. You might compare ads in a men's magazine to those in a women's magazine to see what differences there are in the messages and photography. Take a look, for example, at advertisements for various kinds of drinks: Which seem designed to appeal primarily to men and which to women? What conclusions can you draw about ways of appealing to specific audiences?

**Thinking about Your Own Attention to Purpose and Audience**

Analyze a text you have written or are working on right now.

- Can you state its purpose(s) clearly and succinctly? If not, what can you do to clarify its purpose(s)?
- What other purposes for this piece of writing can you imagine? How would fulfilling some other purpose change the writing?
- Can you tell from reading the piece who the intended audience is? If so, what in your text clearly relates to that audience? If not, what can you add that will strengthen your appeal to this audience?
- What other audiences can you imagine? How would the writing change if you were to address a different audience? How would it change if you were writing to a largely unknown audience, such as people on the Web?
- Does your writing follow the conventions of standard academic English — and if not, how should you revise so that it will?

Note your conclusions about purpose and audience in your own writing.

# Visual Thinking

# 4

Today, we live in a world of words *and* visuals, in which writers routinely accompany email messages with photographs, create graphs and charts to illustrate documents, and animate their writing with many forms of media. But the ability to use color, fancy fonts, and visuals of all kinds presents writers with new challenges. Thinking about how visual information works — including the different messages it sends — will help you decide when to rely on plain old words, when to rely on visual data, and when to rely on both.

## 4a Document design conventions

When you look at a document, its overall appearance — or design — often tells you the kind of document it is. For example, you can spot a standard business letter at a glance just by looking at its layout and seeing the inside address, salutation, and so on. Similarly, many academic essays and résumés have a "look" that makes them instantly identifiable.

You may already recognize the design conventions in the preceding documents, but it is easy to overlook the design features of documents you see every day. As a writer, you'll want to make sure that you are using design conventions appropriately. In other words, you want your lab report in chemistry to *look* like a lab report, just as you want your résumé to identify itself visually as one.

For help with designing your print and online documents, see Chapters 23 and 24. For more on the document conventions of different disciplines, see Chapters 61–66.

## 4b Visuals and their associations

Visual information works by creating associations in readers' minds. When you see a popular company logo, for instance, you often make an immediate connection with the company and its product or service. Notice how quickly you can associate each logo shown in the flag on p. 50 with the company it represents. This Adbusters visual of the American flag is also making a visual argument. (For advice on analyzing visual arguments, see Chapter 10.)

AN IMAGE WITH LOGOS THAT CONVEY ASSOCIATIONS

Regardless of the visual or the words that accompany a message, writers are only partially in control of the messages they send. People will develop their own associations and find their own meaning in the message. For example, the famous golden arches logo associated with McDonald's is interpreted very differently by two students.

**JASON** Instead of a symbol of food, I see the golden arches as a symbol of work. A child may see the "M" and think of fries or toys; I think of sweating, understaffed work crews slaving away in the back of the store.

**DÁNIELLE** When I was a kid, my dad would occasionally sneak me a Happy Meal. My mom must have known since the whole house would end up smelling like hot french fries. When I see the golden arches, I think of having this special secret with my dad and happily eating cheeseburgers and fries.

When you choose visuals for the documents you are creating, remember these lessons and ask what associations readers may already have with a visual you choose.

VISUALS THAT CONVEY DIFFERENT TONES

## 4c Tone

The tone of your writing — the attitude you convey toward your topic and audience — can be conveyed not only by your language but also through the visuals you use in a document. Notice, for example, how each of the visuals of Albert Einstein above conveys a different tone.

A visual appropriate for one type of writing may have the wrong tone for another type of writing. In a serious academic essay about Einstein, for example, you would not use the second and third visuals shown here. When you choose a particular visual, ask yourself if it helps to convey the tone you want to achieve (humorous, serious, impassioned, and so on) and if that tone is appropriate for your audience, purpose, and topic. (For more on tone, see 6g4 and 36f.)

## 4d Pairing words and visuals

Readers and writers today are usually dealing with information presented in both words and visuals. For example, Emily Lesk, the student whose writing process we have been following, used the following words and visuals to help readers "see" the point she was trying to make about Coca-Cola as a cultural icon. (You will see other examples of Emily Lesk's work in Chapters 5 and 6.)

## A STUDENT'S USE OF WORDS AND A VISUAL IN AN ESSAY

Fig. 1. Hebrew Coca-Cola T-shirt. Personal photograph.

Even before setting foot in Israel three years ago, I knew exactly where I could find the Coke T-shirt. The tiny shop in the central block of Jerusalem's Ben Yehuda Street did offer other designs, but the one with a bright white "Drink Coca-Cola Classic" written in Hebrew cursive across the chest was what drew in most of the dollar-carrying tourists. While waiting almost twenty minutes for my shirt (depicted in Fig. 1), I watched nearly every customer ahead of me ask for "the Coke shirt, todah rabah [thank you very much]."

At the time, I never thought it strange that I wanted one, too. After having absorbed sixteen years of Coca-Cola propaganda through everything from NBC's Saturday morning cartoon lineup to the concession stand at Camden Yards (the Baltimore Orioles' ballpark). . . .

Getting words and visuals to work together for maximum effect isn't always easy. In 2001, the U.S. government created a Web site to provide information and to help people prepare for another possible attack. However, some readers found the Web site's visuals unclear — and made their point in a humorous way by rewriting the government's words, as seen below.

**ORIGINAL MESSAGE**

If you become aware of an unusual or suspicious release of an unknown substance nearby, it doesn't hurt to protect yourself.

**REWRITTEN MESSAGE**

Don't get so preoccupied with biological weapons that you forget to put on deodorant.

**ORIGINAL MESSAGE**

**Shielding:** If you have a thick shield between yourself and the radioactive materials, more of the radiation will be absorbed, and you will be exposed to less.

**REWRITTEN MESSAGE**

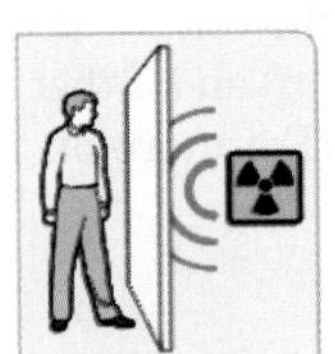

If deadly radiation knocks on your door, do not answer.

To avoid misunderstandings, writers need to integrate all the elements of a document carefully, paying special attention to how well the text and visuals work together and fit the purpose of the writing and the intended audience. In addition, writers need to think carefully about when to put more emphasis on words — and when to put more emphasis on visuals.

## THINKING CRITICALLY ABOUT VISUAL ELEMENTS

Examine a piece of writing you have done recently — an essay, a report, or a term project. First, look at the layout of the text: How visually appealing is it? Is the text easy to read? Do you use subheadings, color, or type size and font in ways that help convey your message? Do you include visuals in this piece of writing? Why, or why not? Consider how visuals (or additional visuals) could be helpful in presenting the information in the most memorable and readable way, and note any other changes that would enhance how your intended audience will perceive this piece of writing.

# 5 Exploring, Planning, and Drafting

Some writers just plunge right into their work, thinking about and developing ideas as they go along. Others find that they can work more effectively by producing detailed blueprints before they ever begin drafting. Still others may jot down lyrics or draw pictures to help them find something new and compelling to say. There are many productive ways to go about exploring, planning, and drafting. The goal is to find strategies that work well for you.

## 5a Exploring a topic

The point is so simple that we often forget it: we write best about topics we know well. One of the most important parts of the entire writing process, therefore, is choosing a topic that will engage your strengths and your interests, surveying what you know about it, and determining what you need to find out. This chapter describes several useful ways to explore a topic, including brainstorming, freewriting, looping, clustering, keeping a journal, questioning, and consulting print as well as electronic sources. Whatever strategies you try, it is a good idea to save your explorations in a computer file or elsewhere. You may want to refer to them later on.

### 1 Brainstorming

One of the best ways to begin exploring a topic is also the most familiar: talk it over with others. Consider beginning with a brainstorming session. Used widely in business and industry, brainstorming means tossing out ideas — either in person or online — to discover new ways to approach a topic. You can also brainstorm by yourself.

1. Within a time limit of five or ten minutes, list every word or phrase that comes to mind about the topic. Just jot down key words and phrases, not sentences. No one has to understand the list but you. Don't worry about whether or not something will be useful — just list as much as you can in this brief span of time.

2. If little occurs to you, try calling out or writing down thoughts about the opposite side of your topic. If you are trying, for instance, to think of reasons to reduce tuition and are coming up blank, try concentrating on reasons to increase tuition. Once you start generating ideas in one direction, you'll find that you can usually move back to the other side fairly easily.
3. When the time is up, stop and read over the lists you have made. If anything else comes to mind, add it to the list. Then reread the list. Look for patterns of interesting ideas or for one central idea that you can begin to explore.

### *Emily Lesk's brainstorming*

Emily Lesk, the student whose work we are following in Chapters 3–6, did some brainstorming with her classmates on the general topic the class was working on: an aspect of American identity affected by one or more media. Here are some of the notes Emily made during the brainstorming session:

- *"American identity" — Don't Americans have more than one identity?*
- *Picking a kind of media could be hard. I like clever ads. Maybe advertising and its influence on us?*
- *Tiger Woods and Nike — a walking ad on the golf course.*
- *Wartime advertising; recruiting ads that promote patriotic themes.*
- *Look at huge American companies like Wal-Mart and Starbucks and how their ads affect the way we view ourselves. Not sure what direction to take. . . .*

## 2 Freewriting

Freewriting is a method of exploring a topic by writing about it for a period of time *without stopping.*

1. Write for ten minutes or so. Begin by thinking about your topic, and then let your mind wander. Write down everything that occurs to you — in complete sentences as much as possible — but don't worry about spelling or grammar. If you get stuck, write anything. Just don't stop.
2. When the time is up, look at what you have written. Much of it will be unusable, but you may discover some important insights and ideas.

## CONSIDERING DISABILITIES: Freespeaking

If you are better at talking out than writing out your ideas, try freespeaking, the talking version of freewriting. Begin by speaking into a tape recorder or into a computer with voice-recognition software, and just keep talking about your topic for at least seven to ten minutes. Say whatever comes to your mind, and don't stop talking. You can then listen to or read the results of your freespeaking and look for an idea to pursue at greater length.

### *Emily Lesk's freewriting*

Here is a portion of the freewriting Emily Lesk did to focus her ideas after the brainstorming session:

> Media and effect on American identity. What media do I want to write about? That would make a big difference — television, radio, Internet — they're all different ways of appealing to Americans. TV shows that say something about American identity? What about magazine or TV advertising? Advertising tells us a lot about what it means to be American. Think about what advertising tells us about American identity. What ads make me think "American"? And why?

### 3 Looping

Looping is a form of directed freewriting that narrows a topic through a series of five-minute stages, or loops.

1. With your topic in mind, spend five minutes freewriting *without stopping*. This is your first loop.
2. Look at what you have written. Find the central or most intriguing thought, and summarize it in a single sentence; it will become the starting point of your next loop. If you are using a computer, simply cut and paste, or copy, your summary to a new page — and continue with your looping.
3. Starting with the summary sentence from your first loop, spend another five minutes freewriting. This second loop focuses on your first loop, just as your first loop focused on your topic. Look for the central idea within your second piece of freewriting, which will form the basis of a third loop.

4. Keep this process going until you discover a clear angle or something about your topic that you can pursue in a full-length piece of writing.

## 4 Clustering

Clustering is a way of generating ideas using a visual scheme or chart. It is especially helpful for understanding the relationships among the parts of a broad topic and for developing subtopics. If you have a software program for clustering, put it to use. If not, follow these steps:

1. Write down your topic in the middle of a blank piece of paper, and circle it.
2. In a ring around the topic circle, write what you see as the main parts of the topic. Circle each part, and draw a line from it to the topic.
3. Think of more ideas, examples, facts, or other details relating to each main part. Write each of these near the appropriate part, circle each one, and draw a line from it to the part.
4. Repeat this process with each new circle until you can't think of any more details. Some trails may lead to dead ends, but you will still have many useful connections among ideas.

### *Emily Lesk's clustering*

Later in her planning and exploring process, Emily Lesk decided to work on the topic of Coca-Cola advertising and American identity (pp. 60–61). After finding a large Coca-Cola advertising archive, she used clustering to help focus her emerging ideas. Her clustering appears on p. 58. (Remember that you may want to explore aspects of your ideas more than once — and exploring may be helpful at any stage as you plan and draft a piece of writing.)

## 5 Keeping a journal

Writers often get their best ideas by jotting down or recording thoughts that come to them randomly. You can use a notebook, a computer, a handheld wireless device, an iPod — we even know of writers who keep a marker and writing board on the shower wall so that they can write down the ideas that come to them while bathing! As you begin thinking about your assignment, taking time to write about or record what you

EMILY LESK'S CLUSTERING

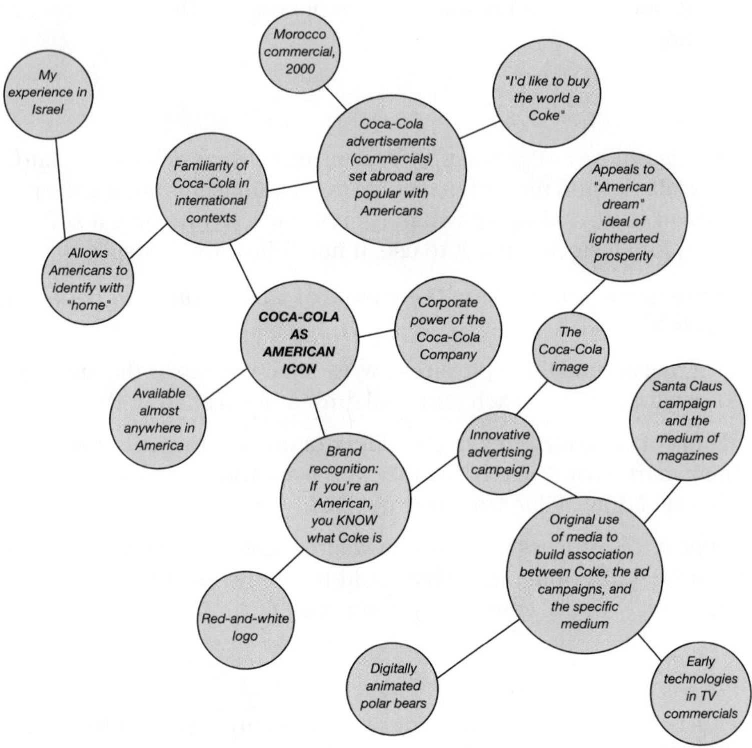


know about your topic and what still puzzles you may lead you to a breakthrough or help you articulate your main idea.

## 6 Asking questions

Another basic strategy for exploring a topic and generating ideas is simply to ask and answer questions. Here are several widely used sets of questions to get you started, either on your own or with one or two others.

### *Questions to describe a topic*

Originally developed by Aristotle, the following questions can help you explore a topic by carefully and systematically describing it:

- *What is it?* What are its characteristics, dimensions, features, and parts? What does it look like?
- *What caused it?* What changes occurred to create your topic? How is it changing? How will it change?
- *What is it like or unlike?* What features differentiate your topic from others? What analogies can you make about your topic?
- *What larger system is your topic a part of?* How does your topic relate to this system?
- *What do people say about it?* What reactions does your topic arouse? What about the topic causes those reactions?

### Questions to explain a topic

The well-known questions *who*, *what*, *when*, *where*, *why*, and *how*, widely used by news reporters, are especially helpful for explaining a topic.

- *Who* is doing it?
- *What* is at issue?
- *When* does it take place?
- *Where* is it taking place?
- *Why* does it occur?
- *How* is it done?

### Questions to persuade

When your purpose is to persuade or convince, the following questions, developed by philosopher Stephen Toulmin, can help you think analytically about your topic (9e and 11i2):

- What *claim* are you making about your topic?
- What *good reasons* support your claim?
- What valid *underlying assumptions* support the reasons for your claim?
- What *backup evidence* can you find for your claim?
- What *refutations* of your claim should you anticipate?
- In what ways should you *qualify* your claim?

## FOR MULTILINGUAL WRITERS: Using your native language to explore ideas

For generating and exploring ideas — the work of much brainstorming, freewriting, looping, clustering, and questioning — consider using your native language; it may help you come up with good ideas quickly and spontaneously. Later in the process of writing, you can choose the best of these ideas and begin working with them in English.

### 7 Consulting print and electronic sources

At the library, browse for a topic you want to learn more about. If you have a short list of ideas, do a quick check of reference works to get overviews of the topics. You can begin with a general encyclopedia or a specialized reference that focuses on a specific area, such as music or psychology (13b3).

Use search engines such as Google and Yahoo! to explore topics and ideas. Many search engines have directories organized by topic that you can browse and explore (such as the "Issues and Causes" page on Yahoo!). Some advanced searches allow you to search only for visual images, current events, or government sites and to otherwise specify your results.

## 5b Narrowing a topic

After exploring ideas, you may have found a topic that interests you and would also be interesting to your audience. The topic, however, may be too large to be manageable. If this is the case, narrow your topic in order to focus on a more workable idea.

### *Emily Lesk's work on narrowing her topic*

After Emily Lesk had settled on her original topic, American advertising, she narrowed this vast topic by asking herself questions.

| | |
|---|---|
| **TOPIC** | American advertising |
| | *Okay, what do I most want to know about this topic? How powerful is advertising? Could advertising be related to how we define "American"?* |

**FIRST FOCUS ATTEMPT** American advertising and national identity

*Hmm . . . I may be onto something. How about portrayals of women and how they affect U.S. identity? Go back to the idea of choosing a large company that might be linked to American identity: McDonald's? Coca-Cola? Wal-Mart?*

**SECOND FOCUS ATTEMPT** Advertising icons that shape American identity

*Yes, but how many icons are there? LOTS — and I just named a few. Should I go with a company — and symbol — that have been around a long time? Better choose one.*

**NARROWED TOPIC** The Coca-Cola logo and American identity

### EXERCISE 5.1

Choose a topic that interests you, and explore it by using two of the strategies described in 5a. When you have generated some material, you might try comparing your results with those of other members of the class to see how effective or helpful each strategy was. If you have trouble choosing a topic, use one of the preliminary working theses in Exercise 5.2.

## 5c Drafting a working thesis

A thesis states the main idea of a piece of writing. Most kinds of college writing contain a thesis statement, often near the beginning, which functions as a promise to readers, letting them know what the writer will discuss. Though you may not have a final thesis when you begin to write, you should establish a tentative working thesis early on in your writing process. The word *working* is important here because the working thesis may well change as you write. Even so, a working thesis focuses your thinking and research and helps keep you on track.

A working thesis should have two parts: a topic part, which states the topic, and a comment part, which makes an important point about the topic.

TOPIC: **The current health care crisis** COMMENT: **arises from three major causes.**

A successful working thesis has three characteristics:

1. It is potentially *interesting* to the intended audience.
2. It is as *specific* as possible.
3. It limits the topic enough to make it *manageable.*

You can assess a working thesis by checking it against each of these characteristics, as in the following example:

**PRELIMINARY WORKING THESIS**

- **Theories about global warming are being debated around the world.**

| | |
|---|---|
| **INTERESTING?** | The topic itself holds interest, but it seems to have no real comment attached to it. The thesis merely states a bare fact, and the only place to go from here is to more bare facts. |
| **SPECIFIC?** | The thesis is not specific. Who is debating these theories? What is at issue in this debate? |
| **MANAGEABLE?** | The thesis is not manageable; it would require research on global warming in many countries. |
| **ASSESSMENT:** | This thesis can be narrowed by the addition of a stronger comment and a sharper focus, as shown here: |

**REVISED WORKING THESIS**

- **Working independently, scientists from several countries have now confirmed that global warming is demonstrably caused by humans.**

### Emily Lesk's working thesis

Before Emily Lesk had narrowed her topic, she wrote this preliminary working thesis: "Advertising icons shape our national identity." When she analyzed this thesis, however, she realized that it was interesting but neither specific nor manageable: she certainly couldn't investigate every advertising symbol. After doing more exploratory work and talking with her instructor, Emily decided to focus on a single icon, the world-famous Coca-Cola logo. Her revised working thesis became "Coca-Cola is a cultural icon that shapes American identity."

### EXERCISE 5.2

Choose one of the following preliminary working theses, and after specifying an audience, evaluate the thesis in terms of its interest, specificity, and manageability. Revise the working thesis as necessary to meet these criteria.

1. Homeland security presents the United States with an ongoing problem.
2. Abortion is a right.

**FOR MULTILINGUAL WRITERS: Stating a thesis explicitly**

In some cultures, stating the main point explicitly may be considered rude or inelegant. In U.S. academic and business practices, however, readers often expect the writer to make key points and positions explicit. Unless your main point is highly controversial or hard for the reader to accept (such as a rejection letter), state your main point early — before presenting the supporting details.

3. Othello is a complex character whose greatest strength is, ironically, also his greatest weakness.
4. White-collar crime poses greater danger to the economy than street crime, even though the latter is more obvious.
5. An educated public is the key to a successful democracy.

### EXERCISE 5.3

Using the topic you chose in Exercise 5.1, write a preliminary working thesis. Evaluate the thesis in terms of its interest, specificity, and manageability. Revise it as necessary to create a satisfactory working thesis.

## 5d Gathering information

Writing often calls for research. An assignment may specify that you conduct research on your topic and cite your sources. Or you may find that you don't know enough about your topic to write about it effectively without doing research. Sometimes you need to do research at various stages of your writing process — early on, to help you understand or define your topic, and later on, to find additional examples and illustrations to support your thesis. Once you have developed a working thesis, consider what additional information you might need.

Basically, you can do three kinds of research to support your thesis: library research, which includes books, periodicals, and databases; online research, which gives you access to texts, visuals, and people on the Internet; and field research, which includes personal observation, interviews, surveys, and other means of gathering information directly. (For more information on conducting research, see Chapter 13.)

## 5e Organizing verbal and visual information

While you're finding information on your topic, think about how you will group or organize that information to make it accessible and persuasive to readers. At the simplest level, writers most often group information in their writing projects according to four principles — space, time, logic, and association.

Whichever of these principles you use to begin organizing an essay or project, take special care in planning for the inclusion of visuals.

- Choose visuals that are closely related to your topic. Visuals shouldn't be just window dressing.
- Consider using visuals when you want to capture readers' attention and interest in a vivid way; emphasize a point you have already made in your text; present information that is difficult to convey in words; or communicate with audiences with different language skills and abilities.
- Plan to place each visual as near as possible to the text it illustrates.
- Remember that, for your final draft, you need to introduce each visual clearly: *As the map to the right depicts. . . .*
- In addition, comment on the significance or effect of the visual: *Figure 1 corroborates the claim made by geneticists: while the human genome may be mapped, it is far from understood.*
- Finally, label each visual appropriately, and cite the source.

### 1 Spatial organization

Organizing according to space directs readers' attention to where the various elements of something appear in physical space. Spatial organization allows the reader to "see" your information and to take a "tour" beginning at one point and moving around in an organized manner — say, from near to far, left to right, or top to bottom. It can be especially useful in description. You might include a map or another graphic that would help readers visualize your description. The example that follows organizes information according to space:

**INFORMATION ORGANIZED SPATIALLY**

I entered the forest cautiously, feeling as if many eyes were watching me. On my left loomed a fairy circle of giant redwoods, the ground below them soft with their needles. On my right, a Douglas fir stood straight and tall. And ahead of me, on the narrow path, I could see small animals scampering back and forth.

## 2 Chronological (time) organization

Organizing according to time means explaining when things happen. You are already familiar with chronological organization, since it is the basic method used in stories, cookbooks, lab reports, and instruction manuals. Writers of such materials group information according to time, putting earliest events first. Chronological order is especially useful in explaining a process, step by step by step, as shown in the following example:

**INFORMATION ORGANIZED CHRONOLOGICALLY**

Heat oil in a skillet over medium heat. Crack four large eggs into a medium bowl. Stir with a whisk. Sprinkle with salt, pepper, parsley, and oregano. Spread egg mixture evenly in pan; top with cheese. Cook until omelet is firm.

## 3 Logical organization

Organizing according to logic means relating pieces of information in ways that make sense. Following is an overview of some of the most commonly used logical patterns: *illustration*, *definition*, *division and classification*, *comparison and contrast*, *cause and effect*, *problem and solution*, *analogy*, and *narration*. The example that follows organizes information logically, according to the principle of division. For other examples of paragraphs organized according to these logical patterns, see 7c1.

**INFORMATION ORGANIZED LOGICALLY**

Burns can be divided into three types or levels: (1) Superficial, or first-degree, burns damage the top layer of skin. They are red and painful. (2) Partial thickness, or second-degree, burns damage the outer layer of skin and the layer just below it. They are very painful and are characterized by blistering, swelling, and redness. (3) Full thickness, or third-degree, burns damage deep tissues. They appear charred and black. The burn area itself is numb, but the surrounding area is very painful.

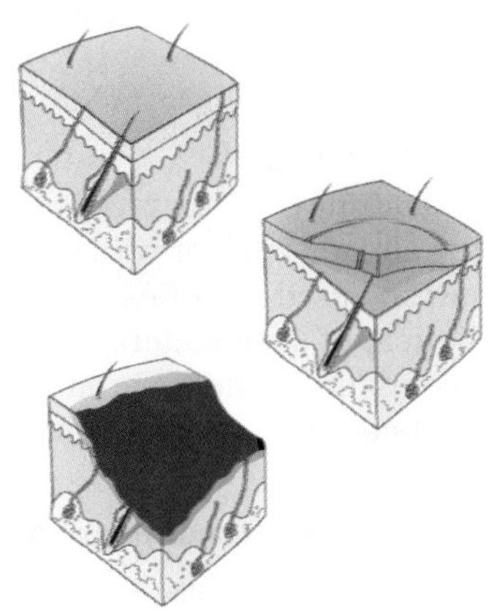

### *Illustration*

You will often gather examples to illustrate a point. An essay discussing how one novelist influenced another might cite a number of examples from the second writer's books that echo themes or characters from the first writer's works. An appeal for donating money to the Red Cross might be organized in a series of examples of how donations are used, along with appropriate illustrations. For maximum effect, arrange your examples and accompanying visuals in order of increasing importance.

### *Definition*

Often a topic can be developed by definition: by saying what something is — or is not — and perhaps by identifying the characteristics that distinguish it from things that are similar or in the same general category.

A magazine article about poverty in the United States, for example, would have to define very carefully what level of income, assets, or other measure defines a person, family, or household as "poor." An essay about Pentecostalism for a religion class might explain what characteristics separate Pentecostalism from related religious movements.

### *Division and classification*

Division means breaking a single topic into separate parts; classification means grouping many separate items of information about a topic according to their similarities. An essay about military recruiting policies might divide the military into different branches — army, navy, air force, and so on — and examine how each recruits volunteers. For a project on women's roles in the eighteenth century, you could organize your notes by classification: information related to women's education, occupations, legal status, and so on.

### *Comparison and contrast*

Comparison focuses on the similarities between two things, whereas contrast highlights their differences, but the two are often used together. If you were asked to analyze two case studies in an advertising text (one on Budweiser ads and the other on ads by Ralph Lauren), you might well organize the response by presenting all the information on Budweiser advertising in one section and all on Ralph Lauren ads in another (block comparison) or by alternating between Budweiser and Ralph Lauren ads as you look at particular characteristics of each (alternating comparison).

### *Cause and effect*

Cause-effect analysis may deal with causes, effects, or both. If you examine why something happens or happened, you are investigating causes. If you explain what has occurred or is likely to occur from a set of conditions, you are discussing effects. An environmental-impact study of the probable consequences of building a proposed dam, for instance, would focus on effects. On the other hand, a newspaper article on the breakdown of authority in inner-city schools might begin with the effects of the breakdown and trace them back to their causes.

### Problem and solution

Moving from a problem to a solution is a natural way to organize certain kinds of information. For example, a student studying motorcycle parking on campus decided to organize his paper in just this way: he identified a problem (the need for more parking) and then offered two possible solutions, along with visuals to help readers imagine the solutions. Many assignments in engineering, business, and economics call for a similar organizational strategy.

### Analogy

An analogy establishes connections between two things or ideas. Analogies are particularly helpful in explaining something new in terms of something very familiar. Likening the human genome to a map, for example, helps explain the complicated concept of the genome to those unfamiliar with it.

### Narration

Narration involves telling a story of some kind. You might, for example, tell the story of how deer ravaged your mother's garden as a way of showing why you support population control measures for wildlife. Narrating calls on the writer to set the story in a context readers can understand, providing any necessary background and descriptive details as well as chronological markers and transitions (*later that day*, *the following morning*, and so on) to guide readers through the story.

## 4 Associational organization

Some writers organize information through a series of associations that grow directly out of their own experiences and memories. In doing so, they may rely on a sensory memory, such as an aroma, a sound, or a scene. Thus, associational organization is common in personal narrative, where writers can use a chain of associations to render an experience vividly for readers. The following example is built on a series of associations:

**INFORMATION ORGANIZED ASSOCIATIONALLY**

Flying from San Francisco to Atlanta, I looked down to see the gentle roll of the Smoky Mountains begin to appear. Almost at once, I was back on Granny's porch, sitting next to her drinking iced tea and eating peaches. Those peaches tasted good — picked ripe, skinned, and eaten with no regard for the sweet juice trickling everywhere. And on special occasions, we'd make ice cream, and Granny would empty a bowl brimming with chopped peaches into the creamy dish. Now — that was the life!

### 5 Combined organizational patterns

In much of your writing, you will want to use two or more principles of organization. You might, for example, combine several passages of narration with vivid examples to make a striking comparison, as one student did in an essay about the dramatic differences between her life in her Zuñi community and her life as a teacher in Seattle. In addition, you may want to include not only visuals but sound and other multimedia effects as well.

### *Emily Lesk's organizational patterns*

Emily Lesk begins the final draft of her essay (p. 106) with what she calls a "confession": *I don't drink Coke.* She follows this opening with an anecdote about a trip to Israel during which she nevertheless bought a T-shirt featuring the Coca-Cola logo. She goes on to explore what lies behind this purchase, relating it to the masterful advertising campaigns of the Coca-Cola Company and illustrating the way that the company's advertising "sells" a certain kind of American identity along with its products. She closes her draft (p. 109) by reflecting on the implications of this relationship between corporate advertising and national identity. Thus her essay, which begins with a personal experience, combines the patterns of narrative with cause-effect and comparison.

## FOR MULTILINGUAL WRITERS: Organizing information

You may know ways of organizing information that differ markedly from those discussed in 5e. A Navajo teacher notes, for example, that explicit linear organization, through chronology or other strictly logical patterns, doesn't ever sound quite right to her. As she puts it, "In traditional Navajo, it's considered rude to get right to the point. Polite conversation or writing between two engaged people always takes a while to get to the point." Although effective organization depends largely on the reader's expectations, it may sometimes make sense to deviate from those expectations. If you choose to organize your writing differently from what your teacher or classmates might expect, consider explaining the reason for your choice — for example, in a cover letter or a footnote.

### EXERCISE 5.4

Using the topic you chose in Exercise 5.1, identify the most effective means of organizing your information. Write a brief paragraph explaining why you chose this particular method (or these methods) of organization.

## 5f Planning

At this point, you will find it helpful to write out an organizational plan or outline. To do so, simply begin with your thesis; review your exploratory notes, research materials, and visual or multimedia sources; and then list all the examples and other good reasons you have to support the thesis.

### *Sample organizational plan*

One informal way to organize your ideas is to figure out what belongs in your introduction, body paragraphs, and conclusion. A student who was writing about solutions to a problem used the following plan:

**WORKING THESIS**

- **Increased motorcycle use demands the reorganization of campus parking lots.**

**INTRODUCTION**

*give background and overview (motorcycle use up dramatically), and use a photograph of overcrowding in a lot*

*state purpose — to fulfill promise of thesis by offering solutions*

**BODY**

*describe the current situation (tell of my research at area parking lots)*

*describe the problem in detail (report on statistics; cars vs. cycles), and include a graph representing findings*

*present two possible solutions (enlarge lots or reallocate space)*

**CONCLUSION**

*recommend against first solution because of cost and space*

*recommend second solution, and summarize benefits of it*

### Formal outline

Even if you have made an informal written plan before drafting, you may wish (or be required) to prepare a more formal outline, which can help you see exactly how the parts of your writing will fit together — how your ideas relate, where you need examples, and what the overall structure of your work will be. Even if your instructor doesn't ask you to make an outline or you prefer to use some other method of sketching out your plans, you may want to come back to an outline later: doing a retrospective outline — one you do after you've already drafted your project — is a great way to see whether you have any big logical gaps or whether parts of the essay are in the wrong place.

It is likely that your word-processing program has an outline feature. (To prepare an outline in Microsoft Word, click on FORMAT, then BULLETS AND NUMBERING, and then OUTLINE NUMBERED.) Most formal outlines follow a conventional format of numbered and lettered headings and subheadings, using roman numerals, capital letters, arabic numerals, and lowercase letters to show the levels of importance of the various ideas and their relationships. Each new level is indented to show its subordination to the preceding level.

Thesis statement

I. First main idea
   A. First subordinate idea
      1. First supporting detail or idea
      2. Second supporting detail or idea
      3. Third supporting detail
   B. Second subordinate idea
      1. First supporting detail or idea
      2. Second supporting detail or idea
II. Second main idea
   A. (continues as above)

Note that each level contains at least two parts, so there is no A without a B, no 1 without a 2. Comparable items are placed on the same level — the level marked by capital letters, for instance, or by arabic numerals. Keep in mind that headings should be stated in parallel form — either all sentences or all grammatically parallel topics.

Formal outlining requires a careful evaluation of your ideas, and this is precisely why it is valuable. (A full-sentence outline will reveal the relationships between ideas — or the lack of relationships — most clearly.) Remember, however, that an outline is at best a means to an end, not an end in itself. Whatever form your plan takes, you may want or need to change it along the way. (For an example of a formal outline, see 17e.)

### EXERCISE 5.5

Write out a plan for an essay supporting the working thesis you developed for Exercise 5.3.

## 5g Drafting

In some sense, drafting begins the moment you start thinking about a topic. At some point, however, you attempt an actual written draft.

### 1 Remaining flexible

No matter how good your planning, investigating, and organizing have been, chances are you will need to return to these activities as you draft. This fact of life leads to the first principle of successful drafting: be flex-

## CONSIDERING DISABILITIES: A talking draft

Using a word processor with voice-recognition software will allow you to speak your ideas, which will then appear onscreen. A "talking" draft of this kind can be a very good way to get your initial draft done, especially if you have difficulty with the physical act of writing. If voice-recognition software isn't available, try to find another student who will work with you to produce talking drafts: as one of you talks, the other types in what is being said. Your school's office of disability services should be able to provide scribes or notetakers as well.

ible. If you see that your organizational plan is not working, do not hesitate to alter it. If some information now seems irrelevant, leave it out, even if you went to great lengths to obtain it. Throughout the drafting process, you may need to refer to points you have already written about. You may learn that you need to do more research, that your whole thesis must be reshaped, or that your topic is still too broad and should be narrowed further.

### 2 Computer drafting

Since it's likely that you will do some or all of your drafting on a computer, take advantage of working with a word processor and using online writing environments, such as email, Web discussion boards, or blogs (see Chapter 22). Here are three ways to manage your drafting:

- *Copy and paste writing from other places.* For example, you may find useful information that you have written for a class discussion list that you can cut and paste into your document. Remember, however, that any material you want to quote from other people's writing on such lists must appear in quotation marks and be cited fully. (See Chapters 15 and 16.)
- *Save and name your files to distinguish among drafts.* Since you will likely change your document over time, you will need to save a copy of each version. If you are sending a copy to classmates for review, give the file a new but related name. For example, for a draft saved as *religion essay 1*, save a copy as *religion essay 2*. Then,

when you receive responses from your classmates, you can leave the copy of your first draft as is and make revisions on *religion essay 2*.

- *Track changes within a file.* Most word processors allow you to track changes you make within a draft — in Word, for example, with the TRACK CHANGES function. This function is useful when you are working on a piece with another writer or when you are working on your own and are not sure which version of a draft you like best. You can take a break from the essay and then come back to it, accepting or rejecting the changes you made earlier.

### *Emily Lesk's computer revision*

Emily Lesk used the TRACK CHANGES function to capture variations so that she could compare them later on. In the following passage, she deleted parts of her early draft (p. 75) and added to a later version, which she ultimately incorporated into her final essay (p. 106).

But while countless campaigns with this general strategy have together shaped the Coca-Cola image, presenting a product as key to a happy life is a fairly typical approach to advertising everything from Allstate insurance to Ziploc bags. Coca-Cola's advertising strategy is unique, however, for the original way the beverage giant has used the specific advertising media of magazines and television to drive home this message. As a result, Coca-Cola has become associated not only with the images of Americana portrayed in specific advertisements but also with the general forms of advertising media that dominate American culture.

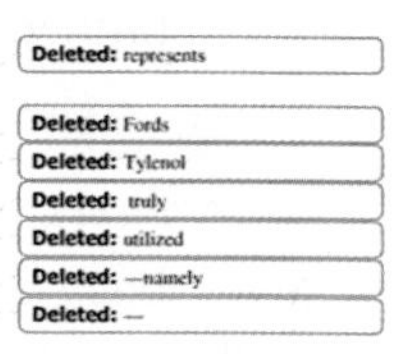


You may feel safer experimenting with different versions if you can still see what you originally wrote.

## 3 Emily Lesk's first draft

Here is Emily Lesk's first draft. She uses brackets and highlighting here to identify questions and sources she will need to cite.

## Guidelines for drafting

- *Set up a computer folder or file for your essay.* Give the file a clear and relevant name, and save to it often.
- *Have all your information close at hand and arranged according to your organizational plan.* Stopping to search for a piece of information can break your concentration or distract you.
- *Keep track of any sources you plan to include.* Keep a working bibliography of sources you are using (14b), and make notes in your draft of any information that comes from your research.
- *Try to write in stretches of at least thirty minutes.* Writing can provide momentum, and once you get going, the task becomes easier.
- *Don't let small questions bog you down.* Just make a note of them in brackets — or in all caps — or make a tentative decision and move on.
- *Remember that first drafts aren't perfect.* Concentrate on getting all your ideas onscreen, and don't worry about anything else.
- *Stop writing at a place where you know exactly what will come next.* Doing so will help you start easily when you return to the draft.

All-Powerful Coke

I don't drink Coke. Call me picky for disliking the soda's saccharine aftertaste. 1
Call me cheap for choosing a water fountain over a twelve-ounce aluminum can that costs a dollar from a vending machine but only pennies to produce. Even call me unpatriotic for rejecting the potable god that over the last century has come to represent all the enjoyment and ease to be found in our American way of life. But don't call me a hypocrite when I admit that I still identify with Coke and the Coca-Cola culture.

I have a favorite T-shirt that says "Drink Coca-Cola Classic" in Hebrew. It's 2
Israel's standard tourist fare, like little nested dolls in Russia or painted horses in Scandinavia, and before setting foot in the Promised Land three years ago, I knew where I could find one. The T-shirt shop in the central block of a Jerusalem shopping center did offer other shirt designs ("Macabee Beer" was a favorite),

but that Coca-Cola shirt was what drew in most of the dollar-carrying tourists. I waited almost twenty minutes for mine, and I watched nearly everyone ahead of me say "the Coke shirt" (and "thanks" in Hebrew).

At the time, I never asked why I wanted the shirt. I do know, though, that 3
the reason I wear it often, despite a hole in the right sleeve, has to do with its power as a conversation piece. Few people notice it without asking something like, "Does that say Coke?" I usually smile and nod. They mumble a compliment and we go our separate ways. But rarely does anyone want to know what language the world's most famous logo is written in. And why should they? Perhaps because Coca-Cola is a cultural icon that shapes American identity.

Throughout the Company's history, marketing strategies have centered on 4
putting Coca-Cola in scenes of the happy, carefree American life we never stop striving for. What 1950's teenage girl wouldn't long to see herself in the soda shop pictured in a Coca-Cola ad appearing in a 1958 issue of *Seventeen* magazine? A clean-cut, handsome man flirts with a pair of smiling girls as they laugh and drink Coca-Colas. And any girls who couldn't put themselves in that perfect, happy scene, could at least buy a Coke for consolation. The malt shop--complete with a soda jerk in a white jacket and paper hat--is a theme that, even today, remains a symbol of Americana. [Use ad? source is *'50s American Magazine Ads* edited by Ikuta.]

But while countless campaigns with this general strategy have together 5
shaped the Coca-Cola image, presenting a product as key to a happy life represents a fairly typical approach to advertising everything from Fords to Tylenol. Coca-Cola's advertising is truly unique, however, for the original way the beverage giant has utilized specific advertising media--namely magazines and television--to drive home this message.

One of the earliest and best known examples of this strategy is artist Haddon 6
Sundblom's masterpiece of Santa Claus. In December 1931, Coca-Cola introduced an advertising campaign featuring Sundblom's depiction of a jolly, Coke-drinking Santa whose face was modeled on Sundblom's own. [Cite "Haddon Sundblom & Coca-Cola" Web site.] [Look for a picture of this original Coke Santa.] But the success of Santa Claus goes far beyond Sundblom's magazine advertisements depicting a warm, happy grandfather figure delighting in an ice cold Coke after a tiring night of delivering presents. The way in which Coca-Cola advertisers presented that inviting image represents Coca-Cola's brilliant manipulation of the medium itself. [Need to cite Pendergrast book here.]

In today's world of CNN, e-journals, and Newsweek.com, it is often easy to 7
forget how pervasive a medium the magazine was prior to the advent of television. Until the late 1950s, American households of diverse backgrounds and geographic

locations subscribed loyally to general subject weeklies and monthlies such as *Life* and the *Saturday Evening Post*. These publications provided the primary source of news, entertainment, and other cultural information to families nationwide. This large and constant group of subscribers enabled Coca-Cola to build a perennial Christmastime advertising campaign that used an extremely limited number of ads ["designs" better word?] [add source], which Americans soon came to look forward to and seek out each holiday season. The marketing strategy was not to capture consumers with a few color drawings, but rather to make them wait eagerly by the mailbox each December so that they could flip through the *Saturday Evening Post* to find the latest scene featuring Santa gulping a Coke. For this strategy to be successful, the advertisements had to be seen by many, but also be just hard enough to come by to be exciting. What better location for this than the December issue of an immensely popular magazine?

There is no denying that this strategy worked brilliantly, as this inviting image 8
of Santa Claus graduated from the pages of the *Saturday Evening Post* to become the central figure of the most celebrated and beloved season of the year. Travel to any strip mall in the United States during December (or even November--that's how much we love Christmas!) and you will no doubt run into Santa clones left and right, punched out of cardboard and sculpted in tinsel hung atop lampposts, all in Coca-Cola red and white. And while, in today's nonmagazine world, Coca-Cola must celebrate Christmas with specially designed diet Coke cans and television commercials, the Coca-Cola Santa Claus will forever epitomize the former power of magazine advertising in America. [Getting off track here?]

In other words, Coca-Cola has hammered itself into our perceptions--both 9
conscious and subconscious--of an American cultural identity by equating itself with media that define American culture. When the omnipresent general magazine that marked the earlier part of the century fell by the wayside under television's power, Coke was there from the beginning. In its 1996 recap of the previous fifty years in industry history, the publication *Beverage Industry* [need to cite] cites Coca-Cola as a frontrunner in the very first form of television advertising: sponsorship of entire programs such as, in the case of Coke, *The Bob Dixon Show* and *The Adventures of Kit Carson*. Just as today we associate sports stadiums with their corporate sponsors, viewers of early television programs will forever equate them with Coke.

When networks switched from offering sponsorships to selling exclusive 10
commercial time in short increments (a format modeled after magazine advertisements), Coca-Cola strove to distinguish itself once again, this time by producing new formats and technologies for these commercials. [This sentence is

way too long!] Early attempts at this--such as choppy "stop motion" animation, where photographs of objects such as Coke bottles move without the intervention of actors--attracted much attention, according to the Library of Congress Motion Picture Archives [need to cite]. Coca-Cola also experimented with color advertisements early enough that the excitement of color advertising technology drew additional attention to these commercials.

But the Coke advertising campaign, that perhaps best illustrates the ability 11
of Coca-Cola advertisers to equate their product with a medium/technology [reword!], did not appear until 1993. Who can forget the completely digitally animated polar bears, that roll, swim, snuggle, slide, and gurgle about, in a computerized South [?] Pole and finish off the playful experience with a swig of Coke? This campaign captured America's attention and held it for six separate commercials, and not because the bears are cute and cuddly. Their main draw--and the reason they remain in our minds--was the groundbreaking technology used to create them. In 1993, two years before the release of *Toy Story*, these were some of the very first widely viewed digital films [cite Library of Congress here]. With these bears, as with other campaigns, Coke didn't just utilize the latest technology--Coke introduced the latest technology.

As a result of this brilliant advertising, a beverage which I do not even let 12
enter my mouth [reword!] is a significant part of my American cultural identity. That's why I spent thirty Israeli shekels and twenty minutes in a tourist trap I would ordinarily avoid buying my Hebrew Coca-Cola shirt. That shirt--along with the rest of the Coca-Cola collectibles industry--demonstrates the power of [something about Coke connecting itself with the American ideal of a life of diversion and lightheartedness]. Seeing the logo that embodies all of this halfway around the world gave me an opportunity to affirm a part of my American identity.

The red-and-white logo's ability to appeal to Americans even in such a 13
foreign context speaks to Coke advertisers' success at creating this association. A 1999 American television commercial described by the Library of Congress archive [need to cite] as highly successful is set in Kenya, with dialogue in a local dialect and English subtitles. In it, two Kenyan boys taste their first Cokes and comment that the experience is much like the way they imagine kissing a girl will be. This image appeals to Americans because it enables us to use the symbol of Coca-Cola to make ourselves comfortable even in the most unfamiliar situations. And if that can't sell your product, nothing can.

(For the works-cited page that Emily Lesk submitted with her final paper, which includes the sources indicated in her notes in this draft, see 6j.)

**bedfordstmartins.com/smhandbook** To see other student drafts, click on **Student Writing.**

### EXERCISE 5.6

Write a draft essay from the plan you produced for Exercise 5.5.

## 5h Your writing process

Once you finish a draft, reflect a bit on your own exploring, planning, and drafting, and make some notes in your writing log if you are keeping one. Jot down what went well, what gave you problems and why, and what you would like to change or improve. You might also use the COMMENT function of your computer to add thoughts about your draft while it is fresh in your mind.

When Emily Lesk reflected in this way, she discovered that brainstorming with her classmates and clustering had been the most fruitful methods for generating ideas and examples and that asking herself questions had helped her narrow her topic. She also recognized that she felt very comfortable with her classmates and her professor (her audience), so writing a first draft felt a lot like talking to them. Wanting to impress an audience she liked, she had worked extra hard to make her essay interesting and clear. The main weaknesses, she decided, were in tone, punctuation, and diction, including some information that got away from her main point. (For a list of questions to use in reviewing your writing process, see 2b.)

### THINKING CRITICALLY ABOUT YOUR WRITING PROCESS

Using the following guidelines, reflect on the process you went through as you prepared for and wrote your draft essay for Exercise 5.6. Make your answers an entry in your writing log if you are keeping one.

1. How did you arrive at your specific topic?
2. When did you first begin to think about the assignment?
3. What kinds of exploring or planning did you do? What kinds of research did you need to do?
4. How long did it take to complete your draft (including the time spent gathering information)?
5. Where did you write your draft? Briefly describe the setting.

6. How did awareness of your audience help shape your draft?
7. What have you learned from your draft about your own rhetorical stance on your topic?
8. What did you learn about your ideas for this topic by exploring, planning, and talking with others about it?
9. What do you see as the major strengths of your draft? What is your favorite sentence, and why?
10. What do you see as the major weaknesses of your draft? What are you most worried about, and why?
11. What would you like to change about your process of exploring, planning, and drafting?

# Reviewing, Revising, and Editing

6

Whether you are writing a wedding invitation, an email to a corporation, or a history essay, make time to get reviews of your work and to revise, edit, and proofread. Reviewing calls for reading your draft with a critical eye and asking others to look over your work. Revising involves reworking your draft on the basis of the review you and others have performed, making sure that the draft is clear and effective and includes all essential information. Editing involves fine-tuning your prose, attending to details of grammar, usage, punctuation, and spelling. Of course, you also need to format and proofread your writing carefully to make it completely ready for public presentation.

## 6a Rereading your draft

The ancient Roman poet Horace advised aspiring writers to get distance from their work by putting it away for nine years. Although impractical, Horace's advice holds a germ of truth: even putting the draft away for a day or two will help clear your mind and give you some objectivity about your writing. After giving yourself — and your draft — a rest, review the draft by rereading it carefully for meaning, recalling your purpose, reconsidering your rhetorical stance, considering your audience, and evaluating your organization and use of visuals.

### 1 Meaning

At this point, don't sweat the small stuff. Instead, concentrate on your message and on whether you have expressed it clearly. Note any places where the meaning seems unclear.

### 2 Purpose

Does your draft achieve its purpose? If you wrote for an assignment, make sure that you have produced what was asked for. If you set out to prove something, make sure you have succeeded. If you intended to propose a solution to a problem, make sure you have set forth a well-supported solution rather than just an analysis of the problem.

## TALKING THE TALK: Revision

"I thought I had revised my assignment, but my instructor said I'd just corrected the typos." It's always a good idea to clarify what *revision* means with a particular instructor. Generally, though, when a writing teacher asks for a revision, minor corrections will not be enough. Plan to review your entire draft, looking first at the big picture — the thesis or overall argument and all the points that support it. After making any necessary changes to improve and strengthen these elements — which can even mean starting over with a very different main idea — examine the structure or organization of your essay to make sure that each paragraph follows logically from the one before and that points are linked with strong transitions. Look for sentence-level errors and typos last, since these may disappear or change as you revise.

### 3 Rhetorical stance

Take time to look at your draft with one central question in mind: where are you coming from in this draft? That is, articulate the rhetorical stance you take, and ask yourself what factors or influences have led you to that position. (For more on rhetorical stance, see 3g.)

### 4 Audience

How appropriate is the essay for your audience? Think carefully about your audience members' experiences and expectations. Will they be interested in and able to follow your discussion? Is the language formal or informal enough for these readers? Have you defined any terms they may not know? What objections might they raise? (For more on audience, see 3h.)

When Emily Lesk reread her draft (5g3), she noticed that she sounded a bit like a know-it-all, especially in the opening of her essay. She decided that her tone was inappropriate, perhaps because she was trying too hard to get her audience's attention, and that she needed to work on this problem in her revision.

#### EXERCISE 6.1

Take twenty to thirty minutes to look critically at the draft you prepared for Exercise 5.6. Reread it carefully, check to see how well the purpose is accomplished, and

consider how appropriate the draft is for the audience. Then write a paragraph about how you would go about revising the draft.

### EXERCISE 6.2

To prepare for a peer review, write a description of your purpose, rhetorical stance, and audience for your reviewer(s) to consider. For example, Emily Lesk might write, "I want to figure out why Coca-Cola seems so American and how the company achieves this effect. My audience is primarily college students like me, learning to analyze their own cultures. I want to sound knowledgeable, and I want this essay to be fun and interesting to read." This type of summary statement can help your reviewers keep your goals in mind as they give you feedback.

### 5 Organization

Look through your draft, paying attention to the way one idea flows into another. Note particularly the first sentence of each new paragraph, and ask yourself how it relates to the paragraph that came before. If you can't immediately see the connection, you probably need to strengthen the transition (see 7e).

Another good way to check your organization is to number the paragraphs in the draft, then read through each one, jotting down the main idea or topic. Do the main ideas clearly relate to the thesis and to each other? Can you identify any confusing leaps from point to point? Have you left out any important points? Does any part of your essay go off track?

### 6 Visuals

Look closely at the visuals you have chosen to use. How do they help support your points and get your ideas across? Make sure that all visuals are clearly labeled with captions and sources, and remember to refer to each visual and comment on its significance in the text. Is there any information in your draft that would be better presented or explained through a visual?

## 6b Peer review

In addition to your own critical appraisal of your draft, you should get responses from friends, classmates, or colleagues you have met in classes or online. If you are part of a peer-review group in your class, use these reviewers to your advantage.

### 1 The role of the peer reviewer

The most helpful reviewers are interested in the topic and the writer's approach to it. They ask questions, make concrete suggestions, report on what is confusing and why, and offer encouragement. Good reviewers give writers a new way to see their drafts so that they can revise effectively. After reading an effective review, writers should feel confident about taking the next step in the writing process.

Peer review is difficult for two reasons. First, offering writers a way to imagine their next draft is just hard work. Unfortunately, there's no formula for giving good writing advice. But you can always do your best to offer your partner a careful, thoughtful response to the draft and a reasonable sketch of what the next version might contain. Second, peer review is challenging because your job as a peer reviewer is not to grade the draft or respond to it as an English instructor would. As a peer reviewer, you will have a chance to think alongside writers whose writing you may consider much better or far worse than your own. Don't dwell on these comparisons. Instead, remember that a thesis is well supported by purposefully arranged details, not by punctuation or impressive vocabulary. Your goal is to read the writer's draft closely enough to hear what he or she is trying to say and to suggest a few strategies for saying it better.

Being a peer reviewer should improve your own writing as you see how other writers approach the same assignment. So make it a point to tell writers what you learned from their drafts; as you express what you learned, you'll be more likely to remember their strategies. Also, you will likely begin reading your own texts in a new way. Although all writers have blind spots when reading their own work, you will gain a better sense of where readers expect cues and elaboration.

#### FOR MULTILINGUAL WRITERS: Understanding peer reviews

If you are not used to giving or receiving criticisms directly, you may find it disturbing when some or most of your classmates take a questioning or even challenging stance toward your work. As long as the questions and suggestions are constructive, however, they are appropriate to peer-review collaboration. Your peers will expect you to join in the critical collaboration, too, so be sure to offer your questions, suggestions, and insights.

## 2 Tools for peer review

Before you get started with your first peer-review assignment, you should become familiar with the tools you can use for responding to a draft. Remember that one of your main goals as a peer reviewer is to help the writer see his or her draft differently. You want to *show* the writer what does and doesn't work about particular aspects of the draft. Visually marking the draft can help the writer know at a glance what revisions the reviewer suggests.

### *Marking up a print draft*

If you are reviewing a hard copy of a draft, write compliments in the left margin and critiques, questions, and suggestions in the right margin. As long as you explain what your symbols mean, you can also use boxes, circles, single and double underlining, highlighting, or other visual annotations to point out patterns to the writer. If an idea is mentioned once in several paragraphs, for example, you can circle those sentences and suggest that the writer use them to form a new paragraph.

### *Marking up a computer draft*

If the draft comes to you as an electronic file, save the document in a peer-review folder under a name you will recognize. It's wise to include the writer's name, the assignment, the number of the draft, and your initials. For example, Ann G. Smith might name the file for the first draft of Javier Jabari's first essay *jabari.essay1.d1.ags.doc*.

You can use the TRACK CHANGES function of your word-processing program to add comments and suggestions and to revise text. If you are working in Microsoft Word, use the REVIEWING toolbar (by selecting TOOLBARS in the VIEW menu). A toolbar similar to the one that follows should appear:

THE REVIEWING TOOLBAR IN MICROSOFT WORD

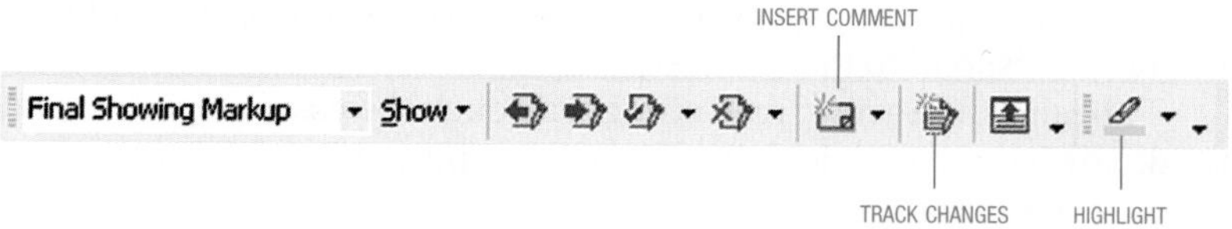

Moving your mouse over the icons will reveal their functions. The critical functions for peer reviewers are TRACK CHANGES, INSERT COMMENT, and HIGHLIGHT.

To review a draft, turn on TRACK CHANGES, which will show your changes to the document in a different color. Insert a comment explaining each revision and suggesting how the writer can build on it in the next draft. The COMMENT function (usually found in the REVIEWING toolbar or the INSERT menu) allows you to type in the margins just as you might write a note in the margins of a printed draft. (If your word processor doesn't have an INSERT COMMENT function, you can use footnotes for comments instead.)

You should also consider using the HIGHLIGHT tool. (If your REVIEWING toolbar does not include the HIGHLIGHT tool, look for it in the FORMATTING toolbar.) If you explain to the writer what the colors mean and use only a few colors, colored highlighting can make a powerful visual statement about what needs to be revised. Here is an example of a key for the writer:

| Color | Revision Suggestion |
|---|---|
| Yellow | Read this sentence aloud, and then revise for clarity. |
| Green | This sentence doesn't fit with the ones around it. Delete or revise it? |
| Blue | This idea isn't clearly connected to your thesis. Cut? |

### 3 The process of peer review

When you respond to a piece of writing, think of the response you are giving — whether orally or in writing — as a letter to the writer of the draft. Your written response should usually have two parts: (1) a personal letter at the end of the draft or on a separate page, and (2) visual markings on the text.

Before you read the draft, ask the writer for any feedback instructions. Take the writer's requests seriously. If, for example, the writer asks you to look at specific aspects of his or her writing and to ignore others, be sure to respond to that request.

To begin your review, read straight through the essay or project and think how you would describe the writer's purpose, audience, stance, thesis, and support.

### *Beginning a letter to the writer*

At the end of the draft, begin your letter by addressing the writer by name (*Dear Javier*). Summarize the main idea(s) of the piece of writing. You might begin your letter by writing *I think the main argument is . . .* or *In this paper, you promise to. . . .* Then outline the main points that support the thesis (5e and f). Once you prepare the outline, your most important work as a peer reviewer can begin. You need to think alongside the writer about how to support the thesis and arrange details most effectively for the audience. Ask yourself the following questions:

- If I heard this topic mentioned in another situation, what would I expect the conversation to include? Would any of those ideas strengthen this paper?
- If I had not read this draft, what order would I expect these ideas to follow?
- Are any ideas or connections missing?

In addition, consult the "Guidelines for peer review" box on p. 91 to generate ideas for your response. Write your suggestions in the letter. You might use sentences like *I didn't understand ______. Could you explain it differently? I think ______ is your strongest point, and I recommend you move ______*. This portion of the letter will help the writer make the most significant changes to the argument and supporting evidence.

### *Marking up the draft*

Next, as you reread the draft, use the mark-up strategies discussed earlier (6b2) to give the writer specific feedback. As you use these strategies, always think about how you would respond to the same markups in your own draft. Avoid an overwhelming number of comments or changes, for example, and don't highlight paragraph after paragraph. In addition, remember that your job in marking up the text is to point out the problems, not to solve them (though you should certainly offer suggestions).

Unlike in the personal letter, where you try to help the writer imagine the next draft, your marginal comments, annotations, and other markings should respond to what is already written. Aim for a balance between compliments and constructive criticism. If you think the author has stated something well, comment on why you like it. If you have trouble understanding or following the writer's ideas, comment on what you

| Compliments | Constructive Criticism |
|---|---|
| • I'd never thought of it that way. Really smart insight.<br>• Your strongest evidence is _______.<br>• You got my attention here by _______.<br>• This example is great because _______.<br>• I like the way you use _______ to tie all these ideas together.<br>• I like this sentence because _______.<br>• I think this approach and your tone is perfect for the audience because _______. | • Here I expected _______ instead of _______.<br>• I think you need more evidence to support your claim that _______.<br>• You might consider adding _______.<br>• What about _______? There are other perspectives on this topic.<br>• I think you need to say this sooner.<br>• I had to read this sentence twice to get what you mean. Simplify it.<br>• Your tone shifts here. Try to sound more _______. |

think may be causing problems. The chart above provides several examples of ways to frame effective marginal comments.

### *Concluding the letter*

After you have added all your mark-ups to the draft, conclude your letter by adding two or three brief paragraphs addressing the following points:

- *The strengths of the current draft.* Refer to the outline you developed and your compliments.
- *Two or three things you think will significantly improve the draft's effectiveness.* Refer to your constructive criticism.
- *Areas on which the writer asked you to focus* (if any).

### FOR MULTILINGUAL WRITERS: Reviewing a draft

Your knowledge of and experience with multiple languages or cultures may give you special insights that help you point out unclear or confusing ideas in your peers' work. Your peers may find questions or comments from your unique perspective helpful in expanding their ideas. Even if you are not used to speaking up in class, remember that you have much to offer!

Read over your comments once more, checking your own tone and clarity. Close by signing your name. Save your response, and send it to the writer using the method recommended by your instructor.

### 4 Responses based on the stage of the draft

You may be asked to review your peers' work at any stage of the writing—after the first draft, during an intermediate stage, or when the paper is close to a final draft. Different stages in the writing process call for different strategies and areas of focus on the part of the peer reviewer.

#### *Responding to early-stage drafts*

Writers of early-stage drafts need direction and options, not editing that focuses on grammar or punctuation. Your goal as a peer reviewer of an early draft is to help the writer think of ways to expand on the ideas. Pose questions and offer examples that will help the writer think of new ways to approach the topic. Try to help the writer imagine what the final draft might be like.

Approach commenting on and marking up an early draft with three types of questions in mind:

- *Fit.* How does this draft fit the assignment? In what areas might the writer struggle to meet the criteria? How does this draft fit the audience? What else does the writer need to remember about the audience's expectations and needs?
- *Potential.* What ideas in this draft are worth developing more? What other ideas or details could inform the argument? Are there other viewpoints on this topic that the writer should explore?
- *Order.* Considering only the parts that are worth keeping, what sequence do you recommend? What new sections do you think need to be added?

#### *Responding to intermediate-stage drafts*

Writers of intermediate-stage drafts need to know where their claims lack sufficient evidence, what ideas confuse readers, and how their approach misses its target audience. They also need to know which parts of their drafts are clear and well written.

Approach commenting on and marking up an intermediate draft with these types of questions in mind:

- *Topic sentences and transitions.* Topic sentences introduce the idea of a paragraph, and transitions move the writing smoothly from one paragraph or section or idea to the next (7b, d, and e). How well does the draft prepare readers for the next set of ideas by explaining how they relate to the overall claim? Look for ideas or details that don't seem to fit into the overall structure. Is the idea or detail out of place because it is not well integrated into this paragraph? If so, recommend a revision or a new transition. Is it out of place because it doesn't support the overall claim? If so, recommend deletion.
- *Supporting details.* Well-developed paragraphs and arguments depend on supporting details (7c). Does the writer include an appropriate number and variety of details? Could the paragraph be improved by adding another example, a definition, a comparison or contrast, a cause-effect relationship, an analogy, a solution to a problem, or a personal narrative?

#### Responding to late-stage drafts

Writers of late-stage drafts need help with first and last impressions, sentence construction, word choice, tone, and format. Their next step is proofreading (6j), and your job as a peer reviewer is to call attention to the sorts of problems writers need to solve before submitting their final work. Your comments and markings should identify the overall strengths of the draft as well as one or two weaknesses that the writer can reasonably improve in a short amount of time.

### 5 Getting the most from reviewers' comments

Remember that your reviewers should be acting as coaches, not judges, and that their job is to help you improve your essay as much as possible. Listen to and read their comments carefully. If you don't understand a particular suggestion, ask for clarification, examples, and so on. Remember, too, that reviewers are commenting on your writing, not on *you*, so be open and responsive to what they recommend. But you are the final authority on your essay; you will decide which suggestions to follow and which to disregard.

## Guidelines for peer review

1. *Overall thoughts.* What are the main strengths and weaknesses of the draft? What might be confusing to readers? What is the single most important thing the writer says in the draft? What will readers want to know more about?
2. *Assignment.* Does the draft carry out the assignment? (6a2)
3. *Title and introduction.* Does the title tell readers what the draft is about? How does it catch their interest? Does the opening make readers want to continue? How else might the draft begin? (6f1 and f2)
4. *Thesis and purpose.* Paraphrase the thesis as a promise: *In this paper, the writer will. . . .* Does the draft fulfill that promise? Why, or why not? Does it carry out the writer's purposes? (6a2 and 6c)
5. *Audience.* How does the draft interest and appeal to its intended audience? (6a4)
6. *Rhetorical stance.* Where does the writer stand? What words or phrases indicate the stance? What influences have likely contributed to that stance? (6a3)
7. *Major points.* List the main points, and review them one by one. Do any points need to be explained more or less fully? Do any seem confusing or boring? Should any points be eliminated or added? How well is each major point supported? (6c)
8. *Visuals.* Do the visuals, if any, add to the key points? Are they clearly referred to in the draft? Are they appropriately labeled? (6a6 and 6e)
9. *Organization and flow.* Is the writing easy to follow? Are the ideas presented in an order that will make sense to readers? Do effective transitions ease the flow between paragraphs and ideas? (6a5 and 6d)
10. *Paragraphs.* Which paragraphs are clearest and most interesting? Which paragraphs need further development, and how might they be improved? (6g1)
11. *Sentences.* Are any sentences particularly effective and well written? Are any sentences weak — confusing, awkward, or uninspired? Are the sentences varied in length and structure? Are the sentence openings varied? (6g2)

*(continued on p. 92)*

*(continued from p. 91)*

12. *Words.* Mark words that draw vivid pictures or provoke strong responses; then mark words that are weak, vague, or unclear. Do any words need to be defined? Are the verbs active and vivid? Are any words potentially offensive? (6g3)
13. *Tone.* What dominant impression does the draft create — serious, humorous, persuasive, something else? Where, specifically, does the writer's attitude come through most clearly? Is the tone appropriate to the topic and the audience? Is it consistent throughout? (6g4)
14. *Conclusion.* Does the draft conclude in a memorable way, or does it seem to end abruptly or trail off into vagueness? How else might it end? (6f3)

You should approach peer reviewers' comments in several stages. First, read straight through everything each reviewer has written. Take a few minutes to digest this feedback and get some distance from your work (6a). Then make a revision plan — as elaborate or simple as you want — that prioritizes the changes needed in your next draft. You might begin by making two lists: (1) areas in which reviewers agree on needed changes and (2) areas in which they disagree. You will then have to make choices about which advice to heed and which to ignore from both lists. Next, rank the suggestions you've chosen to address. Focus on your purpose, audience, stance, thesis, and support. Leave any changes to sentences, words, punctuation, and format for later in the process.

You are now ready to prepare a file for your new draft. If you received a marked-up file from a reviewer as an attachment, you can use that file as the starting point for your next draft, renaming it to indicate that it is your new draft. (For example, Javier Jabari might rename the file *jabari.essay1.d2.doc*, using his name, the assignment, and the number of the draft.) If you did not receive comments as an attachment, you can use your original file as a starting point for your next draft.

In the new file, make the changes you identified in your revision plan. Once you are satisfied that your revisions adequately address major concerns, make corrections to sentences, words, and punctuation. If your file contains a peer reviewer's mark-ups, use the arrows in

the REVIEWING toolbar to move through his or her comments, changes, and highlighting.

You can accept or reject changes by clicking the ACCEPT CHANGE or REJECT CHANGE icon. However, do not click ACCEPT ALL CHANGES IN DOCUMENT before you have reviewed every change. Remove any comments you no longer need by clicking the DELETE COMMENT icon.

THE REVIEWING TOOLBAR IN MICROSOFT WORD

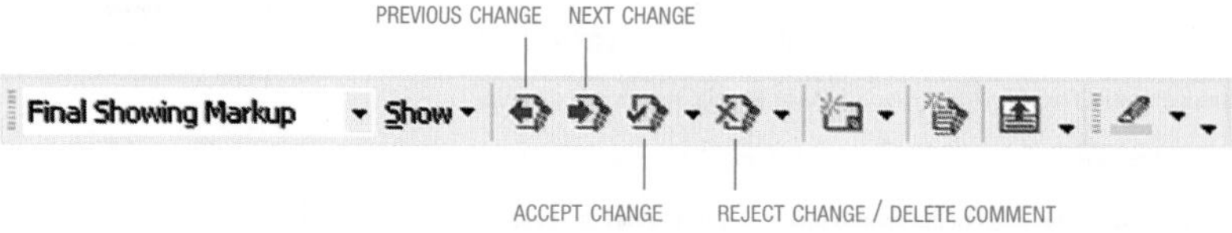


## FOR MULTILINGUAL WRITERS: Asking an experienced writer to review your draft

One good way to make sure that your writing is easy to follow is to have someone else read it. You might find it especially helpful to ask someone who is experienced in the kind of writing you are working on to read over your draft and to point out any words or patterns that are unclear or ineffective.

### 6 Reviews of Emily Lesk's draft

On the following page are the first three paragraphs of Emily Lesk's draft, as reviewed by two students, Beatrice Kim and Nastassia Lopez. Beatrice and Nastassia reviewed the draft separately and combined their comments on the draft they returned to Emily. They also decided to use highlighting for particular purposes: green for material they found particularly effective, yellow for language that seemed unclear, blue for material that could be expanded or made more detailed, and gray for material that could be deleted.

As this review shows, Nastassia and Bea agree on some of the major problems — and good points — in Emily's draft. The comments on the draft, however, reveal their different responses. You, too, will find that

All-Powerful Coke

I don't drink Coke. Call me picky for disliking the soda's saccharine aftertaste. Call me cheap for choosing a water fountain over a twelve-ounce aluminum can that costs a dollar from a vending machine but only pennies to produce. Even call me unpatriotic for rejecting the potable god that over the last century has come to represent all the enjoyment and ease to be found in our American way of life. But don't call me a hypocrite when I admit that I still identify with Coke and the Coca-Cola culture.

I have a favorite T-shirt that says "Drink Coca-Cola Classic" in Hebrew. It's Israel's standard tourist fare, like little nested dolls in Russia or painted horses in Scandinavia, and before setting foot in the Promised Land three years ago, I knew where I could find one. The T-shirt shop in the central block of a Jerusalem shopping center did offer other shirt designs ("Macabee Beer" was a favorite), but that Coca-Cola shirt was what drew in most of the dollar-carrying tourists. I waited almost twenty minutes for mine, and I watched nearly everyone ahead of me say "the Coke shirt" (and "thanks" in Hebrew).

At the time, I never asked why I wanted the shirt. I do know, though, that the reason I wear it often, despite a hole in the right sleeve, has to do with its power as a conversation piece. Few people notice it without asking something like, "Does that say Coke?" I usually smile and nod. They mumble a compliment and we go our separate ways. But rarely does anyone want to know what language the world's most famous logo is written in. And why should they? Perhaps because Coca-Cola is a cultural icon that shapes American identity.

**Comment:** I'm not sure your title says enough about what your essay will argue. NL

**Comment:** This opening sentence is a good attention-getter. Wonder what will come next? NL

**Comment:** The beginning seems pretty abrupt. BK

**Comment:** What does this mean?? Will other members of your audience know? BK

**Comment:** The style of repeating the phrase "call me" is good, but I don't think the first three "call me" statements have much to do with the rest of the paper. NL

**Comment:** It would be cool to show this. BK

**Comment:** Not sure you need all these details. Is any of it going to be important later? BK

**Comment:** one of what? a doll or horse? NL

**Comment:** Say it in Hebrew? BK

**Comment:** This transition works really well. I wasn't sure before about where this was going, but the beginning of the paragraph here starts to clue me in. NL

**Comment:** good detail! Lots of people can relate to a "conversation piece" shirt. NL

**Comment:** I like the question—but is your next sentence really the answer? NL

**Comment:** Is this the thesis? Kind of comes out of nowhere. BK

different readers do not always agree on what is effective or ineffective. In addition, you may find that you simply do not agree with their advice. In examining responses to your writing, you can often proceed efficiently by looking first for areas of agreement (*everyone was confused by this sentence — I'd better revise it*) or strong disagreement (*one person said my conclusion was "perfect," and someone else said it "didn't conclude" — better look carefully at that paragraph again*).

Here is the email message Emily's two peer-review partners wrote to her, giving her some overall comments to accompany those they had written in the margins of her draft:

To: Emily Lesk
From: Beatrice Kim
Subject: Your draft
Attachments: Lesk.essay1.d2.bk_nl.doc

Hi Emily:

We're attaching your draft as a Word document. Good luck on revising!

First, we think this is a great draft. You got us interested right away with the story about your T-shirt and we just wanted to keep on reading. So the introduction seems really good. But the introduction goes on for a while — several paragraphs, we think, and we were beginning to wonder what your point was and when you were going to get to it. And when you get to your thesis, could you make it a little more specific or say a little more about what it means that Coca-Cola is an icon that shapes identity? This last idea wasn't clear to us.

Your stance, though, is very clear, and we liked that you talked about how you were pulled into the whole Coke thing even though you don't particularly like the soda. Sometimes we got bogged down in a ton of details, though, and felt like maybe you were telling us too much.

We were impressed with some of the words you use — we had to look up what a "potable" god is! But sometimes we weren't sure a word was the very best one — we marked some of these words on your draft for you.

See you in class.

Nastassia and Bea

P.S. Could you add a picture of your T-shirt? It would be cool to see what it looks like.

Emily also got advice from her instructor, who suggested that Emily do a careful outline of this draft to check for how one point led to another and to see if the draft stayed on track.

Based on her own review of her work as well as all of the responses she received, Emily decided to (1) make her thesis more explicit, (2) delete some extraneous information and examples, (3) integrate at least one more visual into her text, and (4) work especially hard on the tone and length of her introduction and on word choice.

### EXERCISE 6.3

Using the questions on p. 91 as a guide, analyze the draft you wrote for Exercise 5.6.

## 6c Thesis and support

Once you have sufficient advice on your draft and have studied all the responses, reread the draft once more, paying special attention to your thesis and its support. Make sure your thesis sentence contains a clear statement of the topic and a comment explaining what is particularly significant or noteworthy about the topic (5c). As you read, ask yourself how each paragraph relates to or supports the thesis and how each sentence develops the paragraph topic. Such careful rereading can help you eliminate irrelevant material and identify sections needing further details or examples.

Be particularly careful to note what kinds of evidence, examples, or good reasons you offer in support of your major points. If some points are off topic, look back at your exploratory work (5a). Emily Lesk found, for example, that an entire paragraph in her draft (paragraph 8) did nothing to support her thesis. Thus she deleted the entire paragraph.

### EXERCISE 6.4

After rereading the draft you wrote for Exercise 5.6, evaluate the revised working thesis you produced for Exercise 5.3. Then evaluate its support in the draft. Identify points that need further support, and list those things you must do to provide that support.

**bedfordstmartins.com/smhandbook** For an instructor's response to another student's draft, click on **Student Writing**.

## 6d Organization

One good way to check the organization of a draft is to outline it. After numbering the paragraphs in the draft, read through each one, jotting down its main idea or topic. Then examine your outline, and ask yourself the following questions:

- What overall organizational strategies do you use? spatial? chronological? logical? associational?

- Do the main points clearly relate to the thesis and to one another? Are any of them irrelevant? Should any sections or paragraphs be moved to another part of the draft?
- Can you identify any confusing leaps from point to point? Do you need to provide additional or stronger transitions?
- Do you leave out any important points?

## 6e Visuals

As you check what you've written about your topic, you also need to take a close look at any visuals you have used — and consider whether any need to be added or deleted. Here are some questions to guide you:

- Do the visuals help you make a point?
- Are your visuals clearly labeled and their sources given?
- Do you introduce each visual carefully in the text and comment on its significance?
- Is there any information in your draft that would be better presented as a visual?

### *Emily Lesk's visuals*

When Emily Lesk looked at her draft, she saw a note to herself in paragraph 4 about showing an early Coke ad and another note in paragraph 6 saying, "Look for a picture of this original Coke Santa." Since she was going to post the final draft of her essay on a class Web site that was available to the public, her instructor told her that she would need to obtain permission for these images. When she wrote to the owners of the copyright, however, she learned that she would have to pay a large fee to use the ad and the Santa picture. As a result, she was forced to find other images. Her mother had a button depicting one of Sundblom's Santas, so Emily took a photograph of the button to use in her paper. Emily's peer reviewers had suggested that she include a photo of her Coca-Cola T-shirt, so she took a photo of that as well. Next, she began thinking about how she would integrate these illustrations into her text.

## 6f Title, introduction, and conclusion

Readers remember the first and last parts of a piece of writing better than anything else. For this reason, it is wise to pay careful attention to three important elements — the title, the introduction, and the conclusion.

## 1 Title

A good title gives readers information, draws them into the piece of writing, and may even indicate the writer's view of the topic. The title of Emily Lesk's draft, "All-Powerful Coke," did not provide the link Emily wanted to establish between Coca-Cola and American identity. During the review process, she titled her new draft "Red, White, and Everywhere." This title piques readers' curiosity and suggests that the familiar "red, white, and blue" would be linked to something that is everywhere.

## 2 Introduction

A good introduction accomplishes two important tasks: first, it attracts readers' interest, and, second, it presents the topic and makes some comment on it. It contains, in other words, a strong lead, or hook, and often an explicit thesis as well. Many introductions open with a general statement about the topic and then go into more detail, leading up to a specific thesis at the end. A writer can also begin an introduction effectively with a vivid statement of the problem that led to the thesis or with an intriguing quotation, an anecdote, a question, or a strong opinion. The rest of the introduction then moves from this beginning to a presentation of the topic and the thesis. (For more on introductions, see 7f1.)

In many cases, especially when a writer begins with a quotation or an anecdote, the introduction consists of two or three paragraphs: the first provides the hook, while the next paragraph or two explain the significance of the hook. Emily Lesk used this pattern in her introduction. Her first paragraph contains such a hook, which is followed by a two-paragraph narrative anecdote about a trip to Israel that links Coca-Cola advertising and Americans' sense of identifying with the product. After considering the responses of her peers and analyzing her opening, Emily decided that the introduction took too long to get to the point and that it didn't lead to a clearly articulated thesis. She decided to shorten the introduction and to make her thesis more explicit and detailed.

## 3 Conclusion

A good conclusion leaves readers satisfied that a full discussion has taken place. Many conclusions begin with a restatement of the thesis and end with more general statements that grow out of it: this pattern reverses the common general-to-specific pattern of the introduction. Writers also use other approaches to conclude effectively, including a provocative question, a quotation, a vivid image, a call for action, or a warning.

Emily Lesk's draft two-paragraph conclusion emphasizes the main point of her essay, that the Coke logo now represents America, but it then goes on to discuss the impact of such advertising in other countries, such as Kenya. On reflection, however, Emily decided to cut the paragraph on Kenya because it didn't really draw her essay to a close but rather went off in a different direction. (For more on conclusions, see 7f2.)

**EXERCISE 6.5**

Review Emily Lesk's draft (5g3), and compose an alternative conclusion. Then write a paragraph commenting on the strengths and weaknesses of the two conclusions.

## 6g Paragraphs, sentences, words, and tone

In addition to examining the larger issues of logic, organization, and development, effective writers look closely at the smaller elements: paragraphs, sentences, and words. Many writers, in fact, look forward to this part of revising and editing because its results are often dramatic. Turning a weak paragraph into a memorable one — or finding exactly the right word to express a thought — can yield great satisfaction and self-confidence.

### 1 Paragraphs

Paragraphing serves the reader by visually breaking up long expanses of writing and signaling a shift in focus. Readers expect a paragraph to develop an idea, a process that usually requires several sentences or more. These guidelines can help you revise your paragraphs:

- Look for the topic or main point of each paragraph, whether it is stated or implied. Does every sentence expand, support, or otherwise relate to the topic?
- Check to see how each paragraph is organized — spatially, chronologically, associationally, or by some logical relationship (5e). Is this organization appropriate to the topic of the paragraph?
- Note any paragraphs that have only a few sentences. Do these paragraphs sufficiently develop the topic of the paragraph?

For additional guidelines on editing paragraphs, see p. 137.

Paragraph 5 in Emily Lesk's draft (5g3) contains only two sentences, and they don't lead directly into the next paragraph. In her revision, Emily lengthened (and strengthened) paragraph 5 by adding a sentence that points out the result of Coca-Cola's advertising campaign. (For information on how Emily enlivened her language in this paragraph, see p. 103.)

But while countless campaigns with this general strategy have together shaped the Coca-Cola image, presenting a product as key to a happy life represents a fairly typical approach to advertising everything from Fords to Tylenol. Coca-Cola's advertising is unique, however, for the original way the beverage giant has utilized specific advertising media--namely magazines and television--to drive home this message. <u>As a result, Coca-Cola has come to be associated not only with the images of Americana portrayed in specific advertisements but also with the general forms of advertising media that dominate American culture.</u>

### EXERCISE 6.6

Choose two other paragraphs in Emily Lesk's draft in 5g3, and evaluate them using the guidelines on pp. 91–92. Write a brief paragraph suggesting ways to improve the development or organization of these paragraphs.

## 2 Sentences

As with life, variety is the spice of sentences. You can add variety to your sentences by looking closely at their length, opening patterns, and structure. (See the guidelines for editing sentences in Chapter 44.)

### *Varying sentence length*

Too many short sentences, especially one after another, can sound like a series of blasts on a car horn, whereas a steady stream of long sentences may tire or confuse readers. Most writers aim for some variety of length.

In looking at draft paragraph 9, Emily Lesk found that the sentences were all fairly long, from twenty-two to fifty words. In revising, she

### CONSIDERING DISABILITIES: Technology for revising

Many students with dyslexia and other language-processing disabilities can benefit from the use of assistive technologies. Today, reading and writing software offers active spell checking, word-predictor functions, audio and visual options, and help with mechanics, punctuation, and formatting. You may want to make these technologies a regular part of your revising process.

decided to shorten the second sentence, thereby inserting a short, easy-to-read sentence between two long sentences.

This is just one example of the media strategies Coca-Cola has used to encourage us to equate Coke with the "happy life" element of American identity. As the omnipresent magazine gave way to television, Coke was there from the beginning. In its 1996 recap of the previous fifty years in industry history, the publication *Beverage Industry* cites Coca-Cola as a front runner in the very fast form of television advertising: sponsorship of entire programs such as, in the case of Coke, *The Bob Dixon Show* and *The Adventures of Kit Carson*. Just as we now associate sports stadiums with their corporate sponsors, viewers of early television programs will forever equate them with Coke.

**Deleted:** In other words, Coca-Cola has hammered itself into our perceptions--both conscious and subconscious--of an American cultural identity by equating itself with media that define American culture.

**Deleted:** When

**Deleted:** general

**Deleted:** that marked the earlier part of the century fell by the wayside under television's power.

## *Varying sentence openings*

Most sentences in English follow subject-predicate order and hence open with the subject of an independent clause, as does the sentence you are now reading. But opening sentence after sentence this way results in a jerky, abrupt, or choppy rhythm. You can vary sentence openings by beginning with a dependent clause, a phrase, an adverb, a conjunctive adverb, or a coordinating conjunction (44b).

Emily Lesk's second paragraph tells the story of how she got her Coke T-shirt in Israel. Before she revised, every sentence in this paragraph opened with the subject. Emily deleted some examples and varied her sentence openings for a dramatic and easy-to-read paragraph.

Even before setting foot in the Promised Land three years ago, I knew exactly where I could find the Coke T-shirt. The tiny shop in the central block of Jerusalem's Ben Yehuda Street did offer other shirt designs, but the one with the bright white "Drink Coca-Cola Classic" written in Hebrew cursive across the chest was what drew in most of the dollar-carrying tourists. While waiting almost twenty minutes for my shirt, I watched nearly everyone ahead of me say "the Coke shirt, *todah rabah* [thank you very much]."

**Deleted:** I have a favorite T-shirt that says "Drink Coca-Cola Classic" in Hebrew. It's Israel's standard tourist fare, like little nested dolls in Russia or painted horses in Scandinavia, and

**Deleted:** one

**Deleted:** T-shirt

**Deleted:** a

**Deleted:** shopping center

**Deleted:** ("Macabee Beer" was a favorite).

**Deleted:** that Coca-Cola shirt

**Deleted:** I

**Deleted:** ed

**Deleted:** ine

**Deleted:** and

**Deleted:** "

**Deleted:** (and "thanks" in Hebrew).

### *Checking for sentences opening with* it *and* there

As you go over the sentences of your draft, look especially at those beginning with *it* or *there*. Sometimes these words can create a special emphasis, as in "It was a dark and stormy night." But they can also cause problems. A reader doesn't know what *it* means, for instance, unless the writer has already pointed out exactly what the word stands for. A more subtle problem with these openings, however, is that they may allow a writer to avoid taking responsibility for a statement:

The chancellor believes
**~~It is believed~~ that fees must increase next semester.**
^

The original sentence avoids responsibility by failing to tell us who believes that fees must increase.

### *Varying sentence structure*

Using only simple sentences can be very dull, but overusing compound sentences may result in a singsong or repetitive rhythm. At the same time, strings of complex sentences may sound, well, overly complex. Try to vary your sentence structure (see Chapter 44).

#### EXERCISE 6.7

Find a paragraph in your own writing that lacks variety in sentence length, sentence openings, or sentence structure. Then write a revised version.

## 3 Words

Even more than paragraphs and sentences, word choice — or diction — offers writers an opportunity to put their personal stamp on a piece of writing (see Chapter 29). The following questions will help you become aware of the kinds of words you use:

- Do you use too many abstract and general nouns rather than concrete and specific ones? Saying that you bought a new car is much less memorable than saying you bought a new convertible or a new Volkswagen Bug (29c).
- Are there too many nouns in relation to the number of verbs? The *effect* of the *overuse* of *nouns* in *writing* is the *placing* of too much *strain* on the inadequate *number* of *verbs* and the resultant *prevention* of *movement* of the *thought*. In the preceding sentence, the verb *is* carries the entire weight of all those nouns (in italics). The result is

a heavy, boring sentence. Why not say instead, *Overusing nouns places a big strain on the verbs and slows down the prose*?

- How many verbs are forms of *be* — *be, am, is, are, was, were, being, been*? If *be* verbs account for more than about a third of your total verbs, you are probably overusing them. (See 31b1 and Chapter 32.)
- Are most of your verbs *active* rather than passive? Although the passive voice has many uses (32g), your writing will generally be stronger and more energetic if you use active verbs.
- Are your words *appropriate*? Check to be sure they are not too fancy — or too casual. (See 29a.)

Emily Lesk made a number of changes in word choice. In the second paragraph, she decided to change *Promised Land* to *Israel* since some of her readers might not regard these two as synonymous. She also made her diction more lively, changing *from Fords to Tylenol* in paragraph 5 to *from Allstate insurance to Ziploc bags* to take advantage of the A-to-Z reference.

### 4 Tone

Word choice is closely related to tone, the attitude that a writer's language carries toward the topic and the audience. In examining the tone of your draft, think about the nature of the topic, your own attitude toward it, and that of your intended audience. Check for connotations of words as well as for slang, jargon, emotional language, and your level of formality. Does your language create the tone you want to achieve (humorous, serious, impassioned, and so on)? Is that tone appropriate, given your audience and topic? (For more on creating an appropriate tone through word choice, see Chapter 29.)

Although Emily Lesk's peer reviewers liked the overall tone of her essay, one reviewer had found her opening sentence abrupt. To make her tone friendlier, she decided to preface *I don't drink Coke* with another clause, resulting in *America, I have a confession to make: I don't drink Coke.* Emily also shortened her first paragraph considerably, in part to eliminate the know-it-all attitude she herself had detected.

## 6h Document design

Before you produce a copy for final editing and proofreading, reconsider issues of format and the "look" you want your document to have. You might insert headings in a larger size type or in bold type, for instance, or consider using a different font for examples. You can also improve the design of charts or other illustrations, and perhaps you have the option of presenting your work as a Web text. Whatever your final decisions, now is the time to think carefully about the overall visual appearance of your final draft. (For more on document design, see Chapters 23 and 24.)

## 6i Final editing

Because readers expect a final copy that is clean and correct in every way, you need to make time for careful final editing — checking your use of grammar, punctuation, mechanics, and spelling. If you have not run your spell checker yet, do so now, and check every word the spell checker flags. Remember, however, that spell checkers are limited and that relying too heavily on them can introduce new errors (see 30e1).

To improve your editing of future assignments, keep a personal checklist of the patterns of editing problems you find. Here again, your computer can help: if you notice that you often misuse a certain word, use the FIND function to locate instances of that word, and then check the usage carefully.

### *An editing checklist*

To begin a checklist, jot down all the errors or corrections marked on the last piece of writing you did. Then note the context in which each error appeared, and indicate what you should look for in the future. You can add to this inventory every time you write and edit a draft. Here is an example of one student's checklist:

| ERRORS MARKED | IN CONTEXT | I NEED TO LOOK AT |
|---|---|---|
| fragment | starts with *when* | sentences beginning with *when* |
| missing comma | after *however* | sentences that include *however* |
| missing apostrophe | *company's* | all possessive nouns |
| tense shift | *go* for *went* | my use of the present tense |
| wrong word | *defiantly* for *definitely* | a good dictionary |
| incomplete documentation | no page number | the guidelines for documenting sources |

This writer has begun to isolate patterns, such as her tendency to accept the spell checker's suggestions too readily.

## EXERCISE 6.8

Using several essays you have written, establish your own editing checklist.

## EXERCISE 6.9

Using the guidelines in 6a–g, reread the draft you wrote for Exercise 5.6 with an eye for revising. Try to do this at least one day after you completed the draft. List the things you need or want to address in your revision. At this point, you may want to exchange drafts with one or two classmates and share responses.

# 6j Proofreading the final draft

Take time for one last, careful proofreading, which means reading to correct any typographical errors or other slips, such as inconsistencies in spelling and punctuation. Remember that running the spell checker, while necessary, is *not* the equivalent of thorough proofreading. To proofread most effectively, read through the copy aloud, making sure that you have used punctuation marks correctly and consistently, that all sentences are complete, and that no words are missing. Then go through the copy again, this time reading backward so that you can focus on each word and its spelling.

Student Writer

Emily Lesk

You have already seen and read about a number of the revisions Emily Lesk made to her first draft. On the following pages is the edited and proofread version she turned in to her instructor. If you compare her final draft with her first draft (5g3), you will notice a number of additional changes she made in editing and proofreading. What corrections and improvements can you spot?

## EXERCISE 6.10

Revise, edit, and proofread the draft you wrote for Exercise 5.6.

**bedfordstmartins.com/smhandbook** To see other student writing, click on **Student Writing**.

Emily Lesk
Professor Arraéz
Electric Rhetoric
November 15, 2006

Red, White, and Everywhere

America, I have a confession to make: I don't drink Coke. But don't call me a 1
hypocrite just because I am still the proud owner of a bright red shirt that advertises it. Just call me an American.

Even before setting foot in Israel three years ago, I knew exactly where I 2
could find the Coke T-shirt. The tiny shop in the central block of Jerusalem's Ben Yehuda Street did offer other designs, but the one with a bright white "Drink Coca-Cola Classic" written in Hebrew cursive across the chest was what drew in most of the dollar-carrying tourists. While waiting almost twenty minutes for my shirt (depicted in Fig. 1), I watched nearly every customer ahead of me ask for "the Coke shirt, *todah rabah* [thank you very much]."

Fig. 1. Hebrew Coca-Cola T-shirt. Personal photograph by author.

At the time, I never thought it 3
strange that I wanted one, too. After having absorbed sixteen years of Coca-Cola propaganda through everything from NBC's Saturday morning cartoon lineup to the concession stand at Camden Yards (the Baltimore Orioles' ballpark), I associated the shirt with singing along to the "Just for the Taste of It" jingle and with America's favorite pastime, not with a brown fizzy beverage I refused to consume. When I later realized the immensity of Coke's corporate power, I felt somewhat manipulated, but that didn't stop me from wearing the shirt. I still don it often, despite the growing hole in the right sleeve, because of its power as a conversation piece. Few Americans notice it without asking something like "Does that say Coke?" I usually smile and nod. Then they mumble a one-word compliment, and we go our separate ways. But rarely do they want to know what language the internationally recognized logo is written in. And why should they? They are interested in what they can relate to as Americans: a familiar red-and-white logo, not a foreign language. Through nearly a century of brilliant advertising strategies, the Coca-Cola Company has given Americans not only a thirst-quenching beverage but a cultural icon that we have come to claim as our own.

Throughout the company's history, its marketing strategies have centered on 4
putting Coca-Cola in scenes of the happy, carefree existence Americans are

supposedly striving for. What 1950s teenage girl, for example, wouldn't long to see herself in the Coca-Cola ad that appeared in a 1958 issue of *Seventeen* magazine? A clean-cut, handsome man flirts with a pair of smiling girls as they laugh and drink Cokes at a soda-shop counter. Even a girl who couldn't picture herself in that idealized role could at least buy a Coke for consolation. The malt shop, complete with a soda jerk in a white jacket and paper hat and a Coca-Cola fountain, is a theme that, even today, remains a piece of Americana (Ikuta 74).

But while countless campaigns with this general strategy have together 5
shaped the Coca-Cola image, presenting a product as key to a happy life is a fairly typical approach to advertising everything from Allstate insurance to Ziploc bags. Coca-Cola's advertising strategy is unique, however, for the original way the beverage giant has used the specific advertising media of magazines and television to drive home this message. As a result, Coca-Cola has become associated not only with the images of Americana portrayed in specific advertisements but also with the general forms of advertising media that dominate American culture.

One of the earliest and best-known examples of this strategy is artist Haddon 6
Sundblom's rendering of Santa Claus (see Fig. 2). Using the description of Santa in Clement Moore's poem "A Visit from St. Nicholas"--and his own rosy-cheeked face as a model--Sundblom contributed to the round, jolly image of this American icon, who just happens to delight in an ice-cold Coke after a tiring night of delivering presents ("Haddon Sundblom and Coca-Cola"). Coca-Cola utilized the concept of the magazine to present this inviting image in a brilliant manipulation of the medium (Pendergrast 181).

Fig. 2. Coca-Cola Santa pin. Personal photograph by author.

Today, it's easy to forget how 7
pervasive a medium the magazine was before television became readily available to all. Well into the 1960s, households of diverse backgrounds all across America subscribed loyally to general-subject weeklies and monthlies such as *Life* and the *Saturday Evening Post*, which provided news and entertainment to families nationwide. This large and constant group of subscribers enabled Coca-Cola to build an annual Christmastime campaign that used an extremely limited number of advertisements. According to the Coca-Cola Company's Web site, Sundblom created only around forty images of Santa Claus during

the campaign's duration from 1931 to 1964 ("Coke Lore"). As a result, Americans soon began to seek out the ads each holiday season. The marketing strategy was to make consumers wait eagerly by the mailbox each December to see the latest *Saturday Evening Post* ad featuring Santa gulping a Coke. For this strategy to succeed, the advertisements had to be seen by many, but they also had to be just hard enough to come by to seem special. What better way to achieve these goals than to place an advertisement in the December issue of an immensely popular magazine?

Effective magazine advertising is just one example of the media strategies 8
Coca-Cola has used to encourage us to equate Coke with the "happy life" element of American identity. As the magazine gave way to television, Coke was there. In a 1996 recap of the previous fifty years in industry history, *Beverage Industry* cites Coca-Cola as a frontrunner in the very first form of television advertising: sponsorship of entire programs such as *The Bob Dixon Show* and *The Adventures of Kit Carson* ("Fabulous Fifties" 16). Just as we now associate sports stadiums with their corporate sponsors, viewers of early television programs will forever equate those programs with Coke.

When networks switched from offering sponsorships to selling exclusive 9
commercial time in short increments, Coca-Cola strove to distinguish itself once again, this time by experimenting with new formats and technologies for those commercials. Early attempts--such as choppy "stop motion" animation, where photographs of objects such as Coke bottles move without the intervention of actors--attracted much attention, according to the Library of Congress Motion Picture Archives Web site. Coca-Cola was also a pioneer in color television; after a series of experimental reels, the company produced its first color commercial in 1964 ("Highlights"). While the subject matter of these original commercials was not particularly memorable (Coca-Cola cans and bottles inside a refrigerator), the hype surrounding the use of new technologies helped draw attention to the product.

But the advertising campaign that perhaps best illustrates the ability of 10
Coca-Cola advertisers to tie their product to a groundbreaking technology did not appear until 1993. For the 1994 Winter Olympics, Coke created six television commercials featuring digitally animated polar bears rolling, swimming, snuggling, and sliding about in a computerized North Pole--and finishing off the playful experience with a swig of Coke. In 1993, two years before the release of *Toy Story*, these commercials were some of the very first widely viewed digital films ("Highlights"). As with Sundblom's Santa Clauses, television viewers looked forward to their next sighting of the cute, cuddly, cutting-edge bears, who created a natural association between Coca-Cola and digital animation. Once again, Coke didn't just use the latest technology--Coke defined it.

As a result of all of this brilliant advertising, a beverage I never even drink is a significant part of my American cultural identity. That's why I spent thirty Israeli shekels and twenty minutes in a tourist trap I would ordinarily avoid buying my Hebrew Coca-Cola shirt. That shirt, along with the rest of the enormous Coca-Cola collectibles industry, demonstrates Coke's power to identify itself with the American ideal of a lighthearted life of diversion and pleasure. Standing in line halfway around the world for the logo that embodies these values gave me an opportunity to affirm a part of my American identity. 11

Works Cited

Coca-Cola Santa pin. *Personal photograph by the author*. 9 Nov. 2006.

"Coke Lore." *The Coca-Cola Company: Heritage*. The Coca-Cola Company, 2006. Web. 3 Nov. 2006.

"The Fabulous Fifties." *Beverage Industry* 87.6 (1996): 16. *General OneFile*. Web. 2 Nov. 2006.

"Haddon Sundblom and Coca-Cola." *The History of Christmas*. 10 Holidays, 2004. Web. 2 Nov. 2006.

Hebrew Coca-Cola T-shirt. Personal photograph by the author. 8 Nov. 2006.

"Highlights in the History of Coca-Cola Television Advertising." *Fifty Years of Coca-Cola Television Advertisements: Highlights from the Motion Picture Archives at the Library of Congress*. Motion Picture, Broadcasting, and Recorded Sound Div., Lib. of Cong., 29 Nov. 2000. Web. 5 Nov. 2006.

Ikuta, Yasutoshi, ed. *'50s American Magazine Ads*. Tokyo: Graphic-Sha, 1987. Print.

Pendergrast, Mark. *For God, Country, and Coca-Cola: The Definitive History of the Great American Soft Drink and the Company That Makes It*. 2nd ed. New York: Basic, 2000. Print.

## THINKING CRITICALLY ABOUT YOUR REVIEWING AND REVISING PROCESS

1. How did you begin reviewing your draft?
2. What kinds of comments on or responses to your draft did you have? How helpful were they, and why?
3. How long did revising take? How many drafts did you produce?
4. What kinds of changes did you tend to make? in organization, paragraphs, sentence structure, wording, adding or deleting information? in the use of visuals?
5. What gave you the most trouble as you were revising?
6. What pleased you most? What is your very favorite sentence or passage in the draft, and why?
7. What would you most like to change about your process of revising, and how do you plan to go about doing so?

# 7 Developing Paragraphs

Paragraphs serve as signposts — pointers that help guide readers through a piece of writing. A look through a magazine or novel will show paragraphs working in this way: when a new idea comes up, a new paragraph begins. Within this broad, general guideline, however, paragraph structure is highly flexible, allowing writers to create many different effects. Especially in workplace and online writing, flexibility is paramount as writers create paragraphs for particular purposes and settings.

## 7a Strong paragraphs

Most readers of English come to any piece of writing with certain expectations about paragraphs:

- Paragraphs will begin and end with important information.
- The opening sentence will often let readers know what a paragraph is about.
- The middle of a paragraph will develop what the paragraph is about.
- The end of a paragraph may sum up the paragraph's contents, bringing the discussion of an idea to a close in anticipation of the paragraph that follows.
- A paragraph will make sense as a whole; its words and sentences will be clearly related.
- A paragraph will relate to the paragraphs around it.

Let us look now at the elements in a well-written paragraph — one that is easy for readers to understand and follow.

> I never knew anyone who'd grown up in Jackson without being afraid of Mrs. Calloway, our librarian. She ran the Library absolutely by herself, from the desk where she sat with her back to the books and facing the stairs, her dragon eye on the front door, where who knew what kind of person might come in from the public? SILENCE in big black letters was on signs tacked up everywhere. She herself spoke in her normally commanding voice; every word could be heard all over the

### TALKING THE TALK: Paragraph length

"How long should a paragraph be?" In college writing, paragraphs should address a specific topic or idea and develop that idea with examples and evidence. There is no set rule about how many sentences are required to make a complete paragraph. So write as many as you need — and no more.

> Library above a steady seething sound coming from her electric fan; it was the only fan in the Library and stood on her desk, turned directly onto her streaming face.
>
> — EUDORA WELTY, *One Writer's Beginnings*

This paragraph begins with a general statement of the main idea: that everyone who grew up in Jackson feared Mrs. Calloway. All the other sentences then give specific details about why she inspired such fear. This example demonstrates the three qualities essential to most academic paragraphs: unity, development, and coherence. It focuses on one main idea (unity); its main idea is supported with specifics (development); and its parts are clearly related (coherence).

## 7b Unified paragraphs

An effective paragraph generally focuses on one main idea. A good way to achieve paragraph unity is to state the main idea clearly in one sentence — the topic sentence — and relate all other sentences in the paragraph to that idea. Like the thesis for an essay (5c), the topic sentence includes a topic and a comment on that topic. In the paragraph by Eudora Welty in 7a, the topic sentence opens the paragraph. Its topic is Mrs. Calloway; its comment, that those who grew up in Jackson were afraid of her.

### FOR MULTILINGUAL WRITERS: Being explicit

In U.S. academic contexts, readers often expect paragraphs to be organized around a clearly defined topic and the relationship among ideas signaled by transitional devices (7d). Such step-by-step explicitness may strike you as unnecessary or ineffective, but it helps ensure that the reader understands your point.

## 1 Positioning a topic sentence

A topic sentence often appears at the beginning of a paragraph, but it can come at the end — or it may be implied rather than stated directly.

### *Topic sentence at the beginning*

If you want readers to see your point immediately, open with the topic sentence. This strategy can be particularly useful in letters of application (65b2) or in argumentative writing (Chapter 11). The following paragraph opens with a clear topic sentence (shown in italics), on which subsequent sentences build:

> *Our friendship was the source of much happiness and many memories.* We danced to the tunes of Lenny Kravitz and Sheryl Crow. We sweated together in the sweltering summer sun, trying to win the championship for our softball team. I recall the taste of pepperoni and sausage pizza as we discussed the highlights of our team's victory. Once we even became attracted to the same young man, but luckily we were able to share his friendship.

### *Topic sentence at the end*

When specific details lead up to a generalization, putting the topic sentence at the end of the paragraph makes sense, as in the following paragraph about Alice Walker's "Everyday Use."

> During the visit, Dee takes the pictures, every one of them, including the one of the house that she used to live in and hate. She takes the churn top and dasher, both whittled out of a tree by one of Mama's uncles. She tries to take Grandma Dee's quilts. Mama and Maggie use these inherited items every day, not only appreciating their heritage but living it too. *Dee, on the other hand, wants these items only for decorative use, thus forsaking and ignoring their real heritage.*

### *Topic sentence at the beginning and end*

Sometimes you will want to state a topic sentence at the beginning of a paragraph and then refer to it in a slightly different form at the end. Such an echo of the topic sentence adds emphasis to the main idea. In the following paragraph, the writer begins with a topic sentence announcing a problem:

> *Many of the difficulties we experience in relationships are caused by the unrealistic expectations we have of each other.* Think about it. Women

are expected to feel comfortable doing most of the sacrificing. They are supposed to stay fine, firm, and forever twenty-two while doing double duty, in the home and in the workplace. The burden on men is no easier. They should be tall, handsome, and able to wine and dine the women. Many women go for the glitter and then expect these men to calm down once in a relationship and become faithful, sensitive, supportive, and loving. Let's face it. Both women and men have been unrealistic. *It's time we develop a new sensitivity toward each other and ask ourselves what it is we need from each other that is realistic and fair.*

The last sentence restates the topic sentence as a proposal for solving the problem. This approach is especially appropriate here, for the essay goes on to specify how the problem might be solved.

### *Topic sentence implied but not stated*

Occasionally a paragraph's main idea is so obvious that it does not need to be stated explicitly in a topic sentence. Here is such a paragraph, from an essay about working as an airport cargo handler:

> In winter the warehouse is cold and damp. There is no heat. The large steel doors that line the warehouse walls stay open most of the day. In the cold months, wind, rain, and snow blow across the floor. In the summer the warehouse becomes an oven. Dust and sand from the runways mix with the toxic fumes of fork lifts, leaving a dry, stale taste in your mouth. The high windows above the doors are covered with a thick, black dirt that kills the sun. The men work in shadows with the constant roar of jet engines blowing dangerously in their ears.
>
> — PATRICK FENTON, "Confessions of a Working Stiff"

Here the implied topic sentence might be stated as *Working conditions in the warehouse are uncomfortable, dreary, and hazardous to one's health.* But the writer does not have to state this information explicitly because we can infer it easily from the specific details he provides.

Though implied topic sentences are common in descriptions, many instructors prefer explicit topic sentences in college writing.

### EXERCISE 7.1

Choose an essay you have written, and identify the topic sentence of each paragraph, noting where in the paragraph the topic sentence appears or whether it is implied rather than stated. Experiment with one paragraph, positioning its topic sentence in at least two different places. What difference does the change make? If you have any implied topic sentences, try stating them explicitly. Does the paragraph become easier to read?

### 2 Relating each sentence to the main idea

Whether the main idea of a paragraph is stated in a topic sentence or is implied, each sentence in the paragraph should contribute to the main idea. Look, for example, at the following paragraph, which opens an essay about African American music:

> When I was a teenager, there were two distinct streams of popular music: one was black, and the other was white. The former could only be heard way at the end of the radio dial, while white music dominated everywhere else. This separation was a fact of life, the equivalent of blacks sitting in the back of the bus and "whites only" signs below the Mason-Dixon line. Satchmo might grin for days on "The Ed Sullivan Show" and certain historians hold forth ad nauseam on the black contribution to American music, but the truth was that our worlds rarely twined.
>
> — MARCIA GILLESPIE, "They're Playing My Music, but Burying My Dreams"

The first sentence announces the topic (there were two streams of popular music: black and white), and all of the other sentences back up this idea. The result is a unified paragraph.

#### EXERCISE 7.2

Choose one of the following topic sentences, and spend some time exploring the topic (5a). Then write a paragraph that includes the topic sentence. Make sure that each of the other sentences relates to it. Assume that the paragraph will be part of a letter you are writing to an acquaintance.

1. I found out quickly that college life was not quite what I had expected.
2. Being part of the "in crowd" used to be of utmost importance to me.
3. My work experience has taught me several important lessons.
4. Until recently, I never appreciated my parents fully.
5. I expect my college education to do more than assure me of a job.

#### EXERCISE 7.3

Choose an essay you have written recently, and examine the second, third, and fourth paragraphs. Does each have a topic sentence or strongly imply one? Do all the other sentences in the paragraph focus on its main idea? Would you now revise any of these paragraphs — and, if so, how?

## 7c Paragraph development

In addition to being unified, a paragraph should hold readers' interest and explore its topic fully, using whatever details, evidence, and examples are necessary. Without such development, a paragraph may seem lifeless and abstract.

Most good academic writing not only presents general ideas but also backs up these generalities with specifics. This balance, the shifting between general and specific, is especially important at the paragraph level. If a paragraph contains nothing but specific details, readers may have trouble following the writer's meaning. If, on the other hand, a paragraph contains only general statements, readers may grow bored or may not be convinced.

**A POORLY DEVELOPED PARAGRAPH**

No such thing as human nature compels people to behave, think, or react in certain ways. From the time of our infancy to our death, we are constantly being taught, by the society that surrounds us, the customs, norms, and mores of our distinct culture. Everything in culture is learned, not genetically transmitted.

This paragraph is boring. Although its main idea is clear, it fails to gain our interest or hold our attention because it lacks any specific examples or details. Now look at the paragraph revised to include needed specifics.

**THE SAME PARAGRAPH, REVISED**

Imagine a child in Ecuador dancing to salsa music at a warm family gathering, while a child in the United States is decorating a Christmas tree with bright glass ornaments. Both of these children are taking part in their country's cultures. It is not by instinct that one child knows how to dance to salsa music, nor is it by instinct that the other child knows how to decorate the tree. No such thing as human nature compels people to behave, think, or react in certain ways. Rather, from the time of our infancy to our death, we are constantly being taught, by the society that surrounds us, the customs, norms, and mores of our distinct culture. A majority of people feel that the evil in human beings is human nature. However, the Tasaday, a tribe discovered not long ago in the Philippines, do not even have equivalents in their language for the words *hatred*, *competition*, *acquisitiveness*, *aggression*, and *greed*. Such examples suggest that everything in culture is learned, not genetically transmitted.

## 1 Logical patterns of development

The patterns shown in 5e for organizing essays can also help you develop paragraphs. These logical patterns include narration, description, illustration, definition, division and classification, comparison and contrast, cause and effect, process, problem and solution, analogy, and reiteration.

### *Narration*

Narration tells a story in order to develop a main idea. Although writers usually arrange narrative paragraphs in chronological order, they sometimes use such variations as flashbacks and flash-forwards. Some narratives include dialogue; some gradually lead to a climax, the most dramatic point in the story. Here is one student's narrative paragraph that tells a personal story in order to support a point about the dangers of racing bicycles with flimsy alloy frames. Starting with a topic sentence (shown in italics), the paragraph proceeds chronologically and builds to a climax, saving the most extreme point for last.

> *People who have been exposed to the risk of dangerously designed bicycle frames have paid too high a price.* I saw this danger myself in the 1984 Putney Race. An expensive Stowe-Shimano graphite frame failed, and

the rider was catapulted onto Vermont pavement at fifty miles per hour. The pack of riders behind him was so dense that most other racers crashed into a tangled, sliding heap. The aftermath: four hospitalizations. I got off with some stitches, a bad road rash, and severely pulled tendons. My Italian racing bike was pretzeled, and my racing was over for that summer. Others were not so lucky. An Olympic hopeful, Brian Stone of the Northstar team, woke up in a hospital bed to find that his cycling was over — and not just for that summer. His kneecap had been surgically removed. He couldn't even walk.

### Description

Description uses specific details to create a clear impression. In the following descriptive paragraph, the writer includes details about an old schoolroom to convey the strong impression of a room where "time had taken its toll." Although a topic sentence may be unnecessary in such a paragraph (7b), sometimes a topic sentence at the beginning (as shown in italics) helps set the scene. Notice as well how the writer uses spatial organization (5e1), moving from the ceiling to the floor.

*The professor's voice began to fade into the background as my eyes wandered around the classroom in the old administration building.* The water-stained ceiling was cracked and peeling, and the splitting wooden beams played host to a variety of lead pipes and coils. My eyes followed these pipes down the walls and around corners until I eventually saw the electric outlets. I thought it was strange that they were exposed, not built in, until I realized that there probably had been no electricity when the building was built. Below the outlets the sunshine was falling in bright rays across the hardwood floor, and I noticed how smoothly the floor was worn. Time had taken its toll on this building.

### Illustration

Illustration makes a point with concrete examples or good reasons. To support the topic sentence (shown in italics) in the following illustration paragraph, Mari Sandoz uses one long example about her short hair and short stature.

**A SINGLE EXAMPLE**

*The Indians made names for us children in their teasing way.* Because our very busy mother kept my hair cut short, like my brothers', they called me Short Furred One, pointing to their hair and making the sign for short, the right hand with fingers pressed close together, held upward, back out, at the height intended. With me this was about two feet tall, the Indians laughing gently at my abashed face. I am told that I was given a pair of small moccasins that first time, to clear up my unhappiness at being picked out from the dusk behind the fire and my two unhappy shortcomings made conspicuous. — MARI SANDOZ, "The Go-Along Ones"

In the following excerpt, George Orwell's topic sentence (in italics) begins the paragraph and encourages the reader to ask *why*? Orwell then provides several reasons (also in italics) for and against shooting the elephant.

**SEVERAL REASONS**

*But I did not want to shoot the elephant.* I watched him beating his bunch of grass against his knees, with the preoccupied grandmotherly air that elephants have. *It seemed to me that it would be murder to shoot him.* At that age I was not squeamish about killing animals, but I had never shot an elephant and never wanted to. (Somehow it always seems worse to kill a large animal.) *Besides, there was the beast's owner to be considered.* Alive, the elephant was worth at least a hundred pounds; dead, he would only be worth the value of his tusks, five pounds, possibly. But I had got to act quickly. I turned to some experienced-looking Burmans who had been there when we arrived, and asked them how the elephant had been behaving. They all said the same thing: *he took no notice of you if you left him alone, but he might charge if you went too close to him.*

— GEORGE ORWELL, "Shooting an Elephant"

### Definition

You will often need to write an entire paragraph in order to define a word or concept. In many such instances, however, you will want to combine definition with other patterns of development. In the following paragraph, Timothy Tregarthen starts with a definition of economics (shown in italics) and then uses examples to support it:

*Economics is the study of how people choose among the alternatives available to them.* It's the study of little choices ("Should I take the chocolate or the strawberry?") and big choices ("Should we require a reduction in energy consumption in order to protect the environment?"). It's the study of individual choices, choices by firms, and choices by governments. Life presents each of us with a wide range of alternative uses of our time and other resources; economists examine how we choose among those alternatives.

— TIMOTHY TREGARTHEN, *Economics*

### *Division and classification*

Division breaks a single item into parts. Classification groups many separate items according to their similarities. A paragraph evaluating one history course might divide the course into several segments — textbooks, lectures, assignments — and examine each one in turn. A paragraph giving an overview of many history courses at your college might classify, or group, the courses in a number of ways — by time periods, by geographic areas, by the kinds of assignments demanded, by the number of students enrolled, or by some other criterion. In the following paragraph, note how Aaron Copland divides the listening process into three parts:

**DIVISION**

We all listen to music according to our separate capacities. But, for the sake of analysis, the whole listening process may become clearer if we break it up into its component parts, so to speak. In a certain sense, we all listen to music on three separate planes. For lack of a better terminology, one might name these (1) the sensuous plane, (2) the expressive plane, (3) the sheerly musical plane. The only advantage to be gained from mechanically splitting up the listening process into these hypothetical planes is the clearer view to be had of the way in which we listen.

— AARON COPLAND, *What to Listen for in Music*

In this paragraph, the writer classifies, or separates, fad dieters into two groups:

**CLASSIFICATION**

Two types of people are seduced by fad diets. Those who have always been overweight turn to them out of despair; they have tried everything, and yet nothing seems to work. The second group to succumb appear perfectly healthy but are baited by slogans such as "look good, feel good." These slogans prompt self-questioning and insecurity — do I really look good and feel good? — and, as a direct result, many healthy people fall prey to fad diets. With both types of

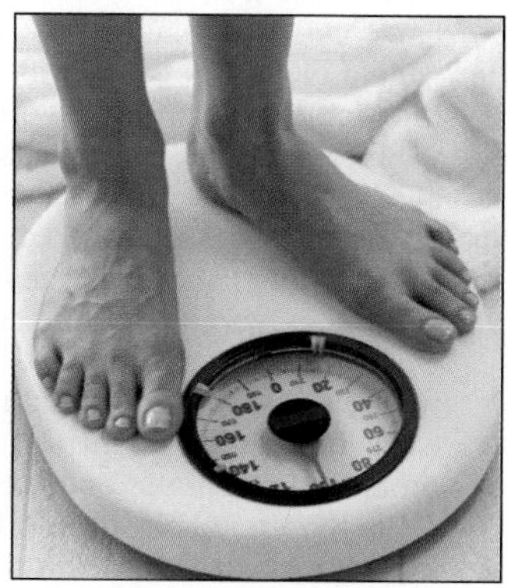

people, however, the problems surrounding such diets are numerous and dangerous. In fact, these diets provide neither intelligent nor effective answers to weight control.

### Comparison and contrast

Comparing two things means looking at their similarities; contrasting means focusing on the differences. You can structure paragraphs that compare and contrast in two different ways. One way is to present all the information about one item and then all the information about the other item (the block method). The other possibility is to switch back and forth between the two items, focusing on particular characteristics of each in turn (the alternating method).

**BLOCK METHOD**

You could tell the veterans from the rookies by the way they were dressed. The knowledgeable ones had their heads covered by kerchiefs, so that if they were hired, tobacco dust wouldn't get in their hair; they had on clean dresses that by now were faded and shapeless, so that if they were hired they wouldn't get tobacco dust and grime on their best clothes. Those who were trying for the first time had their hair freshly done and wore attractive dresses; they wanted to make a good impression. But the dresses couldn't be seen at the distance that many were standing from the employment office, and they were crumpled in the crush. — MARY MEBANE, "Summer Job"

**ALTERNATING METHOD**

Malcolm X emphasized the use of violence in his movement and employed the biblical principle of "an eye for an eye and a tooth for a tooth." King, on the other hand, felt that blacks should use nonviolent civil disobedience and employed the theme of "turning the other cheek," which Malcolm X rejected as "beggarly" and "feeble." The philosophy of Malcolm X was one of revenge, and often it broke the unity of black Americans. More radical blacks supported him, while more conservative ones supported King. King thought that blacks should transcend their humanity. In contrast, Malcolm X thought they should embrace it and reserve their love for one another, regarding whites as "devils" and the "enemy."

King's politics were those of a rainbow, but Malcolm X's rainbow was insistently one color — black. The distance between Martin Luther King Jr.'s thinking and Malcolm X's was the distance between growing up in the seminary and growing up on the streets, between the American dream and the American reality.

### EXERCISE 7.4

Outline the preceding paragraph on Martin Luther King Jr. and Malcolm X, noting its alternating pattern. Then rewrite the paragraph using block organization: the first part of the paragraph devoted to King, the second to Malcolm X. Finally, write a brief analysis of the two paragraphs, explaining which seems more coherent and easier to follow — and why.

### *Cause and effect*

You can often develop paragraphs by detailing the causes of something or the effects that something brings about. The following paragraph discusses how our desire for food that tastes good has affected history:

> The human craving for flavor has been a largely unacknowledged and unexamined force in history. For millennia royal empires have been built, unexplored lands traversed, and great religions and philosophies forever changed by the spice trade. In 1492 Christopher Columbus set sail to find seasoning. Today the influence of flavor in the world marketplace is no less decisive. The rise and fall of corporate empires — of soft-drink companies, snack-food companies, and fast-food chains — is often determined by how their products taste. — ERIC SCHLOSSER, *Fast Food Nation*

### *Process*

You may need to develop a paragraph to explain a process — that is, to describe how something happens or is done: first one step, then the next, and then the next. Every time you give directions or write down a recipe, you are showing a process, usually in chronological order. In college writing, you will probably use process paragraphs most often to tell readers how a process occurs in general — for example, how the Electoral College works or how aerosol sprays destroy the ozone layer of the atmosphere. Here is an example of a process paragraph, with its topic sentence shown in italics:

> *By the late 20s, most people notice the first signs of aging in their physical appearance.* Slight losses of elasticity in facial skin produce the

first wrinkles, usually in those areas most involved in their characteristic facial expressions. As the skin continues to lose elasticity and fat deposits build up, the face sags a bit with age. Indeed, some people have drooping eyelids, sagging cheeks, and the hint of a double chin by age 40 (Whitbourne, 1985). Other parts of the body sag a bit as well, so as the years pass, adults need to exercise regularly if they want to maintain their muscle tone and body shape. Another harbinger of aging, the first gray hairs, is usually noticed in the 20s and can be explained by a reduction in the number of pigment-producing cells. Hair may become a bit less plentiful, too, because of hormonal changes and reduced blood supply to the skin.

— KATHLEEN STASSEN BERGER, *The Developing Person through the Life Span*

### Problem and solution

A paragraph developed in the problem-solution pattern opens with a topic sentence that states a problem or asks a question about a problem; then it offers a solution or answers the question.

*How prepared is America for the next 9/11?* The Bush administration's response to the U.S. intelligence and law-enforcement agencies' failure to communicate is the Terrorist Threat Integration Center. Launched last May, TTIC is an independent body manned with analysts from more than a dozen agencies, including the CIA, FBI, Immigration and Customs Enforcement, the National Security Agency, the Coast Guard, Homeland Security, and the Secret Service. Each day TTIC analysts are supposed to share whatever they hear about potential threats and produce a report that goes to the White House, Pentagon and other major "customers."

— MICHAEL HIRSCH AND MARK HOSENBALL, "Spies: Too Little Sharing"

### Analogy

Analogies (comparisons that explain an unfamiliar thing in terms of a familiar one) can also help develop paragraphs. In the following paragraph, the writer draws an unlikely analogy (shown in italics) — between the human genome and a Thanksgiving dinner — to help readers understand what scientists know about the human genome:

*Think of the human genome as the ingredients list for a massive Thanksgiving dinner.* Scientists long have had a general understanding of how the feast is cooked. They knew where the ovens were. Now, they also have a list of every ingredient. Yet much remains to be discovered. In most cases, no one knows exactly which ingredients are necessary for making, for example, the pumpkin pie as opposed to the cornbread. Indeed, many, if not most, of the recipes that use the genomic ingredients are missing, and there's little understanding why small variations in the quality of the ingredients can "cook up" diseases in one person but not in another.

— *USA TODAY*, "Cracking of Life's Genetic Code Carries Weighty Potential"

### Reiteration

Reiteration is a method of development you may recognize from political speeches or some styles of preaching. In this pattern, the writer states the main point of a paragraph and then restates it, hammering home the point and often building in intensity as well. Martin Luther King Jr.'s mastery of this strategy is obvious in the following example. King reiterates the topic of the paragraph (*We are on the move*) six different ways (shown in italics), repeating the idea like a drumbeat throughout the paragraph:

> *We are on the move now.* The burning of our churches will not deter us. *We are on the move now.* The bombing of our homes will not dissuade us. *We are on the move now.* The beating and killing of our clergymen and young people will not divert us. *We are on the move now.* The arrest and release of known murderers will not discourage us. *We are on the move now.* Like an idea whose time has come, not even the marching of mighty armies can halt us. *We are moving* to the land of freedom.
>
> — MARTIN LUTHER KING JR., "Our God Is Marching On"

### Combining patterns

Most paragraphs combine patterns of development. In the following paragraph, the writer begins with a topic sentence (shown in italics) and then divides his topic (the accounting systems used by American companies) into two subtopics (the system used to summarize a company's overall financial state and the one used to measure internal transactions). Next he develops the second subtopic through illustration (the assessment of costs for a delivery truck shared by two departments) and cause and effect (the system produces some disadvantages).

*Most American companies have basically two accounting systems.* One system summarizes the overall financial state to inform stockholders, bankers, and other outsiders. That system is not of interest here. The other system, called the managerial or cost accounting system, exists for an entirely different reason. It measures in detail all of the particulars of transactions between departments, divisions, and key individuals in the organization, for the purpose of untangling the interdependencies between people. When, for example, two departments share one truck for deliveries, the cost accounting system charges each department for part of the cost of maintaining the truck and driver, so that at the end of the year, the performance of each department can be individually assessed, and the better department's manager can receive a larger raise. Of course, all of this information processing costs money, and furthermore may lead to arguments between the departments over whether the costs charged to each are fair.

— WILLIAM OUCHI, "Japanese and American Workers: Two Casts of Mind"

### EXERCISE 7.5

Choose two of the following topics or two others that interest you, and brainstorm or freewrite about each one for ten minutes (5a1 and 5a2). Then use the information you have produced to determine what method(s) of development would be most appropriate for each topic.

1. the pleasure a hobby has given you
2. the different images of two noted athletes
3. an average Saturday morning
4. why the game Monopoly is an appropriate metaphor for U.S. society
5. the best course you've ever taken

### EXERCISE 7.6

Take an assignment you have written recently, and study the ways you developed each paragraph. For one of the paragraphs, write a brief evaluation of its development. How would you expand or otherwise improve the development?

## 2 Determining paragraph length

Though writers must keep their readers' expectations in mind, paragraph length is determined primarily by content and purpose. Paragraphs should develop an idea, create any desired effects (such as suspense or humor), and advance the larger piece of writing. Fulfilling these aims sometimes requires short paragraphs, sometimes long ones. For example, if you are writing a persuasive essay, you may put all your evidence into one long paragraph to create the impression of a solid, overwhelmingly convincing argument. In a narrative about an exciting event, on the other hand, you may use a series of short paragraphs to create suspense, to keep the reader rushing to each new paragraph to find out what happens next.

Remember that a new paragraph often signals a pause in thought. Just as timing is crucial in telling a joke, so the pause signaled by a paragraph helps readers anticipate what is to follow or gives them a moment to think about the previous paragraph.

### *Reasons to start a new paragraph*

- to turn to a new idea
- to emphasize something (such as a point or an example)
- to change speakers (in dialogue)
- to lead readers to pause
- to take up a subtopic
- to start the conclusion

**EXERCISE 7.7**

Examine the paragraph breaks in something you have written recently. Explain briefly in writing why you decided on each of the breaks. Would you change any of them now? If so, how and why?

## 7d Coherent paragraphs

A paragraph has coherence — or flows — if its details fit together clearly in a way that readers can easily follow. You can achieve paragraph coherence by organizing ideas, by repeating key terms or phrases, and by using parallel structures and transitional devices.

### 1 Organization

When you arrange information in a particular order, you help readers move from one point to another. There are a number of ways to organize details — you might use spatial, chronological, or associational order (5e) or one or more logical patterns, such as illustration, definition, or comparison and contrast (7c). Two other patterns commonly used in paragraphs are general to specific and specific to general.

Paragraphs organized in a general-to-specific pattern usually open with a topic sentence that presents a general idea. The topic sentence is then followed by specific points that support the generalization. In the following paragraph, the topic sentence (shown in italics) presents a general idea about the Black Death, which is then backed up by specific examples:

**GENERAL TO SPECIFIC**

*A massive epidemic, the Black Death of the fourteenth century, brought loss of life in the tens of millions of people and catastrophic debilitation to commerce and agriculture across Eurasia and North Africa.* The bubonic plague seems to have initially irrupted into Chinese populations beginning in the 1320s. It spread in many parts of China until the 1350s with great loss of life. At the same time, it appears to have been carried into Mongolia and across the steppes into Crimea. Two Central Asian areas, one inhabited by the Nestorian Christians and the other by the Uzbek Muslims, were devastated by the plague before it struck in Europe, Southwest Asia, and

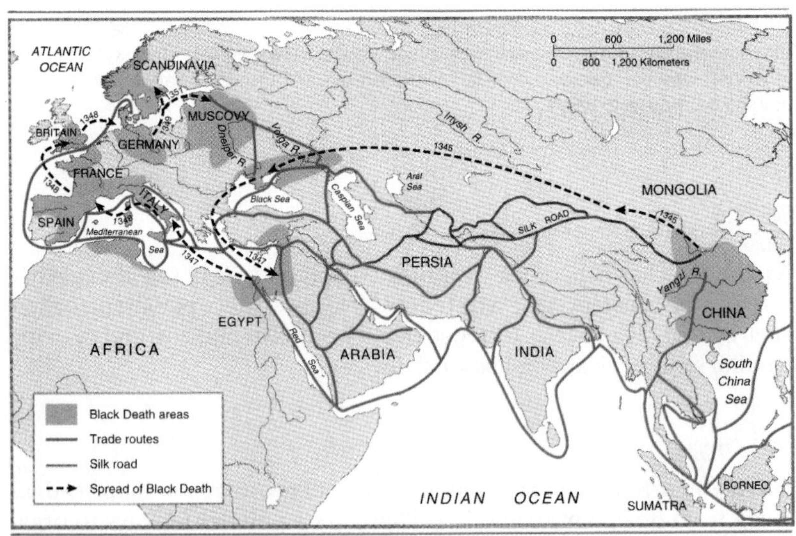


MAP 21.1 *The Spread of Black Death, around 1350.*

Northwest Africa. Travel along Chinese and Central Asian trade routes facilitated the spread of this deadly disease (see Map 21.1).

— LANNY B. FIELDS, RUSSELL J. BARBER, AND CHERYL A. RIGGS, *The Global Past*

Paragraphs can also follow a specific-to-general organization, first providing a series of specific examples or details and then tying them together with a topic sentence that provides a conclusion. The following paragraph begins with specific details about Saturday morning television and ends with a topic sentence (shown in italics):

**SPECIFIC TO GENERAL**

At 8:01 A.M. on Saturday morning, the bright images hawk cereal: Froot Loops, Frosted Flakes, Captain Crunch. At 8:11, it's toy time, as squads of delighted children demonstrate the pleasures of owning Barbie, Ken, or GI Joe. By 8:22, Coca-Cola is quenching thirsts everywhere, and at 8:31, kids declare devotion to their Nikes, ensuring that every child tuned in will want a pair. And so goes Saturday morning children's programming: one part "program" (and that exclusively cartoons) to three parts advertising. *"Children's television" today is simply a euphemism for one long, hard sell, an initiation rite designed to create more and more American consumers.*

## 2 Repetition

A good way to build coherence in paragraphs is through repetition. Weaving in repeated key words and phrases — or pronouns that refer to them — not only links sentences but also alerts readers to the importance of those words or phrases in the larger piece of writing. Notice in the following example how the repetition of italicized key words and the pronoun *they* helps hold the paragraph together:

Over the centuries, *shopping* has changed in function as well as in style. Before the Industrial Revolution, most consumer goods were sold in open-air *markets*, *customers* who went into an actual *shop* were expected to *buy* something, and *shoppers* were always expected to *bargain* for the best possible price. In the nineteenth century, however, the development of the department *store* changed the relationship between buyers and sellers. Instead of visiting several *market* stalls or small *shops*, *customers* could now *buy* a variety of merchandise under the same roof; instead of feeling expected to *buy*, *they* were welcome just to look; and instead of *bargaining* with several merchants, *they* paid a fixed *price* for each *item*. In addition, *they* could return an *item* to the *store* and exchange it for a different one or get their money back. All of these changes helped transform *shopping* from serious requirement to psychological recreation.

### EXERCISE 7.8

Read the following paragraph. Then identify the places where the author uses repetition of key words and phrases, and explain how they bring coherence to the paragraph.

> This is not to say that technology was an unadulterated plus in the '90s. The Information Superhighway was pretty much of a dud. Remember that? By the mid-'90s, just about everybody was hooked up to the vast international computer network, exchanging vast quantities of information at high speeds via modems and fiber-optic cable with everybody else. The problem, of course, was that even though the information was coming a lot faster, the vast majority of it, having originated with human beings, was still wrong. Eventually people realized that the Information Superhighway was essentially CB radio, but with more typing. By late in the decade millions of Americans had abandoned their computers and turned to the immensely popular new VirtuLib 2000, a $14,000 device that enables the user to experience, with uncanny realism, the sensation of reading a book.
>
> — DAVE BARRY, "The '90s"

## 3 Parallel structures

Parallel structures — structures that are grammatically similar — are another effective way to bring coherence to a paragraph. Readers are pulled along by the force of the parallel structures in the following example:

> William Faulkner's "Barn Burning" tells the story of a young boy trapped in a no-win situation. If he betrays his father, he loses his family. If he betrays justice, he becomes a fugitive. In trying to free himself from his trap, he does both.

For more on parallel structures, see Chapter 37.

## 4 Transitional devices

Transitional words and phrases, such as *after all*, *for example*, *indeed*, and *finally*, signal relationships between and among sentences and paragraphs. (For information on linking paragraphs together coherently, see 7e.) Transitions bring coherence to a paragraph by helping readers follow the progression of one idea to the next. To understand how important transitions are in guiding readers, try reading the following paragraph, from which all transitions have been removed:

**A PARAGRAPH WITH NO TRANSITIONS**

> In "The Fly," Katherine Mansfield tries to show us the "real" personality of "the boss" beneath his exterior. The fly helps her to portray this real self.

The boss goes through a range of emotions and feelings. He expresses these feelings to a small but determined fly, whom the reader realizes he unconsciously relates to his son. The author basically splits up the story into three parts, with the boss's emotions and actions changing quite measurably. With old Woodifield, with himself, and with the fly, we see the boss's manipulativeness. Our understanding of him as a hard and cruel man grows.

We can, if we work at it, figure out the relationship of these ideas to one another, for this paragraph is essentially unified by one major idea. But the lack of transitions results in an abrupt, choppy rhythm; the paragraph lurches from one detail to the next, dragging the confused reader behind. See how much easier the passage is to read and understand with transitions added.

**THE SAME PARAGRAPH, WITH TRANSITIONS**

In "The Fly," Katherine Mansfield tries to show us the "real" personality of "the boss" beneath his exterior. The fly *in the story's title* helps her to portray this real self. *In the course of the story*, the boss goes through a range of emotions and feelings. *At the end*, he *finally* expresses these feelings to a small but determined fly, whom the reader realizes he unconsciously relates to his son. *To accomplish her goal*, the author basically splits up the story into three parts, with the boss's emotions and actions changing quite measurably *throughout*. First with old Woodifield, *then* with himself, and *last* with the fly, we see the boss's manipulativeness. *With each part*, our understanding of him as a hard and cruel man grows.

Note that transitions can only clarify connections between thoughts; they cannot create connections. As a writer, you should not expect a transition to provide meaning.

## EXERCISE 7.9

Identify the devices — repetition of key words or phrases, parallel structures, transitional expressions — that make the following paragraph coherent.

I must make two honest confessions to you, my Christian and Jewish brothers. First, I must confess that over the past few years I have been gravely disappointed with the white moderate. I have almost reached the regrettable conclusion that the Negro's great stumbling block on his stride toward freedom is not the White Citizen's Counciler or the Ku Klux Klanner, but the white moderate, who is more devoted to "order" than to justice; who prefers a negative peace which is the absence of tension to a positive peace which is the presence of justice; who constantly says, "I agree with you in the goal you seek, but I cannot agree with your methods of direct action"; who paternalistically

## Commonly used transitions

**To signal sequence**

again, also, and, and then, besides, finally, first . . . second . . . third, furthermore, last, moreover, next, still, too

**To signal time**

after a few days, after a while, afterward, as long as, as soon as, at last, at that time, before, earlier, immediately, in the meantime, in the past, lately, later, meanwhile, now, presently, simultaneously, since, so far, soon, then, thereafter, until, when

**To signal comparison**

again, also, in the same way, likewise, once more, similarly

**To signal contrast**

although, but, despite, even though, however, in contrast, in spite of, instead, nevertheless, nonetheless, on the contrary, on the one hand . . . on the other hand, regardless, still, though, yet

**To signal examples**

after all, even, for example, for instance, indeed, in fact, of course, specifically, such as, the following example, to illustrate

**To signal cause and effect**

accordingly, as a result, because, consequently, for this purpose, hence, so, then, therefore, thus, to this end

**To signal place**

above, adjacent to, below, beyond, closer to, elsewhere, far, farther on, here, near, nearby, opposite to, there, to the left, to the right

**To signal concession**

although it is true that, granted that, I admit that, it may appear that, naturally, of course

**To signal summary, repetition, or conclusion**

as a result, as has been noted, as I have said, as mentioned earlier, as we have seen, in any event, in conclusion, in other words, in short, on the whole, therefore, to summarize believes he can set the timetable for another man's freedom; who lives by a mythical concept of time and who constantly advises the Negro to wait for a "more convenient season." Shallow understanding from people of good will is more frustrating than absolute misunderstanding from people of ill will. Lukewarm acceptance is much more bewildering than outright rejection.

— MARTIN LUTHER KING JR., "Letter from Birmingham Jail"

## 7e Linking paragraphs

The same methods that you use to link sentences and create coherent paragraphs can be used to link paragraphs themselves so that a whole piece of writing flows smoothly. You should include some reference to the previous paragraph, either explicit or implied, in each paragraph after the introduction. As with sentences, you can create this link by repeating or paraphrasing key words and phrases and by using parallel structures and transitional expressions.

### *Repeated key words*

In fact, human offspring remain *dependent on their parents* longer than the young of any other species.

Children are *dependent on their parents* or other adults not only for their physical survival but also for their initiation into the uniquely human knowledge that is collectively called culture. . . .

### *Parallel structures*

Kennedy made an effort to assure non-Catholics that he would respect the separation of church and state, and most of them did not seem to hold his religion against him in deciding how to vote. Since his election, *the church to which a candidate belongs* has become less important in presidential politics.

*The region from which a candidate comes* remains an important factor. . . .

### *Transitional expressions*

While the Indian, in the character of Tonto, was more positively portrayed in *The Lone Ranger*, such a portrayal was more the exception than the norm.

*Moreover, despite this brief glimpse of an Indian as an ever loyal sidekick*, Tonto was never accorded the same stature as the man with the white horse and silver bullets. . . .

### EXERCISE 7.10

Look at the essay you drafted for Exercise 5.6, and identify the ways your paragraphs are linked together. Identify each use of repetition, parallel structures, and transitional expressions, and then evaluate how effectively you have joined the paragraphs.

## 7f Special-purpose paragraphs

Some kinds of paragraphs deserve special attention: opening paragraphs, concluding paragraphs, transitional paragraphs, and dialogue paragraphs.

### 1 Opening paragraphs

Even a good piece of writing may remain unread if it has a weak opening paragraph. In addition to announcing your topic (usually in a thesis statement), an introductory paragraph must engage readers' interest and focus their attention on what is to follow. At their best, introductory paragraphs serve as hors d'oeuvres, whetting the appetite for the following courses.

One common kind of opening paragraph follows the general-to-specific pattern (7d1), in which the writer opens with a general statement and then gets more and more specific, concluding with the thesis (shown here in italics):

> Throughout Western civilization, places such as the ancient Greek agora, the New England town hall, the local church, the coffeehouse, the village square, and even the street corner have been arenas for debate on public affairs and society. Out of thousands of such encounters, "public opinion" slowly formed and became the context in which politics was framed. Although the public sphere never included everyone, and by itself did not determine the outcome of all parliamentary actions, it contributed to the spirit of dissent found in a healthy representative democracy. Many of these public spaces remain, but they are no longer centers for political discussion and action. *They have largely been replaced by television and other forms of media — forms that arguably isolate citizens from one another rather than bringing them together.* — MARK POSTER, "The Net as a Public Sphere"

In this paragraph, the opening sentence introduces a general subject — sites of public debate throughout history; subsequent sentences focus more specifically on political discussion; and the last sentence presents the thesis, which the rest of the essay will develop.

Other effective ways of opening an essay include quotations, anecdotes, questions, and strong opinions.

### Opening with a quotation

*There is a bumper sticker that reads, "Too bad ignorance isn't painful."* I like that. But ignorance is. We just seldom attribute the pain to it or even recognize it when we see it. Take the postcard on my corkboard. It shows a young man in a very hip jacket smoking a cigarette. In the background is a high school with the American flag waving. The caption says, "Too cool for school. Yet too stupid for the real world." Out of the mouth of the young man is a bubble enclosing the words "Maybe I'll start a band." There could be a postcard showing a jock in a uniform saying, "I don't need school. I'm going to the NFL or NBA." Or one showing a young man or woman studying and a group of young people saying, "So you want to be white." Or something equally demeaning. We need to quit it. — NIKKI GIOVANNI, "Racism 101"

### Opening with an anecdote

*I first met Angela Carter at a dinner in honor of the Chilean writer José Donoso at the home of Liz Calder, who then published all of us. My first novel was soon to be published; it was the time of Angela's darkest novel, "The Passion of New Eve." And I was a great fan. Mr. Donoso arrived looking like a Hispanic Buffalo Bill, complete with silver goatee, fringed jacket and cowboy boots, and proceeded, as I saw it, to patronize Angela terribly. His apparent ignorance of her work provoked me into a long expostulation in which I informed him that the woman he was talking to was the most brilliant writer in England. Angela liked that. By the end of the evening, we liked each other, too.* That was almost 18 years ago. She was the first great writer I ever met, and she was one of the best, most loyal, most truth-telling, most inspiring friends anyone could ever have. I cannot bear it that she is dead. — SALMAN RUSHDIE, "Angela Carter"

### Opening with a question

*Why are Americans terrified of using nuclear power as a source of energy?* People are misinformed, or not informed at all, about its benefits and safety. If Americans would take the time to learn about what nuclear power offers, their apprehension and fear might be transformed into hope.

### Opening with a strong opinion

*Men need a men's movement about as much as women need chest hair.* A brotherhood organized to counter feminists could be timely because — let's be honest — women are no more naturally inclined to equality and fairness than men are. They want power and dominion just as much as any group looking out for its own interests. Organizing to protect the welfare of males might make sense. Unfortunately, the current men's movement does not. — JOHN RUSZKIEWICZ, *The Presence of Others*

## 2 Concluding paragraphs

A good conclusion wraps up a piece of writing in a satisfying and memorable way. It reminds readers of the thesis of the essay and leaves them feeling that their expectations have been met. The concluding paragraph is also your last opportunity to get your message across.

A common strategy for concluding uses the specific-to-general pattern (7d1), often beginning with a restatement of the thesis (but not word for word) and moving to more general statements. The following paragraph moves in such a way, opening with a final point of comparison between Generals Grant and Lee (shown in italics), specifying it in several sentences, and then ending with a much more general statement (also in italics):

> *Lastly, and perhaps greatest of all, there was the ability, at the end, to turn quickly from war to peace once the fighting was over.* Out of the way these two men behaved at Appomattox came the possibility of a peace of reconciliation. It was a possibility not wholly realized, in the years to come, but which did, in the end, help the two sections to become one nation again . . . after a war whose bitterness might have seemed to make such a reunion wholly impossible. No part of either man's life became him more than the part he played in this brief meeting in the McLean house at Appomattox. Their behavior there put all succeeding generations of Americans in their debt. Two great Americans, Grant and Lee — very different, yet under everything very much alike. *Their encounter at Appomattox was one of the great moments of American history.*
>
> — BRUCE CATTON, "Grant and Lee: A Study in Contrasts"

Other effective strategies for concluding include questions, quotations, vivid images, calls for action, and warnings.

### *Concluding with a question*

> All so-called "permanent" antifreeze is basically the same. It is made from a liquid known as ethylene glycol, which has two amazing properties: It has a lower freezing point than water, and a higher boiling point than water. It does not break down (lose its properties), nor will it boil away. And every permanent antifreeze starts with it as a base. Also, just about every antifreeze has now got antileak ingredients, as well as antirust and anticorrosion ingre-

dients. Now, let's suppose that, in formulating the product, one of the companies comes up with a solution that is pink in color, as opposed to all the others, which are blue. Presto — an exclusivity claim. "Nothing else looks like it, nothing else performs like it." Or how about, "Look at ours, and look at anyone else's. You can see the difference our exclusive formula makes." Granted, I'm exaggerating. *But did I prove a point?*

— PAUL STEVENS, "Weasel Words: God's Little Helpers"

### Concluding with a quotation

Despite the celebrity that accrued to her and the air of awesomeness with which she was surrounded in her later years, Miss Keller retained an unaffected personality, certain that her optimistic attitude toward life was justified. *"I believe that all through these dark and silent years God has been using my life for a purpose I do not know," she said. "But one day I shall understand and then I will be satisfied."*

— ALDEN WHITMAN, "Helen Keller: June 27, 1880–June 1, 1968"

### Concluding with a vivid image

It is, in any case, finally you that I end up having to trust not to laugh, not to snicker. Even as you regard me in these lines, I try to imagine your face as you read. You who read "Aria," especially those of you with your theme-divining yellow felt pen poised in your hand, you for whom this essay is yet another "assignment," please do not forget that it is my life I am handing you in these pages — *memories that are as personal for me as family photographs in an old cigar box.*

— RICHARD RODRIGUEZ, from a postscript to "Aria"

### Concluding with a call for action

Do we have cause for hope? Many of my friends are pessimistic when they contemplate the world's growing population and human demands colliding with shrinking resources. But I draw hope from the knowledge that humanity's biggest problems today are ones entirely of our own making. Asteroids hurtling at us beyond our control don't figure high on our list of imminent dangers. To save ourselves, we don't need new technology: *we just need the political will to face up to our problems of population and the environment.*

— JARED DIAMOND, "The Ends of the World As We Know Them"

### Concluding with a warning

Because propaganda is so effective, it is important to track it down and understand how it is used. We may eventually agree with what the propagandist says because all propaganda isn't necessarily bad; some advertising, for instance, urges us not to drive drunk, to have regular dental checkups, to contribute to the United Way. Even so, we must be aware that propaganda is being used. *Otherwise, we will have consented to handing over our independence, our decision-making ability, and our brains.*

— ANN MCCLINTOCK, "Propaganda Techniques in Today's Advertising"

### 3 Transitional paragraphs

On some occasions, you may need to alert your readers to a major transition between ideas. To do so in a powerful way, you might use an entire short paragraph, as in the following example from an essay on television addiction. The one-sentence transitional paragraph arrests our attention, announcing that the general characteristics of serious addiction will now be related to television viewing.

Finally a serious addiction is distinguished from a harmless pursuit of pleasure by its distinctly destructive elements. A heroin addict, for instance, leads a damaged life: his increasing need for heroin in increasing doses prevents him from working, from maintaining relationships, from developing in human ways. Similarly an alcoholic's life is narrowed and dehumanized by his dependence on alcohol.

Let us consider television viewing in the light of the conditions that define serious addictions.

— MARIE WINN, *The Plug-In Drug: Television, Children, and the Family*

### 4 Paragraphs to signal dialogue

Dialogue can add life to almost any sort of writing. To set up written dialogue, simply start a new paragraph each time the speaker changes, no matter how short each bit of conversation is. Here is an example:

Whenever I brought a book to the job, I wrapped it in newspaper — a habit that was to persist for years in other cities and under other circumstances. But some of the white men pried into my packages when I was absent and they questioned me.

"Boy, what are you reading those books for?"

"Oh, I don't know, sir."

"That's deep stuff you're reading, boy."

"I'm just killing time, sir."

"You'll addle your brains if you don't watch out."

— RICHARD WRIGHT, *Black Boy*

## Editing the paragraphs in your writing

1. What is the topic sentence of each paragraph? Is it stated or implied? If stated, where in the paragraph does it fall? Should it come at some other point? Would any paragraph be improved by deleting or adding a topic sentence? (7b1)
2. Within each paragraph, how does each sentence relate to the main idea? (7b2)
3. How completely does each paragraph develop its topic sentence? What details and methods of development are used? Are they effective? Do any paragraphs need more detail? What other methods of development might be used? (7c1)
4. Are paragraphs varied in length? Does any paragraph seem too long or too short? (7c2)
5. Is each paragraph organized in a way that is easy for readers to follow? Are sentences within each paragraph clearly linked? Do any of the transitional expressions try to create links between ideas that do not really exist? (7d)
6. Are the paragraphs clearly linked? Do more links need to be added? (7e)
7. How does the introductory paragraph catch readers' interest — with a quotation? an anecdote? a question? a strong opinion? How else might it open? (7f1)
8. How does the last paragraph draw the essay to a conclusion? What lasting impression will it leave with readers? How else might it conclude? (7f2)
9. If you are writing email or creating a Web text, are your paragraphs effective and visually clear? (7g)

## 7g Online paragraphs

Email, online discussion lists, blogs, hypertext — all pose particular challenges for writers trying to create effective paragraphs. Both the limitations of electronic communication (such as lack of indentation in some email software) and the dizzying possibilities (such as ways to arrange hypertext) call for special creativity in writing paragraphs.

### *Messages and postings*

- If your software doesn't allow indentation, create paragraphs by skipping lines every time you introduce a new idea. Remember that long, dense paragraphs make for difficult reading.
- Online readers expect to understand messages quickly, so you may want to state the main point of a paragraph at the beginning.
- Ask yourself whether some information would be easier to read in a list instead of in a paragraph.

### *Web pages and hypertext*

- Take advantage of the many online options for designing paragraphs, but keep your purpose and audience in mind. (See Chapter 24.)
- Design Web paragraphs to guide the reader's eye easily around the page. For an introductory page, you might use few or no paragraphs, opting instead for a strong title, an arresting image, and a list of links. In later pages, you may want to use traditional paragraphs.
- Remember that readers will be working with one screen at a time, so paragraphs should break up text and ease readability.

## THINKING CRITICALLY ABOUT PARAGRAPHS

**Reading with an Eye for Paragraphs**

Read something by a writer you admire. Find one or two paragraphs that impress you in some way, and analyze them, using the guidelines on p. 137. Try to decide what makes them effective paragraphs.

**Thinking about Your Own Use of Paragraphs**

Examine two or three paragraphs you have written, using the guidelines on p. 137, to evaluate the unity, coherence, and development of each one. Identify the topic of each paragraph, the topic sentence (if one is explicitly stated), any patterns of development, and any means used to create coherence. Decide whether or not each paragraph successfully guides your readers, and explain your reasons. Then choose one paragraph, and revise it.

# Working with Others

# 8

The CEO of a successful software business tells an interesting story: twice a year, the company holds a staff retreat to devise a plan for attaining an important new goal or solving a major problem. What surprised the CEO was that effective collaboration was essential for all their improvements. In fact, she noted, no one person was ever the key to what the group had accomplished together.

In a memorable statement, philosopher Hannah Arendt confirms what this CEO discovered: "For excellence, the presence of others is always required." Collaboration, then, is essential not only in business and community work but also in college.

## 8a Collaborating in college

Although you will find yourself working together with many people on campus, your most immediate collaborators will probably be the members of your writing class. You can learn a great deal by comparing ideas with these classmates and by using them as a first audience for your writing (6b). As you talk and write, you will find the ideas they contribute making their way into your writing, and your ideas into theirs. In short, the texts you write are shaped in part by conversations with others. This exchange is one reason citing sources and help from others is so important (see Chapter 16).

In online communication, especially, the roles of "writer" and "reader" and "text" are often interchangeable, as readers become writers and then readers again, and texts constantly change as multiple voices contribute to them. An email message, for example, may carry with it a string of related messages that have accumulated as people have replied to one another. This extended message acts as a portrait of how meaning is made collaboratively.

Whether you are working online or off, however, successful collaboration requires special attention. In college, the two major purposes for collaborating are to improve your individual work and to produce successful group projects.

## TALKING THE TALK: Collaborating or cheating?

"When is asking others for help and opinions acceptable, and when is it cheating?" In academic work, the difference between collaborating and cheating depends almost entirely on context. There will be times — during exams, for example — when instructors will expect you to work alone. At other times, working with others — for a team project, perhaps or peer review — may be required, and getting others' opinions on your writing is always a good habit. You draw the line, however, at having another person do your work for you. Submitting material under your name that you did not write is unacceptable in college writing.

## 8b Group projects

You may often be asked to work as part of a team to produce a group project — a print report, an oral presentation, or a Web document or site. Since group projects are collaborative from the outset, they require additional planning and coordination.

### 1 Starting a group project and seeing it through

Planning goes a long way toward making group collaboration work well. Although you will probably do much group work online, keep in mind that face-to-face meetings can accomplish things that virtual meetings cannot. Some guidelines for a successful group project appear on p. 141.

### 2 Three models for group collaboration

Experienced collaborative writers often use one of three models for setting up the project: an expertise model, a division-of-labor model, or a process model.

*Expertise model.* This model plays to the strengths of each team member. The person who knows the most about graphics and design, for example, takes on all jobs that require those skills, while the person who knows most about the topic takes the lead in drafting.

*Division-of-labor model.* In this model, each group member becomes an expert on one aspect of the project. For example, one person might agree to do print-based research, while another searches online databases, and still another conducts interviews. This model is particularly helpful if a project is large and time is short.

## Guidelines for group projects

1. Establish a regular meeting time, and exchange email addresses and telephone numbers.
2. During your first meeting, discuss the overall project, get to know one another, and establish some ground rules, such as the following, to help your group function smoothly:
   - Every member has an equal opportunity — and responsibility — to contribute.
   - All members agree to be respectful and to listen to the others.
   - Each meeting will have a set agenda.
   - Each person will meet deadlines and due dates.
3. Considering members' expertise and time constraints, establish clear duties for each participant.
4. With final deadlines in mind, write up an overall agenda to organize the project. At each group meeting, take turns writing up notes of what was discussed; review them at the end of the meeting.
5. Use group meetings to work together on difficult problems. If an assignment is complex, have each member explain one section to all others. Check with your instructor if part of the task is unclear to everyone or if members of the group don't agree on what a task requires.
6. Express opinions politely. If disagreements arise, try paraphrasing to see if everyone is hearing the same thing.
7. Remember that constructive conflict is desirable — the goal is not for everyone just to go along. The challenge is to get a really spirited debate going and to argue through all the possibilities.
8. If your project requires a group-written document, divide up the drafting duties. Set reasonable deadlines for each stage of the work. Schedule meetings to iron out the final draft. If your project requires an oral or multimedia presentation, see 8d.
9. Assess the group's effectiveness periodically. What has the group accomplished? What has it done best? What has it been least successful in doing? What has each member contributed? How could the group function more effectively during the rest of the project?

**CONSIDERING DISABILITIES: Accommodating group members' needs**

When you are working with other members of your class to share files for peer review or other group activities, remember to consider differences group members may have. Think of such differences not only in terms of computer compatibility but also in terms of the sensory, physical, or learning abilities of yourself and your classmates. You may have colleagues who wish to receive files in a very large type size, for example, in order to read them with ease. Similarly, you may have a peer who prefers to share files early to read the material or avoid the stress of last-minute preparation. You may have a peer who uses a voice screen reader — these programs work best with files saved as .rtf or .tif rather than as .doc or .pdf. Help your group get off to a good start by making a plan to accommodate everyone's needs.

*Process model.* You can also divide up the project in terms of its chronology: one person gets the project going, presenting an outline for the group to consider and carrying out any initial research; then a second person takes over and begins a draft for the group to review; a third person designs and illustrates the project; and another person takes the job of revising and editing. This model can work well if members are unable to participate equally throughout the entire project. Once the project is completely drafted, however, the whole group needs to work together to create a final version.

## 8c Collaborating on email, blogs, and Web sites

Many college instructors now routinely integrate email or Web sites into their classes. Your writing class may have an email discussion list that lets you send and receive messages from the entire class. If not, you may want to set up a group email, wiki, or blog for yourself and your collaborators. Opposite are guidelines for using such devices for effective collaboration.

If your course has a Web site, it probably offers a space for extending the collaborative work of the classroom. As in other forms of collaboration, your class should establish ground rules to govern participation. When and how often is each member expected to post messages to class discussions? What code of conduct will everyone agree to follow? If you want your text to be read on a Web site, save the files as HTML.

# Part 2



# CRITICAL THINKING AND ARGUMENT

# 9 Analyzing Arguments

How do we come to make up our minds about something? What causes us to give our assent to some ideas but not to others? And how do we seek — and sometimes gain — agreement from others?

The need to explore such questions has never been more pressing than it is today, as language intended to persuade us — to gain our assent (and often our money, our votes, and even our souls) — surrounds us more than ever before. In advertisements, news stories, textbooks, reports, and print and electronic media of all kinds, language competes for our attention and argues for our agreement. Since argument so pervades our lives, we need to be able to recognize and use it effectively — and to question our own arguments as well as those put forth by others.

## 9a Recognizing argument

In one important sense, all language use has an argumentative edge. When you greet friends warmly, you wish to convince them that you are genuinely glad to see them, that you value their presence. Even apparently objective news reporting has strong argumentative overtones. By putting a particular story on the front page, for example, a paper argues that this subject is more important than others; by using emotional language or by focusing on certain details, a newscaster tries to persuade us to view an event in a particular way. Consider the different ways reporters

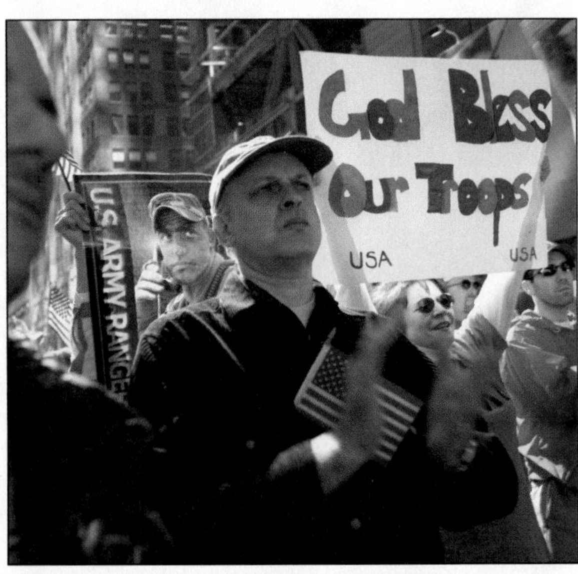

might describe the accompanying image, such as *an outpouring of support for our troops* or *a pro-war rally.*

Emily Lesk's primary purpose in her essay "Red, White, and Everywhere" is to reflect on her own identification with one particular American icon, Coca-Cola (Chapter 7). But her essay clearly has an argumentative edge, asking readers to examine their own cultural identifications and to understand the power of advertising in creating and sustaining such identifications.

It's possible, then, to read any message or text, verbal or visual, as an argument, even if argument is not its primary purpose. In much academic writing, however, *argument* is more narrowly defined as a text that makes a claim (usually in the form of an arguable statement) and supports it fully.

## 9b Critical thinking

Although critical thinking has a number of complex definitions, it is essentially the process by which we make sense of all the information around us. As such, critical thinking is a crucial component of argument, for it guides us in recognizing, formulating, and examining arguments.

Several elements of critical thinking are especially important.

*Playing the believing — and the doubting — game.* Critical thinkers are able to shift stances as they take in an argument, allowing them to gain different perspectives. One good way to begin is to play the *believing game*: that is, put yourself in the position of the person creating the argument, see the topic from that person's point of view as much as possible, and think carefully about how and why that person arrived at the claim(s). Once you have given the argument your sympathetic attention, play the *doubting game*: revisit the argument, looking skeptically at each claim and examining each piece of evidence to see how well (or if) it supports the claim. Eventually, this process of believing and doubting will become natural.

*Asking pertinent questions.* Concentrate on getting to the heart of the matter. Whether you are thinking about others' ideas or about your own, you will want to ask the following kinds of questions:

- What is the writer's agenda — his or her unstated purpose?
- Why does the writer hold these ideas or beliefs? What larger social, economic, political, or other conditions or factors may have influenced him or her?
- What does the writer want readers to do — and why?

- What are the writer's qualifications for making this argument?
- What reasons does the writer offer in support of his or her ideas? Are they good reasons?
- What are the writer's underlying values or unstated assumptions? Are they acceptable — and why or why not?
- What sources does the writer rely on? How current and reliable are they? What agendas do these sources have? Are any perspectives left out?
- What objections might be made to the argument?
- Be especially careful in examining information on the Web. What individual or group is responsible for the site and the argument it makes? (See 14c.)
- Study the visual and audio aspects of arguments, including the use of color, graphics, and all multimedia techniques. How do they appeal to the reader or listener? What do they contribute to the argument? (See Chapter 10 and 11i.)

*Getting information.* To help you decide whether to accept an argument, often you will need to find more information on the topic as well as other perspectives.

*Interpreting and assessing information.* No information that comes to us in language or visuals is neutral; all of it has a perspective — a spin. Your job as a critical thinker is to identify the perspective and to assess it, examining its sources and finding out what you can about its context.

## TALKING THE TALK: Critical thinking

"It seems so impolite to criticize. Why do I have to think critically?" Thinking critically does not require you to be relentlessly negative or impolite. Instead, critical thinking means, first and foremost, asking good questions — not simply accepting an argument at face value. Asking not only what words and images mean but also how meaning gets across, critical thinkers consider why an author makes a particular claim, what an author may be leaving out or ignoring, and how to tell whether evidence is accurate and believable. If you're asking, and answering, questions like these, then you are thinking critically.

Asking pertinent questions will help you examine the interpretations and conclusions drawn by others.

*Making and assessing your own arguments.* The ultimate goal of all critical thinking is to construct your own ideas and reach your own conclusions. These, too, you must question and assess. The rest of this chapter will guide you in the art of assessing arguments.

## 9c Cultural contexts for arguments

If you want to understand as fully as possible the arguments of others, remember that writers come from an astonishing variety of cultural and linguistic backgrounds. Perhaps most important for reading critically, pay attention to clues to cultural context, and be open to the many ways of thinking you will encounter. In short, practice the believing game before you play the doubting game — especially when analyzing an argument influenced by a culture different from your own. In addition, remember that within any given culture there are great differences among individuals. So don't expect that every member of a culture will argue in any one way.

Above all, watch your own assumptions very closely as you read. Just because you assume that the use of statistics as support for your argument holds more water than, say, precedent drawn from religious belief, you can't assume that all writers agree with you. Take a writer's cultural beliefs into account before you begin to analyze an argument. (See Chapter 26.)

## 9d Emotional, ethical, and logical appeals

Aristotle categorized argumentative appeals into three types: emotional appeals that speak to our hearts and values (known to the ancient Greeks as *pathos*), ethical appeals that appeal to character (*ethos*), and logical appeals that involve factual information and evidence (*logos*).

### Emotional appeals

Emotional appeals stir our emotions and remind us of deeply held values. When politicians argue that the country needs more tax relief, they almost always use examples of one or more families they have met, stressing the concrete ways in which a tax cut would improve the quality of their lives. Doing so creates a strong emotional appeal. Some have

RESTAURANT ADVERTISEMENT

Carmelo's Italian Restaurant is Houston's answer to an authentic Sicilian kitchen spiced with continental chic. All the ingredients are here — the pungent smells of garlic, the irresistible sounds of an accordion, a wall-to-wall collection of buildings recreating the village of Taormina where Carmelo was born and, of course, a sundry of the best pasta dishes, seafood, poultry, veal and beef specialties, olive oils, coffees, wines and desserts. Private rooms are available to accommodate anywhere from ten to 230 people. Lunch weekdays and dinner nightly. 14795 Memorial Dr., (281) 531-0696. Also located in Austin. http://www.carmelosrestaurant.com

criticized the use of emotional appeals in argument, claiming that they are a form of manipulation intended to mislead an audience. But emotional appeals are an important part of almost every argument. Critical readers are perfectly capable of "talking back" to such appeals by analyzing them, deciding which are acceptable and which are not. What emotional appeals are at work in the above restaurant advertisement, and how would you analyze their effectiveness?

### Ethical appeals

Ethical appeals support the credibility, moral character, and goodwill of the argument's creator. These appeals are especially important for critical readers to recognize and evaluate. We may respect and admire cyclist Lance Armstrong, for example, but should the credibility he has as an athlete carry over to the argument that we should invest in mutual funds he promotes? To identify ethical appeals in arguments, ask yourself these questions: What is the creator of the argument doing to show that he or she is knowledgeable and credible about the subject — has really done the homework on it? What sort of character does he or she build, and how? More important, is that character trustworthy? What does the creator of the argument do to show that he or she has the best interests of an audience in mind? Do those best interests match your own, and, if not, how does that alter the effectiveness of the argument? Take a look at the following passage, which introduces an argument for viewing the Diné, or Navajo, people as a nation within a nation. As you read, try to identify the ethical appeals within the passage, paying special attention to the writer's identification of himself and the Diné people with the land.

> One of the most remarkable things about this republic is that there exists within its borders a parallel universe known as Dinetah, a nation of more than 155,000 souls who subscribe to a mind-set completely different from the modern American belief that everything in nature is there for the taking. Dinetah is the ancestral homeland of the Diné, more commonly called the Navajo, a misnomer perpetrated by the Spaniards, as are many of the names for the native tribes of the Southwest. An area larger than West Virginia that sprawls out of Arizona into New Mexico and Utah, Dinetah is bounded by four sacred mountains — North Mountain (Debe'nitsaa), in the La Plata Mountains of Colorado; South Mountain (Tso Dzil), or Mount Taylor, near Grants, New Mexico; East Mountain (Sis Naajinæ'i), or Sierra Blanca, in Colorado; and West Mountain (Dook Oslid), in the San Francisco Peaks, near Flagstaff, Arizona — and four sacred rivers (the Colorado, the Little Colorado, the San Juan, and the Rio Grande). It is some of the starkest, most magically open-to-the-sky country anywhere — a sagebrush steppe spotted with juniper and ancient, gnarled piñon trees, occasionally gashed by a yawning canyon or thrust up into a craggy, pine-clad mountain range, a magenta mesa, a blood-red cliff, a tiara of lucent, stress-fractured tan sandstone.
>
> "The land is our Bible," a Navajo woman named Sally once explained to me.
>
> — ALEX SHOUMATOFF, "The Navajo Way"

### *Logical appeals*

Logical appeals are viewed as especially trustworthy: "The facts don't lie," some say. Of course, facts are not the only type of logical appeals, which also include firsthand evidence drawn from observations, interviews, surveys and questionnaires, experiments, and personal experience; and secondhand evidence drawn from authorities, the testimony of others, statistics, and other print and online sources. Critical readers need to examine logical appeals just as carefully as emotional and ethical ones. What is the source of the logical appeal — and is that source trustworthy? Are all terms defined clearly? Has the logical evidence presented been taken out of context, and, if so, does that change the meaning of the data? Look, for example, at the following brief passage:

> [I]t is well for us to remember that, in an age of increasing illiteracy, 60 percent of the world's illiterates are women. Between 1960 and 1970, the number of illiterate men in the world rose by 8 million, while the number of illiterate women rose by 40 million.[1] And the number of illiterate women is increasing.
>
> — ADRIENNE RICH, "What Does a Woman Need to Know?"

As a critical reader, you would question these facts and hence check the footnote to discover the source, which in this case is the UN

*Compendium of Social Statistics*. At this point, you might decide to accept this document as authoritative — or you might decide to look further into the United Nations' publications policy, especially to find out how that body defines *illiteracy*. You would also no doubt wonder why Rich chose the decade from 1960 to 1970 for her example and, as a result, check to see when this essay was written. As it turns out, the essay was written in 1979, so the decade of the sixties would have been the most recent data available on literacy. Nevertheless, you should question the timeliness of these statistics: Are they still meaningful thirty years later? Might the statistics today be even more alarming?

If you attend closely to the emotional, ethical, and logical appeals offered in any argument, you will be well on your way to analyzing — and evaluating — it.

**FOR MULTILINGUAL WRITERS: Appeals in various settings**

You may be familiar with emotional, ethical, or logical appeals that are not discussed in this chapter. If so, consider describing them — and how they work — to members of your class. Doing so would deepen the entire class's understanding of what appeals carry the most power in particular settings.

## 9e The elements of an argument

According to philosopher Stephen Toulmin's framework for analyzing arguments, most arguments contain common features: a *claim* or *claims; reasons* for the claim; *assumptions* (whether stated or unstated) that underlie the argument; *evidence* (facts, authoritative opinion, examples, statistics, and so on); and *qualifiers* that limit the claim in some way. In the following discussion, we will examine each of these elements in more detail. The figure on the following page shows how these elements might be applied to an argument about sex education.

### Claims

Claims (also referred to as arguable statements) are statements of fact, opinion, or belief that form the backbone of arguments. In longer essays,

ELEMENTS OF A SAMPLE SEX-EDUCATION ARGUMENT

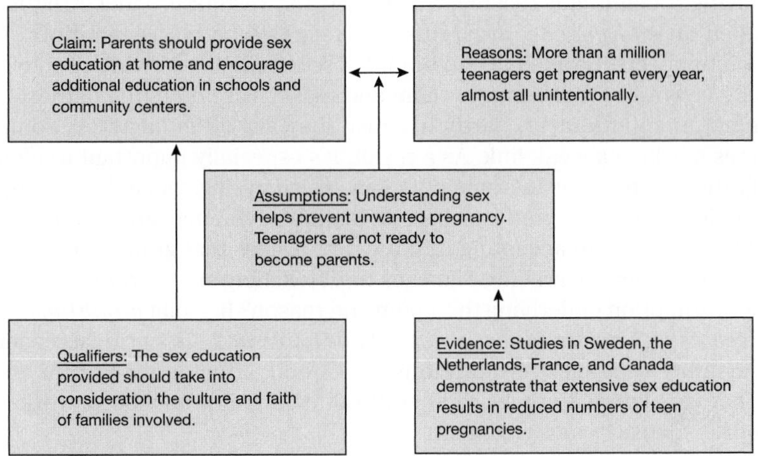


you may detect a series of linked claims or even several separate claims that you need to analyze before you agree to accept them. Claims worthy of arguing are those that are debatable: to say "Ten degrees Fahrenheit is cold" is a claim, but it is probably not debatable — unless you decide that such a temperature in northern Alaska might seem balmy. To take another example, if a movie review you are reading has as its claim "Loved this movie!" is that claim debatable? Almost certainly not, if the reviewer is basing the claim solely on personal taste. But if the reviewer goes on to offer good reasons to love the movie, along with strong evidence to support the reasons, he or she could present a debatable — and therefore arguable — claim.

Claim: Parents should provide sex education at home and encourage additional education in schools and community centers.
Reasons: More than a million teenagers get pregnant every year, almost all unintentionally.
Assumptions: Understanding sex helps prevent unwanted pregnancy. Teenagers are not ready to become parents.
Qualifiers: The sex education provided should take into consideration the culture and faith of families involved.
Evidence: Studies in Sweden, the Netherlands, France, and Canada demonstrate that extensive sex education results in reduced numbers of teen pregnancies.

### Reasons

In fact, a claim is only as good as the reasons attached to it. An essay claiming that grades should be abolished because the writer often earns poor grades is on very thin ice: critical readers will question whether that reason is sufficient to support the claim. As you analyze claims, look for reasons drawn from facts, from authorities, from personal experience, and from examples. Test each reason by asking how directly it supports the claim, how timely it is, and what counter-reasons you could offer to question it.

### Assumptions

Putting a claim and reasons together often results in what Aristotle called an *enthymeme*, an argument that rests on an assumption the writer expects the audience to hold. These assumptions (which Toulmin calls *warrants*) that connect claim and reasons are often the hardest to detect in an argument, partly because they are often unstated, sometimes masking a weak link. As a result, it's especially important to identify the assumptions in arguments you are analyzing. Once the assumption is identified, you can test it against evidence and your own experience before accepting it. If a writer argues that grades should be abolished because grading damages both teaching and learning, what is the assumption underlying this claim and reason? It is that *anything that prevents or hinders education should be abolished.* As a critical reader, remember that such assumptions are deeply affected by culture and belief: ask yourself, then, what cultural differences may be at work in your response to any argument.

### Evidence

Evidence, what Toulmin calls *backing*, also calls for careful analysis in arguments. In an argument about abolishing grades, the writer may offer as evidence several key examples of the damage grading can cause; a statistical analysis of the correlation between grades and later success in life; a historical precedent from the centuries when grading was not used; or psychological studies of grade-related stress on undergraduate students. As a critical reader, you must evaluate each piece of evidence the writer offers, asking specifically how it relates to the claim, whether it is appropriate and timely, and whether it comes from a credible source.

### Qualifiers

Qualifiers offer a way of limiting or narrowing a claim so that it is as precise as possible. Words or phrases that signal a qualification include *few*, *often*, *in these circumstances*, *rarely*, *typically*, and so on. Claims having no qualifiers can sometimes lead to overgeneralizations. For example, the statement *Grading damages learning* is less precise than *Grading can damage learning in some circumstances.* Look carefully for qualifiers in the arguments you analyze, since they will affect the strength and reach of the claim.

## 9f Fallacies

Fallacies have traditionally been viewed as serious flaws that damage the effectiveness of an argument. But arguments are ordinarily fairly complex in that they always occur in some specific rhetorical situation and in some particular place and time; thus what looks like a fallacy in one situation may appear quite different in another. The best advice is to learn to identify fallacies but to be cautious in jumping to quick conclusions about them. Rather than thinking of them as errors you can root out and use to discredit an arguer, you might think of them as barriers to common ground and understanding, since they so often shut off rather than engender debate. If a letter to the editor argues *If this newspaper thinks additional tax cuts are going to help the middle-class family, then this newspaper is run by imbeciles*, it clearly indulges in a fallacy — in this case, an argument ad hominem or argument against character. But the more important point is that this kind of argument shuts down debate: few are going to respond reasonably to being called imbeciles.

You may want to identify fallacies by associating them with the major appeals of argument — ethical, emotional, and logical.

### 1 Ethical fallacies

Some arguments focus not on establishing the credibility of the writer but on destroying the credibility of an opponent. At times, such attacks are justified: if a nominee for the Supreme Court acted in unethical ways in law school, for example, that information is a legitimate argument against the nominee's confirmation. Many times, however, someone attacks a person's character to avoid dealing with the issue at hand. Such unjustified attacks are called ethical fallacies. They take three main forms: ad hominem charges, guilt by association, and appeals to false authority.

Ad hominem (Latin for "to the man") charges directly attack someone's character rather than focusing on the issue at hand, suggesting that because something is "wrong" with this person, whatever he or she says must also be wrong.

- **Patricia Ireland is just a hysterical feminist. We shouldn't listen to her views on abortion.**

Labeling Ireland *hysterical* and linking that label with *feminist* focuses on Ireland's character rather than on her views on the issue.

Guilt by association attacks someone's credibility by linking that person with a person or activity the audience considers bad, suspicious, or untrustworthy.

- **Senator Fleming does not deserve reelection; one of her assistants turned out to be involved with organized crime.**

  Is there any evidence that the senator knew about the organized-crime involvement?

Appeals to false authority occur when someone with authority or expertise in one sphere — sports, films, and so on — testifies to the greatness of a product or idea in another sphere about which the person probably knows very little. You probably recall some fairly obvious appeals to false authority, as when an actor advertises allergy medication or a NASCAR driver sells soft drinks. Some uses of false authority, however, are quite subtle: consider, for example, a politician who argues that her stand on civil rights is based on biblical authority. While the Bible is certainly an authoritative text in many cultures, it is easy to misuse that authority by calling on the Bible in general to support a specific claim. Even if the politician refers specifically to biblical chapter and verse, the matter of interpretation would almost certainly come into play.

## 2 Emotional fallacies

Appeals to the emotions of an audience constitute a valid and necessary part of argument. Unfair or overblown emotional appeals, however, attempt to overcome readers' good judgment. Most common among these emotional fallacies are bandwagon appeal, flattery, in-crowd appeal, veiled threats, and false analogies.

Bandwagon appeal suggests that a great movement is under way and the reader will be a fool or a traitor not to join it.

- **Voters are flocking to candidate X by the millions, so you'd better cast your vote the right way.**

  Why should you jump on this bandwagon? Where is the evidence to support the claim that a vote for X is a vote cast "right"?

Flattery tries to persuade readers to do something by suggesting that they are thoughtful, intelligent, or perceptive enough to agree with the writer.

- **We know you have the taste to recognize the superlative artistry of Bling diamond jewelry.**

  Would buying the jewelry prove that you recognize superlative artistry?

In-crowd appeal, a special kind of flattery, invites readers to identify with an admired and select group.

- **Want to know a secret that more and more of Middletown's successful young professionals are finding out about? It's Mountainbrook Manor, the condominiums that combine the best of the old with the best of the new.**

  Who are these "successful young professionals," and will you become one just by moving to Mountainbrook Manor?

Veiled threats try to frighten readers into agreement by hinting that they will suffer adverse consequences if they don't agree.

- **If Public Service Electric Company does not get an immediate 15 percent rate increase, its services to you, its customers, may be seriously affected.**

  How serious is this possible effect? Is it legal or likely?

False analogies make comparisons between two situations that are not alike in most or important respects.

- **The volleyball team's sudden descent in the rankings resembled the sinking of the *Titanic*.**

  What, other than "descent" and "sinking," do the two have in common?

## 3 Logical fallacies

Although logical fallacies are usually defined as errors in formal reasoning, they can often work very effectively to convince audiences. Common logical fallacies include begging the question, post hoc, non sequitur, either-or, hasty generalization, oversimplification, and straw man.

Begging the question is a kind of circular argument that treats a debatable statement as if it had been proved true.

- **Television news covered that story well; I learned all I know about it by watching TV.**

  That "I learned all I know" about a story from television does not prove that television news covered the story well; the "proof" is just an assumption that the news covered the story well.

The post hoc fallacy, from the Latin *post hoc, ergo propter hoc*, which means "after this, therefore caused by this," assumes that just because B happened *after* A, it must have been *caused* by A.

- **We should not rebuild the town docks because every time we do, a big hurricane comes along and damages them.**

  Does the reconstruction cause hurricanes?

A non sequitur (Latin for "it does not follow") attempts to tie together two or more logically unrelated ideas as if they were related.

- **If we can send a spacecraft to Mars, then we can discover a cure for cancer.**

  These are both scientific goals, but do they have anything else in common? What does achieving one have to do with achieving the other?

The either-or fallacy asserts that a complex situation can have only two possible outcomes, one of which is necessary or preferable.

- **If we do not build the new aqueduct, businesses in the tri-cities area will be forced to shut down because of lack of water.**

  What is the evidence for this claim? Do no other alternatives exist?

A hasty generalization bases a conclusion on too little evidence or on bad or misunderstood evidence.

- **I couldn't understand the lecture today, so I'm sure this course will be impossible.**

  How can the writer be so sure of this conclusion based on only one piece of evidence?

Oversimplification of the relation between causes and effects is another fallacy based on careless reasoning.

**If we prohibit the sale of alcohol, we will get rid of drunkenness.**

This claim oversimplifies the relation between laws and human behavior.

A straw-man argument misrepresents a real opposition argument as a kind of a dummy claim that can easily be refuted.

**My opponent believes that we should offer therapy to the terrorists. I disagree.**

This claim sets up the "straw man" of a plainly ridiculous opposition argument — who would *not* disagree? The opponent's real position is almost certainly more nuanced.

### 4 Visual fallacies

If we live in the age of the image, as many claim we do, it's important to remember that ethical, emotional, and logical fallacies may take the form of images. In fact, the sheer power of images can make them especially difficult to analyze.

Look, for example, at the following photo of a woman struggling through chest-deep water in the aftermath of Hurricane Katrina in New Orleans. When this photograph was published, a caption explained that she was going to "loot a grocery store." In this case, the photo and caption combine to inspire an emotional response that encourages readers to believe the reports of lawlessness that circulated widely in the days just after the hurricane. But because New Orleans residents in heavily flooded areas had no electricity and received inadequate supplies during the emergency, the visual and text commit an emotional fallacy by insisting that a woman in such desperate circumstances must be "looting."

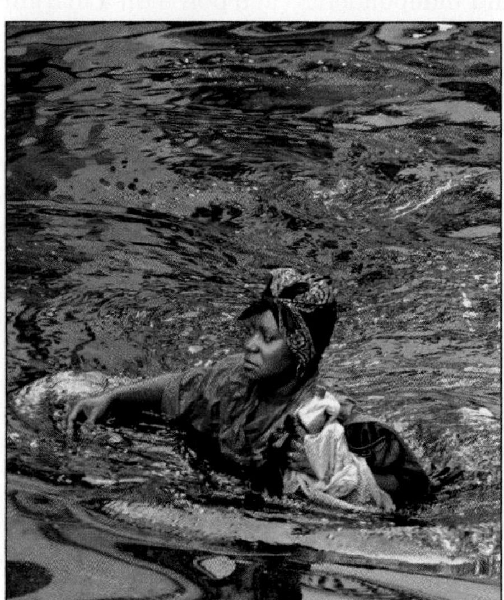

Or take a look at the following bar graph, which purports to deliver a logical argument about how differently Democrats, on the one hand, and Republicans and Independents, on the other, felt about an issue:

GRAPH PRESENTING DATA MISLEADINGLY

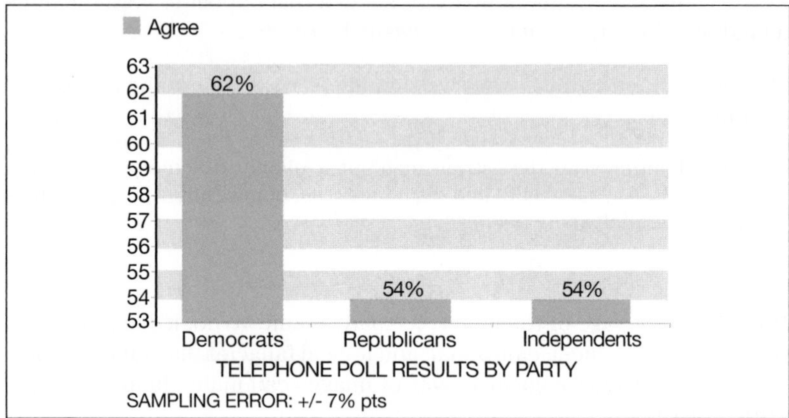


Look closely and you'll see a visual fallacy at work: the vertical axis starts not at zero but at 53 percent, so the visually large difference between the groups is misleading. In fact, a majority of all respondents agree about the issue, and only eight percentage points separate Democrats from Republicans and Independents (in a poll with a margin of error of +/−seven percentage points). Here's how the graph would look if the vertical axis began at zero:

DATA PRESENTED MORE ACCURATELY

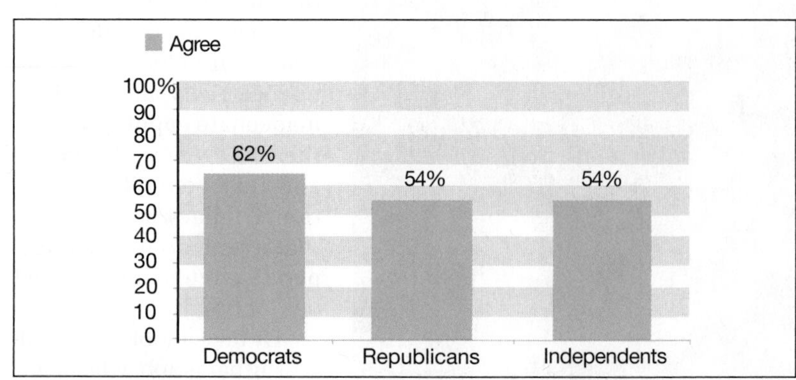

It's not hard to find ethical fallacies that take the form of images as well: think of all the times you've seen a photograph make a politician look really bad — or really good (see below, for example). In these cases, the person who decides to publish the pictures is making an ethical argument that you should examine closely.

### EXERCISE 9.1

Read the following brief essay by Derek Bok, which argues that college administrators should seek to educate and persuade rather than censor students who use speech or symbols that others find deeply offensive. Then carry out an analysis of the argument, beginning with identifying the audience and the author's purpose, then moving to identifying the claim, reason(s), assumption(s), evidence, and qualifiers (if any). As you work, be sure also to identify the emotional, ethical, and logical appeals as well as any fallacies put forward by Bok. You may want to compare your own analysis to the one written by Milena Ateyea in 9g.

For several years, universities have been struggling with the problem of trying to reconcile the rights of free speech with the desire to avoid racial tension. In recent weeks, such a controversy has sprung up at Harvard. Two students hung Confederate flags in public view, upsetting students who equate the Confederacy with slavery. A third student tried to protest the flags by displaying a swastika.

These incidents have provoked much discussion and disagreement. Some students have urged that Harvard require the removal of symbols that offend many members of the community. Others reply that such symbols are a form of free speech and should be protected.

Different universities have resolved similar conflicts in different ways. Some have enacted codes to protect their communities from forms of speech that are deemed to be insensitive to the feelings of other groups. Some have refused to impose such restrictions.

It is important to distinguish between the appropriateness of such communications and their status under the First Amendment. The fact that speech is protected by the First Amendment does not necessarily mean that it is right, proper, or civil. I am sure that the vast majority of Harvard students believe that hanging a Confederate flag in public view — or displaying a swastika in response — is insensitive and unwise because any satisfaction it gives to the students who display these symbols is far outweighed by the discomfort it causes to many others.

I share this view and regret that the students involved saw fit to behave in this fashion. Whether or not they merely wished to manifest their pride in the South — or to demonstrate the insensitivity of hanging Confederate flags, by mounting another offensive symbol in return — they must have known that they would upset many fellow students and ignore the decent regard for the feelings of others so essential to building and preserving a strong and harmonious community.

To disapprove of a particular form of communication, however, is not enough to justify prohibiting it. We are faced with a clear example of the conflict between our commitment to free speech and our desire to foster a community founded on mutual respect. Our society has wrestled with this problem for many years. Interpreting the First Amendment, the Supreme Court has clearly struck the balance in favor of free speech.

While communities do have the right to regulate speech in order to uphold aesthetic standards (avoiding defacement of buildings) or to protect the public from disturbing noise, rules of this kind must be applied across the board and cannot be enforced selectively to prohibit certain kinds of messages but not others.

Under the Supreme Court's rulings, as I read them, the display of swastikas or Confederate flags clearly falls within the protection of the free-speech clause of the First Amendment and cannot be forbidden simply because it offends the feelings of many members of the community. These rulings apply to all agencies of government, including public universities.

Although it is unclear to what extent the First Amendment is enforceable against private institutions, I have difficulty understanding why a university such as Harvard should have less free speech than the surrounding society — or than a public university.

One reason why the power of censorship is so dangerous is that it is extremely difficult to decide when a particular communication is offensive enough to warrant prohibition or to weigh the degree of offensiveness against the potential value of the communication. If we begin to forbid flags, it is only a short step to prohibiting offensive speakers.

I suspect that no community will become humane and caring by restricting what its members can say. The worst offenders will simply find other ways to irritate and insult.

In addition, once we start to declare certain things "offensive," with all the excitement and attention that will follow, I fear that much ingenuity will be exerted trying to test the limits, much time will be expended trying to draw tenuous distinctions, and the resulting publicity will eventually attract more attention to the offensive material than would ever have occurred otherwise.

Rather than prohibit such communications, with all the resulting risks, it would be better to ignore them, since students would then have little reason to create such displays and would soon abandon them. If this response is not possible — and one can understand why — the wisest course is to speak with those who perform insensitive acts and try to help them understand the effects of their actions on others.

Appropriate officials and faculty members should take the lead, as the Harvard House Masters have already done in this case. In talking with students, they should seek to educate and persuade, rather than resort to ridicule or intimidation, recognizing that only persuasion is likely to produce a lasting, beneficial effect. Through such effects, I believe that we act in the manner most consistent with our ideals as an educational institution and most calculated to help us create a truly understanding, supportive community.

— DEREK BOK, "Protecting Freedom of Expression at Harvard"

## Some guidelines for analyzing an argument

Here are some questions that can help you judge the effectiveness of an argument:

- What conclusions about the argument can you reach by playing both the believing and the doubting game? (9b)
- What cultural contexts inform the argument, and what do they tell you about where the writer is coming from? (9b and c)
- What emotional, ethical, and logical appeals is the writer making in support of the argument? (9d)
- How has the writer established credibility to write about the topic? (9d)
- What is the claim (or arguable statement)? Is the claim qualified in any way? (9e)
- What reasons and assumptions support and underlie the claim? (9e)
- What additional evidence backs up the assumption and claim? How current and reliable are the sources? (9e)
- How does the writer use images, graphics, or other visuals to support the argument? (9f4 and Chapter 10)
- What fallacies can you identify, and what effect do they have on the argument's persuasiveness? (9f)
- What is the overall impression you get from analyzing the argument? Are you convinced?

## 9g A student's rhetorical analysis of an argument

For a class assignment, Milena Ateyea was asked to analyze Derek Bok's essay by focusing on the author's use of emotional, ethical, and logical appeals. Her rhetorical analysis follows.

Student Writer

Milena Ateyea

A Curse and a Blessing

*Provocative title suggests Ateyea's mixed response to Bok*

In 1991, when Derek Bok's essay "Protecting Freedom of Expression at Harvard" was first published in the *Boston Globe*, I had just come to America to escape the oppressive Communist regime in Bulgaria. Perhaps my background explains why I support Bok's argument that we should not put arbitrary limits on freedom of expression. Bok wrote the essay in response to a public display of Confederate flags and a swastika at Harvard, a situation that created a heated controversy among the students. As Bok notes, universities have struggled to achieve a balance between maintaining students' right of free speech and avoiding racist attacks. When choices must be made, however, Bok argues for preserving freedom of expression.

*Connects article to her own experience to build credibility (ethical appeal)*

*Provides brief overview of Bok's argument*

*Identifies and states Bok's central claim*

In order to support his claim and bridge the controversy, Bok uses a variety of rhetorical strategies. The author first immerses the reader in the controversy by vividly describing the incident: two Harvard students had hung Confederate flags in public view, thereby "upsetting students who equate the Confederacy with slavery" (51). Another student, protesting the flags, decided to display an even more offensive symbol — the swastika. These actions provoked heated discussions among students. Some students believed that school officials should remove the offensive symbols, whereas others suggested that the symbols "are a form of free speech and should be protected" (51). Bok establishes common ground between the factions: he regrets the actions

*Transition sentence links Bok's claim to strategies he uses to support it*

*Direct quotations show how Bok appeals to emotions through vivid description*

*Shows how Bok establishes common ground between two positions*

of the offenders but does not believe we should prohibit such actions just because we disagree with them.

The author earns the reader's respect because of his knowledge and through his logical presentation of the issue. In partial support of his position, Bok refers to U.S. Supreme Court rulings, which remind us that "the display of swastikas or Confederate flags clearly falls within the protection of the free-speech clause of the First Amendment" (52). The author also emphasizes the danger of the slippery slope of censorship when he warns the reader, "If we begin to forbid flags, it is only a short step to prohibiting offensive speakers" (52). Overall, however, Bok's work lacks the kinds of evidence that statistics, interviews with students, and other representative examples of controversial conduct could provide. Thus, his essay may not be strong enough to persuade all readers to make the leap from this specific situation to his general conclusion.

Emphasizes Bok's credibility and her respect for him (ethical appeal)

Links Bok's credibility to use of logical appeals

Reference to First Amendment serves as assumption to Bok's claim

Comments critically on kinds of evidence Bok's argument lacks

Throughout, Bok's personal feelings are implied but not stated directly. As a lawyer who was president of Harvard for twenty years, Bok knows how to present his opinions respectfully without offending the feelings of the students. However, qualifying phrases like "I suspect that" and "Under the Supreme Court's rulings, as I read them" could weaken the effectiveness of his position. Furthermore, Bok's attempt to be fair to all seems to dilute the strength of his proposed solution. He suggests that one should either ignore the insensitive deeds in the hope that students might change their behavior, or talk to the offending students to help them comprehend how their behavior is affecting other students.

Reiterates Bok's credibility

Identifies qualifying phrases that may weaken claim

Analyzes weaknesses of Bok's proposed solution

Nevertheless, although Bok's proposed solution to the controversy does not appear at first reading to be very strong, it may ultimately be effective. There is enough flexibility in his approach to withstand various tests, and Bok's solution is general enough that it can change with the times and adapt to community standards.

Raises possibility that Bok's imperfect solution may work

Provides reasons why Bok's solution may succeed

In writing this essay, Bok faced a challenging task: to write a short response to a specific situation that represents a very broad and controversial issue. Some people may find

Summarizes Bok's task

that freedom of expression is both a curse and a blessing because of the difficulties it creates. As one who has lived under a regime that permitted very limited, censored expression, I am all too aware that I could not have written this response in 1991 in Bulgaria. As a result, I feel, like Derek Bok, that freedom of expression is a blessing, in spite of any temporary problems associated with it.

Ties conclusion back to title

Concludes by returning to personal experience with censorship and oppression, which argues for accepting Bok's solution

Work Cited

Bok, Derek. "Protecting Freedom of Expression at Harvard." Rpt. in *Current Issues and Enduring Questions*. Ed. Sylvan Barnet and Hugo Bedau. 6th ed. Boston: Bedford, 2002. 51–52. *Boston Globe* 25 May 1991. Print.

## FOR COLLABORATION

Working with a classmate, choose a brief argumentative text — a letter to the editor or an editorial, a "My Turn" essay from *Newsweek* or an essay from *Time*, something from your school newspaper, even an advertisement or editorial cartoon. Then work together to analyze this text, playing both the believing and the doubting game, and identifying claim(s), reason(s), assumption(s), evidence, and qualifiers, as well as emotional, ethical, and logical appeals. Then, still working together, write a two-page double-spaced critical response to the text you have chosen. Finally, bring your chosen text and your critical response to class, and be prepared to present the results of your analysis.

## THINKING CRITICALLY ABOUT ANALYZING ARGUMENTS

For the brief review for *Rolling Stone*, music critic James Hunter recaps five CDs that reissue ten Merle Haggard albums from early in the country star's career. What central claim(s) does Hunter make in this review? What emotional, ethical, and logical appeals does he present in support of his claim (including in the headline and the image of Haggard accompanying the review), and how effective are these appeals?

More than an Okie from Muskogee: Hag in the late Sixties

# Outlaw Classics

*The albums that kept Nashville real in the Sixties and Seventies. By James Hunter*

## Merle Haggard / *Capitol Nashville/EMI*

Merle Haggard wasn't the first outsider to rebuke Nashville prissiness in the Sixties – Johnny Cash, who arrived from Sun Records in Memphis, deserves that honor – but Hag was the most down-to-earth soul that the Music City had seen for some time when he loped onto the scene in the mid to late Sixties. An ex-con from California with Oklahoma roots, he sang eloquently about booze and prison life. His beginnings were in honky-tonk Bakersfield, where he learned first-class musical directness from guys like the great Buck Owens and Wynn Stewart.

For years, Haggard's Sixties and early-Seventies work has been represented chiefly on compilations. This bunch of reissues restores ten of those albums, all with interesting bonus tracks; four of the ten albums have never appeared before on CD. Each showcases Haggard's awesome gifts and inextricable orneriness: There is no Tennessee gothic or flashy Texas ego to this outsider; Haggard was more about subtlety and West Coast calm. A hummable, elastic honky-tonk tune can convey everything he wants to say. His melodies carry a broad range of topics, from cranky love songs ("I'm Gonna Break Every Heart I Can") to prison tunes ("Sing Me Back Home") to perfectly wrought whiskey-and-wine songs, to looks back at his parents' lives. Sometimes, as on the scarily good "I Can't Be Myself," Haggard seems to want to jump out of his own skin; other times, as on "I Threw Away the Rose," he's as centered in his own smooth, crusty tenor as any singer ever has been. In all cases, Haggard sounds like country's coolest customer.

These reissues underscore how Haggard's music far exceeds "Okie From Muskogee," the anti-hippie 1969 smash that made him internationally famous. Cash rocked country up and then went on to become his world's black-clad cultural ambassador. George Jones showed how the field needs at least one opera star, and Willie Nelson yoked local songwriting to American poetry. Haggard proved how crucial it was for a country guy to say what was on his mind – and because he was such a sublime recording artist, he was able to make it stick, right from the start.

KEY TRACKS "I'm Gonna Break Every Heart I Can," "I Can't Be Myself" you can hear them and buy them at *rollingstone.com/merlehaggard*

# 10 Thinking Critically about Visuals

Why make so much of the everyday activity of looking at and responding to visual arguments? Thinking about visual arguments is important precisely because so much contemporary time and space are filled with these images — and because they have very powerful influences on us. When advertisements for sneakers can lead some to attack others in order to steal a pair of the coveted footwear, when five-second sound bites can decide presidential elections, when cartoons can lead to riots, and when photographs of prisoners at Abu Ghraib can horrify the world — it is more than high time to start paying careful attention to visual arguments.

## 10a Visual literacy

The title of a recent book, *The Rise of the Image, the Fall of the Word*, perhaps says it all: visual images now shape or even control our lives at least as much as words do, perhaps even more. The images that bombard us daily influence us to think and behave in certain ways, and images profoundly affect the way we see ourselves and others. So being visually literate — being able to read an image and understand how it aims to persuade or manipulate — is crucial to becoming a critical thinker.

Visual literacy requires you to analyze visuals and the arguments they contain. How do you find out what a visual argument has to say? You do so in much the same way that you analyze any argument. You ask questions to identify the basic elements of the argument — claims, reasons, assumptions, evidence, and so on (9e) — and any ethical, emotional, and logical appeals you can find (9d). You think about the message the visual conveys and the context in which it was presented. You consider the creator(s) of the image and think about why it was created and for whom. You also try to determine what cultural values, such as respect for elders or religious tolerance, are evident and whether different audiences might read the visual differently. But you must also consider the design of the visual argument — whether it is a photograph, advertisement, diagram, cartoon, or some other visual representation — in addition to the other ways it communicates with readers. You should consider, for example, how color, size, shape, texture, layout, sound, and other design elements may affect the effectiveness of the argument.

## 10b Design as a persuasive element

Creators of visual arguments consider the effects of design very carefully. The relative size and placement of various elements and the use of color, sound, or video are some of the design elements to notice. Here are questions to ask yourself as you analyze a visual argument's design:

**QUESTIONS ABOUT DESIGN**

- What detail(s) is your eye first drawn to? Why is your attention drawn to that spot, and what effect does this attention-getting device have on your response to the argument?
- How does the composition of the image affect the argument? What is in the foreground, and what is in the background? Which elements appear close up and which farther away? What is central or at eye level, and what is at the top and at the bottom of the image? Why might the composition be arranged as it is? What effect do the designer's choices have on how you feel about what you see?
- Are the colors appropriate for the argument being made? Does the use of color enhance or conflict with the images and words? Are some parts of the image highlighted with brighter or lighter colors? If so, why? How do you explain the color choices? If black and white are used instead of color, is the choice appropriate for the argument?
- If the visual contains both words and images, what is the relationship between the two in the argument? How well do they work together to make the point? If no words appear, is the visual argument clear without them? Why, or why not?
- Are any words or images repeated? If so, what is the effect of the repetition?
- If sound or video is used, how effective is it in conveying the argument's message?
- What overall impression do you get from the design? What claim does it make? What ethical, emotional, and logical appeals does it use to support the claim?
- How convincing do you find the design of the visual argument?

How an image is designed and formatted affects how others will receive it. Look at the striking image (p. 171) that builds on an analogy between a child and a target, from TurnAround, an organization devoted to helping victims of domestic violence. Note that the design pulls the viewer's eye toward the bull's-eye at the center while also taking advantage of the top left-hand position (where readers of English always begin) for the caption: "A child is not a target." The dramatic combination of words and the image then draws viewers' eyes back over the child-as-bull's-eye target and leads to the demand at the bottom: "Stop the cycle of domestic violence." According to TurnAround, the poster is "intended to strike a chord with abusers as well as their victims." The tension between the words and the image — the child is, in fact, depicted as a target — can make a close look at this poster an unsettling experience.

## 10c Analyzing visual arguments

After you think about how design affects the persuasive power of an image, consider the following questions to analyze the content of a visual argument:

#### QUESTIONS ABOUT THE AUTHORS OR CREATORS

- Who created this visual text? What can you find out about the creator? What other work has he or she done?
- What does the creator's attitude seem to be toward the visual? What effects do you think the creator intends the image to have on viewers?
- What ethical appeals does the creator make (9d)? How does the creator present himself or herself as credible or authoritative?

#### QUESTIONS ABOUT CONTEXT

- Where and in what form was the visual originally published or shown — in a newspaper or magazine, on television or the Internet, on a billboard or poster, or somewhere else?
- What can you infer about the message from the place where the visual first appeared?

#### QUESTIONS ABOUT READERS OR VIEWERS

- What does the visual text assume about its viewers — and about what they know and agree with?

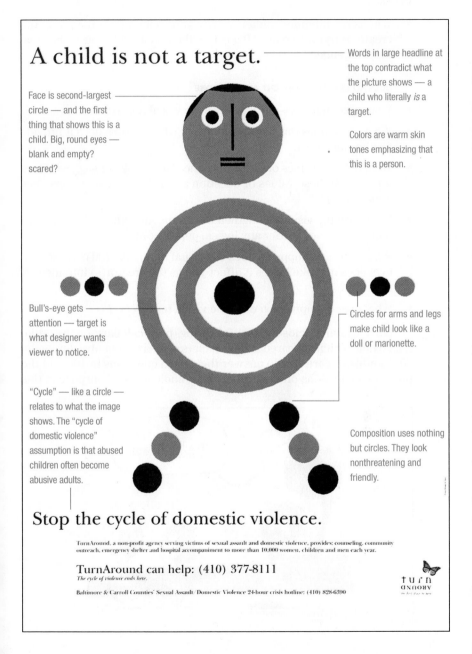

A child is not a target.

Words in large headline at the top contradict what the picture shows — a child who literally *is* a target.

Face is second-largest circle — and the first thing that shows this is a child. Big, round eyes — blank and empty? scared?

Colors are warm skin tones emphasizing that this is a person.

Bull's-eye gets attention — target is what designer wants viewer to notice.

Circles for arms and legs make child look like a doll or marionette.

"Cycle" — like a circle — relates to what the image shows. The "cycle of domestic violence" assumption is that abused children often become abusive adults.

Composition uses nothing but circles. They look nonthreatening and friendly.

Stop the cycle of domestic violence.

TurnAround, a non-profit agency serving victims of sexual assault and domestic violence, provides: counseling, community outreach, emergency shelter and hospital accompaniment to more than 10,000 women, children and men each year.

TurnAround can help: (410) 377-8111

*The cycle of violence ends here.*

Baltimore & Carroll Counties' Sexual Assault/Domestic Violence 24-hour crisis hotline: (410) 828-6390

- Who is the intended audience? Are you a member of the group the creator is trying to reach? If so, does the visual affect you as the creator(s) intended?

**QUESTIONS ABOUT CONTENT AND PURPOSE**

- What argumentative purpose does the visual text convey?
- What claim does the visual text make? What reasons does it provide for the claim (9e)?
- What cultural values or ideals does the visual evoke or suggest? Does it reinforce these values or question them? What assumptions does it make (9e)?
- How does the visual strengthen the argument? What evidence does it present? Does it offer any logical appeals (9d)?
- What emotional appeals does the visual text make (9d)? What feelings does it evoke? Does it affect you as the creator(s) intended? If not, why?
- What overall impression does the visual text create?

Let's examine closely the following political cartoon by Mike Luckovich, which appeared in newspapers across the country during the 2001 anthrax scare. Try to answer the design questions in 10b and the preceding questions on creator, context, audience, and purpose in this

### TALKING THE TALK: Visual texts

"How can a picture be a text?" In its traditional sense, a *text* involves printed words on paper. But in our media-saturated age, we spend at least as much time reading and analyzing images — including moving images — as we spend on printed words. So it makes sense to broaden the definition of *text* to refer to almost anything that sends a message. That's why images are often called *visual texts*.

section. Also consider the claim the cartoon is making (see 9e), and analyze how well the claim supports the argument.

First look at the cartoon's design elements. To which element is your eye first drawn — to Linus in the gas mask, to the words in the bubble, or to something else? Does the landscape look ominous, ordinary, or both? What is the significance of Linus's standing still while the girls are marching along? How well do the words and image work together — that is, would the argument be clearer or more persuasive if it were presented differently?

Next, consider the creator. Even if you are not familiar with the work of Mike Luckovich, a prizewinning political cartoonist, you probably know that the characters in this cartoon were created not by him but by Charles M. Schulz. Think about the attitude Luckovich seems to have toward these borrowed characters. What ethical appeal does he make by including a note below his signature that reads, "Apologies to Schulz"?

You can also ask questions about the medium. This cartoon appeared in nationwide newspapers in the fall of 2001 — what does this suggest about its contents? Who would be the audience for a nationally syndicated newspaper cartoon? Consider, too, what Luckovich expects from his audience. You probably recognize the characters Luckovich depicts and know something about Linus, mentioned in the caption, and the security blanket he carries everywhere in *Peanuts* comics. You may have grown up reading *Peanuts* and watching the popular animated television specials, such as *A Charlie Brown Christmas*, first broadcast in 1965 and still a holiday favorite in the United States. What cultural values does Luckovich invoke by using *Peanuts* characters? What emotional associations does he expect his readers to have with them? What might readers be expected to feel when they see Linus in a gas mask — anger? fear? sadness? nostalgia?

Finally, consider the claim that Luckovich is making — and supporting — in this cartoon. In a discussion with a group of first-year college students about this cartoon, several possible claims emerged.

| | |
|---|---|
| **POSSIBLE CLAIM** | The innocence associated with Charlie Brown's America is no longer possible. |
| **POSSIBLE CLAIM** | A symbolic security blanket can no longer offer protection. |
| **POSSIBLE CLAIM** | In the face of bioterrorism, the best thing to do is continue on as normal. |

All of these claims can be supported by the cartoon. If you choose the first one, how might you support it?

You might word a reason like this: *Because biological or chemical attacks on American soil now seem like a serious threat, the kind of innocence associated with Charlie Brown's America is no longer possible.* You could offer evidence that Charlie Brown's America was a more innocent place where clutching a blanket was enough for Linus to feel secure. You might also note the different meaning *security* has taken on since the fall of 2001 and the widespread view in the United States that further terror attacks are a possibility. You could go on to identify addi-

## Analyzing visual arguments

- How does the design of the visual enhance or hinder the argument? (10b and c)
- What *emotional appeals* does the argument elicit — and how? (9d and 10c)
- What *ethical appeals* make the visual argument credible? Does it call on any authorities or symbols to establish character or credibility? (9d and 10c)
- How does the visual argument make *logical appeals*? Do words and images work together to create a logical cause-effect relationship? How are any examples used? (9d and 10c)
- What *claim(s)* does the visual argument make? (9e and 10c)
- What *reasons* are attached to the claim, and how well are they supported by *evidence*? (9e and 10c)
- What *assumption(s)* underlie the claim and the reasons? (9e and 10c)

tional assumptions and evidence in support of this claim — and you would be well on your way to analyzing this visual argument.

## EXERCISE 10.1

Reproduced below is a page from one of Benetton's public campaigns. Study it carefully. Then, working alone or with one or two other students, make a list of the possible claims the Web site is making.

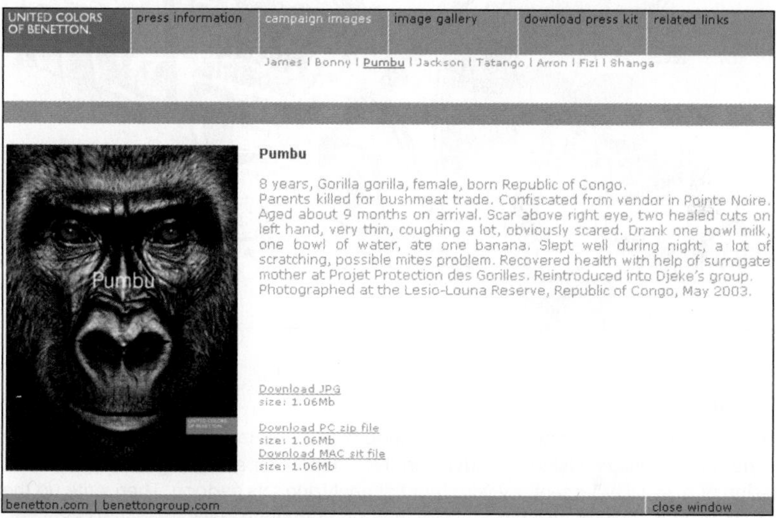

UNITED COLORS OF BENETTON.
press information
campaign images
image gallery
download press kit
related links
James | Bonny | Pumbu | Jackson | Tatango | Arron | Fizi | Shanga
Pumbu
Pumbu
8 years, Gorilla gorilla, female, born Republic of Congo.
Parents killed for bushmeat trade. Confiscated from vendor in Pointe Noire. Aged about 9 months on arrival. Scar above right eye, two healed cuts on left hand, very thin, coughing a lot, obviously scared. Drank one bowl milk, one bowl of water, ate one banana. Slept well during night, a lot of scratching, possible mites problem. Recovered health with help of surrogate mother at Projet Protection des Gorilles. Reintroduced into Djeke's group. Photographed at the Lesio-Louna Reserve, Republic of Congo, May 2003.
Download JPG
size: 1.06Mb
Download PC zip file
size: 1.06Mb
Download MAC sit file
size: 1.06Mb
benetton.com | benettongroup.com
close window


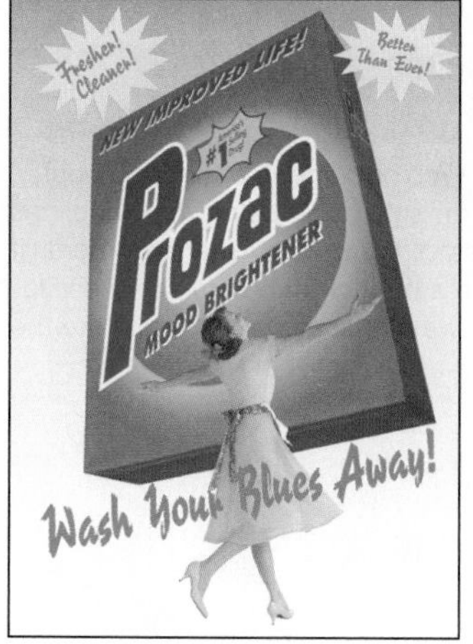


## EXERCISE 10.2

Take a close look at the accompanying image, and use the guidelines in this chapter to analyze its content and design. As a result of your analysis, write a brief (one-page) response explaining how the image achieves its effects and analyzing the values it implicitly holds.

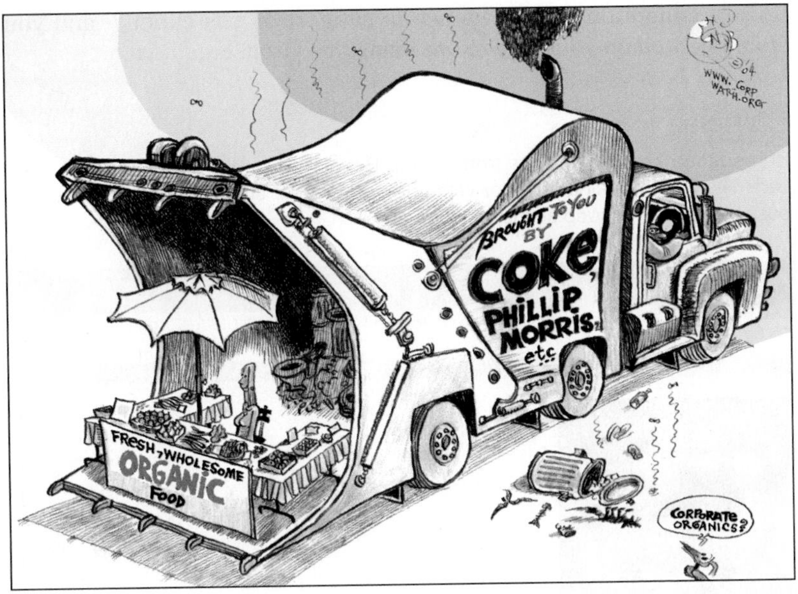

### EXERCISE 10.3

Look at the above cartoon by Khalil Bendib, a frequent contributor to the *San Francisco Chronicle*. Using the advice in this chapter for analyzing the content and design of a visual argument, try your hand at analyzing this cartoon. Then write up the results of your analysis as a set of notes, and bring them to class for discussion.

## THINKING CRITICALLY ABOUT YOUR USE OF VISUAL ARGUMENTS

Take a look at a piece of your writing (an essay, a Web document, a report, a poster, a brochure, and so on) that uses visuals to make an argument. Using the guidelines offered in this chapter, evaluate the effectiveness of your own visual argument. If you have not created such a piece of writing, take a project that does not use visuals to advance its argument and reread it, noting ways that visuals could make the argument more effective.

# Constructing Arguments

# 11

Chances are, you've been making convincing arguments since early childhood, and those around you slowly learned to respond to these arguments. But if family members and friends are not always easy to convince, then the job of making effective arguments to those you don't know presents even more challenges. It is especially difficult to argue with people who are thousands of miles away and are encountering your argument only in cyberspace. You will need to take up those challenges as you craft effective arguments of your own.

## 11a The purposes of argument

Since all language is in some sense argumentative, the purposes of argument will certainly vary widely. For many years, however, traditional notions of argument tended to highlight one purpose — winning. Although winning is still one important purpose of argument, studies of the argument strategies of people from groups historically excluded from public debate — including women and people of color — have demonstrated that it is by no means the only purpose. Nor is winning always going to be *your* purpose. For instance, if you are trying to decide whether to major in business or in chemistry, you may want to consider, or "argue," all sides of the issue. Your purpose is hardly to win out over someone else; instead, it is to understand your choices in order to make a wise decision.

### *To win*

The most traditional purpose of academic argument, arguing *to win* is used in campus debating societies, in political debates, in trials, and often in business. The writer or speaker aims to control the audience, to present a position that prevails over or defeats the positions of others. Presidential debates and trials, for example, focus most often not on changing the opponent's mind but on defeating him or her in order to appeal to someone else — the voting public, the judge, and so on.

### *To convince*

More often than not, out-and-out defeat of another is not only unrealistic but also undesirable. Rather, the goal is *to convince* other persons that they should change their minds about an issue. A writer must provide reasons so compelling that the audience willingly agrees with the writer's conclusion. Such is the goal of advocates of assisted suicide: they well know that they cannot realistically hope to defeat or conquer those who oppose such acts. Rather, they understand that they must provide reasons compelling enough to change people's minds.

### *To reach a decision or explore an issue*

Often, a writer must enter into conversation with others and collaborate in seeking the best possible understanding of a problem, exploring all possible approaches and choosing the best alternative. Argument *to decide or explore* does not seek to conquer or control others or even to convince. Your purpose in many situations — from trying to decide which laptop to buy to exploring with your family the best way to care for an elderly relative — will be to share information and perspectives in order to make informed political, professional, and personal choices.

### *To change yourself*

Sometimes you will find yourself arguing primarily with yourself, and those arguments often take the form of intense meditations on a theme, or even of prayer. In such cases, you may be hoping *to transform something in yourself* or to reach peace of mind on a troubling subject. If

#### TALKING THE TALK: Arguments

"Argument seems so negative — I don't want to attack anybody or contradict what someone else says." In some times and places — law courts, for example — argument may call for attacking the credibility of the opponent. Or you may have used the word *argument* in childhood to describe a conversation in which you voiced nothing more than "I did not!" or "You did too!" But in college writing, you have a chance to reject this narrow definition and to use argument in a much broader way. Instead of attacking or contradicting, you will be expected to explore ideas and to work toward convincing yourself as well as others that these ideas are valuable.

you know a familiar mantra or prayer, for example, think of what it "argues" for and how it uses quiet meditation to help achieve that goal.

## 11b Determining whether a statement can be argued

An early step in an argument intended to convince or decide is to make a statement about a topic and then check to see that the statement can, in fact, be argued. An arguable statement has three characteristics:

1. It attempts to convince readers of something, change their minds about something, or urge them to do something — or it explores a topic in order to make a wise decision.
2. It addresses a problem for which no easily acceptable solution exists or asks a question to which no absolute answer exists.
3. It presents a position that readers might realistically have varying perspectives on.

**ARGUABLE STATEMENT** Advertising in women's magazines contributes to the poor self-image that most young women have.

This statement seeks to convince, addresses a problem — poor self-image among young women — that has no clear-cut solution, and takes a position many could disagree with.

**UNARGUABLE STATEMENT** Women's magazines earn millions of dollars every year from advertising.

This statement does not present a position; it states a fact that can easily be verified and thus offers a poor basis for argument.

### EXERCISE 11.1

Using the three characteristics just listed, decide which of the following statements are arguable and which are not.

1. *The Lord of the Rings* was the best movie of the last decade.
2. The climate of the earth is gradually getting warmer.
3. The United States must further reduce social spending in order to balance the budget.
4. Shakespeare died in 1616.
5. Marlowe really wrote the plays of Shakespeare.

6. Water boils at 212 degrees Fahrenheit.
7. Van Gogh's paintings are the work of a madman.
8. The incidence of breast cancer has risen in the last ten years.
9. The Federal Emergency Management Agency's response to disasters must be radically improved.
10. A fifty-five-mile-per-hour speed limit lowers accident rates.

**bedfordstmartins.com/smhandbook** For additional exercises on recognizing argument, go to Exercise Central and click on **Argument**.

## 11c Formulating a working thesis

Once you have an arguable statement, you need to develop it into a working thesis (5c). One way to do so — often called the Toulmin system — is to identify the elements of an argument (9e and 11i2), which include the following: the claim or arguable statement; one or more reasons for the claim; and assumptions — sometimes unstated — that underlie the claim and reasons. Let's apply these elements to a specific topic — the use of pesticides.

*Begin with an arguable statement (or initial claim).* The following statement is arguable because it aims to convince, it addresses an issue with no one identifiable answer, and it can realistically be disputed.

| | |
|---|---|
| **ARGUABLE STATEMENT (OR INITIAL CLAIM)** | Pesticides should be banned. |

*Attach a good reason.* Although the preceding statement does make a claim — that pesticides should be banned — it offers no reason for doing so. To turn a claim into a working thesis for an argument, you need to include at least one good reason to support the arguable statement.

| | |
|---|---|
| **REASON** | They endanger the lives of farmworkers. |
| **WORKING THESIS (CLAIM WITH REASON ATTACHED)** | Because they endanger the lives of farmworkers, pesticides should be banned. |

*Develop or identify assumptions underlying the claim and reasons.* Once you have a working thesis, examine your assumptions to help test your reasoning and strengthen your argument. Begin by identifying underlying assumptions that support the working thesis.

| | |
|---|---|
| **WORKING THESIS** | Because they endanger the lives of farmworkers, pesticides should be banned. |
| **ASSUMPTION 1** | Workers have a right to a safe working environment. |
| **ASSUMPTION 2** | Substances that endanger the lives of workers deserve to be banned. |

Once you have a working thesis, you may want to use qualifiers to make it more precise and thus less susceptible to criticism. The preceding thesis might be qualified in this way:

- **Because they *often* endanger the lives of farmworkers, *most* pesticides should be banned.**

**bedfordstmartins.com/smhandbook** For additional help with composing arguments, go to Writing Resources/Links and click on **Critical Thinking and Argument.**

## EXERCISE 11.2

Using two arguable statements from Exercise 11.1 or two that you create, formulate two working theses, identifying the claim, reason(s), and assumption(s) for each.

## EXERCISE 11.3

Formulate an arguable statement, and create a working thesis, for two of the following general topics.

1. the Palestinian-Israeli conflict
2. mandatory HIV testing for prison inmates
3. raising the minimum wage
4. reinstatement of a U.S. military draft
5. music downloading

## FOR COLLABORATION

Working with two other members of your class, find two current advertisements you consider particularly eye-catching and persuasive. Then work out what central claim each ad is making, and identify reasons and assumptions in support of the claim. Finally, prepare a brief collaborative report of your findings for the class.

## 11d Finding good reasons

In his *Rhetoric*, Aristotle discusses the various ways one can support a claim. Torture, he notes, makes for a very convincing argument but not one that reasonable people will resort to. In effecting real changes in minds and hearts, we need instead to rely on *good reasons* — reasons that establish our credibility, that appeal to logic, and that appeal to emotion. You can use these appeals to analyze the arguments of others (9d) as well as to construct arguments of your own.

## 11e Ethical appeals

To make your argument convincing, you must first gain the respect and trust of your readers, or establish your credibility with them. The ancient Greeks called this particular kind of character appeal *ethos*, and we refer to it as an ethical appeal (9d). You can establish credibility by demonstrating your knowledge of the topic, by showing that you and your audience share at least some common ground, and by showing yourself to be fair and evenhanded. Visuals can strengthen your ability to make such ethical appeals.

### 1 Personal knowledge about the topic

A writer can establish credibility first by demonstrating his or her knowledge about the topic at hand. You can show that you have some personal experience with the subject: for example, if you are a former preschool teacher, you could mention your teaching background as part of an argument for increased funding of the Head Start program. In addition, showing that you have thought about and researched the subject carefully can help you establish a confident tone.

To determine whether you can effectively present yourself as knowledgeable enough to argue an issue, consider the following questions:

- Can you provide information about your topic from sources other than your own knowledge?
- How reliable are your sources?
- Do any sources contradict one another? If so, can you account for or resolve the contradictions?
- If you have personal experience relating to the issue, would telling about this experience help support your claim?

These questions may help you see what other work you need to do to establish credibility: perhaps you should do more research, resolve contradictions, refocus your working thesis, or even change your topic.

### 2 Common ground

Many arguments between people or groups are doomed to end without resolution because the two sides occupy no common ground, no starting point of agreement. They are, to use an informal phrase, coming from completely different places. Such has often been the case, for example, in India-Pakistan talks, in which the beginning positions of each party have directly conflicted with those of the other side, leaving no room for a settlement that appeases both nations.

Lack of common ground also dooms many arguments that take place in our everyday lives. If you and your roommate cannot agree on how often to clean your apartment, for instance, the difficulty may well be that your definition of a clean apartment conflicts radically with your roommate's. You may find, in fact, that you will not be able to resolve such issues until you can establish common definitions, ones that can turn futile quarrels into constructive arguments. (For more on establishing common ground, see Chapter 27.)

Common ground is just as important in written arguments as it is in diplomatic negotiations or personal disputes. The following questions can help you find common ground in presenting an argument:

- What are the differing perspectives on this issue?
- What common ground can you find — aspects of the issue on which all sides agree?
- How can you express such agreement clearly to all sides?
- How can you discover — and consider — opinions on this issue that differ from your own?
- How can you use language — occupational, regional, or ethnic varieties of English or languages other than English (28c–e) — to establish common ground with those you address?

If you turn to Teal Pfeifer's essay in 11k, you will see that she attempts to establish common ground by assuming that all her readers are concerned about the health and well-being of young women — and by explaining that she, like most women, cannot conform to a magazine's ideal of beauty.

### 3 Fairness toward counterarguments

In arguing a position, writers must demonstrate fairness toward opposing arguments, sometimes called counterarguments (11i2). Audiences are more inclined to give credibility to writers who seem to be fairly considering and representing their opponents' views than to those who seem to be ignoring or distorting such views. Part of your job as an effective writer, then, might involve anticipating possible counterarguments to your writing and establishing yourself as open minded and even-handed. The following questions can help you discover ways of doing so:

- How can you show that you are taking into account all significant points of view?
- How can you demonstrate that you understand and sympathize with points of view other than your own?
- What can you do to show that you have considered evidence carefully, even when it does not support your position?

Some writers, instead of demonstrating fairness, may make unjustified attacks on an opponent's credibility. Such attacks, which are known as ethical fallacies (9f1), should be avoided in your writing.

### 4 Visuals that make ethical appeals

In arguments and in other kinds of writing, visuals that reflect authority can help build credibility. That's why so many universities, nonprofit organizations, and government agencies are following the lead of business and creating "brand-name" images for themselves. The Environmental Protection Agency, for example, includes its seal — and usually its motto, *Protecting human health, safeguarding the natural environment* — on its reports and documents. As shown here, the seal and motto work to establish the ethos or credibility of the agency and its documents.

A VISUAL THAT MAKES AN ETHICAL APPEAL

Visuals that make ethical appeals add to your credibility and fairness as a writer. For college work, you may want to use such visual images. If you build a Web site, consider including a good picture of yourself as well as a brief statement about your background and credentials. If you intend to keep the site going for some time, consider developing a logo for it and using that image to unify the site and help build recognition for it — and for you. Doing so can build your credibility.

## EXERCISE 11.4

List the ways in which the following advertisement for the energy company BP demonstrates knowledge, establishes common ground, and shows fairness. Do you think it succeeds in establishing credibility?

We need more than energy for the future. We need energies.

One form of energy won't secure our needs for the future. It's going to take many–solar, wind, hydrogen, natural gas, and yes, oil. So we're investing $15 billion in the Gulf of Mexico to find and produce new oil and gas supplies. Recently, we announced plans to invest up to $8 billion over 10 years in a new business called BP Alternative Energy that will use a wide range of energy sources to provide low carbon electricity.
It's a start.

bp

beyond petroleum®

bp.com

### EXERCISE 11.5

Using a working thesis you drafted for Exercise 11.2 or 11.3, write a paragraph or two describing how you would go about establishing your credibility in arguing that thesis.

## 11f Logical appeals

While the character a writer presents in writing always exerts a strong appeal (or lack of appeal) in an argument, credibility alone cannot and should not carry the full burden of convincing readers. Indeed, many are inclined to think that the logic of the argument — the reasoning behind it — is as important as its ethos. Logical appeals (9d), known to the ancient Greeks as *logos*, can thus be very effective; particularly useful types of logical appeals include examples, precedents, and narratives; authority and testimony; causes and effects; and inductive and deductive reasoning. In addition, visuals can help you enhance your logical appeals.

### 1 Examples, precedents, and narratives

Just as a picture can sometimes be worth a thousand words, so can a well-conceived example be extremely valuable in arguing a point. Examples are used most often to support generalizations or to bring abstractions to life. In an argument about American mass media and body image, for instance, you might make the general statement that popular media send the message that a woman must be thin to be attractive; you might then illustrate your generalization with these examples:

> At the supermarket checkout, a tabloid publishes unflattering photographs of a young singer and comments on her apparent weight gain in shocked captions that ask "What happened?!?" Another praises a starlet for quickly shedding "ugly pounds" after the recent birth of a child. The cover of *Cosmopolitan* features a glamorously made-up and airbrushed actress in an outfit that reveals her remarkably tiny waist and flat stomach. In every advertisement in the magazine that depicts a woman, the woman is thin — and the context makes it clear that we're supposed to think that she is beautiful.

The generalization would mean far less without the examples.

Examples can also help us understand abstractions. Famine, for instance, may be difficult for us to think about in the abstract, but a graphic description of a drought-stricken community, its riverbed cracked and dry, its people listless, emaciated, and with stomachs bloated by hunger, speaks directly to our understanding.

Precedents are particular kinds of examples taken from the past. The most common use of precedent occurs in law, where an attorney may ask for a certain ruling based on a similar earlier case. Precedent appears in everyday arguments as well. If, as part of a proposal for increasing lighting in the library garage, you point out that the university has increased lighting in four other garages in the past year, you are arguing on the basis of precedent.

In research writing (see Chapters 12–21), you must identify your sources for any examples or precedents not based on your own knowledge.

The following questions can help you check any use of example or precedent:

- How representative are the examples?
- Are they sufficient in strength or number to lead to a generalization?
- In what ways do they support your point?
- How closely does the precedent relate to the point you're trying to make? Are the situations really similar?
- How timely is the precedent? (What would have been applicable in 1920 is not necessarily applicable today.)

Because storytelling is universal, narratives can be very persuasive in helping readers understand and accept the logic of an argument. In arguing for increased funding for the homeless, for instance, you might include a brief narrative about a day in the life of a homeless person to dramatize the issue and help readers see the need for more funding.

Stories drawn from your own experience can appeal particularly to readers, for they not only help make your point in true-to-life, human terms but also help readers know you better and therefore identify with you more closely. In arguing for a stronger government campaign against smoking, for example, former President Clinton often drew on personal stories of his own family's experience with lung cancer.

When you include stories in an argument, ask yourself the following questions:

- Does the narrative support your thesis?
- Will the story's significance to the argument be clear to your readers?

- Is the story one of several good reasons or pieces of evidence — or does it have to carry the main burden of the argument?

In general, do not rely solely on the power of stories to carry your argument, since readers usually expect writers to state and argue their reasons more directly and abstractly as well. An additional danger if you use only your own experiences is that you can seem focused too much on yourself (and perhaps not enough on your readers).

As you develop your own arguments, keep in mind that while narratives can provide effective logical support, they may be used equally effectively for ethical or emotional appeals as well.

**FOR MULTILINGUAL WRITERS: Counting your own experience**

You may have learned that stories based on your own personal experience don't count in academic arguments. If so, reconsider this advice, for showing an audience that you have personal experience with a topic can carry strong persuasive appeal with many English-speaking audiences. As with all evidence used in an argument, however, narratives based on your own experience must be pertinent to the topic, understandable to the audience, and clearly related to your purpose.

### 2 Authority and testimony

Another way to support an argument logically is to cite an authority. In recent decades, the use of authority has figured prominently in the controversy over smoking. Since the U.S. surgeon general's 1964 announcement that smoking is hazardous to health, many Americans have quit smoking, largely persuaded by the authority of the scientists offering the evidence.

But as with other strategies for building support for an argumentative claim, citing authorities demands careful consideration. Ask yourself the following questions to be sure you are using authorities effectively:

- Is the authority timely? (The argument that the United States should pursue a policy just because it was supported by Thomas Jefferson will probably fail because Jefferson's time was so radically different from ours.)

- Is the authority qualified to judge the topic at hand? (To cite a movie star in an essay on linguistics, an appeal to false authority, would not strengthen your argument [9f1].)
- Is the authority likely to be known and respected by readers? (To cite an unfamiliar authority without some identification will lessen the impact of the evidence.)
- Are the authority's credentials clearly stated and verifiable? (Especially with Web-based sources, it is crucial to know whose authority guarantees the reliability of the information.)

Authorities are commonly cited in research writing (see Chapters 12–21), which often relies on the findings of other people. In addition, you may cite authorities in an assignment that asks you to review the literature of any field.

Testimony — the evidence an authority presents in support of a claim — is a feature of much contemporary argument. If testimony is timely, accurate, representative, and provided by a respected authority, then it, like authority itself, can add powerful support to an argument. In an essay for a literature class, for example, you might argue that a new edition of a literary work will open up many new areas of interpretation. You could strengthen this argument by adding a quotation from the author's biographer, noting that the new edition carries out the author's intentions much more closely than the previous edition did.

In research writing (see Chapters 12–21), you should cite your sources for authority and testimony not based on your own knowledge.

### FOR MULTILINGUAL WRITERS: Bringing in other voices

Sometimes quoting authorities will prompt you to use language other than standard academic English. For instance, if you're writing about political relations between Mexico and the United States, you might quote a leader of a Mexican American organization; using that person's own words — which may be partly or entirely in Spanish or a regional variety of English — can carry extra power, calling up a voice from a pertinent community. See Chapter 28 for advice about using varieties of English and other languages.

### 3 Causes and effects

Showing that one event is the cause — or the effect — of another can sometimes help support an argument. Suppose you are trying to explain, in a petition to change your grade in a course, why you were unable to take the final examination. In such a case, you would probably try to trace the causes of your failure to appear (the death of your grandmother followed by the theft of your car, perhaps) so that the committee reading the petition would reconsider the effect (your not taking the examination).

Tracing causes often lays the groundwork for an argument, particularly if the effect of the causes is one we would like to change. In an environmental science class, for example, a student may argue that a national law regulating smokestack emissions from utility plants is needed because (1) acid rain on the East Coast originates from emissions at utility plants in the Midwest, (2) acid rain kills trees and other vegetation, (3) utility lobbyists have prevented midwestern states from passing strict laws controlling emissions from such plants, and (4) in the absence of such laws, acid rain will destroy most eastern forests by 2020. In this case, the first point is that the emissions cause acid rain; the second, that acid rain causes destruction in eastern forests; and the third, that states have not acted to break the cause-effect relationship established by the first two points. The fourth point ties all of the previous points together to provide an overall argument from effect: unless a national law is passed, most eastern forests are doomed.

In fact, a cause-effect relationship is often extremely difficult to establish. Scientists and politicians continue to disagree, for example, over the extent to which acid rain is responsible for the so-called dieback of many eastern forests. If you can show strong evidence that a cause produces an effect, though, you will have a powerful argument at your disposal.

### 4 Inductive and deductive reasoning

Traditionally, logical arguments are classified as using either inductive or deductive reasoning, but in practice, the two types of reasoning usually appear together. Inductive reasoning is the process of making a generalization based on a number of specific instances. If you find you are ill on ten occasions after eating seafood, for example, you will likely draw the inductive generalization that seafood makes you ill. It may not be an absolute certainty that seafood was the culprit, but the probability lies in that direction.

Deductive reasoning, on the other hand, reaches a conclusion by assuming a general principle (known as a major premise) and then applying that principle to a specific case (the minor premise). In practice, this general principle is usually derived from induction. The inductive generalization *Seafood makes me ill*, for instance, could serve as the major premise for the deductive argument *Since all seafood makes me ill, the shrimp on this buffet is certain to make me ill.*

Deductive arguments have traditionally been analyzed as syllogisms — three-part statements containing a major premise, a minor premise, and a conclusion.

| | |
|---|---|
| **MAJOR PREMISE** | All people die. |
| **MINOR PREMISE** | I am a person. |
| **CONCLUSION** | I will die. |

Syllogisms, however, are too rigid and absolute to serve in arguments about questions that have no absolute answers, and they often lack any appeal to an audience. Aristotle's simpler alternative, the enthymeme (9e), calls on the audience to supply the implied major premise. Consider the following example:

> Since violent video games can be addictive and cause psychological harm, players and their parents must carefully evaluate such games and monitor their use.

You can analyze this enthymeme by restating it in the form of two premises and a conclusion.

| | |
|---|---|
| **MAJOR PREMISE** | Games that cause harm to players should be evaluated and monitored. |
| **MINOR PREMISE** | Violent video games cause addiction and psychological harm to players. |
| **CONCLUSION** | These games should be evaluated and monitored. |

Note that the major premise is one the writer can count on an audience agreeing with or supplying: safety and common sense demand that potentially harmful games should be used with great care. As such, this premise is *assumed* rather than stated in the enthymeme. By implicitly asking the audience to supply this premise to the argument, the writer engages the audience's participation.

Note that a deductive conclusion is only as strong as the premises on which it is based. The citizen who argues that *Ed is a crook and shouldn't be elected to public office* is arguing deductively, based on an implied major premise: *No crook should be elected to public office.* Most people would agree with this major premise. So the issue in this argument rests on the minor premise that Ed is a crook. Satisfactory proof of that premise will make us likely to accept the deductive conclusion that Ed shouldn't be elected.

At other times, the unstated premise may be more problematic. The person who says *Don't bother to ask for Ramon's help with physics — he's a jock* is arguing deductively on the basis of an implied major premise: *Jocks don't know anything about physics.* In this case, careful listeners would demand proof of the unstated premise. Because bigoted or prejudiced statements often rest on this kind of reasoning — a type of logical fallacy (9f3) — writers should be particularly alert to it.

A helpful variation on the syllogism and the enthymeme is the Toulmin system (9e, 11c, and 11i2), which looks for claims, reasons, and assumptions rather than major and minor premises.

| | |
|---|---|
| **CLAIM** | Violent video games should be carefully evaluated and their use monitored. |
| **REASON(S)** | Violent video games cause addiction and psychological harm to players. |
| **ASSUMPTION** | Games that cause harm to players should be evaluated and monitored. |

Note that in this system the assumption — which may be unstated — serves the same function as the assumed major premise in an enthymeme.

### 5 Visuals that make logical appeals

Visuals that make logical appeals can be especially useful in arguments, since they present factual information that can be taken in at a glance. Charts, graphs, tables, maps, photographs, and so on can help get your points across. For a report on minority-owned business enterprises, the U.S. Census Bureau used many charts and graphs, including the accompanying pie chart. In the same way, *Business Week* used a simple bar graph to carry a big message about equality of pay for men and women. A quick glance will tell you how long it would take to explain all the information in these charts with words alone. In these instances, pictures can be worth a thousand words.

VISUALS THAT MAKE LOGICAL APPEALS

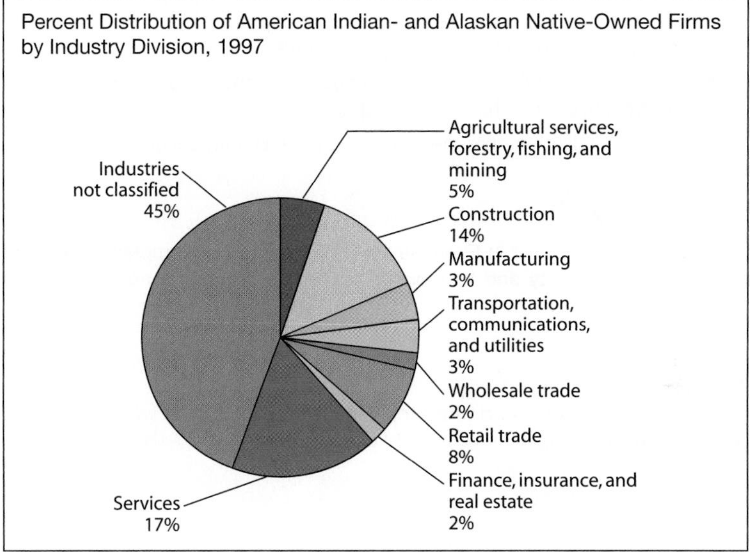
Percent Distribution of American Indian- and Alaskan Native-Owned Firms by Industry Division, 1997
Industries not classified 45%
Agricultural services, forestry, fishing, and mining 5%
Construction 14%
Manufacturing 3%
Transportation, communications, and utilities 3%
Wholesale trade 2%
Retail trade 8%
Finance, insurance, and real estate 2%
Services 17%

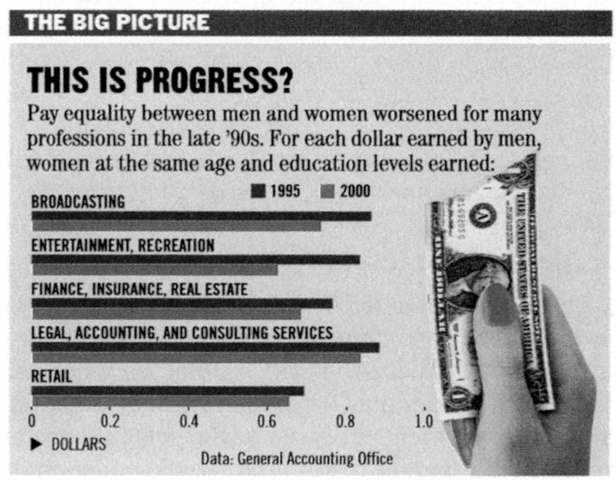
THE BIG PICTURE
THIS IS PROGRESS?
Pay equality between men and women worsened for many professions in the late '90s. For each dollar earned by men, women at the same age and education levels earned:
1995
2000
BROADCASTING
ENTERTAINMENT, RECREATION
FINANCE, INSURANCE, REAL ESTATE
LEGAL, ACCOUNTING, AND CONSULTING SERVICES
RETAIL
0
0.2
0.4
0.6
0.8
1.0
DOLLARS
Data: General Accounting Office

### EXERCISE 11.6

The following sentences contain deductive arguments based on implied major premises. Identify each of the implied premises.

1. Active euthanasia is morally acceptable when it promotes the best interests of everyone concerned and violates no one's rights.
2. Women soldiers should not serve in combat positions because doing so would expose them to a much higher risk of death.
3. Animals can't talk; therefore they can't feel pain as humans do.

### EXERCISE 11.7

Analyze the advertisement in Exercise 11.4 for the use of examples, precedents, and narratives; authority and testimony; causes and effects; and induction and deduction.

### EXERCISE 11.8

Using a working thesis you drafted for Exercise 11.2 or 11.3, write a paragraph describing the logical appeals you would use to support the thesis.

## 11g Emotional appeals

Most successful arguments appeal to our hearts as well as to our minds. Thus, good writers supplement appeals to logic and reason with emotional appeals to their readers. This principle is vividly demonstrated by the AIDS epidemic in Africa. Facts and figures — logical appeals — convince us that the problem is real and serious. What elicits an outpouring of support, however, is the arresting emotional power of stories and images of people with the disease and their families. An effective emotional appeal (*pathos*, to the ancient Greeks) can be made with description and concrete language, with figurative language, and with visuals, as well as by shaping an appeal to a particular audience.

### 1 Description and concrete language

Like photographs, vivid, detailed description can bring a moving immediacy to any argument. A student may amass facts and figures, including diagrams and maps, to illustrate the problem of wheelchair access to the library. Her first draft may be packed with information. But only when the student asks a friend who uses a wheelchair to accompany her to the library does the student writer discover the concrete details necessary to move readers.

The heart of effective description is concrete or specific language (29c). Although the student could have written that her friend "had trouble entering the library," such a general statement would not appeal to readers' emotions. Instead, she uses concrete details: "Maria inched her heavy wheelchair up the narrow, steep entrance ramp, her arms straining to pull up the last twenty feet, her face pinched with the sheer effort."

## 2 Figurative language

Figurative language, or figures of speech (29d), paint detailed pictures that build understanding. They do so by relating something new or unfamiliar to something the audience knows well and by making striking comparisons between something you are writing about and something else that helps a reader visualize, identify with, or understand it.

Figures of speech include metaphors, similes, and analogies. Metaphors compare two things directly: *Richard the Lion-Hearted*; *old age is the evening of life*; *the defensive players are pit bulls on pork chops*. Similes make comparisons using *like* or *as*: *Richard was as brave as a lion*; *old age is like the evening of life*; *the defensive players are like pit bulls on pork chops*. Analogies are extended metaphors or similes that compare an unfamiliar concept or process to a more familiar one to help the reader understand the unfamiliar concept.

> I see the Internet as a city struggling to be built, its laws only now being formulated, its notions of social order arising out of the needs of its citizens and the demands of their environment. Like any city, the Net has its charlatans and its thieves as well as its poets, engineers, and philosophers. . . . Our experience of the Internet will be determined by how we master its core competencies. They are the design principles that are shaping the electronic city.
>
> — PAUL GILSTER, *Digital Literacy*

A student arguing for a more streamlined course-registration process may find good use for an analogy, saying that the current process makes students feel like laboratory rats in a maze. This analogy, which suggests manipulation, frustration, and a clinical coldness, creates a vivid description and adds emotional appeal to the argument. For the analogy to work effectively, however, the student would have to show that the current registration process has a number of similarities to a laboratory maze, such as confused students wandering through complex bureaucratic channels and into dead ends.

As you use analogies or other figurative language to bring emotion into an argument, be careful not to overdo it. Emotional appeals that are unfair or overly dramatic — known as emotional fallacies (9f2) — may serve only to cloud your readers' judgment and ultimately diminish your argument.

### 3 Shaping your appeal to your audience

As with appeals to credibility and logic, appealing to emotions is effective only insofar as it moves your particular audience. A student arguing for increased lighting in campus parking garages, for instance, might consider the emotions such a discussion might raise (fear of attack, for example, or anger at being subjected to danger), decide which emotions the intended audience would be most responsive to, and then look for descriptive and figurative language to carry out such an appeal.

In a leaflet to be distributed on campus or in an online notice to a student listserv, for example, the writer might describe the scene in a dimly lit garage as a student parks her car and then has to walk to an exit alone down shadowy corridors. Parking in the garage might be compared to venturing into a dangerous jungle.

In a proposal to the university administration, on the other hand, the writer might describe past attacks on students in campus garages and the negative publicity and criticism these provoked. For the administration, the writer might compare the lighting in the garages to high-risk gambling, arguing that increased lighting would lower the odds of future attacks.

Notice that shaping your appeal to a specific audience calls on you to consider very carefully the language you use. The student arguing for better lighting in campus parking garages would probably stick to standard academic English in a proposal to the university administration but might well want to use more informal language in a leaflet written for students.

### 4 Visuals that make emotional appeals

Visuals that make emotional appeals can add substance to an argument. Consider, for example, the accompanying photograph of coffins returning from Iraq. This image is undeniably powerful — but exactly what argument does it make? Bush administration officials worked to prevent the publication of photographs like this one, which suggests that they feared the photographs could make an antiwar argument. But some viewers may well see this image as arguing for ideas other than (or in addition to) opposition to the war in Iraq, such as patriotism or respect for the sacrifices made by military troops.

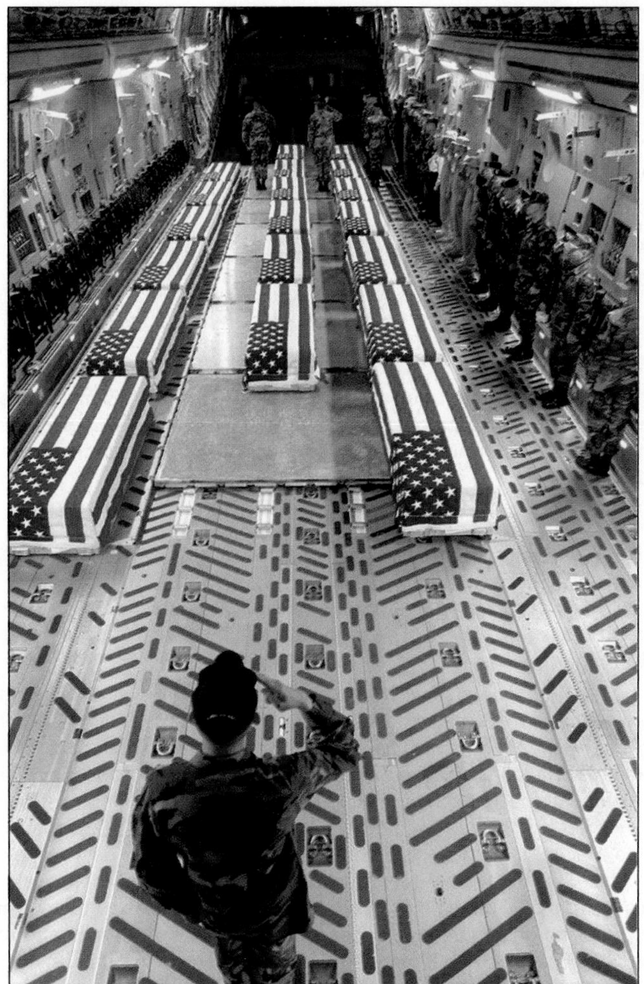

You need to ensure that the visuals you choose to enhance the emotional appeal of your argument will have the intended effect on readers. Test any photos or other visuals you are thinking of using with several potential readers. While images of human suffering can create a vivid emotional appeal, photographs that are profoundly disturbing can backfire, making some readers feel manipulated and thus angry at the person making the argument.

### EXERCISE 11.9

Make a list of common human emotions that might be attached to each of the following topics, and suggest appropriate ways to appeal to those emotions in a specific audience you choose to address.

1. banning drinking on campus
2. airport security
3. disarming land mines
4. attacks on places of worship
5. steroid use among athletes

### EXERCISE 11.10

Using a working thesis you formulated for Exercise 11.2 or 11.3, make a list of the emotional appeals most appropriate to your topic and audience. Then spend ten to fifteen minutes brainstorming, looking for descriptive and figurative language to carry out the appeals.

### FOR COLLABORATION

Working with two or three classmates, read the following paragraph, and then write a paragraph evaluating its use of description and figurative language as well as its appeal to various audiences.

> In 1973, all women in the United States became legally entitled to have abortions performed in hospitals by licensed physicians. Earlier, abortions were frequently performed by persons who bore more resemblance to butchers than to doctors. The all-too-common result was serious complications or death for the woman. If the 1973 Supreme Court decision is completely reversed, abortion will not end. Instead, women will again resort to illegal abortions, and there will be a return to the slaughterhouse. Since abortions are going to take place no matter what the law says, why not have them done safely and legally in hospitals instead of in basements and back alleys? The decision to have an abortion is not an easy one to make, and I believe that a woman who makes it deserves to have her wish carried out in the very safest way possible. Critics of abortion stress the importance of the unborn child's life. At the very least, they should also take the woman's life and safety into consideration.

## 11h Using sources in an argument

In constructing a written argument, it is often essential to use sources. The key to persuading people to accept your argument is good reasons; and even if your assignment doesn't specify that you must consult out-

### CONSIDERING DISABILITIES: Description

Remember that some members of your class or peer group may have difficulty seeing visual arguments or recognizing nuances of color or spacing. Be sure to provide verbal descriptions of visual images. In a video presentation, embed voice descriptions of the visual images for members of the class with visual impairments.

side sources, they are often the most effective way of finding and establishing these reasons. Sources can help you to do the following:

- provide background information on your topic
- demonstrate your knowledge of the topic to readers
- cite authority and testimony in support of your thesis
- find opinions that differ from your own, which can help you sharpen your thinking, qualify your thesis if necessary, and demonstrate fairness to opposing arguments

For a thorough discussion of finding, gathering, and evaluating sources, see Chapters 12–17.

## 11i Organizing an argument

Once you have assembled good reasons and evidence in support of an argumentative thesis, you must organize your material to present the argument convincingly. Although there is no universally favored, one-size-fits-all organizational framework, you may find it useful to try one of the following patterns.

### 1 The classical system

In the classical system of argument — followed by ancient Greek and Roman orators and still in widespread use today, some twenty-five hundred years later — the speaker begins with an introduction, which states the thesis and then gives background information. Next come the different lines of argument and then the consideration of alternative arguments. A conclusion both sums up the argument and makes a final appeal to the audience. You can adapt this format to written arguments, visual arguments, or arguments that combine words and images.

1. Introduction
   - Gain readers' attention and interest.
   - Establish your qualifications to write about your topic.
   - Establish common ground with readers.
   - Demonstrate fairness.
   - State or imply your thesis.
2. Background
   - Present any necessary background information, including pertinent personal narrative.
3. Lines of argument
   - Present good reasons and evidence (including logical and emotional appeals) in support of your thesis.
   - Generally present reasons in order of importance.
   - Demonstrate ways your argument may be in readers' best interest.
4. Consideration of alternative arguments
   - Examine alternative points of view.
   - Note advantages and disadvantages of alternative views.
   - Explain why one view is better than others.
5. Conclusion
   - Summarize the argument if you choose.
   - Elaborate on the implication of your thesis.
   - Make clear what you want readers to think or do.
   - Make a strong ethical or emotional appeal.

### 2 Toulmin's elements of argument

This simplified and systematic form of argument developed by Stephen Toulmin (9e and 11c) can help you organize an argumentative essay:

1. Make your claim or (arguable statement).

   **The federal government should ban smoking.**

2. Qualify your claim, if necessary.

   **The ban would be limited to public places.**

3. Present good reasons to support your claim.

   **Smoking causes serious diseases in smokers.**

   **Nonsmokers are endangered by secondhand smoke.**

4. Explain the underlying assumptions that connect your claim and your reasons. Also provide additional explanations of any controversial assumptions.

| | |
|---|---|
| ASSUMPTION | The Constitution was established to "promote the general welfare." |
| ASSUMPTION | Citizens are entitled to protection from harmful actions by others. |
| ADDITIONAL EXPLANATION | The federal government is supposed to serve the basic needs of the American people, including safeguarding their health. |

5. Provide additional evidence to support your claim (facts, statistics, testimony, and other ethical, logical, or emotional appeals).

| | |
|---|---|
| STATISTICS | Cite the incidence of deaths attributed to secondhand smoke. |
| FACTS | Cite lawsuits won against large tobacco companies. |
| FACTS | Cite bans on smoking already imposed in many municipalities and states. |
| AUTHORITY | Cite the surgeon general. |
| VISUAL APPEAL |  |

6. Acknowledge and respond to possible counterarguments.

| | |
|---|---|
| **COUNTER-ARGUMENTS** | Smoking is legal. Smokers have rights, too. |
| **RESPONSE** | The suggested ban applies only to public places; smokers would be free to smoke in private. A nonsmoker's right not to have to inhale smoke in public places counts for more than a smoker's right to smoke. |

7. State your conclusion in the strongest way possible.

## 11j Designing an argument

As you are well aware, most arguments today no longer appear in black and white or only in print form. Instead, most writers today think of arguments they are writing as documents that must be carefully designed to make the best use of space, font style and type size, color, visuals, and contemporary technology. Chapters 4, 10, 23, and 25 provide extensive information on design issues, and it would be wise to consult those chapters as you design an argument. The following tips will get you thinking about how to produce and design a document that will add to the ethical, logical, and emotional appeals you are making:

- Spend some time deciding on a distinct visual style for your argument, one that will appeal to your intended readers, set a clear voice or tone for your argument, and guide readers through your document (4c and 10b).
- Check out any conventions that may be expected in the kind of argument you are writing. Look for examples of similar arguments, or ask your instructor for information about such conventions (4a).
- Consider the use of white space, titles, and headings and how each page will look. Choose titles, headings, and subheadings that will guide readers from point to point (23c). You may want to set off an especially important part of your argument (such as a list of essential evidence) in a box, carefully labeled.
- Make sure that your visual design is consistent. If you choose a particular color, font, or type style (such as **boldface** or *italic* type) for a particular purpose, such as a second-level heading, make sure that you use the same color, font, or type style for that purpose throughout your paper.

- Be sure to choose readable fonts and font sizes (23b and c).
- Choose colors carefully, keeping in mind that colors call up many responses. In general, you will probably want to stick to black and white for most of your text for readability, reserving color for headings, illustrations, and so on. If you are posting your argument to the Web, remember that you need to have a strong contrast between the background color and print and illustrations (23a and Chapter 24).
- After you have a rough draft of your design, test it out on friends and classmates, asking them to describe how readable it is, how easy it is to follow, and what you need to change to make it more effective. Decide what adjustments you need to make — in format, spacing, alignment, use of color and fonts, and so on.
- Plan where your visuals will go, keeping each one as close to the text it illustrates as possible. Also give each visual a title, label it as a figure or table, and identify the source (see Chapters 18 – 21 and 23d).

## Checklist for constructing an argument

- What is the purpose of your argument — to convince others? to make a good decision? to change yourself? (11a)
- Is the point you want to make arguable? (11b)
- Have you formulated a clear claim and given good reasons for it? (11c and d)
- Have you formulated a strong working thesis, and have you qualified it sufficiently? (11c)
- How have you established your own credibility in the argument? (11e)
- Have you considered, and addressed, counterarguments? (11e3)
- How have you incorporated logical appeals into your argument? (11f)
- How have you used emotional appeals in your argument? (11g)
- How have you used sources in your argument, and how effectively are they integrated into your argument? (11h)
- Is your argument clearly organized? (11i)
- What design elements have you considered in composing your argument? How effective is your design? (11j)

### EXERCISE 11.11

Using the guidelines in this chapter, draft an argument in support of one of the working theses you formulated in Exercise 11.2 or 11.3.

### THINKING CRITICALLY ABOUT CONSTRUCTING ARGUMENTS

Using the checklist on p. 203, analyze an argument you've recently written or the draft you wrote for Exercise 11.11. Decide what you need to do to revise your argument, and write out a brief plan for revision.

## 11k A student argument essay

Student Writer

Teal Pfeifer

Asked to write an essay addressed to her classmates — one that makes an argumentative claim and supports it with good reasons and evidence — Teal Pfeifer argues that images in the media affect how women see themselves, and she offers a solution to the problem she has identified. Her essay has been annotated to point out the various parts of her argument as well as her use of good reasons, evidence, and appeals to logic and emotion.

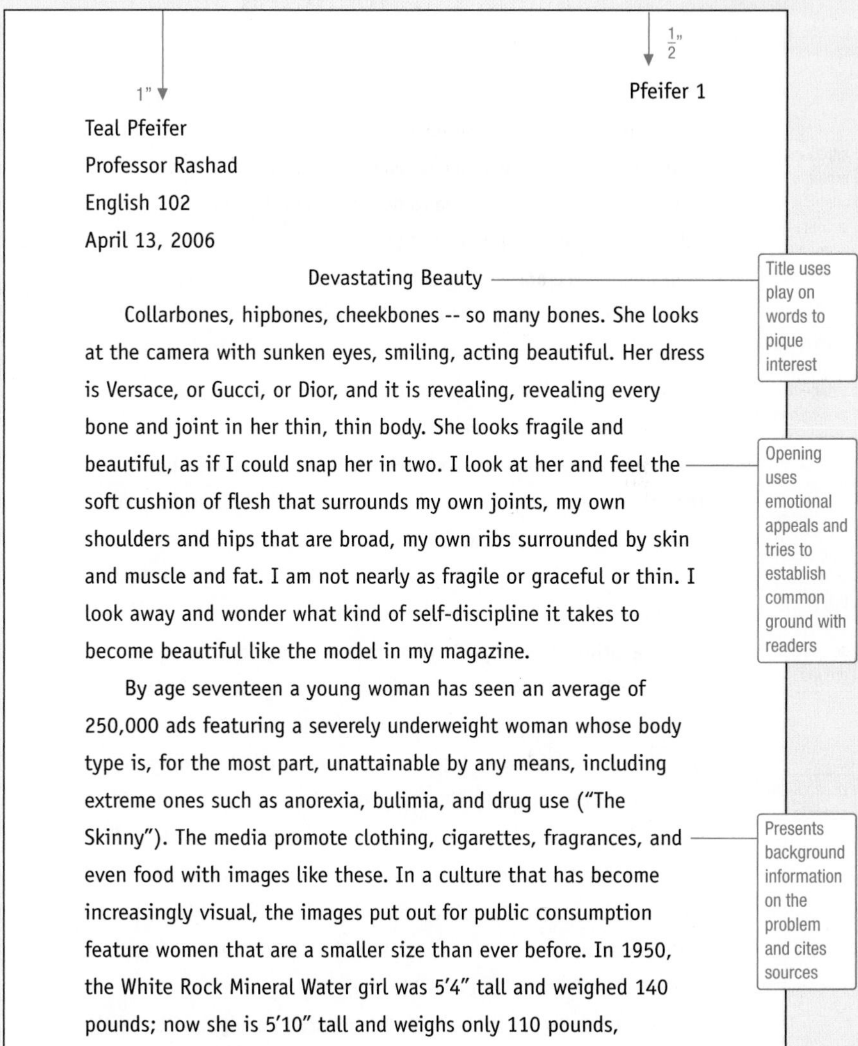
1"
½"
Title uses play on words to pique interest
Opening uses emotional appeals and tries to establish common ground with readers
Presents background information on the problem and cites sources

Pfeifer 1

Teal Pfeifer

Professor Rashad

English 102

April 13, 2006

Devastating Beauty

Collarbones, hipbones, cheekbones -- so many bones. She looks at the camera with sunken eyes, smiling, acting beautiful. Her dress is Versace, or Gucci, or Dior, and it is revealing, revealing every bone and joint in her thin, thin body. She looks fragile and beautiful, as if I could snap her in two. I look at her and feel the soft cushion of flesh that surrounds my own joints, my own shoulders and hips that are broad, my own ribs surrounded by skin and muscle and fat. I am not nearly as fragile or graceful or thin. I look away and wonder what kind of self-discipline it takes to become beautiful like the model in my magazine.

By age seventeen a young woman has seen an average of 250,000 ads featuring a severely underweight woman whose body type is, for the most part, unattainable by any means, including extreme ones such as anorexia, bulimia, and drug use ("The Skinny"). The media promote clothing, cigarettes, fragrances, and even food with images like these. In a culture that has become increasingly visual, the images put out for public consumption feature women that are a smaller size than ever before. In 1950, the White Rock Mineral Water girl was 5'4" tall and weighed 140 pounds; now she is 5'10" tall and weighs only 110 pounds, signifying the growing deviation between the weight of models and that of the normal female population (Pipher 184).

This media phenomenon has had a major effect on the female population as a whole, both young and old. Five to ten million

Pfeifer 2

women in America today suffer from an eating disorder related to poor self-image, and yet advertisements continue to prey on insecurities fueled by a woman's desire to be thin. Current estimates reveal that 80 percent of women are dissatisfied with their appearance and 45 percent of those are on a diet on any given day ("Statistics"). Yet even the most stringent dieting will generally fail to create the paper-thin body so valued in the media, and continuing efforts to do so can lead to serious psychological problems such as depression.

Introduces problem: ads encourage women's poor body image

Good reason for thesis: stringent dieting can cause psychological problems

While many women express dissatisfaction with their bodies, they are not the only victims of the emaciated images so frequently presented to them. Young girls are equally affected by these images, if not more so. Eighty percent of girls under age ten have already been on a diet and expressed the desire to be thinner and more beautiful (*Slim Hopes*). Thus, from a young age, beauty is equated with a specific size. The message girls get is an insidious one: in order to be your best self, you should wear size 0 or 1. The pressure only grows more intense as girls grow up. According to results from the Kaiser Family Foundation Survey "Reflections of Girls in the Media," 16 percent of ten- to seventeen-year-old girls reported that they had dieted or exercised to look like a TV character. Yet two-thirds of teenage girls acknowledged that these thin characters were not an accurate reflection of "real life" (qtd. in Dittrich, "Children" pars. 2–3).

Provides statistical evidence that problem extends across age groups

Uses logical appeals

It is tragic to see so much of the American population obsessed with weight and reaching an ideal that is, for the most part, ultimately unattainable. Equally troubling is the role magazines play in feeding this obsession. When a researcher asked female students from Stanford University to flip through several magazines containing

Good reason for thesis: magazines feed obsession with dieting

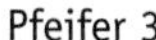

Pfeifer 3

Fig. 1. Young woman reading magazine. Personal photograph by author.

images of glamorized, super-thin models (see Fig. 1), 68 percent of the women felt significantly worse about themselves after viewing the magazine models (qtd. in Dittrich, "Media" par. 16). Another study showed that looking at models on a long-term basis leads to stress, depression, guilt, and lowered self-worth (qtd. in Dittrich, "Media" par. 19). As Naomi Wolfe points out in *The Beauty Myth*, thinking obsessively about fat and dieting has actually been shown to change thought patterns and brain chemistry.

Backs up reasons with research and expert opinion

How do we reject images that are so harmful to the women and young girls who view them? Legislation regarding what can be printed and distributed is not an option because of First

Considers and rejects alternative solutions

Pfeifer 4

Amendment rights. Equally untenable is the idea of appealing to the industries that hire emaciated models. As long as the beauty and clothing industries are making a profit from the physically insecure girls and women who view their ads, nothing will change.

States working thesis: a boycott would effectively solve problem

What, however, might happen if those females stopped buying the magazines that print such destructive images? A boycott is the most effective way to rid the print medium of emaciated models and eliminate the harmful effects they cause. If women stopped buying magazines that target them with such harmful advertising, magazines would be forced to change the kinds of ads they print. Such a boycott would send a clear message: women and girls reject the victimization that takes place every time they look at a skeletally thin model and then feel worse about themselves. Consumers can ultimately control what is put on the market: if we don't buy, funding for such ads will dry up fast.

Good reason: boycotts have been effective

Presents a precedent/ example as evidence

In the past, boycotts have been effective tools for social change. Rosa Parks, often identified as the mother of the modern-day civil rights movement, played a pivotal role in the Montgomery bus boycott in December 1955. When Parks refused to give up her seat to a white bus rider, she was arrested, and this incident inspired the boycott. For more than a year, the vast majority of African Americans in Montgomery chose to walk instead of ride the buses. Many of them were terrorized or harassed, but the boycott was eventually successful: segregation on buses was declared illegal by the U.S. Supreme Court.

Between 1965 and 1973, Cesar Chavez also used boycotts successfully to change wage policies and working conditions for millions of Mexicans and Mexican Americans who were being exploited by growers of grapes and lettuce. In his boycott efforts,

Pfeifer 5

Chavez moved on two fronts simultaneously: he asked the workers to withhold their labor, and he asked consumers to refrain from purchasing table grapes (and later, lettuce) in order to show their support for the workers. In this situation, not only did the boycott force an industry to improve existing conditions, but it also made the public aware of pressing labor issues. Thus a bond was formed between the workers and the community their labor was benefiting.

Presents a second precedent/ example as evidence

As a society, we have much to learn from boycotts of the past, and their lessons can help us confront contemporary social ills. As I have shown, body-image dissatisfaction and eating disorders are rising at an alarming rate among young girls and women in American society. This growing desire for an unrealistically thin body affects our minds and our spirits, especially when we are pummeled dozens of times a day with glamorized images of emaciated and unhealthy women. The resulting anorexia and bulimia that women suffer from are not only diseases that can be cured; they are also ones that can be prevented -- if women will take a solid stand against such advertisements and the magazines that publish them. While we are not the publishers or advertisers who choose the pictures of starving women represented in magazines, we are the ones who decide whether or not these images will be purchased. This is where power lies -- in the hands of those who hand over the dollars that support the glorification of unhealthy and unrealistic bodies. It is our choice to exert this power and to reject magazines that promote such images.

Appeals directly to audience by using "we" in conclusion

Reinforces severity of problem and appeals to emotion

Restates thesis as a call to action

Pfeifer 6

Works Cited

Dittrich, Liz. "About-Face Facts on the Children and the Media." *About-Face*. About-Face, 1996-2008. Web. 10 Mar. 2006.

---. "About-Face Facts on the Media." *About-Face*. About-Face, 1996–2008. Web. 10 Mar. 2006.

Pipher, Mary. *Reviving Ophelia: Saving the Selves of Adolescent Girls*. New York: Ballantine, 1994. Print.

"The Skinny on Media and Weight." *Common Sense Media*. Common Sense Media Inc., 27 Sept. 2005. Web. 15 Mar. 2006.

*Slim Hopes*. Dir. Sut Jhally. Prod. Jean Kilbourne. Media Education Foundation, 1995. Videocassette.

"Statistics." *National Eating Disorders Association*. National Eating Disorders Association, 2005. Web. 14 Mar. 2006.

Wolfe, Naomi. *The Beauty Myth*. New York: Harper, 2002. Print.

Young woman reading magazine. Personal photograph by author. 14 Mar. 2006.

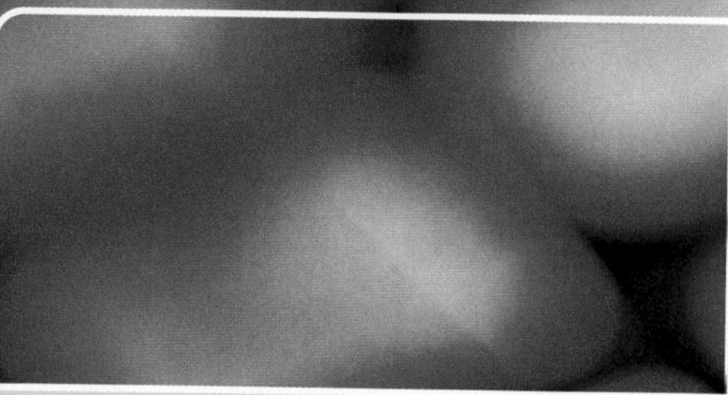

# Part 3

# RESEARCH AND DOCUMENTATION

# 12 Preparing for a Research Project

Your employer asks you to recommend the best software for a particular project. You want to plan a week's vacation in Montreal. Your instructor assigns a term paper about a musician. Each of these situations calls for research, for examining various kinds of sources. Preparing to begin your research means taking a long look at what you already know, the best way to proceed, and the amount of time you have to find out what you need to know. For success in college and beyond, you need to understand how to start the process of academic research.

## 12a Overview of the research process

This chapter rests on five basic assumptions:

1. *You already know something about doing research.* You act as a researcher whenever you investigate something — such as a college course, a cosmetic, a computer, or a comic — by reading up on it, discussing its features with others, or looking closely at the options available.
2. *Good research can make you a genuine expert.* If you approach your research seriously, you may eventually become an expert on a topic that interests you, whether it is a new cancer drug, a political scandal, or Barry Bonds's place in sports history.
3. *Research is usually driven by a purpose.* Researchers usually seek out facts and opinions for a reason. Your main purpose in college research will most often be to fulfill an assignment: for example, to compare literary texts, to trace the causes of a war, or to argue for — or against — mandatory drug testing of athletes.
4. *Your purpose influences the research you do, which in turn refines your purpose.* When you begin any research, it is impossible to know exactly what you will discover. The evidence you gather about global warming, for example, may cause you to advocate a solution to a problem — when you originally had intended only to explain the problem.

5. *Research rarely progresses in a neat line from start to finish.* You begin with a question that you may or may not be able to answer. Then your research may lead you to find other sources. This additional research may narrow your idea even more, leading you to find more specific sources — or to change directions entirely. Wherever the process takes you, however, your overriding goal is to develop a critical understanding of the information you are gathering.

College research may range from a couple of hours spent gathering background about a topic for a brief essay to weeks or months of full-scale exploration for a term project. Chapters 12–17 provide guidelines to help you with any research done for the purpose of writing. In addition, these chapters show examples of work by David Craig, a student whose complete research essay appears in Chapter 18. Other student research essays appear in Chapters 6, 11, 19–21, and 62.

## 12b Analyzing the assignment

For an introductory writing course, David Craig received the following assignment:

> Choose a subject of interest to you, and use it as the basis for a research essay of approximately 2,500 words that makes and substantiates a claim. You should use a minimum of five sources, including at least three print sources.

### 1 Making sure you understand the assignment

Before you begin any research assignment, make sure you understand the requirements and limits of the assignment.

- How many sources should you use?
- Does your instructor require certain kinds of sources? If so, what kinds?
- Will you use images, sound, or video in your assignment?
- Should you work independently or collaborate with others on the project?
- What kind of documentation style does your instructor want you to use? (See Chapters 18–21.)

### TALKING THE TALK: Audience

"Isn't my audience just my teacher?" To write effectively, you must think of your writing as more than just an assignment you go through to get a grade. Recognize that you have something to say — and that in order to get others to pay attention, you have to think about who they are and how to reach them. Of course, your instructor is part of your audience. But who else will be interested in your topic and the unique perspective you bring to it? What does that audience need from you?

- Do you understand what your instructor wants you to do? If not, ask for clarification.

In response to questions, David Craig's instructor clarified that the audience for the project would be members of the writing class. (For information about making a claim, see 9e.)

## 2 The rhetorical situation of the research project

Be sure to consider the rhetorical situation (context) of any research project. Here are detailed questions to think about:

### *Purpose*

- Do you have a choice about the purpose of your assignment? If you can choose the purpose, what would you like to accomplish?
- What do you need to do in this project — explain a situation? weigh opposing viewpoints and make a claim about which is correct? convince the audience to do something? explore the causes or effects of a particular phenomenon? Your purpose will affect the kinds of sources you need to find.
- If you have been assigned a specific research project, keep in mind the key words in that assignment. Does the assignment ask that you *describe*, *survey*, *analyze*, *persuade*, *explain*, *classify*, *compare*, or *contrast*? What do such words mean in this field (3e)?

### Audience

- Who will be the audience for your research project (3h)?
- Who will be interested in the information you gather, and why? What will they want to know? What will they already know?
- What do you know about their backgrounds? What assumptions might they hold about the topic?
- What response do you want to elicit from them?
- What kinds of evidence will you need to convince them?
- What will your instructor expect?

### Rhetorical stance

What is your attitude toward your topic? Are you curious about it? critical of it? Do you like it? dislike it? find it confusing? What influences have shaped your stance? (For more about rhetorical stance, see 3g.)

### Scope

How many and what kind(s) of library or Web sources should you use? What kind(s) of visuals — charts, maps, photographs, and so on — will you need to include? Will you also include sound or video clips? Will you do any field research — interviewing, surveying, or observing? (For more on kinds of sources, see 13a.)

### Length

How long is your project supposed to be? The amount of research and writing time you will need for a five-page essay differs markedly from that for a fifteen-page essay.

### Deadlines

When is the project due? Are any preliminary materials — a working bibliography, a thesis, an outline, a first draft — due before this date? Here is a sample schedule for a research project.

## Scheduling a research project

| | Try to do by: |
|---|---|
| **Date assigned**: ______ | |
| Analyze assignment; decide on primary purpose and audience; choose topic if necessary. | ______ |
| Narrow the topic, and develop research question and tentative hypothesis. | ______ |
| Set aside library time; develop search strategy. | ______ |
| Set up a research log. | ______ |
| Do background reading and online searches; narrow topic further if necessary. | ______ |
| Start working bibliography; track down sources in the library and online. | ______ |
| Develop working thesis and rough outline. | ______ |
| Gather or develop necessary visuals. | ______ |
| If necessary, conduct interviews, make observations, or distribute and collect questionnaires. | ______ |
| Read and evaluate sources; take notes; analyze data from field research. | ______ |
| Draft explicit thesis and outline, storyboard, or map. | ______ |
| Prepare first draft, including all visuals. | ______ |
| **Rough draft due**: | ______ |
| Obtain and evaluate critical responses. | ______ |
| Do more research if necessary. | ______ |
| Revise draft; prepare list of works cited or bibliography. | ______ |
| Edit revised draft; use spell checker. | ______ |
| Prepare final draft. | ______ |
| Do final proofreading. | ______ |
| **Final draft due**: | ______ |

### 3 Choosing a topic

If your assignment, like David Craig's, does not specify a topic, consider the following questions:

- What subjects do you already know something about? Which of them would you like to explore more fully?

- What subjects do you care about? What might you like to become an expert on?
- What subjects evoke a strong reaction from you — intense puzzlement, skepticism, affirmation?

Be sure to get responses about your possible topic from your instructor, classmates, and friends. Ask them whether they would be interested in reading about the topic, whether it seems manageable, and whether they know of any good sources for information on the topic.

David Craig hit on his topic one evening after spending several hours online. As usual, he exchanged instant messages (IMs) with several friends. Like most of the people his age that he knew, David had considered instant messaging (IMing) a regular part of his online experience for years, so he expected his classmates to find the subject intriguing.

**EXERCISE 12.1**

Using the questions in 12b3, come up with at least two topics you would like to carry out research on. Then write a brief response to some key questions about each topic: How much information do you think is available on this topic? What sources on this topic do you know about or have access to? Who would know about this topic — historians, doctors, filmmakers, psychologists, others?

## 12c Narrowing a topic

Any topic you choose to research must be manageable — it must suit the scope, audience, length, and time limits of your assignment. Making a topic manageable often requires narrowing it, but you may also need to find a particular slant and look for a question to guide your research. To arrive at such a question, you might first generate a series of questions about your topic. You can then evaluate them and choose one or two that are both interesting and manageable.

David Craig knew that he had to zero in on some aspect of IMing and take a position on it. He considered researching "the prevalence of IMing worldwide," but he decided that was too vague and unmanageable. He spoke with two instructors about his topic, and both of them criticized IMing for its negative influence on students' writing. Intrigued by this reaction, David decided to focus on instant-message language and its harmful effects on youth literacy.

## 12d Moving from research question to hypothesis

The result of the narrowing process is a research question that can be tentatively answered by a hypothesis, a statement of what you anticipate your research will show. Like a working thesis (5c, 11c), a hypothesis must be manageable, interesting, and specific. In addition, it must be arguable, a debatable proposition that you can prove or disprove with a reasonable amount of research evidence (11b). For example, a statement like this one is not arguable since it merely states a widely known fact: "Senator Joseph McCarthy attracted great attention with his anti-Communist crusade during the 1950s." On the other hand, this statement is an arguable hypothesis because evidence for or against it can be found: "Roy Cohn's biased research while he was an assistant to Senator Joseph McCarthy was partially responsible for McCarthy's anti-Communist crusade."

In moving from a general topic of interest, such as Senator Joseph McCarthy's anti-Communist crusade of the 1950s, to a useful hypothesis, such as the one in the previous paragraph, you first narrow the topic to a single manageable issue: Roy Cohn's role in the crusade, for instance. After background reading, you then raise a question about that issue ("To what extent did Cohn's research contribute to McCarthy's crusade?") and devise a possible answer, your hypothesis.

Here is how David Craig moved from general topic to hypothesis:

| | |
|---|---|
| **TOPIC** | Instant messaging |
| **NARROWED TOPIC** | The language of instant messaging |
| **ISSUE** | The effect of instant messaging on youth literacy |
| **RESEARCH QUESTION** | How has the popularity of instant messaging affected literacy among today's youth? |
| **HYPOTHESIS** | Instant messaging seems to have a negative influence on the writing skills of young people. |

David's hypothesis, which tentatively answers his research question, is precise enough to be supported or challenged by a manageable amount of research.

## 12e Determining what you know

Once you have formulated a hypothesis, determine what you already know about your topic. Here are some strategies for doing so:

- *Brainstorming.* Take five minutes to list everything you think of or wonder about your hypothesis (5a). You may find it helpful to do this in a group with other students.
- *Freewriting about your hypothesis.* For five minutes, write about every reason for believing your hypothesis is true. Then for another five minutes, write down every argument you can think of, no matter how weak, that someone opposed to your hypothesis might make.
- *Freewriting about your audience.* Write for five minutes about your readers, including your instructor. What do you think they currently believe about your topic? What sorts of evidence will convince them to accept your hypothesis? What sorts of sources will they respect?
- *Tapping your memory for sources.* List everything you can remember about *where* you learned about your topic: Web sites, email, books, magazines, courses, conversations, television. What you know comes from somewhere, and that "somewhere" can serve as a starting point for research.

### EXERCISE 12.2

Using the tips provided in 12e, write down as much as you can about one of the topics you identified in Exercise 12.1. Then take some time to reread your notes, and jot down the questions you still need to answer as well as the sources you need to find.

## 12f Preliminary research plan

Once you've considered what you already know about your topic, you can develop a research plan. To do so, answer the following questions:

- What kinds of sources (books, journal articles, databases, Web sites, government documents, specialized reference works, images, videos, and so on) will you need to consult? How many sources should you consult? (For more on different kinds of sources, see Chapter 13.)
- How current do your sources need to be? (For topical issues, especially those related to science, current sources are usually most important. For historical subjects, older sources may offer the best information.)
- How can you determine the location and availability of the kinds of sources you need?
- Do you need to consult sources contemporary with an event or a person's life? If so, how will you get access to those sources?

One goal of your research plan is to begin building a strong working bibliography (see 14b). Carrying out systematic research and keeping careful notes on your sources will make developing your works-cited list or bibliography (Chapters 18 – 21) easier later on.

## 12g Setting up a research log

Keeping a research log — either in print or electronic form — will make the job of writing and documenting your sources more efficient and accurate. You can use your research log to jot down ideas about your topic and possible sources — and to keep track of print and online materials. Whenever you record an online source in your log, include the URL.

Here are a few guidelines for setting up an electronic research log:

1. Create a new folder, and label it with a name that will be easy to identify, such as *Research Log for Project on Instant Messaging.*
2. Within this folder, create subfolders that will help you manage your project. These might include *Project Deadlines*, *Notes on Hypothesis and Thesis*, *Working Bibliography*, *Background Information*, *Organizational Plan*, *Visuals*, *Drafts*, and so on.

You might prefer to begin a Web log (blog) for your research project. You can use it to record your thoughts on the reading you are doing and, especially, add links from there to Web sites, documents, and articles you have found online. You might even find bloggers who are writing about your topic. If so, be sure to check them out carefully before citing information from a blog in support of your research project. (For more on blogs, see 22b3.)

If you prefer not to keep an electronic research log, set up a binder with dividers similar to the subfolders listed above. Whether your log is electronic or not, be sure to carefully distinguish the notes and comments you make from quoted passages you record.

### CONSIDERING DISABILITIES: Dictation

If you have difficulty taking notes either on a computer or in a notebook, consider dictating your notes. You might dictate into a handheld recorder for later playback, into a word processor with voice-recognition capability, or into a phone for podcasting on a Web site.

## 12h Moving from hypothesis to working thesis

As you gather information and begin reading and evaluating sources, you will probably refine your research question and change your hypothesis significantly. Only after you have explored your hypothesis, tested it, and sharpened it by reading, writing, and talking with others does it become a working thesis.

David Craig, for instance, did quite a bit of research on instant-message language, youth literacy, and the possible connection between the two. The more he read, the more he felt that the hypothesis suggested by his discussion with instructors — that instant messaging had contributed to a decline in youth literacy — did not hold up. Thus, he shifted his attention to the positive effects of IMing on communication skills and developed the following working thesis: "Although some educators criticize IMing, it may aid literacy by encouraging young people to use words and to write — even if IMing requires a different kind of writing."

In doing your own research, you may find that your interest shifts, that a whole line of inquiry is unproductive, or that your hypothesis is simply wrong. In each case, the process of research pushes you to learn more about your hypothesis, to make it more precise, to become an expert on your topic.

### THINKING CRITICALLY ABOUT YOUR OWN RESEARCH

If you have done research for an essay or research project before, go back and evaluate the work you did as a researcher and as a writer in light of the principles developed in this chapter. What was the purpose of the research? Who was your audience? How did you narrow and focus your topic? What kinds of sources did you use? Did you use a research log? What about your research and your essay pleased you most? What pleased you least? What would you do differently if you were to revise the essay now?

# 13 Conducting Research

How would you find out where to get the best coffee in town? What would be the best sources for a Web project on a 1930s film star? Where would you get the most recent information about stem-cell research? Whether you are researching Heisenberg's uncertainty principle or haircuts, you need to be familiar with the kinds of sources you are likely to use, the searches you are likely to perform, and the three main types of research you will most often be doing: library, Internet, and field research.

## 13a Kinds of sources

Sources can include data from interviews and surveys, books and articles in print and online, Web sites, film, video, images, and more. Consider these important differences among sources.

### 1 Primary and secondary sources

Primary sources provide firsthand knowledge, while secondary sources report on or analyze the research of others. Primary sources are basic sources of raw information, including your own field research; films, works of art, or other objects you examine; literary works you read; and eyewitness accounts, photographs, news reports, and historical documents (such as letters and speeches). Secondary sources are descriptions or interpretations of primary sources, such as researchers' reports, reviews, biographies, and encyclopedia articles. Often what constitutes a primary or secondary source depends on the purpose of your research. A critic's evaluation of a film, for instance, serves as a secondary source if you are writing about the film but as a primary source if you are studying the critic's writing.

Most research projects draw on both primary and secondary sources. A research-based essay on the effects of steroid use on major league baseball, for example, might draw on primary sources, such as the players' testimony to Congress, as well as secondary sources, such as articles or books by baseball experts.

## 2 Scholarly and popular sources

While nonacademic sources like magazines and personal Web sites can help you get started on a research project, you will usually want to depend more heavily on authorities in a field, whose work generally appears in scholarly journals in print or online. The following list will help you distinguish scholarly and popular sources:

**SCHOLARLY**

- Title often contains the word *Journal*
- Source available mainly through libraries and library databases
- Few commercial advertisements
- Authors identified with academic credentials
- Summary or abstract appears on first page of article; articles are fairly long
- Articles cite sources and provide bibliographies

**POPULAR**

- *Journal* usually does not appear in title
- Source generally available outside of libraries (at newsstands or from a home Internet connection)
- Many advertisements
- Authors are usually journalists or reporters hired by the publication, not academics or experts
- No summary or abstract; articles are fairly short
- Articles may include quotations but do not cite sources or provide bibliographies

### 3 Older and more current sources

Most projects can benefit from both older, historical sources and more current ones. Some older sources are classics in their fields, essential for understanding the scholarship that follows them. Others are simply dated, though even these works can be useful to researchers who want to see what people wrote and read about a topic in the past. Depending on your purpose, you may rely primarily on recent sources (for example, if you are writing about a new scientific discovery), primarily on historical sources (if your project discusses a nineteenth-century industrial accident), or on a mixture of both. Whether a source appeared hundreds of years ago or this morning, evaluate it carefully to determine how useful it will be for you.

## 13b Using the library to get started

Even when you have a general idea of what kinds of sources exist and which kinds you need for your research project, you still have to locate these sources. Many beginning researchers are tempted to assume that all the information they could possibly need is readily available on the Internet from a home connection. However, it is a good idea to begin almost any research project with the sources available in your college library.

### 1 Reference librarians

You might start by getting to know one particularly valuable resource, your library staff — especially reference librarians. You can make an appointment to talk with a librarian about your research project and get specific recommendations about databases and other helpful places to begin your research. In addition, many libraries have online chat environments where students can ask questions about their research and have them answered, in real time, by a reference librarian. To get the most helpful advice, whether online or in person, pose *specific* questions — not "Where can I find information about computers?" but "Where can I find information on the history of instant-message technologies?" If you are having difficulty asking precise questions, you probably need to do some background research on your topic and formulate a sharper hypothesis. A librarian may be helpful in this regard as well.

### CONSIDERING DISABILITIES: Web site accessibility

While the Americans with Disabilities Act stipulates that all government Web sites must be accessible to those with disabilities, these rules have only recently been expanded to cover educational and other Web sites. If you encounter sites that are not accessible to you, ask a reference librarian to help you identify similar sites that may be more accessible. Also consider clicking on the CONTACT US button, if there is one, and letting the sponsors of the site know that some potential users can't get ready access to the information.

## 2 Catalogs and databases

Your library's computers hold many resources not available on the Web or not accessible to students except through the library's system. One of these resources is the library's own catalog of books and other holdings, but most college libraries also subscribe to a large number of databases — electronic collections of information, such as indexes to journal and magazine articles, texts of news stories and legal cases, lists of sources on particular topics, and compilations of statistics — that students can access for free. Many of these databases — such as LexisNexis, MLA Bibiliography, and ERIC — have been screened or compiled by editors, librarians, or other scholars. Your library may also have metasearch software that allows you to search several databases at once.

## 3 Reference works

Consulting general reference works is another good way to get started on a research project. These works are especially helpful for getting an overview of a topic, identifying subtopics, finding more specialized sources, and identifying useful keywords for electronic searches.

### *Encyclopedias*

For general background on a subject, encyclopedias are a good place to begin, particularly because many include bibliographies that can point you to more specialized sources. A librarian can direct you to such

## TALKING THE TALK: Wikis as sources

"Why doesn't my instructor want me to use Wikipedia as a source?" Wikis (the word means "quick" in Hawaiian) are sites that users can add to and edit as they see fit; as a result, their contents are not always reliable. It's true that Wikipedia, a hugely popular site, has such a large and enthusiastic audience that users are likely to catch mistakes and remove deliberately false information fairly quickly. But you can never be certain that a wiki entry has not been tampered with. The best advice is to use wikis as sources only for preliminary research and then to make sure that you double-check any information you find there. If you do not find the same material elsewhere, do not use it; if you do find the same information in a conventionally edited source, cite that source instead.

reference works. Remember that encyclopedias will serve as a place to start your research — not as major sources for a research project.

Specialized encyclopedias, on subjects from ancient history to world drama, provide more detailed articles by authorities in the field as well as extensive bibliographies. For more information on specialized encyclopedias in particular fields, see Chapters 62–64.

### Biographical resources

The lives and historical settings of famous people are the topics of biographical dictionaries and indexes. Besides those listed here, many other volumes are available.

*African American Biographical Database*

*American Men and Women of Science*

*Contemporary Authors*

*Dictionary of American Biography*

*Dictionary of National Biography*

*Webster's New Biographical Dictionary*

*Who's Who*

### Almanacs, yearbooks, and atlases

Almanacs and yearbooks contain data on current events and statistical information.

*American Annual*

*Information Please Almanac*

*Dow Jones–Irwin Business Almanac*

*Facts on File Yearbook*

*The Gallup Poll*

*Statistical Abstracts of the United States* (U.S. Census Bureau)

*UNESCO Statistical Yearbook*

*World Almanac*

Look in an atlas for maps and other geographic data.

*Atlas of World Cultures*

*Encyclopaedia Britannica World Atlas*

*National Atlas of the United States*

*National Geographic Atlas of the World*

## 13c Finding library resources

The library is one of a researcher's best friends, especially in an age of electronic communication. Your college library houses a great number of print materials and gives you access to electronic catalogs, indexes, and databases. But the library may seem daunting to you, especially on your first visit. Experienced student researchers will tell you that the best way to make the library a friend is to get to know it: a good starting place is its Web site, where you can find useful information, including its hours of operation, its floor plan, its collections, and so on; many libraries also have a virtual tour and other tutorials on their Web sites that give you a first-rate introduction to getting the most out of the library's resources.

### 1 Searching catalogs and databases

The most important tools your library offers are its online catalog and databases. Searching these tools will always be easier and more efficient if you use carefully chosen words to limit the scope of your research.

#### *Subject word searching*

Catalogs and databases usually index their contents not only by author and title, but also by subject headings — standardized words and phrases used to classify the subject matter of books and articles. (For books, most U.S. academic libraries use the *Library of Congress Subject Headings*, or LCSH, for this purpose.) When you search the catalog by subject, you need to use the exact subject words.

### Keyword searching

Searches using keywords, on the other hand, make use of the computer's ability to look for any term in any field of the electronic record, including not just subject but also author, title, series, and notes. In article databases, a keyword search will look in abstracts and summaries of articles as well. Keyword searching is less restrictive, but it requires you to put some thought into choosing your search terms in order to get the best results.

### Advanced searching

Many library catalogs and database search engines offer advanced search options (sometimes on a separate page) to help you combine keywords, search for an exact phrase, or exclude items containing particular keywords. Often they limit your search in other ways as well, such as by date, language, country of origin, or location of the keyword within a site.

Many catalogs and databases offer a search option using the Boolean operators AND, OR, and NOT, and some allow you to use parentheses to refine your search or wildcards to expand it. Note that much Boolean decision making is done for you when you use an advanced search

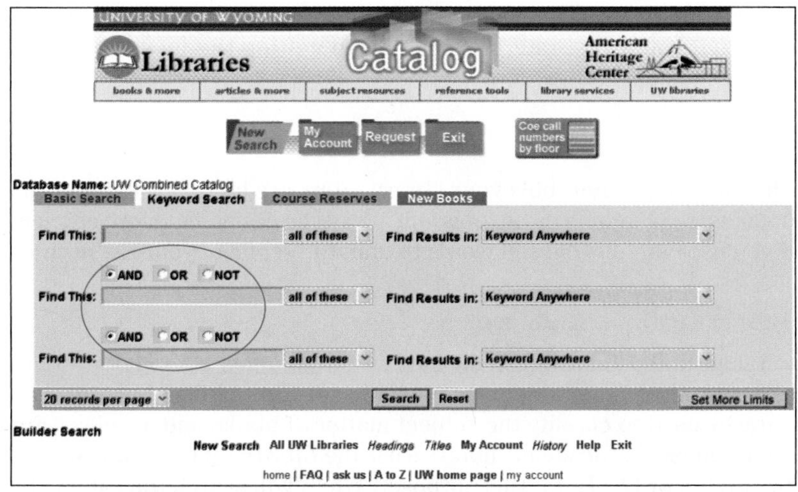


*Advanced search page from a library catalog that incorporates Boolean operators*

option (as on the advanced search page shown on the opposite page). Note, too, that search engines vary in the exact terms and symbols they use to refine searches, so check before you search.

- AND *limits your search.* If you enter the terms *IM* AND *language* AND *literacy*, the search engine will retrieve only those items that contain *all* the terms. Some search engines use a plus sign (+) instead of AND.
- OR *expands your search.* If you enter the terms *IM* OR *language*, the computer will retrieve every item that contains the term *IM* and every item that contains the term *language.*
- NOT *limits your search.* If you enter the terms *IM* NOT *language*, the search engine will retrieve every item that contains *IM* except those that also contain the term *language.* Some search engines use a minus sign (−) or AND NOT instead of NOT.
- *Parentheses customize your search.* Entering *IM* AND (*literacy* OR *linguistics*), for example, will locate items that mention either of those terms in connection with instant messaging.
- *Wildcards expand your search.* Use a wildcard, usually an asterisk (*) or a question mark (?), to find related words that begin with the same letters. Entering *messag** will locate *message*, *messages*, and *messaging.*
- *Quotation marks narrow your search.* Most search engines interpret words within quotation marks as a phrase that must appear with the words in that exact order.

In one of his searches, David Craig used two keywords, *instant messaging* AND *linguistics.* He sometimes narrowed his search further by adding a third term, AND *students* or AND *literacy.* Since search engines don't pick up synonyms automatically, he might also have used the terms *instant messenger*, *language*, and *youth.*

## 2 Books

### *Catalog information*

The library catalog lists all the library's books. Library catalogs follow a standard pattern of organization, with each holding identified by three kinds of entries: one headed by the *author's name*, one by the *title*, and one or (usually) more by the *subject.* If you can't find a particular source under any of these headings, you can search the catalog by using a combination of subject headings and keywords. Such searches may turn up other useful titles as well.

Following are a search page, a page of results for noted linguist and author David Crystal, and a catalog entry for one of his books from a

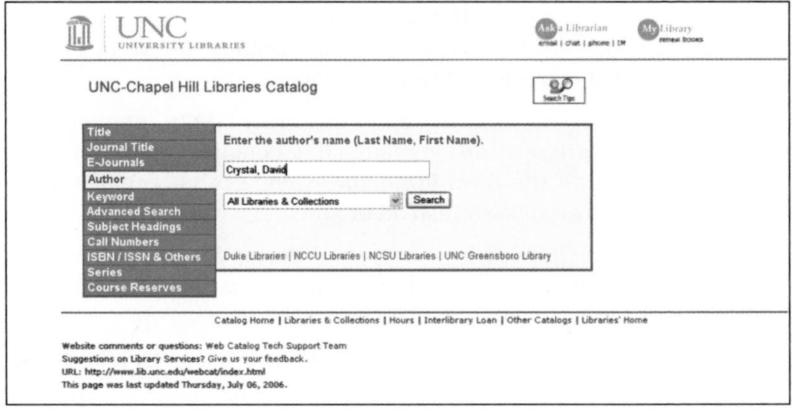


*Library catalog search page*

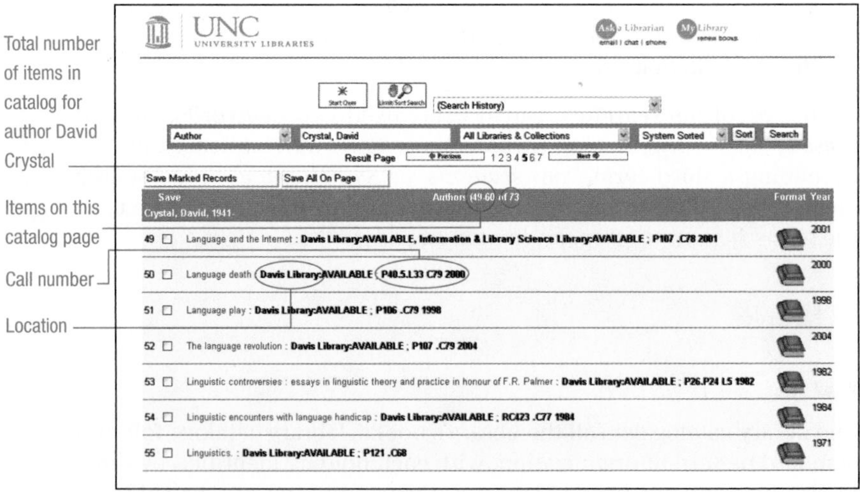


*Results for author search in library catalog database*

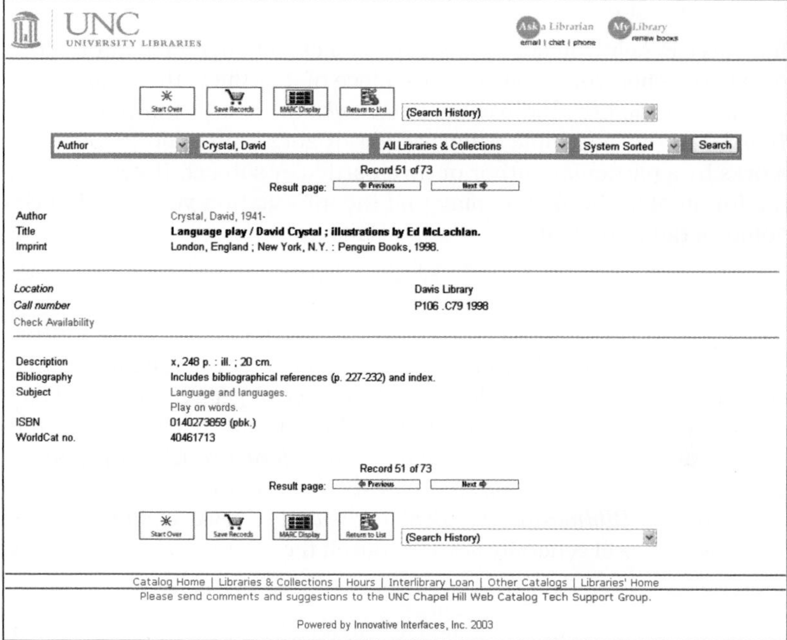


*Catalog entry for a book chosen from author search*

university library catalog. Note that many electronic catalogs indicate whether a book has been checked out and, if so, when it is due to be returned. Sometimes, as in this case, you must click on a link to check the availability of the book.

Catalog entries for books list not only the author, title, subject, and publication information but also a call number that indicates how the book is classified and where it is shelved. Like many online catalogs, the catalog in the preceding examples allows you to save the information about the book while you continue searching and then retrieve the call numbers for all of the books you want to find in one list. Once you have the call number for a book, look for a library map or shelving plan to tell you where the book is housed. Take the time to browse through the books near the call number you are looking for. Often you will find other books related to your topic in the immediate area.

### Book indexes

Indexes can help you quickly locate complete bibliographic information on a book when you know only one piece of it — the author's last name, perhaps, or the title. Indexes such as *Books in Print*, *Cumulative Book Index*, and the electronic database WorldCat can also alert you to other works by a particular author or on a particular subject. If you are looking for an older book, you may find the information you need in print volumes rather than in an electronic database.

### Review indexes

A review index will help you find reviews of books you are interested in so that you can check the relevance of a source or get a thumbnail sketch of its contents before you track it down. Review indexes include *Annual Bibliography of English Language and Literature* (*ABELL*), ARBA Online, *Book Review Digest*, *Book Review Index* (print only), and *International Bibliography of Book Reviews*. For reviews more than ten years old, you will generally need to consult the print version of the index.

## 3 Periodical articles

Titles of periodicals held by a library appear in its catalog, but the titles of individual articles do not. To find the contents of periodicals, you will need to use an index source.

### Periodical indexes

Periodical indexes are databases or print volumes that hold information about articles published in newspapers, magazines, and scholarly journals. Different indexes cover different groups of periodicals; articles written before 1990 may be indexed only in a print volume. Ask a reference librarian for guidance about the most likely index for the subject of your research.

Electronic periodical indexes come in different forms, with some offering the full text of articles and some offering abstracts (short summaries) of the articles. Be sure not to confuse an abstract with a complete article. Full-text databases can be extremely convenient — you can read and print out articles directly from the computer, without the extra step of tracking down the periodical in question. However, don't limit yourself to full-text databases, which may not contain graphics and images that appeared in the print version of the periodical — and which may not include the sources that would benefit your research most. Take advantage of databases that offer abstracts, which give you an overview of the article's contents that can help you decide whether you need to spend time finding and reading the full text.

### General indexes

General indexes of periodicals list articles from general-interest magazines (such as *Time* or *Newsweek*), newspapers, or a combination of these. Many major newspapers, such as the *New York Times*, and other periodicals have online archives, and some of their content can be accessed for free. General indexes usually provide current sources on a topic, but you may need to look further for in-depth articles. Frequently used general indexes include InfoTrac and LexisNexis, which can both be used to access a vast collection of newspapers, magazines, and scholarly journals. Factiva is a good resource for Reuters news agencies and for articles on the financial industry. Databases like WorldCat and FirstSearch can help you locate books in libraries all over the world.

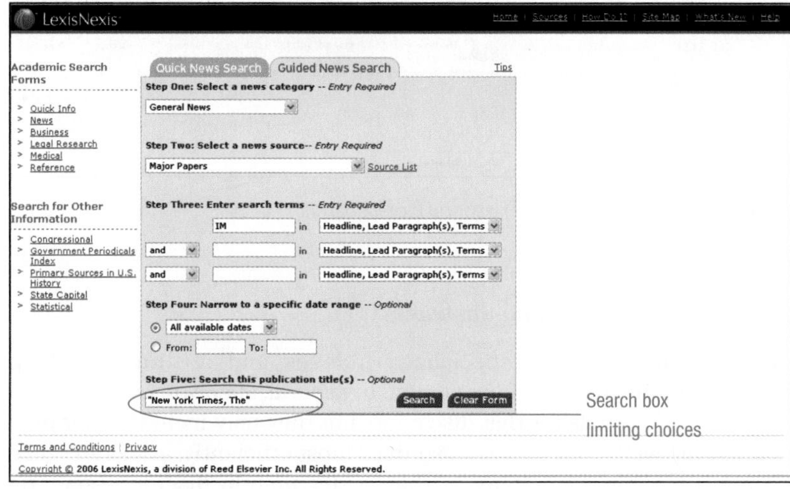


*General index search for articles in the* New York Times

When David Craig began his research, he consulted several general indexes, including LexisNexis, using the keywords *IM* and *instant messenger*. Using the search tools in LexisNexis, David was able to narrow his search to a few helpful articles. His first search using the term *IM* returned over a thousand results in LexisNexis, so he used the GUIDED SEARCH feature to narrow his search. By clicking on the SOURCE LIST link, he limited his search to the *New York Times*. After getting over three hundred results with that search, David used the SEARCH WITHIN RESULTS feature of LexisNexis to narrow his list to six articles. In order to make sure he got as many relevant articles as possible, he chose to display entries from all available dates. Searches can be limited to recent articles as well. He was able to read the full text of each article, and he cited one — on teachers' reactions to instant messaging — in his essay.

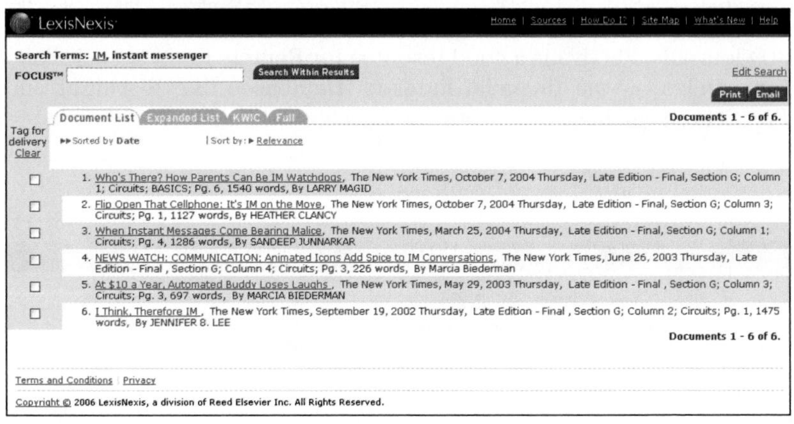


*SEARCH WITHIN RESULTS hits from general index search*

## Specialized indexes and abstracts

Many disciplines have specialized indexes and abstracts to help researchers find detailed information. In general, such works list articles in scholarly journals for that discipline, but they may include other publications as well. To use these resources most efficiently, ask a reference librarian to help you. Many of the most common discipline-specific online databases are listed in the box on page 235. For more specialized

**Discipline-specific online databases**

| HUMANITIES | SOCIAL SCIENCES | NATURAL AND APPLIED SCIENCES |
|---|---|---|
| ABC-CLIO | ERIC | EBSCOhost |
| EBSCOhost | EBSCOhost | General Science Index |
| Humanities Index | Government Documents Catalog Services (GDCS) | JSTOR |
| JSTOR | GPO Access | |
| MLA Bibliography | JSTOR | **BUSINESS** |
| ProjectMuse | PAIS International | EBSCOhost |
| ProQuest | ProQuest | Periodical Abstracts |
| | PsycInfo | ProQuest |
| | Social Science Index | |

indexes in a particular discipline, see Chapters 62–64. For more information on resources in your discipline available at your college library, consult your librarian.

### *Locating indexed periodical articles*

To locate an indexed article that seems promising for your research project, you can check the library catalog to see whether the periodical is available electronically and, if so, whether your library has access to it. Using the library computer network for access can help you avoid paying to view the text of the article that is available online only for subscribers or for a fee.

If the periodical is not available electronically (some scholarly journals, for example, are not), the library catalog also will tell you whether a print version is available in your library's periodicals room. This room probably has recent issues of hundreds or even thousands of newspapers, magazines, and scholarly journals, and it may also contain bound volumes of past issues and microfilm copies of older newspapers.

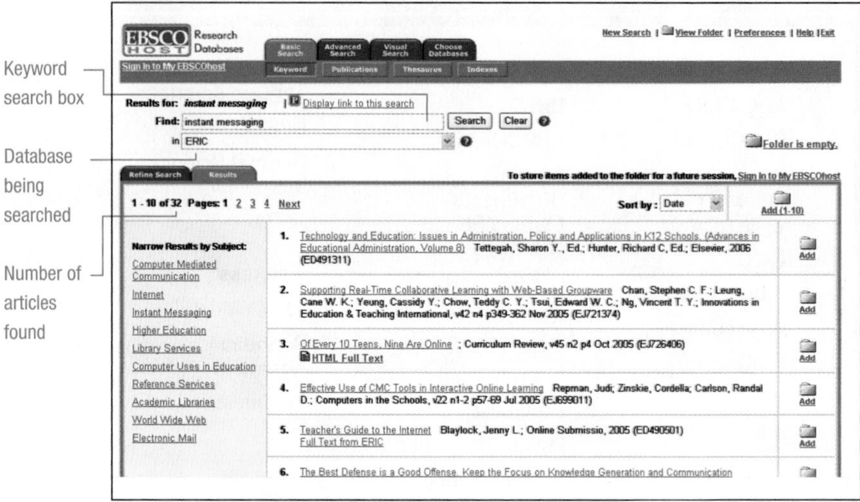


*Results of search in a specialized index*

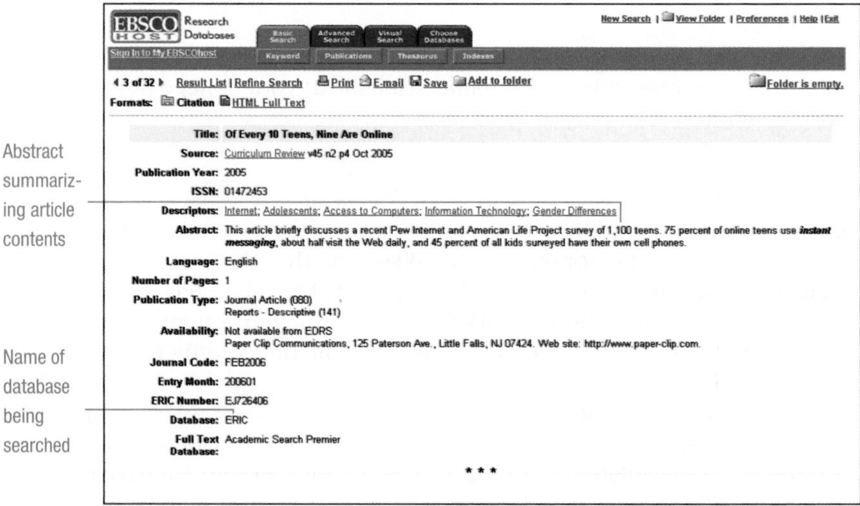


*Article page with abstract from a specialized index search*

David Craig's research on instant messaging required research on educators' opinions on this technology's effect on youth literacy. Therefore, he decided to do a search in ERIC — a database of education-related periodicals. His search on the keywords *instant messaging* gave him the results you see on p. 236. David clicked on an entry that looked like it might pertain to his subject. He was able to read an abstract, and, based on the summary, David thought the article would be helpful. He found the full text in his library's journals collection. Full articles are sometimes accessible in ERIC and other online databases, but you may have to consult your library's periodicals section for a hard copy of the article.

### 4 Bibliographies

Look at any bibliographies (lists of sources) in books or articles you are using for your research; they can lead you to other valuable resources. In addition, check with a reference librarian to find out whether your library has more extensive bibliographies devoted to the area of your research.

### 5 Other library resources

In addition to books and periodicals, libraries give you access to many other useful materials that might be appropriate for your research.

- *Special collections and archives.* Your library may house archives (collections of valuable papers) and other special materials that are often available to student researchers. One student, for example, learned that her university owned a vast collection of twentieth-century posters. With help from a librarian, she was able to use some of these posters as primary sources for her research project on German culture after World War II.
- *Audio, video, multimedia, and art collections.* Many libraries have areas devoted to media and art, where they collect films, videos, paintings, and sound recordings. Some libraries also let students check out laptops and other equipment for classroom presentations.
- *Government documents.* Many libraries have collections of historical documents produced by local or state government offices. Check with a librarian if government publications would be useful sources for your topic. You can also look at the online version of the U.S.

Government Printing Office, known as GPO Access, for electronic versions of government publications from the past decade or so.

- *Interlibrary loans.* To borrow books, videos, or audio materials from another library, use an interlibrary loan. You can also request copies of journal articles from other libraries. Some loans — especially of books — can take time, so be sure to plan ahead.

## 13d Internet research

The Internet is many college students' favorite way of accessing information, and it's true that much information — including authoritative sources identical to those your library provides — can be found online, sometimes for free. However, information in library databases comes from identifiable and professionally edited sources; because no one is responsible for regulating information on the Web, you need to take special care to find out which information online is reliable and which is not. (See Chapter 14 for more on evaluating sources.)

### 1 Internet searches

The Internet offers two ways for you to search for sources: one using subject categories and one using keywords. Most Internet search tools, such as Yahoo! and Google, offer both options. A subject directory allows you to choose a broad category like "Science" and then to click on increasingly narrow categories like "Astronomy" or "The Solar System" until you reach a point where you are given a list of Web sites or the opportunity to do a keyword search. The second option, a search engine, allows you to start right off with a keyword search. Because the Internet contains vastly more material than even the largest library catalog or database, using a search engine requires even more care in the choice and combining of keywords. (See 13c1 for advice on how to combine keywords in order to limit or expand an Internet search.)

### 2 Web browsers

Web browsers, such as Internet Explorer and Mozilla Firefox, not only give you access to powerful search tools but also can provide help in organizing and keeping track of your research.

- *Tracking your searches.* The address bar shows a list of the Web sites you have accessed during your current session. To track your searches over more than one session, find out how to use the browser's HISTORY function. This function can be valuable if you are trying to retrace your steps to find a source you forgot to take notes on or need more information from.
- *Using bookmarks.* Save the URLs — addresses — for sites you want to return to by using the BOOKMARKS (in Firefox) or FAVORITES (in Internet Explorer) function.

## 3 Search tools

Most search tools allow keyword searches as well as subject directory searches (13c1). With a search engine, you simply type in keywords and get results; some metasearch tools use several search engines at once and compile their findings. In a subject directory, on the other hand, you start with general categories and then click on increasingly narrow subcategories. At any point, you can switch to a keyword search to look for specific terms and topics.

GOOGLE'S SUBJECT DIRECTORY

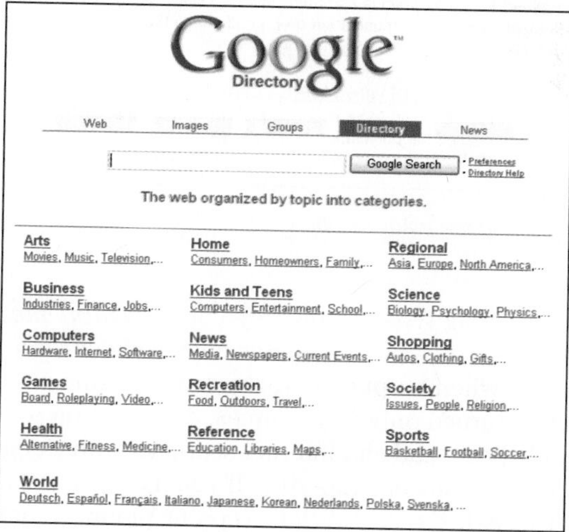

If you decide to use a keyword search in an Internet search engine, you will need to choose keywords carefully in order to get a reasonable number of hits. For example, if you're searching for information on legal issues regarding the Internet and enter *Internet* and *law* as keywords in a Google search, you will get over three million possible sources — a number too huge to be helpful for a researcher. To be useful, then, the keywords you choose — names, titles, authors, concepts — need to lead you to more specific sources. Look for a search engine's search tips or advanced search options for help with refining and limiting a keyword search (13c1).

Google
Web Images Groups News Froogle Maps more »
instant messenger language
Search
Advanced Search
Preferences

**Web** Results **1** - **10** of about **7,120,000** for instant messenger language. (**0.25** seconds)

AIM Acronyms
ATM, As far as I know Away from computer keyboard (for wireless users) AOL **Instant Messenger** As soon as possible Age/Sex/Location At the moment ...
www.aim.com/acronyms.adp?aolp=0 - 21k - Cached - Similar pages

AOL (R) **Instant Messenger** (TM)
(English and Chinese **Language**), (Japanese operating system is required, Japanese **Language**). AOL Latin America · AOL Mexico ...
www.aim.com/international/main.adp - 16k - Cached - Similar pages

LADA POK **Instant** Messaging
IM code **language** allows for quick, precise communication. ... Both America Online and MSN **Instant Messenger** allow for communication over a cell phone that ...
da.co.la.ca.us/pok/im.htm - 29k - Cached - Similar pages

'ru online?': the evolving lexicon of wired teens | csmonitor.com
Mrs. Thomas's oldest son spends about three hours on **instant messenger** each night. ... And while teens have long pushed the boundaries of **language**, ...
www.csmonitor.com/2002/1212/p01s01-ussc.html - 55k - Cached - Similar pages

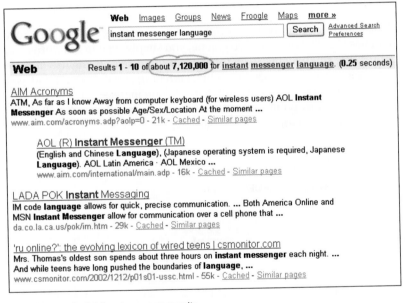

*Google search yielding too many results*

When David Craig typed in the keywords *instant messenger language* for a search on Google, the search engine yielded more than seven million hits. But when he put the three terms in one set of quotation marks, Google returned only fifty sources, as shown on p. 241.

Many people begin and end Internet searches with Google. However, every search tool has unique properties. If you try other search engines — such as AltaVista, Ask, Excite, HotBot, Lycos, or Yahoo! — or a metasearch

Google Web Images Groups News Froogle Maps more »
"instant messenger language" Search Advanced Search Preferences

Web Results 1 - 10 of about 50 for "instant messenger language". (0.33 seconds)

phpBB.com :: Styles
L_AIM, aol **instant messenger language** string, AIM Address. L_YIM, yahoo messenger language string, Yahoo Messenger. L_MSNM, msn **instant messenger language ...**
www.phpbb.com/styles/listvars.php - 199k - Cached - Similar pages

Alohacyberian of Hawaii
You'll also find chatroom and **instant messenger language** translators as well as online dictionaries of computer terms, the American Collegiate Dictionary **...**
keith.martin.home.att.net/vJudaica.html - 22k - Cached - Similar pages

Alohacyberian of Hawaii
There is also a dictionary of computer terminology as well as E-mail, chat room and **instant messenger language** translators. RAINBOWS TO YOU! **...**
keith.martin.home.att.net/vHawaii.html - 40k - Cached - Similar pages

Agnoiologist: This Blog Archives
So, I begin the specifics with a light, more humorous topic: **Instant Messenger language**. "Kids are creating a new slang," they say. **...**
www.agnoiology.com/this_blog/ - 36k - Cached - Similar pages

*Google search using the same keywords in quotation marks*

tool that searches multiple search engines simultaneously — such as Ixquick, WebCrawler, or Zworks — you may find that one of them has capabilities that are particularly helpful for your purposes.

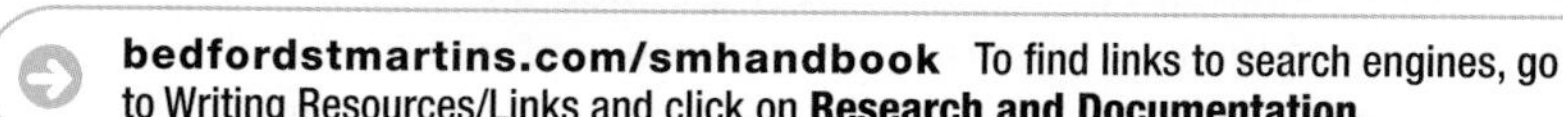
**bedfordstmartins.com/smhandbook** To find links to search engines, go to Writing Resources/Links and click on **Research and Documentation.**

## 4 Authoritative sources online

You can find many sources online that are authoritative and reliable. For example, the Internet enables you to enter virtual libraries that allow access to some collections in libraries other than your own.

Online collections housed in government sites can also be reliable and useful sources. The Library of Congress, the National Institutes of Health, and the U.S. Census Bureau are just a few of the government agencies with large online collections of articles. For current national news, consult online versions of reputable newspapers such as the *New York Times*, the *Washington Post*, the *Los Angeles Times*, or the *Chicago*

*Tribune* or electronic sites for news services such as CNN and C-SPAN. You can also use a search tool like Yahoo!, which has a "News and Media" category you can click on from the main page.

Some scholarly journals (such as those from Berkeley Electronic Press) and general-interest magazines (including *Slate* and *Salon*) are published only on the Web, and many other publications, like *Newsweek*, the *New Yorker*, and the *New Republic*, make at least some of their contents available online for free.

**bedfordstmartins.com/smhandbook** To find links to online governmental collections and sites for newspapers and other media, go to Writing Resources and click on **Reference Resources.**

### 5 Discussion lists

Many other people — friends, classmates, experts, and subscribers to electronic discussion lists — can lead you to sources or serve as sources themselves. For example, if you identify an expert you would like to interview, email that person and ask if she or he would agree to a brief online (or telephone) interview. You might also consider participating in a discussion list that is related to your topic. For example, Google Groups offers discussion groups on a wide variety of general interest topics, and you may also search its archive of Usenet newsgroups, which offers a twenty-year collection of over a billion messages. Your college library probably also subscribes to a number of electronic discussion lists. Remember, though, that not everyone involved in an online discussion will be an expert. As with any kind of research, choose online sources with care.

## 13e Field research

For many research projects, particularly those in the social sciences and business, you will need to collect field data. The "field" may be many things — a classroom, a church, a laboratory, or the corner grocery store. It may even be, as David Craig discovered, a collection of instant messages from the Internet. As a field researcher, then, you need to discover *where* you can find relevant information, *how* to gather it, and *who* might provide the best information.

If you decide to conduct field research, check with your instructor about whether your school has a review board that will need to approve your data-gathering plan.

## 1 Observation

"What," you might ask, "could be easier than observing something?" You just choose a subject, look at it closely, and record what you see and hear. Yet trained observers tell us that making a faithful record of an observation requires intense concentration and mental agility.

Moreover, observation is never neutral. Just as a photographer has a particular angle on a subject, so an observer always has an angle on what he or she is looking at. If, for instance, you decide to conduct a formal observation of your writing class, the field notes you take will reflect your status as an insider. Consequently, you will need to check your observations to see what your participation in the class may have obscured or led you to take for granted. In other instances, when you are not an insider, you still need to aim for optimal objectivity, altering as little as possible the phenomena you are looking at.

### Conducting an observation

1. Determine the purpose of the observation, and be sure it relates to your research question and hypothesis.
2. Brainstorm about what you are looking for, but don't be rigidly bound to your expectations (5a1).
3. If necessary, make appointments and gain permission to observe.
4. Develop an appropriate system for recording data. Consider using a "split" notebook or screen: on one side, record your observations directly; on the other, record your thoughts and interpretations.
5. Record the date, time, and place of the observation.

Before you conduct any observation, decide exactly what you want to find out, and anticipate what you are likely to see. Are you going to observe an action repeated by many people (such as pedestrians crossing a street), a sequence of actions (such as a medical procedure), or the interactions of a group (such as a church congregation)? Also decide exactly what you want to record and how. In a grocery store, for instance, decide whether to observe shoppers or store employees and what you want to note about them — what they say, what they buy, how they are dressed, how they respond to one another, and so on.

## 2 Interviews

Some information is best obtained by interviewing — asking direct questions of other people. If you can talk with an expert in person, on the telephone, or online, you might get information you could not have obtained through any other kind of research. In addition to getting an expert opinion, you might ask for firsthand accounts or suggestions of other places to look or other people to consult.

### Conducting an interview

1. Determine your exact purpose, and be sure it relates to your research question and hypothesis.
2. Set up the interview well in advance. Specify how long it will take, and if you wish to tape-record the session, ask permission to do so.
3. Prepare a written list of factual and open-ended questions. Brainstorming or freewriting can help you come up with questions (5a). Leave plenty of space for notes after each question. If the interview proceeds in a direction that seems fruitful, do not feel that you have to ask all of your prepared questions.
4. Record the subject, date, time, and place of the interview.
5. Even if you are taping, take notes. If you take down quotations, ask your interviewee for permission to use them.
6. Thank those you interview, either in person or in a letter or email.

### Finding people to interview

Check first to see whether your research has generated the names of people you might contact directly. Next, brainstorm for names. In addition to authorities on your topic, consider people in your community—faculty members, war veterans, corporate executives, or others. Once you identify some promising possibilities, write, telephone, or email them to see whether an interview might be arranged.

### Composing questions

To prepare useful questions, you need to know your topic well, and you need to know a fair amount about your interviewee. You will probably want to ask several kinds of questions. Questions about facts and figures (*How many employees do you have?*) elicit specific answers and do not invite expansion or opinion. You can lead the interviewee to think out loud and to give additional details by asking open-ended questions: *How would you characterize the atmosphere at the company just before the union went on strike? How do you feel now about your decision to go to Canada in 1968 rather than be drafted*?

Avoid questions that encourage vague answers (*What do you think of youth today?*) or yes/no answers (*Should the laws governing corporate accounting practices be changed?*). Instead, ask questions that must be answered with supporting details (*Why should the laws governing corporate accounting practices be changed?*).

After discovering a language Web site called the Discouraging Word, David Craig decided to try to set up an interview with the site's anonymous owner, an English literature graduate student at the University of Chicago. Once the owner agreed to an online interview, David drafted a number of specific questions about IM language and other kinds of writing. He eventually used a quotation from the interview in his essay to bolster his thesis.

## 3 Surveys

Although surveys can take the form of interviews, they usually depend on questionnaires. To do survey research, all you need is a representative sample of people and a questionnaire that will elicit the information you need.

How do you choose the people you will survey? In some cases, you might want to survey all members of a small group, such as everyone

### Designing a survey questionnaire

1. Write out your purpose, and review your research question and hypothesis to determine the kinds of questions to ask.
2. Figure out how to reach the respondents you need.
3. Draft potential questions, and make sure that each question calls for a short, specific answer.
4. Test the questions on several people, and revise questions that seem unfair, ambiguous, too hard to answer, or too time consuming.
5. For a questionnaire that is to be mailed, draft a cover letter explaining your purpose. Provide a self-addressed, stamped envelope.
6. Be sure to state a deadline for the respondents to submit the questionnaire.
7. On the final version of the questionnaire, leave adequate space for answers.
8. Proofread the questionnaire carefully.

in one of your classes. More often, however, you'll aim for a random sample of a large group — the first-year class at your university, for example. While a true random sample is probably unattainable, you can aim for a good cross section by, say, emailing every fifth person in the class directory.

On any questionnaire, the questions should be clear and easy to understand and designed so that you will be able to analyze the answers easily. For example, questions that ask respondents to say yes or no or to rank items on a five-point scale are particularly easy to tabulate.

The parking facilities on our campus are adequate.

| Strongly agree | Somewhat agree | Somewhat disagree | Strongly disagree | Don't know |
|---|---|---|---|---|

As you design your questionnaire, think about ways your respondents might misunderstand you or your questions. Adding a category called "other" to a list of options you are asking people about, for example, allows them to fill in information you would not otherwise get.

Because tabulating the responses takes time and because people often resent answering long questionnaires, limit the number of questions to no more than twenty. After tabulating your results, put them in an easily readable format, such as a chart or spreadsheet.

### 4 Data analysis, synthesis, and interpretation

To make sense of the information you have gathered, first try to identify what you want to look at: kinds of language? comparisons between men's and women's responses? The point is to find a focus, since you can't pay equal attention to everything. This step is especially important in analyzing results from observations or survey questionnaires. If you need assistance, see if your instructor can recommend similar research so that you can see how it was analyzed.

Next, synthesize the data by looking for recurring words or ideas that fall into patterns. Establish a system for coding your information, labeling each pattern you identify — a *V* for every use of violent language you observed, for example, or a plus sign for every positive response on a questionnaire. If you ask a few classmates to review your notes or data, they may notice other patterns.

Finally, interpret your data by summing up the meaning of what you have found. What is the significance of your findings? Be careful not to make large generalizations.

### *David Craig's field research — another approach*

If interviews, observations, or opinion surveys aren't quite right for your purposes, consider trying a different kind of field research. A large part of David Craig's paper, for instance, rests on analyzing the data he collected on instant messaging. To determine whether the phrases used in online discussions constitute a language, David obtained and analyzed actual IM conversations from U.S. residents aged twelve to seventeen. After examining over eleven thousand lines of text, David identified four kinds of IM language and was able to use his field research to support his thesis. Details on his research results can be found in his paper (18e).

## THINKING CRITICALLY ABOUT CONDUCTING RESEARCH

Begin to analyze the research project you are now working on by examining the ways in which you conducted your research: What use did you make of primary and secondary sources? What library, online, and field research did you carry out? What aspect of the research process was most satisfying? What was most disappointing or irritating? How could you do research more efficiently? Bring your answers to these questions to class.

# Evaluating Sources and Taking Notes

# 14

On almost any topic you can imagine (Why do mosquitos bite? Who reads fan fiction? What musicians influenced Sonic Youth?), it takes some research — some looking into sources — to answer the question. With most topics, in fact, your problem will be figuring out which sources to consult in the limited time you have available. The difference between a useful source and a poor one depends to a great extent on your topic, purpose, and audience. Once you've found good sources, you will need to take effective notes to use the insights you find to your greatest advantage.

## 14a Purposes for using sources

Why do writers decide to use one source rather than another? Sources serve different purposes, so part of evaluating sources involves deciding what you need the source to provide for your research projects. You may need background information or context that your audience will need to follow your writing; explanations of concepts unfamiliar to your audience; verbal and visual emphasis for your points; authority or evidence for your claims, which can help you create your own authority; other perspectives on your topic; or counter-examples or counter-evidence that you need to consider.

As you begin to work with your sources, make notes in your research log about why you plan to use a particular source. You should also begin your working bibliography.

## 14b Your working bibliography

A working bibliography is a list of sources that you may ultimately use for your project. As you find and begin to evaluate research sources — articles, books, Web sites, and so on — you should record source information for every source you think you might use. (Relevant information includes everything you need to find the source again and cite it correctly; the information you will need varies based on the type of source, whether you found it in a library or not, and whether you consulted it in print or online.) The emphasis here is on *working* because the list will probably include materials that end up not being useful. For this reason, you don't absolutely need to put all entries into the documentation style you will use (see Chapters 18–21). If you do follow the required documentation style, however, that part of your work will be done when you prepare the final draft.

The following lists will help you keep track of the sorts of information you should try to find:

**FOR A BOOK**

Call number
Author(s) or editor(s)
Title and subtitle
Place of publication
Publisher
Year of publication
Other (translator, volume, edition)

**FOR PART OF A BOOK**

Call number
Author(s) of part
Title of part
Author(s) or editor(s) of book
Title of book
Place of publication
Publisher
Year of publication
Inclusive page numbers for part you are using

**FOR A PERIODICAL ARTICLE**

Call number of periodical
Author(s) of article
Title of article
Name of periodical
Volume number
Issue number
Date of issue
Inclusive page numbers for article

**FOR AN ELECTRONIC SOURCE**

Author(s) (if available)
Title of document
Title of site
Editor(s) of site
Sponsor of site
Publication information for print version of source
Name of database or online service
Date of electronic publication or last update
Date you accessed the source
URL

For other kinds of sources (films, recordings, visuals), you should also list the information required by the documentation style you are using (see Chapters 18–21), and note where you found the information.

## TALKING THE TALK: Research with an open mind

"What's wrong with looking for sources that back up what I want to say?" When you start researching a topic, keep an open mind: investigate every important source, even if you think you won't agree with it. If all your sources take the same position you take, you may be doing some pretty selective searching — and you may be missing a big part of the picture. Who knows? You may even change your position after learning more about the topic. And even if you don't, ignoring counterarguments and other points of view harms your credibility, suggesting that you haven't really done your homework.

### *Annotated bibliography*

You might wish to annotate your working bibliography to include your own description and comments as well as publishing information. Even if annotations aren't required, you may want to create them because they can help you understand and remember what the source says. If your instructor requires an annotated bibliography, be sure to ask for the specific guidelines you are to follow in creating the bibliography and then follow them carefully.

Although some annotations can be very detailed — summarizing and evaluating the main points in a source — most annotations students do on their own include fairly brief descriptions and comments.

ANNOTATED BIBLIOGRAPHY ENTRY

Gere, Anne Ruggles. "Kitchen Tables and Rented Rooms: The Extracurriculum of Composition." *Literacy: A Critical Sourcebook*. Ed. Ellen Cushman, Eugene R. Kintgen, Barry M. Kroll, and Mike Rose. Boston: Bedford, 2001. 275-89. Print. This history of writing instruction argues that people teach writing and learn to write--and always have--more often in informal places like kitchens than in traditional writing classrooms. Gere presents numerous examples and comments on their importance to the study of writing today.

**bedfordstmartins.com/smhandbook** For additional examples of annotated bibliographies, click on **Student Writing**.

## 14c Evaluating usefulness and credibility

Since you want the information and ideas you glean from sources to be reliable and persuasive, you must evaluate each potential source carefully. The following guidelines can help you assess the usefulness and credibility of sources you are considering:

- *Your purpose.* What will this source add to your research project? Does it help you support a major point, demonstrate that you have thoroughly researched your topic, or help establish your own credibility through its authority?
- *Relevance.* How closely related is the source to the narrowed topic you are pursuing? You may need to read beyond the title and opening paragraph to check for relevance.
- *Level of specialization and audience.* General sources can be helpful as you begin your research, but you may then need the authority or currency of more specialized sources. On the other hand, extremely specialized works may be very hard to understand. Who was the source originally written for — the general public? experts in the field? advocates or opponents? How does this fit with your concept of your own audience?
- *Credentials of the publisher or sponsor.* What can you learn about the publisher or sponsor of the source you are using? For example, is it a major newspaper known for integrity in reporting, or is it a tabloid? Is it a popular source, whether in print or electronic, or is it sponsored by a professional organization or academic institution (13a2)? If you're evaluating a book, is the publisher one you recognize or can find described on its own Web site? If you are evaluating a Web site, is the site's sponsor a commercial (.com), educational (.edu), governmental (.gov), military (.mil), network (.net), or nonprofit (.org) entity? No hard and fast rules exist for deciding what kind of source to use. But knowing the sponsor's or publisher's credentials can help you determine whether a source is appropriate for your research project.
- *Credentials of the author.* As you do your research, note names that come up from one source to another, since these references may indicate that the author is influential in the field. An author's credentials may also be presented in the article, book, or Web site, or you can search the Internet for information about the author. In U.S. academic writing, experts and those with significant experience in a field have more authority on the subject than others.

- *Date of publication.* Recent sources are often more useful than older ones, particularly in the sciences or other fields that change rapidly. However, in some fields — such as the humanities — the most authoritative works may be older ones. The publication dates of Internet sites can often be difficult to pin down. And even for sites that include dates of posting, remember that the material posted may have been composed some time earlier. Most reliable will be those sites that list the dates of updating regularly.
- *Accuracy of the source.* How accurate and complete is the information in the source? How thorough is the bibliography or list of works cited that accompanies the source? Can you find other sources that corroborate what your source is saying?
- *Stance of the source.* Identify the source's point of view or rhetorical stance, and scrutinize it carefully. Does the source present facts, or does it interpret or evaluate them? If it presents facts, what is included and what is omitted, and why? If it interprets or evaluates information that is not disputed, the source's stance may be obvious, but at other times, you will need to think carefully about the source's goals (14d). What does the author or sponsoring group want? to convince you of an idea? sell you something? call you to action in some way?
- *Cross-references to the source.* Is the source cited in other works? If you see your source cited by others, notice how they cite it and what they say about it to find additional clues to its credibility.

For more on evaluating Web sources and periodical articles, see the Source Maps on pp. 254–57.

### EXERCISE 14.1

Choose two sources that seem well suited to your topic, and evaluate their usefulness and credibility using the criteria presented in this chapter. If possible, analyze one print source and one electronic source. Bring the results of your analysis to class for discussion.

## 14d Critical reading and interpretation

For those sources that you want to analyze more closely, reading with a critical eye can make your research process more efficient. Use the tips on pp. 258–59 to guide your critical reading.

## SOURCE MAP: Evaluating Web sources

**Determine the credibility of the sponsoring organization.**

① Consider the URL, specifically the top-level domain name. (For example, *.edu* may indicate that the sponsor is an accredited college or university; *.org* may indicate it's a nonprofit organization.) Ask yourself whether such a sponsor might be biased about the topic you're researching.

② Look for an *About* page or a link to the home page for background information on the sponsor, including a mission statement. What is the sponsoring organization's stance or point of view? Does the mission statement seem biased or balanced? Does the sponsor seem to take other points of view into account? What is the intended purpose of the site? Is this site meant to inform? Or is it trying to persuade, advertise, or accomplish something?

**Determine the credibility of the author.**

③ Evaluate the author's credentials. On this Web page, the author appears to be a staff writer for the site. Although the author herself may not have a medical background, note that the article was reviewed by a physician and that it includes findings from a respected medical journal. If you suspect that an author may be biased, run a search on the author's name to find any affiliations with interest groups or any leaning toward one side of an issue. Ask yourself if the author seems qualified to write about the issue.

④ Look for the date that indicates when the information was posted or last updated. Here, the date is given at the beginning of the article.

⑤ Check to see if the sources referred to are also up-to-date. This author cites sources from July 2005. Ask yourself if, given your topic, an older source is acceptable or if only the most recent information will do.

**Determine the accuracy of the information.**

⑥ How complete is the information in the source? Examine the works cited by the author. Are sources for statistics included? Do the sources cited seem credible? Is a list of additional resources provided? Here, the author cites the *New England Journal of Medicine* and the National Center for Complementary and Alternative Medicine in addition to two of WebMD's own articles. In some cases, it may be necessary to track down additional sources and corroborate what a source is saying.

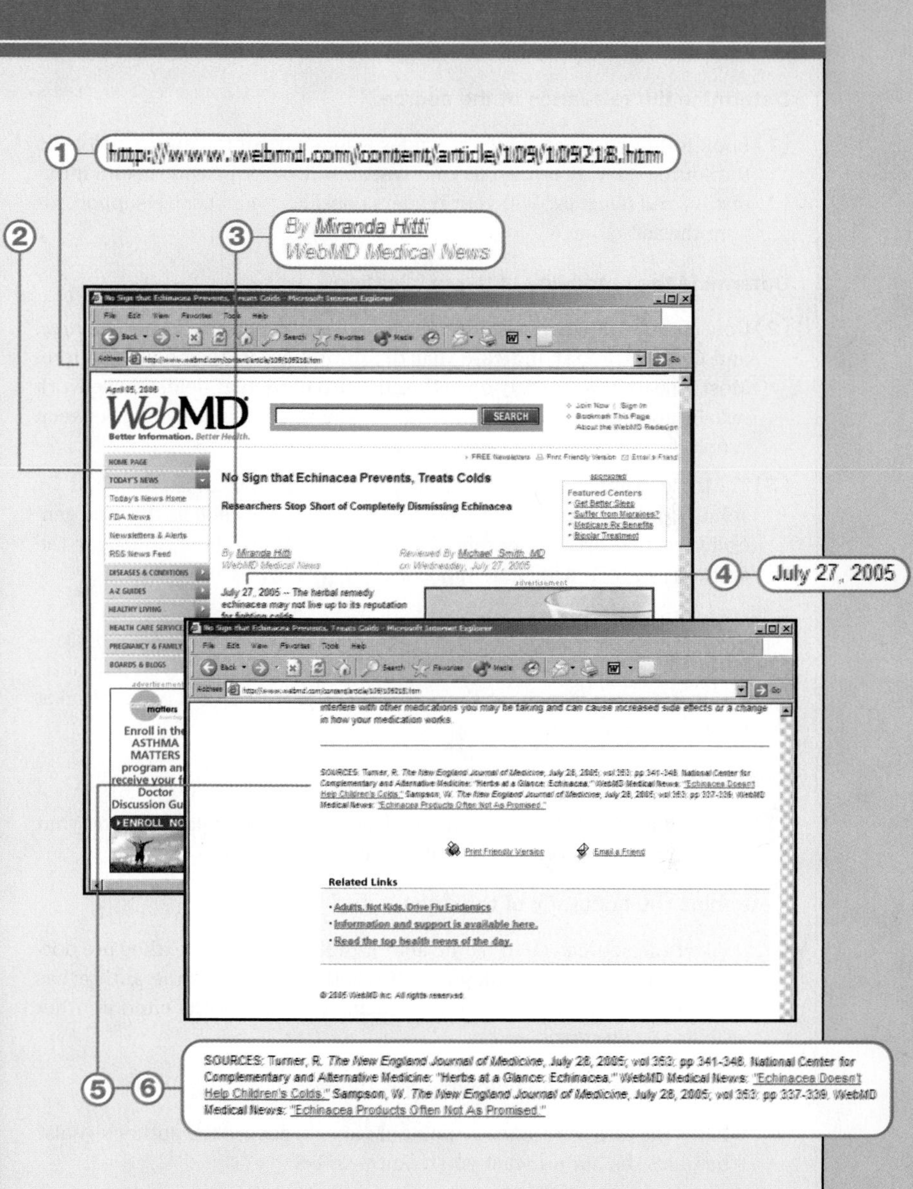

1 http://www.webmd.com/content/article/109/109218.htm
2
3 By Miranda Hitti
WebMD Medical News
4 July 27, 2005
No Sign that Echinacea Prevents, Treats Colds
Researchers Stop Short of Completely Dismissing Echinacea
By Miranda Hitti
WebMD Medical News
Reviewed By Michael Smith, MD
on Wednesday, July 27, 2005
July 27, 2005 -- The herbal remedy echinacea may not live up to its reputation for fighting colds.
Related Links
Adults, Not Kids, Drive Flu Epidemics
Information and support is available here.
Read the top health news of the day.
5 6 SOURCES: Turner, R. The New England Journal of Medicine, July 28, 2005; vol 353: pp 341-348. National Center for Complementary and Alternative Medicine: "Herbs at a Glance: Echinacea." WebMD Medical News: "Echinacea Doesn't Help Children's Colds." Sampson, W. The New England Journal of Medicine, July 28, 2005; vol 353: pp 337-339. WebMD Medical News: "Echinacea Products Often Not As Promised."

## SOURCE MAP: Evaluating articles

**Determine the relevance of the source.**

① Look for an abstract, which provides a summary of the entire article. Is the source directly related to your research? Does it provide useful information and insights? Will your readers consider it persuasive support for your thesis?

**Determine the credibility of the publication.**

② Consider the publication's title. Words in the title such as *Journal*, *Review*, and *Quarterly* may indicate that the periodical is a scholarly source. Most research essays rely on authorities in a particular field, whose work usually appears in scholarly journals. For more on distinguishing between scholarly and popular sources, see 13a2.

③ Try to determine the publisher or sponsor. This journal is published by Johns Hopkins University Press. Academic presses such as this one generally review articles carefully before publishing them and bear the authority of their academic sponsors.

**Determine the credibility of the author.**

④ Evaluate the author's credentials. In this case, they are given in a note, which indicates that the author is a college professor and has written at least two books on related topics.

**Determine the currency of the article.**

⑤ Look at the publication date and think about whether your topic and your credibility depend on your use of very current sources.

**Determine the accuracy of the article.**

⑥ Look at the sources cited by the author of the article. Here, they are documented in footnotes. Ask yourself whether the works the author has cited seem credible and current. Are any of these works cited in other articles you've considered?

**In addition, consider the following questions:**

- What is the article's stance or point of view? What are the author's goals? What does the author want you to know or believe?
- How does this source fit in with your other sources? Does any of the information it provides contradict or challenge other sources?

(2) HUMAN RIGHTS QUARTERLY

# Prisons and Politics in Contemporary Latin America

*Mark Ungar**

**ABSTRACT**

Despite democratization throughout Latin America, massive human rights abuses continue in the region's prisons. Conditions have become so bad that most governments have begun to enact improvements, including new criminal codes and facility decongestion. However, once in place, these reforms are undermined by chaotic criminal justice systems, poor policy administration, and rising crime rates leading to greater detention powers for the police. After describing current prison conditions in Latin America and the principal reforms to address them, this article explains how political and administrative limitations hinder the range of agencies and officials responsible for implementing those changes.

## I. INTRODUCTION

Prison conditions not only constitute some of the worst human rights violations in contemporary Latin American democracies, but also reveal fundamental weaknesses in those democracies. Unlike most other human rights problems, those in the penitentiary system cannot be easily explained with authoritarian legacies or renegade officials. The systemic killing, overcrowding, disease, torture, rape, corruption, and due process abuses all occur under the state's twenty-four hour watch. Since the mid-1990s,

(4) * *Mark Ungar* is Associate Professor of Political Science at Brooklyn College, City University of New York. Recent publications include the books *Elusive Reform: Democracy and the Rule of Law in Latin America* (Lynne Rienner, 2002) and *Violence and Politics: Globalization's Paradox* (Routledge, 2001) as well as articles and book chapters on democratization, policing, and judicial access. He works with Amnesty International USA and local rights groups in Latin America.

*Human Rights Quarterly* 25 (2003) 909–934 © 2003 by The Johns Hopkins University Press

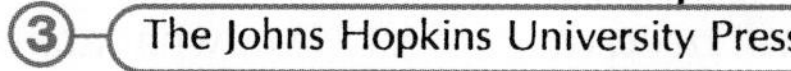


(5) © 2003

915

ezuela, the
jumped to
y agency in
ers, far from
the number
mates form
PCC)—with
In the riots
began in
and spread
s—the PCC
CC leaders.
nd security
naffordable
rgest, some
tiny airless
tes living in
hose in the
az facility of
a Contra el
less cells of
able water,
th rats and
in weapons
ocaine and
on officials,
al Guard in
retribution.
s protesting
colony of El

10. Inspector General de Cárceles, Informe Annual (Caracas: Ministerio de Justicia 1994).
11. *Overcrowding Main Cause of Riots in Latin American Prisons,* AFP, 30 Dec. 1997.
12. Interviews with inmates, speaking on condition of anonymity in San Pedro prison (19 July 2000); Interviews with inmates, speaking on condition of anonymity in La Paz FELCN Prison (20 July 2000).
13. (6) Typhus, cholera, tuberculosis, and scabies run rampant and the HIV rate may be as high as 25 percent. The warden of Retén de la Planta, where cells built for one inmate house three or four, says the prisons "are collapsing" because of insufficient budgets to train personnel. "Things fall apart and stay that way." Interview, Luis A. Lara Roche, Warden of Retén de la Planta, Caracas, Venezuela, 19 May 1995. At El Dorado prison in Bolívar state, there is one bed for every four inmates, cells are infested with vermin, and inmates lack clean bathing water and eating utensils.
14. *La Crisis Penitenciaria,* El Nacional (Caracas), 2 Sept. 1988, at D2. On file with author.

### Guidelines for examining potential sources

Looking quickly at the various parts of a source can provide useful information and help you decide whether to explore that particular source more thoroughly. You are already familiar with some of these basic elements: title and subtitle, title page and copyright page, home page, table of contents, index, footnotes, and bibliography. Be sure to check other items as well.

- *Abstracts* — concise summaries of articles and books — routinely precede journal articles and are often included in indexes and databases.
- A *preface* or *foreword* generally discusses the writer's purpose and thesis.
- *Subheadings* within the text can alert you to how much detail is given on a topic.
- A *conclusion* or *afterword* may summarize or draw the strands of an argument together.
- For an electronic source, click on some of the *links* to see if they're useful, and see if the overall *design* of the site is easy to navigate.

#### *Your research question*

As you read, keep your research question in mind, and ask yourself the following questions:

- How does this material address your research question and support your hypothesis?
- What quotations from this source might help support your thesis?
- Does the source include counterarguments to your hypothesis that you will need to answer? If so, what answers can you provide?

#### *The author's stance and tone*

Even a seemingly factual report, such as an encyclopedia article, is filled with judgments, often unstated. Read with an eye for the author's overall rhetorical stance, or perspective, as well as for facts or explicit opinions. Also pay attention to the author's tone, the way his or her attitude toward the topic and audience is conveyed. The following questions can help:

- Is the author a strong advocate or opponent of something? a skeptical critic? a specialist in the field?
- Are there any clues to why the author takes this stance (3g)? Is professional affiliation a factor?
- How does this stance affect the author's presentation and your reaction to it?
- What facts does the author include? Can you think of any important fact that is omitted?
- What is the author's tone? Is it cautious, angry, flippant, serious, impassioned? What words indicate this tone?

#### *The author's argument and evidence*

Every piece of writing takes a position. Even a scientific report implicitly "argues" that we should accept it and its data as reliable. As you read, look for the main point or the main argument the author is making. Try to identify the reasons the author gives to support his or her position. Then try to determine *why* the author takes this position. Consider these questions:

- What is the author's main point, and what evidence supports it?
- How persuasive is the evidence? Can you think of a way to refute it?
- Can you detect any questionable logic or fallacious thinking (9f)?
- Does this author disagree with arguments you have read elsewhere? If so, what causes the disagreements — differences about facts or about how to interpret facts?

For more on argument, see Chapters 9–11.

## 14e Synthesizing sources

Throughout the research process, you are *synthesizing* — grouping similar pieces of data together, looking for patterns or trends, and identifying the main points of the data. Doing so enables you to use your sources effectively to pursue your research goals.

David Craig grouped the data from his field research into four types of IM language: phonetic replacements, acronyms, abbreviations, and inanities. Recognizing these patterns helped him conclude that instant messaging is in many ways a new language with its own vocabulary. As

David continued his research, he noticed another pattern — that educators, in particular, tend to see IMing as harmful to literacy. He thus put quotations from teachers in a separate subfolder of his research log. David was able to recognize these patterns because he was thinking critically, synthesizing, and comparing his sources.

Often, synthesizing will lead you to make inferences — conclusions that are not explicitly stated but that follow logically from the data given. For example, as David did research on linguistics, he learned that using any kind of language involves wordplay and other analytical abilities. Later on he was able to infer that IM language use can actually aid students in their other writing. (For more on synthesizing sources, see Chapter 15 and 17d.)

## 14f Notes and annotations

Note-taking methods vary greatly from one researcher to another, so you may decide to use a notebook, index cards, or a computer file. Regardless of the method, however, you should (1) record enough information to help you recall the major points of the source; (2) put the information in the form in which you are most likely to incorporate it into your research essay, whether a summary, a paraphrase, or a quotation; and (3) note all the information you will need to cite the source accurately. The following example shows the major items a note should include:

ELEMENTS OF AN ACCURATE NOTE

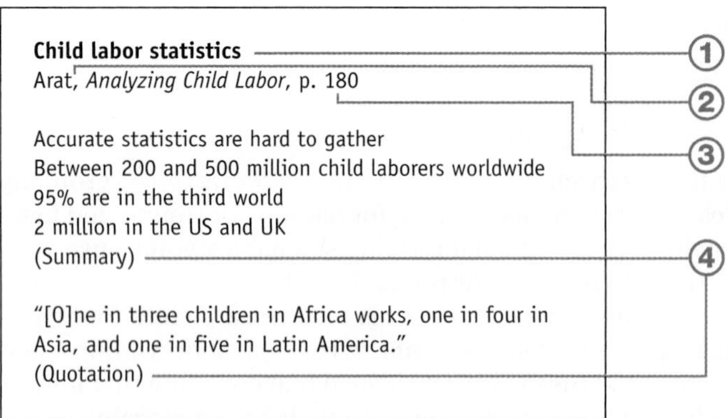

**Child labor statistics**
Arat, *Analyzing Child Labor*, p. 180
Accurate statistics are hard to gather
Between 200 and 500 million child laborers worldwide
95% are in the third world
2 million in the US and UK
(Summary)
"[O]ne in three children in Africa works, one in four in
Asia, and one in five in Latin America."
(Quotation)
1
2
3
4

1. *Use a subject heading*. Label each note with a brief but descriptive subject heading so that you can group similar subtopics together.
2. *Identify the source*. List the author's name and a shortened title of the source. Your working-bibliography entry (14b) for the source will contain the full bibliographic information, so you don't need to repeat it in each note.
3. *Record exact page references (if available)*. For online or other sources without page numbers, record the paragraph, screen, or other section number(s) if indicated.
4. *Indicate whether the note is a direct quotation, paraphrase, or summary* (see below). Make sure quotations are copied accurately. Put square brackets around any change you make, and use ellipses if you omit material.

Taking complete notes will help you digest the source information as you read and incorporate the material into your text without inadvertently plagiarizing the source (see Chapter 16). Be sure to reread each note carefully, and recheck it against the source to make sure quotations, statistics, and specific facts are accurate. (For more information on working with quotations, paraphrases, and summaries, see Chapter 15.)

## 1 Quotations

Some of the notes you take will contain quotations, which give the *exact words* of a source. Here, for example, is a note with a quotation that David Craig planned to use in his research paper:

**Comments from educators** — Subject heading

Lee, "I Think," *NY Times* (Web site) — Author and short title of source (no page number for electronic source)

Melanie Weaver was stunned by some of the term papers she received from a 10th-grade class she recently taught as part of an internship. "They would be trying to make a point in a paper, they would put a smiley face in the end," said Ms. Weaver, who teaches at Alvernia College in Reading, Pa. "If they were presenting an argument and they needed to present an opposite view, they would put a frown."

(Quotation) — Indication that note is direct quotation

### Guidelines for quotations

- Copy quotations carefully, with punctuation, capitalization, and spelling *exactly* as in the original.
- Enclose the quotation in quotation marks; don't rely on your memory to distinguish your own words from those of the source.
- Use square brackets if you introduce words of your own into a quotation or make changes in it, and use ellipses if you omit material. If you later incorporate the quotation into your essay, copy it faithfully — brackets, ellipses, and all. (15b4)
- Record the author's name, the shortened title, and the page number(s) on which the quotation appears. If the note refers to more than one page, use a slash (/) within the quotation to indicate where one page ends and another begins. For sources without page numbers, record the paragraph, screen, or other section number(s), if any.
- Make sure you have a corresponding working-bibliography entry with complete source information. (14b)
- Label the note with a subject heading, and identify it as a quotation.

The above guidelines will help you take accurate notes not only of quotations but also of paraphrases and summaries.

## 2 Paraphrases

A paraphrase accurately states all the relevant information from a passage *in your own words and sentence structures*, without any additional comments or elaborations. A paraphrase is useful when the main points of a passage, their order, and at least some details are important but — unlike passages worth quoting — the particular wording is not. Unlike a summary, a paraphrase always restates *all* the main points of a passage in the same order and often in about the same number of words.

To paraphrase without plagiarizing inadvertently, do not simply substitute synonyms, and do not imitate an author's style. If you wish to cite some of an author's words within a paraphrase, enclose them in quotation marks. The following examples of paraphrases resemble the original either too little or too much:

**ORIGINAL**

Language play, the arguments suggest, will help the development of pronunciation ability through its focus on the properties of sounds and sound contrasts, such as rhyming. Playing with word endings and decoding the syntax of riddles will help the acquisition of grammar. Readiness to play with words and names, to exchange puns and to engage in nonsense talk, promotes links with semantic development. The kinds of dialogue interaction illustrated above are likely to have consequences for the development of conversational skills. And language play, by its nature, also contributes greatly to what in recent years has been called *metalinguistic awareness*, which is turning out to be of critical importance in the development of language skills in general and of literacy skills in particular. — DAVID CRYSTAL, *Language Play* (180)

**UNACCEPTABLE PARAPHRASE: STRAYING FROM THE AUTHOR'S IDEAS**

Crystal argues that playing with language — creating rhymes, figuring out how riddles work, making puns, playing with names, using invented words, and so on — helps children figure out a great deal about language, from the basics of pronunciation and grammar to how to carry on a conversation. Increasing their understanding of how language works in turn helps them become more interested in learning new languages and in pursuing education (180).

This paraphrase starts off well enough, but it moves away from paraphrasing the original to inserting the writer's ideas; Crystal says nothing about learning new languages or pursuing education.

**UNACCEPTABLE PARAPHRASE: USING THE AUTHOR'S WORDS**

Crystal suggests that language play, including rhyme, helps children improve <u>pronunciation ability</u>, that looking at <u>word endings and decoding the syntax of riddles</u> allows them to understand grammar, and that other <u>kinds of dialogue interaction</u> teach conversation. Overall, language play may <u>be of critical importance in the development of language and literacy skills</u> (180).

Because the underlined phrases are either borrowed from the original without quotation marks or changed only superficially, this paraphrase plagiarizes.

**UNACCEPTABLE PARAPHRASE: USING THE AUTHOR'S SENTENCE STRUCTURES**

Language play, Crystal <u>suggests,</u> <u>will improve</u> pronunciation by zeroing in on sounds <u>such as</u> rhymes. <u>Having fun with</u> word endings <u>and analyzing</u> riddle structure <u>will help</u> a person acquire grammar. <u>Being prepared to play with</u> language, <u>to use</u> puns and <u>talk</u> nonsense, <u>improves</u> the ability to use seman-

> tics. These playful methods of communication are likely to influence a person's ability to talk to others. And language play inherently adds enormously to what has recently been known as *metalinguistic awareness*, a concept of great magnitude in developing speech abilities generally and literacy abilities particularly (180).

Although this paraphrase does not rely explicitly on the words of the original, it does follow the sentence structures too closely. Substituting synonyms for the major words in a paraphrase is not enough to avoid plagiarism. The paraphrase must represent your own interpretation of the material and thus must show your own thought patterns.

Here are two paraphrases of the same passage that express the author's ideas accurately and acceptably, the first completely in the writer's own words and the second, from David Craig's notes, including a quotation from the original.

**ACCEPTABLE PARAPHRASE: IN THE STUDENT WRITER'S OWN WORDS**

> Crystal argues that playing with language — creating rhymes, figuring out riddles, making puns, playing with names, using invented words, and so on — helps children figure out a great deal, from the basics of pronunciation and grammar to how to carry on a conversation. This kind of play allows chil-

## Guidelines for paraphrases

- Include all main points and any important details from the original source, in the same order in which the author presents them.
- State the meaning in your own words and sentence structures. If you want to include especially memorable language from the original, enclose it in quotation marks.
- Save your comments, elaborations, or reactions on another note.
- Record the author's name, the shortened title, and the page number(s) on which the original material appears. For sources without page numbers, record the paragraph, screen, or other section number(s), if any.
- Make sure you have a corresponding working-bibliography entry with complete source information. (14b)
- Label the note with a subject heading, and identify it as a paraphrase.

dren to understand the overall concept of how language works, a concept that is key to learning to use — and read — language effectively (180).

**ACCEPTABLE PARAPHRASE: QUOTING SOME OF THE AUTHOR'S WORDS**

Crystal argues that playing with language — creating rhymes, figuring out riddles, making puns, playing with names, using invented words, and so on — helps children figure out a great deal, from the basics of pronunciation and grammar to how to carry on a conversation. This kind of play allows children to understand the overall concept of how language works, or "metalinguistic awareness," a concept that Crystal sees as "of critical importance in the development of language skills in general and of literacy skills in particular" (180).

## 3 Summaries

A summary is a significantly shortened version of a passage or even of a whole chapter or work that captures main ideas *in your own words*. Unlike a paraphrase, a summary uses just enough information to record the main points you wish to emphasize. Your goal is to keep the summary as brief as possible, capturing only the main idea of the original and not distorting the author's meaning.

### Summarizing short pieces

To summarize a short passage, read it carefully and, without looking at the text, write a one- or two-sentence summary. Following is David Craig's note recording a summary of the Crystal passage on p. 263. Notice that it states the author's main points selectively — and without using his words.

**Language development**

Crystal, *Language Play*, p. 180

Crystal argues that various kinds of language play contribute to awareness of how language works and to literacy.

(Summary)

Now read the brief article that follows, and then see a student's note summarizing it:

> One scientist hoarded a rare virus strain for more than a decade, refusing requests to let other researchers study it. Others refused to share biological materials like cloned genes unless they were included as authors of any resulting discoveries, a nice way to boost a résumé. Hundreds of biologists delay publishing their results by more than six months for reasons like applying for a patent or protecting their lead over competitors. The scientific ideal is openness and sharing — describing your experiments in enough detail that others can evaluate their accuracy, and giving even competitors samples of your cell lines and other material so they can replicate your experiment and thus check it — but "ideal" seems to be the operative word here. Now that genetics is big business, researchers are withholding data, refusing to share materials and delaying publication of results in order to commercialize them, finds a new study in the *Journal of the American Medical Association.* Of the 1,240 geneticists whom Eric G. Campbell and colleagues at the Institute for Health Policy at Massachusetts General Hospital surveyed, 47 percent had been denied information, data or materials in the last three years. "The geneticists told us that such denials were slowing research, preventing replication and causing them to abandon promising leads," says Campbell.
>
> — SHARON BEGLEY, "Science Failing to Share"

**Genetics/big business**

Begley, "Science," p. 10

In a perfect world, scientists share their findings freely. But the commercialization of genetics has led scientists to withhold information, sometimes for years, so that they can continue to make money from their research. This tactic has slowed down scientific progress.

(Summary)

### *Summarizing longer pieces*

To summarize a long passage or an entire chapter, skim the headings and topic sentences, and make notes of each; then write your summary in a paragraph or two. For a whole book, you may want to refer to the preface and introduction as well as chapter titles, headings, and topic sen-

## Guidelines for summaries

- Include just enough information to recount the main points you wish to cite. A summary is usually far shorter than the original.
- Use your own words. If you include any language from the original, enclose it in quotation marks.
- Record the author's name, the shortened title, and the page number(s) on which the original material appears. For sources without page numbers, record the paragraph, screen, or other section number(s), if any.
- Make sure you have a corresponding working-bibliography entry with complete source information. (14b)
- Label the note with a subject heading, and identify it as a summary.

tences — and your summary may take a page or more. In general, try to identify the thesis or claim being made, and then look for the subtopics or supports for that claim.

### 4 Other kinds of notes

Many researchers take notes that don't fall into the categories of quotations, paraphrases, or summaries. Some take key-term notes, which might include the topic addressed in the source along with names or short statements — anything to jog their memories when they begin drafting. Others record personal or critical notes — questions, criticisms, or other ideas that come to mind as they read. In fact, an exciting part of research occurs when the materials you are reading spark new ideas in your mind, ideas that may become part of your thesis or argument. Don't let them get away. While you may later decide not to use these ideas, you need to make notes about them just in case.

You may adopt a system particular to your own research project. David Craig analyzed over eleven thousand lines of instant-message conversations as part of his study on IM language and youth literacy. For each conversation, David kept a note on each occurrence of nonstandard English spellings and words and their frequencies. Since he was trying to categorize these occurrences as well as quantify them, David labeled each note with the type of change that he was noticing.

By labeling these notes with subject headings, he could easily determine how often each type of change to the language appeared in his data. Here is one of his notes:

**Phonetic replacement**

Conversation between two teenagers in Texas, line 10.
Teen One: hey i g2g

Writer replaces "to" in abbreviation g2g ["got to go"] with the number 2.

After he had taken notes, David sorted them to see how many related to the category of phonetic replacement; he then placed the notes in the order he planned to use them in his essay. In this case, David's notes not only helped him synthesize his data; they also made it easier for him to present the data in a clear, concise chart (shown on p. 5 of his research paper, which appears at the end of Chapter 18).

Researchers also take field notes, which record their firsthand observations or the results of their surveys or interviews (13e).

Whatever form your notes take, be sure to list the source's title, author, and page number(s) so that you can return to the material easily. In addition, check that you have carefully distinguished your own thoughts and comments from those of the source itself.

## 5 Annotations

Sometimes you may photocopy or print out a source you intend to use. In such cases, you can annotate the photocopies or printouts with your thoughts and questions and highlight interesting quotations and key terms.

If you take notes in a computer file, you may be able to copy online sources electronically, paste them into the file, and annotate them there. Try not to rely too heavily on copying or printing out whole pieces, however; you still need to read the material very carefully. Also resist the temptation to treat copied material as notes, an action that could lead to inadvertent plagiarizing. (In a computer file, using a different color for text pasted from a source will help prevent this problem.)

### EXERCISE 14.2

Choose an online source you are sure you will use in your research project. Then download and print out the source, record all essential publication information for it, and annotate it as you read it.

### THINKING CRITICALLY ABOUT YOUR EVALUATION OF SOURCES

Take a careful look at the sources you have gathered for your research project. How many make points that support your own point of view? How many provide counterarguments to your point of view? Which sources are you relying on most — and why? Which source seems most credible to you — and why? Which sources, if any, are you suspicious of or worried about? Bring the results of this investigation to class for discussion.

# 15 Integrating Sources into Your Writing

The process of absorbing your sources and then integrating them gracefully into your own writing is one of the pleasures of successful research. As you work with these sources and think of using them in your own writing, they become *yours*. Instead of taking over your writing, or drowning out your voice, they work in support of your own good ideas. Integrating sources successfully is key to effective research-based writing.

## 15a Deciding whether to quote, paraphrase, or summarize

You tentatively decided to quote, paraphrase, or summarize material when you took notes on your sources (14f). As you choose which sources to use in your research project and how to use them, however, you may reevaluate those decisions. For example, you may decide to summarize in an essay what you paraphrased in your notes, to use only a quotation you included in the midst of a summary, or not to use a particular quotation at all. The guidelines on p. 271 can help you decide whether to quote, paraphrase, or summarize.

## 15b Working with quotations

Quoting involves using a source's exact words. You might use a direct quotation to catch readers' attention or make an introduction memorable. Quotations from respected authorities can help establish your credibility by showing that you've sought out experts in the field. In addition, quoting authors who disagree with your opinions helps demonstrate your fairness (11e3).

Finally, well-chosen quotations can broaden the appeal of your project by drawing on emotion as well as logic (9d and 11f–g). A student writing on the ethics of bullfighting, for example, might quote Ernest Hemingway's striking comment that "the formal bull-fight is a tragedy, not a sport, and the bull is certain to be killed."

## When to quote, paraphrase, or summarize

**Quote**

- wording that is so memorable or powerful, or expresses a point so perfectly, that you cannot change it without weakening the meaning
- authors' opinions you wish to emphasize
- authors' words that show you are considering varying perspectives
- respected authorities whose opinions support your ideas
- authors whose opinions challenge or vary greatly from those of others in the field

**Paraphrase**

- passages in which the details, but not the exact words, are important to your point

**Summarize**

- long passages in which the main point is important to your point but the details are not

Although quotations can add interest and authenticity to an essay, be careful not to overuse them: your research paper is primarily your own work, meant to showcase your ideas and your argument.

### 1 Brief quotations

Short prose quotations should be run in with your text, enclosed in quotation marks that mark where someone else's words begin and end. When you include such quotations — or other source material — use both signal phrases and parenthetical references or notes, depending on the requirements of the documentation style you are using (see Chapters 18–21). Signal phrases (15b3) introduce the material, often including the author's name. Parenthetical references and notes direct your readers to full bibliographic entries included elsewhere in your text.

The following brief quotation follows Modern Language Association (MLA) style (18b):

> In Miss Eckhart, Welty recognizes a character who shares with her "the love of her art and the love of giving it, the desire to give it until there is no more left" (10).

In this example, the signal phrase that introduces the quotation (*In Miss Eckhart, Welty recognizes*) includes the author's name, so MLA style requires only the page number in parentheses.

## 2 Long quotations

If you are following MLA style, set off a prose quotation longer than four lines. If you are following the style of the American Psychological Association (known as APA style) or *Chicago* style, set off a quotation of more than forty words or more than one paragraph. Begin such a quotation on a new line, and indent every line one inch (MLA), five to seven spaces (APA), or eight spaces (*Chicago*). This indentation sets off the quotation clearly, so quotation marks are unnecessary. Introduce long quotations with a signal phrase or a sentence followed by a colon.

The following long quotation follows MLA style:

> A good seating arrangement can prevent problems; however, "withitness," as defined by Woolfolk, works even better:
>
> > Withitness is the ability to communicate to students that you are aware of what is happening in the classroom, that you "don't miss anything." With-it teachers seem to have "eyes in the back of their heads." They avoid becoming too absorbed with a few students, since this allows the rest of the class to wander. (359)
>
> This technique works, however, only if students actually believe that their teacher will know everything that goes on.

Note that the parenthetical citation comes after the period at the end of the quotation and does not have a period after it.

Though long quotations are often necessary in research projects, use them cautiously. Too many of them may make your writing seem choppy—or suggest that you have not relied enough on your own thinking.

## 3 Integrating quotations smoothly

Carefully integrate quotations into your text so that they flow smoothly and clearly into the surrounding sentences. Use a signal phrase or signal verb, such as those underlined in the following examples. (See also the accompanying box.)

> As Eudora Welty notes, "learning stamps you with its moments. Childhood's learning," she continues, "is made up of moments. It isn't steady. It's a pulse" (9).

> Some instructors claim that the new technology is a threat to the English language. "Abbreviations commonly used in online instant messages are creeping into formal essays that students write for credit, said Debbie Frost, who teaches language arts and social studies to sixth-graders." ("Young Messagers," par. 2)

Remember that the signal verb must be appropriate to the idea you are expressing. In the first example, the verb *notes* tells us that the writer probably agrees with what Welty is saying. If that were not the case, the writer might have chosen a different verb, such as *asserts* or *contends*. In the second example, from David Craig's essay, he uses the signal phrase *Some instructors claim* to introduce the remarks by Frost. The verb *claim* tells readers that Frost's opinion is open to disagreement — that other authorities might disagree with it or that David himself does. If David supported Frost's point, he might have used entirely different wording, such as *Many instructors agree*. Notice that these examples also use neutral signal verbs — *continues* and *said* — where appropriate. The signal verbs you choose allow you to characterize the author's viewpoint or perspective as well as your own, so choose them with care.

### 4 Indicating changes in quotations with square brackets and ellipses

Sometimes you may wish to alter a direct quotation in some way — to make a verb tense fit smoothly into your text, to replace a pronoun with a noun, to eliminate unnecessary detail, to change a capital letter to lowercase or vice versa. Enclose any changed or added words or letters

**Signal verbs**

| | | | |
|---|---|---|---|
| acknowledges | concludes | emphasizes | replies |
| advises | concurs | expresses | reports |
| agrees | confirms | interprets | responds |
| allows | criticizes | lists | reveals |
| answers | declares | objects | says |
| asserts | describes | observes | states |
| believes | disagrees | offers | suggests |
| charges | discusses | opposes | thinks |
| claims | disputes | remarks | writes |

in square brackets (51b), and indicate any deletions with ellipsis points (51f). Do not use ellipses at the beginning or end of a quotation unless the last sentence as you cite it is incomplete.

Here is an example including the original passage and David Craig's note recording a quotation from it. Notice how he uses ellipses to mark omitted words and brackets to show additions or other changes.

**ORIGINAL**

> Even terms that cannot be expressed verbally are making their way into papers. Melanie Weaver was stunned by some of the term papers she received from a 10th-grade class she recently taught as part of an internship. "They would be trying to make a point in a paper, they would put a smiley face in the end," said Ms. Weaver, who teaches at Alvernia College in Reading, Pa. "If they were presenting an argument and they needed to present an opposite view, they would put a frown."
>
> — JENNIFER 8. LEE, "I Think, Therefore IM"

DAVID CRAIG'S NOTE

**IM shortcuts in school assignments**

Lee, "I Think," *NY Times* (Web site)

[Speaker is Melanie Weaver, now prof. at Alvernia College, talking about her students when she taught tenth-grade English as an intern.]

"[When t]hey would be trying to make a point in a paper, they would put a smiley face in the end [☺]. . . . If they were presenting an argument and they needed to present an opposite view, they would put a frown [☹]."

(Quotation)

Here are two examples of quotations that have been altered with bracketed information or ellipsis points and then integrated smoothly into the surrounding text.

> "There is something wrong in the [Three Mile Island] area," one farmer told the Nuclear Regulatory Commission after the plant accident ("Legacy" 33).

The brackets indicate that this information was added by the writer and is not part of the original quotation.

> Economist John Kenneth Galbraith pointed out that "large corporations cannot afford to compete with one another. . . . In a truly competitive market someone loses" (qtd. in Key 17).

Whenever you change a quotation, be careful not to alter its meaning. In addition, use brackets and ellipses sparingly; too many of them make for difficult reading and might suggest that you have removed some of the context for the quotation.

### FOR MULTILINGUAL WRITERS: Identifying sources

While some language communities and cultures expect audiences to recognize the sources of important documents and texts, thereby eliminating the need to cite them directly, conventions for writing in North America call for careful attribution of any quoted, paraphrased, or summarized material. When in doubt, explicitly identify your sources.

### EXERCISE 15.1

Take a source-based piece of writing you have done recently or a research project you are working on now, and examine it to see how successfully you have integrated quotations. Have you used accurate signal verbs and introduced the sources of the quotations? Have you used square brackets and ellipses accurately to indicate changes in quotations?

## 15c Working with paraphrases

Introduce paraphrases clearly in your text, usually with a signal phrase that includes the author of the source. Here are two passages — an original excerpt from a book and a student's integrated paraphrase of it into her text.

**ORIGINAL**

Understanding genderlects makes it possible to change — to try speaking differently — when you want to. But even if no one changes, understanding genderlects improves relationships. Once people realize that their partners have different conversational styles, they are inclined to accept differences without blaming themselves, their partners, or their relationships. The biggest mistake is believing there is one right way to listen, to talk, to have a conversation — or a relationship. Nothing hurts more than being told your intentions are bad when you know they are good, or being told you are doing something wrong when you know you're just doing it your way.

— DEBORAH TANNEN, *You Just Don't Understand: Women and Men in Conversation* (298)

**PARAPHRASE INTEGRATED INTO RESEARCH PAPER**

One observer of the battle of the sexes, linguistics professor Deborah Tannen, is trying to arrange a cease-fire. Tannen illustrates how communication between women and men breaks down and then suggests that an awareness of what she calls "genderlects" can help all speakers realize that there are many ways to communicate with others and that these differing styles of communication have their own validity. Understanding this crucial point can keep speakers from accusing each other of communicating poorly when they are in fact communicating differently (298).

In the preceding passage, notice how the student writer brings authority to the point she makes in the first sentence. She introduces the author by name and title and then paraphrases her work. Note also that a page number is included in parentheses at the end of the paraphrase.

In the following paraphrase, David Craig introduces an authoritative source for his information — the College Board — and then identifies the authors of the College Board's report in parentheses:

The fact remains, however, that youth literacy seems to be declining. What, if not IMing, is the main cause of this phenomenon? According to the College Board, which collects data on several questions from its test takers, enrollment in English composition and grammar classes has decreased in the last decade by 14 percent (Carnahan and Coletti 11).

## 15d Working with summaries

Summaries, too, need to be carefully integrated into your text. Indicate the source of a summary, including the author's name and the page number, if any. Here is how David Craig might have integrated his summary of the passage from David Crystal's book *Language Play* (you can see David's summary note on p. 265 and the entire Crystal passage on p. 263):

David Crystal, an internationally recognized scholar of linguistics at the University of Wales, argues that various kinds of language play contribute to awareness of how language works and to literacy (180).

Note that in this hypothetical example David introduces his source (Crystal), establishes the source's expertise by identifying him as a recognized scholar in the field of linguistics, and uses the signal verb *argues* to characterize Crystal's passage as making a case, not simply offering information. He also includes the page number in parentheses for the passage he has summarized.

Whenever you include summaries, paraphrases, or quotations in your own writing, it is crucially important that you identify the sources of the material; even unintentional failure to cite material that you drew from other sources constitutes plagiarism. Be especially careful with paraphrases and summaries, where there are no quotation marks to remind you that the material is not your own. For more information on acknowledging sources and avoiding plagiarism, see Chapter 16.

## 15e Working with visuals

If you decide to include visuals (photographs, cartoons, paintings, drawings, charts and graphs, or other kinds of images), choose wisely, and integrate them smoothly into your text.

### 1 Choosing effective visuals

Choose visuals that will enhance your research project and pique the interest of your readers.

- *Does each visual make a strong contribution to the written message?* Tangential or decorative visuals weaken the power of your essay.
- *Is each visual appropriate and fair to your subject?* A visual with an obviously biased perspective may be seen by your audience as unfair or manipulative.
- *Is each visual appropriate for and fair to your audience?* Visuals should appeal to various members of your likely audience.

Whenever you post documents containing visuals to the Web, make sure you check for copyright information. While it is considered "fair use" to use a visual in an essay or other project for a college class, once that project is published on the Web, you might infringe copyright protections if you do not ask the copyright holder for permission to use the visual. U.S. copyright law considers the reproduction of works for purposes of teaching and scholarship to be "fair use" not bound by copyright, but the law is open to multiple intepretations. If you have questions about whether your work might infringe on copyright, ask your instructor for help.

## 2 Integrating visuals

Like quotations, paraphrases, and summaries, visuals need to be introduced and commented on in some way.

- Refer to the visual by number in the text (*As Fig. 3 demonstrates . . .*) and position the visual as close as possible after the first reference.
- Explain or comment on the relevance of the visual. This can be done after the visual.
- Label each visual clearly and consistently (*Fig. 1. Chicago skyline*).
- Check the documentation system you are using to make sure you label visuals appropriately; MLA, for instance, asks that you number and title tables and figures (*Table 1: Average Amount of Rainfall by Region*).
- If you are posting your document or essay on a Web site, make sure you have permission to use any visuals that are covered by copyright.

For more on using visuals, see Chapters 4 and 23.

David Craig integrated a chart about SAT scores into his research essay (18e). The chart, which he found in a report published by the

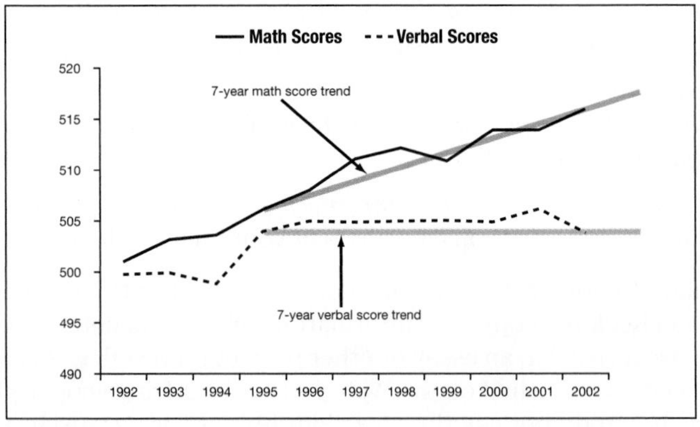


Fig. 1. Comparison of SAT math and verbal scores (1992-2002). Trend lines added. Source: Kristin Carnahan and Chiara Coletti, *Ten-Year Trend in SAT Scores Indicates Increased Emphasis on Math Is Yielding Results; Reading and Writing Are Causes for Concern;* New York: College Board, 2002; print; 9.

### TALKING THE TALK: Saying something new

"What can I say about my topic that experts haven't already said?" All writers — no matter how experienced — face this problem. As you read more about your topic, you will soon see areas of disagreement among experts, who may not be as expert as they first appear. Notice what your sources say and, especially, what they don't say. Consider how your own interests and experiences give you a unique perspective on the topic. Slowly but surely you will identify a claim that you can make about the topic, one related to what others say but taking a new angle or adding something different to the discussion.

College Board, illustrated his point that youth literacy is declining. He added his own trend lines to the chart to make the visual more effective. Following MLA style, David labeled the chart *Fig. 1* and included a descriptive title and source information. In the text of his paper, he included a reference to the chart and a detailed discussion of its data.

## 15f Checking for excessive use of source material

Your text needs to synthesize your research in support of your own argument; it should not be a patchwork of quotations, paraphrases, and summaries from other people. You need a rhetorical stance that represents you as the author. If you cite too many sources, your own voice will disappear, a problem the following passage demonstrates:

> The United States is one of the countries with the most rapid population growth. In fact, rapid population increase has been a "prominent feature of American life since the founding of the republic" (Day 31). In the past, the cause of the high rate of population growth was the combination of large-scale immigration and a high birth rate. As Day notes, "Two facts stand out in the demographic history of the United States: first, the single position as a receiver of immigrants; second, our high rate of growth from natural increase" (31).
>
> Nevertheless, American population density is not as high as in most European countries. Day points out that the Netherlands, with a density of 906 persons per square mile, is more crowded than even the most densely populated American states (33).

Most readers will think that the source, Day, is much too prominent here and that the author of the essay is only secondary. Using three different sources rather than one in this short passage would also overwhelm the writer's voice.

## THINKING CRITICALLY ABOUT YOUR INTEGRATION OF SOURCES

From a research project you have finished or are drafting now, choose three passages that cite sources. Then examine how well these sources are integrated into your text. Consider how you can make that integration smoother, and try your hand at revising one of them.

# Acknowledging Sources and Avoiding Plagiarism

# 16

In some ways, there really is nothing new under the sun, in writing and research as well as in life. Whatever writing you do has in some way been influenced by what you have already read and experienced. As a writer today, you need to understand the concept of intellectual property — those works protected by copyright or alternatives such as a Creative Commons license — and how to acknowledge such works appropriately. You should also take care to avoid plagiarism — using someone else's words and ideas without giving proper credit to the source.

## 16a Reasons to acknowledge sources

Acknowledging the sources you use offers a polite "thank you" for the work of others. In addition, the sources you acknowledge tell your reader that you have tried to gain expertise on your topic, that you are credible, and that you have been fair enough to consider several points of view. Similarly, your sources can help place your research in the context of other thinking. Most of all, you should acknowledge sources in order to help your readers follow your thoughts, understand how your ideas relate to the thoughts of others, and know where to go to find more information.

Acknowledging sources fully and generously, then, is a way to establish your trustworthiness as a researcher. Failure to credit sources can destroy both your own credibility and that of your research.

## 16b Which sources to acknowledge

As you carry out research, you should understand the distinction between materials that require acknowledgment and those that do not.

### 1 Materials that do not require acknowledgment

Information does not need to be credited to a source if it is well known or if you gathered the data yourself.

- *Common knowledge.* If most readers know a fact, you probably do not need to cite a source for it. You do not need to credit a source to say that George Bush was reelected in 2004, for example.
- *Facts available in a wide variety of sources.* If a number of encyclopedias, almanacs, reputable Web sites, or textbooks include a certain piece of information, you usually need not cite a specific source for it. For instance, you would not need to cite a source if you write that the Japanese bombed Pearl Harbor on December 7, 1941.
- *Findings from field research.* If you conduct observations or surveys, announce your findings as your own. Acknowledge people you interview as individuals rather than as part of a survey.

If you are not sure whether a fact, an observation, or a piece of information requires acknowledgment, err on the side of safety, and cite the source.

### 2 Materials that require acknowledgment

For material that does not fall under the preceding categories, credit sources as fully as possible. Follow the conventions of the citation style you are using (see Chapters 18–21), and include each source in a bibliography or list of works cited.

- *Quotations, paraphrases, and summaries.* Whenever you use another person's words, ideas, or opinions, credit the source. Even though the wording of a paraphrase or summary is your own, you should still acknowledge the source (14f and 15b–d).
- *Facts that aren't widely known or claims that are arguable.* If your readers would be unlikely to know a fact, or if an author presents as fact a claim that may or may not be true, cite the source. To claim, for instance, that Switzerland is amassing an offensive nuclear arsenal would demand the citation of a source because Switzerland has long been an officially neutral state. If you are not sure whether a fact will be familiar to your readers or whether a statement is arguable, go ahead and cite the source.
- *Images, statistics, charts, tables, graphs, and other visuals from any source.* Credit all visual and statistical material not derived from your own field research, even if you create your own graph or table from the data provided in a source.

- *Help provided by others.* If an instructor gave you a good idea or if friends responded to your draft or helped you conduct surveys, give credit — usually in a footnote that says something like "Thanks to Kiah Williams, who first suggested this connection."

Here is a quick-reference chart to guide you in deciding whether or not you need to acknowledge a source:

| NEED TO ACKNOWLEDGE | DON'T NEED TO ACKNOWLEDGE |
|---|---|
| quotations | your own words, observations, surveys, and so on |
| paraphrases or summaries of a source | common knowledge |
| ideas you glean from a source | facts available in many sources |
| facts that aren't widely known | drawings or other visuals you create on your own |
| graphs, tables, and other statistical information from a source | |
| photographs, visuals, video, or sound taken from sources | |
| experiments conducted by others | |
| interviews that are not part of a survey | |
| organization or structure taken from a source | |
| help or advice from an instructor or another student | |

**bedfordstmartins.com/smhandbook** For practice identifying when to acknowledge sources, click on **Exercises for Working with Sources**.

## 16c Academic integrity and plagiarism

The principle of academic integrity in intellectual work allows you to trust the sources you use and to demonstrate that your own work is equally trustworthy. While there are many ways to damage academic integrity, two that are especially important are inaccurate or incomplete citation of sources — also called unintentional plagiarism — and plagiarism that is deliberately intended to pass off one writer's work as another's.

Whether intentional or not, plagiarism can bring serious consequences. At some colleges, students who plagiarize fail the course automatically; at others, they are expelled. Academics who plagiarize, even inadvertently, have had their degrees revoked and their books withdrawn from publication. And outside academic life, eminent political, business, and scientific leaders have been stripped of candidacies, positions, and awards because of plagiarism.

### FOR MULTILINGUAL WRITERS: Plagiarism as a cultural concept

Many cultures do not recognize Western notions of plagiarism, which rest on a belief that language and ideas can be owned by writers. Indeed, in many countries outside the United States, and even within some communities in the United States, using the words and ideas of others without attribution is considered a sign of deep respect as well as an indication of knowledge. In academic writing in the United States, however, you should credit all materials except those that are common knowledge, that are available in a wide variety of sources, or that are your own creations (photographs, drawings, and so on) or your own findings from field research.

### 1 Inaccurate or incomplete citation of sources

If your paraphrase is too close to the original wording or sentence structure of the source (even if you identify the source); if you do not identify the source of a quotation (even if you include the quotation marks); or if you fail to indicate clearly the source of an idea that you obviously did not come up with on your own, you may be accused of plagiarism even if your intent was not to plagiarize. Inaccurate or incomplete acknowledgment of sources often results either from carelessness or from not learning how to borrow material properly in the first place. Still, because the costs of even unintentional plagiarism can be severe, it's important to understand how it can happen and how you can guard against it.

In a January 2002 article published in *Time* magazine, historian Doris Kearns Goodwin explains how she made acknowledgment errors in one of her books. The book in question, nine hundred pages long and with thirty-five hundred footnotes, took Goodwin ten years to write. During this time, she says, she took most of her notes by hand, organized them, and later checked her sources to make sure all the material she was using was correctly cited. "Somehow in this process," Goodwin goes on to say, "a few books were not fully rechecked," and thus she omitted some acknowledgments and some quotation marks by mistake. Discovering such carelessness in her own work was very troubling to Goodwin since, as she puts it, "the writing of history is a rich process of building on the work of the past. . . . Through footnotes [and citations] you point the way to future historians."

As a writer of academic integrity, you — like Goodwin — will want to take responsibility for your research and for acknowledging all sources accurately. One easy way to keep track is to keep photocopies or printouts as you do your research; then you can identify needed quotations right on each copy.

### 2 Deliberate plagiarism

Deliberate plagiarism — handing in an essay written by a friend or purchased (or simply downloaded) from an essay-writing company; cutting and pasting passages directly from source materials without marking them with quotation marks and acknowledging your sources; failing to credit the source of an idea or concept in your text — is what most people think of when they hear the word *plagiarism.* This form of plagiarism is particularly troubling because it represents dishonesty and deception: those who intentionally plagiarize present the hard thinking and hard work of someone else as their own, and they deceive readers by claiming knowledge they don't really have.

Deliberate plagiarism is also fairly simple to spot: your instructor will be well acquainted with your writing and likely to notice any sudden shifts in the style or quality of your work. In addition, by typing a few words from an essay into a search engine, your instructor can identify "matches" very easily.

### EXERCISE 16.1

Read the brief original passage that follows, and then look closely at the five attempts to quote or paraphrase it. Decide which attempts are acceptable and which plagiarize, prepare notes on what supports your decision in each case, and bring your notes to class for discussion.

> The strange thing about plagiarism is that it's almost always pointless. The writers who stand accused, from Laurence Sterne to Samuel Taylor Coleridge to Susan Sontag, tend to be more talented than the writers they lift from.
>
> — MALCOLM JONES, "Have You Read This Story Somewhere?"

1. According to Malcolm Jones, writers accused of plagiarism are always better writers than those they are supposed to have plagiarized.
2. According to Malcolm Jones, writers accused of plagiarism "tend to be more talented than the writers they lift from."
3. Plagiarism is usually pointless, says writer Malcolm Jones.
4. Those who stand accused of plagiarism, such as Senator Joseph Biden, tend to be better writers than those whose work they use.
5. According to Malcolm Jones, "plagiarism is . . . almost always pointless."

## 16d Your intellectual property

Although you may not have thought much about it, all of your work in college — including all the research and writing you do, online and off — represents a growing bank of intellectual property. In fact, such original work is automatically copyrighted, even if it lacks the © sym-

### Avoiding plagiarism

- Maintain an accurate and thorough working bibliography. (14b)
- Establish a consistent note-taking system, listing sources and page numbers and clearly identifying all quotations, paraphrases, summaries, statistics, and visuals. (14f)
- Identify all quotations with quotation marks — both in your notes and in your essay. (15b)
- Be sure your summaries and paraphrases use your own words and sentence structures. (15c and d)
- Give a citation or note for each quotation, paraphrase, summary, arguable assertion or opinion, statistic, and visual from a source, including an online source. (For material that needs citation, see 16b; for in-text documentation, see 18b, 19b, 20b, and 21b.)
- Prepare an accurate and complete list of sources cited according to the required documentation style. (See 18d, 19d, 20c, and 21c.)
- Plan ahead on writing assignments so that you can avoid the temptation to take shortcuts.

bol. Here are some tips for making sure that others respect your intellectual property just as you respect theirs:

- Realize that the email messages you send and your posts to discussion groups are public. If you don't want your thoughts and ideas repeated or forwarded, keep them offline. In addition, you may want to let your friends know specifically that you do not want your email passed on to any third parties. In turn, remember that you should not use material from email, discussion groups, or other online forums without asking for permission to do so.
- Be careful with your passwords and with discs or CDs that contain your work. Use a secure storage method so that only you can give someone access to that work.
- Save all your drafts and notes so that you can show where your work has come from should anyone ask you.

## 16e Collaboration

With so much focus on plagiarism and with the advent of online paper mills, you may feel reluctant to share or discuss your work with anyone else. That would be a very unfortunate result, however, since much of our knowledge comes from talking with and learning from others. Indeed, many college projects now require some form of collaboration or teamwork, whether it involves commenting on someone else's draft or preparing a group presentation of research findings.

Collaborative writing projects call for the same kind of acknowledgments you use in a paper or other project you prepare by yourself. In general, cite all sources used by the group, and acknowledge all assistance provided by others. In some cases, you may decide to do this in an endnote rather than in your bibliography or list of works cited.

### THINKING CRITICALLY ABOUT YOUR OWN ACKNOWLEDGMENT OF SOURCES

Look at a recent piece of your writing that incorporates material from sources, and try to determine how completely and accurately you acknowledged them. Did you properly cite every quotation, paraphrase, and summary? every opinion or other idea from a source? every source you used to create visuals? Did you unintentionally plagiarize someone else's words or ideas? Make notes, and bring them to class for discussion.

# 17 Writing a Research Project

Everyday decisions often call for research and writing. In trying to choose between two jobs in different towns, for example, one recent college graduate made a long list of questions to answer: Which company offered the best benefits? Which job location had the lower cost of living? How did the two locations compare in terms of schools, cultural opportunities, major league sports, and so on? After conducting careful research, he was able to send a letter of acceptance to one company and a letter of regret to the other.

In much the same way, when you are working on an academic project, there comes a time to draw the strands of research together and articulate your conclusions in writing.

## 17a Refining your plans

You should by now have notes containing facts, opinions, paraphrases, summaries, quotations, and other material; you probably have some visuals as well. You may also have ideas about how to synthesize these many pieces of information. And you should have some sense of whether your hypothesis has sufficient support. Now is the time to reconsider your purpose, audience, stance, and working thesis.

- What is your central purpose? What other purposes, if any, do you have?
- What is your stance toward your topic (3g)? Are you an advocate, a critic, a reporter, an observer (12b2)?
- What audience(s) are you addressing (3h and 12b2)?
- How much background information or context does your audience need?
- What supporting information will your readers find convincing — examples? quotations from authorities? statistics? graphs, charts, or other visuals? data from your field research?
- Should your tone be that of a colleague, an expert, a student?
- How can you establish common ground with your readers and show them that you have considered points of view other than your own? (See 11e and Chapter 27.)

- What is your working thesis trying to establish? Will your audience accept it?

### 1 Developing an explicit thesis statement

Writing out an explicit thesis statement allows you to articulate your major points and to see how well they carry out your purpose and appeal to your audience. Before you begin a full draft, then, try to develop your working thesis into an explicit statement, which might take the following form:

> **In this research project, I plan to (explain/argue/demonstrate/analyze, and so on) for an audience of ____________________**
> **that ____________________**
> **because/if ____________________.**

David Craig, the student whose research we've been following throughout Part 3, developed the following explicit thesis statement (see Chapter 18):

> In this research project, I plan to demonstrate for an audience of classmates in my first-year writing class that instant messaging seems to be a positive force in the development of youth literacy because it promotes regular contact with words, the use of a written medium for communication, and the development of an alternative form of literacy.

#### FOR MULTILINGUAL WRITERS: Asking an experienced writer to review your thesis

You might find it helpful to ask one or two classmates who have more experience with the particular type of academic writing to look at your explicit thesis. Ask if the thesis is as direct and clear as it can be, and revise accordingly.

### 2 Testing the thesis

Although writing out an explicit thesis will often confirm your research, you may find that your hypothesis is invalid, inadequately supported, or insufficiently focused. In such cases, you need to rethink your original research question and perhaps do further research. To test your thesis, consider the following questions:

- How can you state your thesis more precisely or more clearly (5c)? Should the wording be more specific? Could you use more specific, concrete nouns (29c) or stronger verbs (45a)? Should you add qualifying adjectives or adverbs (Chapter 35)?
- In what ways will your thesis interest your audience? What can you do to increase that interest (3h)?
- Will your thesis be manageable, given your limits of time and knowledge? If not, what can you do to make it more manageable?
- What evidence from your research supports each aspect of your thesis? What additional evidence do you need?

### EXERCISE 17.1

Take the thesis from your current research project, and test it against the questions provided in 17a2. Make revisions if your analysis reveals weaknesses in your thesis.

### 3 Planning design

As you move toward producing a draft, take some time to think about how you want your research essay or project to look. What font size will you use? Should you use color? Do you plan to insert text boxes and visuals? Will you need headings and subheadings? (For more on document design, see Chapter 23.)

## 17b Organizing information

Experienced writers differ considerably in the ways they go about organizing ideas and information, and you will want to experiment until you find a method that works well for you. (For more on organizational strategies, see 5e.) This section will discuss two organizing strategies — grouping material by subject and outlining.

### 1 Grouping notes by subject

Begin by grouping your notes and visuals into subject categories. For example, you can arrange note cards in groups by subject headings, putting the ones with your main topics in the center and any related cards around them. If you have been using a notebook, you can cut the pages apart and group the slips of paper in a similar manner. If your notes are in a computer file, you can sort them by subject headings or cut and paste them into new documents according to category. And if you have access to a software program that allows you to group or map your notes, take advantage of it.

Grouping your notes in this way will help you see how well you can support your thesis and help you see if you have missed any essential points. Do you need to omit any ideas or sources? Do you need to find additional evidence for a main or supporting point? Once you have gathered everything together and organized your materials, you can see how the many small pieces of your research fit together. Make sure that your evidence supports your explicit thesis; if not, you may need to revise it or do additional research — or both.

Once you have established initial groups, skim through the notes and look for ways to organize your draft. Figure out what background your audience needs, what points you need to make first, how much detail and support to offer for each point, and so on.

## 2 Outlining

You can use outlines in various ways and at various stages. Some writers group their notes, write a draft, and then outline the draft to study its tentative structure. Others develop an informal working outline from their notes and revise it as they go along. Still other writers prefer to plot out their organization early on in a formal outline. (For more on outlines, see 5f.)

David Craig drew up a working outline of his ideas while he was still doing research on his topic, thinking that this simple structure would help him focus on the information he still needed to find. Here is his informal outline:

```
Decline of youth literacy
   Lower test scores, other proof (statistics)
   How instant messaging fits in, examples from critics
My research
   Can I show that IM is a language?
   How widespread is it?
Comments from linguists--tie-in to IM language
What is the real cause of declining youth literacy?
```

Because he knew he was required to submit a formal outline with his essay, David Craig kept revising this informal outline as his research and writing progressed. He did not complete his formal outline until after his essay was drafted (see pp. 295–96). At that point, the formal outline helped him analyze and revise the draft.

## 17c Drafting

For most college research projects, drafting should begin *at least* two weeks before the instructor's deadline in case you need to gather more information or do more drafting. Set a deadline for having a complete draft, and structure your work with that date in mind. Gather your notes, outline, and sources, and read through them, getting involved in your topic. Most writers find that some sustained work (two or three hours at a time) pays off at this point. Begin drafting a section that you feel confident about. For example, if you are not sure how you want to introduce the draft but do know how you want to approach a particular point, begin with that, and return to the introduction later. The most important thing is to get started.

The drafting process varies considerably among researchers, and no one else can determine what will work best for you. The tips offered in 5g, however, can help. No matter what approach you take, remember to include sources (for quotations, paraphrases, summaries, and visuals) as you draft; doing so will save time later and help you produce your list of works cited.

Since you probably will be doing most of your drafting with a word-processing program, be sure to take advantage of its outlining and formatting capabilities as well as its numerous other tools (22a).

### 1 Working title and introduction

The title and introduction (6f) play special roles, for they set the context for what is to come. Ideally, the title announces your subject in an intriguing or memorable way. To accomplish these goals, Emily Lesk (the student writer whose work we followed in Part 1) revised the title of her essay from "All-Powerful Coke" (p. 75) to "Red, White, and Everywhere" (6j). David Craig began with the title "Instant Messaging," but he later added the more specific and intriguing subtitle "The Language of Youth Literacy."

The introduction should draw readers in and provide any background they will need to understand the discussion. Here are some tips for drafting an introduction to a research project:

- You may want to *open with a question*, especially your research question, or *with a strong or arresting statement* of some kind. Next, you might explain what you will do to answer the question or to elaborate on the statement. Then *end with your explicit thesis statement* — in essence, the answer to the question or the response to the strong statement.
- Help readers get their bearings by *forecasting your main points.*
- *Establish your own credibility* by revealing how you have become knowledgeable about your topic.
- A *quotation* can be a good attention-getter, but you may not want to open with a quotation from one source if doing so will give that source too much emphasis.

David Craig begins his essay with a strong statement (*The English language is under attack*) that immediately gets readers' attention. He then presents a brief overview of what the critics are saying about youth literacy and brings up instant messaging (IMing) — the general subject of his essay. In his second and third paragraphs, David helps establish his own credibility by including testimony from an educator, a definition of IMing, and an example from his own research. He then summarizes the criticism of IMing, which leads naturally to his explicit thesis statement. Because David had to set the scene and provide necessary background information, he decided to use four paragraphs for his introduction (see pp. 337–38).

## 2 Conclusion

A good conclusion helps readers know what they have learned (6f3 and 7f2). Its job is not to persuade (the body of the essay or project should already have done that) but to contribute to the overall effectiveness of your writing. The following strategies may be helpful:

- Refer to your thesis, and then expand to a more general conclusion that reminds readers of the significance of your discussion.
- If you have covered several main points, you may want to remind readers of them. Be careful, however, to provide more than a mere summary.

- Try to end with something that will have an impact — a provocative quotation or question, a vivid image, a call for action, or a warning. But guard against sounding preachy.

In his conclusion, David Craig briefly recaps his thesis and then summarizes the main point of his argument (p. 346). He ends with a strong assertion: *Although IMing may expose literacy problems, it does not create them.*

## 17d Incorporating source materials

When you reach the point of drafting your research project, a new task awaits: weaving your source materials into your writing. The challenge is to use your sources yet remain the author — to quote, paraphrase, and summarize other voices while remaining the major voice in your work.

Because learning how to effectively integrate source material is so important, Chapter 15 is devoted entirely to this process. Consult that chapter often as you draft.

## 17e Reviewing and getting responses to your draft

Because a research project involves a complex mix of your thoughts and materials from outside sources, it calls for an especially careful review. You should examine the draft yourself as well as seek the comments of other readers. Ask friends and classmates to read and respond to your draft, and get a response from your instructor if possible.

### 1 Reviewing your own draft

As with most kinds of writing, taking a break after drafting is important so that when you reread the draft, you can bring a fresh eye to the task.

#### *Questions for review*

When you do return to the draft, read it straight through without stopping. Then read the draft again slowly, reconsidering your purpose, audience, stance, thesis, and support.

- From your reading of the draft, what do you now see as its *purpose*? How does this compare with your original purpose? Does the draft do what your assignment requires?
- What *audience* does your essay address?
- What is your *stance* toward the topic?
- What is your *thesis*? Is it clearly stated?
- What *evidence* supports your thesis? Is the evidence sufficient?

Answer these questions as best you can, since they are the starting point for revision. If you notice a problem but are unsure how to solve it, write down your concerns so that you can ask readers if they notice the same problem and have ideas about solving it.

### Outline

You might find that outlining your draft (5f and 17b2) helps you analyze it at this point: an outline will reveal the bare bones of your argument and help you see what may be missing or out of place. Here is the formal outline that David Craig prepared after drafting his research paper on instant messaging. (His final essay appears in 18e.)

**Thesis statement:** Instant messaging seems to be a beneficial force in the development of youth literacy because it promotes regular contact with words, the use of a written medium for communication, and the development of an alternative form of literacy.

I. Decline of youth literacy--overview
    A. What many parents, librarians, educators believe
    B. Instant messaging (IMing) as possible cause
        1. Definition of IMing
        2. Example of IM conversation
        3. IMing as beneficial to youth literacy
II. Two background issues
    A. Current state of literacy
        1. Decline in SAT test scores
        2. Decline in writing ability
    B. Prevalence of IMing
        1. Statistics indicating widespread usage
        2. Instant messagers using new vocabulary

III. My field research to verify existence of IM language
    A. Explanation of how research was done
    B. Results of research
        1. Four types of IM language: phonetic replacements, acronyms, abbreviations, inanities
        2. Frequency of IM language use in IM writing
        3. Conclusions about vocabulary
IV. What critics of IMing say
    A. Many problems with student writing, such as incomplete sentences, grammar, and spelling
    B. Students using online abbreviations (smileys) in formal papers
V. What linguists and other supporters of IMing say
    A. Traditional literacy not harmed by IMing
    B. IM use indicative of advanced literacy
        1. Crystal's explanation of metalinguistics and wordplay
        2. Human ability to write in many styles, IM style being only one alternative
        3. IMing helping students shift from language to language
VI. Other possible causes of decline in youth literacy
    A. Lower enrollment in English composition and grammar classes
    B. IMing exposing literacy problems but not causing them

### 2 Getting peer responses

You should seek responses from friends and classmates as your draft evolves. Your reviewers will be best prepared to give you helpful advice and to ask questions specific to your project if they have background information about your writing task.

Tell your reviewers the purpose of your draft, the assignment's criteria, and your target audience. Ask them to explain their understanding of your stance on the topic. Also ask for feedback on your thesis and its support. If you are unsure about whether to include a particular point, how to use a certain quotation, or where to add more examples, ask your reviewers specifically what they think you should do. You should also ask them to identify any parts of your draft that confuse them. Even if you are writing to a target audience with more expertise in the topic than your peer reviewers, you should carefully consider revising the parts they identify as confusing: you may be making too many assumptions about what concepts need to be explained. (For more on peer review, see 6b.)

### 3 Reviewing others' research writing

When you are asked to respond to others' research writing, you may encounter arguments and ideas that are unfamiliar to you. It's tempting to assume that the writer has done a good job and that you are not the right person to give advice. Remember that your job as a peer reviewer is to note whether the writer's thesis, evidence, use of visual and verbal sources, and language are clear and effective.

The writer may direct your attention to specific parts of the draft; be sure to respond to these requests. If the writer does not have specific questions, try to restate the writer's stance, thesis, and key pieces of evidence in your own words. Seeing how someone else summarizes the draft will help the writer assess the effectiveness of the argument (6b). Next, report on what makes sense to you in the draft — and what does not. Pay special attention to these four aspects of the writing:

- *Thesis statement, topic sentences, and transitions.* Were you prepared for the main ideas of the paper and of each paragraph?
- *Organization.* Could you follow the writer's logic? Were the ideas ordered for maximum effect?
- *Amount and quality of evidence, including both visual and verbal sources.* Was there enough credible evidence from reputable sources to be convincing?
- *Sentences.* Could you easily read each sentence and understand its meaning?

The most important part of responding to research writing is deciding that you have something useful to say. Focus on how the text affects you. Even if the ideas are unfamiliar to you, you are not new to learning. If the draft is not helping you think carefully about the topic, identifying the sources of your confusion and doubt will help the writer revise. Many students report that thinking of this response as a letter written directly to the student writer (beginning the response with "Dear X" and concluding with something like "Good luck!") helps them focus on giving concrete criticism and helpful advice (6b3).

## 17f Revising and editing

When you have considered your reviewers' responses and your own analysis, you can turn to revising and editing.

## Guidelines for revising a research project

- *Take responses into account.* Look at specific problems that reviewers think you need to solve or strengths you might capitalize on. For example, if they showed great interest in one point but no interest in another, consider expanding the first and deleting the second.
- *Reconsider your original purpose, audience, and stance.* Have you achieved your purpose? If not, consider how you can. How well have you appealed to your readers? Make sure you satisfy any special concerns of your reviewers. If your rhetorical stance toward your topic has changed, does your draft need to change, too?
- *Assess your research.* Think about whether you have investigated the topic thoroughly and consulted materials with more than one point of view. Have you left out any important sources? Are the sources you use reliable and appropriate for your topic? Have you synthesized your research findings and drawn warranted conclusions?
- *Assess your use of visuals,* making sure that each one supports your argument, is clearly labeled, and is entered on your works-cited list.
- *Gather additional material.* If you need to strengthen any points, first check your notes to see whether you already have the necessary information. In some instances, you may need to do more research.
- *Decide what changes you need to make.* List everything you must do to perfect your draft. With your deadline in mind, plan your revision.
- *Rewrite your draft.* Many writers prefer to revise first on paper rather than on a computer. However you revise, be sure to save copies of each draft. Begin with the major changes, such as adding content or reorganizing. Then turn to sentence-level problems and word choice. Can you sharpen the work's dominant impression?
- *Reevaluate the title, introduction, and conclusion.* Is your title specific and engaging? Does the introduction capture readers' attention and indicate what the work discusses? Does your conclusion help readers see the significance of your argument?
- *Check your documentation.* Make sure you've included a citation in your text for every quotation, paraphrase, and summary you incorporated, following your documentation style consistently. Do the same for all visuals taken from or based on your sources.
- *Edit your draft.* Check grammar, usage, spelling, punctuation, and mechanics. Consider the advice of computer spell checkers (30e1) and grammar checkers (22a) carefully before accepting it.

## 17g Preparing a list of sources

Once your final draft and source materials are in place, you are ready to prepare a list of sources. Follow the guidelines for your documentation style carefully (see Chapters 18–21), creating an entry for each source used. Double-check your work to make sure that you have listed every source mentioned in your draft and (unless you are listing all the sources you consulted) that you have not listed any sources not cited. Most word-processing programs can help you alphabetize and format lists of sources as well as prepare endnotes and footnotes.

## 17h Proofreading your final copy

Your final rough draft may look very rough indeed, so your next step is to create a final, perfectly clean copy. You will submit this version, which represents all your work and effort, to your instructor. At this point, run the spell checker but do not stop there. To make sure that this final version puts your best foot forward, proofread extremely carefully. It's best to work with a hard copy, since reading onscreen often leads to missed typos. Read the copy aloud for content and for the flow of the argument, making sure you haven't mistakenly deleted words, lines, or whole sections. Then read the copy backward from the last sentence to the first, looking for small mistakes such as punctuation problems or missing words. If you are keeping an editing inventory (6i), look for the types of editing problems you have had in the past.

Once you are sure your draft is free of errors, check the design one last time to be sure you are using effective margins, type size, color, boldface and italics, headings, and so on. You want your final copy to be as attractive and readable as possible (see Chapter 23).

After your manuscript preparation and proofreading are complete, celebrate your achievement: your research and hard work have produced a project that you can, and should, take pride in. (To read David Craig's completed research project, see 18e.)

### THINKING CRITICALLY ABOUT RESEARCH PROJECTS

Reflect on the research project you have completed. How did you go about organizing your information? What would you do to improve this process? What problems did you encounter in drafting? How did you solve these problems? How many quotations did you use, and how did you integrate them into your text? When and why did you use summaries and paraphrases? If you used any visuals, how effective were they in supporting your points? What did you learn from revising?

# 18 MLA Style

*Adam was the only man who, when he said a good thing, knew that nobody had said it before him.*

— MARK TWAIN

Since Adam, writers haven't been able to count on being absolutely original and thus have had to understand how to cite sources. In your writing, accurate documentation is essential because it gives credit to those who have influenced your own ideas. The Modern Language Association (MLA) style of formatting manuscripts and documenting sources is widely used in literature, languages, and other fields in the humanities.

For more information on the Modern Language Association style, consult the *MLA Handbook for Writers of Research Papers*, Seventh Edition (2009).

## 18a MLA manuscript format

The MLA recommends the following format for the manuscript of a research-based essay or project. It's always a good idea, however, to check with your instructor about formatting issues before preparing your final draft.

For detailed guidelines on formatting a list of works cited, see 18d. For a sample student essay in MLA style, see 18e.

- *First page and title page.* The MLA does not require a title page. Type each of the following items on a separate line on the first page, beginning one inch from the top and flush with the left margin: your name, the instructor's name, the course name and number, and the date. Double-space between each item; then double-space again and center the title. Double-space between the title and the beginning of the text.
- *Margins and spacing.* Leave one-inch margins at the top and bottom and on both sides of each page. Double-space the entire text, including set-off quotations, notes, and the list of works cited. Indent the first line of a paragraph one-half inch.
- *Page numbers.* Include your last name and the page number on each page, one-half inch below the top and flush with the right margin.
- *Long quotations.* Set off a long quotation (more than four typed lines) in block format by starting

it on a new line and indenting each line one inch from the left margin. Do not enclose the passage in quotation marks (50a1).

- *Headings.* MLA style allows, but does not require, headings. Many students and instructors find them helpful. (See 23c for guidelines on using headings and subheadings.)
- *Visuals.* Place tables, photographs, drawings, charts, graphs, and other figures as near as possible to the relevant text. (See 15e2 and 23d for guidelines on incorporating visuals into your text.) Tables should have a label and number (*Table 1*) and a clear caption. The label and caption should be aligned on the left, on separate lines. Give the source information below the table. All other visuals should be labeled *Figure* (abbreviated *Fig.*), numbered, and captioned. The label and caption should appear on the same line, followed by the source information (see 18d). Remember to refer to each visual in your text, indicating how it contributes to the point(s) you are making.

## 18b In-text citations

MLA style requires documentation in the text of an essay for every quotation, paraphrase, summary, or other material that must be cited (16b). As discussed in Chapter 15, in-text citations document material from other sources with both signal phrases and parenthetical references. Signal phrases introduce the material, often including the author's name. Parenthetical references direct you to full bibliographic entries in a list of works cited at the end of the text.

Keep your parenthetical references short, but include enough information in the parentheses to allow readers to locate the full citation in the works-cited list. Place a parenthetical reference as near the relevant material as possible without disrupting the flow of the sentence. Note in the following examples *where* punctuation is placed in relation to the parentheses. Except for block quotations, place any punctuation mark *after* the closing parenthesis. If you are referring to a quotation, place the parenthetical reference *after* the closing quotation mark but *before* any other punctuation mark. For block quotations, place the reference one space after the final punctuation mark.

## Directory to MLA style for in-text citations



1. AUTHOR NAMED IN A SIGNAL PHRASE Ordinarily, you can use the author's name in a signal phrase that introduces the material and cite the page number(s) in parentheses. You may want to use the full name the first time you cite a source, but use just the last name for later references.

> Herrera indicates that Kahlo believed in a "vitalistic form of pantheism" (328).

2. AUTHOR NAMED IN A PARENTHETICAL REFERENCE When you do not mention the author in a signal phrase, include the author's last name before the page number(s) in the parentheses. Use no punctuation between the author's name and the page number(s).

> In places, Beauvoir "sees Marxists as believing in subjectivity" (Whitmarsh 63).

3. TWO OR THREE AUTHORS Use all the authors' last names in a signal phrase or parenthetical reference.

> Gortner, Hebrun, and Nicolson maintain that "opinion leaders" influence other people in an organization because they are respected, not because they hold high positions (175).

4. FOUR OR MORE AUTHORS Use the names of all authors or the first author's name and *et al.* ("and others") in a signal phrase or parenthetical reference.

As Belenky, Clinchy, Goldberger, and Tarule assert, examining the lives of women expands our understanding of human development (7).

5. ORGANIZATION AS AUTHOR Give the organization's full name or a shortened form of it in a signal phrase or parenthetical reference.

Any study of social welfare involves a close analysis of "the impacts, the benefits, and the costs" of its policies (Social Research Corporation iii).

6. UNKNOWN AUTHOR Use the full title of the work or a shortened version in a signal phrase or parenthetical reference.

"Hype," by one analysis, is "an artificially engendered atmosphere of hysteria" ("Today's Marketplace" 51).

7. AUTHOR OF TWO OR MORE WORKS CITED IN THE SAME PROJECT If your list of works cited has more than one work by the same author, give the title of the work you are citing or a shortened version in a signal phrase or parenthetical reference.

Gardner shows readers their own silliness in his description of a "pointless, ridiculous monster, crouched in the shadows, stinking of dead men, murdered children, and martyred cows" (*Grendel* 2).

8. TWO OR MORE AUTHORS WITH THE SAME LAST NAME Include the author's first *and* last names in a signal phrase or first initial and last name in a parenthetical reference.

Children will learn to write if they are allowed to choose their own subjects, James Britton asserts, citing the Schools Council study of the 1960s (37-42).

9. MULTIVOLUME WORK In a parenthetical reference, note the volume number first and then the page number(s), with a colon and one space between them.

Modernist writers prized experimentation and gradually even sought to blur the line between poetry and prose, according to Forster (3: 150).

If you name only one volume of the work in your list of works cited, include only the page number in the parentheses.

10. LITERARY WORK Literary works are often available in many different editions. For a prose work, cite the page number(s) from the

edition you used followed by a semicolon, and then give other identifying information that will lead readers to the passage in any edition. Indicate the act and/or scene in a play (*37; sc. 1*). For a novel, indicate the part or chapter (*175; ch. 4*).

> Dostoyevsky's character Mitya wonders aloud about the "terrible tragedies realism inflicts on people" (376; bk. 8, ch. 2).

For a poem, instead of page numbers cite the part (if there is one) and line(s), separated by a period. If you are citing only line numbers, use the word *line(s)* in the first reference (*lines 33–34*).

> Whitman speculates, "All goes onward and outward, nothing collapses, / And to die is different from what any one supposed, and luckier" (6.129-30).

For a verse play, give only the act, scene, and line numbers, separated by periods.

> As *Macbeth* begins, the witches greet Banquo as "Lesser than Macbeth, and greater" (1.3.65).

11. WORK IN AN ANTHOLOGY For an essay, short story, or other piece of prose reprinted in an anthology, use the name of the author of the work, not the editor of the anthology, but use the page number(s) from the anthology.

> Narratives of captivity play a major role in early writing by women in the United States, as Silko demonstrates (219).

12. SACRED TEXT To cite a sacred text such as the Qur'an or the Bible, give the title of the edition you used, followed by location information, such as the book, chapter, and verse, separated by a period. In your text, spell out the names of books. In parenthetical references, use abbreviations for books with names of five or more letters (*Gen.* for *Genesis*).

> He ignored the admonition "Pride goes before destruction, and a haughty spirit before a fall" (*New Oxford Annotated Bible*, Prov. 16.18).

13. INDIRECT SOURCE Use the abbreviation *qtd. in* to indicate that you are quoting from someone else's report of a conversation, interview, letter, or the like.

Arthur Miller says, "When somebody is destroyed everybody finally contributes to it, but in Willy's case, the end product would be virtually the same" (qtd. in Martin and Meyer 375).

14. TWO OR MORE SOURCES IN ONE CITATION Separate the information with semicolons.

Some economists recommend that *employment* be redefined to include unpaid domestic labor (Clark 148; Nevins 39).

15. ENTIRE WORK OR ONE-PAGE ARTICLE Include the reference in the text without any page numbers or parentheses.

Michael Ondaatje's poetic sensibility transfers beautifully to prose in *The English Patient*.

16. WORK WITHOUT PAGE NUMBERS If a work has no page numbers or is only one page long, you may omit the page number. If a work uses paragraph numbers instead, use the abbreviation *par.* (or *pars.*). If a parenthetical reference to a work with paragraph numbers includes the author's name, use a comma after the name.

Whitman considered their speech "a source of a native grand opera" (Ellison, par. 13).

17. ELECTRONIC OR NONPRINT SOURCE Give enough information in a signal phrase or parenthetical reference for readers to locate the source in the list of works cited. Usually use the author or title under which you list the source. Specify a source's page, section, paragraph, or screen numbers, if numbered, in parentheses.

Kilgore, the bloodthirsty lieutenant colonel played by Robert Duvall, declares, "I love the smell of napalm in the morning" (*Apocalypse Now*).

As a *Slate* analysis has noted, "Prominent sports psychologists get praised for their successes and don't get grief for their failures" (Engber).

**bedfordstmartins.com/smhandbook** For exercises on working with sources using MLA style, click on **Exercises for Working with Sources**.

## 18c Explanatory and bibliographic notes

MLA style recommends explanatory notes for information or commentary that would not readily fit into your text but is needed for clarification or further explanation. In addition, MLA style permits bibliographic notes for citing several sources for one point and for offering thanks to, information about, or evaluation of a source. Use superscript numbers in the text to refer readers to the notes, which may appear as endnotes (typed under the heading *Notes* on a separate page after the text but before the list of works cited) or as footnotes at the bottom of the page (typed four lines below the last text line).

SUPERSCRIPT NUMBER IN TEXT

Stewart emphasizes the existence of social contacts in Hawthorne's life so that the audience will accept a different Hawthorne, one more attuned to modern times than the figure in Woodberry.[3]

NOTE

[3] Woodberry does, however, show that Hawthorne *was* often an unsociable individual. He emphasizes the seclusion of Hawthorne's mother, who separated herself from her family after the death of her husband, often even taking meals alone (28). Woodberry seems to imply that Mrs. Hawthorne's isolation rubbed off onto her son.

## 18d List of works cited

A list of works cited is an alphabetical list of the sources you have referred to in your essay. (If your instructor asks you to list everything you have read as background, call the list *Works Consulted.*) Here are some guidelines for preparing such a list:

- Start your list on a separate page after the text of your essay and any notes.
- Continue the consecutive numbering of pages.
- Center the heading *Works Cited* an inch from the top of the page; do not underline or italicize it or enclose it in quotation marks. Double-space between the heading and the first entry, and double-space the entire list.

## Directory to MLA style for works-cited entries

### Books



### Periodicals



### Electronic Sources

### Other Sources (Including Online Versions)



- Start each entry flush with the left margin, and indent subsequent lines one-half inch.
- List your sources alphabetically by author's (or editor's) last name. If the author is unknown, alphabetize the source by the first word of the title, disregarding *A*, *An*, or *The*.

## 1 Books

The basic format for a works-cited entry for a book is outlined on pp. 310–11. For an online book, see p. 324.

#### 1. ONE AUTHOR

Winchester, Simon. *The Meaning of Everything: The Story of the Oxford English Dictionary*. New York: Oxford UP, 2003. Print.

2. TWO OR THREE AUTHORS Give the first author listed on the title page, last name first; then list the name(s) of the other author(s) in regular order, with a comma between authors and the word *and* before the last one.

Martineau, Jane, Desmond Shawe-Taylor, and Jonathon Bate. *Shakespeare in Art*. London: Merrill, 2003. Print.

3. FOUR OR MORE AUTHORS Give the first author listed on the title page, followed by a comma and *et al.* ("and others"), or list all the names, since the use of *et al.* diminishes the importance of the other contributors.

Lupton, Ellen, Jennifer Tobias, Alicia Imperiale, Grace Jeffers, and Randi Mates. *Skin: Surface, Substance, and Design*. New York: Princeton Architectural, 2002. Print.

4. ORGANIZATION AS AUTHOR Give the name of the group listed on the title page as the author, even if the same group published the book.

Getty Trust Publications. *Seeing the Getty Center/Seeing the Getty Gardens*. Los Angeles: Getty Trust Publications, 2000. Print.

5. UNKNOWN AUTHOR Begin the entry with the title, and list the work alphabetically by the first word of the title after any initial *A*, *An*, or *The*.

*New Concise World Atlas*. New York: Oxford UP, 2003. Print.

6. TWO OR MORE BOOKS BY THE SAME AUTHOR(S) Arrange the entries alphabetically by title. Include the name(s) of the author(s) in the first entry, but in subsequent entries, use three hyphens followed by a period.

Lorde, Audre. *A Burst of Light*. Ithaca: Firebrand, 1988. Print.

---. *Sister Outsider*. Trumansburg: Crossing, 1984. Print.

If you cite a work by one author who is also listed as the first coauthor of another work you cite, list the single-author work first, and then repeat the author's name in the entry for the coauthored work. Also repeat the author's name if you cite a work in which that author is listed as the first of a different set of coauthors. In other words, use three hyphens only when the work is by *exactly* the same author(s) as the previous entry.

7. EDITOR Treat an editor as an author, but add a comma and *ed.* (or *eds.*).

## SOURCE MAP: Citing books using MLA style

Take information from the book's title page and copyright page (on the reverse side of the title page), not from the book's cover or a library catalog.

(1) *Author.* List the last name first, followed by a comma, the first name, and the middle initial (if given). Omit titles such as *MD*, *PhD*, or *Sir;* include suffixes after the name and a comma (*O'Driscoll, Gerald P., Jr.*). End with a period.

(2) *Title.* Italicize the title and any subtitle; capitalize all major words. End with a period. (See 52c for more on capitalizing titles.)

(3) *City of publication.* If more than one city is given, use the first one listed. For foreign cities that may be unfamiliar to your readers, add an abbreviation of the country or province (*Cork, Ire.*). Follow it with a colon.

(4) *Publisher.* Give a shortened version of the publisher's name (*Harper* for *HarperCollins Publishers; Harcourt* for *Harcourt Brace; Oxford UP* for *Oxford University Press*). Follow it with a comma.

(5) *Year of publication.* Consult the copyright page. If more than one copyright date is given, use the most recent one. End with a period.

(6) *Medium of publication.* End with the medium (*Print*) followed by a period.

**For a book by one author, use the following format:**

Last name, First name. *Title of book*. City: Publisher, Year. Medium.

**A citation for the book on p. 311 would look like this:**

For more on using MLA style to cite books, see 18d1. (For guidelines and models for using APA style, see 19d1; for *Chicago* style, see 20c1; for CSE style, see 21c1.)

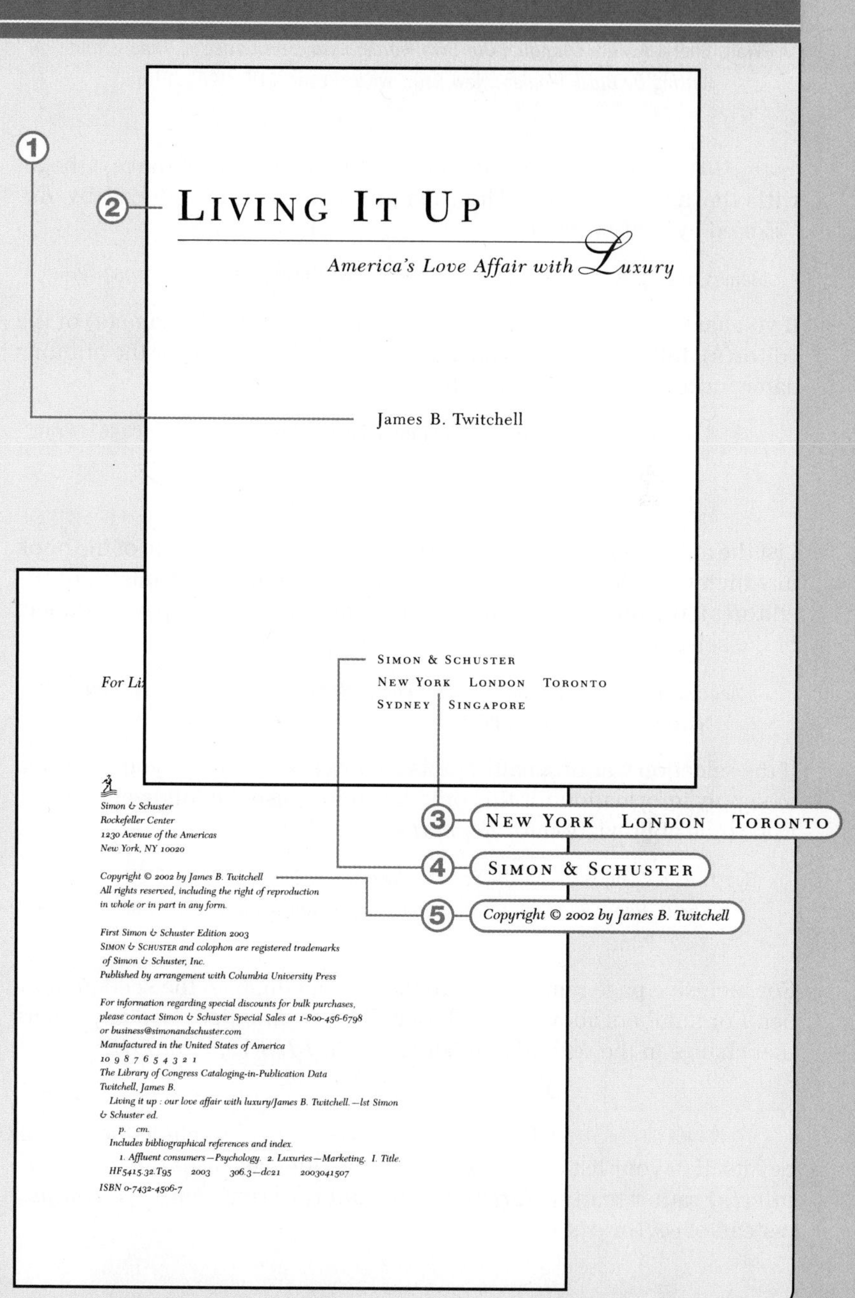

LIVING IT UP

*America's Love Affair with Luxury*

James B. Twitchell

SIMON & SCHUSTER
NEW YORK LONDON TORONTO
SYDNEY SINGAPORE

*For Li*

*Simon & Schuster*
*Rockefeller Center*
*1230 Avenue of the Americas*
*New York, NY 10020*

*Copyright © 2002 by James B. Twitchell*
*All rights reserved, including the right of reproduction in whole or in part in any form.*

*First Simon & Schuster Edition 2003*
*SIMON & SCHUSTER and colophon are registered trademarks of Simon & Schuster, Inc.*
*Published by arrangement with Columbia University Press*

*For information regarding special discounts for bulk purchases, please contact Simon & Schuster Special Sales at 1-800-456-6798 or business@simonandschuster.com*
*Manufactured in the United States of America*
*10 9 8 7 6 5 4 3 2 1*
*The Library of Congress Cataloging-in-Publication Data*
*Twitchell, James B.*
*Living it up : our love affair with luxury/James B. Twitchell.—lst Simon & Schuster ed.*
*p. cm.*
*Includes bibliographical references and index.*
*1. Affluent consumers—Psychology. 2. Luxuries—Marketing. I. Title.*
*HF5415.32.T95 2003 306.3—dc21 2003041507*
*ISBN 0-7432-4506-7*

Wall, Cheryl A., ed. *Changing Our Own Words: Essays on Criticism, Theory, and Writing by Black Women*. New Brunswick: Rutgers UP, 1989. Print.

8. AUTHOR AND EDITOR If you have cited the body of the text, begin with the author's name. Then list the editor(s), introduced by *Ed.* ("Edited by"), after the title.

James, Henry. *Portrait of a Lady*. Ed. Leon Edel. Boston: Houghton, 1963. Print.

If you have cited the editor's contribution, begin with the name(s) of the editor(s), followed by a comma and *ed.* (or *eds.*). Then list the author's name, introduced by *By*, after the title.

Edel, Leon, ed. *Portrait of a Lady*. By Henry James. Boston: Houghton, 1963. Print.

9. WORK IN AN ANTHOLOGY OR CHAPTER IN A BOOK WITH AN EDITOR List the author(s) of the selection or chapter; its title; the title of the book in which the selection or chapter appears; *Ed.* and the name(s) of the editor(s); the publication information; and the inclusive page numbers of the selection or chapter.

Komunyakaa, Yusef. "Facing It." *The Seagull Reader*. Ed. Joseph Kelly. New York: Norton, 2000. 126-27. Print.

If the selection was originally published in a periodical and you are asked to supply information for this original source, use the following format. *Rpt.* is the abbreviation for *Reprinted*.

Byatt, A. S. "The Thing in the Forest." *New Yorker* 3 June 2002: 80-89. Rpt. in *The O. Henry Prize Stories 2003*. Ed. Laura Furman. New York: Anchor, 2003. 3-22. Print.

For inclusive page numbers up to 99, note all digits in the second number. For numbers above 99, note only the last two digits and any others that change in the second number (*115-18*, *1378-79*, *296-301*).

10. TWO OR MORE ITEMS FROM AN ANTHOLOGY Include the anthology itself in your list of works cited. If the title page uses the term *compiler(s)* rather than *editor(s)*, use the abbreviation *comp.* (or *comps.*) instead of *ed.* (or *eds.*).

Walker, Dale L., ed. *Westward: A Fictional History of the American West*. New York: Forge, 2003. Print.

Also list each selection separately by its author and title, followed by a cross-reference to the anthology. Alphabetize all entries.

Estleman, Loren D. "Big Tim Magoon and the Wild West." Walker 391-404. Print.

Salzer, Susan K. "Miss Libbie Tells All." Walker 199-212. Print.

11. TRANSLATION Begin with the author's name, and give the translator's name, preceded by *Trans.* ("Translated by"), after the title.

Hietamies, Laila. *Red Moon over White Sea*. Trans. Borje Vahamaki. Beaverton, OR: Aspasia, 2000. Print.

If you cite a translated selection from an anthology, add *Trans.* and the translator's name before the title of the anthology.

Horace. *The Art of Poetry*. Trans. Smith Palmer Bovie. *The Critical Tradition: Classic Texts and Contemporary Trends*. Ed. David H. Richter. 2nd ed. Boston: Bedford, 1998. 68-78. Print.

12. BOOK IN A LANGUAGE OTHER THAN ENGLISH If necessary, you may provide a translation of the book's title in brackets. You may also choose to give the English name of a foreign city in brackets.

Benedetti, Mario. *La borra del café [The Coffee Grind]*. Buenos Aires: Sudamericana, 2000. Print.

13. EDITION OTHER THAN THE FIRST Add the information, in abbreviated form, after the title.

Walker, John A. *Art in the Age of Mass Media*. 3rd ed. London: Pluto, 2001. Print.

14. MULTIVOLUME WORK If you cite only one volume, give the volume number after the title, using the abbreviation *Vol.* You may give the number of volumes in the complete work at the end of the entry, using the abbreviation *vols.*

Ch'oe, Yong-Ho, Peter Lee, and William Theodore De Barry, eds. *Sources of Korean Tradition*. Vol. 2. New York: Columbia UP, 2000. Print. 2 vols.

If you cite two or more volumes, give the number of volumes in the complete work after the title.

Ch'oe, Yong-Ho, Peter Lee, and William Theodore De Barry, eds. *Sources of Korean Tradition*. 2 vols. New York: Columbia UP, 2000. Print.

15. PREFACE, FOREWORD, INTRODUCTION, OR AFTERWORD Begin with the author of the item and the item title (not underlined, italicized, or in quotation marks). Then give the title of the book and the book's author (preceded by the word *By*) or editor (preceded by *Ed.*). If the same person wrote or edited both the book and the cited item, use just the last name after *By* or *Ed.* List the page numbers of the item at the end of the entry.

Atwan, Robert. Foreword. *The Best American Essays 2002*. Ed. Stephen Jay Gould. Boston: Houghton, 2002. viii-xii. Print.

16. ENTRY IN A REFERENCE WORK List the author of the entry, if known. If no author is identified, begin with the title. For a well-known reference work, just note the edition number and year of publication or designate the edition by its year of publication. If the entries in the work are in alphabetical order, you need not give volume or page numbers. (For an electronic version of a reference work, see p. 325.)

"Hero." *Merriam-Webster's Collegiate Dictionary*. 11th ed. 2003. Print.

Kettering, Alison McNeil. "Art Nouveau." *World Book Encyclopedia*. 2002 ed. Print.

17. BOOK THAT IS PART OF A SERIES Cite the series name as it appears on the title page, followed by any series number.

Nichanian, Marc, and Vartan Matiossian, eds. *Yeghishe Charents: Poet of the Revolution*. Costa Mesa: Mazda, 2003. Print. Armenian Studies Ser. 5.

18. REPUBLICATION To cite a modern edition of an older book, add the original publication date, followed by a period, after the title.

Scott, Walter. *Kenilworth*. 1821. New York: Dodd, 1956. Print.

19. PUBLISHER'S IMPRINT If a book is published under a publisher's imprint (indicated on the title page), hyphenate the imprint and the publisher's name.

Gilligan, Carol. *The Birth of Pleasure: A New Map of Love*. New York: Vintage-Random, 2003. Print.

20. BOOK WITH A TITLE WITHIN THE TITLE Do not italicize the title of a book within the title of a book you are citing. Enclose in quotation marks the title of a short work within a book title, and italicize it as you do the rest of the title.

Mullaney, Julie. *Arundhati Roy's* The God of Small Things: *A Reader's Guide*. New York: Continuum, 2002. Print.

Rhynes, Martha. *"I, Too, Sing America": The Story of Langston Hughes*. Greensboro: Morgan, 2002. Print.

21. SACRED TEXT To cite individual published editions of sacred books, begin with the title. If a specified version is not part of the title, list the version after the title.

**bedfordstmartins.com/smhandbook** For exercises on working with sources using MLA style, click on **Exercises for Working with Sources**.

## 2 Periodicals

The basic format for a works-cited entry for a periodical article appears on pp. 316–17.

22. ARTICLE IN A JOURNAL Follow the journal title with the volume number, a period, the issue number (if given), and the year (in parentheses).

Gigante, Denise. "The Monster in the Rainbow: Keats and the Science of Life." *PMLA* 117.3 (2002): 433-48. Print.

23. ARTICLE IN A JOURNAL WITH MORE THAN ONE SERIES Give the appropriate designation—whether the number of the series (*2nd*, *3rd*, etc.) or the abbreviation *os* (for "old series") or *ns* (for "new series")—between the title and the volume number.

Fertel, Randy. "Katrina Five Ways." *Kenyon Review* ns 28.3 (2006): 71-84. Print.

24. ARTICLE THAT SKIPS PAGES When an article skips pages, give only the first page number and a plus sign.

Tyrnauer, Matthew. "Empire by Martha." *Vanity Fair* Sept. 2002: 364+. Print.

## SOURCE MAP: Citing articles from periodicals using MLA style

(1) *Author.* List the last name first, followed by a comma, the first name, and the middle initial (if given). Omit titles such as *MD*, *PhD*, or *Sir;* include suffixes after the name and a comma (*O'Driscoll, Gerald P., Jr.*). End with a period.

(2) *Article title.* Enclose the title and any subtitle in quotation marks, and capitalize all major words. The closing period goes inside the closing quotation mark. (See 52c for more on capitalizing titles.)

(3) *Periodical title.* Italicize the title (excluding initial *A(n)* or *The*), and capitalize major words. For journals, give the volume and issue number.

(4) *Date of publication.* For journals, list the year in parentheses, and a colon. For monthly magazines, list the month and year. For weekly magazines and newspapers, list the day, month, and year.

(5) *Inclusive page numbers.* For page numbers up to 99, note all digits in the second number. For numbers above 99, note only the last two digits and any others that change in the second number (*115-18, 1378-79, 296-301*). Include section letters for newspapers. End with a period.

(6) *Medium of publication.* End with the medium of publication (*Print*) followed by a period.

**For a journal article, use the following format:**

Last name, First name. "Title ." *Journal* Volume number (year): Page number(s). Medium.

**For a newspaper article, use the following format:**

Last name, First name. "Title." *Newspaper* Date, Edition (if any): Section number (if any): Page number(s) (including section letter, if any). Medium.

**For a magazine article, use the following format:**

Last name, First name. "Title of article." *Magazine* Date: Page number(s). Medium.

**A citation for the magazine article on p. 317 would look like this:**

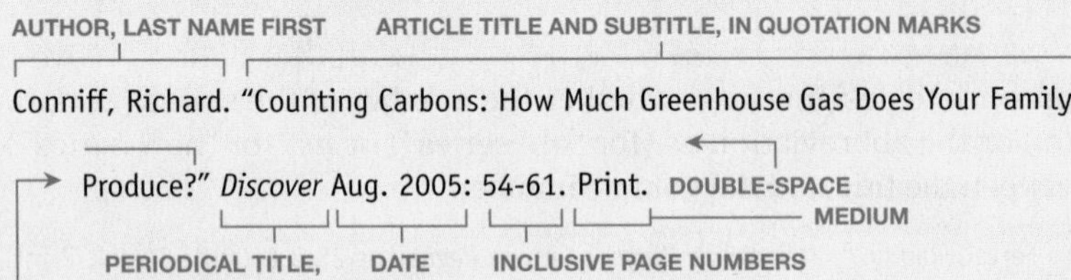


For more on using MLA style to cite periodical articles, see 18d2. (For guidelines and models for using APA style, see 19d2; for *Chicago* style, see 20c2; for CSE style, see 21c2.)

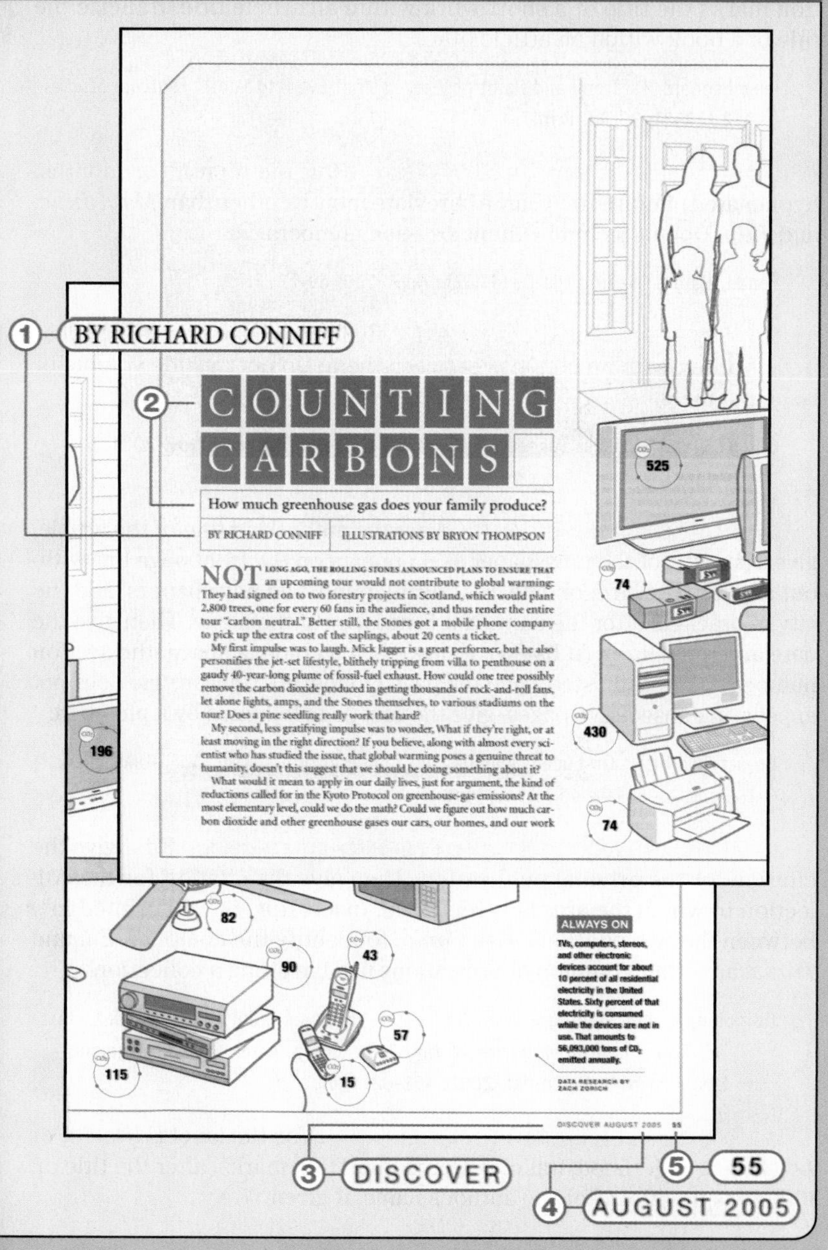



# COUNTING CARBONS

How much greenhouse gas does your family produce?

BY RICHARD CONNIFF | ILLUSTRATIONS BY BRYON THOMPSON

NOT LONG AGO, THE ROLLING STONES ANNOUNCED PLANS TO ENSURE THAT an upcoming tour would not contribute to global warming: They had signed on to two forestry projects in Scotland, which would plant 2,800 trees, one for every 60 fans in the audience, and thus render the entire tour "carbon neutral." Better still, the Stones got a mobile phone company to pick up the extra cost of the saplings, about 20 cents a ticket.

My first impulse was to laugh. Mick Jagger is a great performer, but he also personifies the jet-set lifestyle, blithely tripping from villa to penthouse on a gaudy 40-year-long plume of fossil-fuel exhaust. How could one tree possibly remove the carbon dioxide produced in getting thousands of rock-and-roll fans, let alone lights, amps, and the Stones themselves, to various stadiums on the tour? Does a pine seedling really work that hard?

My second, less gratifying impulse was to wonder, What if they're right, or at least moving in the right direction? If you believe, along with almost every scientist who has studied the issue, that global warming poses a genuine threat to humanity, doesn't this suggest that we should be doing something about it?

What would it mean to apply in our daily lives, just for argument, the kind of reductions called for in the Kyoto Protocol on greenhouse-gas emissions? At the most elementary level, could we do the math? Could we figure out how much carbon dioxide and other greenhouse gases our cars, our homes, and our work



**ALWAYS ON**

TVs, computers, stereos, and other electronic devices account for about 10 percent of all residential electricity in the United States. Sixty percent of that electricity is consumed while the devices are not in use. That amounts to 56,093,000 tons of $CO_2$ emitted annually.

DATA RESEARCH BY ZACH ZORICH

DISCOVER AUGUST 2005 55

25. ARTICLE WITH A TITLE WITHIN THE TITLE Enclose in single quotation marks the title of a short work within an article title. Italicize the title of a book within an article title.

Frey, Leonard H. "Irony and Point of View in 'That Evening Sun.'" *Faulkner Studies* 2 (1953): 33-40. Print.

26. ARTICLE IN A MONTHLY MAGAZINE Put the month (or months, hyphenated) before the year. Abbreviate months other than *May*, *June*, and *July*. Do not include volume or issue numbers.

Fonda, Daren. "Saving the Dead." *Life* Apr. 2000: 69-72. Print.

27. ARTICLE IN A WEEKLY MAGAZINE Include the day, month, and year in that order, with no commas between them. Do not include volume or issue numbers.

Gilgoff, Dan. "Unusual Suspects." *US News and World Report* 26 Nov. 2001: 51. Print.

28. ARTICLE IN A NEWSPAPER After the author and title of the article, give the name of the newspaper as it appears on the front page but without any initial *A*, *An*, or *The*. For locally published newspapers, add the city in brackets after the name if it is not part of the name. Then give the date and the edition (if listed), followed by a colon, a space, the section number or letter (if listed), and the page number(s). If the article does not appear on consecutive pages, give the first page followed by a plus sign.

Bernstein, Nina. "On Lucille Avenue, the Immigration Debate." *New York Times* 26 June 2006, late ed.: A1+. Print.

29. ARTICLE IN A COLLECTION OF REPRINTED ARTICLES First give the citation for the original publication. Then give the citation for the collection in which the article is reprinted. Insert *Rpt. in* ("Reprinted in") between the two citations. Use *Comp.* to identify the compiler. *Ed.* and *Trans.* are other common abbreviations used in citing a collection.

Quindlen, Anna. "Playing God on No Sleep." *Newsweek* 2 July 2001: 64. Rpt. in *The Best American Magazine Writing 2002*. Comp. Amer. Soc. of Magazine Eds. New York: Perennial, 2002. 458-62. Print.

30. EDITORIAL OR LETTER TO THE EDITOR Use the label *Editorial* or *Letter*, not underlined, italicized, or in quotation marks, after the title or, if there is no title, after the author's name, if given.

Magee, Doug. "Soldier's Home." Editorial. *Nation* 26 Mar. 1988: 400-01. Print.

31. REVIEW List the reviewer's name and the title of the review, if any, followed by *Rev. of* and the title and author, director, or other creator of the work reviewed. Then add the publication information.

Franklin, Nancy. "Dead On." Rev. of *Deadwood,* by David Milch. *New Yorker* 12 June 2006: 158-59. Print.

32. UNSIGNED ARTICLE Begin with the article title, alphabetizing the entry according to the first word after any initial *A*, *An*, or *The*.

"Performance of the Week." *Time* 6 Oct. 2003: 18. Print.

**bedfordstmartins.com/smhandbook** For exercises on working with sources using MLA style, click on **Exercises for Working with Sources**.

## 3 Electronic sources

Electronic sources such as Web sites differ from print sources in the ease with which they can be — and frequently are — changed, updated, or even eliminated. In addition, the various electronic media do not organize their works the same way.

The most commonly cited electronic sources are documents from Web sites and databases. The entry for such a source may include up to five basic elements, as in the following list, but must always include the last two:

- *Author*. List the last name first, followed by a comma and the first name, and end with a period. If no author is given, begin the entry with the title.
- *Title*. Enclose the title and subtitle of the document in quotation marks unless you are citing an entire site or an online book, both of which should be italicized. Capitalize all major words, and end with a period inside the closing quotation marks. (For more on capitalizing titles, see 52c.)
- *Print publication information*. Give any information the document provides about a previous or simultaneous publication in print, using the guidelines in 18d1 and 18d2.
- *Electronic publication information*. List all of the following items that you can find, with a period after each one: the title of the site, italicized, with all major words capitalized; the editor(s) of the site,

preceded by *Ed.*; and the name of any sponsoring institution or organization. Then add the date of electronic publication or of the latest update, with the month, if any, abbreviated except for *May*, *June*, and *July*; and end with the medium consulted (*Web*).

- *Access information.* Give the most recent date you accessed the source.
- *URLs.* Include a URL only if you think your readers will have difficulty finding your source without one. If you do include a URL, put it after the period following the date of access, enclose it in angle brackets, and put a period after the closing bracket.

Further guidelines for citing electronic sources can be found in the *MLA Handbook for Writers of Research Papers* and online at www.mla.org.

33. ARTICLE FROM AN ONLINE DATABASE OR A SUBSCRIPTION SERVICE
The basic format for citing a work from a database appears on pp. 322–23.

For a work from an online database, provide all of the following elements that are available: the author's name, if given; the title of the work in quotation marks; any print publication information; the name of the online database, italicized; the medium consulted (*Web*); and the date of access.

Goldman, William. "*The Princess Bride* Shooting Draft." 1987. *Internet Movie Script Database*. Web. 12 June 2008.

For a work from a subscription service, include the same information as for an online database; after the information about the work, give the name of the database, italicized; the medium consulted (*Web*); and the date of access.

Collins, Ross F. "Cattle Barons and Ink Slingers: How Cow Country Journalists Created a Great American Myth. "*American Journalism* 24.3 (2007); 7-29. *Communication and Mass Media Complete*. Web. 7 Feb. 2008.

34. WORK FROM A WEB SITE For basic information on citing a work from a Web site, see pp. 326–27. Include all of the following elements that are available: the author; the title of the document in quotation marks; the name of the Web site, italicized; the name of the publisher or sponsor (if none is available, use *N.p.*); the date of publication (if not available, use *n.d.*); the medium consulted (*Web*); and the date of access.

"Hands Off Public Broadcasting." *Media Matters for America*. Media Matters for America 24 May 2005. Web. 31 May 2005.

Stauder, Ellen Keck. "Darkness Audible: Negative Capability and Mark Doty's 'Nocturne in Black and Gold.'" *Romantic Circles Praxis Series*. U of Maryland, 2003. Web. 28 Sept. 2003.

35. ENTIRE WEB SITE Follow the guidelines for a specific work from the Web, beginning with the name of the author, editor, compiler, director, narrator, or translator, followed by the title of the Web site, italicized; the name of the sponsor or publisher (if none, use *N.p.*); the date of publication or last update; the medium of publication (*Web*); and the date of access.

Bernstein, Charles, Kenneth Goldsmith, Martin Spinelli, and Patrick Durgin, eds. *Electronic Poetry Corner*. SUNY Buffalo, 2003. Web. 26 Sept. 2006.

*Weather.com*. Weather Channel Interactive. 2006. Web. 13 Mar. 2006.

For a personal Web site, include the name of the person who created the site; the title, italicized, or (if there is no title) a description such as *Home page*, not italicized; the publisher or sponsor of the site (if none, use *N.p.*); the date of the last update; the medium of publication (*Web*); and the date of access.

Lunsford, Andrea A. Home page. Stanford U, 27 Mar. 2003. Web. 17 May 2006.

36. ACADEMIC COURSE OR DEPARTMENT WEB SITE For a course site, include the name of the instructor, the title of the course in quotation marks, a description such as *Course home page*, the dates of the course, the department name, the institution, the medium consulted (*Web*), and the access information.

Creekmur, Corey K., and Philip Lutgendorf. "Topics in Asian Cinema; Popular Hindi Cinema." Depts. of English, Cinema, and Comparative Literature, U of Iowa, 2004. Web. 13 Mar. 2007.

For a department Web site, give the department name, a description such as *Home page*, the institution, the medium (*Web*), and the access information.

Dept. of English. Home page. Amherst Coll., n.d. Web. 5 Apr. 2006.

## SOURCE MAP: Citing articles from databases using MLA style

Library subscriptions—such as InfoTrac, EBSCOhost, ProQuest, and Lexis-Nexis—provide access to huge databases of articles.

(1) *Author.* List the last name first.

(2) *Article title.* Enclose the title and any subtitle in quotation marks.

(3) *Periodical title.* Italicize it. Exclude any initial *A*, *An*, or *The*.

(4) *Print publication information.* List the volume and issue number, if any; the date of publication, including the day (if given), month, and year, in that order; and the inclusive page numbers.

(5) *Name of database.* Provide the name of the database, italicized.

(6) *Medium.* For an online database, use *Web*.

(7) *Date of access.* Give the day, month, and year, then a period.

**For an article from a database, use the following format:**

[Citation format for journal, magazine, or newspaper article — see pp. 315–19]. *Name of database*. Medium. Date accessed.

**A citation for the article on p. 323 would look like this:**

For more on using MLA style to cite articles from databases, see 18d3. (For guidelines and models for using APA style, see 19d3; for *Chicago* style, see 20c3; for CSE style, see 21c3.)

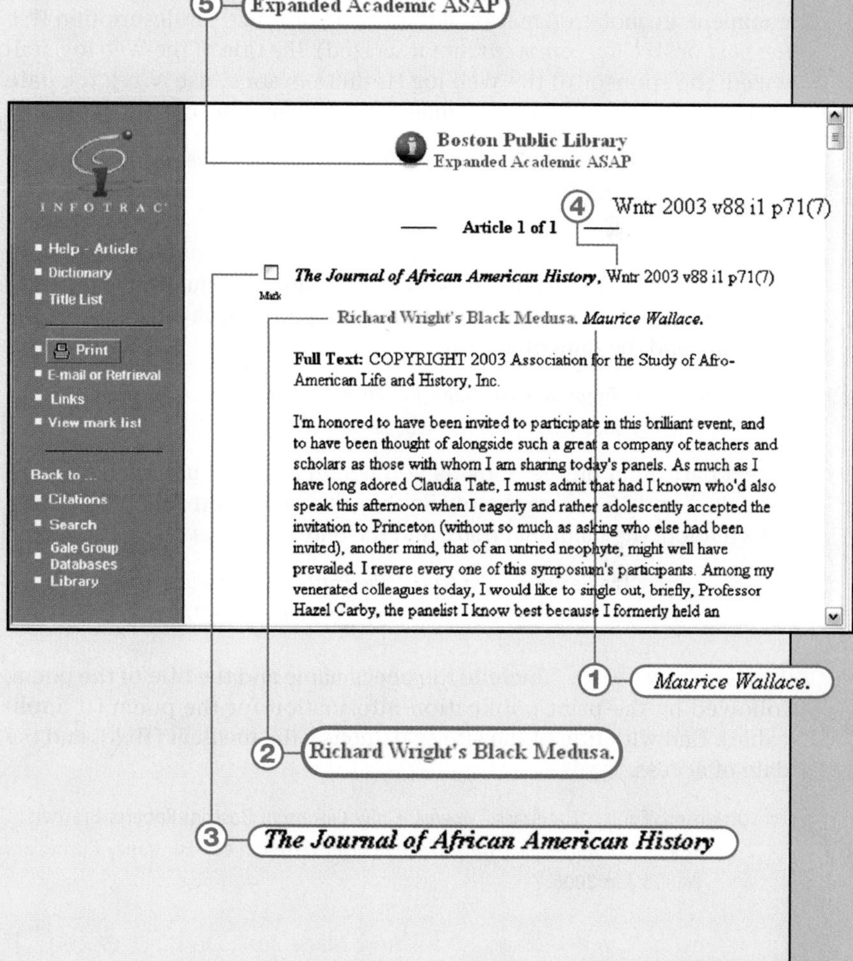

Expanded Academic ASAP
INFOTRAC
Help - Article
Dictionary
Title List
Print
E-mail or Retrieval
Links
View mark list
Back to ...
Citations
Search
Gale Group Databases
Library
Boston Public Library
Expanded Academic ASAP
Wntr 2003 v88 i1 p71(7)
Article 1 of 1
Mark
The Journal of African American History, Wntr 2003 v88 i1 p71(7)
Richard Wright's Black Medusa. Maurice Wallace.
Full Text: COPYRIGHT 2003 Association for the Study of Afro-American Life and History, Inc.
I'm honored to have been invited to participate in this brilliant event, and to have been thought of alongside such a great a company of teachers and scholars as those with whom I am sharing today's panels. As much as I have long adored Claudia Tate, I must admit that had I known who'd also speak this afternoon when I eagerly and rather adolescently accepted the invitation to Princeton (without so much as asking who else had been invited), another mind, that of an untried neophyte, might well have prevailed. I revere every one of this symposium's participants. Among my venerated colleagues today, I would like to single out, briefly, Professor Hazel Carby, the panelist I know best because I formerly held an
Maurice Wallace.
Richard Wright's Black Medusa.
The Journal of African American History

37. WEB LOG (BLOG) For an entire Web log, give the author's name; the title of the Web log, italicized; the sponsor or publisher of the Web log (if there is none, use *N.p.*); the date of the most recent update; the medium (*Web*); and the date of access.

Atrios. *Eschaton*. N.p., 27 June 2006. Web. 27 June 2006.

For a post or comment on a Web log, follow the guidelines for a short work from a Web site. Give the author's name; the title of the post or comment, in quotation marks (if there is no title, use the description *Web log post* or *Web log comment*, not italicized); the title of the Web log, italicized; the sponsor of the Web log (if there is none, use *N.p.*); the date of the most recent update; the medium (*Web*); and the date of access.

Parker, Randall. "Growth Rate for Electric Hybrid Vehicle Market Debated." *FuturePundit*. N.p., 20 May 2005. Web. 24 May 2005.

38. ONLINE BOOK Cite an online book as you would a print book (see models 1–21). After the print publication information (city, publisher, and year), if any, give the electronic publication information, the medium, and the date of access.

Euripides. *The Trojan Women*. Trans. Gilbert Murray. New York: Oxford UP, 1915. *Internet Sacred Text Archive*. Web. 12 Oct. 2008.

Cite a part of an online book as you would a part of a print book (see models 9 and 15). Give the available print and electronic publication information, the medium (*Web*), and the date of access.

Riis, Jacob. "The Genesis of the Gang." *The Battle with the Slum*. New York: Macmillan, 1902. *Bartleby.com: Great Books Online*. 2000. Web. 31 Mar. 2005.

39. ONLINE POEM Include the poet's name and the title of the poem, followed by the print publication information for the poem (if applicable). End with title of the site or database, the medium (*Web*), and the date of access.

Dickinson, Emily. "The Grass." *Poems: Emily Dickinson*. Boston: Roberts Brothers, 1891. *Humanities Text Initiative American Verse Project*. Ed. Nancy Kushigian. Web. 6 Jan 2006.

40. ARTICLE IN AN ONLINE JOURNAL, MAGAZINE, OR NEWSPAPER If the journal, magazine, or newspaper also appears in print, include print

publication information, if it is available (see models 22–28). If the print article includes page numbers and the online version does not provide that information, use *n. pag.* Then give the medium (*Web*) and the date of access.

Gallaher, Brian. "Greta Garbo Is Sad: Some Historical Reflections on the Paradoxes of Stardom in the American Film Industry, 1910-1960." *Images: A Journal of Film and Popular Culture* 3 (1997): n. pag. Web. 7 Oct. 2007.

If the print publication information is not available, or if the article appears online only, do the following: after the title of the journal, magazine, or newspaper, give the publisher or sponsor's name (if unavailable, use *N. p.*), a comma, and the date of online publication (if unavailable, use *n.d.*). Then give the medium (*Web*) and the date of access.

Burt, Stephen. "The True Legacy of Marianne Moore, Modernist Monument." *Slate*. Washingtonpost.Newsweek Interactive Co., LLC, 11 Nov. 2003. Web. 12 Nov. 2008.

Shea, Christopher. "Five Truths about Tuition." *New York Times*. New York Times, 9 Nov. 2003. Web. 11 Apr. 2009.

41. ONLINE EDITORIAL OR LETTER TO THE EDITOR Include the word *Editorial* or *Letter* after the author (if given) and title (if any). End with the periodical name, the sponsor of the Web site, the date of electronic publication, the medium, and the access date.

"The Funding Gap." Editorial. *Washington Post.* Washington Post, 5 Nov. 2003. Web. 9 Nov. 2003.

Piccato, Pablo. Letter. *New York Times.* New York Times, 9 Nov. 2003. Web. 9 Nov. 2003.

42. ONLINE REVIEW Cite an online review as you would a print review (see model 31). End with the name of the Web site, the sponsor, the date of electronic publication, the medium, and the date of access.

O'Hehir, Andrew. "The Nightmare in Iraq." Rev. of *Gunner Palace*, dir. Michael Tucker and Petra Epperlein. *Salon.* Salon Media Group, 4 Mar. 2005. Web. 24 May 2005.

43. ENTRY IN AN ONLINE REFERENCE WORK Cite the entry as you would an entry from a print reference work (see model 16). Follow with

## SOURCE MAP: Citing works from Web sites using MLA style

You may need to browse other parts of a site to find some elements, and some sites may omit elements. Uncover as much information as you can.

1. *Author of the work.* List the last name first, followed by a comma, the first name, and the middle initial (if given). End with a period. If no author is given, begin with the title.
2. *Title of the work.* Enclose the title and any subtitle of the work in quotation marks.
3. *Title of the Web site.* Give the title of the entire Web site, italicized. Where there is no clear title, use *Home page* without italicizing it.
4. *Name of publisher or sponsoring organization.* Look for the sponsor's name at the bottom of the home page. If no information is available, write *N.p.* and follow it with a comma.
5. *Date of publication or latest update.* Give the most recent date, followed by a period. If no date is available, use *n.d.*
6. *Medium consulted.* Use *Web* and follow it with a period.
7. *Date of access.* Give the date you accessed the work. End with a period.

**For a work from a Web site, use the following format:**

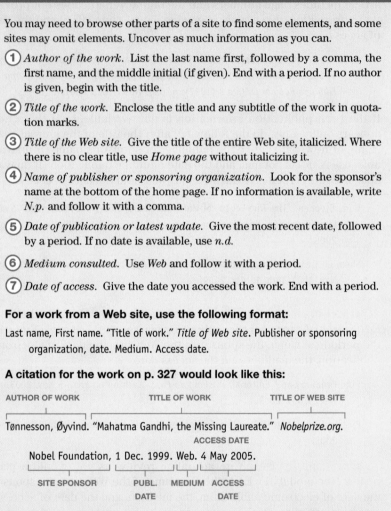

Last name, First name. "Title of work." *Title of Web site*. Publisher or sponsoring organization, date. Medium. Access date.

**A citation for the work on p. 327 would look like this:**

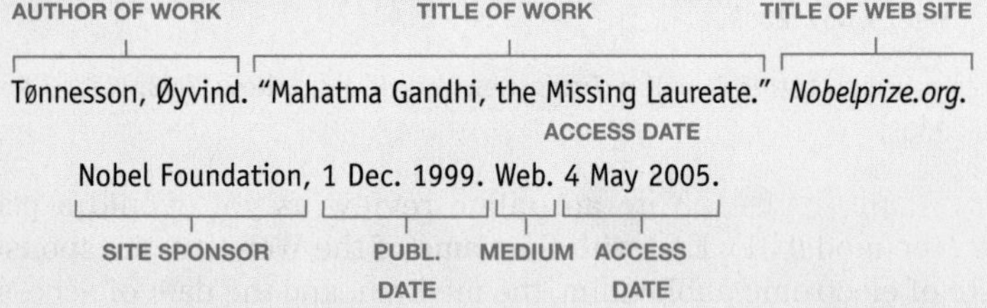


For more on using MLA style to cite Web documents, see 18d3. (For guidelines and models for using APA style, see 19d3; for *Chicago* style, see 20c3; for CSE style, see 21c3.)

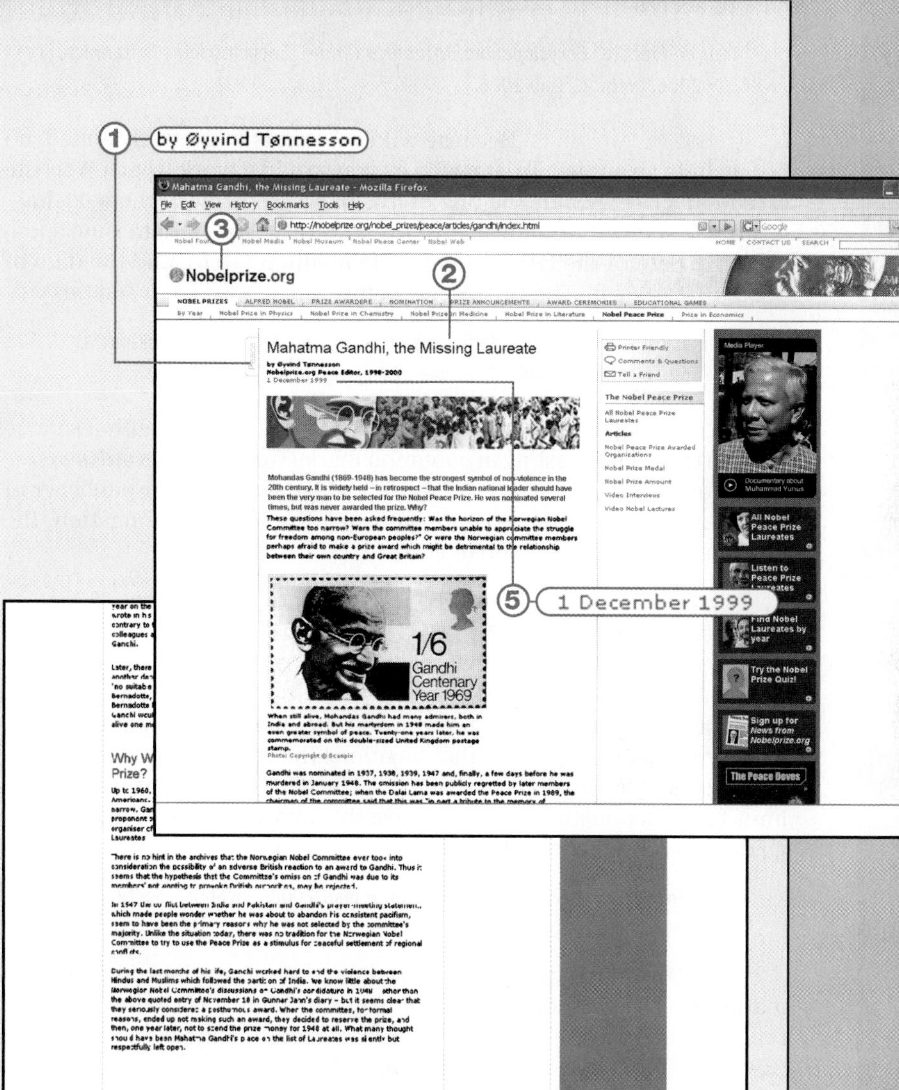

1 by Øyvind Tønnesson
2
3
4 The Official Web Site of the Nobel Foundation
5 1 December 1999
Mahatma Gandhi, the Missing Laureate - Mozilla Firefox
http://nobelprize.org/nobel_prizes/peace/articles/gandhi/index.html
Nobelprize.org
Mahatma Gandhi, the Missing Laureate
by Øyvind Tønnesson
Nobelprize.org Peace Editor, 1998-2000
1 December 1999
Mohandas Gandhi (1869-1948) has become the strongest symbol of non-violence in the 20th century. It is widely held – in retrospect – that the Indian national leader should have been the very man to be selected for the Nobel Peace Prize. He was nominated several times, but was never awarded the prize. Why?
These questions have been asked frequently: Was the horizon of the Norwegian Nobel Committee too narrow? Were the committee members unable to appreciate the struggle for freedom among non-European peoples?" Or were the Norwegian committee members perhaps afraid to make a prize award which might be detrimental to the relationship between their own country and Great Britain?
1/6 Gandhi Centenary Year 1969
When still alive, Mohandas Gandhi had many admirers, both in India and abroad. But his martyrdom in 1948 made him an even greater symbol of peace. Twenty-one years later, he was commemorated on this double-sized United Kingdom postage stamp.
Photo: Copyright © Scanpix
Gandhi was nominated in 1937, 1938, 1939, 1947 and, finally, a few days before he was murdered in January 1948. The omission has been publicly regretted by later members of the Nobel Committee; when the Dalai Lama was awarded the Peace Prize in 1989, the
There is no hint in the archives that the Norwegian Nobel Committee ever took into consideration the possibility of an adverse British reaction to an award to Gandhi. Thus it seems that the hypothesis that the Committee's omission of Gandhi was due to its members' not wanting to provoke British authorities, may be rejected.
In 1947 the conflict between India and Pakistan and Gandhi's prayer-meeting statements, which made people wonder whether he was about to abandon his consistent pacifism, seem to have been the primary reasons why he was not selected by the committee's majority. Unlike the situation today, there was no tradition for the Norwegian Nobel Committee to try to use the Peace Prize as a stimulus for peaceful settlement of regional conflicts.
During the last months of his life, Gandhi worked hard to end the violence between Hindus and Muslims which followed the partition of India. We know little about the Norwegian Nobel Committee's discussions on Gandhi's candidature in 1948 other than the above quoted entry of November 18 in Gunnar Jahn's diary – but it seems clear that they seriously considered a posthumous award. When the committee, for formal reasons, ended up not making such an award, they decided to reserve the prize, and then, one year later, not to spend the prize money for 1948 at all. What many thought should have been Mahatma Gandhi's place on the list of Laureates was silently but respectfully left open.
The Official Web Site of the Nobel Foundation

the name of the Web site, the sponsor, date of publication, medium, and date of access.

"Tour de France." *Encyclopaedia Britannica Online*. Encyclopaedia Britannica, 2006. Web. 21 May 2006.

44. ENTRY IN A WIKI Because wiki content is collectively edited, do not include an author. Treat a wiki as you would a work from a Web site (see model 34). Include the title of the entry; the name of the wiki, italicized; the sponsor or publisher of the wiki (use *N.p.* if there is no sponsor); the date of the latest update; the medium (*Web*); and the date of access. Check with your instructor before using a wiki as a source.

"Fédération Internationale de Football Association." *Wikipedia*. Wikipedia Foundation, 27 June 2006. Web. 27 June 2006.

45. POSTING TO A DISCUSSION GROUP Begin with the author's name and the title of the posting in quotation marks (or the words *online posting*). Follow with the name of the Web site, the sponsor or publisher of the site (use *N.p.* if there is no sponsor), the date of publication, the medium (*Web*), and the date of access.

Daly, Catherine. "Poetry Slams." *Poetics Discussion List*. SUNY Buffalo, 29 Aug. 2003. Web. 1 Oct. 2003.

46. POSTING ON A SOCIAL NETWORKING SITE To cite a message on Facebook or another social networking site, include the writer's name, a description of the posting that mentions the recipient, the date of the message, and the medium of delivery. (The MLA does not provide guidelines for citing postings on such sites; this model is based on the MLA's guidelines for citing email.)

Ferguson, Sarah. Message to the author. 6 Mar. 2008. Facebook posting. 8 Mar. 2008.

47. EMAIL Include the writer's name; the subject line, in quotation marks; *Message to* (not italicized or in quotation marks) followed by the recipient's name; the date of the message; and the medium of delivery (*E-mail*). (MLA style hyphenates *e-mail.*)

Harris, Jay. "Thoughts on Impromptu Stage Productions." Message to the author. 16 July 2006. E-mail.

48. COMPUTER SOFTWARE OR GAME Include the title, italicized, version number (if given), and publication information. If you are citing downloaded software, replace the publication information with the medium and the date of access.

*The Sims 2*. Redwood City: Electronic Arts, 2004. CD-ROM.

*Web Cache Illuminator.* Vers. 4.02. NorthStar Solutions, n.d. Web. 12 Nov. 2003.

49. PERIODICALLY REVISED CD-ROM For a periodically revised CD-ROM, begin with the author, title, and any available print publication information. Then give the place of publication, the name of the company or group producing it, the electronic publication date (month and year, if available), and the medium (*CD-ROM*).

Ashenfelter, Orley, and Kathryn Graddy. "Auctions and the Price of Art." *Journal of Economic Literature* 41.3 (2003): 763-87. Nashville: Amer. Economic Assn., Sept. 2003. CD-ROM.

50. SINGLE-ISSUE CD-ROM Cite a CD-ROM like a book if it is not regularly updated.

*Cambridge Advanced Learner's Dictionary*. Cambridge: Cambridge UP, 2003. CD-ROM.

51. MULTIDISC CD-ROM If the CD-ROM includes more than one disc, include either the total number of discs (*3 discs*) or, if you used material from only one, the number of that disc.

*IRIS: Immigration Research Information Service, LawDesk*. Disc 2. Eagon, MN: West, 2003. CD-ROM.

**bedfordstmartins.com/smhandbook** For more information on citing electronic sources using MLA style, go to Documenting Sources and click on **MLA Style**.

## 4 Other sources (including online versions)

If an online version is not shown here, use the appropriate model for the source and then end with the medium and date of access.

52. REPORT OR PAMPHLET Cite a report or pamphlet by following the guidelines for a print or an online book.

Allen, Katherine, and Lee Rainie. *Parents Online*. Washington: Pew Internet and Amer. Life Project, 2002. Print.

Environmental Working Group. *Dead in the Water*. Washington: Environmental Working Group, 2006. Web. 24 Apr. 2006.

53. GOVERNMENT PUBLICATION Begin with the author, if identified. Otherwise, start with the name of the government, followed by the agency and any subdivision. Use abbreviations if they can be readily understood. Then give the title. For congressional documents, cite the number, session, and house of Congress (using *S* for Senate and *H* or *HR* for House of Representatives); the type (*Report*, *Resolution*, *Document*) in abbreviated form; and the number of the material. If you cite the *Congressional Record*, give only the date and page number(s). Otherwise, end with the publication information. For print versions, the publisher is often the Government Printing Office (GPO). For online versions, follow the models for a work from a Web site (model 34) or an entire Web site (model 35).

Gregg, Judd. *Report to Accompany the Genetic Information Act of 2003*. US 108th Cong., 1st sess. S. Rept. 108-22. Washington: GPO, 2003. Print.

Kinsella, Kevin, and Victoria Velkoff. *An Aging World: 2001*. US Bureau of the Census. Washington: GPO, 2001. Print.

United States. Environmental Protection Agency. Office of Emergency and Remedial Response. *This Is Superfund*. Environmental Protection Agency, 2000. Web. 16 Aug. 2002.

54. PUBLISHED PROCEEDINGS OF A CONFERENCE Cite proceedings as you would a book. If the title doesn't include enough information about the conference, add necessary information after the title.

Cleary, John, and Gary Gurtler, eds. *Proceedings of the Boston Area Colloquium in Ancient Philosophy 2002*. Boston: Brill Academic, 2003. Print.

55. UNPUBLISHED DISSERTATION OR THESIS Enclose the title in quotation marks. Add the label *Diss.*, the school, and the year the work was

accepted. If you are citing a thesis, use a label such as *MA thesis* (or whatever is appropriate) instead of *Diss.*

LeCourt, Donna. "The Self in Motion: The Status of the (Student) Subject in Composition Studies." Diss. Ohio State U, 1993. Print.

56. PUBLISHED DISSERTATION Cite a published dissertation as a book, adding the identification *Diss.* and the university. If the dissertation was published by University Microfilms International, end the entry with *Ann Arbor: UMI*, the year, and medium.

Yau, Rittchell Ann. *The Portrayal of Immigration in a Selection of Picture Books Published since 1970*. Diss. U of San Francisco, 2003. Ann Arbor: UMI, 2003. Print.

57. DISSERTATION ABSTRACT To cite the abstract of a dissertation using *Dissertation Abstracts International* (*DAI*), include the *DAI* volume, year (in parentheses), and page number.

Huang-Tiller, Gillian C. "The Power of the Meta-Genre: Cultural, Sexual, and Racial Politics of the American Modernist Sonnet." Diss. U of Notre Dame, 2000. *DAI* 61 (2000): 1401. Print.

58. UNPUBLISHED OR PERSONAL INTERVIEW List the person interviewed, and then use the label *Telephone interview*, *Personal interview*, or *E-mail interview*. End with the date(s) the interview took place.

Freedman, Sasha. Personal interview. 10 Nov. 2006.

59. PUBLISHED OR BROADCAST INTERVIEW List the person interviewed and then the title of the interview. If the interview has no title, use the label *Interview* and name the interviewer, if relevant. Then identify the source.

Ebert, Robert. Interview with Matthew Rothschild. *Progressive*. Progressive Magazine, Aug. 2003. Web. 5 Oct. 2003.

Taylor, Max. "Max Taylor on Winning." *Time* 13 Nov. 2000: 66. Print.

To cite a broadcast interview, end with information about the program, the date(s) the interview took place, and the medium.

Revkin, Andrew. Interview by Terry Gross. *Fresh Air*. Natl. Public Radio. WNYC, New York, 14 June 2006. Radio.

60. UNPUBLISHED LETTER Cite a published letter as a work in an anthology (see model 9). If the letter is unpublished, follow this form:

Anzaldúa, Gloria. Letter to the author. 10 Sept. 2002. MS.

61. MANUSCRIPT OR OTHER UNPUBLISHED WORK Begin with the author's name and the title or, if there is no title, a description of the material. Then note the form of the material (such as *MS.* for *manuscript* or *TS.* for *typescript*) and any identifying numbers assigned to it. End by giving the name and location of the library or research institution housing the material, if applicable.

Woolf, Virginia. "The Searchlight." N.d. TS. Ser. III, Box 4, Item 184. Papers of Virginia Woolf, 1902-1956. Smith Coll., Northampton.

62. LEGAL SOURCE To cite a legal case, give the name of the case, the number of the case (using the abbreviation *No.*), the name of the court, and the date of the decision.

Eldred v. Ashcroft. No. 01-618. Supreme Ct. of the US. 15 Jan. 2003. Print.

To cite an act, give the name of the act followed by its Public Law (*Pub. L.*) number, the date the act was enacted, and its Statutes at Large (*Stat.*) cataloging number.

Museum and Library Services Act of 2003. Pub. L. 108-81. 25 Sept. 2003. Stat. 117.991. Print.

63. FILM, VIDEO, OR DVD If you cite a particular person's work, start the entry with that person's name. In general, start with the title, italicized; then name the director, the distributor, and the year of release. Other contributors, such as writers or performers, may follow the director. If you cite a video or DVD instead of a theatrical release, include the original film release date (if relevant) and the label *Videocassette* or *DVD*. For material found on a Web site, give the name of the site or database, the medium (*Web*), and the access date.

Moore, Michael, dir. *Bowling for Columbine*. 2002. *BowlingforColumbine.com*. Web. 30 Sept. 2005.

*Spirited Away*. Dir. Hiyao Miyazaki. Perf. Daveigh Chase, Suzanne Pleshette, and Jason Marsden. 2001. Walt Disney Video, 2003. DVD.

*Water*. Dir. Deepa Mehta. Fox Searchlight, 2006. Film.

64. TELEVISION OR RADIO PROGRAM In general, begin with the title of the program, italicized. Then list any important contributors (narrator, writer, director, actors); the network; the local station and city, if any; the broadcast date; and the medium. To cite a particular person's work, begin the entry with that name. To cite a particular episode, begin with the episode title, in quotation marks.

*Box Office Bombshell: Marilyn Monroe*. Writ. Andy Thomas, Jeff Schefel, and Kevin Burns. Dir. Bill Harris. Narr. Peter Graves. A&E Biography. Arts and Entertainment Network, 23 Oct. 2002. Television.

"The Fleshy Part of the Thigh." *The Sopranos*. Writ. Diane Frolov and Andrew Schneider. Dir. Alan Taylor. HBO, 2 Apr. 2006. Television.

Komando, Kim. "E-mail Hacking and the Law." *CBS Radio*. CBS Radio Inc., 28 Oct. 2003. Web. 11 Nov. 2003.

65. SOUND RECORDING Begin with the name of the person or group you wish to emphasize (such as the composer, conductor, or band). Then give the title of the recording or musical composition; the artist(s), if appropriate; the manufacturer; and the year of issue. Give the medium (such as *CD*, *MP3* file, or *LP*) at the end. If you are citing a particular song or selection, include its title, in quotation marks, before the title of the recording. If you are citing a piece of instrumental music (such as a symphony) that is identified *only* by form, number, and key, do not underline, italicize, or enclose it in quotation marks.

Fountains of Wayne. "Bright Future in Sales." *Welcome Interstate Managers*. S-Curve, 2003. CD.

Grieg, Edvard. Concerto in A minor, op. 16. Cond. Eugene Ormandy. Philadelphia Orch. RCA, 1989. LP.

Sonic Youth. "Incinerate." *Rather Ripped*. Geffen, 2006. MP3 file.

66. MUSICAL COMPOSITION When you are *not* citing a specific published version, first give the composer's name, followed by the title. Italicize the title of an opera, a ballet, or a piece of instrumental music that is identified by name.

Mozart, Wolfgang Amadeus. *Don Giovanni*, K527.

Mozart, Wolfgang Amadeus. Symphony no. 41 in C major, K551.

Cite a published score as you would a book. If you include the date when the composition was written, do so immediately following the title.

Schoenberg, Arnold. *Chamber Symphony No. 1 for 15 Solo Instruments, Op. 9*. 1906. New York: Dover, 2002. Print.

67. LECTURE OR SPEECH List the speaker, the title in quotation marks, the name of the sponsoring institution or group, the place, the date, and the medium. If the speech is untitled, use a label such as *Lecture* or *Keynote speech*.

Colbert, Stephen. Speech. White House Correspondents' Association Dinner. *YouTube*. YouTube, LLC, 29 Apr. 2006. Web. 20 May 2006.

Eugenides, Jeffrey. Portland Arts and Lectures. Arlene Schnitzer Concert Hall, Portland, OR. 30 Sept. 2003. Lecture.

68. LIVE PERFORMANCE List the title, other appropriate details (composer, writer, performer, or director), the place, and the date. To cite a particular person's work, begin the entry with that name.

*Anything Goes*. By Cole Porter. Perf. Klea Blackhurst. Shubert Theater, New Haven. 7 Oct. 2003. Performance.

69. PODCAST Include all of the following that are relevant and available: the speaker, the title of the podcast, the title of the program, the host or performers, the title of the site, the site's sponsor, the date of posting, the medium (such as *MP3* file or *Web*), and the acess date. (This model is based on MLA guidelines for a short work from a Web site.)

"Seven Arrested in U.S. Terror Raid." *Morning Report*. Host Krishnan Guru-Murthy. *4 Radio*. Channel 4 News, 23 June 2006. MP3 file. 27 June 2006.

70. WORK OF ART OR PHOTOGRAPH List the artist or photographer; the work's title, italicized; the date of composition (if unknown, use *n.d.*); and the medium of composition (*Oil on canvas*, *Bronze*). Then cite the name of the museum or other location and the city. To cite a reproduction in a book, add the publication information. To cite artwork found online, omit the medium of composition, and after the location, add the title of the database or Web site, italicized; the medium consulted (*Web*); and the date of access.

Chagall, Marc. *The Poet with the Birds*. 1911. Minneapolis Inst. of Arts. *artsmia.org*. Web. 6 Oct. 2003.

*General William Palmer in Old Age*. 1810. Oil on canvas. National Army Museum, London. *White Mughals: Love and Betrayal in Eighteenth-Century India.* William Dalrymple. New York: Penguin, 2002. 270. Print.

Kahlo, Frida. *Self-Portrait with Cropped Hair. 1940.* Oil on canvas. Museum of Mod. Art, New York.

71. MAP OR CHART Cite a map or chart as you would a book or a short work within a longer work and include the word *Map* or *Chart* after the title. Add the medium of publication. For an online source, end with the date of access.

"Australia." Map. *Perry-Castañeda Library Map Collection*. U of Texas, 1999. Web. 4 Nov. 2003.

*California*. Map. Chicago: Rand, 2002. Print.

72. CARTOON OR COMIC STRIP List the artist's name; the title (if any) of the cartoon or comic strip, in quotation marks; the label *Cartoon* or *Comic strip*; and the usual publication information for a print periodical (see models 22–28) or a work from a Web site (model 34).

Johnston, Lynn. "For Better or for Worse." Comic strip. *FBorFW.com*. Lynn Johnston Publications, 30 June 2006. Web. 20 July 2006.

Lewis, Eric. "The Unpublished Freud." Cartoon. *New Yorker* 11 Mar. 2002: 80. Print.

73. ADVERTISEMENT Include the label *Advertisement* after the name of the item or organization being advertised.

Microsoft. Advertisement. *Harper's* Oct. 2003: 2-3. Print.

Microsoft. Advertisement. *New York Times*. New York Times, 11 Nov. 2003. Web. 11 Nov. 2003.

**bedfordstmartins.com/smhandbook** For more information on citing sources using MLA style, go to Documenting Sources and click on **MLA Style**.

## 18e A student research essay, MLA style

David Craig's final essay appears on the following pages. In preparing this essay, he followed the MLA guidelines described in this chapter. Note that the essay has been reproduced in a narrow format to allow for annotation. (For other MLA-style student research essays in this book, see 6j, 11k, and 62d.)

**bedfordstmartins.com/smhandbook** For additional student research writing, click on **Student Writing**.

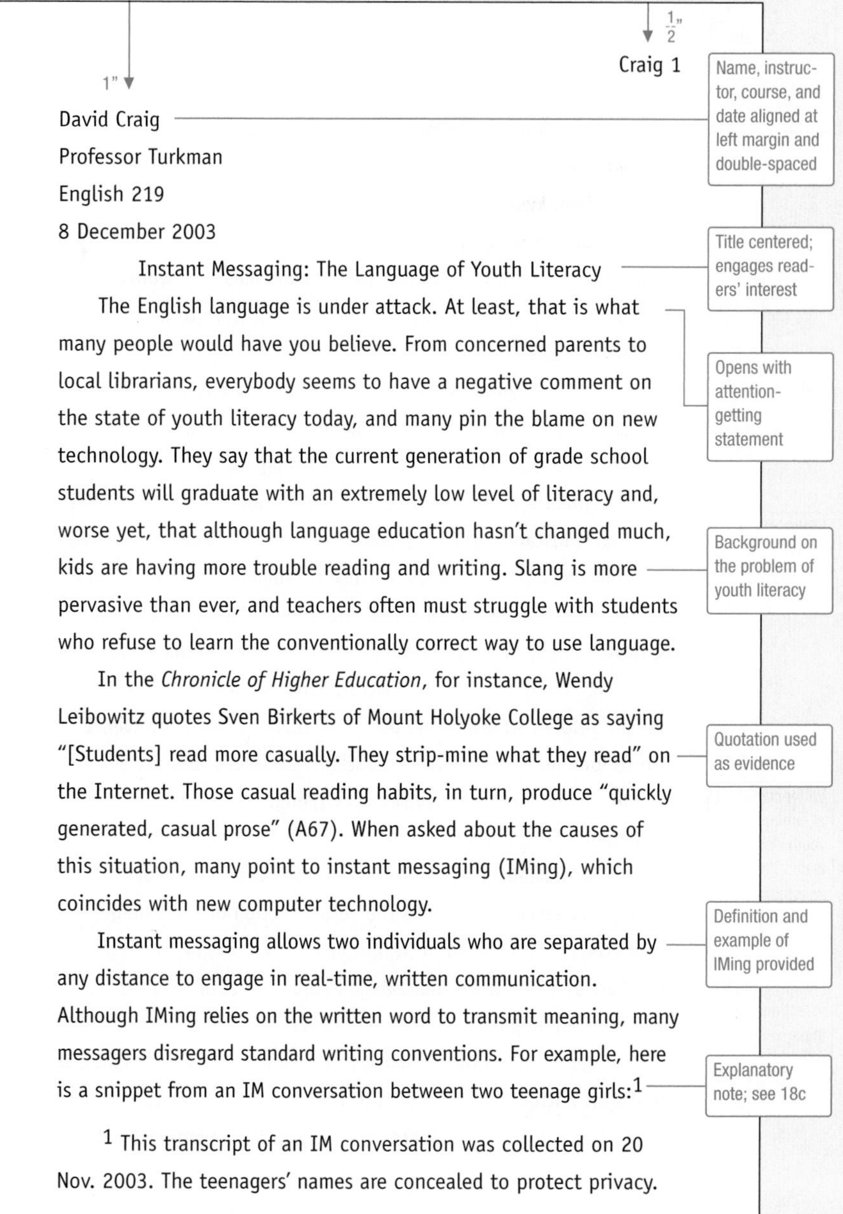


Craig 1

David Craig

Professor Turkman

English 219

8 December 2003

Instant Messaging: The Language of Youth Literacy

The English language is under attack. At least, that is what many people would have you believe. From concerned parents to local librarians, everybody seems to have a negative comment on the state of youth literacy today, and many pin the blame on new technology. They say that the current generation of grade school students will graduate with an extremely low level of literacy and, worse yet, that although language education hasn't changed much, kids are having more trouble reading and writing. Slang is more pervasive than ever, and teachers often must struggle with students who refuse to learn the conventionally correct way to use language.

In the *Chronicle of Higher Education*, for instance, Wendy Leibowitz quotes Sven Birkerts of Mount Holyoke College as saying "[Students] read more casually. They strip-mine what they read" on the Internet. Those casual reading habits, in turn, produce "quickly generated, casual prose" (A67). When asked about the causes of this situation, many point to instant messaging (IMing), which coincides with new computer technology.

Instant messaging allows two individuals who are separated by any distance to engage in real-time, written communication. Although IMing relies on the written word to transmit meaning, many messagers disregard standard writing conventions. For example, here is a snippet from an IM conversation between two teenage girls:[1]

[1] This transcript of an IM conversation was collected on 20 Nov. 2003. The teenagers' names are concealed to protect privacy.

Last name and page number in upper right-hand corner

Craig 2

Teen One: sorry im talkinto like 10 ppl at a time

Teen Two: u izzyful person

Teen Two: kwel

Teen One: hey i g2g

As this brief conversation shows, participants must use words to communicate via IMing, but their words do not have to be in standard English.

Overview of the criticism of IMing

Instant messaging, according to many, threatens youth literacy because it creates and compounds undesirable reading and writing habits and discourages students from learning standard literacy skills. Passionate or not, however, the critics' arguments don't hold up. In fact, instant messaging seems to be a beneficial force in the development of youth literacy because it promotes regular contact with words, the use of a written medium for communication, and the development of an alternative form of literacy. Perhaps most important, IMing can actually help students learn conventional English. Before turning to the pros and cons of IMing, however, I wish to look more closely at two background issues: the current state of literacy and the prevalence of IMing.

Explicit thesis stated

Writer considers argument that youth literacy is in decline

Regardless of one's views on IMing, the issue of youth literacy does demand attention because standardized test scores for language assessments, such as the verbal section of the College Board's SAT, have declined in recent years. This trend is illustrated in a chart distributed by the College Board as part of its 2002 analysis of aggregate SAT data (see Fig. 1).

Figure explained in text and cited in parenthetical reference

The trend lines, which I added to the original chart, illustrate a significant pattern that may lead to the conclusion that youth literacy is on the decline. These lines display the seven-year paths

Craig 3

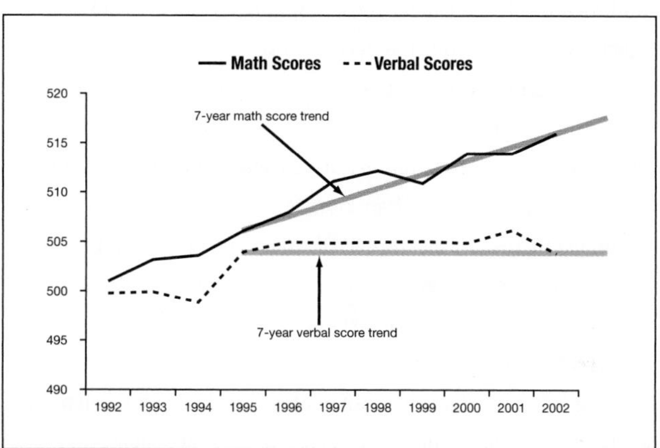

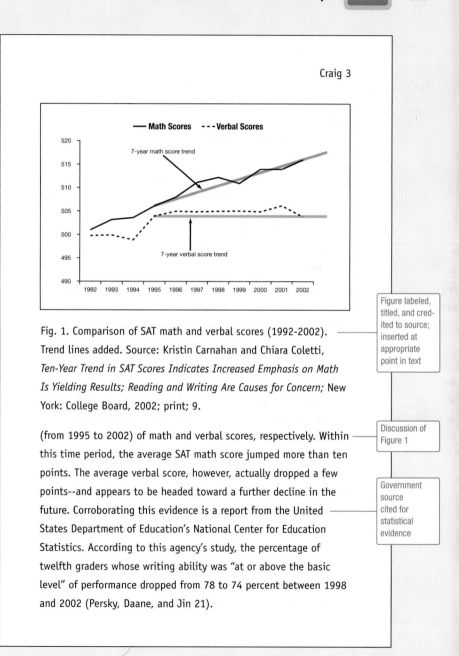


Fig. 1. Comparison of SAT math and verbal scores (1992-2002). Trend lines added. Source: Kristin Carnahan and Chiara Coletti, *Ten-Year Trend in SAT Scores Indicates Increased Emphasis on Math Is Yielding Results; Reading and Writing Are Causes for Concern;* New York: College Board, 2002; print; 9.

Figure labeled, titled, and credited to source; inserted at appropriate point in text

(from 1995 to 2002) of math and verbal scores, respectively. Within this time period, the average SAT math score jumped more than ten points. The average verbal score, however, actually dropped a few points--and appears to be headed toward a further decline in the future. Corroborating this evidence is a report from the United States Department of Education's National Center for Education Statistics. According to this agency's study, the percentage of twelfth graders whose writing ability was "at or above the basic level" of performance dropped from 78 to 74 percent between 1998 and 2002 (Persky, Daane, and Jin 21).

Discussion of Figure 1

Government source cited for statistical evidence

Craig 4

Writer acknowledges part of critics' argument; transition to next point

Based on the preceding statistics, parents and educators appear to be right about the decline in youth literacy. And this trend is occurring while IM usage is on the rise. According to the Pew Internet and American Life Project, 54 percent of American youths aged twelve to seventeen have used IMing (qtd. in Lenhart and Lewis 20). This figure translates to a pool of some thirteen million young instant messagers. Of this group, Pew reports, half send instant messages every time they go online, with 46 percent spending between thirty and sixty minutes messaging and another 21 percent spending more than an hour. The most conservative estimate indicates that American youths spend, at a minimum, nearly three million hours per day on IMing. What's more, they seem to be using a new vocabulary, and this is one of the things that bothers critics. In order to have an effect on youth literacy, however, this new vocabulary must actually exist, so I set out to determine if it did.

Statistical evidence cited

Writer's field research introduced

In the interest of establishing the existence of IM language, I analyzed 11,341 lines of text from IM conversations between youths in my target demographic: US residents aged twelve to seventeen. Young messagers voluntarily sent me chat logs, but they were unaware of the exact nature of my research. Once all of the logs had been gathered, I went through them, recording the number of times IM language was used in place of conventional words and phrases. Then I generated graphs to display how often these replacements were used.

During the course of my study, I identified four types of IM language: phonetic replacements, acronyms, abbreviations, and inanities. An example of phonetic replacement is using *ur* for *you are*.

Craig 5

Another popular type of IM language is the acronym; for a majority of the people in my study, the most common acronym was *lol*, a construction that means *laughing out loud*. Abbreviations are also common in IMing, but I discovered that typical IM abbreviations, such as *etc.*, are not new to the English language. Finally, I found a class of words that I call "inanities." These words include completely new words or expressions, combinations of several slang categories, or simply nonsensical variations of other words. My favorite from this category is *lolz*, an inanity that translates directly to *lol* yet includes a terminating *z* for no obvious reason.

Findings of field research presented

In the chat transcripts that I analyzed, the best display of typical IM lingo came from the conversations between two thirteen-year-old Texan girls, who are avid IM users. Figure 2 is a graph showing how often they used certain phonetic replacements and abbreviations. On the *y*-axis, frequency of replacement is plotted, a calculation that compares the number of times a word or phrase is used in IM language with the total number of times that it is

Figure introduced and explained

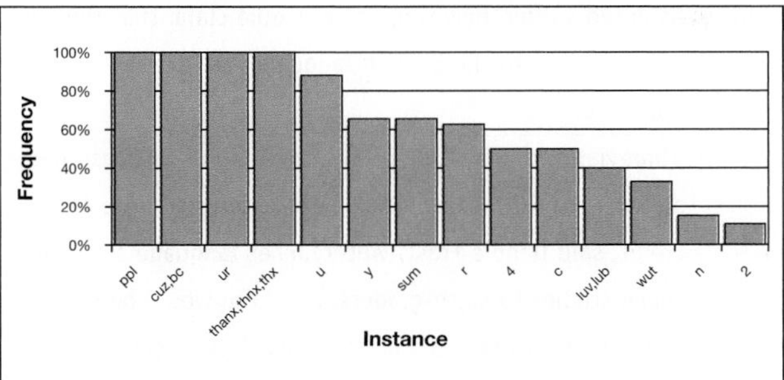


Fig. 2. Usage of phonetic replacements and abbreviations in IMing.

Figure labeled and titled

Craig 6

communicated in any form. On the *x*-axis, specific IM words and phrases are listed.

Discussion of findings presented in Figure 2

My research shows that the Texan girls use the first ten phonetic replacements or abbreviations at least 50 percent of the time in their normal IM writing. For example, every time one of them writes *see*, there is a parallel time when *c* is used in its place. In light of this finding, it appears that the popular IM culture contains at least some elements of its own language. It also seems that much of this language is new: no formal dictionary yet identifies the most common IM words and phrases. Only in the heyday of the telegraph or on the rolls of a stenographer would you find a similar situation, but these "languages" were never a popular medium of youth communication. Instant messaging, however, is very popular among young people and continues to generate attention and debate in academic circles.

Writer returns to opposition argument

Signal verb introduces quotation

My research shows that messaging is certainly widespread, and it does seem to have its own particular vocabulary, yet these two factors alone do not mean it has a damaging influence on youth literacy. As noted earlier, however, some people claim that the new technology is a threat to the English language, as revealed in the following passage:

Block quotation; quotation within a quotation

> Abbreviations commonly used in online instant messages are creeping into formal essays that students write for credit, said Debbie Frost, who teaches language arts and social studies to sixth-graders. . . . "You would be shocked at the writing I see. It's pretty scary. I don't get cohesive thoughts, I don't get sentences, they don't capitalize, and they have a lot of misspellings and bad grammar," she

Craig 7

> said. "With all those glaring mistakes, it's hard to see the content." ("Young Messagers")

Parenthetical reference uses brief title — author unknown

Echoing Frost's concerns is Melanie Weaver, a professor at Alvernia College, who taught a tenth-grade English class as an intern. In an interview with the *New York Times*, she said, "[When t]hey would be trying to make a point in a paper, they would put a smiley face in the end [:)]. . . . If they were presenting an argument and they needed to present an opposite view, they would put a frown [:(]" (qtd. in Lee).

The critics of instant messaging are numerous. But if we look to the field of linguistics, a central concept--metalinguistics--challenges these criticisms and leads to a more reasonable conclusion--that IMing has no negative impact on a student's development of or proficiency with traditional literacy.

Transition to support of thesis and refutation of critics

Scholars of metalinguistics offer support for the claim that IMing is not damaging to those who use it. As noted earlier, one of the most prominent components of IM language is phonetic replacement, in which a word such as *everyone* becomes *every1*. This type of wordplay has a special importance in the development of an advanced literacy, and for good reason. According to David Crystal, an internationally recognized scholar of linguistics at the University of Wales, as young children develop and learn how words string together to express ideas, they go through many phases of language play. The singsong rhymes and nonsensical chants of preschoolers are vital to their learning language, and a healthy appetite for such wordplay leads to a better command of language later in life (182).

Linguistic authority cited in support of thesis

As justification for his view of the connection between language play and advanced literacy, Crystal presents an argument

Evidence to support connection between wordplay and advanced literacy

Craig 8

for metalinguistic awareness. According to Crystal, *metalinguistics* refers to the ability to "step back" and use words to analyze how language works. "If we are good at stepping back," he says, "at thinking in a more abstract way about what we hear and what we say, then we are more likely to be good at acquiring those skills which depend on just such a stepping back in order to be successful--and this means, chiefly, reading and writing. . . . [T]he greater our ability to play with language, . . . the more advanced will be our command of language as a whole" (181).

Ellipses indicate omissions in quotation

If we accept the findings of linguists such as Crystal that metalinguistic awareness leads to increased literacy, then it seems reasonable to argue that the phonetic language of IMing can also lead to increased metalinguistic awareness and, therefore, increases in overall literacy. As instant messagers develop proficiency with a variety of phonetic replacements and other types of IM words, they should increase their subconscious knowledge of metalinguistics.

Writer links Crystal's views to thesis about IMing

Metalinguistics also involves our ability to write in a variety of distinct styles and tones. Yet in the debate over instant messaging and literacy, many critics assume that *either* IMing *or* academic literacy will eventually win out in a person and that the two modes cannot exist side by side. This assumption is, however, false. Human beings ordinarily develop a large range of language abilities, from the formal to the relaxed and from the mainstream to the subcultural. Mark Twain, for example, had an understanding of local speech that he employed when writing dialogue for *Huckleberry Finn*. Yet few people would argue that Twain's knowledge of this form of English had a negative impact on his ability to write in standard English.

Another refutation of critics' assumptions

Example from well-known work of literature used as support

Craig 9

However, just as Mark Twain used dialects carefully in dialogue, writers must pay careful attention to the kind of language they use in any setting. The owner of the language Web site *The Discouraging Word*, who is an anonymous English literature graduate student at the University of Chicago, backs up this idea in an e-mail to me:

> What is necessary, we feel, is that students learn how to shift between different styles of writing--that, in other words, the abbreviations and shortcuts of IM should be used online . . . but that they should not be used in an essay submitted to a teacher. . . . IM might even be considered . . . a different way of reading and writing, one that requires specific and unique skills shared by certain communities.

Email correspondence cited in support of claim

The analytical ability that is necessary for writers to choose an appropriate tone and style in their writing is, of course, metalinguistic in nature because it involves the comparison of two or more language systems. Thus, youths who grasp multiple languages will have a greater natural understanding of metalinguistics. More specifically, young people who possess both IM and traditional skills stand to be better off than their peers who have been trained only in traditional or conventional systems. Far from being hurt by their online pastime, instant messagers can be aided in standard writing by their experience with IM language.

Writer synthesizes evidence for claim

The fact remains, however, that youth literacy seems to be declining. What, if not IMing, is the main cause of this phenomenon? According to the College Board, which collects data on several questions from its test takers, enrollment in English

Transition to writer's final point

Craig 10

Alternate explanation for decline in literacy

composition and grammar classes has decreased in the last decade by 14 percent (Carnahan and Coletti 11). The possibility of instant messaging causing a decline in literacy seems inadequate when statistics on English education for US youths provide other evidence of the possible causes. Simply put, schools in the United States are not teaching English as much as they used to. Rather than blaming IMing alone for the decline in literacy and test scores, we must also look toward our schools' lack of focus on the teaching of standard English skills.

Transition to conclusion

Concluding paragraph sums up argument and reiterates thesis

I found that the use of instant messaging poses virtually no threat to the development or maintenance of formal language skills among American youths aged twelve to seventeen. Diverse language skills tend to increase a person's metalinguistic awareness and, thereby, his or her ability to use language effectively to achieve a desired purpose in a particular situation. The current decline in youth literacy is not due to the rise of instant messaging. Rather, fewer young students seem to be receiving an adequate education in the use of conventional English. Unfortunately, it may always be fashionable to blame new tools for old problems, but in the case of instant messaging, that blame is not warranted. Although IMing may expose literacy problems, it does not create them.

left margin and do not use quotation marks. Place the page reference in parentheses one space after the final punctuation.

- *Abstract.* If your instructor asks for an abstract with your paper — a one-paragraph summary of your major thesis and supporting points — it should go on a separate page immediately after the title page. Center the word *Abstract* about an inch from the top of the page. Double-space the text of the abstract, and begin the first line flush with the left margin. APA recommends that an abstract not exceed 120 words.
- *Headings.* Headings are used within the text of many APA-style papers. In papers with only one or two levels of headings, center the main headings; italicize the subheadings and position them flush with the left margin. Capitalize all major words; however, do not capitalize articles, short prepositions, or coordinating conjunctions unless they are the first word or follow a colon.
- *Visuals.* Tables should be labeled *Table*, numbered, and captioned. All other visuals (charts, graphs, photographs, and drawings) should be labeled *Figure*, numbered, and captioned with a description and the source information. Remember to refer to each visual in your text, stating how it contributes to the point(s) you are making. Tables and figures should generally appear near the relevant text; check with your instructor for guidelines on placement of visuals.

## 19b In-text citations

APA style requires parenthetical references in the text to document quotations, paraphrases, summaries, and other material from a source (see Chapters 15 and 16). These citations include the year of publication and correspond to full bibliographic entries in the list of references at the end of the text.

Note that APA style generally calls for past-tense signal verbs (*Baker showed*) in literature reviews or when describing a past action that occurred at a definite time. Use the present perfect tense (*Baker has shown*) for actions or conditions that are ongoing or didn't happen at a specific time. Use the present tense to discuss results (*the second experiment corroborates*) or widely accepted information (*researchers agree*).

## Directory to APA style for in-text citations



1. AUTHOR NAMED IN A SIGNAL PHRASE In most instances, use the author's name in a signal phrase to introduce the cited material, and place the date, in parentheses, immediately after the author's name. For a quotation, the page number, preceded by *p.*, appears in parentheses after the quotation.

> As Fanderclai (2001) observed, older siblings play an important role in the development of language and learning skills.

> Chavez (2003) noted that "six years after slim cigarettes for women were introduced, more than twice as many teenage girls were smoking" (p. 13).

For electronic texts or other works with paragraph numbers but no page numbers, use the paragraph number preceded by the abbreviation *para.*

> Weinberg (2000) has claimed that "the techniques used in group therapy can be verbal, expressive, or psychodramatic" (para. 5).

If paragraph numbers are not given, cite the heading and number of the paragraph in that section, if any: (*Types of Groups section, para. 1*). For a long, set-off quotation (one having more than forty words), place the page reference in parentheses one space after the final punctuation.

2. AUTHOR NAMED IN A PARENTHETICAL REFERENCE When you do not mention the author in a signal phrase in your text, give the author's

name and the date, separated by a comma, in parentheses at the end of the cited material.

> One study found that 17% of adopted children in the United States are of a different race than their adoptive parents (Peterson, 2003).

3. TWO AUTHORS Use both names in all citations. Join the names with *and* in a signal phrase, but use an ampersand (&) instead in a parenthetical reference.

> Babcock and Laschever (2003) have suggested that many women do not negotiate their salaries and pay raises as vigorously as their male counterparts do.

> A recent study has suggested that many women do not negotiate their salaries and pay raises as vigorously as their male counterparts do (Babcock & Laschever, 2003).

4. THREE TO FIVE AUTHORS List all the authors' names for the first reference.

> Safer, Voccola, Hurd, and Goodwin (2003) reached somewhat different conclusions by designing a study that was less dependent on subjective judgment than were previous studies.

In subsequent references, use just the first author's name plus *et al.* ("and others").

> Based on the results, Safer et al. (2003) determined that the apes took significant steps toward self-expression.

5. SIX OR MORE AUTHORS Use only the first author's name and *et al.* ("and others") in every citation, including the first.

> As Soleim et al. (2002) demonstrated, advertising holds the potential for manipulating "free-willed" consumers.

6. CORPORATE OR GROUP AUTHOR If the name of the organization or corporation is long, spell it out the first time you use it, followed by an abbreviation in brackets. In later references, use the abbreviation only.

| | |
|---|---|
| **FIRST CITATION** | (Centers for Disease Control and Prevention [CDC], 2006) |
| **LATER CITATIONS** | (CDC, 2006) |

7. UNKNOWN AUTHOR Use the title or its first few words in a signal phrase or in parentheses. Italicize a book or report title; place an article title in quotation marks.

> The school profiles for the county substantiate this trend (*Guide to secondary schools*, 2003).

8. TWO OR MORE AUTHORS WITH THE SAME LAST NAME If your list of references includes works by different authors with the same last name, include the authors' initials in each citation.

> G. Jones (2001) conducted the groundbreaking study on teenage childbearing.

9. TWO OR MORE WORKS BY AN AUTHOR IN A SINGLE YEAR Assign lowercase letters (*a*, *b*, and so on) alphabetically by title, and include the letters after the year.

> Gordon (2004b) examined this trend in more detail.

10. TWO OR MORE SOURCES IN ONE PARENTHETICAL REFERENCE List sources by different authors in alphabetical order by authors' last names, separated by semicolons; list works by the same author in chronological order, separated by commas.

> (Cardone, 2004; Lai, 2002)

> (Lai, 2000, 2002)

11. SPECIFIC PARTS OF A SOURCE Use abbreviations (*chap.*, *p.*, *para.*, and so on) in a parenthetical reference to name the part of a work you are citing.

> Mogolov (2003, chap. 9) has argued that his research yielded the opposite results.

12. EMAIL AND OTHER PERSONAL COMMUNICATION Cite any personal letters, email messages, electronic postings, telephone conversations, or interviews with the person's initial(s) and last name, the identification *personal communication*, and the date. Do not include personal communications in the reference list.

> R. Tobin (personal communication, November 4, 2005) supported his claims about music therapy with new evidence.

13. ELECTRONIC DOCUMENT Cite a Web or electronic document as you would a print source, using the author's name and date; indicating the chapter or figure, as appropriate; and giving a full citation in your list of references. To cite a quotation, include the page or paragraph numbers, if available.

In her report, Zomkowski stressed the importance of "ensuring equitable access to the Internet" (2003, para. 3).

## 19c Content notes

APA style allows you to use content notes to expand or supplement your text. Indicate such notes in the text by superscript numerals ([1]). Type the notes themselves on a separate page after the last page of the text, under the heading *Footnotes*, which should be centered at the top of the page. Double-space all entries. Indent the first line of each note one-half inch (or five to seven spaces), but begin subsequent lines at the left margin.

SUPERSCRIPT NUMBER IN TEXT

The age of the children involved in the study was an important factor in the selection of items for the questionnaire.[1]

FOOTNOTE

[1]Marjorie Youngston Forman and William Cole of the Child Study Team provided great assistance in identifying appropriate items for the questionnaire.

## 19d List of references

The alphabetical list of the sources cited in your document is called *References*. (If your instructor asks that you list everything you have read as background — not just the sources you cite — call the list *Bibliography*.) Here are guidelines for preparing a list of references:

- Start your list on a separate page after the text of your document but before any appendices or notes. Identify each page with the short title and page number, continuing the numbering of the text.
- Type the heading *References*, neither italicized nor in quotation marks, centered one inch from the top of the page.

- Double-space, and begin your first entry. Unless your instructor suggests otherwise, do not indent the first line of each entry, but indent subsequent lines one-half inch or five to seven spaces. Double-space the entire list.
- List sources alphabetically by authors' (or editors') last names. If the author is unknown, alphabetize the source by the first major word of the title, disregarding *A*, *An*, or *The*. If the list includes two or more works by the same author, see the examples on pp. 357 and 360.

APA style specifies the treatment and placement of four basic elements — author, publication date, title, and other publication information.

- *Author.* List all authors' last names first, and use only initials for first and middle names. Separate the names of multiple authors with commas, and use an ampersand (&) before the last author's name.
- *Publication date.* Enclose the date in parentheses. Use only the year for books and journals; use the year, a comma, and the month or month and day for magazines; use the year, a comma, and the month and day for newspapers. Do not abbreviate.
- *Title.* Italicize titles and subtitles of books and periodicals. Do not enclose titles of articles in quotation marks. For books and articles, capitalize only the first word of the title and subtitle and any proper nouns or proper adjectives. Capitalize all major words in a periodical title.
- *Publication information.* For a book, list the city and state of publication (or country), a colon, and the publisher's name, dropping any *Inc.*, *Co.*, or *Publishers*. For a periodical, follow the periodical title with a comma, the volume number (italicized), the issue number (if appropriate) in parentheses and followed by a comma, and the inclusive page numbers of the article. For newspaper articles and for articles or chapters in books, include the abbreviation *p.* ("page") or *pp.* ("pages") before the page numbers.

The sample entries that start on p. 356 use a hanging indent format, in which the first line aligns on the left and the subsequent lines indent one-half inch or five to seven spaces. This is the customary APA format for final copy, including student papers.

## Directory to APA style for references

### Books



### Periodicals



### Electronic Sources



### Other Sources (Including Online Versions)

## 1 Books

The basic format for a reference-list entry for a book is outlined on pp. 358–59.

### 1. ONE AUTHOR

Lightman, A. P. (2002). *The diagnosis*. New York, NY: Vintage Books.

### 2. TWO OR MORE AUTHORS

Walsh, M. E., & Murphy, J. A. (2003). *Children, health, and learning: A guide to the issues*. Westport, CT: Praeger.

### 3. CORPORATE OR GROUP AUTHOR

Committee on Abrupt Climate Change, National Research Council. (2002). *Abrupt climate change: Inevitable surprises*. Washington, DC: National Academies Press.

Use the word *Author* as the publisher when the organization is both the author and the publisher.

Resources for Rehabilitation. (2003). *A woman's guide to coping with disability*. London, England: Author.

### 4. UNKNOWN AUTHOR

*National Geographic atlas of the Middle East*. (2003). Washington, DC: National Geographic Society.

### 5. EDITOR

Dickens, J. (Ed.). (1995). *Family outing: A guide for parents of gays, lesbians, and bisexuals*. London, England: Peter Owen.

### 6. SELECTION IN A BOOK WITH AN EDITOR

Burke, W. W., & Nourmair, D. A. (2001). The role of personality assessment in organization development. In J. Waclawski & A. H. Church (Eds.), *Organization development: A data-driven approach to organizational change* (pp. 55–77). San Francisco, CA: Jossey-Bass.

### 7. TRANSLATION

Al-Farabi, A. N. (1998). *On the perfect state* (R. Walzer, Trans.). Chicago, IL: Kazi.

8. EDITION OTHER THAN THE FIRST

Moore, G. S. (2002). *Living with the earth: Concepts in environmental health science* (2nd ed.). New York, NY: Lewis.

9. MULTIVOLUME WORK

Barnes, J. (Ed.). (1995). *Complete works of Aristotle* (Vols. 1–2). Princeton, NJ: Princeton University Press.

10. ARTICLE IN A REFERENCE WORK If no author is listed, begin with the title.

Dean, C. (1994). Jaws and teeth. In *The Cambridge encyclopedia of human evolution* (pp. 56–59). Cambridge, England: Cambridge University Press.

11. REPUBLICATION

Piaget, J. (1952). *The language and thought of the child*. London, England: Routledge & Kegan Paul. (Original work published 1932)

12. TWO OR MORE WORKS BY THE SAME AUTHOR(S) List two or more works by the same author in chronological order (if the works appear in a single year, see model 21). Repeat the author's name in each entry.

Goodall, J. (1999). *Reason for hope: A spiritual journey*. New York, NY: Warner Books.

Goodall, J. (2002). *Performance and evolution in the age of Darwin: Out of the natural order*. New York, NY: Routledge.

## 2 Periodicals

The basic format for a reference-list entry for an article in a periodical is outlined on pp. 362–63.

13. ARTICLE IN A JOURNAL PAGINATED BY VOLUME

O'Connell, D. C., & Kowal, S. (2003). Psycholinguistics: A half century of monologism. *The American Journal of Psychology, 116,* 191–212.

14. ARTICLE IN A JOURNAL PAGINATED BY ISSUE

Hall, R. E. (2000). Marriage as vehicle of racism among women of color. *Psychology: A Journal of Human Behavior, 37*(2), 29–40.

## SOURCE MAP: Citing books using APA style

Take information from the book's title page and copyright page (on the reverse side of the title page), not from the book's cover or a library catalog.

① *Author*. List all authors' last names first, and use only initials for first and middle names. Separate the names of multiple authors with commas, and use an ampersand (&) before the last author's name.

② *Publication year*. Enclose the year of publication in parentheses.

③ *Title*. Italicize the title and subtitle. Capitalize only the first word of the title and the subtitle and any proper nouns or proper adjectives.

④ *City of publication*. List the city and state (or country) of publication followed by a colon.

⑤ *Publisher*. Give the publisher's name, dropping any *Inc.*, *Co.*, or *Publishers*.

**For a book by one author, use the following format:**

Last name, initial(s). (Year). *Title of book: Subtitle*. City, ST: Publisher.

**A citation for the book on p. 359 would look like this:**

For more on using APA style to cite books, see 19d1. (For guidelines and models for using MLA style, see 18d1; for *Chicago* style, see 20c1; for CSE style, see 21c1.)

2
2004
GODZILLA ON MY MIND
Copyright © William Tsutsui, 2004.
All rights reserved. No part of this book may be used or reproduced in any manner whatsoever without written permission except in the case of brief quotations embodied in critical articles or reviews.
First published 2004 by
PALGRAVE MACMILLAN™
175 Fifth Avenue, New York, N.Y. 10010 and
Houndmills, Basingstoke, Hampshire, England RG21 6XS.
Companies and representatives throughout the world.
4
New York, N.Y.
3
GODZILLA® ON MY MIND
Fifty Years of the King of Monsters
1
WILLIAM TSUTSUI
5
palgrave macmillan

15. ARTICLE IN A MAGAZINE

Ricciardi, S. (2003, August 5). Enabling the mobile work force. *PC Magazine, 22,* 46.

16. ARTICLE IN A NEWSPAPER

Faler, B. (2003, August 29). Primary colors: Race and fundraising. *The Washington Post*, p. A5.

17. EDITORIAL OR LETTER TO THE EDITOR

Zelneck, B. (2003, July 18). Serving the public at public universities [Letter to the editor]. *The Chronicle Review*, p. B18.

18. UNSIGNED ARTICLE

Annual meeting announcement. (2003, March). *Cognitive Psychology*, *46*, 227.

19. REVIEW

Ringel, S. (2003). [Review of the book *Multiculturalism and the therapeutic process*]. *Clinical Social Work Journal, 31*, 212–213.

20. PUBLISHED INTERVIEW

Smith, H. (2002, October). [Interview with A. Thompson]. *The Sun*, pp. 4–7.

21. TWO OR MORE WORKS BY THE SAME AUTHOR IN THE SAME YEAR

List the works alphabetically by title, and place lowercase letters (*a*, *b*, etc.) after the dates.

Shermer, M. (2002a). On estimating the lifetime of civilizations. *Scientific American*, *287*(2), 33.

Shermer, M. (2002b). Readers who question evolution. *Scientific American*, *287*(1), 37.

## 3 Electronic sources

The *APA Style Guide to Electronic References* (2007) includes guidelines for citing various kinds of electronic resources. Updated guidelines are maintained at the APA's Web site (www.apa.org).

The basic entry for most sources accessed via the Internet should include the following elements:

- *Author*. Give the author's name, if available.

- *Publication date.* Include the date of electronic publication or of the latest update, if available. Use *n.d.* ("no date") when the publication date is unavailable.
- *Title.* List the title of the document or subject line of the message, neither italicized nor in quotation marks.
- *Publication information.* For articles from online journals, newspapers, or reference databases, give the publication title and other publishing information as you would for a print periodical.
- *Retrieval information.* For a work from a database, do the following: If the article has a DOI (digital object identifier), include that number after publication information; do not include the name of the database. If there is no DOI, write *Retrieved from* followed by the URL for the journal's home page (not the database URL). For a work found on a Web site, write *Retrieved from* and include the URL.

22. ARTICLE FROM AN ONLINE PERIODICAL Give the author, date, title, and publication information as you would for a print document. Include both the volume and issue numbers for all journal articles. If the article has a DOI, include it. If there is no DOI, include the URL for the periodical's home page or for the article (if the article is difficult to find from the home page). For newspaper articles accessible from a searchable Web site, give the site URL only.

Barringer, F. (2008, February 7). In many communities, it's not easy going green. *The New York Times.* Retrieved from http://www.nytimes.com

Cleary, J. M., & Crafti, N. (2007). Basic need satisfaction, emotional eating, and dietary restraint as risk factors for recurrent overeating in a community sample. *E-Journal of Applied Psychology 2*(3), 27–39. Retrieved from http://ojs.lib.swin.edu.au/index.php/ejap/article/view/90/116

23. ARTICLE OR ABSTRACT FROM A DATABASE (See pp. 366–67 for the basic format for citing an article from a database.) Give the author, date, title, and publication information as you would for a print document. Include both the volume and issue numbers for journal articles. If the article has a DOI, include it. If there is no DOI, write *Retrieved from* and the URL of the journal's home page (not the URL of the database).

## SOURCE MAP: Citing articles from periodicals using APA style

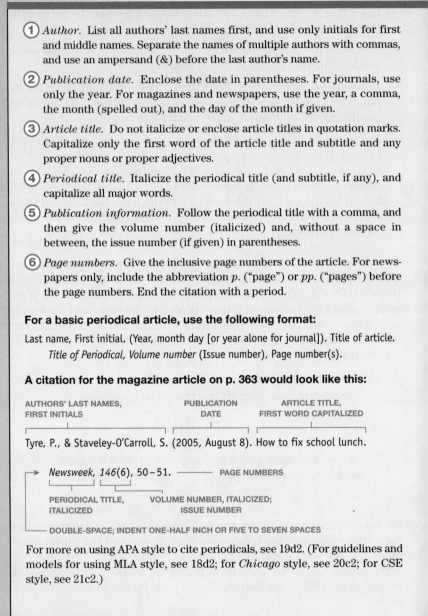

① *Author.* List all authors' last names first, and use only initials for first and middle names. Separate the names of multiple authors with commas, and use an ampersand (&) before the last author's name.

② *Publication date.* Enclose the date in parentheses. For journals, use only the year. For magazines and newspapers, use the year, a comma, the month (spelled out), and the day of the month if given.

③ *Article title.* Do not italicize or enclose article titles in quotation marks. Capitalize only the first word of the article title and subtitle and any proper nouns or proper adjectives.

④ *Periodical title.* Italicize the periodical title (and subtitle, if any), and capitalize all major words.

⑤ *Publication information.* Follow the periodical title with a comma, and then give the volume number (italicized) and, without a space in between, the issue number (if given) in parentheses.

⑥ *Page numbers.* Give the inclusive page numbers of the article. For newspapers only, include the abbreviation *p.* ("page") or *pp.* ("pages") before the page numbers. End the citation with a period.

**For a basic periodical article, use the following format:**

Last name, First initial. (Year, month day [or year alone for journal]). Title of article.
*Title of Periodical, Volume number* (Issue number), Page number(s).

**A citation for the magazine article on p. 363 would look like this:**

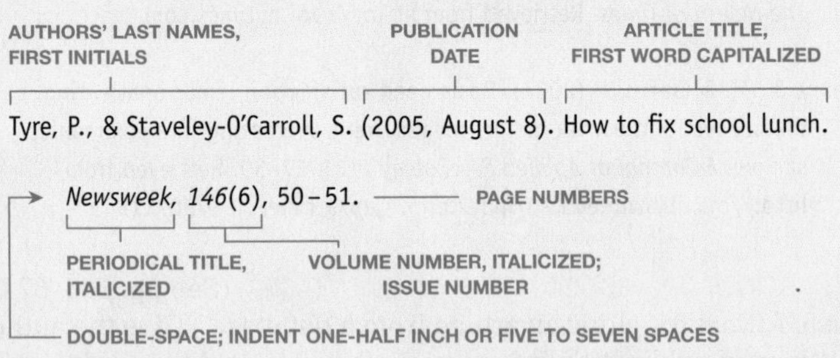


For more on using APA style to cite periodicals, see 19d2. (For guidelines and models for using MLA style, see 18d2; for *Chicago* style, see 20c2; for CSE style, see 21c2.)

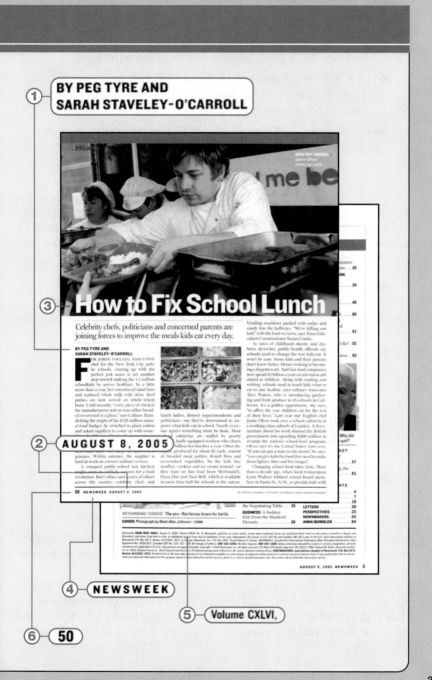

① BY PEG TYRE AND SARAH STAVELEY-O'CARROLL

HEALTHY CHOICE: Jamie Oliver serves up lunch

③ How to Fix School Lunch

Celebrity chefs, politicians and concerned parents are joining forces to improve the meals kids eat every day.

BY PEG TYRE AND SARAH STAVELEY-O'CARROLL

FOR JORGE COLLAZO, EXECUTIVE chef for the New York City public schools, coming up with the perfect jerk sauce is yet another step toward making the 1.1 million schoolkids he serves healthier. In a little more than a year, he's introduced salad bars and replaced whole milk with skim. Beef patties are now served on whole-wheat buns. Until recently, "every piece of chicken the manufacturers sent us was either breaded or covered in a glaze," says Collazo. Brandishing the might of his $125 million annual food budget, he switched to plain cutlets and asked suppliers to come up with some- [illegible] grimace. Within minutes, the supplier is hard at work on a lower-sodium version.

A cramped public-school test kitchen might seem an unlikely outpost for a food revolution. But Collazo and scores of others across the country—celebrity chefs and lunch ladies, district superintendents and politicians—say they're determined to improve what kids eat in school. Nearly everyone agrees something must be done. Most school cafeterias are staffed by poorly [illegible], badly equipped workers who churn [illegible] billion hot lunches a year. Often the meals, produced for about $1 each, consist of breaded meat patties, french fries and overcooked vegetables. So the kids buy muffins, cookies and ice cream instead—or they feast on fast food from McDonald's, Pizza Hut and Taco Bell, which is available in more than half the schools in the nation. Vending machines packed with sodas and candy line the hallways. "We're killing our kids" with the food we serve, says Texas Education Commissioner Susan Combs.

As rates of childhood obesity and diabetes skyrocket, public-health officials say schools need to change the way kids eat. It won't be easy. Some kids and their parents don't know better. Home cooking is becoming a forgotten art. And fast-food companies now spend $3 billion a year on television ads aimed at children. Along with reading and writing, schools need to teach kids what to eat to stay healthy, says culinary innovator Alice Waters, who is introducing gardening and fresh produce to 16 schools in California. It's a golden opportunity, she says, "to affect the way children eat for the rest of their lives." Last year star English chef Jamie Oliver took over a school cafeteria in a working-class suburb of London. A documentary about his work shamed the British government into spending $500 million to revamp the nation's school-food program. Oliver says it's the United States' turn now. "If you can put a man on the moon," he says, "you can give kids the food they need to make them lighter, fitter and live longer."

Changing school food takes time. More than a decade ago, when local restaurateur Lynn Walters lobbied school-board members in Santa Fe, N.M., to provide kids with

② AUGUST 8, 2005



RETHINKING CHOICE: The pro-*Roe* forces brace for battle

COVER: Photograph by Mark Allen Johnson—ZUMA





④ NEWSWEEK

⑤ Volume CXLVI,

⑥ 50

Crook, S. (2003). Change, uncertainty and the future of sociology. *Journal of Sociology, 39*(1), 7 – 14. Retrieved from http://jos.sagepub.com

McCall, R. B. (1998). Science and the press: Like oil and water? *American Psychologist, 43*(2), 87 – 94. Abstract retrieved from http://www.apa.org /journals/amp/

Morley, N.J., Ball, L.J., & Ormerod, T.C. (2006). How the detection of insurance fraud succeeds and fails. *Psychology, Crime, & Law, 12*(2), 163–180. doi: 10.1080/10683160512331316325

24. DOCUMENT FROM A WEB SITE (See pp. 368–69 for the basic format for citing a work from a Web site.) Include information as you would for a print document, followed by information about its retrieval. If no author is identified, give the title of the document followed by the date (if available).

Hacker, J. S. (2006). The privatization of risk and the growing economic insecurity of Americans. *Items and Issues, 5*(4), 16–23. Retrieved from http://publications.ssrc.org/items/items5.4/Hacker.pdf

What parents should know about treatment of behavioral and emotional disorders in preschool children. (2006). *APA Online*. Retrieved from http://www.apa .org/releases/kidsmed.html

25. CHAPTER OR SECTION OF A WEB DOCUMENT After the chapter or section title, type *In* and give the document title, with identifying information, if any, in parentheses. End with the date of access and the URL.

Salamon, Andrew. (n.d.). War in Europe. In *Childhood in times of war* (chap. 2). Retrieved April 11, 2005, from http://remember.org/jean

26. EMAIL MESSAGE OR REAL-TIME COMMUNICATION Do not include entries for email messages or real-time communications (such as IMs) in the list of references; instead, cite these sources in your text as forms of personal communication (see in-text model 12 on p. 352).

27. ONLINE POSTING List an online posting in the references list only if the message is retrievable from a mailing list's archive. Give the author's name and the posting's date and subject line. Include the

description *[Electronic mailing list message]* in square brackets. End with the words *Retrieved from* and the URL of the archived message.

Troike, R. C. (2001, June 21). Buttercups and primroses [Electronic mailing list message]. Retrieved from http://listserv.linguistlist.org/archives/ads-l.html

For a newsgroup posting, use the label *[Online forum comment]*.

Wittenberg, E. (2001, July 11). Gender and the Internet [Online forum comment]. Retrieved from news://comp.edu.composition

28. SOFTWARE OR COMPUTER PROGRAM

PsychMate [Computer software]. (2003). Available from Psychology Software Tools: http://pstnet.com/products/psychmate

## 4 Other sources (including online versions)

29. GOVERNMENT PUBLICATION

Office of the Federal Register. (2003). *The United States government manual 2003/2004*. Washington, DC: U.S. Government Printing Office.

For an online government document, add the date of access and the URL.

U.S. Public Health Service. (1999). *The surgeon general's call to action to prevent suicide*. Retrieved November 5, 2003, from http://www.mentalhealth.org/suicideprevention/calltoaction.asp

30. DISSERTATION ABSTRACT If you retrieve a dissertation from a database, give the database name and the accession number, if one is assigned.

Bandeji, N. (2003). Embedded economies: Foreign direct investment in Central and Eastern Europe. Retrieved from ProQuest Digital Dissertations. (6900033)

31. UNPUBLISHED DISSERTATION If you retrieve a dissertation from a Web site, give the type of dissertation, the institution, and year, and provide a retrieval statement.

Meeks, M. G. (2006). *Between abolition and reform: First-year writing programs, e-literacies, and institutional change* (Doctoral dissertation, University of North Carolina). Retrieved from http://dc.lib.unc.edu/etd

## SOURCE MAP: Citing articles from databases using APA style

Libraries pay for services—such as InfoTrac, EBSCOhost, ProQuest, and LexisNexis—that provide access to large databases of electronic articles.

1. *Author.* If available, include the author's name as you would for a print source. List all authors' last names first, and use only initials for first and middle names. Separate the names of multiple authors with commas, and use an ampersand (&) before the last author's name.
2. *Publication date.* Enclose the date in parentheses. For journals, use only the year. For magazines and newspapers, use the year, a comma, the month (spelled out), and the day of the month if given.
3. *Article title.* Do not italicize or enclose article titles in quotation marks. Capitalize only the first word of the article title and the subtitle and any proper nouns or proper adjectives.
4. *Periodical title.* Italicize the periodical title (and subtitle, if any), and capitalize all major words.
5. *Publication information.* Follow the periodical title with a comma, and then give the volume number (italicized) and, without a space in between, the issue number (if given) in parentheses.
6. *Page numbers.* Give inclusive page numbers of the article. For newspapers, include abbreviation *p.* ("page") or *pp.* ("pages") before the page numbers.
7. *Retrieval information.* If the article has a DOI, include it after publication information; do not include the database name. If there is no DOI, write *Retrieved from* followed by the URL of the home page of the journal (not the database URL).

**For a journal article retrieved from a database, use the following format:**

Last name, First initial. (Year). Title of article. *Title of Journal, Volume number*(Issue number), Page number(s). DOI or Retrieved from Database name (Document number, if available).

**A citation for the article on p. 367 would look like this:**

AUTHORS' LAST NAMES, INITIALS

YEAR OF PUBLICATION

ARTICLE TITLE AND SUBTITLE, FIRST WORD OF EACH CAPITALIZED

VOLUME NUMBER, ITALICIZED, AND ISSUE NUMBER, IF GIVEN

Chory-Assad, R. M., & Tamborini, R. (2004). Television sitcom exposure and aggressive communication: A priming perspective. *North American Journal of Psychology, 6*(3), 415–422. Retrieved from http://najp.8m.com/

PERIODICAL TITLE, ITALICIZED

PAGE NUMBERS

PERIODICAL HOME PAGE

DOUBLE-SPACE; INDENT ONE-HALF INCH OR FIVE SPACES

For more on using APA style to cite articles retrieved from databases, see 19d3. (For guidelines and models for using MLA style, see 18d3; for *Chicago* style, see 20c3; for CSE style, see

## SOURCE MAP: Citing works from Web sites using APA style

① *Author.* If available, include the author's name as you would for a print source. List all authors' last names first, and use only initials for first and middle names. Separate the names of multiple authors with commas, and use an ampersand (&) before the last author's name. In some cases, the site's host or sponsoring organization may be the author. If no author is identified, begin the citation with the title of the document or Web site.

② *Publication date.* Include the date of Internet publication or latest update, if available. Use *n.d.* ("no date") when the publication date is unavailable.

③ *Title.* Do not italicize or enclose document titles in quotation marks. Capitalize only the first word of the title and subtitle and any proper nouns or proper adjectives.

④ *Retrieval information.* Write *Retrieved from* and include the URL. If the work seems likely to be updated or has no date of publication, include the retrieval date.

**For a document found on a Web site with one author, use the following format:**

Last name, First initial. (Internet publication date). Title of document. Retrieved from URL

**A citation for the Web document on p. 369 would look like this:**

For more on using APA style to cite works from Web sites, see 19d3. (For guidelines and models for using MLA style, see 18d3; for *Chicago* style, see 20c3; for CSE style, see 21c3.)

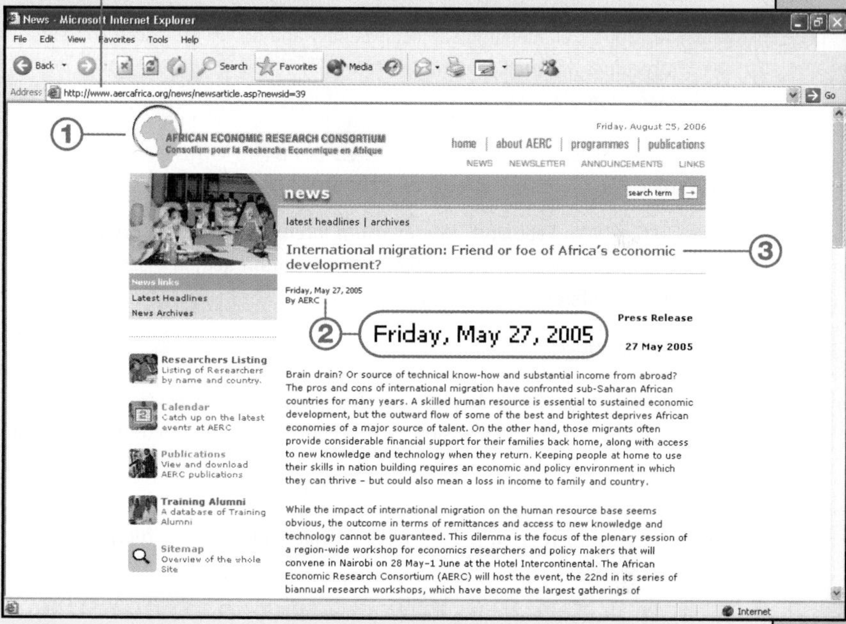

④ http://www.aercafrica.org/news/newsarticle.asp?newsid=39
News - Microsoft Internet Explorer
File Edit View Favorites Tools Help
Address http://www.aercafrica.org/news/newsarticle.asp?newsid=39
①
AFRICAN ECONOMIC RESEARCH CONSORTIUM
Consortium pour la Recherche Economique en Afrique
Friday, August 25, 2006
home | about AERC | programmes | publications
NEWS NEWSLETTER ANNOUNCEMENTS LINKS
news
latest headlines | archives
International migration: Friend or foe of Africa's economic development?
③
Friday, May 27, 2005
By AERC
② Friday, May 27, 2005
Press Release
27 May 2005
News links
Latest Headlines
News Archives
Researchers Listing
Listing of Researchers by name and country.
Calendar
Catch up on the latest events at AERC
Publications
View and download AERC publications
Training Alumni
A database of Training Alumni
Sitemap
Overview of the whole Site
Brain drain? Or source of technical know-how and substantial income from abroad? The pros and cons of international migration have confronted sub-Saharan African countries for many years. A skilled human resource is essential to sustained economic development, but the outward flow of some of the best and brightest deprives African economies of a major source of talent. On the other hand, those migrants often provide considerable financial support for their families back home, along with access to new knowledge and technology when they return. Keeping people at home to use their skills in nation building requires an economic and policy environment in which they can thrive – but could also mean a loss in income to family and country.
While the impact of international migration on the human resource base seems obvious, the outcome in terms of remittances and access to new knowledge and technology cannot be guaranteed. This dilemma is the focus of the plenary session of a region-wide workshop for economics researchers and policy makers that will convene in Nairobi on 28 May–1 June at the Hotel Intercontinental. The African Economic Research Consortium (AERC) will host the event, the 22nd in its series of biannual research workshops, which have become the largest gatherings of
Internet

32. TECHNICAL OR RESEARCH REPORT Give the report number, if available, in parentheses after the title.

McCool, R., Fikes, R., & McGuinness, D. (2003). *Semantic web tools for enhanced authoring* (Report No. KSL-03-07). Stanford, CA: Knowledge Systems Laboratory.

33. CONFERENCE PROCEEDINGS

Mama, A. (2001). Challenging subjects: Gender and power in African contexts. In *Proceedings of Nordic African Institute Conference: Rethinking power in Africa*. Uppsala, Sweden, 9–18.

34. PAPER PRESENTED AT A MEETING OR SYMPOSIUM, UNPUBLISHED Cite the month of the meeting if it is available.

Jones, J. G. (1999, February). *Mental health intervention in mass casualty disasters*. Paper presented at the Rocky Mountain Region Disaster Mental Health Conference, Laramie, WY.

35. POSTER SESSION

Barnes, Young, L. L. (2003, August). *Cognition, aging, and dementia*. Poster session presented at the 2003 Division 40 APA Convention, Toronto, Ontario, Canada.

36. FILM, VIDEO, OR DVD

Moore, M. (Director). (2003). *Bowling for Columbine* [Motion picture]. United States: MGM.

37. TELEVISION PROGRAM, SINGLE EPISODE

Imperioli, M. (Writer), & Buscemi, S. (Director). (2002). Everybody hurts [Television series episode]. In D. Chase (Executive Producer), *The Sopranos*. New York, NY: HBO.

38. PODCAST

O'Brien, K. (Writer). (2008, January 31). Developing countries. *KUSP's life in the fast lane* [Audio podcast]. Retrieved from http://www.kusp.org/shows/fast.html

## 19e A student research-based essay, APA style

On the following pages is a paper by Merlla McLaughlin that conforms to the APA guidelines described in this chapter. Note that this essay has been reproduced in a narrow format to allow for annotation.

**bedfordstmartins.com/smhandbook** For additional student research writing, click on **Student Writing**.

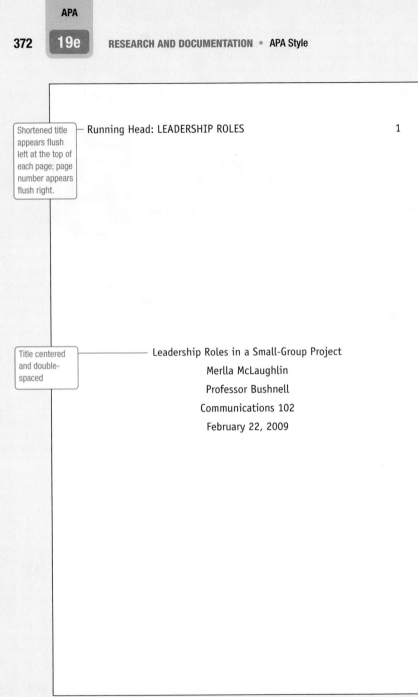

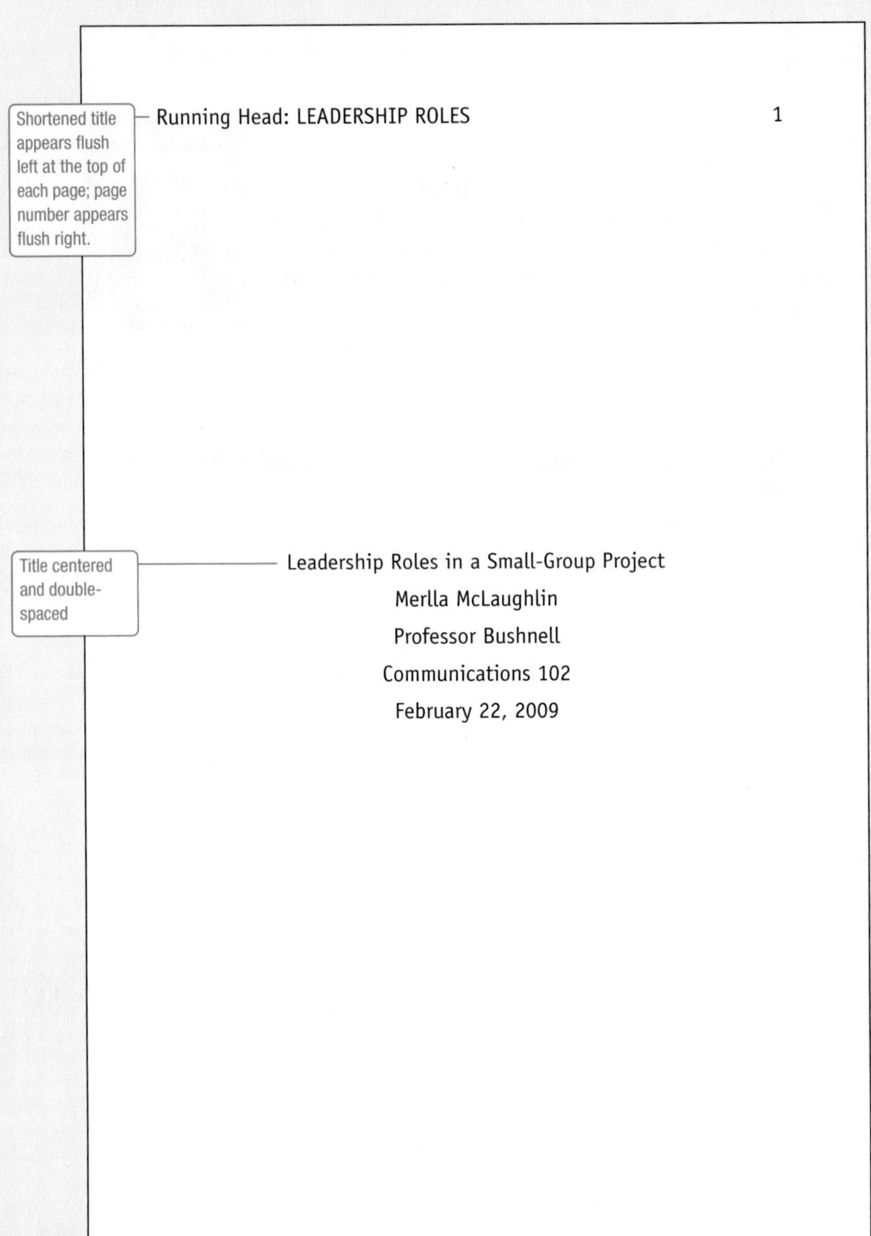
Shortened title appears flush left at the top of each page; page number appears flush right.
Running Head: LEADERSHIP ROLES
1
Title centered and double-spaced
Leadership Roles in a Small-Group Project
Merlla McLaughlin
Professor Bushnell
Communications 102
February 22, 2009

LEADERSHIP ROLES 2

Abstract

Using the interpersonal communications research of J. K. Brilhart and G. J. Galanes as well as that of W. Wilmot and J. Hocker, along with T. Hartman's Personality Assessment, I observed and analyzed the leadership roles and group dynamics of my project collaborators in a communications course. Based on results of the Hartman Personality Assessment, I predicted that a single leader would emerge. However, complementary individual strengths and gender differences encouraged a distributed leadership style, in which the group experienced little confrontation. Conflict, because it was handled positively, was crucial to the group's progress.

Heading centered

No indentation

Study described

Key points of report discussed

Double spacing throughout

Full title, centered

Paragraphs indented

Questions indicate the focus of the essay

Headings help organize the report

APA-style parenthetical reference

Background information about team members' personality types

First observations about leadership roles

Quotation defines key term for this study

LEADERSHIP ROLES 3

Leadership Roles in a Small-Group Project

Although classroom lectures provide students with volumes of information, many experiences can be understood only by living them. So it is with the workings of a small, task-focused group. What observations can I make after working with a group of peers on a class project? And what have I learned as a result?

**Leadership Expectations and Emergence**

The six members of this group were selected by the instructor; half were male and half were female. By performing the Hartman Personality Assessment (Hartman, 1998) in class, we learned that Hartman has associated key personality traits with the colors red, blue, white, and yellow (see Table 1). The assessment identified most of us as "Blues," concerned with intimacy and caring. Because of the bold qualities associated with "Reds," I expected that Nate, our only "Red" member, might become our leader. (Kaari, the only "White," seemed poised to become the peacekeeper.) However, after Nate missed the first two meetings, it seemed that Pat, who contributed often during our first three meetings, might emerge as leader. Pat has strong communications skills, a commanding presence, and displays sensitivity to others. I was surprised, then, when our group developed a *distributed style* of leadership (Brilhart & Galanes, 1998). The longer we worked together, however, the more I was convinced that this approach to leadership was best for our group.

As Brilhart and Galanes have noted, "distributed leadership explicitly acknowledges that the leadership of a group is spread among members, with each member expected to move the group toward its goal" (p. 175). These researchers divide positive

LEADERSHIP ROLES 4

Table 1

*Hartman's Key Personality Traits*

| Trait category | Color: Red | Blue | White | Yellow |
|---|---|---|---|---|
| Motive | Power | Intimacy | Peace | Fun |
| Strengths | Loyal to tasks | Loyal to people | Tolerant | Positive |
| Limitations | Arrogant | Self-righteous | Timid | Uncommitted |

*Note*. Table is adapted from information found at The Hartman Personality Profile, by N. Hayden. Retrieved from http://students.cs.byu.edu/~nhayden/Code/index.php

Table displays information concisely and is referred to in preceding text

Source of table listed

communicative actions into two types: *task functions* that affect a group's productivity and *maintenance functions* that influence the interactions of group members. One of our group's most immediate task-function needs was decision-making, and as we made our first major decision — what topic to pursue — our group's distributed-leadership style began to emerge.

Minimum of one-inch margin on all sides

**Decision-Making Methods**

Our choice of topic — the parking services at Oregon State University (OSU) — was the result not of a majority vote but of negotiated consensus. During this decision-making meeting, several of us argued that a presentation on parking services at OSU would interest most students, and after considerable discussion, the other group members agreed. Once we had a topic, other decisions came naturally.

Discussion of the group's decision-making supports claim of distributed-leadership style

**Roles Played**

Thanks in part to the distributed leadership that our group developed, the strengths of individual group members became

Another example of distributed-leadership style

increasingly apparent. Although early in our project Pat was the key initiator and Nate was largely an information seeker, all group members eventually took on these functions in addition to serving as recorders, gathering information, and working on our questionnaire. Every member coordinated the group's work at some point; several made sure that everyone could speak and be heard, and one member was especially good at catching important details the rest of us were apt to miss. Joe, McKenzie, Kaari, and I frequently clarified or elaborated on information, whereas Pat, Kaari, and Nate were good at contributing ideas during brainstorming sessions. Nate, Joe, and McKenzie brought tension-relieving humor to the group.

Transition to gender influences

Just as each member brought individual strengths to the group, gender differences also made us effective. For example, the women took a holistic approach to the project, looking at the big picture and making intuitive leaps in ways that the men generally did not. The men preferred a more systematic process. Brilhart and Galanes have suggested that men working in groups dominated by women may display "subtle forms of resistance to a dominant presence of women" (p. 98). Although the men in our group did not attend all the meetings and the women did, I did not find that the men's nonattendance implied male resistance any more than the women's attendance implied female dominance. Rather, our differing qualities complemented each other and enabled us to work together effectively.

**Social Environment**

Writer returns to categories defined earlier

As previously noted, most of our group members were Blues on the Hartman scale, valuing altruism, intimacy, appreciation, and having a moral conscience (Hayden). At least three of the four

LEADERSHIP ROLES 6

Blues had White as their secondary color, signifying the importance of peace, kindness, independence, and sacrifice (Hayden). The presence of these traits may explain why our group experienced little confrontation and conflict. Nate (a Red) was most likely to speak bluntly. The one time that Nate seemed put off, it was not his words but his body language that expressed his discomfort. This was an awkward moment, but a rare one given our group's generally positive handling of conflict.

**Conclusion**

Perhaps most important is the lesson I learned about conflict. Prior to participating in this group, I always avoided conflict because, as Wilmot and Hocker (1998) have suggested, most people think "harmony is normal and conflict is abnormal" (p. 9). Now I recognize that some kinds of conflict are essential for increasing understanding between group members and creating an effective collaborative result. It was essential, for instance, that our group explore different members' ideas about possible topics for our project, and this process inevitably required some conflict. The end result, however, was a positive one.

In her concluding section, writer clearly answers question posed in the introduction

Constructive conflict requires an open and engaging attitude among group members, encourages personal growth, and ends when the issue at hand is resolved. Most important for our group, such conflict encouraged cooperation (pp. 47–48) and increased the group's cohesiveness. All the members of our group felt, for instance, that their ideas about possible topics were seriously considered. Once we decided on a topic, everyone fully committed to it. Thus our group effectiveness was enhanced by constructive conflict.

LEADERSHIP ROLES 7

Conclusion looks toward future

As a result of this project, I have a better sense of when conflict is — and isn't — productive. My group used conflict productively when we hashed out our ideas, and we avoided the kind of conflict that creates morale problems and wastes time. Although all groups operate somewhat differently, I now feel more prepared to understand and participate in future small-group projects.

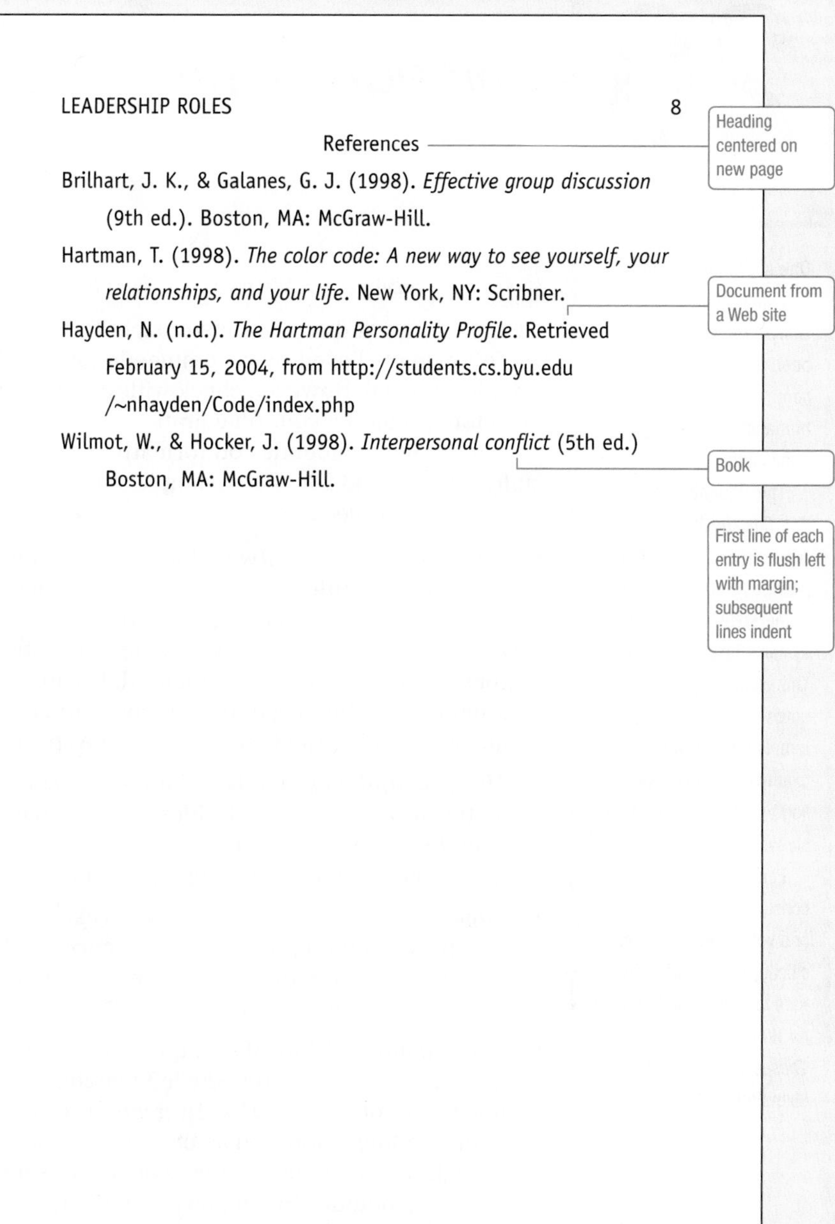
LEADERSHIP ROLES 8

References

Brilhart, J. K., & Galanes, G. J. (1998). *Effective group discussion* (9th ed.). Boston, MA: McGraw-Hill.

Hartman, T. (1998). *The color code: A new way to see yourself, your relationships, and your life*. New York, NY: Scribner.

Hayden, N. (n.d.). *The Hartman Personality Profile*. Retrieved February 15, 2004, from http://students.cs.byu.edu/~nhayden/Code/index.php

Wilmot, W., & Hocker, J. (1998). *Interpersonal conflict* (5th ed.) Boston, MA: McGraw-Hill.

# 20 *Chicago* Style

One of the oldest formal documentation systems, *Chicago* style has long been used in history and some other fields in the humanities, as well as in publishing.

The Fifteenth Edition of *The Chicago Manual of Style*, published in 2003, provides a complete guide to this style, including two systems for citing sources. This chapter presents the notes and bibliography system. For easy reference, examples of notes and bibliographic references are shown together in 20c.

For further reference, consult *The Chicago Manual* or a volume intended specifically for student writers, Kate L. Turabian's *A Manual for Writers of Term Papers, Theses, and Dissertations*, Sixth Edition (1996).

## 20a *Chicago* manuscript format

*Chicago* does not discuss student-paper formats, so the following is based on recommendations in the Turabian manual. However, check with your instructor before preparing your final draft.

For detailed guidelines on formatting a bibliography, see 20b and 20c. For a sample student essay in *Chicago* style, see 20d.

- *Title page.* About halfway down the title page, center the full title of your paper and your name. Unless otherwise instructed, at the bottom of the page also list the course name, the instructor's name, and the date submitted. Do not type a number on this page, but do count it; consequently, number the first page of text as page 2.
- *Margins and spacing.* Leave one-inch margins at the top, bottom, and sides of your pages. Double-space the entire text, including block quotations, notes, and bibliographic entries.
- *Page numbers.* Number all pages (except the title page) in the upper right-hand corner. Also use a short title or your name before page numbers.
- *Long quotations.* Indent long quotations one-half inch (or five spaces) from the left margin, and do not use quotation marks. In general, *Chicago* defines a long quotation as one hundred words or eight lines, though you may decide to set off shorter quotations for emphasis (see 50a).

- *Headings. Chicago* style allows, but does not require, headings. Many students and instructors find them helpful. (See 23c for guidelines on using headings and subheadings.)
- *Visuals.* Visuals (photographs, drawings, charts, graphs, and tables) should be placed as near as possible to the relevant text. Tables should be labeled *Table*, numbered, and captioned. All other visuals should be labeled *Figure* (abbreviated *Fig.*), numbered, and captioned. Remember to refer to each visual in your text, explaining how it contributes to the point(s) you are making.

## 20b In-text citations, notes, and bibliography

In *Chicago* style, use superscript numbers ([1]) to mark citations in the text. Sequentially numbered citations throughout the text correspond to notes that contain either publication information about the source cited or explanatory or supplemental material not included in the main text. Place the superscript material for each note near the cited material — at the end of the relevant quotation, sentence, clause, or phrase. Type the number after any punctuation mark except the dash, and leave no space between the superscript and the preceding letter or punctuation mark. When you use signal phrases to introduce quotations or other source material, note that *Chicago* style requires you to use the present tense (*citing Bebout's studies, Meier points out*).

The notes themselves can be footnotes (each typed at the bottom of the page on which the superscript for it appears in the text) or endnotes (all typed on a separate page at the end of the text under the heading *Notes*). Be sure to check your instructor's preference. The first line of each note is indented like a paragraph (three to five spaces) and begins with a number followed by a period, one space, and the first word. All remaining lines of the entry are typed flush with the left margin. Footnotes and endnotes should be double-spaced.

IN THE TEXT

Sweig argues that Castro and Che Guevara were not the only key players in the Cuban Revolution of the late 1950s.[19]

IN THE FIRST NOTE

19. Julia Sweig, *Inside the Cuban Revolution* (Cambridge, MA: Harvard University Press, 2002), 9.

After giving complete information the first time you cite a work, shorten any additional references to that work: list only the author's last name followed by a comma, a shortened version of the title, a comma, and the page number. If the reference is to the same source cited in the previous note, you can use the Latin abbreviation *Ibid.* (for "in the same place") instead of the name and title.

IN SUBSEQUENT NOTES

19. Julia Sweig, *Inside the Cuban Revolution* (Cambridge, MA: Harvard University Press, 2002), 9.
20. Ibid., 13.
21. Ferguson, "Comfort of Being Sad," 63.
22. Sweig, *Cuban Revolution*, 21.

The alphabetical list of the sources in your paper is usually titled *Bibliography* in *Chicago* style. You may instead use the title *Sources Consulted*, *Works Cited*, or *Selected Bibliography* if it better describes your list.

In the bibliographic entry for a source, include the same information as in the first note for that source, but omit the specific page reference. However, give the *first* author's last name first, followed by a comma and the first name; separate the main elements of the entry with periods rather than commas; and do not enclose the publication information for books in parentheses. Type the first line flush with the left margin, and indent the subsequent lines of each entry three to five spaces.

IN THE BIBLIOGRAPHY

Sweig, Julia. *Inside the Cuban Revolution*. Cambridge, MA: Harvard University Press, 2002.

Start the bibliography on a separate page after the main text and any endnotes. Continue the consecutive numbering of pages. Center the title *Bibliography* (without underlining, italics, or quotation marks) one inch below the top of the page. List sources alphabetically by authors' last names or, if an author is unknown, by the first major word in the title. Double-space the entire list.

## 20c Notes and bibliographic entries

### Directory to *Chicago* style



The following examples demonstrate how to format both notes and bibliographic entries according to *Chicago* style. The note, which is numbered, appears first; the bibliographic entry, which is not numbered, appears below the note.

### 1 Books

For the basic format for citing a book in *Chicago* style, see pp. 386–87. The note for a book typically includes four elements: the author's name, the title and subtitle, the publication information, and the page number(s) to which the note refers. The bibliographic entry for a book usually includes the first three of these elements, but they are styled somewhat differently.

1. ONE AUTHOR

1. James S. Hirsch, *Riot and Remembrance: The Tulsa Race War and Its Legacy* (Boston: Houghton Mifflin, 2002), 119.

Hirsch, James S. *Riot and Remembrance: The Tulsa Race War and Its Legacy*. Boston: Houghton Mifflin, 2002.

2. MULTIPLE AUTHORS

2. Margaret Macmillan and Richard Holbrooke, *Paris 1919: Six Months That Changed the World* (New York: Random House, 2003), 384.

Macmillan, Margaret, and Richard Holbrooke. *Paris 1919: Six Months That Changed the World*. New York: Random House, 2003.

When there are more than three authors, you may give the first-listed author followed by *et al.* or *and others* in the note. In the bibliography, however, list all the authors' names.

2. Stephen J. Blank and others, *Conflict, Culture, and History: Regional Dimensions* (Miami: University Press of the Pacific, 2002), 276.

Blank, Stephen J., Lawrence E. Grinter, Karl P. Magyar, Lewis B. Ware, and Bynum E. Weathers. *Conflict, Culture, and History: Regional Dimensions*. Miami: University Press of the Pacific, 2002.

3. ORGANIZATION AS AUTHOR

3. World Intellectual Property Organization, *Intellectual Property Profile of the Least Developed Countries* (Geneva: World Intellectual Property Organization, 2002), 43.

World Intellectual Property Organization. *Intellectual Property Profile of the Least Developed Countries*. Geneva: World Intellectual Property Organization, 2002.

4. UNKNOWN AUTHOR

4. *Broad Stripes and Bright Stars* (Kansas City, MO: Andrews McMeel, 2002), 10.

*Broad Stripes and Bright Stars*. Kansas City, MO: Andrews McMeel, 2002.

5. EDITOR

5. James H. Fetzer, ed., *The Great Zapruder Film Hoax: Deceit and Deception in the Death of JFK* (Chicago: Open Court, 2003), 56.

Fetzer, James H., ed. *The Great Zapruder Film Hoax: Deceit and Deception in the Death of JFK*. Chicago: Open Court, 2003.

6. SELECTION IN AN ANTHOLOGY OR CHAPTER IN A BOOK, WITH AN EDITOR

6. Denise Little, "Born in Blood," in *Alternate Gettysburgs*, ed. Brian Thomsen and Martin H. Greenberg (New York: Berkley Publishing Group, 2002), 245.

Give the inclusive page numbers of the selection or chapter in the bibliographic entry.

Little, Denise. "Born in Blood." In *Alternate Gettysburgs*, edited by Brian Thomsen and Martin H. Greenberg, 242–55. New York: Berkley Publishing Group, 2002.

7. TRANSLATION

7. Suetonius, *The Twelve Caesars*, trans. Robert Graves (London: Penguin Classics, 1989), 202.

Suetonius. *The Twelve Caesars*. Translated by Robert Graves. London: Penguin Classics, 1989.

8. EDITION OTHER THAN THE FIRST

8. Charles G. Beaudette, *Excess Heat: Why Cold Fusion Research Prevailed*, 2nd ed. (South Bristol, ME: Oak Grove Press, 2002), 313.

Beaudette, Charles G. *Excess Heat: Why Cold Fusion Research Prevailed*. 2nd ed. South Bristol, ME: Oak Grove Press, 2002.

9. MULTIVOLUME WORK

9. John Watson, *Annals of Philadelphia and Pennsylvania in the Olden Time*, vol. 2 (Washington, DC: Ross & Perry, 2003), 514.

Watson, John. *Annals of Philadelphia and Pennsylvania in the Olden Time*. Vol. 2. Washington, DC: Ross & Perry, 2003.

## SOURCE MAP: Citing books using *Chicago* style

Take information from the book's title page and copyright page (on the reverse side of the title page), not from the book's cover or a library catalog.

1. *Author.* In a note, list author first name first. In a bibliographic entry, list the first author last name first, followed by a comma; list other authors first name first.
2. *Title.* Italicize title and subtitle, and capitalize major words. In a note, put a comma before the title. In the bibliography, place a period before and after the title.
3. *City of publication.* List the city (and country or state abbreviation for an unfamiliar city) followed by a colon. In a note only, city, publisher, and year appear in parentheses.
4. *Publisher.* Drop *Inc., Co., Publishing,* or *Publishers.* Follow with a comma.
5. *Publication year.* In a note, end with parentheses, comma, page number, and period. In the bibliography, end with a period.

**For a book by one author, use the following formats:**

*Endnote*

Note number. First name Last name, *Title of Book* (City: Publisher, Year), Page number(s).

*Bibliographic entry*

Last name, First name. *Title of Book*. City: Publisher, Year.

**Citations for the book on p. 387 would look like this:**

*Endnote*

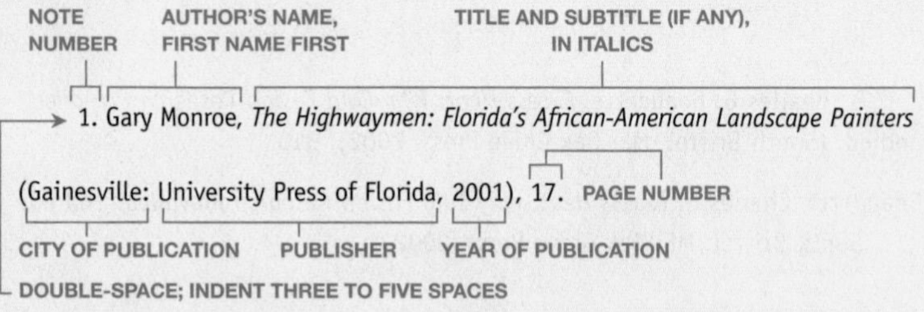


*Bibliographic entry*

Monroe, Gary. *The Highwaymen: Florida's African-American Landscape Painters.*

Gainesville: University Press of Florida, 2001.

For more on using *Chicago* style to cite books, see 20c1. (For guidelines and models for using MLA style, see 18d1; for APA style, see 19d1; for CSE style, see 21c1.)

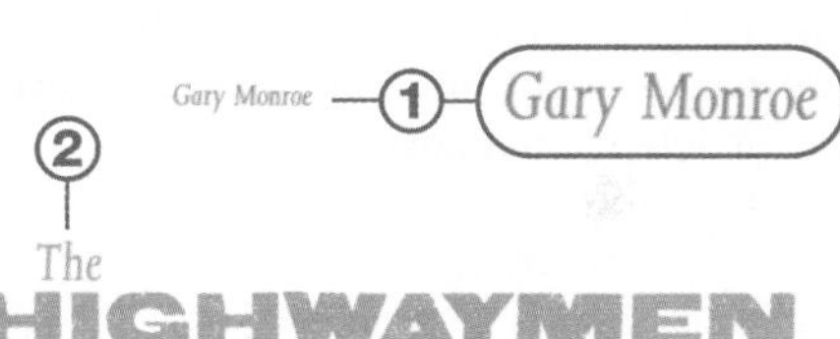


Copyright 2001 by Gary Monroe
Printed in Hong Kong on acid-free paper
All rights reserved

Page i, by Hezekiah Baker; pages ii and iii, diptych by Alfred Hair

06 05 04 03 6 5 4

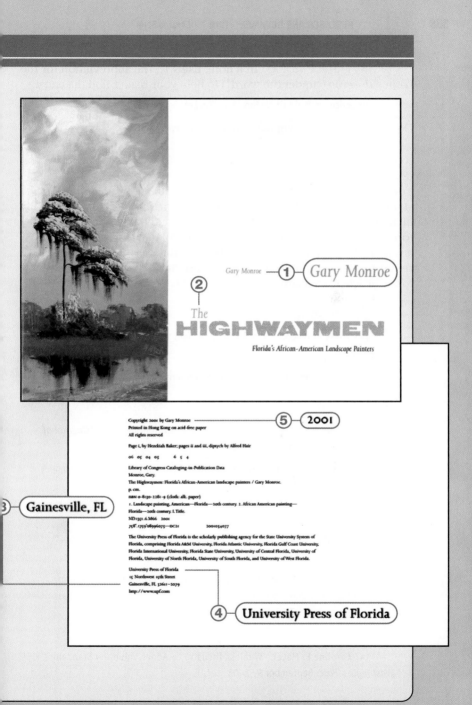

Library of Congress Cataloging-in-Publication Data
Monroe, Gary.
The Highwaymen: Florida's African-American landscape painters / Gary Monroe.
p. cm.
ISBN 0-8130-2281-9 (cloth: alk. paper)
1. Landscape painting, American—Florida—20th century. 2. African American painting—Florida—20th century. I. Title.
ND1351.6.M66 2001
758'.1759'08996073—DC21 2001034077

The University Press of Florida is the scholarly publishing agency for the State University System of Florida, comprising Florida A&M University, Florida Atlantic University, Florida Gulf Coast University, Florida International University, Florida State University, University of Central Florida, University of Florida, University of North Florida, University of South Florida, and University of West Florida.

University Press of Florida
15 Northwest 15th Street
Gainesville, FL 32611–2079
http://www.upf.com

5 2001

3 Gainesville, FL

4 University Press of Florida

10. REFERENCE WORK In a note, use *s.v.*, the abbreviation for the Latin *sub verbo* ("under the word") to help your reader find the entry.

10. *Encarta World Dictionary*, s.v. "carpetbagger."

Do not list reference works in your bibliography.

## 2 Periodicals

For the basic format for citing an article from a periodical in *Chicago* style, see pp. 390–91. The note for an article in a periodical typically includes the author's name, the article title, and the periodical title. The format for other information, including the volume and issue numbers (if any), the date of publication, and the page number(s) to which the note refers, varies according to the type of periodical. In a bibliographic entry for an article from a periodical, also give the inclusive page numbers.

11. ARTICLE IN A JOURNAL PAGINATED BY VOLUME

11. Linda Hutcheon, "She Do the President in Different Voices," *PMLA* 116 (2001): 518.

Hutcheon, Linda. "She Do the President in Different Voices." *PMLA* 116 (2001): 518.

12. ARTICLE IN A JOURNAL PAGINATED BY ISSUE

12. Karin Lützen, "The Female World: Viewed from Denmark," *Journal of Women's History* 12, no. 3 (2000): 36.

Lützen, Karin. "The Female World: Viewed from Denmark." *Journal of Women's History* 12, no. 3 (2000): 34–38.

13. ARTICLE IN A MAGAZINE

13. Douglas Brinkley and Anne Brinkley, "Lawyers and Lizard-Heads," *Atlantic Monthly*, May 2002, 56.

Brinkley, Douglas, and Anne Brinkley. "Lawyers and Lizard-Heads." *Atlantic Monthly*, May 2002, 55–61.

14. ARTICLE IN A NEWSPAPER

14. Caroline E. Mayer, "Wireless Industry to Adopt Voluntary Standards," *Washington Post*, September 9, 2003, sec. E.

Mayer, Caroline E. "Wireless Industry to Adopt Voluntary Standards." *Washington Post*, September 9, 2003, sec. E.

## 3 Electronic sources

15. ARTICLE FROM A DATABASE For the basic format for citing an article from a database in *Chicago* style, see pp. 392–93.

15. Peter DeMarco, "Holocaust Survivors Lend Voice to History," *Boston Globe*, November 2, 2003, http://www.lexisnexis.com (accessed November 19, 2003).

DeMarco, Peter. "Holocaust Survivors Lend Voice to History." *Boston Globe,* November 2, 2003. http://www.lexisnexis.com (accessed November 19, 2003).

16. ONLINE BOOK

16. Janja Bec, *The Shattering of the Soul* (Los Angeles: Simon Wiesenthal Center, 1997), http://motlc.wiesenthal.com/resources/books/shatteringsoul/index.html (accessed November 6, 2005).

Bec, Janja. *The Shattering of the Soul*. Los Angeles: Simon Wiesenthal Center, 1997. http://motlc.wiesenthal.com/resources/books/shatteringsoul/index.html (accessed November 6, 2005).

17. ARTICLE IN AN ELECTRONIC JOURNAL

17. Damian Bracken, "Rationalism and the Bible in Seventh-Century Ireland," *Chronicon* 2 (1998), http://www.ucc.ie/chronicon/bracfra.htm (accessed November 1, 2004).

Bracken, Damian. "Rationalism and the Bible in Seventh-Century Ireland." *Chronicon* 2 (1998). http://www.ucc.ie/chronicon/bracfra.htm (accessed November 1, 2004).

If a scholarly journal has both print and online versions and page numbers are shown online, give the inclusive pages of the article, after the publication date, in the bibliographic reference only: *(May 2006): 432–58.*

18. ARTICLE IN AN ONLINE MAGAZINE

18. Kim Iskyan, "Putin's Next Power Play," *Slate*, November 4, 2003, http://slate.msn.com/id/2090745 (accessed November 7, 2005).

(*continued on p. 396*)

## SOURCE MAP: Citing articles from periodicals using *Chicago* style

1. *Author.* In a note, list author first name first. In a bibliographic entry, list the first author last name first, comma, first name; list other authors' names first name first.
2. *Article title.* Enclose title and subtitle (if any) in quotation marks, and capitalize major words. In the notes section, put a comma before and after the title. In the bibliography, put a period before and after.
3. *Periodical title.* Italicize title and subtitle and capitalize major words. Follow the title with a comma, unless it is a journal.
4. *Journal volume and issue numbers.* For journals only, include the volume number, a comma, the abbreviation *no.*, and the issue number.
5. *Publication date.* For journals, enclose the publication year in parentheses and follow with a colon. For other periodicals, give the month and year or the month, day, and year followed by a comma.
6. *Page numbers.* In the notes section, give the page number. In the bibliography, give inclusive page numbers. For newspapers, write *sec.* and give the section number or letter. End with a period.

**For a magazine article by one author, use the following formats:**

*Endnote*

1. First name Last name, "Title of Article," *Title of Magazine*, month year or month day, year, page number(s).

*Bibliographic entry*

Last name, First name. "Title of Article." *Title of Magazine*, month year or month day, year, page number(s).

**Citations for the magazine article on p. 391 would look like this:**

*Endnote*

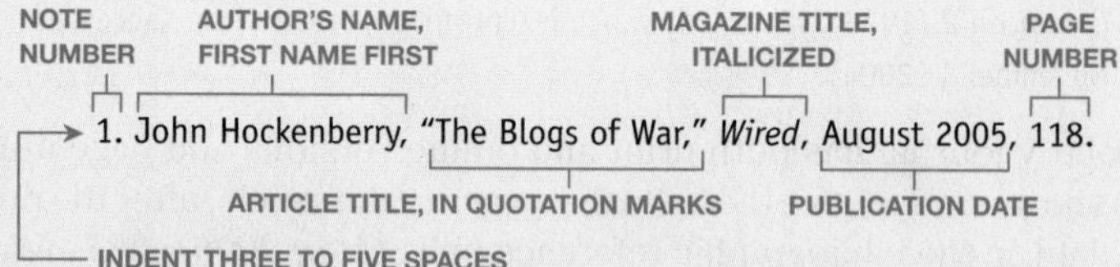


*Bibliographic entry*

Hockenberry, John. "The Blogs of War." *Wired*, August 2005, 118-35.

For more on using *Chicago* style to cite articles from periodicals, see 20c2. (For guidelines and models for using MLA style, see 18d2; for APA style, see 19d2; for CSE style, see 21c2.)

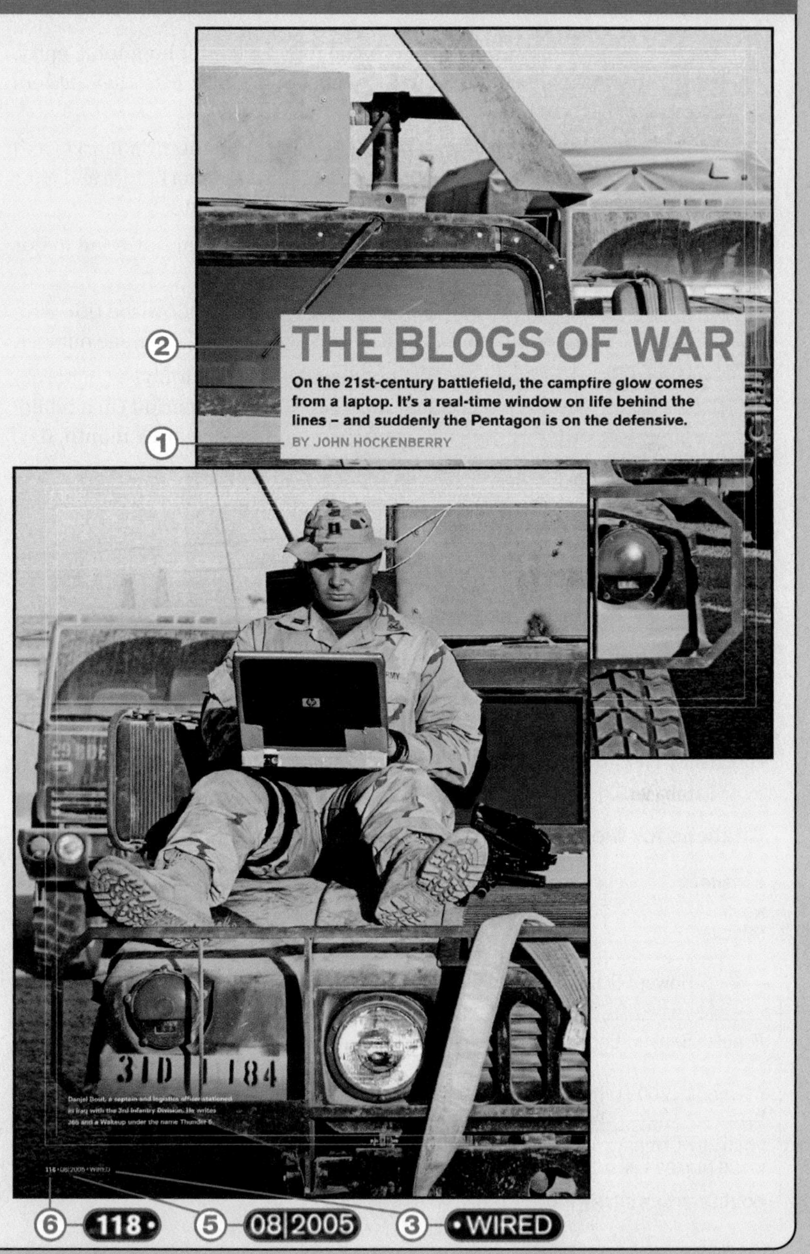

2
THE BLOGS OF WAR
On the 21st-century battlefield, the campfire glow comes from a laptop. It's a real-time window on life behind the lines – and suddenly the Pentagon is on the defensive.
1
BY JOHN HOCKENBERRY
3ID 1 184
Daniel Bout, a captain and logistics officer stationed in Iraq with the 3rd Infantry Division. He writes 365 and a Wakeup under the name Thunder 6.
118 • 08|2005 • WIRED
6
118•
5
08|2005
3
•WIRED

## SOURCE MAP: Citing articles from databases using *Chicago* style

① *Author.* In a note, list author first name first. In the bibliographic entry, list the first author last name first, comma, first name; list other authors first name first.

② *Article title.* Enclose title and subtitle (if any) in quotation marks, and capitalize major words. In the notes section, put a comma before and after the title. In the bibliography, put a period before and after.

③ *Periodical title.* Italicize the title and subtitle, and capitalize all major words. Follow with a comma, unless it is a journal.

④ *Journal volume and issue numbers.* For journals, follow the title with the volume number, a comma, the abbreviation *no.*, and the issue number.

⑤ *Publication date.* For journals, enclose the publication year in parentheses and follow with a comma (in a note) or with a period (in a bibliography). For other periodicals, give the month and year or month, day, and year, followed by a comma.

⑥ *Retrieval information.* Give the brief URL for the database, followed, in parentheses, by the word *accessed* and the access date. End with a period.

**For an article accessed from a database, use the following formats:**

*Endnote*

1. First name Last name, "Title of Article," *Periodical Title* Volume, no. Issue (Year), Database URL (accessed Date).

*Bibliographic entry*

Last name, First name. "Title of Article." *Periodical Title* Volume, no. Issue (Year). Database URL (accessed Date).

**Citations for the article on p. 393 would look like this:**

*Endnote*

NOTE NUMBER — AUTHORS' NAMES — ARTICLE TITLE, IN QUOTATION MARKS

1. Howard Schuman, Barry Schwartz, and Hannah D'Arcy, "Elite Revisionists and Popular Beliefs: Christopher Columbus, Hero or Villain?" *Public Opinion Quarterly* 69, no. 1 (2005), http://elibrary.bigchalk.com (accessed October 15, 2005).

PERIODICAL TITLE, ITALICIZED

VOLUME NUMBER; ISSUE NUMBER (IF GIVEN) — PUBLICATION DATE — DATABASE URL — DATE OF ACCESS

DOUBLE-SPACE ENTRY; INDENT THREE TO FIVE SPACES

*Bibliographic entry*

Schuman, Howard, Barry Schwartz, and Hannah D'Arcy. "Elite Revisionists and Popular Beliefs: Christopher Columbus, Hero or Villain?" *Public Opinion Quarterly* 69, no. 1 (2005). http://elibrary.bigchalk.com (accessed October 15, 2005).

For more on using *Chicago* style to cite articles from databases, see 20c3. (For guidelines and models for using MLA style, see 18d3; for APA style, see 19d3; for CSE style, see 21c3.)

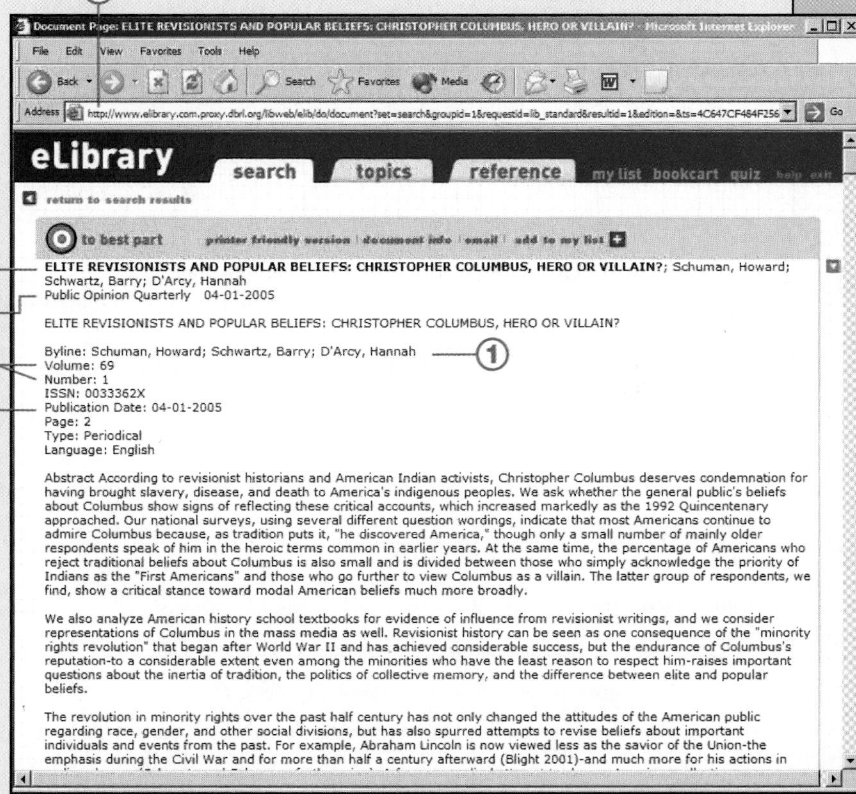

Document Page: ELITE REVISIONISTS AND POPULAR BELIEFS: CHRISTOPHER COLUMBUS, HERO OR VILLAIN? - Microsoft Internet Explorer

File Edit View Favorites Tools Help

Address http://www.elibrary.com.proxy.dbrl.org/libweb/elib/do/document?set=search&groupid=1&requestid=lib_standard&resultid=1&edition=&ts=4C647CF484F256

eLibrary search topics reference my list bookcart quiz

return to search results

to best part printer friendly version | document info | email | add to my list

ELITE REVISIONISTS AND POPULAR BELIEFS: CHRISTOPHER COLUMBUS, HERO OR VILLAIN?; Schuman, Howard; Schwartz, Barry; D'Arcy, Hannah
Public Opinion Quarterly 04-01-2005

ELITE REVISIONISTS AND POPULAR BELIEFS: CHRISTOPHER COLUMBUS, HERO OR VILLAIN?

Byline: Schuman, Howard; Schwartz, Barry; D'Arcy, Hannah
Volume: 69
Number: 1
ISSN: 0033362X
Publication Date: 04-01-2005
Page: 2
Type: Periodical
Language: English

Abstract According to revisionist historians and American Indian activists, Christopher Columbus deserves condemnation for having brought slavery, disease, and death to America's indigenous peoples. We ask whether the general public's beliefs about Columbus show signs of reflecting these critical accounts, which increased markedly as the 1992 Quincentenary approached. Our national surveys, using several different question wordings, indicate that most Americans continue to admire Columbus because, as tradition puts it, "he discovered America," though only a small number of mainly older respondents speak of him in the heroic terms common in earlier years. At the same time, the percentage of Americans who reject traditional beliefs about Columbus is also small and is divided between those who simply acknowledge the priority of Indians as the "First Americans" and those who go further to view Columbus as a villain. The latter group of respondents, we find, show a critical stance toward modal American beliefs much more broadly.

We also analyze American history school textbooks for evidence of influence from revisionist writings, and we consider representations of Columbus in the mass media as well. Revisionist history can be seen as one consequence of the "minority rights revolution" that began after World War II and has achieved considerable success, but the endurance of Columbus's reputation-to a considerable extent even among the minorities who have the least reason to respect him-raises important questions about the inertia of tradition, the politics of collective memory, and the difference between elite and popular beliefs.

The revolution in minority rights over the past half century has not only changed the attitudes of the American public regarding race, gender, and other social divisions, but has also spurred attempts to revise beliefs about important individuals and events from the past. For example, Abraham Lincoln is now viewed less as the savior of the Union-the emphasis during the Civil War and for more than half a century afterward (Blight 2001)-and much more for his actions in

## SOURCE MAP: Citing works from Web sites using *Chicago* style

① *Author.* In a note, list author first name first. In a bibliographic entry, list the first author last name first, comma, first name; list additional authors first name first. Note that the host may serve as the author.

② *Document title.* Enclose the title in quotation marks, and capitalize all major words. In a note, put a comma before and after the title. In the bibliography, put a period before and after.

③ *Title of Web site.* Italicize the title and capitalize all major words. In the notes section, put a comma after the title. In the bibliography, put a period after the title.

④ *Retrieval information.* Give the URL for the Website, followed, in parentheses, by the word *accessed* and the access date. End with a period.

### When citing works from Web sites, use the following formats:

*Endnote*

1. First name Last name, "Title of Document," *Title of Web Site*, URL (accessed Date).

*Bibliographic entry*

Last name, First name. "Title of Document." *Title of Web Site*. URL (accessed Date).

### Citations for the Web site on p. 395 would look like this:

*Endnote*

NOTE NUMBER — AUTHOR'S NAME, FIRST NAME FIRST — DOCUMENT TITLE, IN QUOTATION MARKS — TITLE OF WEB SITE, IN ITALICS

1. Douglas Linder, "The Scopes Trial: An Introduction," *Famous Trials, University of Missouri-Kansas City School of Law*, http://www.law.umkc.edu/faculty/projects/FTrials/scopes/scopes.htm (accessed September 24, 2006). — RETRIEVAL INFORMATION

INDENT THREE TO FIVE SPACES

*Bibliographic entry*

Linder, Douglas. "The Scopes Trial: An Introduction." *Famous Trials, University of Missouri-Kansas City School of Law*. http://www.law.umkc.edu/faculty/projects/FTrials/scopes/scopes.htm (accessed September 24, 2006).

For more on using *Chicago* style to cite works from Web sites, see 20c3. (For guidelines and models for using MLA style, see 18d3; for APA style, see 19d3; for CSE style, see 21c3.)

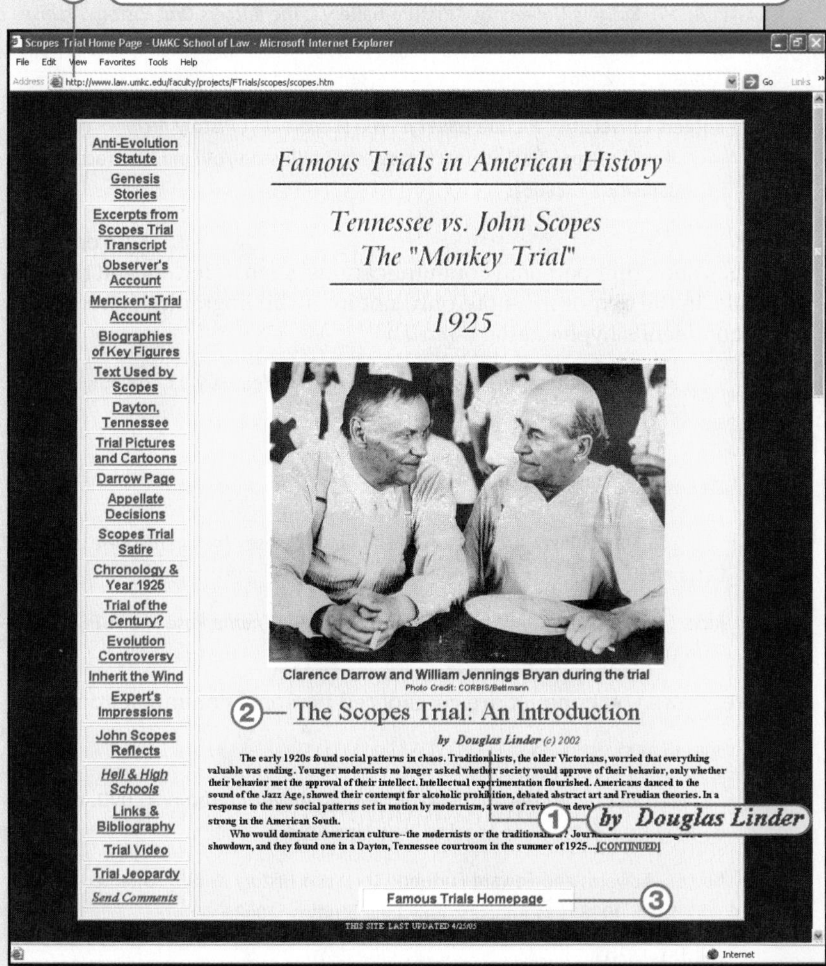
4 http://www.law.umkc.edu/faculty/projects/FTrials/scopes/scopes.htm
Scopes Trial Home Page - UMKC School of Law - Microsoft Internet Explorer
File Edit View Favorites Tools Help
Address http://www.law.umkc.edu/faculty/projects/FTrials/scopes/scopes.htm
Go Links
Anti-Evolution Statute
Genesis Stories
Excerpts from Scopes Trial Transcript
Observer's Account
Mencken'sTrial Account
Biographies of Key Figures
Text Used by Scopes
Dayton, Tennessee
Trial Pictures and Cartoons
Darrow Page
Appellate Decisions
Scopes Trial Satire
Chronology & Year 1925
Trial of the Century?
Evolution Controversy
Inherit the Wind
Expert's Impressions
John Scopes Reflects
Hell & High Schools
Links & Bibliography
Trial Video
Trial Jeopardy
Send Comments
Famous Trials in American History
Tennessee vs. John Scopes
The "Monkey Trial"
1925
Clarence Darrow and William Jennings Bryan during the trial
Photo Credit: CORBIS/Bettmann
2 The Scopes Trial: An Introduction
by Douglas Linder (c) 2002
1 by Douglas Linder
[CONTINUED]
Famous Trials Homepage 3
Internet

Iskyan, Kim. "Putin's Next Power Play." *Slate*, November 4, 2003. http://slate.msn.com/id/2090745 (accessed November 7, 2005).

19. ARTICLE FROM A WEB SITE For the basic format for citing an article from a Web site, see pp. 394–95.

19. Rutgers University, "Picture Gallery," *The Rutgers Oral History Archives of World War II*, http://fas-history.rutgers.edu/oralhistory/orlhom.htm (accessed January 17, 2006).

Rutgers University. "Picture Gallery." *The Rutgers Oral History Archives of World War II*. http://fas-history.rutgers.edu/oralhistory/orlhom.htm (accessed January 17, 2006).

20. EMAIL AND OTHER PERSONAL COMMUNICATIONS Cite email messages and other personal communications, such as letters and telephone calls, in the text or in a note only, not in the bibliography. (*Chicago* style recommends hyphenating *e-mail.*)

20. Kareem Adas, e-mail message to author, February 11, 2006.

## 4 Other sources

21. PUBLISHED OR BROADCAST INTERVIEW

21. Condoleezza Rice, interview by Charlie Rose, *The Charlie Rose Show*, PBS, October 30, 2003.

Rice, Condoleezza. Interview by Charlie Rose. *The Charlie Rose Show*. PBS, October 30, 2003.

Interviews you conduct are considered personal communications.

22. VIDEO OR DVD

22. Edward Norton and Edward Furlong, *American History X*, DVD, directed by Tony Kaye (1998; Los Angeles: New Line Studios, 2002).

Norton, Edward, and Edward Furlong. *American History X*. DVD. Directed by Tony Kaye, 1998. Los Angeles: New Line Studios, 2002.

23. CD-ROM

23. *The Civil War*, CD-ROM (Fogware, 2000).

*The Civil War*. CD-ROM. Fogware, 2000.

24. PAMPHLET, REPORT, OR BROCHURE Information about the author or publisher may not be readily available, but give enough information to identify your source.

24. Jamie McCarthy, *Who Is David Irving?* (San Antonio, TX: Holocaust History Project, 1998).

McCarthy, Jamie. *Who Is David Irving?* San Antonio, TX: Holocaust History Project, 1998.

25. GOVERNMENT DOCUMENT

25. U.S. House Committee on Ways and Means, *Report on Trade Mission to Sub-Saharan Africa*, 108th Cong., 1st sess. (Washington, DC: U.S. Government Printing Office, 2003), 28.

U.S. House Committee on Ways and Means. *Report on Trade Mission to Sub-Saharan Africa*. 108th Cong., 1st sess. Washington, DC: U.S. Government Printing Office, 2003.

## 20d A student research essay, *Chicago* style

On the following pages is an essay by Amanda Rinder that conforms to the *Chicago* guidelines described in this chapter. Note that this essay has been reproduced in a narrow format to allow for annotation.

Student Writer

Amanda Rinder

**bedfordstmartins.com/smhandbook** For additional student research writing, click on **Student Writing**.

Title and writer's name centered about halfway down title page

Sweet Home Chicago: Preserving the Past,
Protecting the Future of the Windy City
Amanda Rinder

Title announces topic clearly and succinctly

Course title, instructor's name, and date centered at bottom of title page

Twentieth-Century U.S. History
Professor Goldberg
November 27, 2006

Rinder 2

Only one city has the "Big Shoulders" described by Carl Sandburg: Chicago (fig. 1). So renowned are its skyscrapers and celebrated building style that an entire school of architecture is named for Chicago. Presently, however, the place that Frank Sinatra called "my kind of town" is beginning to lose sight of exactly what kind of town it is. Many of the buildings that give Chicago its distinctive character are being torn down in order to make room for new growth. Both preserving the classics and encouraging new creation are important; the combination of these elements gives Chicago architecture its unique flavor. Witold Rybczynski, a professor of urbanism at the University of Pennsylvania, told the *New York Times*, "Of all the cities we can think of . . . we associate Chicago with new things, with building new. Combining that with preservation is a difficult task, a tricky thing. It's hard to find the

Paper refers to each figure by number

Double-spaced text

Fig. 1. Chicago skyline, circa 1940s. (Postcard courtesy of Minnie Dangberg.)

Figure caption includes number, short title, and source

Rinder 3

Source cited using superscript numeral

middle ground in Chicago."[1] Yet finding a middle ground is essential if the city is to retain the original character that sets it apart from the rest. In order to maintain Chicago's distinctive identity and its delicate balance between the old and the new, the city government must provide a comprehensive urban plan that not only directs growth, but calls for the preservation of landmarks and historic districts as well.

Opening paragraph concludes with thesis statement

Chicago is a city for the working man. Nowhere is this more evident than in its architecture. David Garrard Lowe, author of *Lost Chicago*, notes that early Chicagoans "sought reality, not fantasy, and the reality of America as seen from the heartland did not include the pavilions of princes or the castles of kings."[2] The inclination toward unadorned, sturdy buildings began in the late nineteenth century with the aptly named Chicago School, a movement led by Louis Sullivan, John Wellborn Root, and Daniel Burnham and based on Sullivan's adage, "Form follows function."[3] Burnham and Root's Reliance Building (fig. 2) epitomizes this vision: simple, yet possessing a unique angular beauty.[4] The early skyscraper, the very symbol of the Chicago style, represents the triumph of function and utility over sentiment, America over Europe, and perhaps even the frontier over the civilization of the East Coast.[5] These ideals of the original Chicago School were expanded upon by architects of the Second Chicago School. Frank Lloyd Wright's legendary organic style and the famed glass and steel constructions of Mies van der Rohe are often the first images that spring to mind when one thinks of Chicago.

Second paragraph provides background

Yet the architecture that is the city's defining attribute is being threatened by the increasing tendency toward development.

Clear transition from previous paragraph

Rinder 4

Fig. 2. The Reliance Building. (Photo courtesy of The Art Institute of Chicago.)

The root of Chicago's preservation problem lies in the enormous drive toward economic expansion and the potential in Chicago for such growth. The highly competitive market for land in the city means that properties sell for the highest price if the buildings on them can be obliterated to make room for newer, larger developments. Because of this preference on the part of potential buyers, the label "landmark" has become a stigma for property owners. "In other cities, landmark status is sought after — in Chicago, it's avoided at all costs," notes Alan J. Shannon of the *Chicago Tribune*.[6] Even if owners wish to keep their property's original structure, designation as a landmark is still undesirable as it limits the renovations that can be made to a building and thus

Signal verb "notes" introduces quotation

Rinder 5

decreases its value. Essentially, no building that has even been recommended for landmark status may be touched without the approval of the Commission on Chicago Historical and Architectural Landmarks, a restriction that considerably diminishes the appeal of the real estate. "We live in a world where the owners say, 'If you judge my property a landmark you are taking money away from me.' And in Chicago the process is stacked in favor of the economics," says former city Planning Commissioner David Mosena.[7]

The Berghoff buildings, which house the Berghoff Restaurant and its facilities, are a prime example of this problem. The restaurant has been a feature of the Loop for more than ninety years. But when the building was proposed for official designation in 1991, the City Council voted against it after considerable urging from the Berghoff family. Neil King, a real estate valuation expert who testified before the Landmark Preservation Committee, stated that "no developer is going to buy this property once it's designated."[8] The LaSalle National Bank told the Berghoffs that it would foreclose on a mortgage for more than $2.7 million if the Council named the Berghoff buildings landmarks.[9] The Berghoff conflict illustrates that the problem of overbearing development cannot be solved simply by assigning landmark status to historic buildings; it is an ongoing struggle between yesterday's creations and today's economic prosperity.

Example of complicated economics of preservation

Nowhere is this clash more apparent than on North Michigan Avenue—Chicago's Magnificent Mile. The historic buildings along this block are unquestionably some of the city's finest works. In addition, the Mile is one of Chicago's most prosperous districts, with a massive volume of shoppers traveling there daily. The

"Magnificent Mile" illustrates conflict between development and preservation

Rinder 6

small-scale, charming buildings envisioned by Arthur Rubloff, the prominent real estate developer who first conceived of the Magnificent Mile in the late 1940s, could not accommodate the crowds. Numerous high-rises, constructed to accommodate the masses that flock to Michigan Avenue, interrupt the cohesion and unity envisioned by the original planners of the Magnificent Mile. In *Chicago's North Michigan Avenue*, John W. Stamper says that with the standard height for new buildings on the avenue currently at about sixty-five stories, the "pleasant shopping promenade" has become a "canyon-like corridor."[10]

Evidence supports claim made in paragraph's topic sentence

Many agree that the individual style of Michigan Avenue is being lost. In 1995, the same year that the Landmarks Preservation Council of Illinois declared the section of Michigan Avenue from Oak Street to Roosevelt Road one of the state's ten most endangered historic sites, the annual sales of the Magnificent Mile ran around $1 billion and were increasing at an annual rate of about five to seven percent.[11] Clearly, the property's potential as part of a commercial hub is taking priority over its architectural and historic value. The future of this district rests on a precarious balance between Chicago's responsibility for its own heritage and Chicagoans' desire for economic gain. Stamper notes, "What made North Michigan Avenue such an attractive focus of activity in the 1920s is being incrementally destroyed in the interest of maximizing return on the investment."[12]

Perhaps the best single example of the conflict between preservation and development in Chicago is the case of the McCarthy Building (fig. 3). Built in 1872, the McCarthy was designed by John M. Van Osdel, Chicago's first professional

Additional example introduced

Rinder 7

Source of image quoted in figure caption

Fig. 3. The McCarthy Building. (From the University of Illinois at Chicago, *Chicago Imagebase*, http://www.uic.edu/depts/ahaa/imagebase.)

architect. Paul Gapp, a *Chicago Tribune* architecture critic, described it as "a stunningly appealing relic from Chicago's 19th century Renaissance era."[13] The McCarthy was made a landmark in 1984, but it wasn't long before developers recognized the potential of the property, situated on Block 37 of State Street, directly across from Marshall Field's. With plans for a $300 million retail and office complex already outlined, developers made a $12.3 million bid for the property, promising to preserve the McCarthy and integrate it into the complex. The city readily agreed. However, a series of modifications over the next two years completely transformed the original plan. With the old structure now useless to the project, developers made subsequent proposals to preserve just the facade, or even to move the entire McCarthy Building to another location. When these propositions didn't work out, the developers began offering to preserve other buildings in exchange for permission to

Rinder 8

demolish the McCarthy. Gapp admitted that the city was caught in a difficult situation: if it protected the McCarthy, it would be impeding development in an important urban renewal area, and if it allowed demolition, Chicago's landmark protection ordinance would be completely devalued. He nonetheless urged city officials to choose the "long view" and preserve the McCarthy.[14] However, the developers' offer to buy and restore the Reliance Building, at a cost of between $7 million and $11 million, and to contribute $4 million to other preservation efforts, prevailed. In September 1987, the Chicago City Council voted to revoke the McCarthy's landmark status.

Introduction of counterevidence that large number of significant buildings diminishes value of each

Ironically, Chicago's rich architectural heritage may work against its own preservation. With so many significant buildings, losing one does not seem as critical as perhaps it should. The fact that Chicago boasts some forty-five Mies buildings, seventy-five Frank Lloyd Wright buildings, and numerous other buildings from the first and second Chicago Schools may inspire a nonchalant attitude toward preservation.[15] The public seems to justify the demolition of quality architecture by citing Chicago's vast number of such works. Excusing the razing of Chicago's Arts Club, noted for having the only known interior designed by Mies himself, and other buildings on Michigan Avenue, the city's Planning and Development Commissioner, Valerie Jarrett, told the *Chicago Sun-Times*, "We are a city that is rich in our architectural heritage . . . we do a yeoman's job of preserving those buildings."[16] This rationale is careless; each building is an original creation and should be evaluated as one, not as a faceless member of the group.

The razing of the McCarthy Building in 1987 exposes the problems inherent in Chicago's landmark policy. But the real

Rinder 9

tragedy is that none of the plans for development of the property were ever carried out. Block 37 remains vacant to this day. Clearly, the city needs creative and vigilant urban planning. Yet some have questioned the importance of such planning, arguing that it stifles innovation and creative advances. Jack Guthman, a Chicago lawyer representing a group of property owners, told the *Chicago Tribune* that he opposed landmark designation: "What [those proposing designation are] saying is a clear indictment of today's architecture—that we can't improve on the past."[17] Proponents of this viewpoint, however, neglect one important fact. The city has an extensive history of urban planning, dating back to Burnham's original Chicago Plan of 1909, which posed no hindrance to the likes of Mies and Wright. In addition, just one look at the rapid and disorderly growth of North Michigan Avenue makes it clear that unlimited development is not the answer.

Call for planning to address economic costs of preservation

To uphold Chicago's reputation as an architectural jewel, the city must participate in urban planning. The most important municipal duty in managing development is to ease the economic burdens that preservation entails. Some methods that have been suggested for this are property tax breaks for landmark owners and transferable development rights, which would give landmark owners bonuses for developing elsewhere. Overall, however, the city's planning and landmarks commissions simply need to become more involved, working closely with developers throughout the entire design process. If both parties outline their needs, restrictions, and priorities and then negotiate until mutually satisfied, a middle ground can be reached. Of course, there are some demands on which the city should not compromise, such as the significance of landmark

Rinder 10

Fig. 4. Union Station, circa 1925. (Postcard courtesy of Minnie Dangberg.)

status. But added cooperation on other fronts could help to mitigate a few strict policies and achieve a practical, productive balance.

The effectiveness of an earnest but open-minded approach to urban planning has already been proven in Chicago. Union Station (fig. 4) is one project that worked to the satisfaction of both developers and preservationists. Developers U.S. Equities Realty Inc. and Amtrak proposed replacing the four floors of outdated office space above the station with more practical high-rise towers. This offer allowed for the preservation of the Great Hall and other public spaces within the station itself. "We are preserving the best of the historical landmark . . . and at the same time creating an adaptive reuse that will bring back some of the old glory of the station," Cheryl Stein of U.S. Equities told the *Tribune*.[18] The city responded to this magnanimous offer in kind, upgrading zoning on

Example of successful planning introduced

the site to permit additional office space and working with developers to identify exactly which portions of the original structure needed to be preserved. Today, the sight of Union Station, revitalized and bustling, is proof of the sincere endeavors of developers and city planners alike.

Conclusion offers hope of a solution

In the midst of abandonment and demolition, buildings such as Union Station and the Reliance Building offer Chicago some hope for a future that is as architecturally rich as its past. The key to achieving this balance of preserving historic treasures and encouraging new development is to view the city not so much as a product, but as a process. Robert Bruegmann, author of *The Architects and the City*, defines a city as "the ultimate human artifact, our most complex and prodigious social creation, and the most tangible result of the actions over time of all its citizens."[19] Nowhere is this sentiment more relevant than in Chicago. Comprehensive urban planning will ensure that the city's character, so closely tied to its architecture, is preserved.

Rinder 12

Notes

1. Tracie Rozhon, "Chicago Girds for Big Battle over Its Skyline," *New York Times*, November 12, 2000, http://www.lexisnexis.com (accessed November 7, 2006).

2. David Garrard Lowe, *Lost Chicago* (New York: Watson-Guptill Publications, 2000), 112.

3. *Microsoft Encarta Encyclopedia 2000*, s.v. "Sullivan, Louis Henri," CD-ROM (Microsoft, 2000).

Encyclopedia entry; appears in notes but not in bibliography

4. Lowe, *Lost Chicago*, 123.

Second reference to source

5. Daniel Bluestone, *Constructing Chicago* (New Haven: Yale University Press, 1991), 105.

6. Alan J. Shannon, "When Will It End?" *Chicago Tribune*, September 11, 1987, quoted in Karen J. Dilibert, *From Landmark to Landfill* (Chicago: Chicago Architectural Foundation, 2000), 11.

7. Steve Kerch, "Landmark Decisions," *Chicago Tribune*, March 18, 1990, sec. 16.

8. Patrick T. Reardon, "'No' Vote Makes It a Landmark Day for the Berghoff," *Chicago Tribune*, April 5, 1991, sec 1.

9. Ibid.

Reference to preceding source

10. John W. Stamper, *Chicago's North Michigan Avenue* (Chicago: University of Chicago Press, 1991), 215.

11. Nancy Stuenkel, "Success Spoiling the Magnificent Mile?" *Chicago Sun-Times*, April 9, 1995, http://www.lexisnexis.com (accessed November 8, 2006).

12. Stamper, *North Michigan Avenue*, 215.

13. Paul Gapp, "McCarthy Building Puts Landmark Law on a Collision Course with Developers," *Chicago Tribune*, April 20, 1986,

Rinder 13

quoted in Karen J. Dilibert, *From Landmark to Landfill* (Chicago: Chicago Architectural Foundation, 2000), 4.

14. Ibid.

15. Rozhon, "Chicago Girds for Big Battle."

16. Rich Hein, "Preservationists Rally behind 'Mies and Moe's,'" *Chicago Sun-Times*, November 4, 1994, http://www.lexisnexis.com (accessed November 10, 2006).

17. David Mendell and Gary Washburn, "Daley Acts to Protect Michigan Ave. Skyline," *Chicago Tribune*, March 8, 2001.

18. Kerch, "Landmark Decisions."

19. Robert Bruegmann, *The Architects and the City* (Chicago: University of Chicago Press, 1997), 443.

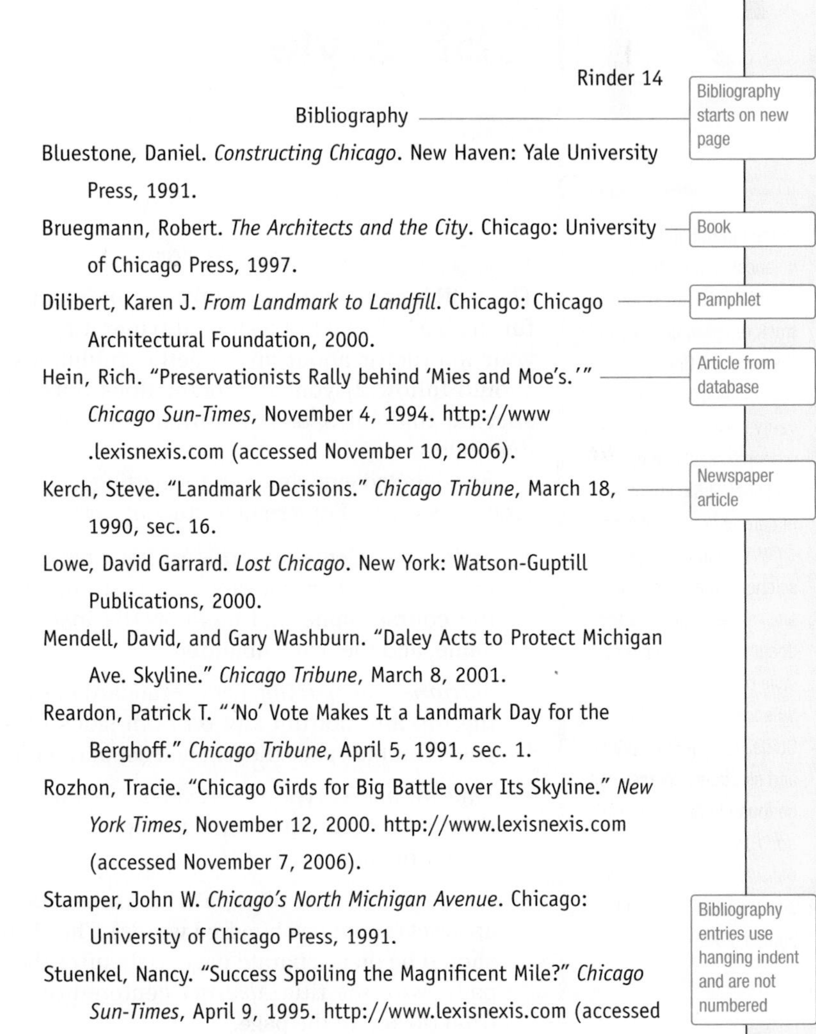

Rinder 14

Bibliography

Bluestone, Daniel. *Constructing Chicago*. New Haven: Yale University Press, 1991.

Bruegmann, Robert. *The Architects and the City*. Chicago: University of Chicago Press, 1997.

Dilibert, Karen J. *From Landmark to Landfill*. Chicago: Chicago Architectural Foundation, 2000.

Hein, Rich. "Preservationists Rally behind 'Mies and Moe's.'" *Chicago Sun-Times*, November 4, 1994. http://www.lexisnexis.com (accessed November 10, 2006).

Kerch, Steve. "Landmark Decisions." *Chicago Tribune*, March 18, 1990, sec. 16.

Lowe, David Garrard. *Lost Chicago*. New York: Watson-Guptill Publications, 2000.

Mendell, David, and Gary Washburn. "Daley Acts to Protect Michigan Ave. Skyline." *Chicago Tribune*, March 8, 2001.

Reardon, Patrick T. "'No' Vote Makes It a Landmark Day for the Berghoff." *Chicago Tribune*, April 5, 1991, sec. 1.

Rozhon, Tracie. "Chicago Girds for Big Battle over Its Skyline." *New York Times*, November 12, 2000. http://www.lexisnexis.com (accessed November 7, 2006).

Stamper, John W. *Chicago's North Michigan Avenue*. Chicago: University of Chicago Press, 1991.

Stuenkel, Nancy. "Success Spoiling the Magnificent Mile?" *Chicago Sun-Times*, April 9, 1995. http://www.lexisnexis.com (accessed November 8, 2006).

Bibliography starts on new page

Book

Pamphlet

Article from database

Newspaper article

Bibliography entries use hanging indent and are not numbered

# 21 CSE Style

In the natural and physical sciences and mathematics, it's often very important to track reported findings to their source. Because scientists need to be able to verify — or repudiate — research results, they understand the importance of careful documentation.

Writers in the physical sciences, the life sciences, and mathematics use the documentation and format style of the Council of Science Editors (CSE). Guidelines for citing print and electronic sources can be found in *Scientific Style and Format: The CSE Manual for Authors, Editors, and Publishers*, Seventh Edition (2006).

## 21a CSE manuscript format

The CSE manual does not make recommendations for the basic format of a student paper. Check with your instructor about any specific guidelines you should follow. If your instructor does not require specific guidelines, use the formatting suggestions that follow.

For detailed guidelines on formatting a list of references, see 21c. For a sample student essay, see 21d.

- *Title page.* Center the title of your paper, your name, and other relevant information, such as the course name and number, the instructor's name, and the date submitted.
- *Margins and spacing.* Leave standard margins at the top and bottom and on both sides of each page. Double-space the text and list of references.
- *Page numbers.* Type a short version of the paper's title and the page number in the upper right-hand corner of each page.
- *Abstract.* CSE style often calls for a one-paragraph abstract (about one hundred words). The abstract should be on a separate page, right after the title page, with the title *Abstract* centered one inch from the top of the page.
- *Headings.* CSE style does not require headings, but it notes that they can help readers quickly find a specific section of a paper.
- *Tables and figures.* Tables and figures must be labeled *Table* or *Figure* and numbered separately,

one sequence for tables and one for figures. Give each table and figure a short, informative title.

## 21b In-text citations

In CSE style, citations within an essay follow one of three formats.

- The *citation-sequence format* calls for a superscript number or a number in parentheses after any mention of a source. The sources are numbered in the order they appear. Each number refers to the same source every time it is used. The first source mentioned in the paper is numbered *1*, the second source is numbered *2*, and so on.
- The *citation-name format* also calls for a superscript number or a number in parentheses after any mention of a source. The numbers are added after the list of references is completed and alphabetized, so that the source numbered *1* is alphabetically first in the list of references, *2* is alphabetically second, and so on.
- The *name-year format* calls for the last name of the author and the year of publication in parentheses after any mention of a source. If the last name appears in a signal phrase, the name-year format allows for giving only the year of publication in parentheses.

Before deciding which system to use, check a current journal in the field or ask an instructor about the preferred style in a particular course or discipline.

### 1. IN-TEXT CITATION USING CITATION-SEQUENCE OR CITATION-NAME FORMAT

VonBergen[12] provides the most complete discussion of this phenomenon.

For the citation-sequence and citation-name formats, you would use the same superscript[(12)] for each subsequent citation of this work by VonBergen.

### 2. IN-TEXT CITATION USING NAME-YEAR FORMAT

VonBergen (2003) provides the most complete discussion of this phenomenon.

Hussar's two earlier studies of juvenile obesity (1995, 1999) examined only children with diabetes.

The classic examples of such investigations (Morrow 1968; Bridger et al. 1971; Franklin and Wayson 1972) still shape the assumptions of current studies.

## 21c List of references

The citations in the text of an essay correspond to items on a list titled *References*, which starts on a new page at the end of the essay. Continue to number the pages consecutively, center the title *References* one inch from the top of the page, and double-space before beginning the first entry.

The order of the entries depends on which CSE format you follow:

- *Citation-sequence format*: number and list the references in the order the references are first cited in the text.
- *Citation-name format*: list and number the references in alphabetical order.
- *Name-year format*: list the references, unnumbered, in alphabetical order.

In the following examples, you will see that the citation-sequence and citation-name formats call for listing the date after the publisher's name in references for books and after the periodical name in references for articles. The name-year format calls for listing the date immediately after the author's name in any kind of reference.

CSE style also specifies the treatment and placement of the following basic elements in the list of references:

- *Author*. List all authors last name first, and use only initials for first and middle names. Do not place a comma after the author's last name, and do not place periods after or spaces between the initials. Use a period after the last initial of the last author listed.
- *Title*. Do not italicize or underline titles and subtitles of books and titles of periodicals. Do not enclose titles of articles in quotation marks. For books and articles, capitalize only the first word of the title and any proper nouns or proper adjectives. Abbreviate and capitalize all major words in a periodical title.

As you refer to these examples, pay attention to how publication information (publishers for books, details about periodicals for articles) and other specific elements are styled and punctuated.

## Directory to CSE style for references



## 1 Books

For the basic format for citing a book, see pp. 416–17.

#### 1. ONE AUTHOR

CITATION-SEQUENCE AND CITATION-NAME

1. Buchanan M. Nexus: small worlds and the groundbreaking theory of networks. New York: Norton; 2003.

NAME-YEAR

Buchanan M. 2003. Nexus: small worlds and the groundbreaking theory of networks. New York: Norton.

#### 2. TWO OR MORE AUTHORS

CITATION-SEQUENCE AND CITATION-NAME

2. Wojciechowski BW, Rice NM. Experimental methods in kinetic studies. 2nd ed. St. Louis (MO): Elsevier Science; 2003.

## SOURCE MAP: Citing books using CSE style

Note that, depending on whether you are using the citation-sequence or citation-name format or the name-year format, the date placement will vary.

1. *Author.* List authors' last names first, and use initials for first and middle names. Do not place periods after or spaces between initials. Use a period after the last initial of the last author.

2, 6. *Publication year.* In name-year format, put the year of publication immediately after the author name(s). In citation-sequence or citation-name format, put the year of publication after the publisher's name.

3. *Title.* Do not italicize, underline, or put quotation marks around titles and subtitles of books. Capitalize only the first word of the title and any proper nouns or proper adjectives.

4. *City of publication.* List the city of publication (and the country or state abbreviation for unfamiliar cities) followed by a colon.

5. *Publisher.* Give the publisher's name. In citation-sequence or citation-name format, follow with a semicolon. In name-year format, follow with a period.

**For a book by one author with no middle initial, use one of the following formats:**

*Citation-sequence or citation-name format*

1. Last name and first initial(s). Title of book: subtitle. City: Publisher; Year.

*Name-year format*

Last name and first initial(s). Year. Title of book: subtitle. City: Publisher.

**A citation for the book on p. 417 would look like this:**

*Citation-sequence or citation-name format*

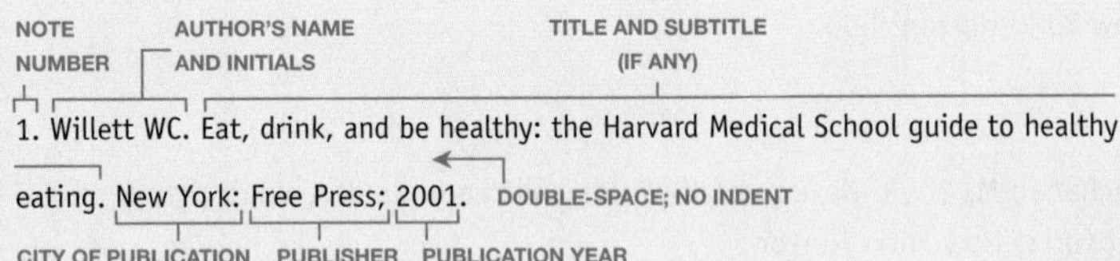

*Name-year format*

Willett WC. 2001. Eat, drink, and be healthy: the Harvard Medical School guide to healthy eating. New York: Free Press.

For more on using CSE style to cite books, see 21c1. (For guidelines and models for using MLA style, see 18d1; for APA style, see 19d1; for *Chicago* style, see 20c1.)

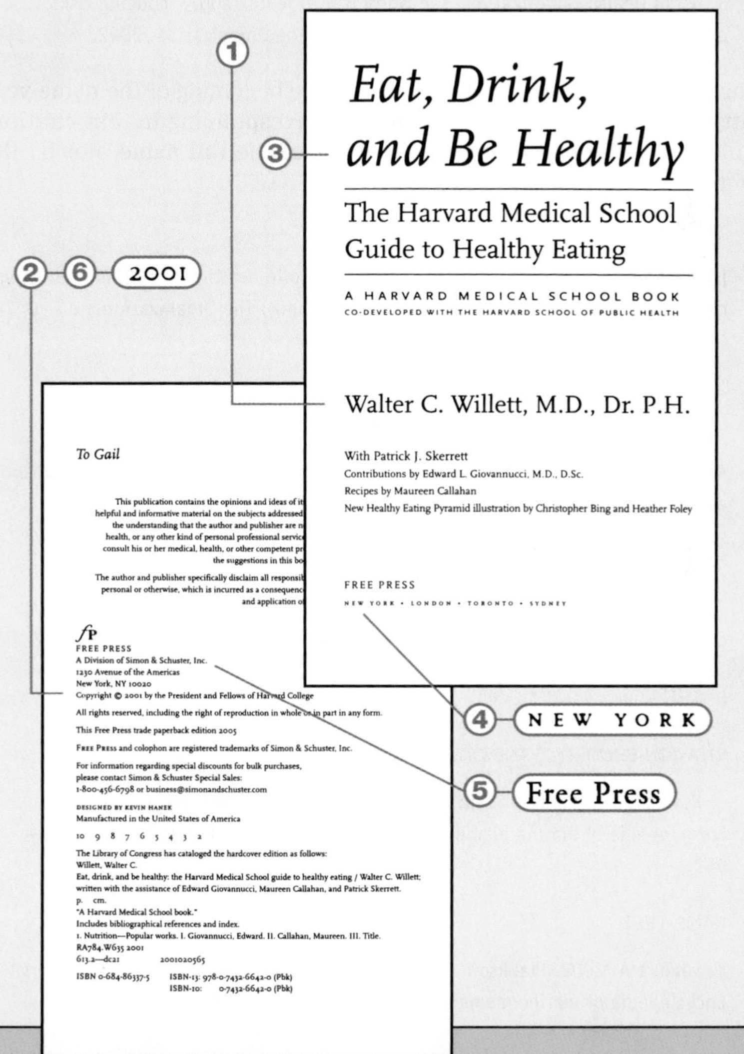


*Eat, Drink, and Be Healthy*

The Harvard Medical School Guide to Healthy Eating

A HARVARD MEDICAL SCHOOL BOOK
CO-DEVELOPED WITH THE HARVARD SCHOOL OF PUBLIC HEALTH

Walter C. Willett, M.D., Dr. P.H.

With Patrick J. Skerrett
Contributions by Edward L. Giovannucci, M.D., D.Sc.
Recipes by Maureen Callahan
New Healthy Eating Pyramid illustration by Christopher Bing and Heather Foley

FREE PRESS
NEW YORK • LONDON • TORONTO • SYDNEY

*To Gail*

This publication contains the opinions and ideas of it
helpful and informative material on the subjects addressed
the understanding that the author and publisher are n
health, or any other kind of personal professional servic
consult his or her medical, health, or other competent pr
the suggestions in this bo

The author and publisher specifically disclaim all responsib
personal or otherwise, which is incurred as a consequenc
and application o

*fp*
FREE PRESS
A Division of Simon & Schuster, Inc.
1230 Avenue of the Americas
New York, NY 10020

This Free Press trade paperback edition 2005
FREE PRESS and colophon are registered trademarks of Simon & Schuster, Inc.
For information regarding special discounts for bulk purchases,
please contact Simon & Schuster Special Sales:
1-800-456-6798 or business@simonandschuster.com
DESIGNED BY KEVIN HANEK
Manufactured in the United States of America
10 9 8 7 6 5 4 3 2
The Library of Congress has cataloged the hardcover edition as follows:
Willett, Walter C.
Eat, drink, and be healthy: the Harvard Medical School guide to healthy eating / Walter C. Willett;
written with the assistance of Edward Giovannucci, Maureen Callahan, and Patrick Skerrett.
p. cm.
"A Harvard Medical School book."
Includes bibliographical references and index.
1. Nutrition—Popular works. I. Giovannucci, Edward. II. Callahan, Maureen. III. Title.
RA784.W635 2001
613.2—dc21 2001020565
ISBN 0-684-86337-5 ISBN-13: 978-0-7432-6642-0 (Pbk)
ISBN-10: 0-7432-6642-0 (Pbk)

NAME-YEAR

Wojciechowski BW, Rice NM. 2003. Experimental methods in kinetic studies. 2nd ed. St. Louis (MO): Elsevier Science.

### 3. ORGANIZATION AS AUTHOR

CITATION-SEQUENCE AND CITATION-NAME

3. World Health Organization. The world health report 2002: reducing risks, promoting healthy life. Geneva (Switzerland): The Organization; 2002.

Place the organization's abbreviation at the beginning of the name-year entry, and use the abbreviation in the corresponding in-text citation. Alphabetize the entry by the first word of the full name, not by the abbreviation.

NAME-YEAR

[WHO] World Health Organization. 2002. The world health report 2002: reducing risks, promoting healthy life. Geneva (Switzerland): The Organization.

### 4. BOOK PREPARED BY EDITOR(S)

CITATION-SEQUENCE AND CITATION-NAME

4. Torrence ME, Isaacson RE, editors. Microbial food safety in animal agriculture: current topics. Ames: Iowa State University Press; 2003.

NAME-YEAR

Torrence ME, Isaacson RE, editors. 2003. Microbial safety in animal agriculture: current topics. Ames: Iowa State University Press.

### 5. SECTION OF A BOOK WITH AN EDITOR

CITATION-SEQUENCE AND CITATION-NAME

5. Kawamura A. Plankton. In: Perrin MF, Wursig B, Thewissen JGM, editors. Encyclopedia of marine mammals. San Diego: Academic Press; 2002. p. 939–942.

NAME-YEAR

Kawamura A. 2002. Plankton. In: Perrin MF, Wursig B, Thewissen JGM, editors. Encyclopedia of marine mammals. San Diego: Academic Press. p. 939–942.

6. CHAPTER OF A BOOK

CITATION-SEQUENCE AND CITATION-NAME

6. Honigsbaum M. The fever trail: in search of the cure for malaria. New York: Picador; 2003. Chapter 2, The cure; p. 19–38.

NAME-YEAR

Honigsbaum M. 2003. The fever trail: in search of the cure for malaria. New York: Picador. Chapter 2, The cure; p. 19–38.

7. PAPER OR ABSTRACT IN CONFERENCE PROCEEDINGS

CITATION-SEQUENCE AND CITATION-NAME

7. Gutierrez AP. Integrating biological and environmental factors in crop system models [abstract]. In: Integrated Biological Systems Conference; 2003 Apr 14–16; San Antonio, TX. Beaumont (TX): Agroeconomics Research Group; 2003. p. 14–15.

NAME-YEAR

Gutierrez AP. 2003. Integrating biological and environmental factors in crop system models [abstract]. In: Integrated Biological Systems Conference; 2003 Apr 14–16; San Antonio, TX. Beaumont (TX): Agroeconomics Research Group. p. 14–15.

## 2 Periodicals

For the basic format for an article from a periodical, see pp. 420–21. For newspaper and magazine articles, include the section designation and column number, if any, in addition to the date and the inclusive page numbers. For rules on abbreviating journal titles, consult the CSE manual, or ask an instructor to suggest other examples.

8. ARTICLE IN A JOURNAL

CITATION-SEQUENCE AND CITATION-NAME

8. Mahmud K, Vance ML. Human growth hormone and aging. New Engl J Med. 2003;348(2):2256–2257.

NAME-YEAR

Mahmud K, Vance ML. 2003. Human growth hormone and aging. New Engl J Med. 348(2):2256–2257.

## SOURCE MAP: Citing articles from periodicals using CSE style

Note that date placement will vary, depending on whether you are using the citation-sequence or citation-name format or the name-year format.

(1) *Author.* List all authors' last names first, and use only initials for first and middle names. Do not place periods after or spaces betwen the initials. Use a period after the last initial of the last author.

(2), (5) *Publication date.* In name-year format, put publication date after author name(s). In citation-sequence or citation-name format, put publication date after periodical title. For journals, use only the year; use the year and month (and day) for publications without volume numbers.

(3) *Title and subtitle of article.* Capitalize only the first word of the title and any proper nouns or proper adjectives.

(4) *Title of periodical.* Capitalize all major words and end with a period. Follow the guidelines in the CSE manual for abbreviating journal titles.

(6) *Publication information.* For articles from scholarly journals, give the volume number, the issue number if available (in parentheses), and then a colon.

(7) *Page numbers.* Give the inclusive page numbers, and end with a period.

### For an article in a scholarly journal, use one of the following formats:

*Citation-sequence or citation-name format*

1. Last name first initial. Title of article. Journal abbreviation. Year;Volume(Issue):Pages.

*Name-year format*

Last name first initial. Year. Title of article. Journal abbreviation. Volume(Issue):Pages.

### Citations for the article on p. 421 would look like this:

*Citation-sequence or citation-name format*

NOTE NUMBER — AUTHOR'S LAST NAME AND INITIAL — ARTICLE TITLE AND SUBTITLE (IF ANY)

1. Narechania A. Hearing is believing: ivory-billed sightings leave field biologists wanting to hear more. Am Scholar. 2005;74(3):84-97.

DOUBLE-SPACE; NO INDENT

JOURNAL TITLE ABBREVIATED — PUBLICATION YEAR — VOLUME AND ISSUE NUMBERS — PAGE NUMBERS

*Name-year format*

Narechania A. 2005. Hearing is believing: ivory-billed sightings leave field biologists wanting to hear more. Am Scholar. 74(3):84-97.

For more on using CSE style to cite articles in periodicals, see 21c2. (For guidelines and models for using MLA style, see 18d2; for APA style, see 19d2; for *Chicago* style, see 20c2.)

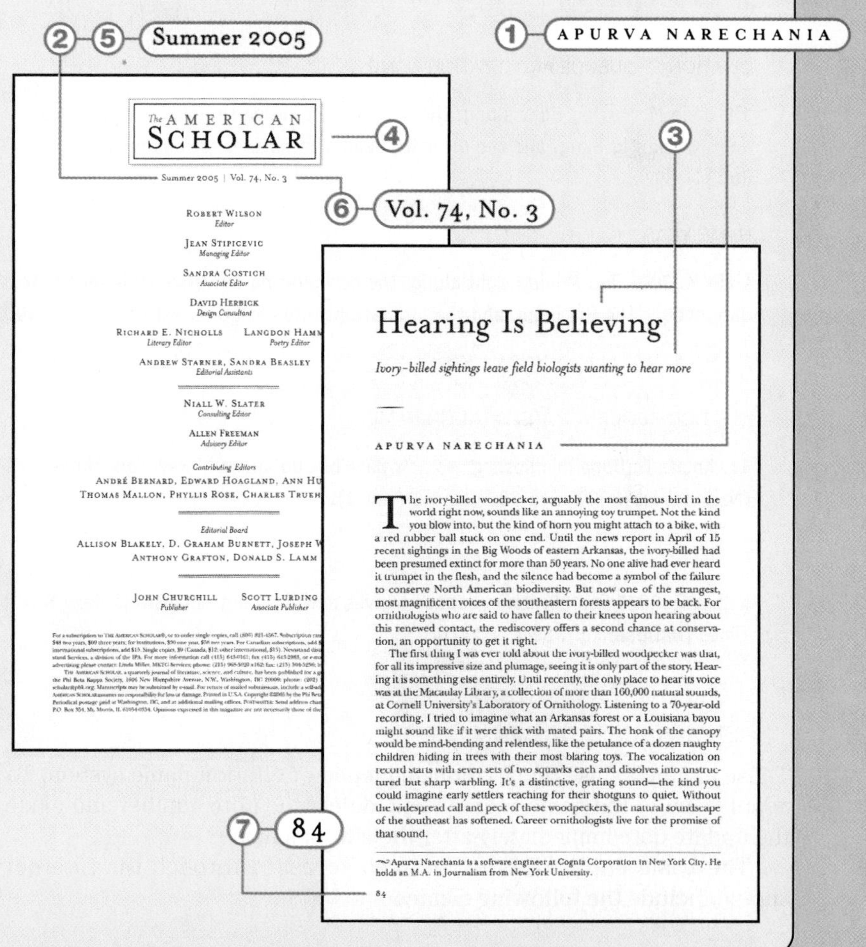


The AMERICAN SCHOLAR

Summer 2005 | Vol. 74, No. 3



# Hearing Is Believing

*Ivory-billed sightings leave field biologists wanting to hear more*

APURVA NARECHANIA

The ivory-billed woodpecker, arguably the most famous bird in the world right now, sounds like an annoying toy trumpet. Not the kind you blow into, but the kind of horn you might attach to a bike, with a red rubber ball stuck on one end. Until the news report in April of 15 recent sightings in the Big Woods of eastern Arkansas, the ivory-billed had been presumed extinct for more than 50 years. No one alive had ever heard it trumpet in the flesh, and the silence had become a symbol of the failure to conserve North American biodiversity. But now one of the strangest, most magnificent voices of the southeastern forests appears to be back. For ornithologists who are said to have fallen to their knees upon hearing about this renewed contact, the rediscovery offers a second chance at conservation, an opportunity to get it right.

The first thing I was ever told about the ivory-billed woodpecker was that, for all its impressive size and plumage, seeing it is only part of the story. Hearing it is something else entirely. Until recently, the only place to hear its voice was at the Macaulay Library, a collection of more than 160,000 natural sounds, at Cornell University's Laboratory of Ornithology. Listening to a 70-year-old recording, I tried to imagine what an Arkansas forest or a Louisiana bayou might sound like if it were thick with mated pairs. The honk of the canopy would be mind-bending and relentless, like the petulance of a dozen naughty children hiding in trees with their most blaring toys. The vocalization on record starts with seven sets of two squawks each and dissolves into unstructured but sharp warbling. It's a distinctive, grating sound—the kind you could imagine early settlers reaching for their shotguns to quiet. Without the widespread call and peck of these woodpeckers, the natural soundscape of the southeast has softened. Career ornithologists live for the promise of that sound.

Apurva Narechania is a software engineer at Cognia Corporation in New York City. He holds an M.A. in Journalism from New York University.

84

### 9. ARTICLE IN A WEEKLY JOURNAL

CITATION-SEQUENCE AND CITATION-NAME

9. Holden C. Future brightening for depression treatments. Science. 2003 Oct 31:810–813.

NAME-YEAR

Holden C. 2003. Future brightening for depression treatments. Science. Oct 31:810–813.

### 10. ARTICLE IN A MAGAZINE

CITATION-SEQUENCE AND CITATION-NAME

10. Livio M. Moving right along: the accelerating universe holds secrets to dark energy, the Big Bang, and the ultimate beauty of nature. Astronomy. 2002 Jul:34–39.

NAME-YEAR

Livio M. 2002 Jul. Moving right along: the accelerating universe holds secrets to dark energy, the Big Bang, and the ultimate beauty of nature. Astronomy. 34–39.

### 11. ARTICLE IN A NEWSPAPER

CITATION-SEQUENCE AND CITATION-NAME

11. Kolata G. Bone diagnosis gives new data but no answers. New York Times (National Ed.). 2003 Sep 28;Sect. 1:1 (col. 1).

NAME-YEAR

Kolata G. 2003 Sep 28. Bone diagnosis gives new data but no answers. New York Times (National Ed.). Sect. 1:1 (col. 1).

## 3 Electronic sources

These examples use the citation-sequence or citation-name system. To adapt them to the name-year system, delete the note number and place the update date immediately after the author's name.

The basic entry for most sources accessed through the Internet should include the following elements:

- *Author.* Give the author's name, if available, last name first, followed by the initial(s) and a period.
- *Title.* For book, journal, and article titles, follow the style for print materials. For all other types of electronic material, reproduce the title that appears on the screen.
- *Medium.* Indicate, in brackets, that the source is not in print format by using designations such as [Internet].
- *Place of publication.* The city usually should be followed by the two-letter abbreviation for state. No state abbreviation is necessary for well-known cities such as New York, Chicago, Boston, and London or for a publisher whose location is part of its name (for example, University of Oklahoma Press). If the city is inferred, put the city and state in brackets. If the city cannot be inferred, use the words *place unknown* in brackets.
- *Publisher.* For Web sites, pages on Web sites, and online databases, include the individual or organization that produces or sponsors the site. If no publisher can be determined, use the words *publisher unknown* in brackets. No publisher is necessary for online journals or journals accessed online.
- *Dates.* Cite three important dates if possible: the date the publication was placed on the Internet or the copyright date; the latest date of any update or revision; and the date the publication was accessed by you.
- *Page, document, volume, and issue numbers.* When citing a portion of a larger work or site, list the inclusive page numbers or document numbers of the specific item being cited. For journals or journal articles, include volume and issue numbers. If exact page numbers are not available, include in brackets the approximate length in computer screens, paragraphs, or bytes: [2 screens], [10 paragraphs], [332K bytes].
- *Address.* Include the URL or other electronic address; use the phrase *Available from:* to introduce the address. Only URLs that end with a slash are followed by a period.

12. MATERIAL FROM AN ONLINE DATABASE For the basic format for citing an article from a database, see pp. 424–25. (Because CSE does not provide guidelines for citing an article from an online database, this

## SOURCE MAP: Citing articles from databases using CSE style

Note that date placement will vary depending on whether you are using the citation-sequence or citation-name format or the name-year format.

① *Author.* List all authors' last names first, and use only initials for first and middle names.

②, ⑤ *Publication date.* For name-year format, put publication date after author name(s). For citation-sequence or citation-name format, put it after periodical title. Use year only (for journals) or year month day (for other periodicals).

③ *Title of article.* Capitalize first word and proper nouns/adjectives.

④ *Title of periodical.* Capitalize major words. Abbreviate journal titles. Follow with [*Internet*] and a period.

⑥ *Date of access.* In brackets, write *cited* and year, month, and day. End with a semicolon.

⑦ *Publication information for article.* Give volume number, issue number (in parentheses), a colon, and page numbers. End with a period.

⑧ *Name of database.* End with a period.

⑨ *Publication information for database.* Include the city, the state abbreviation in parentheses, a colon, the publisher's name, and a period.

⑩ *Web address.* Write *Available from* and give the brief URL.

⑪ *Document number.* Write *Document no.* and identifying number.

(Adapted from the CSE guidelines for citing an online journal.)

**For an article in a database, use the following formats:**

*Citation-sequence or citation-name format*

1. Last name first initial(s). Title of article. Journal abbreviation [Internet]. Year [cited year month day]; Volume(Issue):Pages. Name of database. City of database publication: Database Publisher. Available from: URL Document No.: number.

*Name-year format*

Last name first initial(s). Title of article. Journal abbreviation [Internet]. Year [cited year month day]; Volume(Issue):Pages. Name of database. City of database publication: Database Publisher. Available from: URL Document No.: number.

**A citation for the article on p. 425 would look like this:**

p. 425

*Citation-sequence or citation-name format*

NOTE NO. AUTHOR'S LAST NAME, INITIALS ARTICLE TITLE

1. Miller AL. Epidemiology, etiology, and natural treatment of seasonal affective disorder.

JOURNAL ABBREV. PUBL. YEAR DATE OF ACCESS NAME OF DATABASE

Altern Med Rev [Internet]. 2005 [cited 2006 Aug 9]; 10(1):5-13. Expanded Academic

PAGE NUMBERS

DATABASE PUBL. CITY DATABASE PUBL.

VOLUME AND ISSUE NUMBER

ASAP. Farmington Hills (MI): Thomson Gale. Available from: http://find.galegroup.com

DOCUMENT NUMBER URL

Document No.: A131086129.

*Name-year format*

Miller AL. 2005. Epidemiology, etiology, and natural treatment of seasonal affective disorder. Altern Med Rev [Internet]. [cited 2006 Aug 9]; 10(1):5-13. Expanded Academic ASAP. Farmington Hills (MI): Thomson Gale. Available from: http://find.galegroup.com Document No.: A131086129.

For more on using CSE style to cite articles in a database, see 21c3. (For guidelines and models for using MLA style, see 18d3; for APA style, see 19d3; for *Chicago* style, see 20c3.)

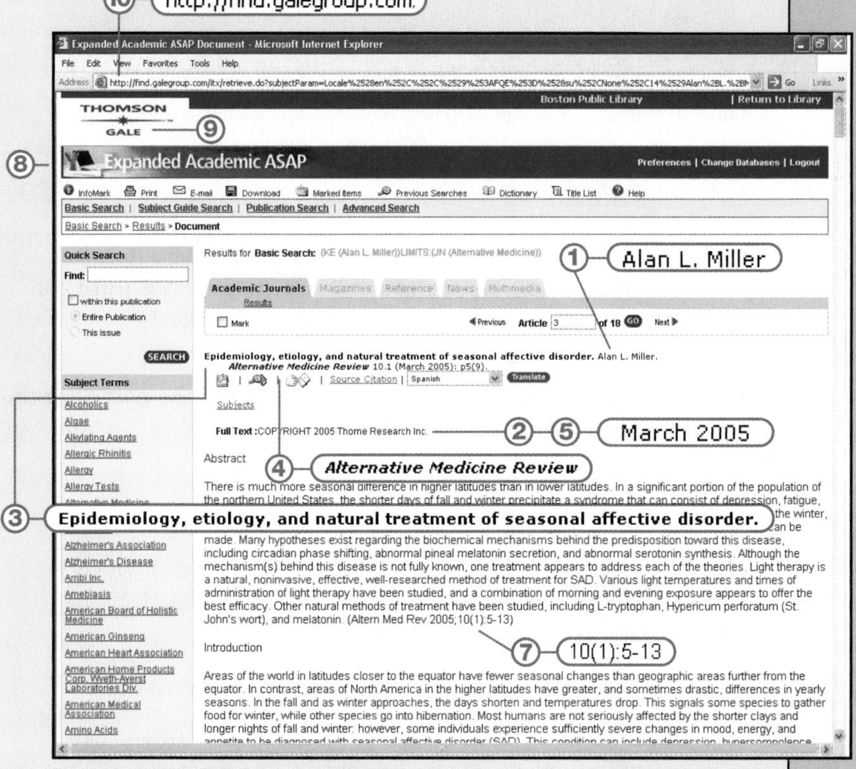

model has been adapted from CSE guidelines for citing an online journal article.)

12. Shilts E. Water wanderers. Can Geographic [Internet]. 2002 [cited 2004 Jan 27];122(3):72–77. Expanded Academic ASAP. Farmington Hills (MI): Thomson Gale. Available from: http://web4.infotrac.galegroup.com/itw/ Document No.: A86207443.

#### 13. ARTICLE IN AN ONLINE JOURNAL

13. Perez P, Calonge TM. Yeast protein kinase C. J Biochem [Internet]. 2002 Oct [cited 2003 Nov 3];132(4):513–517. Available from: http://edpex104 .bcasj.or.jp/jb-pdf/132-4/jb132-4-513.pdf

#### 14. ARTICLE IN AN ONLINE NEWSPAPER

14. Brody JE. Reasons, and remedies, for morning sickness. New York Times Online [Internet]. 2004 Apr 27 [cited 2004 Apr 30]. Available from: http://www.nytimes.com/2004/04/27/health/27BROD.html

#### 15. ONLINE BOOK

15. Patrick TS, Allison JR, Krakow GA. Protected plants of Georgia [Internet]. Social Circle (GA): Georgia Department of Natural Resources; c1995 [cited 2003 Dec 3]. Available from: http://www.georgiawildlife.com/content/ displaycontent.asp?txtDocument=89&txtPage=9

To cite a portion of an online book, give the name of the part after the publication information: *Chapter 6, Encouraging germination.* See model 6.

#### 16. WEB SITE

16. Geology and public policy [Internet]. Boulder (CO): Geological Society of America; c2003 [updated 2003 Apr 8; cited 2003 Apr 13]. Available from: http://www.geosociety.org/science/govpolicy.htm

#### 17. GOVERNMENT WEB SITE

17. Health disparities: minority cancer awareness [Internet]. Atlanta (GA): Centers for Disease Control and Prevention (US); [updated 2004 Apr 27; cited 2005 May 1]. Available from: http://www.cdc.gov/cancer/ minorityawareness.htm

## 21d A student paper, CSE style

The following research proposal by Tara Gupta conforms to the citation-sequence format in the CSE guidelines described in this chapter. Note that these pages have been reproduced in a narrow format to allow for annotation.

Student Writer

Tara Gupta

**bedfordstmartins.com/smhandbook** For additional student research writing, click on **Student Writing**.

Specific and informative title, name, and other relevant information centered on title page

Field Measurements of
Photosynthesis and Transpiration
Rates in Dwarf Snapdragon
(*Chaenorrhinum minus* Lange):
An Investigation of Water Stress
Adaptations

Tara Gupta

Proposal for a
Summer Research
Fellowship
Colgate University
February 25, 2003

Water Stress Adaptations 2

Shortened title appears next to page number

Introduction

Headings throughout help organize the proposal

Dwarf snapdragon (*Chaenorrhinum minus*) is a weedy pioneer plant found growing in central New York during spring and summer. Interestingly, the distribution of this species has been limited almost exclusively to the cinder ballast of railroad tracks [1] and to sterile strips of land along highways [2]. In these harsh environments, characterized by intense sunlight and poor soil water retention, one would expect *C. minus* to exhibit anatomical features similar to those of xeromorphic plants (species adapted to arid habitats).

Introduction states scientific issue, gives background information; documentation follows CSE citation-sequence format

However, this is not the case. T. Gupta and R. Arnold (unpublished) have found that the leaves and stems of *C. minus* are not covered by a thick, waxy cuticle but rather with a thin cuticle that is less effective in inhibiting water loss through diffusion. The root system is not long and thick, capable of reaching deeper, moister soils; instead, it is thin and diffuse, permeating only the topmost (and driest) soil horizon. Moreover, in contrast to many xeromorphic plants, the stomata (pores regulating gas exchange) are not found in sunken crypts or cavities in the epidermis that retard water loss from transpiration.

Despite a lack of these morphological adaptations to water stress, *C. minus* continues to grow and reproduce when morning dew has been its only source of water for up to 5 weeks (2002 letter from R. Arnold to me). Such growth involves fixation of carbon by photosynthesis and requires that the stomata be open to admit sufficient carbon dioxide. Given the dry, sunny environment, the time required for adequate carbon fixation must also mean a significant loss of water through transpiration as open stomata exchange carbon dioxide with water. How does *C. minus* balance the need for carbon with the need to conserve water?

Personal communication cited in parentheses within text but not included in references

Purposes of the Proposed Study

States purposes and scope of proposed study

The above observations have led me to an exploration of the extent to which *C. minus* is able to photosynthesize under conditions of low water availability. It is my hypothesis that *C. minus* adapts to these conditions by photosynthesizing in the early morning and late afternoon, when leaf and air temperatures are lower and transpirational water loss is reduced. During the middle of the day, its photosynthetic rate may be very low, perhaps even zero, on hot, sunny afternoons. Similar diurnal changes in photosynthetic rate in response to midday water deficits have been described in crop plants [3,4]. There appear to be no comparable studies on noncrop species in their natural habitats.

Significance of study noted

Relates proposed research project to future research

Thus, the research proposed here aims to help explain the apparent paradox of an organism that thrives in water-stressed conditions despite a lack of morphological adaptations. This summer's work will also serve as a basis for controlled experiments in a plant growth chamber on the individual effects of temperature, light intensity, soil water availability, and other environmental factors on photosynthesis and transpiration rates. These experiments are planned for the coming fall semester.

Methods and Timeline

Briefly describes methodology to be used

Provides timeline

Simultaneous measurements of photosynthesis and transpiration rates will indicate the balance *C. minus* has achieved in acquiring the energy it needs while retaining the water available to it. These measurements will be taken daily from June 22 to September 7, 2003, at field sites in the Hamilton, NY, area, using an LI-6220 portable photosynthesis system (LICOR, Inc., Lincoln, NE). Basic methodology and use of correction factors will be similar to that described in related studies [5–7]. Data will be collected at regular intervals throughout the daylight hours and will be related to measurements of ambient air temperature, leaf temperature, relative humidity, light intensity, wind velocity, and cloud cover.

Budget

| | |
|---|---|
| 1 kg soda lime, 4-8 mesh<br>(for absorption of $CO_2$ in photosynthesis analyzer) | $70 |
| 1 kg anhydrous magnesium perchlorate<br>(used as desiccant for photosynthesis analyzer) | $130 |
| SigmaScan software (Jandel Scientific Software, Inc.)<br>(for measurement of leaf areas for which photosynthesis and transpiration rates are to be determined) | $195 |
| Estimated 500 miles travel to field sites in own car @ $0.28/mile | $140 |
| $CO_2$ cylinder, 80 days rental @ $0.25/day<br>(for calibration of photosynthesis analyzer) | $20 |
| TOTAL REQUEST | $555 |

Budget provides itemized details

Includes all published works cited; numbers correspond to order in which sources are first mentioned

Article from government Web site

Article in weekly journal

Article in journal

Water Stress Adaptations 5

References

1. Wildrlechner MP. Historical and phenological observations of the spread of *Chaenorrhinum minus* across North America. Can J Bot. 1983;61(1):179–187.

2. Dwarf Snapdragon [Internet]. Olympia (WA): Washington State Noxious Weed Control Board; 2001 [updated 2001 Jul 7; cited 2003 Jan 25]. Available from: http://www.wa.gov/agr/weedboard/weed_info/dwarfsnapdragon.html

3. Boyer JS. Plant productivity and environment. Science. 1982 Nov 6:443–448.

4. Manhas JG, Sukumaran NP. Diurnal changes in net photosynthetic rate in potato in two environments. Potato Res. 1988;31:375–378.

5. Doley DG, Unwin GL, Yates DJ. Spatial and temporal distribution of photosynthesis and transpiration by single leaves in a rainforest tree, *Argyrodendron peralatum*. Aust J Plant Physiol. 1988;15(3):317–326.

6. Kallarackal J, Milburn JA, Baker DA. Water relations of the banana. III. Effects of controlled water stress on water potential, transpiration, photosynthesis and leaf growth. Aust J Plant Physiol. 1990;17(1):79–90.

7. Idso SB, Allen SG, Kimball BA, Choudhury BJ. Problems with porometry: measuring net photosynthesis by leaf chamber techniques. Agron. 1989;81(4):475–479.

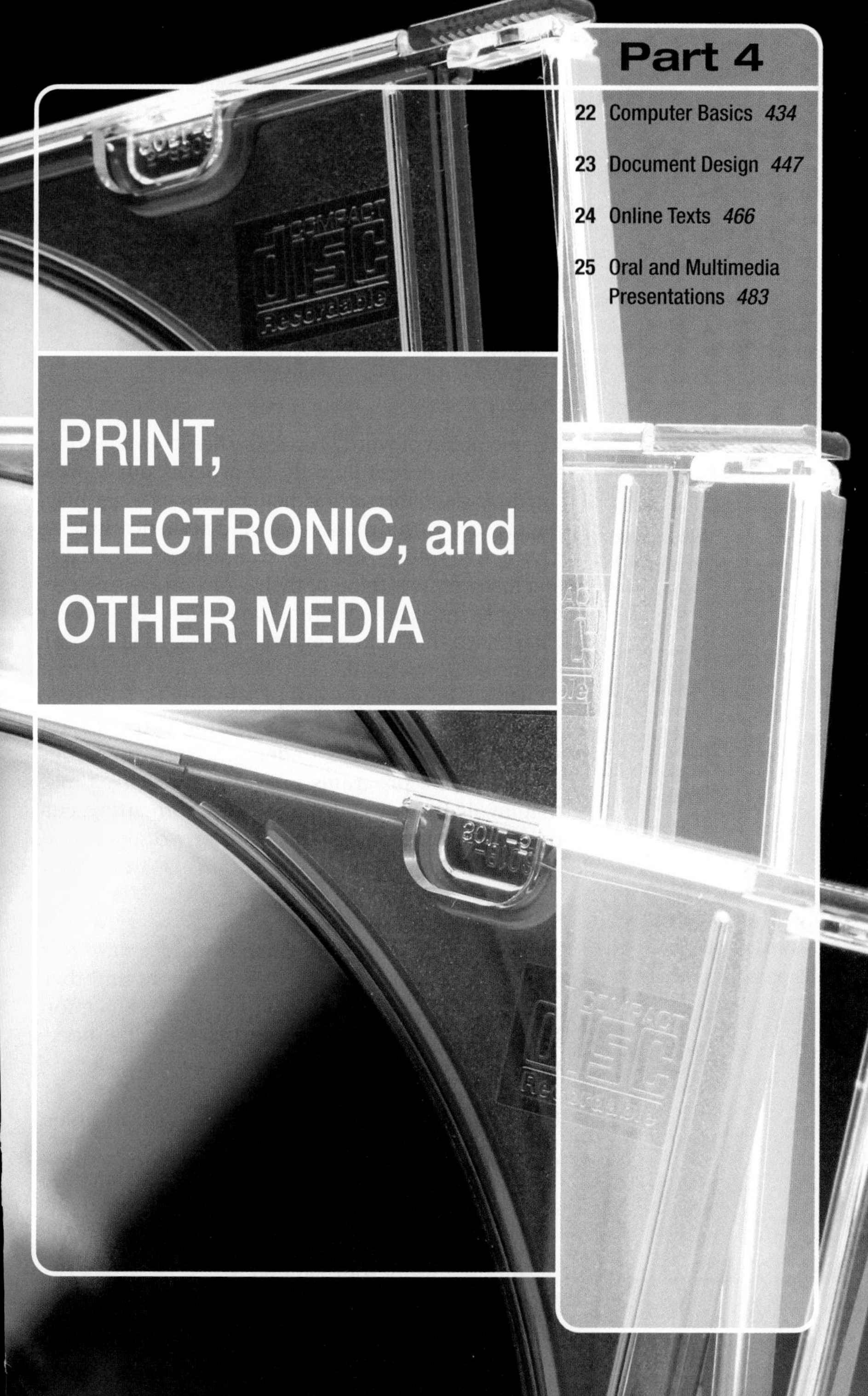

# Part 4



# PRINT, ELECTRONIC, and OTHER MEDIA

# 22 Computer Basics

Writers use computers in all kinds of ways and combinations. Many writers use a word processor to draft and revise essays from start to finish; use the Web and online library databases for research; read and write email and instant messages; keep a blog that is personal, professional, or both; visit chat rooms to keep in touch with colleagues, family, and friends or to meet new people; and use sound, images, animation, and video as part of their compositions. For many writers, the computer is the tool they turn to first to present their ideas.

## 22a Word processing

The metaphor of word *processing* deserves attention: we use computers literally to process our words, organizing and formatting them in various ways, playing around with organization and stylistic choices. This active role we ascribe to computers is one reason many writers think of their word-processing programs as integral to writing today: film critic Roger Ebert says that "the computer keyboard is now an extension of my mind."

However, getting word-processing programs to work efficiently and effectively for you calls for some care. It requires understanding the various tools that the programs provide, especially those that involve saving and sharing files, formatting, cutting and pasting, and improving your writing.

### Saving and sharing files

In most word processors, you can choose NEW from the file menu to create a new document and then save it as a file. You will save yourself time and effort later on, when you're looking for a particular document, by assigning each file a clear name (*Rhetorical Analysis draft 1*, for example, instead of *Paper 1*). Here are some other tips for saving and sharing files:

- Create a master folder for your writing course, labeled with the name of the course (*Writing and Rhetoric*). Within that folder, create folders labeled *My Drafts* and *Peer Drafts*. Then save files in the appropriate folder.

- Remember to use SAVE AS to record every draft you write, changing the file name to keep track of each draft and each peer review you do. If your instructor asks you to submit a CD of all your drafts and peer comments, it will be easy to copy your folders to the CD for submission.
- If you are handing in your draft electronically to an instructor or giving a copy to someone else, include your name in the file name, along with other pertinent information (Mamta Ahluwalia's essay might be saved as *Mamta Ahluwalia rhet analysis draft 1*, for example). The use of your full name in the file makes it easier for an instructor to see if you've handed in the work and to distinguish it from that of other students.
- Always check on the file type another person can receive before sending a draft electronically, since not all users will have the same edition or type of software you have. Remember that adding visuals and multimedia will increase the file size, and some email accounts limit the size of files. For sharing one file with a group of people, you can choose SAVE AS and select RICH TEXT FORMAT (as long as you are not using graphics or complicated tables in the file).
- Set your word processor to save automatically, or remember to save your files every five minutes or right after you've made an important change. Few things are more frustrating to writers than losing part of their work.
- Take the extra precaution of saving a second copy of every file and giving it a slightly different name (*Rhetorical Analysis draft 1 dup*) on a disc or in another location.

## CONSIDERING DISABILITIES: Accessible files

When you are working with other members of your class to share files for peer review or other group activities, remember to consider differences group members may have, not only in terms of computer compatibility but in terms of varying abilities as well. You may have classmates who wish to receive files in a very large type size, for example, in order to read them with ease. You can help your group get off to a good start by making a plan for accommodating everyone's needs.

### Formatting

When formatting a document (23b), make use of the tools your word-processing program provides. The advantage of using specific formatting tools is that your formatting choices will remain intact even if you change the content. The following list of format recommendations includes keywords (in *italics*) that you can search for in your word processor's HELP menu to learn how to use each feature:

- Most word processors set the default *margins* at 1 inch for top and bottom and 1.25 inches for left and right sides. You may need to adjust the default margins for some documents by changing the default settings.
- For text you want to *indent*, highlight the text, and then use the FORMAT menu or ruler bar to align the text as needed.
- Use the word processor to insert *page numbers* automatically and to adjust them if you add or delete pages. Include additional information with the page number, such as your name or the paper's title, by adding *headers* or *footers*. You can also add and number *footnotes* or *endnotes*.
- Try using the FORMAT menu to add *bullets*, *numbering*, or *columns*. Highlight the text you want to be bulleted or numbered or formatted in columns before you choose the appropriate command.
- Most word processors include graphics tools for creating charts, graphs, tables, and other illustrations. Your word processor may also have an INSERT function for easily adding a *picture*, *symbol*, or *hyperlink* into your document.
- Use the PRINT PREVIEW function in the FILE menu to see what your document will look like before it is printed.
- Use the ZOOM function to increase or decrease the size of the type for more comfortable reading on the screen.
- Review the TOOLBARS function to see how you can customize the toolbar to include the features you use most often.

### Cutting and pasting

Your word-processing program offers CUT, COPY, and PASTE tools (in the toolbar and the EDIT menu) to help you revise. When you highlight and then cut or copy text, the word-processing program saves the text in its clipboard memory and lets you paste it in another location, including other files or programs. Note that the clipboard-stored text will be replaced whenever you highlight and cut or copy a new selection of text. Be careful to paste the first bit somewhere before you cut or copy another bit; otherwise, you will lose that first bit of text. Following are additional tips to help you use the CUT, COPY, and PASTE functions efficiently:

- When you copy text that you are thinking of moving elsewhere, the copied text will stay where it was in your document while you experiment. If the passage fits better somewhere else, you can paste it there and then go back and delete it from its original location.
- If you plan to revise the organization of a document extensively (perhaps after getting feedback from a classmate), use SAVE AS to give the document a new file name and then work from the new copy before making additions, cutting, copying, pasting, and so on.
- If you think you might want to use text you're cutting for some future writing project, open a new file for these scraps and give it a name associated with the draft you're working on (for example, *Cuts from rhet analysis dr 2*). You will then be able to retrieve the text if you decide to use it later.
- Remember that too much cutting and pasting can quickly result in an incoherent text. After cutting and pasting, reread your document to make sure it still moves logically from point to point.

### *Basic tools for improving writing*

Several other word-processing tools may help you improve the quality of your writing. For starters, your campus writing center or computer lab may have a software program that helps you begin a piece of writing by asking you a series of questions, giving a set of prompts, or allowing you to create idea maps. Many students find brainstorming and talking with others (online or off) more effective than such programs, but if one is available to you, try it out and use it if it seems helpful. Here are some other word-processing tools that may help:

- Use the OUTLINE function to check the logical connections in a document you create. An outline can be extremely useful after your entire draft is complete: looking at only the main points of your draft allows you to focus on transitions between points as well as overall logic.

- The COMPARE AND MERGE tool allows you to see how your draft has changed between versions. Seeing a visual representation of your revision can be enlightening — but it can also be confusing in a long document with many changes, so you may want to experiment with this tool on less complex revisions.
- Spell checkers can go a long way toward identifying typos and other misspellings. But a spell checker will not pick up many kinds of mistakes: wrong words that are spelled correctly, misspelled proper names, and confused homonyms (*there*, *their*, *they're*). A spell checker set to accept suggestions automatically can even introduce new errors. The bottom line is that there is no substitute for careful proofreading. (See 30e.)
- Grammar and style checkers can be problematic: they are looking at your text out of context, without knowing your purpose, audience, or rhetorical situation. Furthermore, grammar and style checkers sometimes give the wrong advice. Although grammar checkers can help you spot some grammatical errors, you should use them with caution.
- If you're using Microsoft Word, experiment with the TRACK CHANGES and COMMENT tools. TRACK CHANGES records changes, in color, and

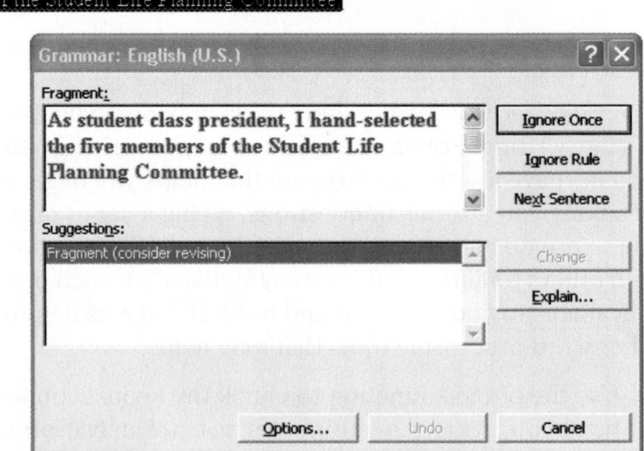


*Grammar checkers may give the wrong advice.*

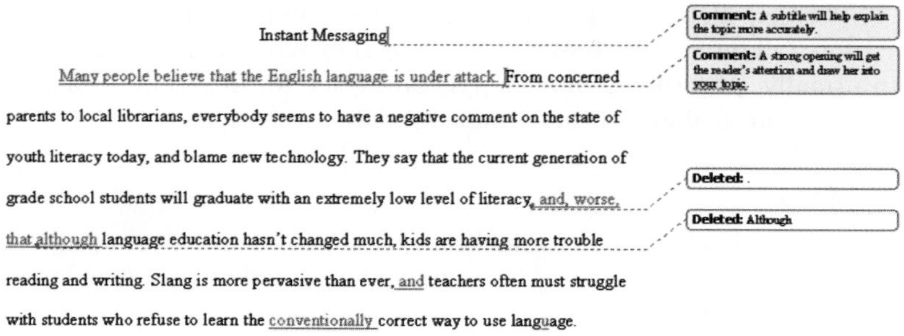

Instant Messaging

Many people believe that the English language is under attack. From concerned parents to local librarians, everybody seems to have a negative comment on the state of youth literacy today, and blame new technology. They say that the current generation of grade school students will graduate with an extremely low level of literacy, and, worse, that although language education hasn't changed much, kids are having more trouble reading and writing. Slang is more pervasive than ever, and teachers often must struggle with students who refuse to learn the conventionally correct way to use language.

**Comment:** A subtitle will help explain the topic more accurately.

**Comment:** A strong opening will get the reader's attention and draw her into your topic.

**Deleted:** .

**Deleted:** Although

TRACK CHANGES *and* COMMENT *tools help with revision*

allows you to accept or reject them later. Both of these tools are useful for revising and working collaboratively; different users' changes and comments appear in different colors.

- Use the FIND and REPLACE functions to help you search for certain kinds of errors or overused words. For example, if you tend to mistype *it's* for *its*, you can search for all uses of *it's* and correct them as necessary.

### EXERCISE 22.1

Take an assignment you are working on, and experiment with the TRACK CHANGES editing function in Microsoft Word (under TOOLS). Practice editing your text, using this function to highlight additions and to cross out material that needs to be changed. Print out a page of your revision, and bring it to class for comparison with other students' work.

## 22b Electronic communication

Much of our communication today takes place electronically — via email, instant messaging, discussion forums, listservs, blogs, and so on. So prevalent is this form of communication in our daily lives that we may stop thinking about it consciously. Computers and text-messaging devices allow people to remain in constant, and seemingly effortless, contact.

Because electronic communication is so common, however, many writers fall into habits based on the way they write most often — very informally. By failing to adjust style and voice for different occasions and audiences, they may undermine their own intentions.

## 1 Email

As with any kind of writing, email calls on you to consider your purpose and audience. The following tips can help ensure that your email messages are effective:

- Use a subject line that states your purpose accurately and clearly — whether you are writing an email message or responding to one. Remember to change the subject line if you are writing about something different from the original subject.
- Take care not to offend or irritate your reader. Avoid flaming — using intentionally rude language — and remember that even if your intentions are good, tone is hard to convey in online messages: what you intend as a joke may come across as an insult. In addition, many readers find messages in ALL CAPS irritating, as if someone were shouting at them.
- Be pertinent. Give your readers only the information they need. The length and style of your messages will vary, depending on the subject at hand and your recipients' expectations. For example, a teacher might expect short and to-the-point messages, whereas readers of a scholarly discussion list might expect long, analytical messages.
- Break your long paragraphs into shorter paragraphs, and when a message has several points, create sections with headings.
- Use a more formal tone along with a formal greeting and closing when posting a message to someone you don't know or to an authority, such as a supervisor or instructor (*Dear Ms. Aulie* rather than *Hello*).
- Except in very informal situations, use the conventions of academic English (28b). If you want your messages to be taken seriously, be sure they are clearly written and error free. Proofread email messages just as you would other writing.
- Check to make sure you are responding to the appropriate person or persons. Most email programs allow you to click on REPLY to respond to the person who sent you the message or on REPLY TO ALL

to reach the whole group. People often send very personal messages meant for one person to whole groups or to an entire discussion list because they forget to check where the reply is going. This can be extremely embarrassing.

- Use *Cc:* ("carbon copy") to copy someone other than the main recipient of your message. Use *Bcc:* ("blind carbon copy") when you want to free a recipient — for instance, an employer or instructor — from REPLY TO ALL threads in response to your message.
- Remember that the Internet is public and that online readers can easily print or forward your messages. When privacy is important, think twice before communicating by email, and always ask permission before forwarding a sensitive message from someone else.
- Consider email permanent and always findable. Even if you delete it from your inbox or hard drive, a copy will likely exist on your senders' or receivers' machines or on the server you or they use; many people have been embarrassed (or worse, prosecuted) because of email trails.
- Before attaching text or graphics files, check with your recipients to make sure they will be able to download them. If you are sending a document as an attachment, save it as RICH TEXT FORMAT (RTF), or copy and paste your text into your email message. (If you copy and paste, you may lose formatting.)
- Avoid using color fonts or other special formatting unless you know the formatting will appear as you intend on your reader's screen.
- Conclude your message with your name and email address. Your email program likely includes a command that lets you place this information in a signature file.

**bedfordstmartins.com/smhandbook** For more information on effective electronic communication, click on **Online Writing**.

## EXERCISE 22.2

Choose several email messages you have sent recently — at least one of which is more formal than the others. Take a critical look at the messages you have chosen, noting differences and similarities and thinking about how easily readers could follow them. Bring your findings to class for discussion.

EMAIL

To: Andrea Lunsford [lunsford@stanford.edu]

From: Rudy Rubio [alofides@stanford.edu]

Subject: Letter of recommendation

Attachment: GSGLrec.doc; Rubio_2007.doc; Rubio_WCS.doc

---

Dear Professor Lunsford:

I am writing with some great news: I am now a finalist for the Goldman Sachs Global Leaders Program. The program now asks that I seek two letters of recommendation that will speak to the "specific qualities of the nominee."

I am attaching the recommender form that the program sent to me this week along with my application, a copy of my current résumé, and a summary of the work that I did in your Writing Center Seminar class.

If you will agree to write this letter of recommendation, I can pick it up from you, in an envelope with your signature across the back flap. The due date is June 1, 2007.

Thank you very much for considering this request, Professor Lunsford. I will be sure to keep you posted as I continue with the nomination process.

Sincerely yours,

Rudy

Rudy Rubio

alofides@stanford.edu

## 2 Lists and discussion forums

When you participate in a discussion list (sometimes called a listserv) or in a discussion forum, you are part of an ongoing electronic conversation. As members post and respond to one another, the messages accumulate, creating a chain or thread that is read, and created, by many people. When you are part of such an electronic discussion, keep the following tips in mind:

## FOR MULTILINGUAL WRITERS: Email conventions

Email conventions are still evolving, and they differ from one cultural context to another. Especially if you do not know the recipients of your email, stick to a more formal tone (*Dear Ms. Ditembe* and *Sincerely yours*, for example), and follow the conventions of print letter writing — complete sentences, regular capitalization, and so on. If you have special knowledge about conventions of email use in a particular culture, draw on that knowledge, and share it with others in your class.

- Avoid unnecessary criticism of spelling or other obvious language errors. These kinds of comments are often taken as flames. If a typo makes a message unclear, ask politely for a clarification. If you disagree with an assertion of fact, offer what you believe to be the correct information, but don't insult the writer for making the mistake.
- If you think you've been flamed, give the writer the benefit of the doubt. Replying with patience establishes your credibility and helps you come across as mature and fair.
- Decide whether to reply off-list to the sender of a message or to the whole group, and be careful to use REPLY or REPLY TO ALL accordingly.
- Include only those parts of the original message that you will be addressing, and delete the rest. If you need to, quote from the original message, but only quote as needed, and make sure to set off the quotations from your writing.
- In general, follow the conventions of the particular forum regarding the use of a growing number of acronyms (such as *IOW* for "in other words"). If readers might not understand a particular acronym, write it out.
- Keep in mind that many discussion forums and listservs are archived and that more people than you think may be reading your messages. Remember that your postings create an impression of you.

### 3 Web logs (blogs) and social networking spaces

You have probably run into more than a few Web logs, or blogs. Current figures estimate that there are now over 70 million blogs online worldwide. In fact, you may be taking one or more classes that use a blog as

### DISCUSSION LIST POSTINGS

Subject line provides specific information

Tone is engaged, friendly, and polite

Includes first name and initial only; audience is closed discussion list for class

Author: Kristen Convery
Subject: Class discussion of "self"

I've been thinking about our class discussion on the self. Carl Rogers theorized that people do things in line with their concept of themselves in order to avoid having to rework that self-concept. For instance, if I think of myself as an artist and not as a musician, even if I want to go to a concert, I might go to the art museum instead so that I do not have to change my view of myself.

We seem to feel as if we must fit one mold, and that that mold blocks out all other concepts of the self. How many families do you know where the parents proudly introduce a child as "the scientist (artist/musician/whatever) of the family"? And how does this inhibit other siblings who might also want to be scientists, artists, or musicians but fear taking over someone else's place?

Kristen C.

Opens with point of agreement

Quotations from earlier post clarify what is being discussed

Politely questions conclusions of another writer

Author: Yazmin Guerrero
Subject: Re: Class discussion of "self"

I think Kristen is right when she says that siblings might be inhibited from following up on an interest in science when parents introduce another child as "the scientist of the family." But is that really an example of "people [who] do things in line with their concept of themselves in order to avoid having to rework that self-concept"? Aren't these siblings trying to avoid conflict with their parents' idea of who they are and who their brothers and sisters are? If a child likes science but avoids becoming a scientist in order not to displace her brother as "the scientist of the family," isn't she actually reworking her self-concept in order to keep order in the family?

Yazmin

part of class activity and discussion. For those writing and reading them, blogs provide an ongoing record of thinking, one that is easily recoverable: think of an interactive electronic journal you write in as often as possible. Many online sites allow you to create a blog easily.

Blogs are not the only public online spaces that allow users to say almost anything about themselves or to comment freely on the postings of others. Social networking sites such as Facebook, MySpace, LiveJournal, and many others are the online versions of printed journals, diaries, yearbooks signed by friends and acquaintances, and the like. Many users think of these online spaces as relatively private and safe, intended — like diaries and signed yearbooks — to be seen by only a small circle of friends and acquaintances. Nothing could be further from the truth, however: almost anyone can access social networking sites, and those who use them to post information that they prefer not to share with the world are likely to regret their openness.

A WEB LOG (BLOG)

Here are some basic tips for using blogs and online social networking technologies effectively:

- If you are composing a blog or online journal, remember that it, like email (22b1), is public — what you wish to remain private should not be posted in such spaces.
- To comment on a blog or journal, follow the same conventions you would for a discussion-list posting (22b2). In addition, experienced bloggers recommend that you become familiar with the conversation before you add a comment of your own and that you avoid commenting on entries that are several days old.
- Remember that a blog can serve as a personal journal, as a place to comment on other blogs, as a research log, or as a way to share your writing with classmates. A blog makes it easy to post writing to the Web, but how you use a blog is determined by your purpose and audience — as well as your imagination.

**bedfordstmartins.com/smhandbook** For more information on creating a blog, click on **Online Writing**.

## THINKING CRITICALLY ABOUT WRITING WITH COMPUTERS

Take at least one day and note down every time you use a computer for writing anything at all, from an IM or a casual email to a Facebook entry, Web site update, or notes in a Word document for an upcoming assignment. At the end of the day, make an inventory of all your uses, and then stop to think critically about them. What kinds of writing do you use the computer for most often? How is the writing you do on the computer related to reading? to speaking? What differences can you note between the informal writing you do on a computer and the more formal or academic writing? How would you describe the tone and voice of your online writing — and how do you differ from one audience to the next?

# Document Design

23

In the ancient Greek world, a speaker's delivery (known as *actio*) was an art every educated person needed to master; how a speaker delivered a speech — tone and volume of voice, use of gestures, and so on — had a great impact on how the speech would be received. Today, the electronic revolution has dramatically affected the delivery of information. Computers make it easy for us to use color, headings, lists, graphics, and other visuals in print and online texts. Because these visual elements can be fundamental to readability and to helping us get and keep a reader's attention, they bring a whole new dimension to writing — what some refer to as *visual rhetoric*.

## 23a Visual structure

Effective writers think of their print and Web-based documents as visual structures to which they can apply basic principles of design. Even the most basic essay — all text, on paper — has a visual structure, with certain margins and spacing, a centered title, paragraphs indented on the first line, and so on. A fairly simple manuscript format incorporates many visual rhetoric principles, and computers offer more complex design choices such as varied fonts and inserted images. However visually rich the document, however, the writer's goals are to make each page look inviting and to lead readers smoothly from one part of the text to the next.

### 1 Mode of delivery

When you prepare a print or a Web-based document, remember that there are important differences between these two media. In general, print documents are easily portable and more familiar than Web documents. In addition, the tools for producing print texts are highly developed and stable. For the most part, pages you print will look just the way they looked in the PRINT PREVIEW function, whereas the look of Web-based pages often varies depending on your browser or your reader's browser. Nevertheless, Web-based documents have significant advantages: publishing on the Web is still fairly inexpensive; color, sound, and other illustrative materials are often available at no extra cost; updates are easy to make; distribution is fast and efficient; and feedback can be swift. Whether you are working to produce a print or a Web document, however, you should rely on several important principles of design.

## 2 Design principles

Most design experts begin with several very simple principles that guide the design of print and Web-based texts. These principles are illustrated in the Web pages shown on pp. 448 – 50. (For more information on the design of nonprint documents, see Chapter 24.)

### Contrast

Contrast attracts your eye to elements on a page and guides you around it, helping you follow an argument or find information. You may achieve contrast through the use of color, icons, boldface or large type size, headings, and so on. Begin with a focus point — the dominant point, image, or words on the page where you want your reader's eye to go first — and structure the flow of your visual information from this point.

*The* National Geographic *Web site uses high-contrast yellow and blue effectively.*

### Proximity

Parts of the page that are closely related should appear together (*proximate* to one another). Your goal is to position related points, text, and visuals near one another and to use clear headings to identify these clusters.

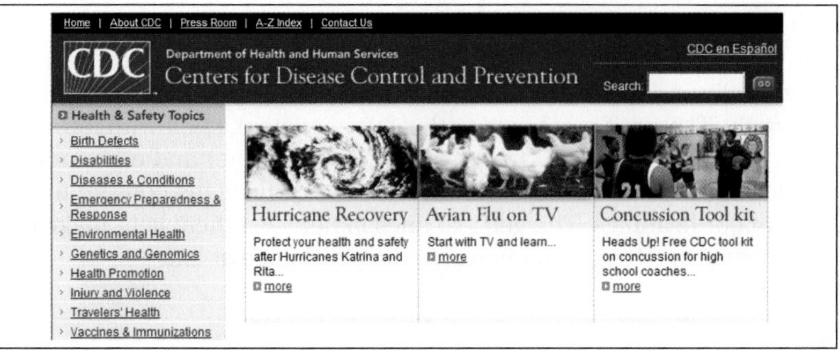


*The Centers for Disease Control and Prevention site demonstrates proximity by placing each image above its label and supporting text.*

### *Repetition*

Readers are guided by the repetition of key words or elements. You can take advantage of this design principle by using a consistent design throughout your document for such elements as color, typeface, and images. Bartleby.com's navigation tabs at the top of every page on the site are repeated in the sidebar.

*Repetition is used in the sidebar and top navigation menus on Bartleby.com.*

### Alignment

This principle refers to how images and text on a page are lined up, both horizontally and vertically. The overall guideline is not to mix alignments arbitrarily. That is, if you begin with a left alignment, stick with it for the major parts of your page. The result will be a cleaner and more organized look. The U.S. Postal Service site effectively aligns content under three major headings. The vertical lines in between them help make the alignment clear. Text under each heading is aligned at left.

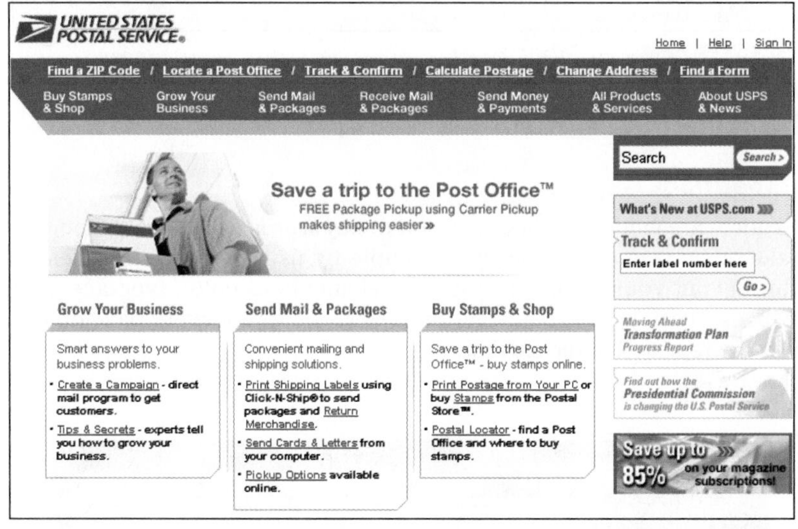


*The U.S. Postal Service site aligns content under headings.*

### Consistent overall impression

Aim for a design that creates the appropriate overall impression or mood for your document. For an academic essay, you will probably make conservative choices that strike a serious scholarly note. In a newsletter for a campus group, you might choose bright colors and arresting images.

## 23b Formatting

With so many options available, it's important to spend some time thinking about the most appropriate formatting elements for a document. Although the following formatting guidelines often apply, remember that

REPORT USING WHITE SPACE EFFECTIVELY

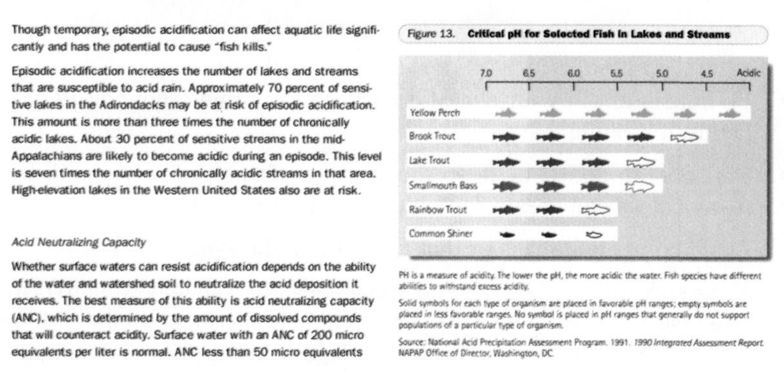

Though temporary, episodic acidification can affect aquatic life significantly and has the potential to cause "fish kills."

Episodic acidification increases the number of lakes and streams that are susceptible to acid rain. Approximately 70 percent of sensitive lakes in the Adirondacks may be at risk of episodic acidification. This amount is more than three times the number of chronically acidic lakes. About 30 percent of sensitive streams in the mid-Appalachians are likely to become acidic during an episode. This level is seven times the number of chronically acidic streams in that area. High-elevation lakes in the Western United States also are at risk.

*Acid Neutralizing Capacity*

Whether surface waters can resist acidification depends on the ability of the water and watershed soil to neutralize the acid deposition it receives. The best measure of this ability is acid neutralizing capacity (ANC), which is determined by the amount of dissolved compounds that will counteract acidity. Surface water with an ANC of 200 micro equivalents per liter is normal. ANC less than 50 micro equivalents

Figure 13. **Critical pH for Selected Fish in Lakes and Streams**



PH is a measure of acidity. The lower the pH, the more acidic the water. Fish species have different abilities to withstand excess acidity.

Solid symbols for each type of organism are placed in favorable pH ranges; empty symbols are placed in less favorable ranges. No symbol is placed in pH ranges that generally do not support populations of a particular type of organism.

Source: National Acid Precipitation Assessment Program. 1991. *1990 Integrated Assessment Report.* NAPAP Office of Director, Washington, DC.

print documents, Web pages, slide shows, videos, or radio essays will each have their own formatting conventions.

### White space

Use white space, or negative space, to emphasize and direct readers to parts of the page. White space determines a page's density—the distance between information bits. You consider white space at the page level (margins), paragraph level (space between paragraphs), and sentence level (space between sentences). Within the page, you can also use white space around particular content, such as a graphic or list, to make it stand out. The report above uses white space between paragraphs, before a heading, and below the visual.

### Color

Decisions about color depend to a large extent not only on the kind of equipment you are using—and, for printing, who's paying for the color ink cartridges—but also on the purpose(s) of your document and its intended audience. As you design your documents, keep in mind that some colors can evoke powerful responses, so take care that the colors you use match the message you are sending. Here are some other tips about the effective use of color:

- Use color to draw attention to elements you want to emphasize: headings, bullets, text boxes, or parts of charts or graphs.

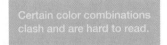

| Certain color combinations clash and are hard to read. | Other combinations are easier on the eyes. |
|---|---|

- Be consistent in your use of color; use the same color for all subheads, for example.
- For most documents, keep the number of colors fairly small; too many colors can create a jumbled or confused look.
- Avoid colors that clash or that are hard on the eyes.
- Make sure all color visuals and text are legible. You may want to print one test page; often what appears readable on the screen — where colors can be sharper — may be less legible in the printed document.

### CONSIDERING DISABILITIES: Color for contrast

Remember when you are using color that not everyone will see it as you do. Some individuals do not perceive color at all; others perceive color in a variety of ways, especially colors like blue and green, which are close together on the color spectrum. When putting colors next to one another, then, use those on opposite sides of the color spectrum, such as purple and gold, in order to achieve high contrast. Doing so will allow readers to see the contrast, if not the nuances, of color.

### *Paper*

The quality of the paper affects the overall look and feel of print documents. Although inexpensive paper is fine for your earlier drafts, use 8½" x 11" good-quality white bond paper for your final presentation. For résumés, you may wish to use parchment or cream-colored bond. For brochures and posters, colored paper may be most appropriate. Use the best-quality printer available to you for your final product.

### *Pagination*

Your instructor may ask that you follow a particular pagination format (for MLA, APA, *Chicago*, and CSE styles, see Chapters 18, 19, 20, and 21); if not, beginning with the first page of text, place your last name and a number in the upper-right-hand corner of the page.

## FOR MULTILINGUAL WRITERS: Reading patterns

In documents written in English and other Western languages, information tends to flow from left to right and top to bottom — since that is the way English texts are written. For a quick example of this principle at work, log on to cnn.com and note that the name of the company appears in the top left corner of the page, where CNN expects readers' eyes to look first. In some languages, which may be written from right to left or vertically, documents may be arranged from top right to bottom left. Understanding the reading patterns of the language you are working in will help you design your documents most effectively.

### *Type*

Most computers allow writers to choose among a great variety of type sizes and typefaces, or fonts. For most college writing, the easy-to-read 11- or 12-point type size is best.

This is 12-point Times New Roman
This is 11-point Times New Roman

A serif font, as is used in the main text of this book, is generally easier to read than a sans serif font. Although unusual fonts might seem attractive at first glance, readers may find such styles distracting and hard to read over long stretches of material.

Remember that typefaces help you create the tone of a document, so consider your audience and purpose when selecting type.

*Different fonts convey different feelings.*
**Different fonts convey different feelings.**
**DIFFERENT FONTS CONVEY DIFFERENT FEELINGS.**
Different fonts convey different feelings.

Most important, be consistent in the size and style of typeface you use, especially for the main part of your text. Unless you are striving for some special effect, shifting sizes and fonts within a document can give an appearance of disorderliness.

### *Spacing*

Final drafts for most of your college writing should be double-spaced, with the first line of paragraphs indented five spaces. Certain kinds of writing for certain disciplines may call for different spacing. Letters, memorandums, and Web texts, for example, are usually single-spaced, with no paragraph indentation. Some long reports may be printed with one-and-a-half-line spacing to save paper. Other kinds of documents, such as flyers and newsletters, may call for multiple columns of print. If in doubt, consult your instructor.

In general, leave one space after all punctuation except in the following cases:

- Leave no space before or after a dash (*Please respond—right away—to this message*).
- Leave no space before or after a hyphen (*a red-letter day*).
- Leave no space between punctuation marks ("*on my way*,").

Computers allow you to decide whether or not you want both side margins justified, or squared off — as they are on this page. Except in posters and other writing where you are trying to achieve a distinctive visual effect, you should always justify the left margin, though you may decide to indent lists and blocks of text that are set off. However, most readers — and many instructors — prefer the right margin to be "ragged," or unjustified.

## 23c Headings

For brief essays and reports, you may need no headings at all. For longer documents, however, these devices call attention to the organization of the text and thus aid comprehension. Some kinds of reports use set headings (like *Abstract* or *Summary*), which readers expect and writers therefore must provide; see 19e for an example. When you use headings, you need to decide on type size and style, wording, and placement.

### *Type size and style*

This book, which is a long and complex document, uses various levels of headings. These levels of headings are distinguished by type sizes and fonts as well as by color.

In a college paper, you will usually distinguish levels of headings using only type — for example, all capitals for the first-level headings, capitals and lowercase boldface for the second level, capitals and lowercase italics for the third level, and so on.

FIRST-LEVEL HEADING
**Second-Level Heading**
*Third-Level Heading*

### *Consistent headings*

Look for the most succinct and informative way to word headings. In general, state a topic in a single word, usually a noun (*Toxicity*); in a phrase, usually a noun phrase (*Levels of Toxicity*) or a gerund phrase (*Measuring Toxicity*); in a question that will be answered in the text (*How Can Toxicity Be Measured?*); or in an imperative that tells readers what steps to take (*Measure the Toxicity*). Whichever structure you choose, make sure you use it consistently for all headings of the same level.

### *Positioning*

Be sure to position each level of heading consistently throughout the text. And remember not to put a heading at the very bottom of a page, since readers would have to turn to the next page to find the text that the heading is announcing.

## 23d Visuals

Because scanners, image archives, image-editing software, digital cameras, drawing programs, and other tools make it easier than ever to find or create visuals, preparing for the use of visuals and creating a visual design may be part of your process of generating ideas and planning for a complete document. Visuals can both draw readers into your argument and help persuade them to accept your claim. In some cases, visuals may even be the primary text you present. In every case, they can help make a point vividly and emphatically by presenting information more succinctly and more clearly than words alone could.

Visuals fall into two categories: tables, which present information in columns and rows of numbers or words, and figures, which include all other visuals — pie, bar, and line charts; line and bar graphs; photographs; maps; drawings; and other illustrations.

For print manuscripts, label and number your visuals (tables and figures should be numbered separately), and give them informative titles.

In some instances, you may need to provide captions to give readers additional data such as source information.

> Figure 1. College Enrollment for Men and Women by Age, 2005 (in millions)
>
> Table 1. Word Choice by Race: *Seesaw and Teeter-totter,* Chicago 1996

In deciding when and where to use visuals, the best rule of thumb is simply to use ones that will make your points most emphatically and will most help your readers understand your document. Researchers who have studied the use of visuals offer tips about when particular types of visuals are most appropriate (see the chart on p. 458).

### *Analyzing and altering visuals*

Because of the technical tools available to writers and designers today, many people can create and publish visuals on the Web. Sometimes, however, the visuals are manipulated or taken out of context. For example, the image below on the far left was circulated widely via email as a *National Geographic* Photo of the Year. The National Geographic Society had to step in to clarify that the picture was a prank and not real. Instead, the photograph was a collage a digital artist had made of two separate pictures — the photo in the middle, from *National Geographic,* and the photo on the right, from the U.S. Air Force Web site.

As you would with any source material, carefully assess any visuals you find online for effectiveness, appropriateness, and validity. Here are additional tips for evaluating visuals:

- Check the context in which the visual appears. Is it part of an official government, company, or library site?

- If the visual is a photograph, is the date, time, place, and setting shown or explained? If the visual is a chart, graph, or diagram, are the numbers and labels explained? Are the sources of the data given?
- Is biographical and contact information for the designer, artist, or photographer given?

If you *do* alter a visual, do so ethically:

- Make sure the visual does not attempt to mislead readers. Show things as accurately as possible.
- Tell your audience what changes you have made.
- Include all relevant data and information about the visual, including the source.

### EXERCISE 23.1

Take an essay or other writing assignment you have done recently, one that makes little use of visuals or the other design elements discussed in this chapter. Reevaluate the effectiveness of your text, and make a note of all the places where visuals and other design elements (color, different type size, and so on) would help you get your ideas across more effectively.

## 23e Sample documents

Interested in creating a flyer advertising your services as a tutor? Want to put together a newsletter for a campus group you belong to? Need to design a portfolio, including an eye-catching cover, for a course you are taking? Such documents are now easier to design and create than ever before. Many word-processing programs or desktop-publishing programs, such as Microsoft Publisher, have templates and step-by-step wizards to help you get started on your document designs. These can be useful invention and design learning tools for getting started. However, don't hesitate to adjust the default designs and elements in a program's preset templates to better fit your needs.

Because it's now easy to make many different document types, college instructors may encourage (or require) you to respond to assignments in ways that go beyond the traditional essay or lab report. Beginning on p. 460 is a catalog of documents collected from college students and others, along with some tips and annotations that should help you create similar documents for your own projects.

**Type of Visual** — **When to Use It**

---

Pie Chart

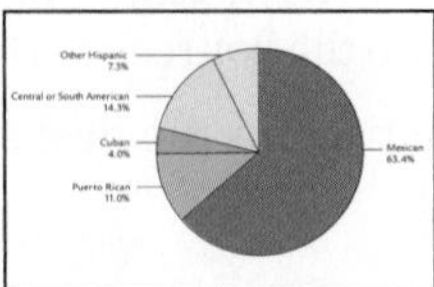


Use *pie charts* to compare a part to the whole.

---

Bar Graph

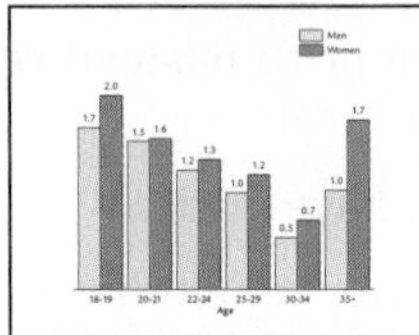


Use *bar graphs* and *line graphs* to compare one element with another, to compare elements over time, to demonstrate correlations, and to illustrate frequency.

---

Table

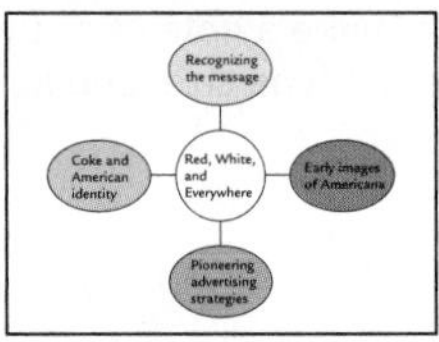

TABLE 10: Commuter Rail Schedule: Reading/Haverhill Line, Boston 2004

| | Train 223 | Train 227 | Train 231 |
|---|---|---|---|
| North Station | 3:00 PM | 4:36 PM | 5:15 PM |
| Reading | 3:38 PM | 4:54 PM | 5:42 PM |
| Haverhill | 4:04 PM | 5:31 PM | 6:21 PM |

Use *tables* to draw attention to particular numerical information.

---

Diagram

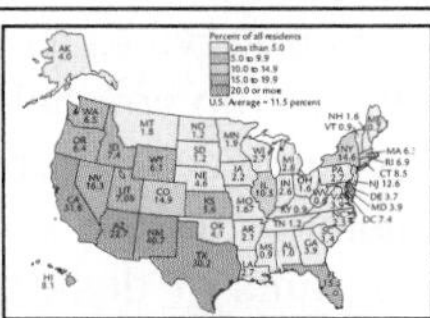


Use *drawings* or *diagrams* to draw attention to dimensions and to details.

---

Map

Use *maps* to draw attention to location and to spatial relationships.

---

Cartoon

Use *cartoons* to illustrate or emphasize a point dramatically or comically.

---

Photo

Use *photographs* to draw attention to a graphic scene (such as devastation following an earthquake) or to depict people or objects.

## Guidelines for using visuals

- Use visuals as a part of your text, not as decoration.
- In print texts, refer to the visual before it actually appears. For example: *As Table 1 demonstrates, the cost of a college education has risen dramatically in the past decade.*
- Tell readers explicitly what the visual demonstrates, especially if it presents complex information. Do not assume readers will "read" the visual the way you do; your commentary on it is important.
- Number and title all visuals. Number and label tables and figures separately.
- Follow established guidelines for documenting visual sources, and ask permission for use, if necessary. (Chapter 16)
- Use clip art sparingly, if at all. Clip art is so easy to cut and paste that you may be tempted to slip it in everywhere, but resist this urge.
- Get responses to your visuals in an early draft. If readers can't follow them or are distracted by them, revise accordingly.
- Do a test-run printout of all visuals to make sure your printer is adequate for the job.
- Use scanners, digital cameras, and image editors to grab, crop, size, and set print and color resolution for any drawings, photographs, or other illustrations that you want to insert into your document. But remember to edit ethically.

**bedfordstmartins.com/smhandbook** For additional models of student writing in various formats, click on **Student Samples**.

NEWSLETTER

- Organization logo uses distinctive visual
- Sponsoring organization identified
- Question used as attention-getting title
- Italics signal overview of problem
- Text wraps around appropriate visual
- Double spacing between sections of text
- Bullets call out important statistics
- Visuals indicate what's coming up inside the newsletter

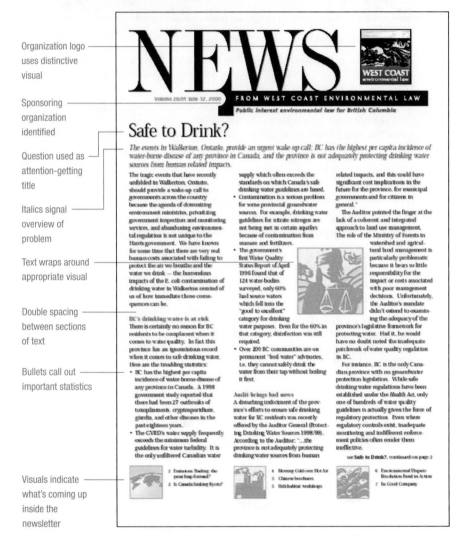

# NEWS

Volume 26:01 June 12, 2000

FROM WEST COAST ENVIRONMENTAL LAW

*Public interest environmental law for British Columbia*

## Safe to Drink?

*The events in Walkerton, Ontario, provide an urgent wake-up call: BC has the highest per capita incidence of water-borne disease of any province in Canada, and the province is not adequately protecting drinking water sources from human related impacts.*

The tragic events that have recently unfolded in Walkerton, Ontario, should provide a wake-up call to governments across the country because the agenda of downsizing environment ministries, privatizing government inspection and monitoring services, and abandoning environmental regulation is not unique to the Harris government. We have known for some time that there are very real human costs associated with failing to protect the air we breathe and the water we drink — the horrendous impacts of the E. coli contamination of drinking water in Walkerton remind of us of how immediate those consequences can be.

### BC's drinking water is at risk

There is certainly no reason for BC residents to be complacent when it comes to water quality. In fact this province has an ignominious record when it comes to safe drinking water. Here are the troubling statistics:

- BC has the highest per capita incidence of water-borne disease of any province in Canada. A 1998 government study reported that there had been 27 outbreaks of toxoplasmosis, cryptosporidium, giardia, and other diseases in the past eighteen years.
- The CVRD's water supply frequently exceeds the minimum federal guidelines for water turbidity. It is the only unfiltered Canadian water supply which often exceeds the standards on which Canada's safe drinking water guidelines are based.
- Contamination is a serious problem for some provincial groundwater sources. For example, drinking water guidelines for nitrate-nitrogen are not being met in certain aquifers because of contamination from manure and fertilizers.
- The government's first Water Quality Status Report of April 1996 found that of 124 water-bodies surveyed, only 60% had source waters which fell into the "good to excellent" category for drinking water purposes. Even for the 60% in that category, disinfection was still required.
- Over 200 BC communities are on permanent "boil water" advisories, i.e. they cannot safely drink the water from their tap without boiling it first.

### Audit brings bad news

A disturbing indictment of the province's efforts to ensure safe drinking water for BC residents was recently offered by the Auditor General (Protecting Drinking Water Sources 1998/99). According to the Auditor: "...the province is not adequately protecting drinking water sources from human related impacts, and this could have significant cost implications in the future for the province, for municipal governments and for citizens in general."

The Auditor pointed the finger at the lack of a coherent and integrated approach to land use management. The role of the Ministry of Forests in watershed and agricultural land management is particularly problematic because it bears so little responsibility for the impact or costs associated with poor management decisions. Unfortunately, the Auditor's mandate didn't extend to examining the adequacy of the province's legislative framework for protecting water. Had it, he would have no doubt noted the inadequate patchwork of water quality regulation in BC.

For instance, BC is the only Canadian province with no groundwater protection legislation. While safe drinking water regulations have been established under the *Health Act*, only one of hundreds of water quality guidelines is actually given the force of regulatory protection. Even where regulatory controls exist, inadequate monitoring and indifferent enforcement policies often render them ineffective.

see **Safe to Drink?**, continued on page 2

FIRST PAGE OF A REPORT (ON THE WEB)

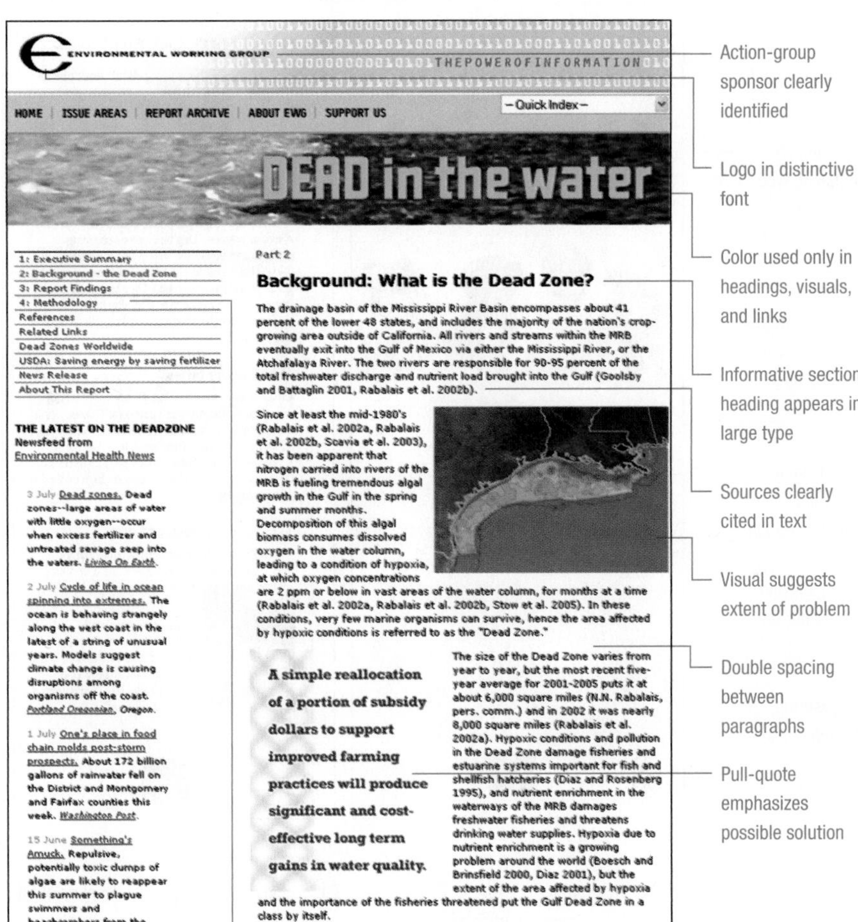

ENVIRONMENTAL WORKING GROUP THEPOWEROFINFORMATION

HOME | ISSUE AREAS | REPORT ARCHIVE | ABOUT EWG | SUPPORT US — Quick Index —

DEAD in the water

1: Executive Summary
2: Background - the Dead Zone
3: Report Findings
4: Methodology
References
Related Links
Dead Zones Worldwide
USDA: Saving energy by saving fertilizer
News Release
About This Report

**THE LATEST ON THE DEADZONE**
Newsfeed from
Environmental Health News

3 July Dead zones. Dead zones--large areas of water with little oxygen--occur when excess fertilizer and untreated sewage seep into the waters. *Living On Earth*.

2 July Cycle of life in ocean spinning into extremes. The ocean is behaving strangely along the west coast in the latest of a string of unusual years. Models suggest climate change is causing disruptions among organisms off the coast. *Portland Oregonian*, Oregon.

1 July One's place in food chain molds post-storm prospects. About 172 billion gallons of rainwater fell on the District and Montgomery and Fairfax counties this week. *Washington Post*.

15 June Something's Amuck. Repulsive, potentially toxic clumps of algae are likely to reappear this summer to plague swimmers and beachcombers from the

Part 2

**Background: What is the Dead Zone?**

The drainage basin of the Mississippi River Basin encompasses about 41 percent of the lower 48 states, and includes the majority of the nation's crop-growing area outside of California. All rivers and streams within the MRB eventually exit into the Gulf of Mexico via either the Mississippi River, or the Atchafalaya River. The two rivers are responsible for 90-95 percent of the total freshwater discharge and nutrient load brought into the Gulf (Goolsby and Battaglin 2001, Rabalais et al. 2002b).

Since at least the mid-1980's (Rabalais et al. 2002a, Rabalais et al. 2002b, Scavia et al. 2003), it has been apparent that nitrogen carried into rivers of the MRB is fueling tremendous algal growth in the Gulf in the spring and summer months. Decomposition of this algal biomass consumes dissolved oxygen in the water column, leading to a condition of hypoxia, at which oxygen concentrations are 2 ppm or below in vast areas of the water column, for months at a time (Rabalais et al. 2002a, Rabalais et al. 2002b, Stow et al. 2005). In these conditions, very few marine organisms can survive, hence the area affected by hypoxic conditions is referred to as the "Dead Zone."

**A simple reallocation of a portion of subsidy dollars to support improved farming practices will produce significant and cost-effective long term gains in water quality.**

The size of the Dead Zone varies from year to year, but the most recent five-year average for 2001-2005 puts it at about 6,000 square miles (N.N. Rabalais, pers. comm.) and in 2002 it was nearly 8,000 square miles (Rabalais et al. 2002a). Hypoxic conditions and pollution in the Dead Zone damage fisheries and estuarine systems important for fish and shellfish hatcheries (Diaz and Rosenberg 1995), and nutrient enrichment in the waterways of the MRB damages freshwater fisheries and threatens drinking water supplies. Hypoxia due to nutrient enrichment is a growing problem around the world (Boesch and Brinsfield 2000, Diaz 2001), but the extent of the area affected by hypoxia and the importance of the fisheries threatened put the Gulf Dead Zone in a class by itself.

BROCHURE

"Don't worry, they won't bite."
"Don't worry, they won't bite..."
While that's true for the vast majority of dogs, even the cuddliest, fuzziest, sweetest pup can bite if provoked.
Unwisely, some owners actually promote aggression in their dogs as symbols of power.
From nips to bites to actual attacks, dog bites are a serious problem. Dog bite victims requiring medical attention in the United States number 500,000 to 1 million annually. Countless more bites go unreported and untreated. On average, about a dozen people die each year from dog bites.
Fortunately, there are steps we can take to address this problem.
Who's being bitten?
Children make up more than 60 percent of all dog bite victims. The national Centers for Disease Control and Prevention estimates half of all children 12 and younger have been bitten by a dog.
The elderly and home service people — like mail carriers and meter readers — also are high on the list of frequent dog bite victims.
What's a dog owner to do?
Carefully consider your pet selection. Before and after selection, your veterinarian is the best source for information about behavior and suitability.
Make sure your pet is socialized as a young puppy, so it feels at ease around people and other animals. Expose your puppy to a variety of situations a little at a time and under
Title in eye-catching type
Appropriate illustration in central spot
Ample space surrounds title and illustration
Long, narrow trifold design
Reassuring, friendly images
Simple design draws attention to important information
Clear, bold headings
Explanation of title and definition of problem

PORTFOLIO COVER

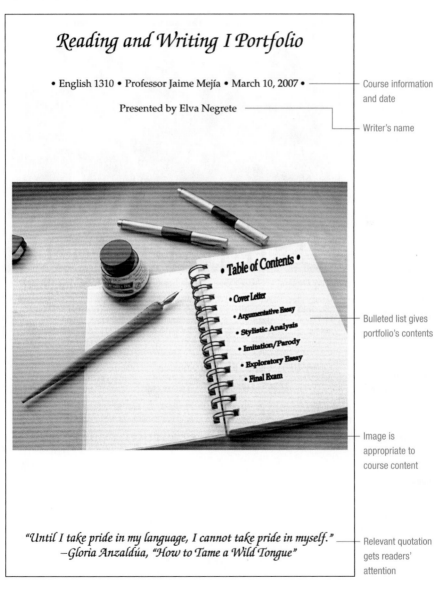

*Reading and Writing I Portfolio*

• English 1310 • Professor Jaime Mejía • March 10, 2007 • — Course information and date

Presented by Elva Negrete — Writer's name

Bulleted list gives portfolio's contents

Image is appropriate to course content

*"Until I take pride in my language, I cannot take pride in myself."*
*–Gloria Anzaldúa, "How to Tame a Wild Tongue"*

Relevant quotation gets readers' attention

FLYER

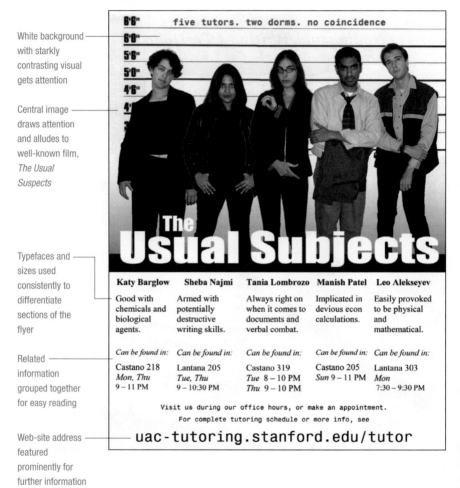

6'6" five tutors. two dorms. no coincidence

6'0"

5'6"

5'0"

4'6"

The Usual Subjects

| Katy Barglow | Sheba Najmi | Tania Lombrozo | Manish Patel | Leo Alekseyev |
|---|---|---|---|---|
| Good with chemicals and biological agents. | Armed with potentially destructive writing skills. | Always right on when it comes to documents and verbal combat. | Implicated in devious econ calculations. | Easily provoked to be physical and mathematical. |
| *Can be found in:* | *Can be found in:* | *Can be found in:* | *Can be found in:* | *Can be found in:* |
| Castano 218<br>*Mon, Thu*<br>9 – 11 PM | Lantana 205<br>*Tue, Thu*<br>9 – 10:30 PM | Castano 319<br>*Tue* 8 – 10 PM<br>*Thu* 9 – 10 PM | Castano 205<br>*Sun* 9 – 11 PM | Lantana 303<br>*Mon*<br>7:30 – 9:30 PM |

Visit us during our office hours, or make an appointment.
For complete tutoring schedule or more info, see

uac-tutoring.stanford.edu/tutor

White background with starkly contrasting visual gets attention

Central image draws attention and alludes to well-known film, *The Usual Suspects*

Typefaces and sizes used consistently to differentiate sections of the flyer

Related information grouped together for easy reading

Web-site address featured prominently for further information

## FOR COLLABORATION

Gather up at least five documents you have received in other classes, through groups you belong to, or through the mail. (These might be reports, newsletters, brochures, flyers, or other kinds of documents.) Then, working with one or two other class members, choose two of the documents to analyze according to the advice presented in this chapter. Decide which features make the documents successful or unsuccessful in their delivery of information, and consider how each document's design makes a mediocre point of information stronger or more compelling — or does just the opposite. Bring reports of your analysis to class for discussion.

## THINKING CRITICALLY ABOUT THE DESIGN OF YOUR DOCUMENT

Take a look at a piece of writing or a document you have recently finished writing. (If you have created a flyer or one of the other kinds of documents shown in this chapter, choose that one.) Using the advice in this chapter, assess your use of visual structure and page design, consistent use of conventions for guiding readers through your document, and the use of headings, color, font size, and visuals for emphasis. Then write a paragraph reflecting on how well your piece of writing or document is designed and how you could improve it.

# 24 Online Texts

The uses of online texts are expanding dramatically. In school, you read, analyze, and in many cases create online texts for your classes. Even if you simply save an essay you've written as HTML and post it to a class Web site for others to read and respond to, you've created an online text. And if you include any links in your essay, you've made a basic hypertext. In addition to creating online projects for classwork, you may be among the millions of people who develop online texts on their jobs or for organizations they belong to — or just to add to, or start, a conversation on a topic that interests them.

## 24a Features of online texts

Web sites present writers with new opportunities and demands. Unlike print texts — which proceed in a linear, sequential way from beginning to end — the hypertext that makes up a Web site allows the writer to organize elements as a cluster of associations; links can take readers to other parts of the site or to other sites. Unlike a print text, an online text is dynamic and relatively easy to change in order to accommodate new information.

Online texts have other capabilities that print texts do not. They can include audio and video files as well as printed words. Written words are important in online texts, but writing for the Web often requires brief, scannable chunks. Finally, while space can sometimes be an issue on a Web site (especially when a document contains large files), online texts may have fewer space limitations than a printed page.

### *Sample Web pages*

The Web pages shown on pp. 467–68 illustrate some common features of Web texts. The first page profiles the author of an online student journal. Links across the bottom of the page allow readers to navigate to this student's journal entries or to visit other students' journals on the site. Links in the left navigation menu take readers to other key sections of the site as well as to related pages. The introductory text is brief, and readers can scroll through the words while

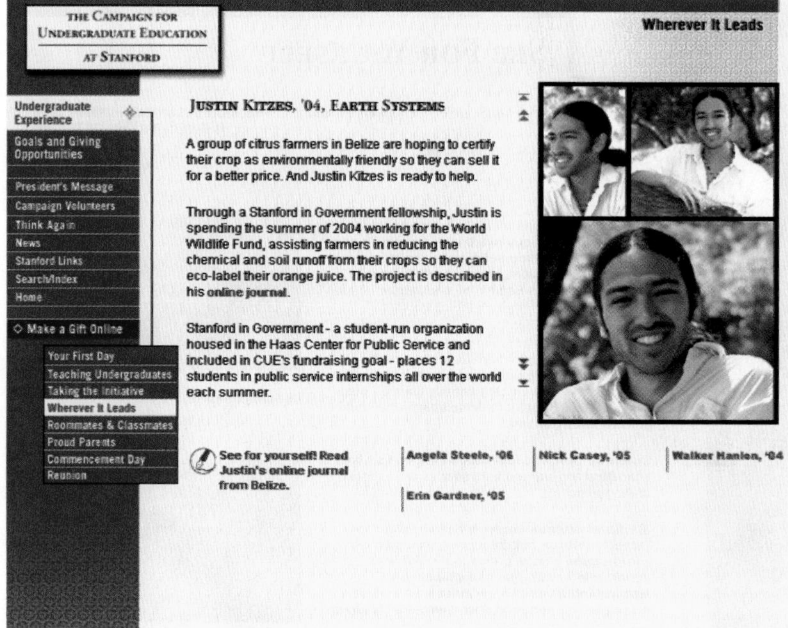


the photographs and navigation remain static, maintaining the balance of text, images, and white space on the page.

The second page, an online journal entry from the same site, visually resembles the first profile page. From this entry, readers can link to the home page of the sponsoring organization, look at the student's other entries, return to his profile, send him an email, or go to another student journal. The writer has included photographs that he took to accompany his short, scannable report, and readers can scroll down to read more without having to move to another page.

### *Evaluating others' Web texts*

Before planning a Web text, take some time to look at and evaluate others' sites on the Web. Examine, for example, the Google Maps page on p. 469. Some of its most useful features are annotated. As you find sites you admire, notice any elements that you find particularly effective. How might you adapt features that you admire for your own Web text?

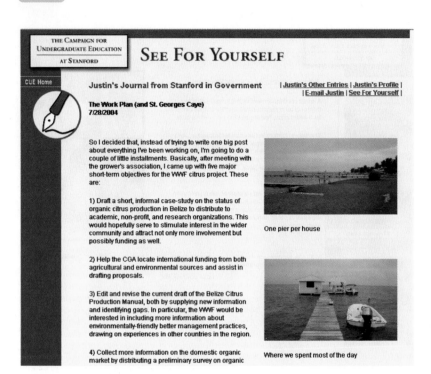

THE CAMPAIGN FOR UNDERGRADUATE EDUCATION AT STANFORD

SEE FOR YOURSELF

CUE Home

Justin's Journal from Stanford in Government | Justin's Other Entries | Justin's Profile | | E-mail Justin | See For Yourself |

The Work Plan (and St. Georges Caye)
7/28/2004

So I decided that, instead of trying to write one big post about everything I've been working on, I'm going to do a couple of little installments. Basically, after meeting with the grower's association, I came up with five major short-term objectives for the WWF citrus project. These are:

One pier per house

1) Draft a short, informal case-study on the status of organic citrus production in Belize to distribute to academic, non-profit, and research organizations. This would hopefully serve to stimulate interest in the wider community and attract not only more involvement but possibly funding as well.

2) Help the CGA locate international funding from both agricultural and environmental sources and assist in drafting proposals.

Where we spent most of the day

3) Edit and revise the current draft of the Belize Citrus Production Manual, both by supplying new information and identifying gaps. In particular, the WWF would be interested in including more information about environmentally-friendly better management practices, drawing on experiences in other countries in the region.

4) Collect more information on the domestic organic market by distributing a preliminary survey on organic

## 24b Planning a Web text

Plan a Web text as you would any piece of writing. Answer questions about your purpose, audience, topic, and rhetorical stance, address time-management concerns, choose appropriate tools, make decisions about your organization and design before you begin, and get feedback on your draft.

### 1 Audience, purpose, topic, and stance

As with any writing you do, pay very careful attention to your audience, purpose, topic, and rhetorical stance when planning a Web text. Let's look at some of these factors, which will help you plan the shape and scope of your Web text.

- *Who is the audience for your text* (3h)? Identifying your intended audience as clearly as possible will help you decide on appropriate

GOOGLE MAPS PAGE

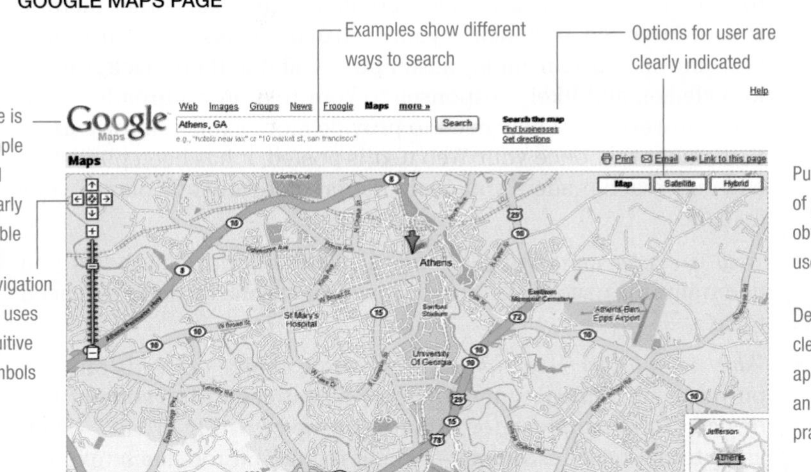


## Guidelines for evaluating a Web text

- Does the Web text accomplish its purpose? Is every page relevant to the topic? (24b1)
- How credible is the site? What makes it useful (or not useful)? (14c)
- What is the creator's stance toward the topic? (24b1)
- Who is the intended audience? Does the home page invite those readers in? (3h and 24b1)
- Does the home page clearly introduce the topic and give an overview of the contents of the site? (24b4)
- How effective is the organization? Is it easy to navigate? (24b4)
- Is the site's design appealing? Do the words, visuals, and white space in the Web document strike an appropriate balance? (23b and 24c3)
- Does the creator's name or contact information appear on every page? Is it clear when the site was last updated? (24b5)
- Are all links clear? Does every link work? (24c2 and 24d)
- Do the visuals and multimedia elements help convey the intended meaning? (24b1 and 24c3)

tone, diction, graphic styles, level of detail, and many other factors. If your intended audience is your instructor, classmates, or others you know, you can make assumptions about their background, knowledge, and likely responses to your text. For a broader audience, however, you may need to provide more explicit information. Remember that once your Web text is posted, it has been published and may reach readers you could not predict would be part of your audience.

- *Why are you creating the text?* Considering purpose helps you determine the page's overall format and length and the links you need to create.
- *What is your Web text about?* Your topic choice depends on your purpose and audience, and the topic will affect a site's content and design. For example, a topic that is vague or overly broad — such as "International Terrorism" — might require far too much text and too many links to make it useful to others. Narrow your topic, and clarify your stance on it until you have something with a more practical scope: "A Proposal to Resist Terrorism: What College Students Can Do."
- *How do you relate to your topic?* Your rhetorical stance (3g) determines how your audience will see you. Will you present yourself as an expert, as a colleague, or as a novice seeking information and input from others? What information will you need to provide about yourself to seem credible and persuasive to your audience in any of these or other possible stances?
- *What overall impression do you intend to create?* Do you want your text to be bold, soothing, serious — or something else? Articulating this impression clearly can guide your decisions about how much text to include, what kinds of navigation aids to use, and what images, colors, video and sound clips, and so on will help you create that effect.

### 2 Time management

You already know that time management is crucial for your success in any writing situation. How well you can manage decisions will be affected both by your deadline and how much time you can squeeze out of your other interests and responsibilities to meet that deadline. How much technical expertise do you have, and how much will you need to learn in order to create the Web document? It's important to allow enough time for that learning to take place. Also consider how much research you will have to do and how long you will need to scan or resize images and insert them into your Web document. Finally, consider how much time you will need to seek permission to use any images or other texts in your document (see Chapter 16). Then make up a timeline for your Web-document project.

### 3 Web tools

The World Wide Web and hypertext use codes called hypertext markup language (HTML) that tell a Web browser how to interpret the various elements on a page. These codes can indicate **boldface** or *italic* type, create links to other pages, load images, and call up files or ancillary programs (called plug-ins) that work with a browser. Plug-ins create even more options, allowing you, for example, to read documents in Adobe's Portable Document Format (PDF), listen to an audio file such as a Podcast, or view an animation.

Other programs help you create and manage the content of your Web document. Current versions of WordPerfect, Microsoft Word, and PowerPoint all allow you to save documents in the HTML format (click on FILE and then SAVE AS). Or you can use a simple text editor to write a Web page and enter all the HTML codes manually. You can also use an HTML editor (24c4) such as Microsoft FrontPage, Netscape Composer, Dreamweaver, or a shareware or freeware program such as Nvu that lets you see each page as you create it.

The tools you choose will be determined by the computer you are using and the software available on it, the programs you already know how to use, the context and requirements you need to meet, and the complexity of the site you have in mind, among other factors.

**bedfordstmartins.com/smhandbook** For more information on tools for constructing a Web site, click on **Working Online**.

### 4 Structure

Just as you might outline an essay, you should develop a clear structure for your Web text. Think of a Web text as a collection of pages that will be mapped and linked in a way that matches your purpose, audience, topic, and rhetorical stance. The pattern you choose should allow readers to find what they are looking for as quickly and intuitively as possible. Many Web sites are organized according to one of three basic patterns: linear, hierarchical, or spoke-and-hub.

LINEAR ORGANIZATION

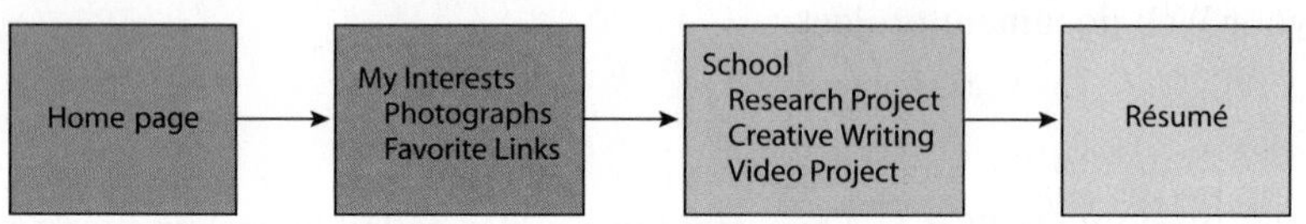


Linear, or sequential, organization orders pages in a sequence that leads readers through the text one page at a time.

A hierarchical structure begins with general information and takes readers to more and more specific content.

HIERARCHICAL ORGANIZATION

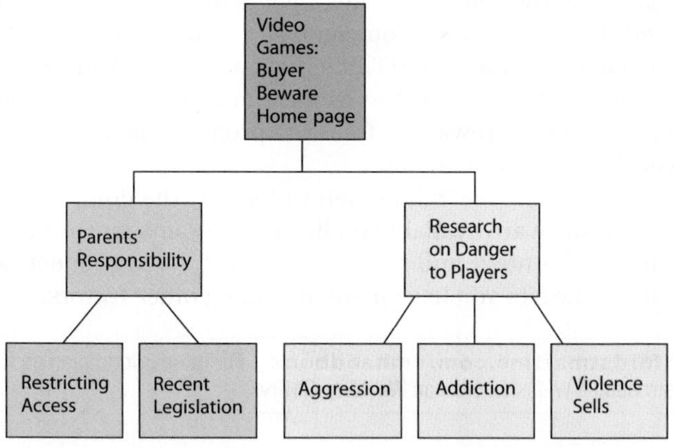


A spoke-and-hub structure allows readers to move from place to place in no particular order. This organization works well when all topics are roughly equal in importance and when all the information necessary for readers to understand the topics can appear on the home page.

SPOKE-AND-HUB ORGANIZATION

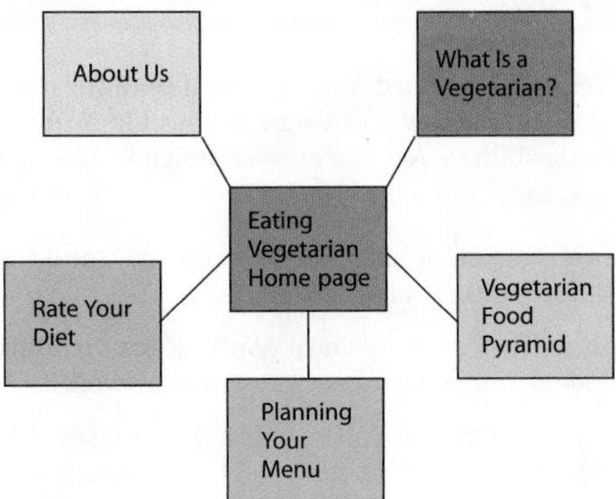


The following tips should be helpful as you organize your Web text:

- Look at the content you have, and make a note of what you still need to find or create — text, visuals, audio clips, and so on.
- Map or storyboard your Web document. To do so, draw the arrangement and types of pages you have in mind, and be ready to move the elements around in order to improve the organization. As you work on your map or storyboard, start planning the underlying page design so that you can create a template for consistent layout of pages or sections (23a–d and 24b5).
- As your Web map progresses, consider any navigation menus you might use and how detailed they will need to be.
- Remember that Web texts can be dynamic rather than static — they are capable of being changed at any point — so if you expect to update the site regularly, plan for a structure that makes it possible to keep track of your changes and to let readers know when new content has been added.

## EXERCISE 24.1

Use a search engine to find a Web page you haven't visited before but that addresses a topic you know something about. Using the guidelines in 24b, determine the following: What is the purpose of the Web page? Who is its intended audience? What rhetorical stance does it take? What overall impression does the page create, and how are color, visuals, and multimedia used to create that impression?

## CONSIDERING DISABILITIES: Accessible Web sites

Much on the Web remains hard to access and read for persons with disabilities. For details on how to design accessible Web texts, visit the Americans with Disabilities Act site at www.ada.gov. Here are a few of the ADA's design tips:

- Organize information simply and consistently, and make sure that important information is easy to find.
- Choose colors that create a sharp contrast for visibility. Do not rely on color alone to carry meaning: add words as well.
- Provide brief descriptions of all visuals to assist visually impaired readers using software that reads onscreen text aloud. If you use tables to convey data, identify the header cells in the rows and columns. Include a caption and summary with each table. Screen readers read from left to right, which will render the tables themselves meaningless.
- Give each link a descriptive name such as "Return to the home page."
- Provide alternative text for all pictures, photos, graphics, and decorative filters. If graphic material is important to the page, include an identifying tag or a title for each graphic. If the graphic is used for design or formatting, consider alternatives.
- Punctuate appropriately; screen readers pause for punctuation.
- For deaf or hearing-impaired readers, provide captions for any sound on your Web site. Do not rely on sound — even with captions — to carry the central or singular meaning of your text. Provide a transcript or other written text of a Podcast or other audio file.
- For many readers, using a mouse may be problematic. If you are using forms or other interactive elements, make sure it's possible to move from field to field in the form by using the TAB and ENTER keys.
- If, after your best efforts, the site cannot be made accessible, provide a text-only alternative and ensure that it is updated with the main page.

### 5 Design

Each page of your text will contain two main areas: navigation areas (such as menus or links to offsite pages elsewhere on the Web) and content areas (where the words, images, and other elements combine to convey your ideas and information). Your goal is to make these two areas readily distinguishable from each other and to make sure that content is easy to find and not overwhelmed by menus or other navigational elements. Finally, remember that the most important navigation and content information should be viewable from the very first page.

### Templates

Consider using an existing design template or creating one of your own. A template can serve as a model for all the pages of your Web document, helping give consistency to your pages and making them easier to read. Basically, a template sets the background color, heading information, navigation buttons, and contact information — all the elements you want to appear on every page.

If you are creating your own template, sketch out a basic design that answers the following questions:

- How will the site title look, and where will you place it on the page?
- Where will the page title appear, and how will it look?
- What graphics will appear on each page? What features will be unique to a particular page?
- Where will you place the navigation menu — horizontally across the top or vertically on the left? Will your navigation require graphics or just text?
- Will there be NEXT and BACK buttons on the page? If so, where? (Generally, you will want all sections of your Web text to link to the home page.)
- Where will your name and contact information be placed? Where will the date of the last update be placed?
- Where will you place the most important text or images? (For most readers of English and other Western languages, the most visible positions are at the top left and the lower right.)

### Design conventions

Although the conventions for designing Web texts are still evolving, it's pretty clear what doesn't work well. The Yale Center for Advanced Instructional Media, for example, uses the term *clown's pants pages* to refer to the kind of haphazard use of color, clip art, and fonts characteristic of many Web texts. So whether or not you use a design template, remember to follow these basic principles of good document design (23a2):

- Differentiate parts of the page and text or visuals from the background (*contrast*).
- Group related items together (*proximity*).
- Guide readers by using color, layout, and other elements consistently (*repetition*).
- Arrange elements to line up with other elements for a clean look (*alignment*).

You can also help your readers by choosing an easy-to-read font and by using white space effectively (23b). When appropriate, organize information with lists and headings (23c). Always give considerable thought to the use of color, remembering that colors carry emotional associations: reds get attention, greens may evoke images of nature, blues can seem comforting, oranges or yellows may evoke sunshine but can be hard to read, and grays seem dignified and serious.

Ultimately, the organization and look of each page depend on what you are trying to achieve. You should make decisions about page length, color, visuals, multimedia, and interactive elements based on rhetorical choices (your audience, purpose, topic, and stance) and on practical constraints (the time and tools available).

### *A sample home-page design*

Opposite is the home page for the DePaul University Writing Centers. Note that its design is fairly simple and that menu items are listed below the main heading. Clear, simple links from the main page provide information about locations, services, and programs, for example.

## 6 Feedback

Before you do additional work on your Web text, ask readers to review and respond to a rough draft of your pages, especially the home page. Direct your reviewers to specific questions you would like addressed: How understandable or readable are the pages? How easy are they to navigate? How effective is the use of color, fonts, visuals, sound, and so on? What additional content is needed?

HOME PAGE FOR THE DEPAUL UNIVERSITY WRITING CENTERS

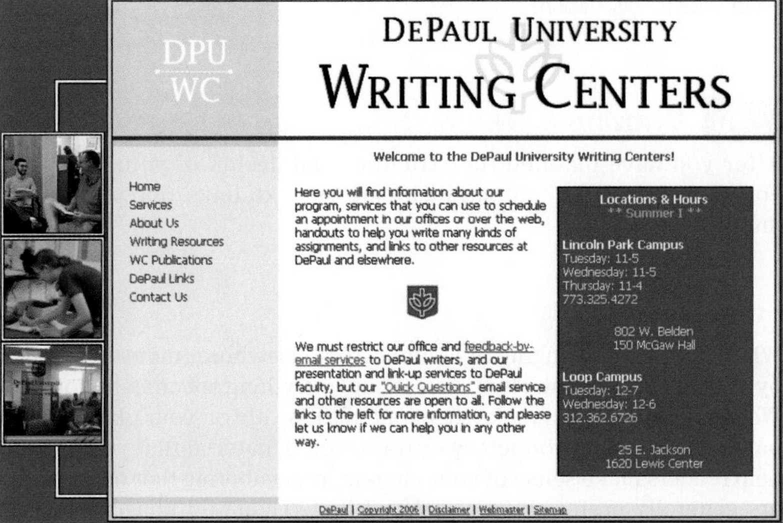


## CONSIDERING DISABILITIES: Signaling changes

Remember that some of your readers may not be able to go from one link to another if the links are marked by graphic icons that can't be read by textreader software. For this reason, use vertical lines to signal these changes. The vertical lines before and after links can be read by the text-reader, making it easier for users with impaired vision to click on the words between lines.

### EXERCISE 24.2

You can practice learning to read Web texts critically by comparing several sites. To begin, search for a site that is fairly unregulated and unedited — a fan site, for instance, for a writer, a book, an actor, a television show, or a film. What on this site indicates credibility? Who is responsible for the site, and how can you tell?

Next, compare it to the site of a major government agency, such as the Library of Congress, or a national broadcaster, such as PBS or CNN. What kinds of connections do you see between the sponsoring organization and the Web site?

Finally, working alone or with another member of your class, analyze the sites you have looked at for trust, credibility, and authority. Bring the results of your analysis to class for discussion.

## 24c Drafting a Web text

After you have planned the structure and design of your Web site, you should draft its content, including the text, links, and visuals and multimedia.

### 1 Text

Whether you are bringing in content from elsewhere (material created by you or by someone else) or creating everything specifically for your Web text, take care to make that content fit neatly on your planned Web pages. Draft any introductory or transitional material that you need to help readers make sense of your content, remembering that online readers generally prefer short chunks of text. Then add image captions, sound transcripts (if you are featuring an audio file such as a Podcast), and so on. Be sure to obtain permission to use any material from another source (see Chapter 16) if your work will be posted to a server that is available to the public.

### 2 Links

The success of any hypertext is tied to the effectiveness of the links within it, both those to other pages in the same site (internal links) and those to other sites (external links). Links add depth and texture to the hypertext: the opening page(s) provide an overview and announce the general purpose of the document, but the links bring this aim to life. Use links for complex explanations, lists of supporting statistics, bibliographies, referenced Web sites, or additional readings.

Like all elements of a Web document, each link should have a clear rhetorical purpose and be in an appropriate location. If, for example, you put a link in the middle of a paragraph on a page, be aware that readers may go to the linked page before finishing what's before them — and remember that if that link takes them to an external site, they may never come back! If that's a choice you want to offer, then link away; however, if it's important for users to read the whole paragraph, move the link to the end of it. Another alternative to sending readers to content elsewhere is to have the link call up a small pop-up window that provides more information, as a footnote does in an essay or a sidebar does in a magazine article.

To signal a link, you may use underlining, color, **boldface**, icons (▶), labeling (*for more readings on taboos, click here*), or a combination of these devices. Regardless of the signal you use, make sure readers will understand the purpose of the link and, if it's an external link, who created it. Indeed, you may create much of the text for links, just as you would create the text in footnotes to add information or explain a concept.

### 3 Visuals and multimedia

The Web offers a dizzying array of ways to present your ideas through the use of visuals (borders, icons, graphs and charts, maps, photographs, and illustrations of all kinds) and multimedia, including sound (Podcasts and other MP3s) and video files. But the number of possibilities can prove daunting, especially to beginning Web-text designers. The following tips will help you think carefully about how to incorporate visuals and multimedia into your Web document:

- Remember that, except in special circumstances (such as comics or photo essays), visuals add to but do not substitute for text, so integrate the written words and accompanying images very carefully, and never use visuals for mere decoration.
- Don't expect readers to instantly see the connection between a visual and text: you need to make the relationship clear in the text or through labels and captions.
- To consider readers who may have slower connections and lack the time necessary to download your documents, limit each image to 30 to 40 kilobytes, or use a smaller thumbnail image and link users to the original, larger file.
- If you have not taken a photograph or created a graphic yourself, you will need to see if it is copyrighted and, if so, to ask permission to scan or download and use it on a public Web site (see Chapter 16).
- Free icons, clip art, and other visuals are widely available, but be aware that clip art can be tiresome and clichéd. Don't use it unless it contributes something to your text.

- Use lines, boxes, and icons carefully and consistently so that they emphasize information rather than detract from it.
- Use white space (23b) to emphasize and direct readers to parts of the page and to keep the page from appearing uninvitingly dense. You can emphasize different kinds of content, such as text, lists, and graphics, by using white space carefully.

### 4 Coding

Essentially, codes tell a Web browser how to interpret the various elements on a page. One set of codes (usually called document tags) governs the larger aspects of the text (such as title, body elements, background color, and so on), while another set (usually called appearance tags) governs smaller aspects (italics, boldface, underlining, and so on). The figures on p. 481 show part of a student's Web text and the HTML code used to produce it. You're no doubt familiar with HTML code, but richer and more complex markup languages — such as XHTML, SMGL, and XML — are becoming increasingly popular.

As noted earlier, you can write your own code from scratch, save your document in HTML format, or use an HTML editor. Microsoft FrontPage, Netscape Composer, PageMill, Dreamweaver, the open-source software Nvu, and other Web development tools do the bulk of the hard work for you and let you review each page as it is created.

## 24d Reviewing, revising, and editing a Web text

As with any text, you should check the draft of your Web document carefully. Make sure that visuals serve your purpose effectively and that you have given credit for any material you did not create yourself. Check the navigation of the site, verifying that all links work as they should and that readers can find their way around with ease. If possible, check the site using several different browsers to be sure the pages display properly.

After resolving any problems that you find, seek additional feedback from readers. Then, after addressing your reviewers' concerns, proofread every page, looking for typos, other errors, and confusing passages, and make final corrections to your text.

When you are satisfied that your document is as good as you can make it — and that it is ready for the general public to view — post your text to the Web.

## A STUDENT WEB PAPER AND ITS HTML CODE

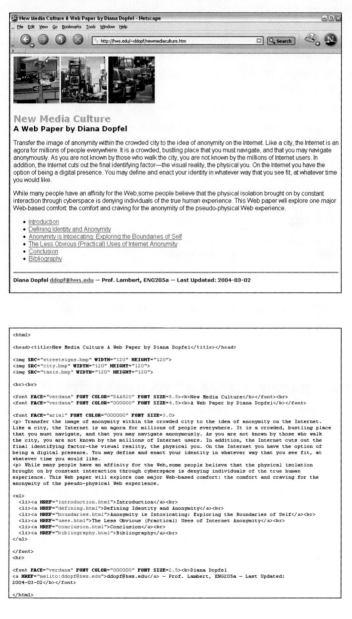

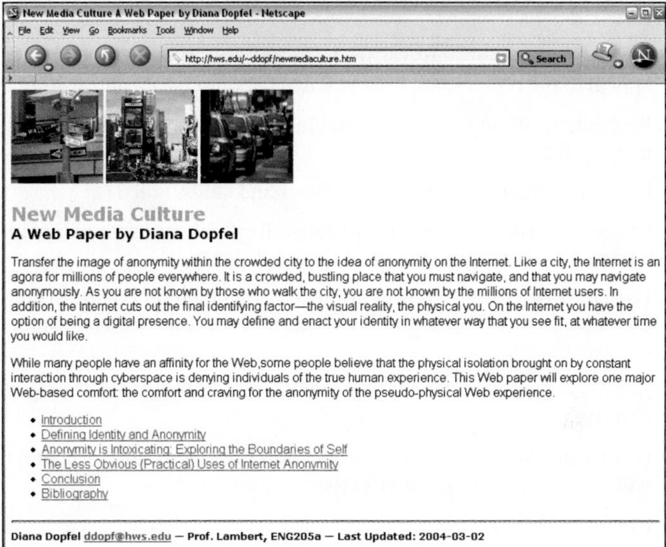


New Media Culture
A Web Paper by Diana Dopfel

Transfer the image of anonymity within the crowded city to the idea of anonymity on the Internet. Like a city, the Internet is an agora for millions of people everywhere. It is a crowded, bustling place that you must navigate, and that you may navigate anonymously. As you are not known by those who walk the city, you are not known by the millions of Internet users. In addition, the Internet cuts out the final identifying factor—the visual reality, the physical you. On the Internet you have the option of being a digital presence. You may define and enact your identity in whatever way that you see fit, at whatever time you would like.

While many people have an affinity for the Web,some people believe that the physical isolation brought on by constant interaction through cyberspace is denying individuals of the true human experience. This Web paper will explore one major Web-based comfort: the comfort and craving for the anonymity of the pseudo-physical Web experience.

- Introduction
- Defining Identity and Anonymity
- Anonymity is Intoxicating: Exploring the Boundaries of Self
- The Less Obvious (Practical) Uses of Internet Anonymity
- Conclusion
- Bibliography

Diana Dopfel ddopf@hws.edu — Prof. Lambert, ENG205a — Last Updated: 2004-03-02

```
<html>

<head><title>New Media Culture A Web Paper by Diana Dopfel</title></head>

<img SRC="streetsigns.bmp" WIDTH="120" HEIGHT="120">
<img SRC="city.bmp" WIDTH="120" HEIGHT="120">
<img SRC="taxis.bmp" WIDTH="120" HEIGHT="120">

<br><br>

<font FACE="verdana" FONT COLOR="DAA520" FONT SIZE=5.5><b>New Media Culture</b></font><br>
<font FACE="verdana" FONT COLOR="000000" FONT SIZE=4.5><b>A Web Paper by Diana Dopfel</b></font>

<font FACE="arial" FONT COLOR="000000" FONT SIZE=3.0>
<p> Transfer the image of anonymity within the crowded city to the idea of anonymity on the Internet.
Like a city, the Internet is an agora for millions of people everywhere. It is a crowded, bustling place
that you must navigate, and that you may navigate anonymously. As you are not known by those who walk
the city, you are not known by the millions of Internet users. In addition, the Internet cuts out the
final identifying factor-the visual reality, the physical you. On the Internet you have the option of
being a digital presence. You may define and enact your identity in whatever way that you see fit, at
whatever time you would like.
<p> While many people have an affinity for the Web,some people believe that the physical isolation
brought on by constant interaction through cyberspace is denying individuals of the true human
experience. This Web paper will explore one major Web-based comfort: the comfort and craving for the
anonymity of the pseudo-physical Web experience.

<ul>
  <li><a HREF="introduction.html">Introduction</a><br>
  <li><a HREF="defining.html">Defining Identity and Anonymity</a><br>
  <li><a HREF="boundaries.html">Anonymity is Intoxicating: Exploring the Boundaries of Self</a><br>
  <li><a HREF="uses.html">The Less Obvious (Practical) Uses of Internet Anonymity</a><br>
  <li><a HREF="conclusion.html">Conclusion</a><br>
  <li><a HREF="bibliography.html">Bibliography</a><br>
</ul>

</font>
<hr>

<font FACE="verdana" FONT COLOR="000000" FONT SIZE=2.5><b>Diana Dopfel
<a HREF="mailto:ddopf@hws.edu">ddopf@hws.edu</a> - Prof. Lambert, ENG205a - Last Updated:
2004-03-02</b></font>

</html>
```

## Guidelines for creating a Web document

- Consider audience, purpose, topic, and stance. How can your Web text appeal to the right readers? How will it accomplish its purpose? (24b1)
- Be realistic about the time available for the project, and plan accordingly. (24b2)
- Use appropriate tools for your project and skills. (24b3)
- Choose a structure that makes sense for the way users will want to navigate your content. (24b4)
- Use contrast, proximity, repetition, and alignment to create an appealing design, or choose a template that follows basic design principles. (24b5)
- Ask reviewers to evaluate your draft site plans, design, and navigation. (24b6)
- Draft your Web text, and create or find images, sound, or video that will help make your point effectively. (24c)
- Create links. (24c2)
- Get final responses from reviewers; then proofread carefully and check that navigation and links function correctly. (24d)
- Post your Web text online.

## THINKING CRITICALLY ABOUT YOUR WEB TEXTS

Take some time to reflect on a Web text you have produced — it might be an assignment you posted to a course Web site, a single-page site intended for your family and friends, or a major multiple-page Web site. Go back through this chapter, reviewing the advice for designing effective Web texts, and then evaluate your own efforts. Conclude by drawing up a list of tips for future — and better — Web texts.

# Oral and Multimedia Presentations

# 25

When the Gallup Poll reports on what U.S. citizens say they fear most, the findings are always the same: public speaking is apparently even scarier than an attack from outer space. Perhaps it is not surprising, then, that students who use this handbook have consistently asked for information on giving oral presentations.

Successful speakers point to four elements crucial to their effectiveness:

- *a thorough knowledge of the subject at hand*
- *careful attention to the interactive nature of speaking and thus to the needs of the audience*
- *careful integration of verbal and visual information*
- *practice, practice, and more practice*

## 25a Class discussions

You may give some of the most important oral presentations of your college career when you participate in classroom discussions. The challenge is to contribute to such discussions without losing track of the overall conversation or aims of the class and without monopolizing the discussion. Especially if you are also taking notes, you may find yourself straining to manage all these tasks at once. Here are a few tips for making effective contributions to class discussions:

- Be prepared so that the comments you make will relate to the work of the class.
- Listen purposefully, jotting down related points and following the flow of the conversation.
- If you think you might lose track of your ideas while speaking, jot down key words to keep you on track.
- Make your comments count by asking a key question to clarify a point, by taking the conversation in a more productive direction, or by analyzing or summarizing what has been said.
- Respond to questions or comments by others as specifically as possible (*The passage on p. 42 provides evidence to support your point* rather than *I agree*).
- Offer a brief analysis of a problem, issue, or text, one that leaves room for others to build on.

- If you have trouble participating frequently in class discussions, try making one comment a day. You might also speak with your instructor about ways to contribute to the conversation.
- Remember that there is no direct correlation between talking in class and being intellectually engaged: many students are participating actively, whether or not they are speaking.

**FOR MULTILINGUAL WRITERS: Speaking up in class**

Speaking up in class is viewed as inappropriate or even rude in some cultures. In the United States, however, doing so is expected and encouraged. Indeed, some instructors assign credit for such class participation.

## 25b Assignment, purpose, and audience

You will be wise to begin preparing for a presentation as soon as you get the assignment. Think about how much time you have to prepare; how long the presentation is to be; whether you will use written-out text or note cards; whether visual aids, handouts, or other materials are called for; and what equipment you will need. If you are making a group presentation, you will need time to divide duties and practice (8b2). Make sure that you understand the criteria for evaluation — how will the presentation be graded or assessed?

Consider the purpose of your presentation. Are you to lead a discussion? teach a lesson? give a report? engage a group in an activity? Also consider the audience (3h). If your instructor is a member of the audience, what will he or she expect you to do — and do well? What do audience members know about your topic? What opinions do they already hold about it? What do they need to know to follow your presentation and perhaps accept your point of view? Finally, consider your own stance toward your topic and audience. Are you an expert? novice? well-informed observer? peer?

## 25c Effective oral presentations

More and more students report that formal oral presentations are becoming part of their work both in and out of class. As you plan for such a presentation, consider these issues:

- How much time will you have for the presentation, and how much information will you be able to present in that time?
- Will you present most comfortably using a fully written-out text, notes, or note cards?
- What visual aids and handouts will make your presentation most successful? What kind of visuals make the most sense for your presentation? A statistical pie chart may be appropriate in one presentation, whereas photographs might be more appropriate in another.
- Can you use presentation software? What equipment will you need?
- Where will you make your presentation — in a lecture hall? in an informal sitting area? in a Webcast? Will you have a lectern? Will you sit or stand? move around or stay in one place? Will the lighting need to be adjusted?
- How will your presentation be evaluated?

## CONSIDERING DISABILITIES: Accessible presentations

Remember that some members of your audience may not be able to see your presentation or may have trouble hearing it, so do all you can to make your presentation accessible.

- Be sure to face any audience members who rely on lipreading to understand your words. For a large audience, request an ASL (American Sign Language) interpreter.
- Do not rely on color or graphics alone to get across information — some audience members may be unable to pick up these visual cues.
- For presentations you publish on the Web, provide brief textual descriptions of your visuals (p. 474).
- If you use video, provide labels for captions to explain any sounds that won't be audible to some audience members, and embed spoken captions to explain images to those who cannot see them. Be sure that the equipment you'll be using is caption capable.
- Remember that students have very different learning styles and abilities. You may want to provide a written overview of your presentation or put the text of your presentation on slides or transparencies for those who learn better by reading *and* listening.

## 1 Writing to be heard — and remembered

To be heard and remembered, write a memorable introduction and conclusion; use explicit structures, helpful signpost language, straightforward syntax, and concrete diction, and give the presentation effectively.

### *A memorable introduction and conclusion*

Remember that listeners, like readers, tend to remember beginnings and endings most readily, so work extra hard to make these elements memorable (6f). Consider, for example, using a startling statement, opinion, or question; a vivid anecdote; a powerful quotation; or a vivid visual image. Shifting language, especially into a variety of language that your audience will identify with, is another effective way to catch their attention (see Chapter 28). Whenever you can link your subject to the experiences and interests of your audience, do so.

Writer Amy Tan began a 1989 presentation to the Language Symposium in San Francisco with a puzzling statement, especially given that she was addressing a group of language scholars:

> I am not a scholar of English or literature. I cannot give you much more than personal opinions on the English language and its variations in this country or others.
>
> — AMY TAN

Tan's statement not only got the attention of her audience but also served as a springboard to address her audience's interests.

### *Explicit structure and signpost language*

Organize your presentation clearly and carefully, and give an overview of your main points toward the beginning of your presentation. (You may wish to recall these points again toward the end of the talk.) Throughout your presentation, pause between major points, and use signpost language as you move from one topic to the next. Such signposts act as explicit transitions in your talk and should be clear and concrete: *The second crisis point in the breakup of the Soviet Union occurred hard on the heels of the first* instead of *The breakup of the Soviet Union came to another crisis point. . . .* In addition to such explicit transitions (7d4) as *next*, *on the contrary*, and *finally*, you can offer signposts to your listeners by carefully repeating key words and ideas as well as by sticking to concrete topic sentences to introduce each new idea.

### *Syntax and diction*

Avoid long, complicated sentences, and use straightforward sentence structure (subject-verb-object) as much as possible. Listeners prefer action verbs and concrete nouns to abstractions. You may need to deal with abstract ideas, but try to provide concrete examples for them (29c).

### *Making your presentation memorable*

Memorable presentations call on the power of figures of speech and other devices of language, such as careful repetition, parallelism, and climactic order.

You can see an example of all of these devices in the following passage from Barack Obama's 2004 speech at the Democratic National Convention. Obama contrasts what he identifies as the ideas of "those who are preparing to divide us" with memorable references to common ground and unity, including parallel references to the United States (italicized below) as he builds to his climactic point:

> Now even as we speak, there are those who are preparing to divide us — the spin masters, the negative ad peddlers who embrace the politics of anything goes. Well, I say to them tonight, there is not a liberal America and a conservative America — *there is the United States of America.* There is not a black America and a white America and Latino America and an Asian America — *there's the United States of America.* The pundits like to slice and dice our country into Red States and Blue States: Red States for Republicans, Blue States for Democrats. But I've got news for them, too. We worship an awesome God in the Blue States, and we don't like federal agents poking around in our libraries in the Red States. We coach Little League in the Blue States and yes, we've got some gay friends in the Red States. There are patriots who opposed the war in Iraq and there are patriots who supported the war in Iraq. *We are one people, all of us pledging allegiance to the stars and stripes, all of us defending the United States of America.*
>
> — BARACK OBAMA

### *Turning writing into a full script for a presentation*

Even though you will rely on some written material, you will need to adapt it for speech. Depending on the assignment, the audience, and your personal preferences, you may even speak from a full script. If so, double- or triple-space it, and use fairly large print so that it will be easy to read. Try to end each page with the end of a sentence so that you won't have to pause while you turn a page. In addition, you may decide to mark spots where you want to pause and to highlight words you want to emphasize.

Look carefully at the following paragraphs. The first is from an essay about the importance of thinking critically before choosing a course of study. The second paragraph presents the same information, this time revised for an oral presentation.

A PARAGRAPH FROM A WRITTEN ESSAY

The decision about a major or other course of study is crucial because it determines both what we study and how we come to think about the world. The philosopher Kenneth Burke explains that we are inevitably affected not only by our experiences but also by the terminologies through which our perceptions of those experiences are filtered. Burke calls these filters "terministic screens" and says that they affect our perception, highlighting some aspects of an experience while obscuring others. Thus the terminologies (or languages) we use influence how we see the world and how we think about what we see.

THE PARAGRAPH REVISED AS A FULL SCRIPT FOR AN ORAL PRESENTATION

Why is our decision about a major so crucial? I can give two important reasons. First, our major determines what we study. [PAUSE] Second, it determines how we come to think about the world. The philosopher Kenneth Burke explains these influences this way: our experience, he says, influences what we think about ideas and the world. But those experiences are always filtered through language, through words and terminologies. [PAUSE] Burke calls these terminologies "terministic screens," a complicated-sounding term for a pretty simple idea. Take, for example, the latest hike in student fees on our campus. The Board of Trustees and the administration use one kind of term to describe the hike: "modest and reasonable," they call it. Students I know use entirely different terms: "exorbitant and unjust," they call it. Why the difference? Because their terministic screens are entirely different. [PAUSE] Burke says we all have such screens made up of language, and these screens act to screen out some things for us and to screen in, or highlight, others. Burke's major point is this: the terms and screens we use have a big influence on how we see the world and how we think about what we see.

Note that the revised paragraph presents the same information, but this time it is written to be heard. The revision uses helpful signpost language, some repetition, simple syntax, and the example of student fees to help listeners follow along and keep them interested. Note how the writer has marked her text for emphasis and pauses.

### *Speaking from notes*

If you decide to speak from notes rather than from a full script, here are some tips for doing so effectively:

- In general, use one note card for each point in your presentation, beginning with the introduction and ending with the conclusion.
- Number the cards so that you can quickly find the next part of your presentation if your cards are out of order.
- On each card, include the major point you want to make in large bold text. Include subpoints in a bulleted list below the main point, again printed large enough for you to see easily. You can use full sentences or phrases, as long as you include enough information to remind you of what you have planned to say.
- Include signpost language on each note so that you will be sure to use it to guide your listeners.
- Practice your presentation using the notes at least twice.
- Time your presentation very carefully so that you will be sure not to go overtime. If you think you may run out of time, use color or brackets to mark material in your notes that you can skip. If your presentation is too long, move past the marked material so that you can end with your planned conclusion.

The following note card for the introduction to a presentation reminds the student to emphasize her title and her three points about the origins of graphic novels. Notice how she has highlighted her signpost language as well as the card's number.

NOTE CARD FOR AN ORAL PRESENTATION

> [1] Title: The Rise of the Graphic Novel
>
> **Graphic novels are everywhere — but where do they come from?**
>
> - First, from "funnies" in early American newspapers
> - Second, from comics, esp. great-adventure comic books
> - Finally, from focus on images and visuals throughout society

### 2 Using visuals

Visuals may be an integral part of an oral presentation, and they should be prepared with great care. Think of them not as add-ons but as a major means of conveying information. Many speakers use presentation software throughout a presentation to help keep themselves on track and to guide their audience. Transparencies, posters, flip charts, chalkboards, and whiteboards can make strong visual statements as well.

Because of their importance, visuals must be large enough to be easily seen and read by your audience. Be sure the information is simple, clear, and easy to read and understand. And remember *not* to read from visuals such as PowerPoint slides (25d) or to turn your back on the audience while you refer to visuals.

Most important, make sure your visuals engage and help your listeners rather than distract them from your message. One good way to test the effectiveness of the visuals you plan to use is by trying them out on classmates, friends, or roommates. If these colleagues do not clearly grasp the meaning of the visuals, revise them and try again.

You may also want to prepare handouts for your audience: pertinent bibliographies, for example, or text too extensive to be presented otherwise. Unless the handouts include material you want your audience to use while you speak, distribute them at the end of the presentation.

### 3 Practicing the presentation

In oral presentations, as with many other things in life, practice makes perfect. Prepare a draft of your presentation, including visuals, far enough in advance to allow for several run-throughs. If possible, have yourself videotaped, and then examine the tape in detail. You can also make an audio recording or practice in front of a mirror or in front of friends. Do whatever works for you — just as long as you practice!

Make sure you can be heard clearly. If you are soft-spoken, concentrate on projecting your voice. If your voice tends to rise when you are in the spotlight, practice lowering your pitch. If you speak rapidly, practice slowing down and enunciating words clearly. Remember that tone of voice affects listeners, so aim for a tone that conveys interest in and commitment to your topic and listeners. If you practice with friends or classmates, ask them how well they can hear you and what advice they have for making your voice clearer and easier to listen to.

One student who taped her rehearsal found, to her great surprise, that she had used the word *like* thirty-two times in her eight-minute presentation, even though the word never appeared in her notes. In this case, it took a lot of practice to break the *like* habit.

Once you are comfortable giving the presentation, make sure you will stay within the allotted time. One good rule of thumb is to allow roughly two and a half minutes per double-spaced 8½" × 11" page of text (or one and a half minutes per note card). The only way to be sure about your time, however, is to time yourself as you practice. Knowing that your presentation is neither too short nor too long will help you relax and gain self-confidence; and when the members of your audience sense your self-confidence, they will become increasingly receptive to your message.

### 4 Making the presentation

Experienced speakers say they always expect to feel some anxiety before an oral presentation — and they develop strategies for dealing with it. In addition, they note that some nervousness can act to a speaker's advantage: adrenaline, after all, can help you perform well.

The best strategy seems to be to know your material. Having confidence in your own knowledge will go a long way toward making you a confident presenter. In addition to doing your homework, however, you may be able to use the following strategies to good advantage:

- Consider how you will dress and how you will move around. In each case, your choices should be appropriate for the situation. Most experienced speakers like to dress simply and comfortably for easy movement. But they are seldom overly casual — dressing up a little signals your pride in your appearance and your respect for your audience.

- Go over the scene of your presentation in your mind, and think it through completely, in order to feel more comfortable during it.
- Get some rest before the presentation, and avoid consuming an excessive amount of caffeine.
- Try to relax while you wait to begin. You might want to do some deep-breathing exercises.

Most speakers make a stronger impression standing than sitting. You can move around the room if you are comfortable doing so. If you are more comfortable in one spot, then stand with both feet flat on the floor. If you are standing at a lectern, rest your hands lightly on it. Many speakers find that this stance keeps them from fidgeting.

Pause before you begin your presentation, concentrating on your opening lines. During your presentation, interact with your audience as much as possible. You can do so by facing the audience at all times and making eye contact as often as possible. You may want to choose two or three people to look at and "talk to," particularly if you are addressing a large group. Allow time for the audience to ask questions. Try to keep your answers short so that others may participate in the conversation. When you conclude, remember to thank your audience.

### EXERCISE 25.1

Attend a lecture or presentation on your campus, and analyze its effectiveness. How does the speaker capture and hold your interest? What signpost language and other guides to listening can you detect? How well are visuals integrated into the presentation? How do the speaker's tone of voice, dress, and eye contact affect your understanding and appreciation (or lack of it)? What is most memorable about the presentation, and why? Bring your analysis to class and report your findings.

## 25d Multimedia for oral presentations

As you learn to create Web pages (see Chapter 24), you will probably wish to incorporate some of their qualities into your presentations for college classes as well as for work or community-related projects. Among the most popular forms of multimedia presentation are those that use presentation software and those that use posters.

### 1 Presentation software

Presentation software such as PowerPoint allows you to prepare slides you want to display and even to enhance the images with sound. Before you begin designing your presentation, find out if the computer equipment and projector you need will be available. As you design presentation slides, keep some simple principles in mind (for more on principles of visual design, see Chapter 23):

- For captions or any other print text, use fonts for emphasis, and make sure your audience can read them: 44- to 50-point type for titles, for example, or 30- to 34-point type for subheads.
- For slides that contain print text, use bulleted or numbered points rather than running text. Keep these items as concise as possible, and use clear language. If you are using the points to guide your own discussion, think carefully about the number of points you wish to include on each slide. Make sure that these points will actually guide both you and the audience.
- Don't try to put too much information on one slide — a good rule of thumb is to use no more than three to five bullet points or no more than fifty words.
- Create a clear contrast between any print text or illustration and the background. As a general rule, light backgrounds work better in a darkened room, dark backgrounds in a lighted one.
- Be careful of becoming overly dependent on presentation-software templates such as those provided by PowerPoint's AutoContent Wizard. The choices of color, font, and so on offered by such templates may not always match your goals or fit with your topic.
- As a general rule, use slides for illustrating what you are saying or for talking points. Never simply read the text of the slides to your audience; this technique, guaranteed to bore your listeners, has been called "death by PowerPoint."
- Choose visuals — photographs, paintings, graphs, and so on — that will reproduce sharply, and make sure they are large enough to be clearly visible to your audience.
- If you add sound or video clips, make sure that they are audible and that they relate directly to your topic. Especially if sound is to be used as background, make sure it does not distract from what you are trying to say.

Following are the full script and the PowerPoint slides prepared by student Jennifer Bernal for a class presentation. Her assignment was to analyze a graphic novel. Note that she cites the source of each image on the slide where it appears and that she includes a list of her sources on the final slide in the presentation.

[slide 1] Hello, I'm Jennifer Bernal. And I've been thinking about the voice of the child narrator in the graphic novel *Persepolis* by Marjane Satrapi, an autobiographical narrative of a young girl's coming of age in Iran during the Islamic revolution. My research questions seemed fitting for a child: what? how? why? What is the "child's voice"? How is it achieved? Why is it effective? The child's voice in this book is characterized by internal conflict: the character sometimes sounds like a child and sometimes like an adult. She truly is a child on the threshhold of adulthood. I'm going to show how Satrapi expresses the duality of this child's voice, not only through content but also through her visual style.

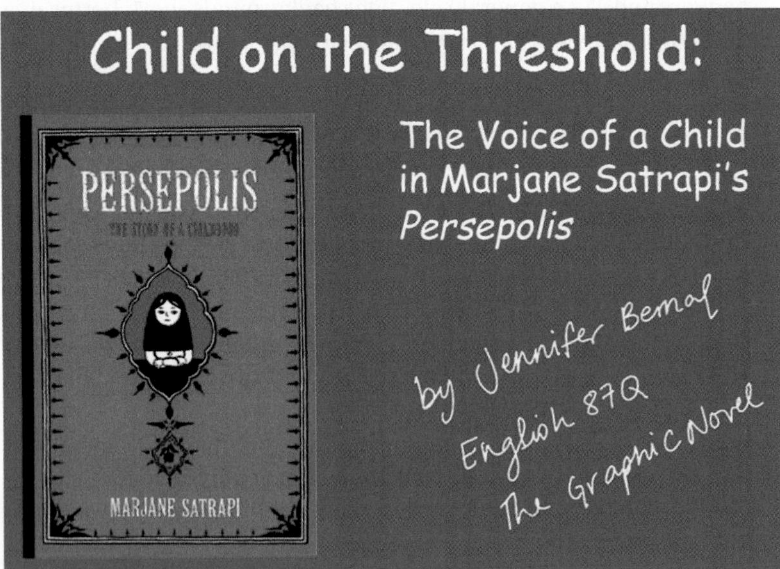

[slide 2] The main character, Marjane, faces a constant conflict between childhood and adulthood. But the struggle takes place not only between the child and the adults in her society but also between the child and the adult *within Marjane herself*. For example, Marjane is exposed to many ideas and experiences as she tries to understand the world around her. Here [first image] we see her suprising an adult by discussing Marx. But we also see her being a kid. Sometimes, like all children, she is unthinkingly cruel: here [second image] we see her upsetting another little girl with the horrifying (and, as it turns out, incorrect) "truth" about her father's absence.

[slide 3] In her review of *Persepolis* for the *Village Voice*, Joy Press says that "Satrapi's supernaive style . . . persuasively communicates confusion and horror through the eyes of a precocious preteen." It seems to me that this simple visual style is achieved through repetition and filtering. Let's take a look at this. [point to slide] First, there's *repetition* of elements. We often see the same images being used over and over. Sometimes [point to first image] the repetition suggests the sameness imposed by the repressive government. At other times similar images are repeated throughout the book for emphasis. For example [point to examples], on several occasions we see her raising her finger

The Child's Voice through Visual Style: Repetition

Fig. 3 from Marjane Satrapi, *Persepolis* (New York: Pantheon, 2003) 96.

Figs. 4, 5, 6 - from Satrapi 19, 114, 117.

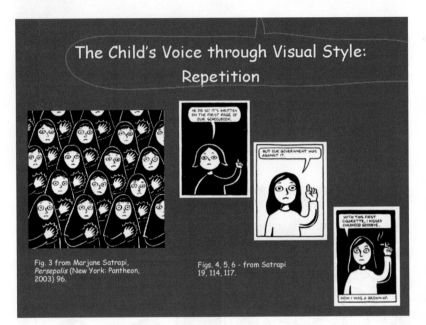

and speaking directly to the reader to make an emphatic point. The repetition throughout *Persepolis* makes it look and feel more like a children's book. [slide 4] In addition to simplification through repetition, there's a second simplifying process, that of *filtering*. *Persepolis* is filled with violent elements. One good example is the torture and execution of guerilla fighter Ahmadi. Marjane recounts, "In the end he was cut to pieces." The dismemberment is one of the most violent images that we see in the book. However, Satrapi's representation filters the horror. [point to illustration] This figure doesn't seem real — it looks neatly sectioned and hollow, like a doll. We see the image presented as a child might imagine it.

So, let me conclude by answering *why* Satrapi's visual voice is so effective. Remember, she is connecting to the world of childhood through comics. Her story seems very grim and adult — too grim for children. But it *is* a child's story, or rather the story of a character standing on the threshhold of the adult world. So the graphic novel is an ideal way to reveal both the conflicting aspects of the child's voice and the balance between these aspects. For the author to explain the child Marjane's particular, slightly uncomfortable vantage point, the in-between genre of the graphic novel is a perfect fit.
[slide 5] Thanks! Are there any questions?

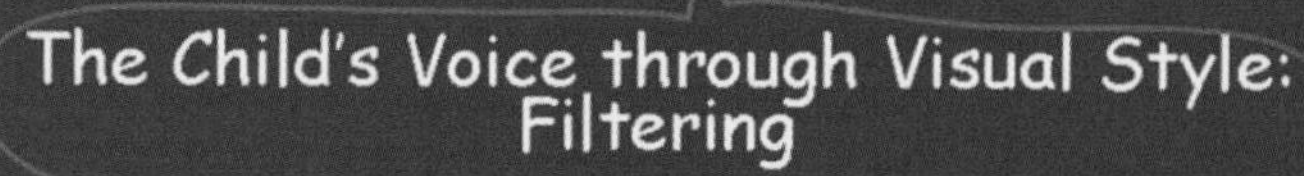


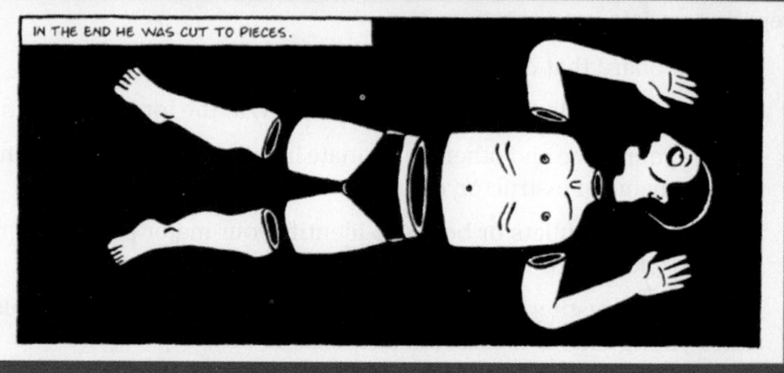

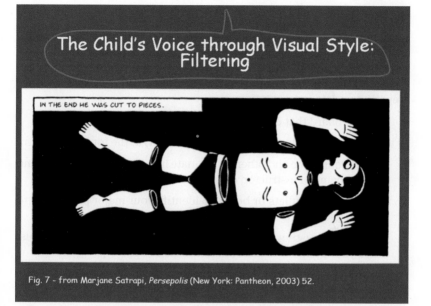

Fig. 7 - from Marjane Satrapi, *Persepolis* (New York: Pantheon, 2003) 52.

## Works Cited

Press, Joy. "Veil of Tears." Rev. of *Persepolis* by Marjane Satrapi. *Village Voice*. Village Voice Media Holdings LLC, 2 May 2003. Web. 30 Jan. 2006.

Satrapi, Marjane. *Persepolis: The Story of a Childhood*. New York: Pantheon Books, 2003. Print.

### 2 Posters

Many college courses and conferences now call on students to make poster presentations. During the class or conference session, the presenter uses a poster board as background while talking through the presentation and answering questions. Follow these tips if you are preparing a poster presentation:

- Create a board that can be read from at least three feet away.
- Include a clear title (at least two inches high) at the top of the board.
- Include your name and other appropriate information: course title and number, name of instructor, conference title or session, and so on.
- Use a series of bullets or boxes to identify your major points and to lead the audience through the presentation.
- Include an arresting image or an important table or figure if it illustrates your points in a clear and memorable way.
- Consider using a provocative question toward the bottom of the poster to focus attention and anticipate your conclusion.
- Remember that simple, uncluttered posters are usually easier to follow and therefore more effective than overly complex ones.
- Practice the oral part of the presentation until you are comfortable referring to the poster while keeping your full attention on the audience.

Page 499 shows the poster prepared by Amanda Rinder for a presentation based on her research (20d).

## 25e Webcasts

This chapter on oral and multimedia presentations has thus far assumed that you will be speaking before an audience in the same room with you. Increasingly, however, the presentations you make will be live, but you won't actually be in the same physical space as the audience. Instead, you'll make your presentation over the Web, speaking into a camera that captures your presentation (and perhaps your image) and relays it, via the Internet, to attendees who might be anywhere in the world.

As you learn to adapt to Webcast environments, most of the strategies that work in oral and multimedia presentations for an audience that

# Sweet Home Chicago:

**Preserving the Past, Protecting the Future of the Windy City**

- What happens when architectural preservation impedes new development?
- Why should Chicago invest in saving historically significant—but economically inefficient—buildings?
- How can Chicago balance the desire to preserve its rich architectural past with continued growth and prosperity?

Preservation Growth

Amanda Rinder
Sixteenth National Conference
on Undergraduate Research

January 6, 2007
Salisbury State University
Salisbury, Maryland

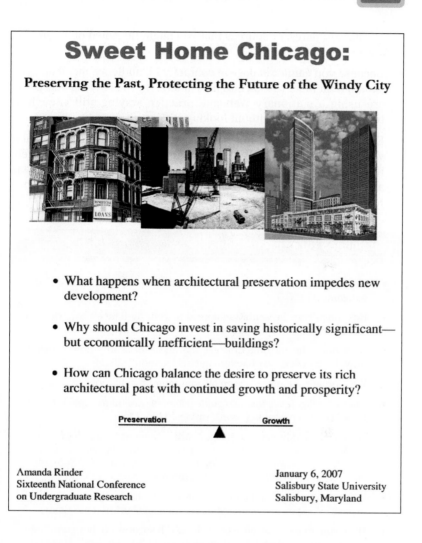

is actually present will continue to serve you well. But there are some significant differences:

- Practice is even more important in Webcasts, since you need to make sure that you can immediately access everything you need online — a set of slides, for example, or a document or video clip, as well as any names, dates, or sources that you might be called on to provide during the Webcast.

- Because you cannot make eye contact with audience members, you should remember to look into the camera, if you are using one. If you are using a stationary Webcam, practice staying still enough to remain in the frame without looking stiff.
- Even though your audience may not be visible to you, assume that if you are on camera, the Web-based audience can see you quite well; if you slouch, they'll notice. Also assume that your microphone is always live — don't say anything that you don't want your audience to hear.

## Guidelines for presentations

- How does your presentation accomplish the specifications of the assignment? (25b)
- How does your presentation appeal to your audience's experiences and interests? Does it achieve your purpose? (25b)
- How does the introduction get the audience's attention? Does it provide any necessary background information? (25c1)
- What organizational structure informs your presentation? (25c1)
- Check for signposts that can guide listeners. Are there explicit transitions? Do you repeat key words or ideas? (25c1)
- Have you used mostly straightforward sentences? Consider revising any long or complicated sentences to make your talk easier to follow. Check your words as well for too much abstraction. Substitute concrete words for abstract ones as often as you can. (25c1)
- Have you marked your text for pauses and emphasis? Have you marked material that you can omit if you find yourself short of time? (25c1)
- Have you prepared all necessary visuals? If so, how do they contribute to your presentation? Are they large enough to be seen? Have you followed the principles of good design? (25c2 and 23a2)
- If you have not prepared visuals, can you identify any information that would be enhanced by them? (23d and 25c)
- Have you practiced your presentation so that you will appear confident and knowledgeable? (25c3 and e)

### THINKING CRITICALLY ABOUT ORAL AND MULTIMEDIA PRESENTATIONS

Study the text of an oral or multimedia presentation you've prepared or given. Using the advice in this chapter, see how well your presentation appeals to your audience. Look in particular at how well you catch and hold their attention. How effective is your use of signpost language or other structures that help guide your listeners? How helpful are the visuals (PowerPoint slides, posters) in conveying your message? What would you do to improve this presentation?

# Part 5



# EFFECTIVE LANGUAGE

# 26 Writing to the World

People today often communicate instantaneously across vast distances and cultures. Businesspeople complete multinational transactions with ease, students take online classes at distant universities, and grandparents check in with family members across multiple time zones.

In this era of extreme communication, you might find yourself writing to (or with) students throughout the country or even across the globe — and you may well be in classes with people from other cultures, language groups, and countries. In business, government, and education, writers increasingly operate on an international stage and must become *world writers*, able to communicate across cultures.

## 26a Thinking about what seems "normal"

How do you decide what is "normal" in a given situation? Your judgment may be based on assumptions you are not even aware of. But remember: behavior that is considered out of place in one community may appear perfectly normal in another. If you want to communicate with people across cultures, try to learn something about the norms in those cultures and, even more important, be aware of the norms that guide your own behavior.

- Remember that most of us tend to see our own way as the normal or right way to do things. How do your own values and assumptions guide your thinking and behavior? Keep in mind that if your ways seem inherently right, then — even without thinking about it — you may assume that other ways are somehow less than right.
- Know that most ways of communicating are influenced by cultural contexts and differ widely from one culture to the next.
- Pay close attention to the ways that people from cultures other than your own communicate, and be flexible and open to their ways.
- Pay attention to and respect the differences among individual people within a given culture. Don't assume that all members of a community behave in just the same way or value exactly the same things. Perhaps most important, don't

overgeneralize. For example, just because empathy — as opposed to explicit criticism — is a preferred method of persuasion for some Asians does not mean this cultural pattern holds true for all Asians.

## 26b Clarifying meaning

When an instructor called for "originality" in his students' essays, what did he mean? A Filipina student thought *originality* meant going to an original source and explaining it; a student from Massachusetts thought *originality* meant coming up with an idea entirely on her own. The professor, however, expected students to read multiple sources and develop a critical point of their own about those sources. In subsequent classes, this professor defined *originality* and gave examples of student work he judged original.

This brief example points to the challenges all writers face in trying to communicate across space, across languages, across cultures. While there are no foolproof rules, here are some tips for communicating with people from cultures other than your own:

- Listen carefully. Don't hesitate to ask people to explain or even repeat a point if you're not absolutely sure you understand.
- Take care to be explicit about the meanings of the words you use.
- Invite response — ask whether you're making yourself clear. This kind of back-and-forth is particularly easy (and necessary) in email.

## 26c Your authority as a writer

In the United States, students are often asked to establish authority in their writing — by drawing on certain kinds of personal experience, by reporting on research they or others have conducted, or by taking a position for which they can offer strong evidence and support. But this expectation about writerly authority is by no means universal. Indeed, some cultures view student writers as novices whose job is to reflect what they learn from their teachers — those who hold the most important knowledge, wisdom, and, hence, authority. One Japanese student, for example, said he was taught that it's rude to challenge a teacher: "Are you ever so smart that you should challenge the wisdom of the ages?"

As this student's comment reveals, a writer's tone also depends on his or her relationship with listeners and readers. In this student's case, the valued relationship is one of respect and deference, of what one Indonesian student called "good modesty." As a world writer, you need to remember that those you're addressing may hold very different attitudes about authority.

- Whom are you addressing, and what is your relationship to him or her? (See 3h.)
- What knowledge are you expected to have? Is it appropriate for or expected of you to demonstrate that knowledge — and, if so, how?
- What is your goal — to answer a question? to make a point? to agree? something else? (See 3d and e.)
- What tone is appropriate? If in doubt, show respect: politeness is rarely if ever inappropriate. (See 6g.)

## 26d Audience expectations

In the United States, many audiences (and especially those in the academic and business worlds) expect a writer to get to the point as directly as possible and to take on the major responsibility of articulating that point efficiently and unambiguously. But not all audiences have such expectations. For instance, a Chinese student with an excellent command of English found herself struggling in her American classes. Her writing, U.S. teachers said, was "vague," with too much "beating around the bush." As it turned out, teachers prized this kind of indirectness in China, where readers are expected to read between the lines to understand the message.

The point of this story (and note how swiftly that point is made!) is that world writers must think carefully about whether audience members expect the writer to make the meaning of a text explicitly clear or whether they expect to do some of the work themselves. A typical U.S. academic report, for example, puts the responsibility on the writer to present an unambiguous message. Such a report begins with a clear overview of all the major points to be covered, follows with an orderly discussion of each point, and ends with a brief summary. In many other cultures, however, writers organize information differently because the audience takes more responsibility for figuring out what is being said. Here are tips for thinking about reader and writer responsibility:

- What general knowledge do members of your audience have about your topic? What information do they expect — or need — you to provide?
- Do members of your audience tend to be very direct, saying explicitly what they mean? Or are they more subtle, less likely to call a spade a spade? Look for cues to determine how much responsibility you have as the writer.

## 26e Persuasive evidence

How do you decide what evidence will best support your ideas? The answer depends, in large part, on how you define *evidence*. American academics generally give great weight to factual evidence. In doing research at a U.S. university, a Chinese student reports she was told time and time again by her instructors that "facts, and facts alone, provide the sure route to truth." While she learned to document her work in ways her U.S. professors found persuasive, she also continued to value the kinds of evidence often favored in China, especially those based on authority and on allusion.

Differing concepts of what counts as evidence can lead to arguments that go nowhere. Consider, for example, how rare it is for a believer in creationism to be persuaded by what the theory of evolution presents as evidence — or how rare for a supporter of evolutionary theory to be convinced by what creationists present as evidence. A person who regards biblical authority as the supreme evidence in any argument may never see eye to eye with a person who views religion and science as occupying separate spheres, each of which offers its own kind of truth. Think carefully about how you use evidence in writing, and pay attention to what counts as evidence to members of other groups.

- Should you rely on facts? concrete examples? firsthand experience?
- Should you include the testimony of experts? Which experts are valued most, and why?
- Should you cite religious or philosophical texts? proverbs or everyday wisdom? other sources?

- Should you use analogies as support? How much will they count?
- Once you determine what counts as evidence in your own thinking and writing, think about where you learned to use and value this kind of evidence. You can ask these same questions about the use of evidence by members of other cultures.

## 26f Organization

As you make choices about how to organize your writing, remember that cultural influences are at work here as well: the patterns that you find pleasing are likely to be ones that are deeply embedded in your own culture. For example, the organizational pattern favored by U.S. engineers, highly explicit and leaving little or nothing unsaid or unexplained, is probably familiar to most U.S. students: introduction and thesis, necessary background, overview of the parts to follow, systematic presentation of evidence, consideration of other viewpoints, and conclusion. If a piece of writing follows this pattern, American readers ordinarily find it "well organized" or "coherent."

But writers who value different organizational patterns may not. To some, the writing done by U.S. engineers may seem overly simple. One writer from Chile, for instance, reports that this pattern of writing strikes her as downright childlike: " 'This is a watch; the watch is brown; the watch tells time; yadda yadda.' For us, that's funny. I think that, for Americans, it must be funny the way I describe things." This writer is accustomed to writing that is more elaborate, sometimes digressing from the main point and not spelling out every connection from point A to point B.

In cultures that value indirection and subtlety, writers tend to use patterns of organization that display these values. One common pattern in Korean writing, for instance, includes an introduction; a topic with development; a tangential topic, again with development; and then a conclusion — with the thesis appearing only at the end.

Some cultures value repetition. Some Arabic readers, for example, expect a writer to reiterate a major point from several different perspectives as a way of making that point.

When writing for world audiences, then, think about how you can organize material to get your message across effectively. One expert in international business communication recommends, for example, that businesspeople writing to others in Japan should state their requests indirectly — and only after a formal and respectful opening. There are no hard and fast rules to help you organize your writing for effectiveness across cultures, but here are a couple of options to consider:

- Determine when to state your thesis — at the beginning? at the end? somewhere else? not at all?
- Consider whether digressions are a good idea, a requirement, or best avoided with your intended audience.

## 26g Style

As with beauty, good style is most definitely in the eye of the beholder — and thus is always affected by language, culture, and rhetorical tradition. In fact, what constitutes effective style varies broadly across cultures and depends on the rhetorical situation — purpose, audience, and so on (see Chapter 3). Even so, there is one important style question to consider when writing across cultures: what level of formality is most appropriate? In most writing to a general audience in the United States, a fairly informal style is often acceptable, even appreciated. Many cultures, however, tend to value a more formal approach. When in doubt, it may be wise to err on the side of formality in writing to people from other cultures, especially to elders or to those in authority.

- Be careful to use proper titles:

  Dr. Beverly Moss        Professor Jaime Mejía

- Avoid slang and informal structures such as fragments.
- Do not use first names in correspondence (even in email) unless invited to do so. Note, however, that an invitation to use a first name could come indirectly; if someone signs an email message or letter to you with his or her first name, you are implicitly invited to do the same.
- For international business email (as with print letters), use complete sentences and words; avoid contractions. Open with the salutation "Dear Mr./Ms. ______" or the person's title, if you know it. Write dates by listing the day before the month and spelling out the name of the month rather than using a numeral (*7 June 2006*). For more information on style in email, see Chapter 24.

## Editing to communicate across cultures

- Recognize what you consider "normal." Examine your own customary behaviors and assumptions, and think about how they may affect what you think and say (and write). (26a)
- Listen closely to someone from another culture, and ask for clarification if necessary. Carefully define your terms. (26b)
- Consider your authority as a writer. Should you sound like an expert? a subordinate? something else? (26c)
- Think about your audience's expectations. How explicit does your writing need to be? (26d)
- What kind of evidence will count most with your audience? (26e)
- Organize your writing with your audience's expectations in mind. (26f)
- If in doubt, use formal style. (26g)

Beyond formality, other stylistic preferences vary widely. Many writers of Spanish, for example, prefer long, complex sentences and ornate language (which members of some cultures might find overdone — and others might find understated!). Japanese writing tends to be very polite and diplomatic, perhaps because the Japanese language has three forms — the honorific, the polite, and the everyday.

World writers, then, should take nothing about language for granted. To be an effective world writer, you will want to recognize and respect stylistic differences as you move from culture to culture.

### THINKING CRITICALLY ABOUT ASSUMPTIONS IN YOUR WRITING

Choose one or two recent essays or other pieces of writing, and examine them carefully, noting what you assume about what counts as persuasive evidence, good organization, and effective style. How do you represent yourself in relation to your audience? What other unstated assumptions about good writing can you identify?

# Language That Builds Common Ground

# 27

As a child, you may have learned to "do to others what you would have them do to you." To that golden rule, we could add "say to others what you would have them say to you." The words we select have the power to praise, delight, inspire — and also to hurt, offend, or even destroy. That's why we refer to "a *stinging* rebuke" or "a *cutting* remark." Words that offend break the golden rule of language use, preventing others from identifying with you or even considering your ideas.

Few absolute guidelines exist for using language that shows respect for differences and builds common ground. Two general rules, however, can help: consider the sensitivities and preferences of others, and watch for words that carry stereotypes and betray your assumptions, even though you have not directly stated them.

## 27a Stereotypes and generalizations

Children like cartoons; U.S. citizens value freedom; people who drop out of high school do not get good jobs. These broad statements contain stereotypes, standardized or fixed ideas about a group. To some extent, we all think in terms of stereotypes, and sometimes they can be helpful in making a generalization. Stereotyping any individual on the basis of generalizations about a group, however, can lead to inaccurate and even hurtful conclusions.

For example, an instructor who notes a fraternity member's absence from class on the morning after a big frat party and remarks, "Ah, he must be nursing a hangover," is stereotyping the student on the basis of assumptions about fraternity men. But such stereotyping may be far off the mark with this particular student — and with many other fraternity members. By indulging in it, this instructor may well be alienating some of her students and undermining her effectiveness as a teacher.

Because stereotypes are often based on half-truths, misunderstandings, and hand-me-down prejudices, they can lead to intolerance, bias, and bigotry. But even positive stereotypes — for example, *Jewish doctors are the best*, or neutral ones, for example, *college students like pizza* — can hurt, for they inevitably ignore the uniqueness of an individual.

Other kinds of unstated assumptions also destroy common ground by ignoring the differences between others and ourselves. For example, a student in a religion seminar who uses *we* to refer to

Christians and *they* to refer to members of other religions had better be sure that everyone in the class is Christian, or some people present may feel left out of the discussion.

Sometimes assumptions even lead writers to call special attention to a group affiliation when it is not relevant to the point, as in *a woman bus driver* or *a white basketball player.* Decisions about whether to generalize about a group or to describe an individual as a member of a group are often difficult for writers. Think about how your language can build — rather than destroy — common ground.

## 27b Assumptions about gender

An elementary teacher in Toronto got increasingly tired of seeing hands go up every time the children sang the line in Canada's national anthem, "True patriot love in all thy sons command." "When do we get to the part about the daughters?" the children inevitably asked. These children's questions point to the ways in which powerful gender-related words can subtly affect our thinking and our behavior. For instance, many young women at one time were discouraged from pursuing careers in medicine or engineering at least partially because speakers commonly referred to hypothetical doctors or engineers as *he* (and then labeled any woman who worked as a doctor a *woman doctor,* as if to say, "She's an exception; doctors are normally men"). Similarly, a label like *male nurse* may offend by reflecting stereotyped assumptions about proper roles for men. Equally problematic is the traditional use of *man* and *mankind* to refer to people of both sexes and the use of *he, him, his,* and *himself* to refer to people of unknown sex. Because such usage ignores half the human race, it hardly helps a writer build common ground.

*Who is a nurse and who is a doctor? Be careful not to make assumptions based on gender stereotypes.*

### *Revising sexist language*

Sexist language, those words and phrases that stereotype or ignore members of either sex or that unnecessarily call attention to gender, can usually be revised fairly easily. There are several alternatives to using masculine pronouns to refer to persons of unknown sex. (See also 34g.)

One option is to recast the sentence using plural forms.

- **~~A lawyer~~ [Lawyers] must pass the bar exam before ~~he~~ [they] can begin to practice.**

Another option is to substitute *he or she*, *him or her*, and so on.

- **A lawyer must pass the bar exam before he [or she] can begin to practice.**

Yet another way to revise the sentence is to eliminate the pronouns.

- **A lawyer must pass the bar exam before ~~he can begin~~ [beginning] to practice.**

You should also try to eliminate words that make assumptions about gender or emphasize it for no good reason.

| INSTEAD OF | TRY USING |
|---|---|
| anchorman, anchorwoman | anchor |
| businessman | businessperson, business executive |
| chairman, chairwoman | chair, chairperson |
| congressman | member of Congress, representative |
| fireman | firefighter |
| mailman | mail carrier |
| male secretary | secretary |
| man, mankind | humans, human beings, humanity, the human race, humankind |
| manpower | workers, personnel |
| mothering | parenting |
| policeman, policewoman | police officer |
| salesman | salesperson |
| woman engineer | engineer |

## EXERCISE 27.1

The following excerpt is taken from the 1968 edition of Dr. Benjamin Spock's *Baby and Child Care*. Read it carefully, noting any language we might now consider sexist. Then try bringing it up-to-date by revising the passage, substituting nonsexist language as necessary.

> When you suggest something that doesn't appeal to your baby, he feels he *must* assert himself. His nature tells him to. He just says No in words or actions, even about things that he likes to do. The psychologists call it "negativism"; mothers

call it "that terrible No stage." But stop and think what would happen to him if he never felt like saying No. He'd become a robot, a mechanical man. You wouldn't be able to resist the temptation to boss him all the time, and he'd stop learning and developing. When he was old enough to go out into the world, to school and later to work, everybody else would take advantage of him, too. He'd never be good for anything.

**bedfordstmartins.com/smhandbook** For more exercises on avoiding sexist language, go to Exercise Central and click on **Language That Builds Common Ground**.

## 27c Assumptions about race and ethnicity

Generalizations about racial and ethnic groups can result in especially harmful stereotyping. To build common ground, then, avoid language that ignores differences not only among individual members of a race or ethnic group but also among subgroups. Writers must be aware, for instance, of the diverse places from which Americans of Spanish-speaking ancestry have come.

### *Using preferred terms*

When writing about an ethnic or racial group, how can you refer to that group in terms that its members actually desire? Doing so is sometimes not an easy task, for terms can change often and vary widely.

The word *colored*, for example, was once widely used in the United States to refer to Americans of African ancestry. By the 1950s, the preferred term had become *Negro*. This changed in the 1960s, however, as *black* came to be preferred by most, though certainly not all, members of that community. Then, in the late 1980s, some leaders of the American black community urged that *black* be replaced by *African American*.

The word *Oriental*, once used to refer to people of East Asian descent, is now often considered offensive. At the University of California at Berkeley, the Oriental Languages Department is now known as the East Asian Languages Department. One advocate of the change explained that *Oriental* is appropriate for objects — like rugs — but not for people.

Once widely preferred, the term *Native American* is being challenged by those who argue that the most appropriate way to refer to indigenous peoples is by the specific name of the tribe or pueblo, such as *Chippewa* or *Diné*. Many indigenous peoples once referred to as *Eskimos* now prefer *Inuit* or a specific term such as *Tlingit*. It has also become fairly common for tribal groups to refer to themselves as *Indians* or *Indian tribes*.

Among Americans of Spanish-speaking descent, the preferred terms of reference are many: *Chicano/Chicana*, *Hispanic*, *Latin American*, *Latino/Latina*, *Mexican American*, *Dominican*, and *Puerto Rican*, to name but a few.

Clearly, then, ethnic terminology changes often enough to challenge the most careful writers. Consider your words carefully, seek information about ways members of groups refer to themselves (or ask them their preferences), and check any term you are unsure of in a current dictionary. The *Random House Webster's College Dictionary* includes particularly helpful usage notes about racial and ethnic designations.

## 27d Other kinds of difference

Gender, race, and ethnicity are among the most frequent challenges to a writer seeking to find common ground with readers, but you will face many others as well.

### 1 Age

Mention age if it is relevant, but be aware that age-related terms can carry derogatory connotations (*matronly*, *well-preserved*, and so on). Although describing Mr. Fry as *elderly but still active* may sound polite to you, chances are Mr. Fry would prefer being called *an active seventy-eight-year-old* — or just *a seventy-eight-year-old*, which eliminates the unstated assumption of surprise that he is active at his age.

### 2 Class

Take special care to examine your words for assumptions about class. In a *New York Times* column, for example, a young woman wrote about losing her high-paying professional job. Unable to find other "meaningful work," as she put it, she was forced to accept "absurd" jobs like cleaning houses and baby-sitting.

The column provoked a number of angry letters to the *Times*, including this one: "So the young and privileged are learning what we of the working classes have always understood too well: there is no entitlement in life. We have always taken the jobs you label 'absurd.' Our mothers are the women who clean your mothers' houses."

As a writer, then, do not assume that all your readers share your background or values — that your classmates all own cars, for instance. And avoid using any words — *redneck*, *blue blood*, and the like — that might alienate members of an audience.

### 3 Geographic area

You should not assume that geography determines personality, politics, or lifestyle. New Englanders are not all thrifty and tight-lipped; people in "red states" may hold liberal social and political views; midwesterners are not always polite. Check your writing carefully to be sure it doesn't make such simplistic assumptions.

Check also that you use geographic terms accurately:

| | |
|---|---|
| **AMERICA, AMERICAN** | Although many people use these words to refer to the United States alone, such usage will not necessarily be acceptable to people from Canada, Mexico, and Central or South America. |
| **BRITISH, ENGLISH** | Use *British* to refer to the island of Great Britain, which includes England, Scotland, and Wales, or to the United Kingdom of Great Britain and Northern Ireland. In general, do not use *English* for these broader senses. |
| **ARAB** | This term refers only to people of Arabic-speaking descent. Note that Iran is not an Arab nation; its people speak Farsi, not Arabic. Note also that *Arab* is not synonymous with *Muslim* or *Moslem* (a believer in Islam). Most (but not all) Arabs are Muslims, but many Muslims (those in Pakistan, for example) are not Arab. |

### 4 Physical ability or health

When writing about a person with a serious illness or disability, ask yourself whether mentioning the disability is relevant to your discussion and whether the words you use carry negative connotations. You might choose, for example, to say someone *uses* a wheelchair rather than to say he or she is *confined to* one. Similarly, you might note a subtle but meaningful difference between calling someone *a person with AIDS* rather than *an AIDS victim*. Mentioning the person first and the dis-

## CONSIDERING DISABILITIES: Know your readers

The American Council on Education reports that nearly 10 percent of all first-year college students — some 155,000 — identify themselves as having one or more disabilities. As this figure suggests, living with a disability is more the norm than many previously thought. And the actual figure may well be higher, since many students with disabilities do not identify themselves as disabled. Effective writers learn as much as possible about their readers so that they can find ways to build common ground.

ability second, such as referring to a *child with diabetes* rather than a *diabetic child* or a *diabetic*, is always a good idea. In addition, remember that people with disabilities may well resent the use of euphemisms like "physically challenged" because such terms can minimize the importance of a disability.

**bedfordstmartins.com/smhandbook** For more information, go to Links and click on **Considering Disabilities**.

### 5 Religion

Religious stereotypes are very often inaccurate and unfair. For example, Roman Catholics hold a wide spectrum of views on abortion, Muslim women do not all wear veils, and many Baptists are not fundamentalists. In fact, many people do not believe in or practice a religion at all, so be careful of such assumptions. As in other cases, do not use religious labels if they are not relevant.

### 6 Sexual orientation

If you wish to build common ground, do not assume that readers all share one sexual orientation — that everyone is attracted to the opposite sex, for example. As with any label, reference to sexual orientation should be governed by context. Someone writing about Representative Barney Frank's economic views would probably have little or no reason to refer to his sexual orientation. On the other hand, someone writing about diversity in U.S. government might find it important to note that Frank has long made his homosexuality public.

## Editing for language that builds common ground

- What stereotypes and other assumptions might come between you and your readers? Look, for instance, for language implying approval or disapproval and for the ways you use *we*, *you*, and *they*. (27a)
- Avoid potentially sexist language, and omit irrelevant references to gender. Be careful not to assume gender based on occupation, and use gender-neutral nouns when you may be referring to either men or women (*firefighters* instead of *firemen*, for instance). Avoid using a masculine pronoun such as *he* or *him* to refer to a person who may be female. (27b)
- Make sure your references to race, religion, gender, sexual orientation, physical ability, age, and so on are relevant or necessary to your discussion. (27b–d)
- Are the terms you use to refer to groups accurate and acceptable? Pay attention to the terms that members of the group prefer. (27c and d)

## THINKING CRITICALLY ABOUT HOW LANGUAGE CAN BUILD COMMON GROUND

Below is the opening paragraph of a "My Turn" column in *Newsweek*, along with the photograph of the author that accompanied the piece. In both the photograph and essay, the author appeals to readers to empathize with the destruction of the environment he grew up in. What views and values do you think he expects his readers to share with him? Note the strategies the writer uses to establish common ground with his readers in this paragraph and image.

I grew up in the mountains of East Tennessee, on a modest farm where we raised a lot of what we ate, watched sunsets on the porch and had supper together every night. For nine generations, mine included, both sides of my family have lived and died in the shadows of the surrounding peaks.

—**ABE WHALEY, "Once Unique, Soon a Place Like Any Other"**

# Language Variety

28

As comedian Dave Chappelle has said with pointed irony, "Every black American is bilingual. We speak street vernacular, and we speak job interview." As Chappelle understands, English comes in many varieties that differ from one another in pronunciation, vocabulary, rhetoric, and grammar. You probably already adjust the variety of English you use depending on how well — and how formally — you know the audience you are addressing. If you speak another language in addition to English, you may also find yourself using different languages for different situations. Adding language variety to your writing can improve your communication with your audience if you think carefully about the effect you want to achieve.

## 28a Varieties of language in academic writing

How do writers decide *when* to use another language or *when* to use a particular variety of English — when to insert eastern Tennessee dialect or African American vernacular patterns into a formal essay, for example? Even writers who are perfectly fluent in several languages must think carefully before switching linguistic gears. The key to shifting among varieties of English and among languages is appropriateness: you need to consider when such shifts will help you connect with your audience, get their attention, make a particular point, or represent the actual words of someone you are writing about.

Sometimes writers' choices are limited by various kinds of pressures. One example is the tendency of many to discriminate against those who fail to use an expected variety of English. Not only do some discriminate against those who don't speak "standard" English; people in other communities may reject those who sound affected or too proper. Used appropriately and wisely, however, *all* varieties of English can serve good purposes.

## 28b Standard varieties of English

One variety of English, often referred to as the "standard" or "standard academic," is taught prescriptively in schools, represented in this and most other textbooks, used in the national media, and written and spoken widely by those wielding the most social and economic power. As the language used in business and most public institutions, standard English is a variety you will want to be completely familiar with — while recognizing that it is only one of many effective and powerful varieties of our language.

Even standard English is hardly a monolith, however; the standard varies according to purpose and audience, from the very formal style used in academic writing to the informal style characteristic of casual conversation. Thus there is usually more than one "standard" way to say or write something. Nevertheless, recognizable practices and conventions do exist, and they go by the shorthand name of standard English. (For more on academic conventions, see Chapter 1.)

**FOR MULTILINGUAL WRITERS: Global English**

Like other world languages, English is used in many countries, so it has many global varieties. For example, British English differs somewhat from U.S. English in certain vocabulary (*bonnet* for *hood* of a car), syntax (*to hospital* rather than *to the hospital*), spelling (*centre* rather than *center*), and pronunciation. If you have learned a non-American variety of English, you will want to recognize the ways in which it differs from the variety widely used in U.S. academic settings.

## 28c Ethnic varieties of English

Whether you are American Indian or trace your ancestry to Europe, Asia, Latin America, Africa, or elsewhere, your ethnic heritage lives on in the diversity of the English language. See how one Hawaiian writer uses an ethnic variety of English to paint a picture of young teens hearing a "chicken skin" story from their grandmother.

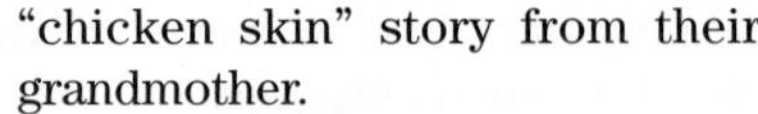

"—So, rather dan being rid of da shark, da people were stuck with many little ones, for dere mistake."

Then Grandma Wong wen' pause, for dramatic effect, I guess, and she wen' add, "Dis is one of dose times. Dis is da time of da mano." She wen' look at my kid brother 'Analu and said, "Da time of da sharks."

> Those words ended another of Grandma's chicken skin stories. The stories she told us had been passed on to her by her grandmother, who had heard them from *her* grandmother. Always skipping a generation.
>
> — RODNEY MORALES, "When the Shark Bites"

Notice how the narrator of the story uses both standard and ethnic varieties of English — presenting information necessary to the story line mostly in standard English and using a local, ethnic variety to represent spoken language.

Zora Neale Hurston's work often mixes African American vernacular with standard English.

> My grandmother worried about my forward ways a great deal. She had known slavery and to her my brazenness was unthinkable.
>
> "Git down offa dat gate-post! You li'l sow, you! Git down! Setting up dere looking dem white folks right in de face! They's gowine to lynch you, yet. And don't stand in dat doorway gazing out at 'em neither. Youse too brazen to live long."
>
> Nevertheless, I kept right on gazing at them, and "going a piece of the way" whenever I could make it. — ZORA NEALE HURSTON, *Dust Tracks on a Road*

In each of these examples, one important reason for the shift from standard English is to demonstrate that the writer is a member of the community whose language he or she is representing and thus to build credibility with others in the community.

Take care, however, in using the language of communities other than your own. When used inappropriately, such language can have an opposite effect, perhaps destroying credibility and alienating your audience.

## 28d Regional varieties of English

> "Ever'body says words different," said Ivy. "Arkansas folks says 'em different from Oklahomy folks says 'em different. And we seen a lady from Massachusetts, an' she said 'em differentest of all. Couldn' hardly make out what she was sayin'." — JOHN STEINBECK, *The Grapes of Wrath*

### FOR MULTILINGUAL WRITERS: Appropriate words

If you are unsure about what words are most appropriate in U.S. English — or if you are unfamiliar with particular regional, occupational, or social varieties — talk with your instructor or ask your classmates for advice.

Like Ivy — and every other speaker of English — your language has been affected by region. Using regional language is an effective way to evoke a character or place.

Garrison Keillor, for instance, has become famous for his Lake Wobegon stories, which are peppered with the English spoken in parts of Minnesota. When Keillor says "Gimme a Wendy's," he refers not to a kind of hamburger but to Saint Wendell's beer, "brewed by the Dimmers family at the Old Dimmers Brewery in nearby Saint Wendell's for five generations."

Look at the following piece of dialogue from an essay about Vermont:

> "There'll be some fine music on the green tonight, don't ya know?"
> "Well, I sure do want to go."
> "So don't I!"

In both these instances, the regional English creates a homespun effect and captures some of the language used in a particular place.

See how an anthropologist weaves together regional and standard academic English in writing about one Carolina community.

> For Roadville, schooling is something most folks have not gotten enough of, but everybody believes will do something toward helping an individual "get on." In the words of one oldtime resident, "Folks that ain't got no schooling don't get to be nobody nowadays."
>
> — SHIRLEY BRICE HEATH, *Ways with Words*

Notice that the researcher takes care to let a resident of Roadville speak her mind — and in her own words.

### EXERCISE 28.1

Identify the purpose and audience for one of this chapter's examples of ethnic or regional English. Then rewrite the passage to remove all evidence of any variety of English other than the so-called standard. Compare your revised version with the original and with those produced by some of your classmates. What differences do you notice in tone (is it more formal? more distant? something else?) and in overall impression? Which version seems most appropriate for the intended audience and purpose? Which do you prefer — and why?

**bedfordstmartins.com/smhandbook** For more on using varieties of English, go to Links and click on **Language Variety**.

**CONSIDERING DISABILITIES: American Sign Language**

One variety of language that is becoming increasingly popular on college campuses is American Sign Language (ASL), a fairly young language that began in this country around 1817. Some colleges now offer ASL courses that satisfy a second language requirement — and also introduce hearing students to Deaf culture.

## 28e Other languages

You might use a language other than English for the same reasons you might use different varieties of English: to represent the actual words of a speaker, to make a point, to connect with your audience, or to get their attention.

See how Gerald Haslam uses Spanish to capture his great-grandmother's words as well as to make a point about his relationship to her.

"*Expectoran su sangre!*" exclaimed Great-grandma when I showed her the small horned toad I had removed from my breast pocket. I turned toward my mother, who translated: "They spit blood."

"*De los ojos,*" Grandma added. "From their eyes," mother explained, herself uncomfortable in the presence of the small beast.

I grinned, "Awwwwwww."

But my Great-grandmother did not smile. "*Son muy tóxicos,*" she nodded with finality. Mother moved back an involuntary step, her hands suddenly busy at her breast. "Put that thing down," she ordered.

"His name's John," I said.

— GERALD HASLAM, *California Childhood*

In the following passage, notice how the novelist Michele Herman uses Yiddish to evoke her grandmother's world:

"Skip *shabes*?" Rivke chuckled. "I don't think this is possible. Once a week comes *shabes*. About this a person doesn't have a choice."

"What I *mean*" — Myra's impatience was plain — "is skip the preparation. It's too much for you, it tires you out."

"Ach," Rivke said. "Too much for me it isn't." This wasn't true. For some time she had felt that it really was too much for her. It was only for *shabes* that she cooked; the rest of the week she ate cold cereal, fruit, pot cheese, crackers.

— MICHELE HERMAN, *Missing*

In this passage, Rivke's syntax — the inversion of word order (*Once a week comes shabes*, for example, and *Too much for me it isn't*) — reflects Yiddish rhythms. In addition, the use of the Yiddish *shabes* carries a strong association with a religious institution, one that would be lost if it were translated to "sabbath." It is not "sabbath" to Rivke; it is *shabes*.

In the following passage, a linguist uses Spanish — and English translations — in her discussion of literacy in a Mexican community in Chicago:

*Gracia* (grace, wit) is used to refer to wittiness in talk; people who *tiene gracia* (have grace, are witty) are seen as clever and funny. Not everyone illustrates this quality, but those who do are obvious from the moment they speak. As one middle-aged male said,

*. . . cuando ellos empiezan a hablar, desde el momento que los oyes hablar, tienen gracia. Entonces, la gente que tiene gracia, se va juntando gente a oírlos. Y hay gente más desabrida, diría yo. No tiene, no le quedan sus chistes. Aunque cuente uno una charrita . . . ya no te vas a reír igual.*

(. . . when they start to speak, from the moment that you hear them speak, they are witty. So then, the people who are witty begin to have a listening crowd gather about them. And then there are people who are more boring, I would say. They don't have, their jokes just don't make it. Even though they may tell a joke . . . you're not going to laugh in the same manner.)

— MARCIA FARR, "Essayist Literacy and Other Verbal Performances"

Here, Farr provides a translation of the Spanish, for she expects that many of her readers will not know Spanish. She evokes the language of the community she describes, however, by presenting the Spanish first.

In general, you should not assume that all your readers will understand another language. So, in most cases, including a translation (as Marcia Farr does) is appropriate. Occasionally, however, the words from the other language will be clear from the context (as is *shabes* in Michele Herman's passage). At other times, a writer might leave something untranslated to make a point — to let readers know what it's like not to understand, for example.

## Checklist for language variety

Standard (28b), ethnic (28c), and regional varieties of English (28d), as well as other languages (28e), can all be used very effectively for the following purposes in your writing:

- to repeat someone's exact words
- to evoke a person, place, or activity
- to establish your credibility and build common ground
- to make a strong point
- to get your audience's attention

## THINKING CRITICALLY ABOUT LANGUAGE VARIETY

The following description of a meal features English that is characteristic of the Florida backwoods in the 1930s. Using this passage as an example, write a description of a memorable event from your daily life. Try to include some informal dialogue. Then look at the language you used — do you use more than one variety of English? What effect does your use of language have on your description?

> Jody heard nothing; saw nothing but his plate. He had never been so hungry in his life, and after a lean winter and a slow spring . . . his mother had cooked a supper good enough for the preacher. There were poke-greens with bits of white bacon buried in them; sandbuggers made of potato and onion and the cooter he had found crawling yesterday; sour orange biscuits and at his mother's elbow the sweet potato pone. He was torn between his desire for more biscuits and another sandbugger and the knowledge, born of painful experience, that if he ate them, he would suddenly have no room for pone. The choice was plain.
>
> — MARJORIE KINNAN RAWLINGS, *The Yearling*

# 29 Word Choice

Deciding which word is the right word can be a challenge. English has borrowed and absorbed words from other languages for centuries, so it's not unusual to find many words that have similar but subtly different meanings — and choosing one instead of another can make a very different impression on the audience. For instance, the "pasta with marinara sauce" served in a restaurant may look and taste much like the "macaroni and gravy" served at an Italian American family dinner, but in each case the choice of words says something not only about the food but also about the people serving it — and about the people they expect to serve it to.

## 29a Choosing words carefully

To choose clear and appropriate words, writers need to think about purpose, topic, and audience. What is appropriate for one region or occupation, for example, may not be appropriate for another. Also, a writer's level of formality will vary because of topic and audience. In an email or letter to a friend or close associate, informal language is often appropriate. But for most academic and professional writing, more formal language is appropriate because you are addressing people you do not know well. Compare these responses to a request for information about a job candidate:

**EMAIL TO SOMEONE YOU KNOW WELL**

Maisha is great — hire her if you can!

**LETTER OF RECOMMENDATION TO SOMEONE YOU DO NOT KNOW**

I am pleased to recommend Maisha Fisher. She will bring good ideas and extraordinary energy to your organization.

In deciding on the right words to use in a particular piece of writing, a writer needs to be aware of the possibilities and pitfalls of different kinds of language, including slang and colloquial language; technical and occupational language; and pompous language, euphemisms, and doublespeak.

### 1 Slang and colloquial language

Slang, or extremely informal language, is often confined to a relatively small group and usually becomes

## TALKING THE TALK: Instant-message shortcuts

"Can I use IM shortcuts when I email my teacher?" Instant-message slang may be second nature for many students, but using IM shortcuts, such as *u* for *you*, when communicating with an instructor can be a serious mistake. On an IM thread or in a text message, IM slang can indeed be conventional usage. But at least some of your instructors are likely to view such informal shortcuts as disrespectful, unprofessional, or simply sloppy writing. Unless you are working to create a special effect for a special purpose and audience, keep to the conventions of standard English for college writing — even in email.

obsolete rather quickly, though some slang gains wide use (*duh*, *dot-com*). Colloquial language, such as *a lot*, *in a bind*, or *snooze*, is less informal, more widely used, and longer lasting than most slang.

Writers who use slang and colloquial language run the risk of not being understood or of not being taken seriously. If you are writing for a general audience about gun-control legislation, for example, and you use terms like *gat* or *Mac* to refer to types of weapons, some readers may not know what you mean, and others may be irritated by what they see as a frivolous reference to a deadly serious subject.

### EXERCISE 29.1

Choose something or someone to describe — a favorite cousin, a stranger on the bus, an automobile, a musical instrument, whatever strikes your fancy. Describe your subject using colloquial language and slang. Then rewrite the description, this time using neither of these. Read the two passages aloud, and note what different effects each creates.

### 2 Technical and occupational language

Those who work — or play — in particular fields sometimes create their own technical language. Businesspeople talk about *greenmail* and *upside movement*, biologists about *nucleotides* and *immunodestruction*, and baseball fans about *fielder's choices* and *suicide bunts*. If you use any technical or occupation-specific language, make sure that your audience will understand your terms, and replace or define those that they will not. Technical and occupational language can be divided into two overlapping categories: neologisms and jargon.

### *Neologisms*

Defined as new words that have not yet found their way into dictionaries, neologisms can be especially helpful to writers in the sciences and applied disciplines. Terms like *nanotechnology*, for example, could not be easily replaced except by a much more complex explanation. Some neologisms, however, do not meet a real need. Existing words could replace a word like *ginormous*.

### *Jargon*

Jargon is the special vocabulary of a trade or profession, enabling members to speak and write concisely to one another. Reserve jargon for an audience that will understand your terms. In the first example that follows, jargon is used inappropriately in writing addressed to general readers. The revision eliminates or defines the jargon terms.

**JARGON**

The VDTs in composition were down last week, so we had to lay out on dummies and crop and size the art with a wheel.

**REVISED FOR A GENERAL AUDIENCE**

The video display terminals were not working last week in the composing room, where models of the newspaper pages are made up for printing, so we had to arrange the contents of each page on a large cardboard sheet and use a wheel, a kind of circular slide rule, to figure out the size and shape of the pictures and other illustrations.

Like all jargon, the terms emerging in the digital age can be irritating and incomprehensible — or extremely helpful. If the jargon is specific, it can provide a useful shorthand for an otherwise lengthy explanation. Saying "I'm currently limited to asynchronous communication" sends a clearer message than "I'm currently limited to the kinds of electronic communication in which there's a delay between the sending and receiving of messages."

Writers should know frequently used online terms (such as *asynchronous communication* and *email*). Other terms, like the jargon in this sentence — *Savvy wavelet compression is the fiber signpost of the virtual chillout room* — may be appropriate for techies talking to one another, but not for those trying to communicate with a nontechnical or general audience. Before you use technical jargon, remember your readers: if they will not understand the terms, or if you don't know them well enough to judge, then say what you need to say in everyday language.

### 3 Pompous language, euphemisms, and doublespeak

Stuffy or pompous language is unnecessarily formal for the purpose, audience, or topic. It gives writing an insincere or unintentionally humorous tone, making a writer's ideas seem insignificant or even unbelievable.

**POMPOUS**

Pursuant to the August 9 memorandum regarding petroleum supply exigencies, it is incumbent upon us to endeavor to make maximal utilization of telephonic communication in lieu of personal visitation.

**REVISED**

As noted in the August 9 memo, please make telephone calls rather than personal visits whenever possible because of the gasoline shortage.

As these examples illustrate, some writers use words in an attempt to sound expert or important, and these puffed-up words can easily backfire.

| INSTEAD OF | TRY USING |
|---|---|
| ascertain | find out |
| commence | begin |
| finalize | finish or complete |
| functionality | function |
| impact (as a verb) | affect |
| methodology | method |
| operationalize | start; put into operation |
| optimal | best |
| parameters | boundaries |
| peruse | look at |
| ramp up | increase |
| utilize | use |

Euphemisms are words and phrases that make unpleasant ideas seem less harsh. *Your position is being eliminated* seeks to soften the blow of being fired or laid off. Other euphemisms include *pass on* for *die* and *sanitation engineer* for *garbage collector.* Although euphemisms can sometimes show that the writer is considerate of people's feelings, such language can also sound insincere or evasive.

Doublespeak, a word coined from the *Newspeak* and *doublethink* of George Orwell's novel *1984*, is language used to hide or distort the truth. During massive layoffs and cutbacks in the business world, companies speak of layoffs as *work reengineering, employee repositioning, proactive downsizing*, and *special reprogramming.* Nevertheless, most people — and particularly those who have lost jobs — recognize these terms as doublespeak.

## FOR MULTILINGUAL WRITERS: Avoiding fancy language

In writing standard academic English, which is fairly formal, students are often tempted to use many "big words" instead of simple language. Although learning impressive words can be a good way to expand your vocabulary, it is usually best to avoid flowery or fancy language in college writing. Academic writing at U.S. universities tends to value clear, concise prose.

### EXERCISE 29.2

Revise each of these sentences to use formal language consistently. Example:

> Although I can ~~get all enthused~~ be enthusiastic about writing, ~~but~~ as soon as I sit down to write, ~~and~~ my mind goes ~~right to sleep.~~ blank.

1. Desdemona is a wimp; she just lies down and dies, accepting her death as inevitable.
2. Some people feel that "The Star-Spangled Banner," which is kind of obsessed with war, should be dumped as our national anthem in favor of "America the Beautiful."
3. Finding all that loot in King Tut's tomb was one of the biggest archeological scores of the twentieth century.
4. The more she freaked out about his actions, the more he rebelled and continued doing what he pleased.
5. My family lived in Trinidad for the first ten years of my life, and we went through a lot, but when we came to the United States, we thought we had it made.

**bedfordstmartins.com/smhandbook** For more exercises on levels of formality, go to Exercise Central and click on **Using Appropriate Language.**

## 29b Denotation and connotation

To understand the distinction between denotation and connotation, think of denotation — the general meaning of a word — as a stone tossed into a pool, and of connotation — the associations that accompany the word — as the ripples spreading out from it, circle by circle.

Words with similar denotations may have connotations that vary widely. The words *enthusiasm*, *passion*, and *obsession*, for instance, all denote roughly the same thing. But the connotations are quite different: an *enthusiasm* is a pleasurable and absorbing interest; a *passion* has a strong emotional component and may affect someone positively or negatively; an *obsession* is an unhealthy attachment that excludes other interests. *Pushy* and *assertive* also have similar denotations but different connotations — one negative, the other neutral or positive.

Take special care to use words with the appropriate connotations for your intended meaning. Note the differences in connotation among the following three statements:

- **Students Against Racism (SAR) erected a temporary barrier on the campus oval. They say it symbolizes "the many barriers to those discriminated against by university policies."**
- **Left-wing agitators threw up an eyesore right on the oval to try to stampede the university into giving in to their every demand.**
- **Supporters of human rights for all students challenged the university's investment in racism by erecting a protest barrier on campus.**

The first statement is the most neutral, merely stating facts (and quoting the assertion about university policy to represent it as someone's words rather than as facts); the second, by using words with negative connotations (*agitators, eyesore, stampede*), is strongly critical; the third, by using words with positive connotations (*supporters of human rights*) and presenting assertions as facts (*the university's investment in racism*), gives a favorable slant to the group and its actions.

### EXERCISE 29.3

From the parentheses, choose the word with the denotation that makes most sense in the context of the sentence. Use a dictionary if necessary.

1. She listened (*apprehensively/attentively*) to the lecture and took notes.
2. The telemarketers were told to (*empathize/emphasize*) more expensive items.
3. The interns were (*conscientious/conscious*) workers who listened carefully and learned fast.
4. Franklin advised his readers to be (*feudal/frugal*) and industrious.

### EXERCISE 29.4

Study the italicized words in each of the following passages, and decide what each word's connotations contribute to your understanding of the passage. Think of a synonym for each word, and see if you can decide what difference the new word would make on the effect of the passage.

1. If boxing is a sport, it is the most *tragic* of all sports because, more than any human activity, it consumes the very excellence it *displays*: Its very *drama* is this consumption. — JOYCE CAROL OATES, "On Boxing"

2. Then one evening Miss Glory told me to serve the ladies on the porch. After I set the tray down and turned toward the kitchen, one of the women asked, "What's your name, *girl*?" — MAYA ANGELOU, *I Know Why the Caged Bird Sings*

3. The Kiowas are a summer people; they *abide* the cold and keep to themselves; but when the season *turns* and the land becomes warm and *vital*, they cannot *hold still*. — N. SCOTT MOMADAY, "The Way to Rainy Mountain"

**bedfordstmartins.com/smhandbook** For more exercises on denotation and connotation, go to Exercise Central and click on **Appropriate Language**.

## 29c General and specific language

Effective writers move their prose along by balancing general words, which name or describe groups or classes of things, with specific words, which refer to individual items. Some general words are abstractions, referring to qualities or ideas, things that the five senses cannot perceive. Specific words are often concrete words, referring to things we can see, hear, touch, taste, or smell. We can seldom draw a clear-cut line between general or abstract words on the one hand and specific or concrete ones on the other. Instead, most words fall somewhere between these two extremes.

| GENERAL | LESS GENERAL | SPECIFIC | MORE SPECIFIC |
|---|---|---|---|
| book | dictionary | abridged dictionary | my 2004 edition of *The American Heritage College Dictionary* |

| ABSTRACT | LESS ABSTRACT | CONCRETE | MORE CONCRETE |
|---|---|---|---|
| culture | visual art | painting | van Gogh's *Starry Night* |

Passages that contain too many general terms or abstractions demand that readers supply the specific details with their imaginations, making such writing hard to read. But writing that is full of specifics can also be hard to follow if the main point is lost amid a flood of details. Strong writing usually provides readers both with a general idea or overall picture and with specific examples or concrete details to fill in that picture. In the following passage, the author might have simply made a general statement — *their breakfast was always liberal and good* — or simply described the breakfast. Instead, he is both general and specific.

> There would be a brisk fire crackling in the hearth, the old smoke-gold of morning and the smell of fog, the crisp cheerful voices of the people and their ruddy competent morning look, and the cheerful smells of breakfast, which was always liberal and good, the best meal that they had: kidneys and ham and eggs and sausages and toast and marmalade and tea.
>
> — THOMAS WOLFE, *Of Time and the River*

Here a student writer balances a general statement (*My next-door neighbor is a nuisance*) with specific details:

> My next-door neighbor is a nuisance, poking and prying into my life, constantly watching me as I enter and leave my house, complaining about the noise when I am having a good time, and telling my parents whenever she sees me kissing my date.

### EXERCISE 29.5

Rewrite each of the following sentences to be more specific and concrete.

1. The entryway of the building was dirty.
2. The sounds at dawn are memorable.
3. Our holiday dinner tasted good.
4. The attendant came toward my car.
5. I woke up.

**bedfordstmartins.com/smhandbook** For more exercises on specific language, go to Exercise Central and click on **Appropriate Language**.

## 29d Figurative language

Figurative language, or figures of speech, can paint pictures in our minds, allowing us to "see" a point readily and clearly. For example, an economist might explain that if you earned one dollar per second, you would need nearly thirty-two years to become a billionaire. When scientists compare certain genetic variants to typographical errors, they too are giving us a picture to help us grasp a difficult concept. Far from being mere decoration, then, figurative language is crucial to understanding.

In important ways, all language is metaphoric, referring to something beyond the word itself for which the word is a symbol. Particularly helpful in building understanding are specific types of figurative language, including similes, metaphors, and analogies.

**FOR MULTILINGUAL WRITERS: Idioms**

Why do you wear a diamond *on* your finger but *in* your ear? (See 60a.)

### *Similes*

Similes use *like*, *as*, *as if*, or *as though* to make an explicit comparison between two things.

- **The comb felt as if it was raking my skin off.**

  — MALCOLM X, "My First Conk"

- **You can tell the graphic-novels section in a bookstore from afar, by the young bodies sprawled around it like casualties of a localized disaster.**

  — PETER SCHJELDAHL

### *Metaphors*

Metaphors are implicit comparisons, omitting the *like*, *as*, *as if*, or *as though* of similes.

- **The Internet is the new town square.** — REP. JEB HENSARLING

Often, metaphors are more elaborate.

- **Black women are called, in the folklore that so aptly identifies one's status in society, "the mule of the world," because we have been handed the burdens that everyone else — everyone else — refused to carry.** — ALICE WALKER, *In Search of Our Mothers' Gardens*

### Analogies

Analogies compare similar features of two dissimilar things; they explain something unfamiliar by relating it to something familiar. Analogies are often several sentences or paragraphs in length. In the first passage that follows, the writer draws an analogy between a bear trainer and the animals he works with:

- **Raised from childhood with a love for the wilderness, 63-year-old Doug Seus is distinctly bearlike himself, with a voice that growls and a penchant for grabbing visitors in an affectionate bear hug.** — ROGER TOLL, "The Claws in His Contract"

- **One Hundred and Twenty-fifth Street was to Harlem what the Mississippi was to the South, a long traveling river always going somewhere, carrying something.** — MAYA ANGELOU, *The Heart of a Woman*

Before you use an analogy, make sure that the two things you are comparing have enough points of similarity to justify the comparison.

### Clichés and mixed metaphors

Just as effective figurative language can create the right impression, *ineffective* figures of speech — such as clichés and mixed metaphors — may wind up boring, irritating, or unintentionally amusing readers.

A cliché is a frequently used expression such as *busy as a bee* or *children are the future*. By definition, we use clichés all the time, especially in speech, and many serve usefully as shorthand for familiar ideas. If you use too many clichés in your writing, however, readers may conclude that what you are saying is not very new or interesting — or true. For example, if you write that a group of schoolgirls looked *pretty as a picture*, this clichéd simile may sound false or insincere. A more original figure of speech, such as *pretty as brand-new red shoes*, might be more effective.

Since people don't always agree on what is a cliché and what is a fresh image, how can you check your writing for clichés? Here is a rule to follow: if you can predict exactly what the upcoming word(s) in a phrase will be, it is probably a cliché.

Mixed metaphors are comparisons that are not consistent. Instead of creating a clear impression, they confuse the reader by pitting one image against another.

**The lectures were brilliant comets streaking through the night sky, ~~showering~~ dazzling listeners with ~~a torrential rain~~ flashes of insight.**

The images of streaking light and heavy precipitation are inconsistent; in the revised sentence, all of the images relate to light.

### *Allusions*

Allusions are indirect references to cultural works, people, or events. When a sports commentator said, *If the Georgia Tech men have an Achilles heel, it is their inexperience, their youth*, he alluded to the Greek myth in which the hero Achilles was fatally wounded in his single vulnerable spot, his heel.

You can draw allusions from history, literature, sacred texts, common wisdom, or current events. Many movies and popular songs are full of allusions. The *Simpsons* episode called "Pranksta Rap," for example, alludes to the musical genre of "gangsta rap." Remember, however, that allusions work only if your audience recognizes them.

### *Signifying*

One distinctive use of figurative language found extensively in African American English is signifying, in which a speaker cleverly needles or insults the listener. In the following passage, two African American men (Grave Digger and Coffin Ed) signify on their white supervisor (Anderson), who ordered them to discover the originators of a riot:

> "I take it you've discovered who started the riot," Anderson said.
> "We knew who he was all along," Grave Digger said.
> "It's just nothing we can do to him," Coffin Ed echoed.
> "Why not, for God's sake?"
> "He's dead," Coffin Ed said.
> "Who?"

"Lincoln," Grave Digger said.

"He hadn't ought to have freed us if he didn't want to make provisions to feed us," Coffin Ed said. "Anyone could have told him that."

— CHESTER HIMES, *Hot Day, Hot Night*

Coffin Ed and Grave Digger demonstrate the major characteristics of effective signifying: indirection, ironic humor, fluid rhythm — and a surprising twist, the revelation that Abraham Lincoln caused the riot by ending slavery. This twist leaves the supervisor speechless — and gives Grave Digger and Coffin Ed the last word.

## EXERCISE 29.6

Return to the description you wrote in Exercise 29.1. Note any words that carry strong connotations, and identify the concrete and abstract language as well as any use of figurative language. Revise any inappropriate language you find.

**bedfordstmartins.com/smhandbook** For more exercises on using words appropriately, go to Exercise Central and click on **Appropriate Language**.

## Editing for appropriate and precise language

- Check to see that your language reflects the appropriate level of formality and courtesy for your audience, purpose, and topic. If you use informal language (such as *yeah*), is it appropriate? (29a)
- Unless you are writing for a specialized audience that will understand jargon, either define the jargon or replace it with words that will be understood. (29a2)
- Revise any pompous language, inappropriate euphemisms, or double-speak. (29a3)
- Consider the connotations of words carefully. If you say someone is *pushy*, be sure you mean to be critical; otherwise, use a word like *assertive*. (29b)
- Be sure to use both general and specific words. If you are writing about the general category of "beds," for example, do you give enough concrete detail (*an antique four-poster bed*)? (29c)
- Look for clichés, and replace them with fresher language. (29d)

## THINKING CRITICALLY ABOUT WORD CHOICE

Read the following brief poem. What dominant feeling or impression does the poem produce in you? Identify the specific words and phrases that help create that impression.

What happens to a dream deferred?

Does it dry up
Like a raisin in the sun?
Or fester like a sore —
And then run?
Does it stink like rotten meat?
Or crust and sugar over —
Like a syrupy sweet?

Maybe it just sags
Like a heavy load.

Or does it explode?

— LANGSTON HUGHES, "Harlem (A Dream Deferred)"

# Dictionaries, Vocabulary, and Spelling

# 30

Think back to a time when you learned the word for something new. Before that time, this thing did not exist for you; yet curiously enough, once you knew its name, you began to see it all around you. Such is the power of vocabulary to enrich not only our personal language but our lives as well.

Expanding your vocabulary — which includes finding out about words in reference books like dictionaries — can expand your ability to communicate with a wide variety of audiences. To communicate most effectively, pay careful attention to the meaning, and to the spelling, of the words you use.

## 30a Information in dictionaries

A good dictionary packs a surprising amount of information about words into a relatively small space, sometimes containing a dozen or more kinds of information about a word. Spelling, word division, pronunciation, grammatical functions, irregular forms (if any), the language(s) the word comes from, and its meaning(s) are all discussed in most dictionary entries.

### *Usage notes and labels*

Usage notes in dictionaries, such as the following note from *Merriam-Webster's Online Dictionary* about the nonstandard word *irregardless*, often provide extensive information about how a particular usage may affect readers:

> *Irregardless* originated in dialectal American speech in the early 20th century. Its fairly widespread use in speech called it to the attention of usage commentators as early as 1927. The most frequently repeated remark about it is that "there is no such word." There is such a word, however. It is still used primarily in speech, although it can be found from time to time in edited prose. Its reputation has not risen over the years, and it is still a long way from general acceptance. Use *regardless* instead.

Many dictionaries include usage labels, which let readers know that some or all meanings of a particular word are nonstandard or inappropriate in certain contexts. An explanation of such labels usually

## SOURCE MAP: Finding information in a dictionary

The following kinds of information appear in many dictionary entries. The entries here come from the online and print versions of *The American Heritage Dictionary of the English Language*, Fourth Edition.

1. *Spelling*, including alternative spellings if they exist.
2. *Word division*, with bars, dots, or spaces separating syllables and showing where a word may be divided at the end of a line.
3. *Pronunciation*, including alternative pronunciations. Online dictionaries often provide an audio link to a recording of the pronunciation; many print dictionaries give a pronunciation key at the bottom of each page or every other page.
4. *Grammatical functions and irregular forms* (if any), including plurals of nouns, principal parts of verbs, and comparative and superlative forms of adjectives and adverbs.
5. *Etymology*, the languages and words that the word comes from.
6. *Meanings*, in order of either development or frequency of use.
7. *Examples* of the word in the context of a phrase or sentence.
8. *Usage notes and labels* (see p. 539), indicating usage that is nonstandard or inappropriate in certain contexts. A dictionary's philosophy about usage is generally explained in an essay preceding the entries.
9. *Field labels*, indicating that a word has a special meaning in a particular field of knowledge or activity.
10. *Synonyms and antonyms*, showing words with similar or opposite meanings.
11. *Related words* and their grammatical functions.
12. *Idioms* in which the word appears and their meanings.

**letter** (1)

SYLLABICATION: let·ter (2)

PRONUNCIATION: lĕt′ər

(3)

NOUN: (4) **1a.** A written symbol or character representing a speech sound and being a component of an alphabet. **b.** A written symbol or character used in the graphemic representation of a word, such as the *h* in *Thames*. See Note at **Thames**. **2.** A written or printed communication directed to a person or organization. **3.** A certified document granting rights to its bearer. Often used in the plural. **4.** Literal meaning: *had to adhere to the letter of the law*. **5. letters** *(used with a sing. verb)* **a.** Literary culture; belles-lettres. **b.** Learning or knowledge, especially of literature. **c.** Literature or writing as a profession. **6.** *Printing* **a.** A piece of type that prints a single character. **b.** A specific style of type. **c.** The characters in one style of type. **7.** An emblem in the shape of the initial of a school awarded for outstanding performance, especially in varsity athletics. (8) (9)

VERB: Inflected forms: **let·tered, let·ter·ing, let·ters** (6)

TRANSITIVE VERB: **1.** To write letters on. **2.** To write in letters. (7)

INTRANSITIVE VERB: **1.** To write or form letters. **2.** To earn a school letter, as for outstanding athletic achievement: *She lettered in three collegiate sports.*

(5)

IDIOM: **to the letter** To the last detail; exactly: *followed instructions to the letter.*

ETYMOLOGY: Middle English, from Old French *lettre*, from Latin *littera*, perhaps from Etruscan, from Greek *diphtherā*, hide, leather, writing surface.

OTHER FORMS: **let′ter·er** — noun (11)

SYNONYMS: *letter, epistle, missive, note* These nouns denote a written communication directed to another: *received a letter of complaint; the Epistles of the New Testament; a missive of condolence; a thank-you note.* (10) (12)

(2)

(3) **let•ter** (lĕt′ər) *n.* **1a.** A written symbol or character representing a speech sound and being a component of an alphabet. **b.** A written symbol or character used in the graphemic representation of a word, such as the *h* in *Thames*. See Note at **Thames**. **2.** A written or printed communication directed to a person or organization. **3.** A certified document granting rights to its bearer. Often used in the plural. **4.** Literal meaning: *had to adhere to the letter of the law*. **5. letters** *(used with a sing. verb)* **a.** Literary culture; belles-lettres. **b.** Learning or knowledge, especially of literature. **c.** Literature or writing as a profession. **6.** *Printing* **a.** A piece of type that prints a single character. **b.** A specific style of type. **c.** The characters in one style of type. **7.** An emblem in the shape of the initial of a school awarded for outstanding performance, especially in varsity athletics. ❖ *v.* **-tered, -ter•ing, -ters** — *tr.* **1.** To write letters on. **2.** To write in letters. — *intr.* **1.** To write or form letters. **2.** To earn a school letter, as for outstanding athletic achievement: *She lettered in three collegiate sports.* **—*idiom:* to the letter** To the least detail; exactly: *followed instructions to the letter.* [Middle English, from Old French *lettre*, from Latin *littera*, perhaps from Etruscan, from Greek *diphtherā*, hide, leather, writing surface.] — **let′ter•er** *n.*

(6) (8) (9) (4) (12) (7) (5)

(10) ***Synonyms*** *letter, epistle, missive, note* These nouns denote a written communication directed to another: *received a letter of complaint; read the Epistles of the New Testament; sent a missive of condolence; mailed a thank-you note.* (11)

### FOR MULTILINGUAL WRITERS: Idioms in the dictionary

When you encounter an unfamiliar phrase that seems to involve an idiom, you might find help at the end of a word's dictionary definition, where idioms often are defined. For example:

> **point** (point) *n.* 1. The sharp or tapered end of something. 2. An object having a sharp or tapered end, as a knife or needle. ***idioms*:** **beside the point**. Irrelevant. **to the point**. Pertinent.

For more help with idioms, see 60a.

appears at the beginning of the dictionary. Here are some of the labels *Webster's New World Dictionary* uses:

1. *Archaic*: rarely used today except in specialized contexts
2. *Obsolete* or *obs.*: no longer used
3. *Colloquial* or *colloq.*: characteristic of conversation and informal writing
4. *Slang*: extremely informal
5. *Dialect*: used mostly in a particular geographic or linguistic area, often one that is specified, such as Scotland or New England

### EXERCISE 30.1

Look up the spelling, syllable division, and pronunciation of the following words in your dictionary. Note any variants in spelling and pronunciation.

1. heinous
2. exigency
3. schedule
4. greasy
5. macabre
6. mature

### EXERCISE 30.2

Look up the etymology of the following words in your dictionary.

1. rhetoric
2. student
3. tobacco
4. crib
5. cinema
6. okra

**bedfordstmartins.com/smhandbook** For more information on dictionaries, go to Writing Resources/Links and click on **Effective Language**.

## 30b Types of dictionaries

Become familiar with the most common kinds of dictionaries.

### 1 Abridged dictionaries

Abridged, or "abbreviated," dictionaries are popular with college writers and are widely available in print and online. The most helpful abridged dictionaries include *Random House Webster's College Dictionary* and *The American Heritage College Dictionary.*

*Random House Webster's College Dictionary*, updated annually, has more than 207,000 entries, including words new to the language, from *hotlink* to *identity theft*. This work is notable for its usage notes that warn users about offensive or disparaging terms and its appendix "Avoiding Insensitive and Offensive Language."

*The American Heritage College Dictionary*, Fourth Edition (Houghton, 2002), has more than 200,000 listings, plus 5,000 scientific and technical terms and more than 3,000 illustrations. This dictionary lists meanings in the order of most to least common and includes extensive notes on usage. Introductory essays about usage are in the form of a debate.

#### *Online dictionaries*

Free access to dictionaries is widely available on the Internet. Some dictionary sites, such as Dictionary.com and RhymeZone, are online only. However, many dictionaries available electronically — such as the *Compact Oxford English Dictionary*, *Merriam-Webster's Online Dictionary*, *Cambridge Dictionary of American English*, and *The American Heritage Dictionary of the English Language* — are online versions of print dictionaries. Libraries allow users access to many fee-based online dictionaries.

### 2 Unabridged dictionaries

Unabridged, or "unabbreviated," dictionaries are the most complete and thorough dictionaries of English. They are large and often multivolume; you may not want to own one, but you may want to consult one from time to time in a library. Among the leading unabridged dictionaries are *The Oxford English Dictionary* (OED) and *Webster's Third New International Dictionary of the English Language.*

### FOR MULTILINGUAL WRITERS: A learner's dictionary

In addition to using a good college dictionary, you may want to invest in one of the following dictionaries intended especially for learners of English. The *Longman Dictionary of American English* presents the English spoken in the United States; the *Oxford Advanced Learner's Dictionary* covers British and American English.

These dictionaries provide information about count and noncount nouns, idioms and phrasal verbs, grammatical usage, and other topics important to learners of English. Bilingual dictionaries (such as English-Spanish) can be helpful for quick translations of common words but rarely give information about usage or related idioms. Many multilingual writers find it helpful to use multiple dictionaries to get a range of information about a word and its usage.

*The Oxford English Dictionary* began in Britain in the nineteenth century as an attempt to give a full history of each English word: a record of its entry into the language and the development of the word's various meanings with dated quotations in chronological order. The Second Edition (Oxford UP, 1989) traces more than half a million words and is unparalleled in its historical account of changes in word meanings and spellings.

*Webster's Third New International Dictionary of the English Language* (Merriam-Webster, 2002) contains nearly half a million entries, with a special section covering fourteen thousand new words and meanings. This one-volume work stirred considerable controversy at its publication because of its tendency to *describe* the way people actually use words rather than to *prescribe* standards of correct and incorrect usage. *Webster's Third* lists meanings in order of their entry into the language and quotes from authors to illustrate words in context.

## 3 Specialized dictionaries

Sometimes you will need to turn to specialized dictionaries, especially if you are seeking more information on usage, synonyms, or slang. Like standard dictionaries, many specialized dictionaries are available online.

### *Dictionaries of usage*

In cases where usage is disputed or where you feel unsure of your own usage, you may wish to consult *The New Fowler's Modern English Usage*, Third Edition, which is the most widely used specialized dictionary of usage. Note, however, that its focus is more on British than American usage.

### Dictionaries of synonyms and the thesaurus

If you are stuck for just the right word, a dictionary of synonyms or a thesaurus is a friend indeed. In these works, each entry is followed by words whose meanings are similar to that of the entry. A useful source is *Merriam Webster's Dictionary of Synonyms.*

A thesaurus provides antonyms as well as synonyms. Two thesauri are particularly helpful: *Merriam Webster's Collegiate Thesaurus* and *The New American Roget's Thesaurus in Dictionary Form.*

Remember, however, to use such dictionaries carefully, because rarely can two English words be used interchangeably in radically different contexts. As Mark Twain put it, the difference between the right word and the almost-right word is the difference between lightning and the lightning bug.

**bedfordstmartins.com/smhandbook** For online thesauri, go to Writing Resources/Links and click on **Effective Language**.

### Dictionaries for specific disciplines

If you need information about how a word is used in a particular discipline, you may want to consult a dictionary that specializes in usage in that discipline. *Black's Law Dictionary*, for example, is a specialized source for legal terminology. Ask your instructor or a librarian for help finding standard references in a field that is new to you. (See also Chapter 61.)

### Dictionaries of etymology, regional English, slang, and neologisms

If you need to investigate the origins of a word, look up a term used in only one area of the country, or understand a word that may be slang or jargon, the following specialized dictionaries can help you:

*Dictionary of American Regional English.* Ed. Frederic G. Cassidy. Cambridge: Belknap-Harvard UP, Vol. 1, 1985; Vol. 2, 1991; Vol. 3, 1996.

*Dictionary of Computer and Internet Words.* New York: Houghton, 2001.

*NTC's Dictionary of American Slang and Colloquial Expressions.* 3rd ed. New York: NTC/McGraw, 2000.

*The Oxford Dictionary of English Etymology.* Ed. C. T. Onions. New York: Oxford UP, 1966.

## 30c Vocabulary building blocks

At its largest, your vocabulary includes all the words whose meanings you either recognize or can deduce from context. This group of words, called your *processing vocabulary*, allows you to interpret the meanings of many passages whose words you might not use yourself. Your *producing vocabulary*, on the other hand, is more limited, made up of words you actually use in writing or speaking.

An important intellectual goal is to consciously strengthen your producing vocabulary — to begin to use in your own speech and writing more of the words you understand in context. To accomplish this goal, you must become an investigative reporter of your own language and the language of others.

### *The history of English*

English, like one-third of all languages in the world, descends from Indo-European, a language spoken by groups of people whose original home was in some part of north-central Europe. Scholars began to consider Indo-European a "common source" when they noted striking resemblances among words in a number of languages.

| ENGLISH | LATIN | SPANISH | FRENCH | GREEK | GERMAN | DUTCH | SWEDISH |
|---|---|---|---|---|---|---|---|
| *three* | *tres* | *tres* | *trois* | *treis* | *drei* | *drie* | *tre* |

A version of Indo-European was brought to Britain by the Germanic invasions following 449. This early language, called Anglo-Saxon or Old English, was influenced by Latin and Greek when Christianity was reintroduced into England beginning in 597, was later shaped by the Viking invasions beginning in the late 700s, and was transformed by French after the Norman Conquest (1066).

Although English continued to evolve in the centuries after the conquest, Latin and French were then the languages of the learned — of the church and court. In the late 1300s, it was Geoffrey Chaucer, writing *The Canterbury Tales* in the language of the people, who helped establish what is now called Middle English as the political, legal, and literary language of Britain. And after the advent of printing in the mid-1400s, that language became more accessible and more standardized. By about 1600, it had essentially become the Modern English we use today.

In the past four hundred years, English has continued borrowing from many languages and, as a result, now has one of the world's largest vocabularies. Modern English, then, is a plant growing luxuriously in the soil of multiple language sources.

*This image of Chaucer appears in a manuscript of* The Canterbury Tales.

## 1 Word roots

As its name suggests, a root is a word from which other words grow, usually through the addition of prefixes or suffixes. From the Latin root *-dic-* or *-dict-* ("speak"), for instance, grows a whole range of words in English: *contradict*, *dictate*, *dictator*, *diction*, *edict*, *predict*, *dictaphone*, and others. Here are some other Latin (L) and Greek (G) roots and examples of words derived from them.

| ROOT | MEANING | EXAMPLES |
|---|---|---|
| -audi- (L) | to hear | audience, audio |
| -bene- (L) | good, well | benevolent, benefit |
| -bio- (G) | life | biography, biosphere |
| -duc(t)- (L) | to lead or to make | ductile, reproduce |
| -gen- (G) | race, kind | genealogy, gene |
| -geo- (G) | earth | geography, geometry |
| -graph- (G) | to write | graphic, photography |
| -jur-, -jus- (L) | law | justice, jurisdiction |
| -log(o)- (G) | word, thought | biology, logical |
| -luc- (L) | light | lucid, translucent |
| -manu- (L) | hand | manufacture, manual |
| -mit-, -mis- (L) | to send | permit, transmission |

| ROOT | MEANING | EXAMPLES |
|---|---|---|
| -path- (G) | feel, suffer | empathy, pathetic |
| -phil- (G) | love | philosopher, bibliophile |
| -photo- (G) | light | photography, telephoto |
| -port- (L) | to carry | transport, portable |
| -psych- (G) | soul | psychology, psychopath |
| -scrib-, -script- (L) | to write | scribble, manuscript |
| -sent-, -sens- (L) | to feel | sensation, resent |
| -tele- (G) | far away | telegraph, telepathy |
| -tend- (L) | to stretch | extend, tendency |
| -terr- (L) | earth | inter, territorial |
| -vac- (L) | empty | vacant, evacuation |
| -vid-, -vis- (L) | to see | video, envision, visit |

### EXERCISE 30.3

Using the preceding list of roots, try to figure out the meaning of each of the following words. Write a potential definition for each one, and compare it with your dictionary's definition.

1. terrestrial
2. vacuous
3. graphology
4. pathogenic
5. scriptorium

## 2 Prefixes

Originally individual words, prefixes are groups of letters added to the beginning of words or to roots to create new words. Prefixes modify or extend the meaning of the original word or root. Recognizing common prefixes can help you decipher the meaning of unfamiliar words.

### *Prefixes of negation or opposition*

| PREFIX | MEANING | EXAMPLES |
|---|---|---|
| a-, an- | without, not | amoral, anemia |
| anti- | against | antibody, antiphonal |
| contra- | against | contravene, contradict |
| de- | from, take away from | demerit, declaw |

| | | |
|---|---|---|
| dis- | apart, away | disappear, discharge |
| il-, im-, in-, ir- | not | illegal, immature, indistinct, irreverent |
| mal- | wrong | malevolent, malpractice |
| mis- | wrong, bad | misapply, misanthrope |
| non- | not | nonentity, nonsense |
| un- | not | unbreakable, unable |

### *Prefixes of quantity*

| PREFIX | MEANING | EXAMPLES |
|---|---|---|
| bi- | two | bipolar, bilateral |
| milli- | thousand | millimeter, milligram |
| mono- | one, single | monotone, monologue |
| omni- | all | omniscient, omnipotent |
| semi- | half | semicolon, semiconductor |
| tri- | three | tripod, trimester |
| uni- | one | unitary, univocal |

### *Prefixes of time and space*

| PREFIX | MEANING | EXAMPLES |
|---|---|---|
| ante- | before | antedate, antebellum |
| circum- | around | circumlocution, circumnavigate |
| co-, col-, com-, con-, cor- | with | coequal, collaborate, commiserate, contact, correspond |
| e-, ex- | out of | emit, extort, expunge |
| hyper- | over, more than | hypersonic, hypersensitive |
| hypo- | under, less than | hypodermic, hypoglycemia |
| inter- | between | intervene, international |
| mega- | enlarge, large | megalomania, megaphone |
| micro- | tiny | micrometer, microscopic |
| neo- | recent | neologism, neophyte |
| post- | after | postwar, postscript |

| PREFIX | MEANING | EXAMPLES |
|---|---|---|
| pre- | before | previous, prepublication |
| pro- | before, onward | project, propel |
| re- | again, back | review, re-create |
| sub- | under, beneath | subhuman, submarine |
| super- | over, above | supercargo, superimpose |
| syn- | at the same time | synonym, synchronize |
| trans- | across, over | transport, transition |

### 3 Suffixes

Like prefixes, suffixes modify and extend meanings. Suffixes, which are attached to the end of words or roots, often alter the grammatical function or part of speech of the original word — for example, turning the verb *create* into a noun, an adjective, or an adverb.

| | |
|---|---|
| **VERB** | create |
| **NOUNS** | creat*or*/creat*ion*/creat*ivity*/creat*ure* |
| **ADJECTIVE** | creat*ive* |
| **ADVERB** | creative*ly* |

#### *Noun suffixes*

| SUFFIX | MEANING | EXAMPLES |
|---|---|---|
| -acy | state or quality | democracy, privacy |
| -al | act of | dismissal, refusal |
| -ance, -ence | state or quality of | maintenance, eminence |
| -dom | place or state of being | freedom, kingdom |
| -er, -or | one who | trainer, investor |
| -ism | doctrine or belief characteristic of | liberalism, Taoism |
| -ist | one who | organist, physicist |
| -ity | quality of | veracity, opacity |
| -ment | condition of | payment, argument |
| -ness | state of being | watchfulness, cleanliness |

| | | |
|---|---|---|
| -ship | position held | professorship, fellowship |
| -sion, -tion | state of being or action | digression, transition |

### *Verb suffixes*

| SUFFIX | MEANING | EXAMPLES |
|---|---|---|
| -ate | cause to be | concentrate, regulate |
| -en | cause to be or become | enliven, blacken |
| -ify, -fy | make or cause to be | unify, terrify, amplify |
| -ize | cause to become | magnetize, civilize |

### *Adjective suffixes*

| SUFFIX | MEANING | EXAMPLES |
|---|---|---|
| -able, -ible | capable of being | readable, edible |
| -al | pertaining to | regional, political |
| -esque | reminiscent of | picturesque, statuesque |
| -ful | having much of a quality | colorful, sorrowful |
| -ic | pertaining to | poetic, mythic |
| -ious, -ous | of or characterized by | famous, nutritious |
| -ish | having the quality of | prudish, clownish |
| -ive | having the nature of | festive, creative, massive |
| -less | without | endless, senseless |

#### EXERCISE 30.4

Using the preceding lists of prefixes and suffixes, figure out the meaning of each of the following words. (Use your dictionary if necessary.) Then choose two of the words, and use each one in a sentence.

1. contemplative
2. fanciful
3. impairment
4. hyperbole
5. progenitor

## 30d Vocabulary in context

In addition to using prefixes and suffixes, you can increase your vocabulary by analyzing contexts, reading actively, and learning the vocabulary of your field.

### Tips for building your vocabulary

- If you encounter an unfamiliar word or phrase, try to write a definition of it. Then check the dictionary to see how accurate you were.
- Practice naming the opposites of words. If you see *abbreviation*, for example, can you think of *enlargement* or *elaboration*?
- As you read, try to come up with better words than the authors have used.
- While reading a work by a writer you admire, identify several words you like but do not yet use. Investigate the meanings of these words, and then try using them in your speech or writing.

## 1 Context analysis

If a word is at first unfamiliar to you, look carefully at its context, paying attention to all the clues the context provides; often, you will be able to deduce the meaning. For instance, if the word *accouterments* is unfamiliar in the sentence *We stopped at a camping-supply store to pick up last-minute accouterments*, the context — *a camping-supply store* and *last-minute* — suggests strongly that *equipment* or some similar word fits the bill. And that is what *accouterments* means.

### EXERCISE 30.5

Identify the contextual clues that help you understand any unfamiliar words in the following sentences. Then write paraphrases of three of the sentences.

1. Before Prohibition, the criminal fringe in the United States had been a self-effacing, scattered class with little popular support.
2. The judge failed to recuse himself from the trial, even though he had a vested interest in the case's outcome.
3. The community's reaction to the preternatural creature in Shelley's *Frankenstein* shows that people are often more monstrous than a monster is.
4. My fifth-grade teacher was the epitome of what I wanted to be, and I began to imitate him scrupulously.
5. Health officials warned the population of an extremely virulent strain of flu next season and urged those with compromised immune systems to be vaccinated.

### 2 The vocabulary of a field

All occupations, professions, and disciplines rely on characteristic jargon. The vocabulary of medical fields, for example, includes technical terms such as *hematoma* and *carcinoid*, which the layperson might refer to simply as a "bruise" and a "tumor." In physics, the term *charm* indicates the quantum property assigned to the "charmed" quark. And in copyright law, the word *original* carries much more specific meanings than those associated with the word in everyday use. You may want to keep a log of the language of your chosen field, noting both meanings and examples of each term's use. (See also 61d.)

## 30e Checking spelling

Words work best for you, of course, when they are spelled correctly.

**bedfordstmartins.com/smhandbook** For exercises on commonly misspelled words, go to Exercise Central and click on **Spelling**.

### 1 Spell checkers

Research conducted for this textbook shows that students are using spell checkers extensively. In fact, spell checking is now second nature to many writers. Unfortunately, however, spell checkers alone can't correct *all* spelling errors. To make spell checkers work best for you, you need to learn to adapt them to your own needs.

- Always proofread carefully, even after you have used the spell checker. The more important the message or document, the more careful you should be about its accuracy and clarity.
- Keep a dictionary near your computer or bookmark a good online dictionary, and look up any word the spell checker highlights that you are not absolutely sure of.
- If your spell checker's dictionary allows you to add new words, enter any proper names, non-English words, or specialized language you use regularly and have trouble spelling.
- Remember that spell checkers do not recognize homonym errors (misspelling *there* as *their*, for example). If you know that you

## TALKING THE TALK: Spell checkers and wrong-word errors

"Can I trust spell checkers to give me the correct alternative for a word that I have spelled wrong?" In a word, no. The spell checker may suggest bizarre substitutes for many proper names and specialized terms (even when you spell them correctly) and for certain typographical errors, thus introducing wrong words into your paper if you accept its suggestions automatically. For example, a student who had typed *fantic* instead of *frantic* found that the spell checker's first choice was to substitute *fanatic* — a replacement word that made no sense in context. Wrong-word errors are the most common surface error in college writing today (see p. 2), and spell checkers are partly to blame. So be careful not to take a spell checker's recommendation without paying careful attention to the replacement word.

## Today's most common spelling problems

Research conducted for this book shows that spelling errors have changed dramatically in the past twenty years — and the reason is spell checkers. But although these programs have weeded out many once-common misspellings, they are not foolproof. Spell checkers still allow typical *kinds* of errors that you should look out for.

- *Homonyms*. Spell checkers cannot differentiate among words such as *affect* and *effect* that sound alike but are spelled differently (see the opposite page and pp. 558–9 for a list of confusing homonyms). Proofread especially carefully for these words.
- *Proper nouns*. You can add names and other proper nouns to your spell checker's dictionary so that the spell checker will not flag these words as incorrect, but first be certain you have spelled the names correctly.
- *Compound words written as two words*. Spell checkers will not identify a problem, for example, when *nowhere* is incorrectly written as *no where*. When in doubt, check a dictionary.
- *Typos*. The spell checker will not flag *heat*, even if you meant to type *heart*. Careful proofreading is still essential.

mix up certain words, check for them after running your spell checker (30e2).

- Remember that spell checkers are not usually sensitive to capitalization. If you write "president bush," the spell checker won't question it.
- Do *not* automatically accept the spell checker's suggestions: doing so can lead you to choose a word you really don't want.

### 2 Homonyms

English has many homonyms — words that sound alike but have different spellings and meanings. But a relatively small number of them, just eight groups, cause student writers frequent trouble. If you tend to confuse any of these words, create a special memory device to help you remember the differences: "the *weather* will dictate *whether* I wear a jacket."

In addition, pay close attention to homonyms that may be spelled as one word or as two, depending on the meaning.

- **Of course, they did not wear *everyday* clothes *every day* of the year.**
- **Though we were *all ready* to dance, our dates had *already* departed.**
- **Sonya *may be* on time for the meeting, or *maybe* she'll be late.**

#### The most troublesome homonyms

| | |
|---|---|
| accept (to take or receive)<br>except (to leave out) | to (in the direction of)<br>too (in addition; excessive)<br>two (number between *one* and *three*) |
| affect (an emotion; to have an influence)<br>effect (a result; to cause to happen) | weather (climatic conditions)<br>whether (if) |
| its (possessive form of *it*)<br>it's (contraction of *it is* or *it has*) | who's (contraction of *who is* or *who has*)<br>whose (possessive form of *who*) |
| their (possessive form of *they*)<br>there (in that place)<br>they're (contraction of *they are*) | your (possessive form of *you*)<br>you're (contraction of *you are*) |

### EXERCISE 30.6

Choose the appropriate word in parentheses to fill each blank.

If _______ (*your/you're*) looking for summer fun, _______ (*accept/except*) the friendly _______ (*advice/advise*) of thousands of happy adventurers: spend three _______ (*weaks/weeks*) kayaking _______ (*thorough/threw/through*) the inside passage _______ (*to/too/two*) Alaska. For ten years, Outings, Inc., has _______ (*lead/led*) groups of novice kayakers _______ (*passed/past*) some of the most breathtaking scenery in North America. The group's goal is simple: to give participants the time of _______ (*their/there/they're*) lives and show them things they don't see _______ (*every day/everyday*). As one of last year's adventurers said, "_______ (*Its/It's*) a trip that is _______ (*already/all ready*) one of my favorite memories. It _______ (*affected/effected*) me powerfully."

**bedfordstmartins.com/smhandbook** For additional exercises on homonyms, go to Exercise Central and click on **Spelling**.

## 3 Spelling and pronunciation

Pronunciation often leads spellers astray. Not only do we pronounce words differently if we live in different regions, but we also tend to blur letters or syllables when we speak. To link spelling and pronunciation, try to pronounce words mentally the way they look, including every letter and syllable (so that, for example, you hear the *b* at the end of *crumb*). Doing so will help you "see" words with unpronounced letters or syllables, such as those listed here. The frequently unpronounced letters or syllables are italicized.

| | | |
|---|---|---|
| can*d*idate | forei*g*n | prob*ab*ly |
| condem*n* | gover*n*ment | quan*t*ity |
| diff*e*rent | int*e*rest | rest*au*rant |
| drastic*al*ly | lib*r*ary | sep*a*rate (adjective) |
| enviro*n*ment | marr*i*age | su*r*prise |
| Feb*r*uary | mus*c*le | We*d*nesday |

In English words, *a*, *i*, and *e* often sound alike in syllables that are not stressed. Hearing the word *definite*, for instance, gives us few clues as to whether the vowels in the second and third syllables should be *i*'s or *a*'s. In this case, remembering the related word *finite* helps us know that the *i*'s are correct. If you are puzzled about how to spell a word with unstressed vowels, try to think of a related word, and then check your

### FOR MULTILINGUAL WRITERS: American spellings

You have likely noticed that different varieties of English often use different spelling conventions. If you have learned British or Indian English, for example, you will want to be aware of some of the more common spelling differences in American English. For example, words ending in *-yse* or *-ise* in British and Indian English (*analyse, criticise*) usually end in *-yze* or *-ize* in American English (*analyze, criticize*); words ending in *-our* in British/Indian English (*colour, labour*) usually end in *-or* in American English (*color, labor*); and words ending in *-re* in British/Indian English (*theatre, centre*) usually end in *-er* in American English (*theater, center*).

dictionary. You can also use memory cues, or mnemonic devices, to master words that tend to trip you up. Here are two memory cues one student made up:

| WORD | MISSPELLING | CUE |
|---|---|---|
| government | goverment | Government should serve those it *governs*. |
| separate | seperate | *Separate* rates two *a*'s. |

## 30f Spelling rules

This section focuses on some general spelling rules that can be of enormous help to writers.

### 1 *i* before *e*

Here is a slightly expanded version of the "*i* before *e*" rule:

> *i* before *e* except after *c* or when pronounced "ay" as in *neighbor* and *weigh*, or in *weird* exceptions like *either* and *species*

| | |
|---|---|
| ***I* BEFORE *E*** | ach*ie*ve, br*ie*f, f*ie*ld, fr*ie*nd |
| **EXCEPT AFTER C** | c*ei*ling, conc*ei*vable, dec*ei*t, rec*ei*ve |
| **OR WHEN PRONOUNCED "AY"** | *ei*ghth, n*ei*ghbor, r*ei*gn, w*ei*gh |
| **OR IN WEIRD EXCEPTIONS** | anc*ie*nt, consc*ie*nce, *ei*ther, for*ei*gn, h*ei*ght, l*ei*sure, n*ei*ther, s*ei*ze, spec*ie*s, w*ei*rd |

## Other homonyms and frequently confused words

advice (suggestion)
advise (to suggest [to])

all ready (fully prepared)
already (previously)

allude (refer indirectly [to])
elude (avoid or escape)

allusion (indirect reference)
illusion (false idea or appearance)

altar (sacred platform or table)
alter (change)

are (form of *be*)
our (belonging to us)

bare (uncovered; to uncover)
bear (animal; to carry or endure)

brake (device for stopping; to stop)
break (interruption; to fragment)

buy (purchase)
by (near; beside; through)

capital (principal city)
capitol (legislators' building)

cite (refer to)
sight (seeing; something seen)
site (location)

coarse (rough or crude)
course (plan of study; path)

complement (something that completes; to complete)
compliment (praise; to praise)

conscience (moral sense)
conscious (mentally aware)

council (leadership group)
counsel (advice; to advise)

dairy (source of milk)
diary (journal)

desert (dry area; to abandon)
dessert (course at end of a meal)

device (something planned or invented)
devise (plan or invent)

elicit (draw forth)
illicit (illegal)

every day (each day)
everyday (daily; ordinary)

forth (forward; out into view)
fourth (between *third* and *fifth*)

hear (perceive with the ears)
here (in this place)

heard (past tense of *hear*)
herd (group of animals)

hoarse (sounding rough)
horse (animal)

know (understand)
no (opposite of *yes*)

lead (a metal; to go before)
led (past tense of *lead*)

loose (not tight; not confined)
lose (to misplace; to fail to win)

may be (might be)
maybe (perhaps)

meat (flesh used as food)
meet (encounter)

passed (went by; received a passing grade)
past (beyond; events that have already occurred)

patience (quality of being patient)
patients (persons under medical care)

peace (absence of war)
piece (part)

personal (private or individual)
personnel (employees)

plain (simple, not fancy; flat land)
plane (airplane; tool; flat surface)

presence (condition of being)
presents (gifts; gives)

principal (most important; head of a school)
principle (fundamental truth)

rain (precipitation)
reign (period of rule; to rule)
rein (strap; to control)

right (correct; opposite of *left*)
rite (ceremony)
write (produce words on a surface)

road (street or highway)
rode (past tense of *ride*)

scene (setting; view)
seen (past participle of *see*)

stationary (unmoving)
stationery (writing paper)

than (as compared to)
then (at that time; therefore)

thorough (complete)
threw (past tense of *throw*)
through (in one side and out the other; by means of)

waist (part of the body)
waste (trash; to squander)

weak (feeble)
week (seven days)

wear (put onto the body)
where (in what place)

which (what; that)
witch (person with supernatural power)

## 2 Prefixes

Prefixes are groups of letters placed at the beginning of words to add to or qualify their meaning (30c2). A prefix does not change the spelling of the word it is added to, even when the last letter of the prefix and the first letter of the word are the same.

dis- + service = disservice    over- + rate = overrate

Some prefixes require the use of hyphens (see 55b).

### 3 Suffixes

Suffixes are placed at the end of words to form related words (30c3). A suffix may change the spelling of the word it is added to.

#### *Words ending in a silent* e

In general, drop the final silent *e* on a word when you add a suffix that starts with a vowel.

exercise + -ing = exercising    imagine + -able = imaginable

Keep the final silent *e* if the suffix starts with a consonant.

force + -ful = forceful    state + -ly = stately

**SOME EXCEPTIONS** argument, changeable, courageous, judgment, ninth, noticeable, truly

#### -ally *and* -ly

Use *-ally* if the base word ends in *ic*, *-ly* if it does not.

drastic, drastically    tragic, tragically
apparent, apparently    quick, quickly

**EXCEPTION** publicly

#### -cede, -ceed, *and* -sede

Use *-ceed* only for *exceed, proceed, succeed.* Use *-sede* only for *supersede.* All other such words use the spelling *-cede.*

accede    intercede    recede
concede    precede    secede

#### *Words ending in* y

When you add a suffix to words ending in *y*, you generally change the *y* to *i* if it is preceded by a consonant.

bounty, bountiful    busy, busily    try, tried

## CONSIDERING DISABILITIES: Spelling

While some English spellings are hard for anyone to learn, spelling is especially difficult for those who have trouble processing letters and/or sounds in sequence. If spelling seems to be particularly difficult or nearly impossible for you, some technologies can help, including "talking pens" that read words aloud when they're scanned or voice-recognition computer programs that take and transcribe dictated text.

Keep the *y* if it is preceded by a vowel, if it is part of a proper name, or if the suffix begins with *i*.

| | | |
|---|---|---|
| employ, employed | Kennedy, Kennedyesque | dry, drying |
| **EXCEPTIONS** | daily, dryly, gaily, shyer, wryness | |

### *Words ending in a consonant*

When you add a suffix beginning with a vowel to a word that ends in a consonant, double the final consonant if the word contains only one syllable or ends in an accented syllable.

| | | |
|---|---|---|
| stop, stopping | begin, beginning | occur, occurrence |

Do not double the consonant if it is preceded by more than one vowel, by a consonant and a vowel, or by another consonant; if the suffix begins with a consonant; if the word is not accented on the last syllable; or if the accent shifts from the last to the first syllable when the suffix is added.

| | | |
|---|---|---|
| sleep, sleeping | start, started | ship, shipment |
| fit, fitness | benefit, benefiting | prefer, preference |

## 4 Plurals

Making singular nouns plural calls for the use of several different spelling guidelines. For most words, simply add *-s*. For words ending in *s*, *ch*, *sh*, *x*, or *z*, add *-es*.

| | | |
|---|---|---|
| pencil, pencils | book, books | computer, computers |
| Jones, Joneses | fox, foxes | flash, flashes |
| bus, buses | church, churches | buzz, buzzes |

### Words ending in o

Add *-es* if the *o* is preceded by a consonant. Add *-s* if the *o* is preceded by a vowel.

| | | |
|---|---|---|
| potato, potatoes | hero, heroes | veto, vetoes |
| rodeo, rodeos | patio, patios | zoo, zoos |

**EXCEPTIONS**

| | | |
|---|---|---|
| memo, memos | piano, pianos | solo, solos |

### Words ending in f or fe

For some words ending in *f* or *fe*, change *f* to *v*, and add *-s* or *-es*.

| | | |
|---|---|---|
| calf, calves | life, lives | leaf, leaves |
| half, halves | wife, wives | hoof, hooves |
| self, selves | shelf, shelves | knife, knives |

### Words ending in y

For words ending in *y*, change *y* to *i* and add *-es* if the *y* is preceded by a consonant. Keep the *y* and add *-s* if the *y* is preceded by a vowel or if the word is a proper name.

| | | |
|---|---|---|
| theory, theories | guy, guys | O'Malley, O'Malleys |

### Irregular plurals

Memorize irregular plurals you do not already know.

| | | |
|---|---|---|
| woman, women | bacterium, bacteria | deer, deer |
| sheep, sheep | medium, media | criterion, criteria |

### Compound words

For compound nouns written as one word, make the last part of the compound plural (*briefcases, mailboxes*). For compound nouns written as separate or hyphenated words, make the most important part plural.

| | |
|---|---|
| brothers-in-law | lieutenant governors |

For plurals of numbers, letters, symbols, and words used as terms, see 49c.

## THINKING CRITICALLY ABOUT DICTIONARIES, VOCABULARY, AND SPELLING

**Reading with an Eye for Vocabulary**

In his autobiography, Malcolm X says that he taught himself to write by reading and copying the dictionary. You can teach yourself to be a better writer by paying careful attention to the way other writers use words. Choose a writer whose work you admire, and read that author's work for at least thirty minutes, noting six or seven words that you would not ordinarily have thought to use. Do a little dictionary investigative work on these words, and bring your results to class for discussion.

**Thinking about Your Own Vocabulary and Spelling**

Read over a piece of your recent writing. Underline any words you think could be improved on, and come up with several possible substitutes. Then look for any words whose meanings are not absolutely clear to you, and check them in your dictionary. Finally, double-check spelling throughout. What do you notice about the words you use?

# Part 6

# SENTENCE GRAMMAR

# 31 Grammatical Sentences

The grammar of our first language comes to us almost automatically. Listen in on a conversation between two four-year-olds.

AUDREY: **My new bike that Aunt Andrea got me has a red basket and a loud horn, and I love it.**

SOFI: **Can I ride it?**

AUDREY: **Yes, as soon as I take a turn.**

This simple conversation features sophisticated grammar — the subordination of one clause to another, a compound object, and a number of adjectives — used effortlessly. Though native speakers know the basic grammatical rules, these rules can produce a broad range of sentences, some more effective and artful than others. Understanding grammatical structures can help you produce sentences that are grammatical — and appropriate and effective as well.

## 31a The basic grammar of sentences

A sentence is a grammatically complete group of words that expresses a thought. It must contain both a subject and a predicate. The subject identifies what the sentence is about, and the predicate says or asks something about the subject or tells the subject to do something.

| SUBJECT | PREDICATE |
|---|---|
| I | have a dream. |
| The rain in Spain | stays mainly in the plain. |
| Harry Potter, the young wizard, | studies at Hogwarts. |

Some sentences contain only a one-word predicate with an implied, or understood, subject (for example, *Stop!*). Most sentences, however, contain words that expand the basic subject and predicate. In the preceding example, for instance, the subject might have been simply *Harry Potter*; the words *the young wizard* say more about the subject. Similarly, the predicate of that sentence could be *studies*; the words *at Hogwarts* expand the predicate by telling us where Harry studies.

### EXERCISE 31.1

Identify the subject and the predicate in each of the following sentences, underlining the subject once and the predicate twice. Example:

The roaring lion at the beginning of old MGM films is part of movie history.

**TALKING THE TALK: Grammatical terms**

"I never learned any grammar." You may lack *conscious* knowledge of grammar and grammatical terms (and if so, you are not alone — American students today rarely study English grammar). But you probably understand the ideas that grammatical terms such as *auxiliary verb* and *direct object* represent, even if the terms themselves are unfamiliar. Brushing up on the terms commonly used to talk about grammar will make it easier for you and your instructor — as well as other readers and reviewers — to share a common language when you discuss the best ways to get your ideas across clearly and with few distractions.

1. My foot got tangled in the computer cord.
2. Her first afternoon as a kindergarten teacher had left her exhausted.
3. The Croatian news media is almost entirely owned by the state.
4. Our office manager, a stern taskmaster with a fondness for Chanel suits, has been terrifying interns since 1992.
5. Making bread on a dreary winter day always cheers me up.

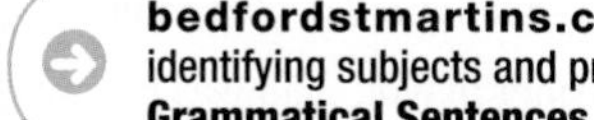

**bedfordstmartins.com/smhandbook** For more exercises on identifying subjects and predicates, go to Exercise Central and click on **Grammatical Sentences.**

## 31b The parts of speech

The central elements of subjects and predicates are nouns and verbs.

SUBJECT — PREDICATE

NOUN VERB

**A solitary figure waited on the platform.**

Nouns and verbs are two of the grammatical categories called parts of speech. The other parts of speech are pronouns, adjectives, adverbs, prepositions, conjunctions, and interjections. Many English words can function as more than one part of speech. Take the word *book*: when you *book an airplane flight*, it is a verb; when you *take a good book to the beach*, it is a noun; and when you have *book knowledge*, it is an adjective.

## PARTS OF SPEECH

**1. Verbs show action, occurrence, or being.**

Roy is running for mayor, and maybe he will win. Hey, who knows? This could finally be his big chance. He is honest—unlike the former mayor, who was caught in a financial scandal that made the newspapers shortly before he resigned.

Verb phrases: *is running*—present progressive tense; *will win*—future tense; *could be*—present tense (*could* is a modal auxiliary); *was caught*—past tense of irregular verb *catch*, in the passive voice. Verbs: *knows*—present tense; *is*—present tense (third-person singular of *be*); *had*—simple past tense of *have*; *made*—simple past tense of irregular verb *make*; *resigned*—simple past of regular verb *resign*.

**2. Nouns name persons, places, things, or concepts.**

Roy is running for mayor, and maybe he will win. Hey, who knows? This could finally be his big chance. He is honest—unlike the former mayor, who was caught in a financial scandal that made the newspapers shortly before he resigned.

Proper noun: *Roy*—subject. Common nouns: *mayor* (first use)—object of preposition *for*; *chance*—subject complement; *mayor* (second use)—object of preposition *unlike*; *scandal*—object of preposition *in*; *newspapers*—direct object of verb.

**3. Pronouns substitute for nouns.**

Roy is running for mayor, and maybe he will win. Hey, who knows? This could finally be his big chance. He is honest—unlike the former mayor, who was caught in a financial scandal that made the newspapers shortly before he resigned.

Personal pronouns: *he* (all three uses)—subject. Interrogative pronoun: *who* (first use). Demonstrative pronoun: *this* (refers to the fact that Roy is running for mayor). Possessive pronouns: *his*. Relative pronouns: *who* (second use—refers to *the former mayor*) and *that* (refers to *a financial scandal*).

**4. Adjectives modify nouns or pronouns.**

Roy is running for mayor, and maybe he will win. Hey, who knows? This could finally be his big chance. He is honest—unlike the former mayor, who was caught in a financial scandal that made the newspapers shortly before he resigned.

Articles: *the* (both uses); *a*. Subject complement: *honest*. Other adjectives: *big*—modifies *chance*; *former*—modifies *mayor*; *financial*—modifies *scandals*.

5. **Adverbs modify verbs, adjectives, other adverbs, or entire clauses.**

Roy is running for mayor, and maybe he will win. Hey, who knows? This could finally be his big chance. He is honest—unlike the former mayor, who was caught in a financial scandal that made the newspapers shortly before he resigned.

*Maybe*—modifies the clause *he will win*; *finally*—modifies the verb phrase *could be*; *shortly*—modifies the clause *before he resigned*.

6. **Prepositions express relationships between nouns or pronouns and other words.**

Roy is running for mayor, and maybe he will win. Hey, who knows? This could finally be his big chance. He is honest—unlike the former mayor, who was caught in a financial scandal that made the newspapers shortly before he resigned.

For—object is the noun *mayor*; *unlike*—object is the noun phrase *the former mayor*; *in*—object is the noun phrase *a financial scandal*.

7. **Conjunctions join words or groups of words.**

Roy is running for mayor, and maybe he will win. Hey, who knows? This could finally be his big chance. He is honest—unlike the former mayor, who was caught in a financial scandal that made the newspapers shortly before he resigned.

Coordinating conjunction: *and*. Subordinating conjunction: *before*.

8. **Interjections express surprise or emotion and do not relate grammatically to other parts of speech.**

Roy is running for mayor, and maybe he will win. **Hey,** who knows? This could finally be his big chance. He is honest—unlike the former mayor, who was caught in a financial scandal that made the newspapers shortly before he resigned.

Here is the paragraph again, with each of the eight parts of speech identified as above.

Roy is running for mayor, and maybe he will win. **Hey**, who knows? This could finally be his big chance. He is honest—unlike the former mayor, who was caught in a financial scandal that made the newspapers shortly before he resigned.

### 1 Verbs

Verbs move the meaning of sentences along by showing action (*glance*, *speculate*), occurrence (*become*, *happen*), or being (*be*, *seem*). Verbs change form to show *time*, *person*, *number*, *voice*, and *mood* (32a, g–h and 33a.)

| | |
|---|---|
| **TIME** | we *work*, we *worked* |
| **PERSON** | I *work*, she *works* |
| **NUMBER** | one person *works*, two people *work* |
| **VOICE** | she *asks*, she *is asked* |
| **MOOD** | we *see*, if I *were to see* |

Auxiliary verbs (or helping verbs) combine with other verbs (or main verbs) to create verb phrases. Auxiliaries include the forms of *be*, *do*, and *have*, which are also used as main verbs, and *can*, *could*, *may*, *might*, *must*, *shall*, *should*, *will*, and *would* (32b).

- **I *could have danced* all night.**
- **She *would prefer* to learn Italian rather than Spanish.**

#### EXERCISE 31.2

Underline each verb or verb phrase in the following sentences. Example:

Terence should sing well in Sunday's performance.

1. After the holidays, I will ask for a pay raise.
2. The faucet had been leaking all day.
3. I agree; the office does need a new copy machine.
4. Ideally, you should drink eight cups of water each day.
5. A job at an animal hospital would be great.

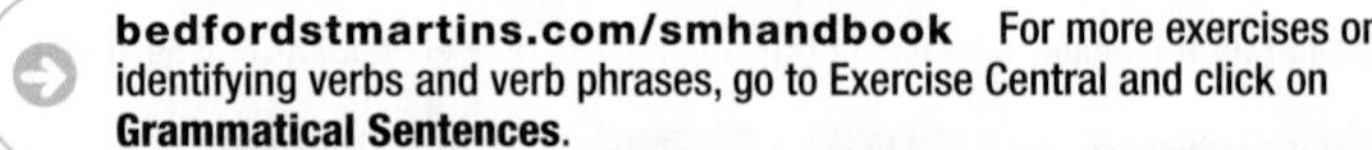
**bedfordstmartins.com/smhandbook** For more exercises on identifying verbs and verb phrases, go to Exercise Central and click on **Grammatical Sentences.**

### 2 Nouns

Nouns name persons (*aviator*, *child*), places (*lake*, *library*), things (*truck*, *suitcase*), or concepts (*happiness*, *balance*). Proper nouns name specific persons, places, things, or concepts: *Bill*, *Iowa*, *Supreme Court*,

*Buddhism*. Proper nouns are capitalized (52b). Collective nouns (33d and 34f2) name groups: *flock, jury*.

Most nouns change from singular (one) to plural (more than one) when you add *-s* or *-es*: *horse, horses*; *kiss, kisses*. Some nouns, however, have irregular plural forms: *woman, women*; *mouse, mice*; *deer, deer*. Noncount nouns (58a) cannot be made plural because they name things that cannot easily be counted: *dust, peace, prosperity*.

The possessive form of a noun shows ownership. Possessive forms add an apostrophe plus *-s* to most singular nouns or just an apostrophe to most plural nouns: *the horse's owner, the boys' department*.

Nouns are often preceded by the article (or determiner) *a, an*, or *the*: *a rocket, an astronaut, the launch* (58d).

### FOR MULTILINGUAL WRITERS: Count and noncount nouns

Do people conduct *research* or *researches*? See 58a for a discussion of count and noncount nouns.

### EXERCISE 31.3

Identify the nouns and the articles in each of the following sentences. Underline the nouns once and the articles twice. Example:

> The Puritans hoped for a different king, but Charles II regained his father's throne.

1. After Halloween, the children got sick from eating too much candy.
2. Although June is technically the driest month, severe flooding has occurred in the late spring.
3. Manuel, an avid gardener, has a vegetable garden with tomatoes, lettuce, and sweet corn.
4. A sudden frost turned the ground into a field of ice.
5. In the front row sat two people, a man with slightly graying hair and a young woman in jeans.

**bedfordstmartins.com/smhandbook** For more exercises on identifying nouns and articles, go to Exercise Central and click on **Grammatical Sentences**.

### 3 Pronouns

Pronouns often take the place of nouns or other words functioning as nouns so that you do not have to repeat words that have already been mentioned. A word or word group that a pronoun replaces or refers to is called the *antecedent* of the pronoun (34f). In the following example, the antecedent of *she* is *Caitlin*:

- ***Caitlin* refused the invitation even though *she* wanted to go.**

Pronouns fall into several categories.

Personal pronouns (*I*, *you*, *he*, *she*, *it*, *we*, *they*) refer to specific persons or things. Each can take several different forms (for example, *I*, *me*, *my*, *mine*) depending on how it functions in a sentence (34a).

- **When Keisha saw the dogs again, *she* called *them*, and *they* ran to *her*.**

Possessive pronouns (*my*, *mine*, *your*, *yours*, *her*, *hers*, *his*, *its*, *our*, *ours*, *their*, *theirs*) are personal pronouns that show ownership (34a3 and 49a).

- ***My* roommate lost *her* keys.**

Reflexive pronouns refer to the subject of the sentence or clause in which they appear. They end in *-self* or *-selves*.

- **The seals sunned *themselves* on the warm rocks.**

Intensive pronouns, which also end in *-self* or *-selves*, emphasize their antecedents.

- **He decided to paint the apartment *himself*.**

Indefinite pronouns do not refer to specific nouns, although they may refer to identifiable persons or things (33e and 34k). The following is a partial list: *all*, *anybody*, *both*, *each*, *everything*, *few*, *most*, *none*, *one*, and *some*.

- ***Everybody* screamed, and *someone* fainted, when the lights went out.**

Demonstrative pronouns (*this*, *that*, *these*, *those*) identify or point to specific nouns.

- ***These* are Peter's books.**

Interrogative pronouns (*who*, *which*, *what*) ask questions.

- ***Who* can help set up the chairs for the meeting?**

Relative pronouns (*who*, *which*, *that*, *what*, *whoever*, *whichever*, *whatever*) introduce dependent clauses (31c4) and relate the clause to the rest of the sentence. The pronouns *who* and *whoever* have different forms depending on how they are used in a sentence (34b).

- **Agnetha, *who* hires interns, is the manager *whom* you should contact.**

Reciprocal pronouns (*each other*, *one another*) refer to individual parts of a plural antecedent.

- **The business failed because the partners distrusted *each other*.**

### EXERCISE 31.4

Identify the pronouns and any antecedents in each of the following sentences, underlining the pronouns once and any antecedents twice. Example:

As identical twins, they really do understand each other.

1. He told the volunteers to help themselves to the leftovers.
2. Kiah is the only one who understands the telephone system, and she is on vacation.
3. Who is going to buy the jeans and wear them if the designer himself finds them uncomfortable?
4. They have only themselves to blame.
5. Those people who claim they don't have to study for exams aren't fooling anyone.

**bedfordstmartins.com/smhandbook** For more exercises on identifying pronouns and antecedents, go to Exercise Central and click on **Grammatical Sentences.**

## 4 Adjectives

Adjectives modify (limit the meaning of) nouns and pronouns, usually by describing, identifying, or quantifying those words (see Chapter 35). Adjectives that identify or quantify are sometimes called *determiners* (58d).

- **The *red* Corvette ran off the road.** [describes]
- ***That* Corvette needs to be repaired.** [identifies]
- **We saw *several other* Corvettes race by.** [quantifies]

In addition to their basic forms, most descriptive adjectives have other forms that allow you to make comparisons: *small*, *smaller*, *smallest*; *foolish*, *more foolish*, *most foolish*, *less foolish*, *least foolish*.

- **This year's attendance was *smaller* than last year's.**

Adjectives usually precede the words they modify, though they may follow linking verbs: *The car was defective.* Many pronouns (31b3) can function as identifying adjectives when they are followed by a noun.

- ***That* is a dangerous intersection.** [pronoun]
- ***That* intersection is dangerous.** [identifying adjective]

Other kinds of adjectives that identify or quantify are the articles *a*, *an*, and *the* (58e) and numbers (*three*, *sixty-fifth*, *five hundred*).

Proper adjectives form from or relate to proper nouns (*Egyptian*, *Emersonian*). Proper adjectives are capitalized (52b).

### 5 Adverbs

Adverbs modify verbs, adjectives, other adverbs, or entire clauses (see Chapter 35). Many adverbs end in *-ly*, though some do not (*always*, *never*, *very*, *well*), and some words that end in *-ly* are not adverbs but adjectives (*friendly*, *lovely*). One of the most common adverbs is *not*.

- **Jabari *recently* visited his roommate's family in Maine.** [modifies the verb *visited*]
- **He had an *unexpectedly* exciting trip.** [modifies the adjective *exciting*]
- **He *very* soon discovered lobster.** [modifies the adverb *soon*]
- ***Frankly*, he would have liked to stay another month.** [modifies the independent clause that makes up the rest of the sentence]

Adverbs often answer the questions *when? where? why? how? to what extent?*

Many adverbs, like many adjectives, take different forms when making comparisons: *forcefully, more forcefully, most forcefully, less forcefully, least forcefully.*

**Of all the candidates, she speaks the *most forcefully*.**

Conjunctive adverbs modify an entire clause and express the connection in meaning between that clause and the preceding clause (or sentence). Conjunctive adverbs include *however, furthermore, therefore,* and *likewise* (31b7).

### EXERCISE 31.5

Identify the adjectives and adverbs in each of the following sentences, underlining the adjectives once and the adverbs twice. Remember that articles and some pronouns are used as adjectives. Example:

Inadvertently, the two agents misquoted their major client.

1. An empty subject line and a somewhat familiar sender's name tricked me into opening the seemingly innocent email.
2. Nevertheless, her teenage son eventually overcame his poor study habits.
3. Koalas are generally quiet creatures that make loud grunting noises during mating season.
4. The huge red tomatoes looked lovely, but they tasted disappointingly like cardboard.
5. The youngest dancer in the troupe performed a brilliant solo.

**bedfordstmartins.com/smhandbook** For more exercises on identifying adjectives and adverbs, go to Exercise Central and click on **Grammatical Sentences**.

## 6 Prepositions

Prepositions express relationships — in space, time, or other senses — between nouns or pronouns and other words in a sentence.

**We did not want to leave *during* the game.**

**The contestants waited nervously *for* the announcement.**

**Drive *across* the bridge and go *down* the avenue *past* three stoplights.**

**SOME COMMON PREPOSITIONS**

| | | | | |
|---|---|---|---|---|
| about | at | down | near | since |
| above | before | during | of | through |
| across | behind | except | off | toward |
| after | below | for | on | under |
| against | beneath | from | onto | until |
| along | beside | in | out | up |
| among | between | inside | over | upon |
| around | beyond | into | past | with |
| as | by | like | regarding | without |

**SOME COMPOUND PREPOSITIONS**

| | | |
|---|---|---|
| according to | except for | instead of |
| as well as | in addition to | next to |
| because of | in front of | out of |
| by way of | in place of | with regard to |
| due to | in spite of | |

If you are not sure which preposition to use, consult your dictionary. *Funk and Wagnalls Standard Handbook of Synonyms, Antonyms, and Prepositions* is one good source.

A prepositional phrase (see Chapter 60) begins with a preposition and ends with the noun or pronoun it connects to the rest of the sentence.

## EXERCISE 31.6

Identify and underline the prepositions in the following sentences. Example:

<u>In</u> the dim interior <u>of</u> the hut crouched an old man.

1. The transportation board of the county is planning to add limited bus service from midnight until 5:00 AM.
2. He ran swiftly through the brush, across the beach, and into the sea.
3. Instead of creating a peaceful new beginning, the tribunal factions are constantly fighting among themselves.
4. After some hard thinking on a weeklong camping trip, I decided to quit my job and join the peace corps for two years.
5. The nuclear power plant about ten miles from the city has the worst safety record in the country.

**bedfordstmartins.com/smhandbook** For more exercises on identifying prepositions, go to Exercise Central and click on **Grammatical Sentences**.

## 7 Conjunctions

Conjunctions connect words or groups of words to each other.

### *Coordinating conjunctions*

Coordinating conjunctions join equivalent structures — two or more nouns, pronouns, verbs, adjectives, adverbs, prepositions, conjunctions, phrases, or clauses.

- **A strong *but* warm breeze blew across the desert.**
- **Please print *or* type the information on the application form.**
- **Taiwo worked two shifts today, *so* she is tired tonight.**

**COORDINATING CONJUNCTIONS**

| | | | | | | |
|---|---|---|---|---|---|---|
| and | but | for | nor | or | so | yet |

### *Correlative conjunctions*

Correlative conjunctions join equal elements, and they come in pairs.

- ***Both* Bechtel *and* Kaiser submitted bids on the project.**
- **Maisha *not only* sent a card *but also* visited me in the hospital.**

**CORRELATIVE CONJUNCTIONS**

| | | |
|---|---|---|
| both . . . and | just as . . . so | not only . . . but also |
| either . . . or | neither . . . nor | whether . . . or |

### *Subordinating conjunctions*

Subordinating conjunctions introduce adverb clauses and signal the relationship between the adverb clause and another clause, usually an independent clause. For instance, in the following sentence, the subordinating conjunction *while* signals a time relationship, letting us know that the two events in the sentence happened simultaneously:

- **Sweat ran down my face *while* I frantically searched for my child.**

**SOME COMMON SUBORDINATING CONJUNCTIONS**

| | | |
|---|---|---|
| after | if | unless |
| although | in order that | until |
| as | once | when |
| as if | since | where |
| because | so that | while |
| before | than | |
| even though | though | |

### *Conjunctive adverbs*

Conjunctive adverbs connect independent clauses and often act as transitional expressions (46e). As their name suggests, conjunctive adverbs can act as both adverbs and conjunctions because they modify the second clause in addition to connecting it to the preceding clause. Like many other adverbs yet unlike other conjunctions, they can move to different positions in a clause.

- **The cider tasted bitter; *however*, each of us drank a tall glass of it.**
- **The cider tasted bitter; each of us, *however*, drank a tall glass of it.**

**SOME CONJUNCTIVE ADVERBS**

| | | |
|---|---|---|
| also | indeed | now |
| anyway | instead | otherwise |
| besides | likewise | similarly |
| certainly | meanwhile | still |
| finally | moreover | then |
| furthermore | namely | therefore |
| however | nevertheless | thus |
| incidentally | next | undoubtedly |

Independent clauses connected by a conjunctive adverb must be separated by a semicolon or a period, not just a comma (38c).

- **Some of these problems could occur at any company; *still*, many could happen only here.**

### EXERCISE 31.7

Underline the coordinating, correlative, and subordinating conjunctions as well as the conjunctive adverbs in each of the following sentences. Example:

We used sleeping bags, even though the cabin had sheets and blankets.

1. After waiting for an hour and a half, both Jenny and I were disgruntled, so we went home.
2. The facilities were not only uncomfortable but also dangerous.
3. We were going to have a yard sale because we had so much junk in our garage and needed more space; however, we decided to donate everything to charity.
4. Although I live in a big city, my neighborhood has enough trees and raccoons to make me feel as if I live in the suburbs.
5. Enrique was not qualified for the job because he knew one of the programming languages but not the other; still, the interview encouraged him.

**bedfordstmartins.com/smhandbook** For more exercises on identifying conjunctions, go to Exercise Central and click on **Grammatical Sentences**.

### 8 Interjections

Interjections express surprise or emotion: *oh*, *ouch*, *hey*. Interjections often stand alone. Even when they are included in a sentence, they do not relate grammatically to the rest of the sentence.

- ***Hey*, no one suggested that we would find an easy solution.**

## 31c The parts of a sentence

Knowing a word's part of speech helps you understand how to use that word, but you also have to look at the part it plays in a particular sentence. Every sentence has a grammatical pattern or structure, and certain parts of speech — nouns, pronouns, and adjectives — can function in more than one way, depending on this structure.

SUBJECT
- **This *description* conveys the ecology of the Everglades.**

DIRECT OBJECT
- **I read a *description* of the ecology of the Everglades.**

*Description* is a noun in both of these sentences, yet in the first it serves as the subject of the verb *conveys*, while in the second it serves as the direct object of the verb *read*.

### 1 Subjects

Almost every sentence has a stated subject, which identifies whom or what the sentence is about. The simple subject consists of one or more nouns or pronouns; the complete subject consists of the simple subject (SS) with all its modifiers.

## Basic sentence patterns

1. **Subject/verb**

   S V
   Babies drool.

2. **Subject/verb/subject complement**

   S V SC
   Babies smell sweet.

3. **Subject/verb/direct object**

   S V DO
   Babies drink milk.

4. **Subject/verb/indirect object/direct object**

   S V IO DO
   Babies give grandparents pleasure.

5. **Subject/verb/direct object/object complement**

   S V DO OC
   Babies keep parents awake.

SS
- ***Baseball*** **is a summer game.**

COMPLETE SUBJECT
SS
- ***Sailing over the fence, the ball*** **crashed through Mr. Wilson's window.**

COMPLETE SUBJECT
SS
- ***Those who sit in the bleachers*** **have the most fun.**

A compound subject contains two or more simple subjects joined with a coordinating conjunction (*and*, *but*, *or*) or a correlative conjunction (*both...and*, *either...or*, *neither...nor*, *not only...but also*). (See 31b7.)

- ***Baseball and softball*** **developed from cricket.**
- ***Both baseball and softball*** **developed from cricket.**

The subject usually comes before the predicate, or verb, but sometimes writers reverse this order to achieve a particular effect.

- **Up to the plate stepped *Casey*.**

In imperative sentences, which express requests or commands, the subject *you* is usually implied but not stated.

- **(*You*) Keep your eye on the ball.**

In questions and certain other constructions, the subject usually appears between the auxiliary verb and the main verb.

- **Did *Casey* save the game?**
- **Never have *I* felt so angry.**

In sentences beginning with *there* or *here* followed by a form of the verb *be*, the subject always follows the verb. *There* and *here* are never the subject.

- **There was no *joy* in Mudville.**

### EXERCISE 31.8

Identify the complete subject and the simple subject in each sentence. Underline the complete subject once and the simple subject twice. Example:

The tall, powerful woman defiantly blocked the doorway.

1. That container of fried rice has spent six weeks in the back of the refrigerator.
2. Did the new tour guide remember to stop in the ancient Greek gallery?
3. There goes my favorite car.
4. Japanese animation, with its cutting-edge graphics and futuristic plots, has earned many American admirers.
5. Some women worried about osteoporosis take calcium supplements.

**bedfordstmartins.com/smhandbook** For more exercises on subjects, go to Exercise Central and click on **Grammatical Sentences.**

## 2 Predicates

In addition to a subject, every sentence has a predicate, which asserts or asks something about the subject or tells the subject to do something. The hinge, or key word, of most predicates is a verb. The simple predicate of a sentence is the main verb and any auxiliaries; the complete predicate includes the simple predicate (SP) and any modifiers of the verb and any objects or complements and their modifiers.

▶ **Both of us *are planning to major in history.***

A compound predicate contains two or more verbs that have the same subject and that are usually joined by a coordinating or a correlative conjunction.

▶ **Omar *shut the book, put it back on the shelf, and sighed.***

On the basis of how they function in predicates, verbs can be divided into three categories: linking, transitive, and intransitive.

### *Linking verbs*

A linking verb links, or joins, a subject with a subject complement (SC), a word or word group that identifies or describes the subject.

S V SC
▶ **Christine is a single mother.**

S V SC
▶ **She is patient.**

If it identifies the subject, the complement is a noun or pronoun (*a single mother*). If it describes the subject, the complement is an adjective (*patient*).

The forms of *be*, when used as main verbs, are linking verbs (like *are* in this sentence). Other verbs, such as *appear, become, feel, grow, look, make, seem, smell,* and *sound*, can also function as linking verbs, depending on the sense of the sentence.

S V SC
▶ **The abandoned farmhouse had become dilapidated.**

### *Transitive verbs*

A transitive verb expresses action that is directed toward a noun or pronoun, called the direct object of the verb.

S V DO
▶ **He peeled all the rutabagas.**

In the preceding example, the subject and verb do not express a complete thought. The direct object completes the thought by saying *what* he peeled.

A direct object may be followed by an object complement, a word or word group that describes or identifies it. Object complements may be adjectives, as in the next example, or nouns, as in the second example.

S V DO OC
- **I find cell-phone conversations in restaurants very annoying.**

S V DO OC
- **Alana considers Keyshawn her best friend.**

A transitive verb may also be followed by an indirect object, which tells to whom or what, or for whom or what, the verb's action is done. You might say the indirect object is the recipient of the direct object.

S V IO DO
- **The sound of the traffic all night long gave me a splitting headache.**

### *Intransitive verbs*

An intransitive verb expresses action that is not directed toward an object. Therefore, an intransitive verb does not have a direct object.

S V
- **The Red Sox persevered.**

S V
- **Their fans watched anxiously.**

The action of the verb *persevered* has no object (it makes no sense to ask, *persevered what?* or *persevered whom?*), and the action of the verb *watched* is directed toward an object that is implied but not expressed.

Some verbs that express action can be only transitive or only intransitive, but most can be used both ways, with or without a direct object.

S V DO
- **A maid wearing a uniform opened the door.** [transitive]

S V
- **The door opened silently.** [intransitive]

### EXERCISE 31.9

Underline the predicate in each of the following sentences. Then label each verb as linking (LV), transitive (TV), or intransitive (IV). Finally, label all subject and object complements and all direct and indirect objects. Example:

TV DO OC
We considered city life unbearable.

1. He is proud of his heritage.
2. The horrifying news story made me angry.
3. A hung jury seems likely in this case.
4. Rock and roll will never die.
5. Advertisers promise consumers the world.

**bedfordstmartins.com/smhandbook** For more exercises on predicates, go to Exercise Central and click on **Grammatical Sentences**.

## 3 Phrases

A phrase is a group of words that lacks either a subject or a predicate or both.

- **The new law will restrict smoking *in most public places*.**

The basic subject of this sentence is a noun phrase, *the new law*; the basic predicate is a verb phrase, *will restrict smoking*. The prepositional phrase *in most public places* functions here as an adverb, telling where smoking will be restricted.

This section will discuss the various kinds of phrases: noun, verb, prepositional, verbal, absolute, and appositive.

### Noun phrases

Made up of a noun and all its modifiers, a noun phrase can function in a sentence as a subject, object, or complement.

- SUBJECT: ***Delicious, gooey peanut butter* is surprisingly healthful.**
- OBJECT: **Dieters prefer *green salad with plenty of fresh vegetables*.**
- COMPLEMENT: **A tuna sandwich is *a popular lunch*.**

### Verb phrases

A main verb and its auxiliary verbs make up a verb phrase, which functions in a sentence in only one way: as a predicate.

- **Frank *had been depressed* for some time.**
- **His problem *might have been caused* by tension between his parents.**

### Prepositional phrases

A prepositional phrase begins with a preposition and includes a noun or pronoun (called the object of the preposition) and any modifiers of the object. Prepositional phrases usually function as adjectives or adverbs.

**ADJECTIVE** Our house *in Maine* was a cabin.

**ADVERB** *From Cadillac Mountain*, you can see the northern lights.

### Verbal phrases

Verbals are verb forms that do not function as verbs. Instead, they function as nouns, adjectives, or adverbs. A verbal phrase includes a verbal and any modifiers, objects, or complements. There are three kinds of verbals: participles, gerunds, and infinitives.

#### Participles and participial phrases

The present participle is the *-ing* form of a verb (*spinning*). The past participle of most verbs ends in *-ed* (*accepted*), but some verbs have an irregular past participle (*worn, frozen*). Participles function as adjectives (35a).

- **A kiss awakened the *dreaming* princess.**

- **The cryptographers deciphered the *hidden* meaning in the message.**

Participial phrases consist of a present participle or a past participle and any modifiers, objects, or complements. Participial phrases always function as adjectives.

- ***Irritated by the delay,* Luisa complained.**

- **A dog *howling at the moon* kept me awake.**

#### Gerunds and gerund phrases

The gerund has the same form as the present participle but functions as a noun.

**SUBJECT** *Writing* takes practice.

**OBJECT** The organization promotes *recycling*.

Gerund phrases consist of a gerund and any modifiers, objects, or complements. Gerund phrases function as nouns.

SUBJECT

- ***Opening their eyes to the problem* was not easy.**

DIRECT OBJECT

- **They suddenly heard *a loud wailing from the sandbox.***

### Infinitives and infinitive phrases

The infinitive is the *to* form of a verb (*to dream, to be*). An infinitive can function as a noun, an adjective, or an adverb.

| | |
|---|---|
| **NOUN** | She wanted *to write.* |
| **ADJECTIVE** | They had no more time *to waste.* |
| **ADVERB** | The corporation was ready *to expand.* |

Infinitive phrases consist of an infinitive and any modifiers, objects, or complements. They can function as nouns, adjectives, or adverbs.

NOUN/SC

- **My goal is *to be a biology teacher.***

ADJECTIVE

- **A party would be a good way *to end the semester.***

ADVERB

- ***To perfect a draft*, always proofread carefully.**

## Absolute phrases

An absolute phrase usually includes a noun or pronoun and a participle. It modifies an entire sentence rather than a particular word and is usually set off from the rest of the sentence with commas (46c).

- **I stood on the deck, *the wind whipping my hair.***
- ***My fears laid to rest*, I climbed into the plane for my first solo flight.**

When the participle is *being*, it is often omitted.

- **The ambassador, *her head* (*being*) *high*, walked out of the room.**

## Appositive phrases

An appositive phrase is a noun phrase that renames the noun or pronoun that immediately precedes it (46c3).

- **The report, *a hefty three-volume work*, included ninety recommendations.**
- **We had a single desire, *to change the administration's policies*.**

## EXERCISE 31.10

Read the following sentences, and identify and label all of the prepositional, verbal, absolute, and appositive phrases. Notice that one kind of phrase may appear within another kind. Example:

ABSOLUTE (His voice breaking with emotion), PREP (with emotion), PREP (for the award)

His voice breaking with emotion, Ed thanked us for the award.

1. Chantelle, the motel clerk, hopes to be certified as a river guide.
2. Countertops made of granite will last the longest.
3. My stomach doing flips, I answered the door.
4. Floating on my back, I ignored my practice requirements.
5. Learning to drive a car with a manual transmission takes time and patience.

**bedfordstmartins.com/smhandbook** For more exercises on phrases, go to Exercise Central and click on **Grammatical Sentences**.

### 4 Clauses

A clause is a group of words containing a subject and a predicate. There are two kinds of clauses: independent and dependent. Independent clauses (also known as main clauses) can stand alone as complete sentences.

- **The window is open.**

Pairs of independent clauses may be joined with a coordinating conjunction and a comma (31b7 and 46b).

- **The window is open, *so* we'd better be quiet.**

Like independent clauses, dependent clauses (also known as subordinate clauses) contain a subject and a predicate. They cannot stand alone as complete sentences, however, for they begin with a subordinating word — a subordinating conjunction (31b7) or a relative pronoun (31b3) — that connects them to an independent clause.

- ***Because the window is open*, the room feels cool.**

In this combination, the subordinating conjunction *because* transforms the independent clause *the window is open* into a dependent clause. In doing so, it indicates a causal relationship between the two clauses.

Dependent clauses function as nouns, adjectives, or adverbs.

### Noun clauses

Noun clauses can function as subjects, direct objects, subject complements, or objects of prepositions. Thus, they are always contained within another clause. They usually begin with a relative pronoun (*that*, *which*, *what*, *who*, *whom*, *whose*, *whatever*, *whoever*, *whomever*, *whichever*) or with *when*, *where*, *whether*, *why*, or *how*.

S

- ***That he had a college degree*** **was important to her.**

DO

- **She asked *where he went to college.***

SC

- **The real question was *why she wanted to know.***

OBJ OF PREP

- **She was looking for *whatever information was available.***

Notice that in each of these sentences the noun clause is an integral part of the independent clause that makes up the sentence; for example, in the second sentence the independent clause is not just *She asked* but *She asked where he went to college.*

### Adjective clauses

Adjective clauses modify nouns and pronouns in another clause. Usually they immediately follow the words they modify.

- **The surgery, *which took three hours*, was a complete success.**
- **It was performed by the surgeon *who had developed the procedure.***
- **The hospital was the one *where I was born.***

Sometimes the relative pronoun introducing an adjective clause may be omitted, as in the following example:

- **That is one book [*that*] *I intend to read.***

### *Adverb clauses*

Adverb clauses modify verbs, adjectives, or other adverbs. They begin with a subordinating conjunction (31b7). Like adverbs, they usually tell when, where, why, how, or to what extent.

- **We hiked *where there were few other hikers.***
- **My backpack felt heavier *than it ever had.***
- **I climbed as swiftly *as I could under the weight of my backpack.***

#### EXERCISE 31.11

Identify the independent and dependent clauses and any subordinating conjunctions and relative pronouns in each of the following sentences. Example:

> DEPENDENT CLAUSE — INDEPENDENT CLAUSE
> If I were going on a really long hike, I would carry a lightweight stove.
>
> *If* is a subordinating conjunction.

1. The hockey game was postponed because one of the players collapsed on the bench.
2. She immediately recognized the officer who walked into the coffee shop.
3. After completing three advanced drawing classes, Jason was admitted into the fine arts program, and he immediately rented a small studio space.
4. The trip was longer than I had remembered.
5. I could see that he was very tired, but I had to ask him a few questions.

**bedfordstmartins.com/smhandbook** For more exercises on clauses, go to Exercise Central and click on **Grammatical Sentences.**

#### EXERCISE 31.12

Expand each of the following sentences by adding at least one dependent clause to it. Be prepared to explain how your addition improves the sentence. Example:

> As the earth continued to shake, the
> ~~The~~ books tumbled from the shelves.
> ^

1. News of the virus was beginning to frighten the public.
2. Simone waited nervously by the phone.

3. The new computer made a strange noise.
4. Rob always borrowed money from friends.
5. The crowd grew louder and more disorderly.

## 31d Classifying sentences

Like words, sentences can be classified in different ways: grammatically, functionally, or rhetorically. Grammatical classification groups sentences according to how many and what types of clauses they contain. Functional classification groups sentences according to whether they make a statement, ask a question, issue a command, or express an exclamation. Rhetorical classification groups sentences according to where in the sentence the main idea is located. These methods of classification can help you analyze and assess your sentences as you write and revise.

### 1 Grammatical classification

Grammatically, sentences may be classified as simple, compound, complex, and compound-complex.

#### *Simple sentences*

A simple sentence consists of one independent clause and no dependent clause. The subject or the predicate, or both, may be compound.

- **The trailer is surrounded by a wooden deck.**
- **Both my roommate and I had left our keys in the room.**
- **At the country club, the head pro and his assistant give lessons, run the golf shop, and try to keep the members content.**

#### *Compound sentences*

A compound sentence consists of two or more independent clauses and no dependent clause. The clauses may be joined by a comma and a coordinating conjunction (31b7) or by a semicolon.

- **Occasionally a car goes up the dirt trail, and dust flies everywhere.**
- **Alberto is obsessed with soccer; he eats, breathes, and lives the game.**

### Complex sentences

A complex sentence consists of one independent clause and at least one dependent clause.

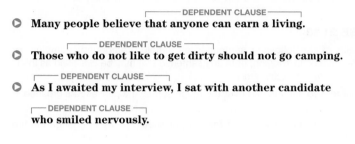

DEPENDENT CLAUSE
- **Many people believe that anyone can earn a living.**

DEPENDENT CLAUSE
- **Those who do not like to get dirty should not go camping.**

DEPENDENT CLAUSE
- **As I awaited my interview, I sat with another candidate**

  DEPENDENT CLAUSE
  **who smiled nervously.**

### Compound-complex sentences

A compound-complex sentence consists of two or more independent clauses and at least one dependent clause.

IND CLAUSE DEP CLAUSE
- **I complimented Joe when he finished the job, and**

  IND CLAUSE
  **he seemed pleased.**

IND CLAUSE
- **Sister Lucy tried her best to help Martin,**

  IND CLAUSE
  **but he was an undisciplined boy**

  DEP CLAUSE
  **who drove many teachers to despair.**

## 2 Functional classification

In terms of function, sentences can be classified as declarative (making a statement), interrogative (asking a question), imperative (giving a command), or exclamatory (expressing strong feeling).

| | |
|---|---|
| **DECLARATIVE** | He sings with the Grace Church Boys' Choir. |
| **INTERROGATIVE** | How long has he sung with them? |
| **IMPERATIVE** | Comb his hair before the performance starts. |
| **EXCLAMATORY** | What voices those boys have! |

### 3 Rhetorical classification

Some sentences can be classified rhetorically as either cumulative or periodic sentences. (See 44c3 for an explanation of these patterns.)

#### EXERCISE 31.13

Classify each of the following sentences as simple, compound, complex, or compound-complex. In addition, note any sentence that may be classified as interrogative, imperative, or exclamatory.

1. The boat rocked and lurched over the rough surf as the passengers groaned in agony.
2. How long would he have to wait for help, or should he try to change the tire himself?
3. Hoping for an end to the rain, we huddled together in the shop doorway, unwilling to get drenched.
4. Keeping in mind the terrain, the weather, and the length of the hike, decide what you need to take.
5. The former prisoner, who was cleared by DNA evidence, has lost six years of his life, and he needs a job right away.

**bedfordstmartins.com/smhandbook** For more exercises on classifying sentences, go to Exercise Central and click on **Grammatical Sentences**.

#### THINKING CRITICALLY ABOUT SENTENCES

The following sentences come from the openings of well-known works. Identify the independent and dependent clauses in each sentence. Then choose one sentence, and write a sentence of your own imitating its structure, clause for clause and phrase for phrase. Example:

> Ten days after the war ended, my sister Laura drove a car off a bridge.
>
> — MARGARET ATWOOD, *The Blind Assassin*

A few minutes before the detectives arrived, our friend Nastassia found a passageway behind the wall.

1. We observe today not a victory of party but a celebration of freedom, symbolizing an end as well as a beginning, signifying renewal as well as change.
   — JOHN F. KENNEDY, Inaugural Address
2. Once in a long while, four times so far for me, my mother brings out the metal tube that holds her medical diploma.
   — MAXINE HONG KINGSTON, "Photographs of My Parents"

# Verbs

# 32

Restaurant menus often spotlight verbs in action. One famous place in Boston, for instance, offers to bake, broil, pan-fry, deep-fry, poach, sauté, fricassée, blacken, or scallop any of the fish entrées on its menu. To someone ordering — or cooking — at this restaurant, the distinctions lie entirely in the verbs.

Used skillfully, verbs can be the heartbeat of prose, moving it along, enlivening it, carrying its action: the little girl *skipped* in, *bouncing* a red rubber ball and *smiling* from ear to ear.

## 32a Verb forms

Except for *be*, all English verbs have five possible forms.

| BASE FORM | PAST TENSE | PAST PARTICIPLE | PRESENT PARTICIPLE | *-S* FORM |
|---|---|---|---|---|
| talk | talked | talked | talking | talks |
| adore | adored | adored | adoring | adores |

The base form is the one listed in the dictionary. For all verbs except *be*, use the base form to indicate an action or condition in the present when the subject is plural or when the subject is *I* or *you*.

- **During the ritual, the women *go* into trances.**

Use the past tense to indicate an action or condition that occurred entirely in the past. For most verbs, it is formed by adding *-ed* or *-d* to the base form. Some verbs, however, have irregular past-tense forms. *Be* has two past-tense forms, *was* and *were* (p. 595).

- **The Globe *was* the stage for many of Shakespeare's works.**
- **In 1613, it *caught* fire and burned to the ground.**

Use the past participle to form perfect tenses and the passive voice (32g). A past participle usually has the same form as the past tense, though some verbs have irregular past participles. (See 32c.)

- **She *had accomplished* the impossible.** [past perfect]
- **No one *was injured* in the explosion.** [passive voice]

The present participle is constructed by adding *-ing* to the base form. Use it with auxiliary verbs to indicate a continuing action or condition.

- **Many students *are competing* in the race.** [continuing action]

Present participles sometimes function as adjectives or nouns (gerunds), and past participles can also serve as adjectives; in such cases they are not verbs but verbals (31c3).

Except for *be* and *have*, the *-s* form consists of the base form plus *-s* or *-es*. This form indicates an action in the present for third-person singular subjects. All singular nouns; *he*, *she*, and *it*; and many other pronouns (such as *this* and *someone*) are third-person singular.

| | SINGULAR | PLURAL |
|---|---|---|
| FIRST PERSON | I *wish* | we *wish* |
| SECOND PERSON | you *wish* | you *wish* |
| THIRD PERSON | he/she/it *wishes* | they *wish* |
| | Joe *wishes* | children *wish* |
| | someone *wishes* | many *wish* |

The third-person singular form of *have* is *has*.

## Editing for -*s* and -*es* endings

If you tend to leave off or misuse the *-s* and *-es* verb endings in academic writing, you should check for them systematically.

1. Underline every verb, and then circle all verbs in the present tense.
2. Find the subject of every verb you circled.
3. If the subject is a singular noun; *he*, *she*, or *it*; or a singular indefinite pronoun, be sure the verb ends in *-s* or *-es*. If the subject is not third-person singular, the verb should not have an *-s* or *-es* ending.
4. Be careful with auxiliary verbs such as *can* or *may* (59b). These auxiliaries are used with the base form, never with the *-s* or *-es* form.

## 1 Forms of *be*

*Be* has three forms in the present tense (*am*, *is*, *are*) and two in the past tense (*was*, *were*).

### *Present tense*

| | SINGULAR | PLURAL |
|---|---|---|
| FIRST PERSON | I *am* | we *are* |
| SECOND PERSON | you *are* | you *are* |
| THIRD PERSON | he/she/it *is* | they *are* |
| | Juan *is* | children *are* |
| | somebody *is* | many *are* |

### *Past tense*

| | SINGULAR | PLURAL |
|---|---|---|
| FIRST PERSON | I *was* | we *were* |
| SECOND PERSON | you *were* | you *were* |
| THIRD PERSON | he/she/it *was* | they *were* |
| | Juan *was* | children *were* |
| | somebody *was* | many *were* |

## 2 Absence of *be*; habitual *be*

- **My sister at work. She be there every day 'til five.**

The preceding sentences illustrate common usages of *be*. The first sentence shows the absence of *be*; the second shows the use of "habitual *be*," indicating that something is always or almost always the case. (The same sentences rephrased in academic English would read, "My sister is at work. She is there every day until five.")

Many African American speakers regularly and systematically use *be* in these ways. You may want to quote dialogue featuring these patterns in your own writing to evoke particular regions or communities (see Chapter 28). Most academic writing, however, calls for academic English.

## 32b Auxiliary verbs

Use auxiliary verbs with a base form, present participle, or past participle to create verb phrases. The base form or participle in a verb phrase is the main verb. The most common auxiliaries, forms of *be*, *do*, and *have*, indicate completed or continuing action, the passive voice, emphasis, questions, and negative statements.

- **We *have considered* all viewpoints.** [completed action]
- **The college *is building* a new dormitory.** [continuing action]
- **We *were warned* to stay away.** [passive voice]
- **I *do respect* your viewpoint.** [emphasis]
- ***Do* you *know* the answer?** [question]
- **He *does* not *like* wearing a tie.** [negative statement]

Modal auxiliaries — *can, could, might, may, must, ought to, shall, will, should, would* — indicate future action, possibility, necessity, obligation, and so on.

- **They *will explain* the procedure.** [future action]
- **You *can see* three states from the top of the mountain.** [possibility]
- **I *must try* harder to go to bed early.** [necessity]
- **She *should visit* her parents more often.** [obligation]

### FOR MULTILINGUAL WRITERS: Modal auxiliaries

Why do we *not* say "Alice can to read Latin"? For a discussion of *can* and other modal auxiliaries, see 59b.

## 32c Regular and irregular verbs

A verb is regular when its past tense and past participle are formed by adding *-ed* or *-d* to the base form.

| BASE FORM | PAST TENSE | PAST PARTICIPLE |
|---|---|---|
| love | loved | loved |
| honor | honored | honored |
| obey | obeyed | obeyed |

## Editing for *-ed* or *-d* endings

Speakers who delete the *-ed* or *-d* endings in conversation may forget to include them in academic writing. If you tend to drop these endings, make a point of checking for them when proofreading. Underline all the verbs, and then underline a second time any that are past tense or past participles. Check each of these for an *-ed* or *-d* ending. Unless the verb is irregular (see the following list), it should end in *-ed* or *-d*.

### *Irregular verbs*

A verb is irregular when it does not follow the *-ed* or *-d* pattern. If you are unsure about whether a verb is regular or irregular, or what the correct form is, consult the following list or a dictionary. Dictionaries list any irregular forms under the entry for the base form.

## Some common irregular verbs

| BASE FORM | PAST TENSE | PAST PARTICIPLE |
|---|---|---|
| arise | arose | arisen |
| be | was/were | been |
| bear | bore | borne, born |
| beat | beat | beaten |
| become | became | become |
| begin | began | begun |
| bite | bit | bitten, bit |
| blow | blew | blown |
| break | broke | broken |
| bring | brought | brought |
| broadcast | broadcast | broadcast |
| build | built | built |
| burn | burned, burnt | burned, burnt |
| burst | burst | burst |
| buy | bought | bought |
| catch | caught | caught |

*(continued on next page)*

*(continued from p. 597)*

| BASE FORM | PAST TENSE | PAST PARTICIPLE |
|---|---|---|
| choose | chose | chosen |
| come | came | come |
| cost | cost | cost |
| cut | cut | cut |
| dig | dug | dug |
| dive | dived, dove | dived |
| do | did | done |
| draw | drew | drawn |
| dream | dreamed, dreamt | dreamed, dreamt |
| drink | drank | drunk |
| drive | drove | driven |
| eat | ate | eaten |
| fall | fell | fallen |
| feel | felt | felt |
| fight | fought | fought |
| find | found | found |
| fly | flew | flown |
| forget | forgot | forgotten, forgot |
| freeze | froze | frozen |
| get | got | gotten, got |
| give | gave | given |
| go | went | gone |
| grow | grew | grown |
| hang (suspend)[1] | hung | hung |
| have | had | had |
| hear | heard | heard |
| hide | hid | hidden |
| hit | hit | hit |
| keep | kept | kept |
| know | knew | known |
| lay | laid | laid |
| lead | led | led |
| leave | left | left |
| lend | lent | lent |

[1]*Hang* meaning "execute by hanging" is regular: *hang, hanged, hanged.*

| BASE FORM | PAST TENSE | PAST PARTICIPLE |
|---|---|---|
| let | let | let |
| lie (recline)[2] | lay | lain |
| lose | lost | lost |
| make | made | made |
| mean | meant | meant |
| meet | met | met |
| pay | paid | paid |
| prove | proved | proved, proven |
| put | put | put |
| read | read | read |
| ride | rode | ridden |
| ring | rang | rung |
| rise | rose | risen |
| run | ran | run |
| say | said | said |
| see | saw | seen |
| send | sent | sent |
| set | set | set |
| shake | shook | shaken |
| shoot | shot | shot |
| show | showed | showed, shown |
| shrink | shrank | shrunk |
| sing | sang | sung |
| sink | sank | sunk |
| sit | sat | sat |
| sleep | slept | slept |
| speak | spoke | spoken |
| spend | spent | spent |
| spread | spread | spread |
| spring | sprang, sprung | sprung |
| stand | stood | stood |
| steal | stole | stolen |
| strike | struck | struck, stricken |
| swim | swam | swum |
| swing | swung | swung |

*(continued on next page)*

[2]*Lie* meaning "tell a falsehood" is regular: *lie, lied, lied.*

*(continued from p. 599)*

| BASE FORM | PAST TENSE | PAST PARTICIPLE |
|---|---|---|
| take | took | taken |
| teach | taught | taught |
| tear | tore | torn |
| tell | told | told |
| think | thought | thought |
| throw | threw | thrown |
| wake | waked, woke | waked, woken |
| wear | wore | worn |
| win | won | won |
| wind | wound | wound |
| write | wrote | written |

## EXERCISE 32.1

Complete each of the following sentences by filling in each blank with the past tense or past participle of the verb listed in parentheses. Example:

They had already _eaten_ (eat) the entrée; later they _ate_ (eat) the dessert.

1. The babysitter ______ (let) the children play with my schoolbooks, and before I ______ (come) home, they had ______ (tear) out several pages.
2. After she had ______ (make) her decision, she ______ (find) that her constant anxiety was gone.
3. The process of hazing ______ (begin) soon after fraternities were formed.
4. My parents ______ (plant) a tree for me in the town where I was born, but I have never ______ (go) back to see it.
5. Some residents ______ (know) that the levee was leaking long before the storms, but public officials ______ (ignore) the complaints.
6. I ______ (wake) up with a start because I was convinced that something had ______ (fly) through the window.
7. When the buzzer sounded, the racers ______ (spring) into the water and ______ (swim) toward the far end of the pool.
8. We had ______ (assume) for some time that surgery was a possibility, and we had ______ (find) an excellent facility.
9. Once the storm had ______ (pass), we could see that the old oak tree had ______ (fall).
10. Some high-level employees ______ (decide) to speak publicly about the cover-up before the company's official story had ______ (be) released to the media.

**bedfordstmartins.com/smhandbook** For more exercises on regular and irregular verbs, go to Exercise Central and click on **Verbs**.

## 32d *Lay* and *lie*, *sit* and *set*, *raise* and *rise*

*Lay* and *lie*, *sit* and *set*, and *raise* and *rise* cause problems for many writers because both verbs in each pair have similar-sounding forms and related meanings. In each pair, one of the verbs is transitive, meaning that it takes a direct object; the other is intransitive, meaning that it does not take an object. The best way to avoid confusing the two is to memorize their forms and meanings. All these verbs except *raise* are irregular.

| BASE FORM | PAST TENSE | PAST PARTICIPLE | PRESENT PARTICIPLE | -S FORM |
|---|---|---|---|---|
| lie (recline) | lay | lain | lying | lies |
| lay (put) | laid | laid | laying | lays |
| sit (be seated) | sat | sat | sitting | sits |
| set (put) | set | set | setting | sets |
| rise (get up) | rose | risen | rising | rises |
| raise (lift) | raised | raised | raising | raises |

*Lie* is intransitive and means "recline" or "be situated." *Lay* is transitive and means "put" or "place." This pair is especially confusing because *lay* is also the past-tense form of *lie*.

**INTRANSITIVE** He *lay* on the floor when his back ached.

**TRANSITIVE** I *laid* the cloth on the table.

*Sit* is intransitive and means "be seated." *Set* usually is transitive and means "put" or "place."

**INTRANSITIVE** She *sat* in the rocking chair.

**TRANSITIVE** We *set* the bookshelf in the hallway.

*Rise* is intransitive and means "get up" or "go up." *Raise* is transitive and means "lift" or "cause to go up."

**INTRANSITIVE** He *rose* up in bed and glared at me.

**TRANSITIVE** He *raised* his hand eagerly.

### EXERCISE 32.2

Underline the appropriate verb form in each of the following sentences. Example:

The guests (*raised/rose*) their glasses to the happy couple.

1. Sometimes she just (*lies/lays*) and stares at the ceiling.
2. The chef (*lay/laid*) his knives carefully on the counter.
3. The two-year-old walked carefully across the room and (*set/sat*) the glass vase on the table.
4. Grandpa used to love (*sitting/setting*) on the front porch and telling stories of his childhood.
5. The submarine began to (*raise/rise*) to the surface.

**bedfordstmartins.com/smhandbook** For more exercises on regular and irregular verbs, go to Exercise Central and click on **Verbs**.

## 32e Verb tenses

Tenses show when the action or condition expressed by a verb occurs. The three simple tenses are present tense, past tense, and future tense.

| | |
|---|---|
| **PRESENT TENSE** | I *ask, write* |
| **PAST TENSE** | I *asked, wrote* |
| **FUTURE TENSE** | I *will ask, will write* |

More complex aspects of time are expressed through progressive, perfect, and perfect progressive forms of the simple tenses. (Although this terminology sounds complicated, you regularly use all these forms.)

| | |
|---|---|
| **PRESENT PROGRESSIVE** | she *is asking, is writing* |
| **PAST PROGRESSIVE** | she *was asking, was writing* |
| **FUTURE PROGRESSIVE** | she *will be asking, will be writing* |
| **PRESENT PERFECT** | she *has asked, has written* |
| **PAST PERFECT** | she *had asked, had written* |
| **FUTURE PERFECT** | she *will have asked, will have written* |
| **PRESENT PERFECT PROGRESSIVE** | she *has been asking, has been writing* |

| | |
|---|---|
| **PAST PERFECT PROGRESSIVE** | she *had been asking, had been writing* |
| **FUTURE PERFECT PROGRESSIVE** | she *will have been asking, will have been writing* |

The simple tenses locate an action only within the three basic time frames of present, past, and future. Progressive forms express continuing actions; perfect forms express actions completed before another action or time in the present, past, or future; perfect progressive forms express actions that continue up to some point in the present, past, or future.

### 1 Present-tense forms

The simple present indicates actions or conditions occurring at the time of speaking as well as those occurring habitually. In addition, with appropriate time expressions, the simple present can be used to indicate a scheduled future event.

- **They *are* very angry about the decision.**
- **I *eat* breakfast every day at 8:00 AM.**
- **Love *conquers* all.**
- **Classes *begin* next week.**

Write about general truths or scientific facts in the simple present, even when the predicate of the sentence is in the past tense.

- **Pasteur demonstrated that his boiling process ~~made~~ [makes] milk safe.**

Use the simple present, not the past tense, when writing about action in literary works.

- **Ishmael slowly ~~realized~~ [realizes] all that ~~was~~ [is] at stake in the search for the white whale.**

In general, use the simple present when you are quoting, summarizing, or paraphrasing someone else's writing.

- **Keith Walters ~~wrote~~ [writes] that the "reputed consequences and promised blessings of literacy are legion."**

But in an essay using APA (American Psychological Association) style (see Chapter 19), report your experiments or another researcher's work in the past tense (*wrote*, *noted*) or the present perfect (*has reported*).

- **Comer (1995) ~~notes~~ *noted* that protesters who deprive themselves of food are seen not as dysfunctional but rather as "caring, sacrificing, even heroic" (p. 5).**

Use the present progressive to indicate actions that are ongoing or continuous in the present. It typically describes an action that is happening at the moment of speaking, in contrast to the simple present, which more often indicates habitual actions.

| | |
|---|---|
| PRESENT PROGRESSIVE | You *are driving* too fast. |
| SIMPLE PRESENT | I always *drive* carefully. |

With an appropriate expression of time, you can also use the present progressive to indicate a scheduled event in the future.

- **We *are having* friends over for dinner tomorrow night.**

Use the present perfect to indicate actions begun in the past and either completed at some unspecified time in the past or continuing into the present.

- **Uncontrolled logging *has destroyed* many tropical forests.**

Use the present perfect progressive to indicate actions begun in the past and continuing into the present.

- **The two sides *have been trying* to settle the case out of court.**

## 2 Past-tense forms

Use the simple past to indicate actions or conditions that occurred at a specific time and do not extend into the present.

- **Germany *invaded* Poland on September 1, 1939.**

Use the past progressive to indicate continuing actions or conditions in the past, often with specified limits.

- **Lenin *was living* in exile in Zurich when the tsar was overthrown.**

Use the past perfect to indicate actions or conditions completed by a specific time in the past or before some other past action occurred.

- **By the fourth century, Christianity *had become* the state religion.**

Use the past perfect progressive to indicate continuing actions or conditions in the past that began before a specific time or before some other past action began.

- **Carter *had been planning* a naval career until his father died.**

### 3 Future-tense forms

Use the simple future to indicate actions or conditions that have not yet begun.

- **The exhibition *will come* to Washington in September.**

Use the future progressive to indicate continuing actions or conditions in the future.

- **The loans *will be coming* due over the next two years.**

Use the future perfect to indicate actions or conditions that will be completed by or before some specified time in the future.

- **By next summer, she *will have published* the results of the study.**

Use the future perfect progressive to indicate continuing actions or conditions that will be completed by some specified time in the future.

- **In May, I *will have been living* in Tucson for five years.**

#### EXERCISE 32.3

Complete each of the following sentences by filling in the blank with an appropriate form of the verb listed in parentheses. Since more than one form will sometimes be possible, be prepared to explain the reasons for your choices. Example:

The supply of a product _rises_ (rise) when the demand is great.

1. History ______ (show) that physical torture does not make prisoners tell the truth.
2. Ever since the first nuclear power plants were built, opponents ______ (fear) disaster.

3. Thousands of Irish peasants _______ (emigrate) to America after the potato famine of the 1840s.
4. *The Da Vinci Code* _______ (be) on the bestseller list for 138 weeks.
5. Olivia _______ (direct) the play next year.
6. While they _______ (eat) in a neighborhood restaurant, they witnessed a minor accident.
7. By this time next week, each of your clients _______ (receive) an invitation to the opening.
8. By the time a child born today enters first grade, he or she _______ (watch) thousands of television commercials.
9. In one of the novel's most famous scenes, Huck _______ (express) his willingness to go to hell rather than report Jim as an escaped slave.
10. Traffic jams usually _______ (last) longer in August, when many tourists come to the area.

**bedfordstmartins.com/smhandbook** For more exercises on verb forms, go to Exercise Central and click on **Verbs**.

## 32f Verb tense sequence

Careful and accurate use of tenses is important to clear writing. Even the simplest narrative describes actions that take place at different times; when you use the appropriate tense for each action, readers can follow such time changes easily.

### Editing verb tenses

Errors in verb tenses take several forms. If you have trouble with verb tenses, check for common errors as you proofread.

- Errors of verb form (32c): for example, writing *seen* for *saw*, which confuses the past participle and past-tense forms
- Omitted auxiliary verbs (32b and e): for example, using the simple past (*Uncle Charlie arrived*) when meaning requires the present perfect (*Uncle Charlie has arrived*)
- Regional or ethnic variety of English in situations calling for academic English (see p. 595 and Chapter 28): for example, writing *they eat it all up* when the situation requires *they ate it all up*

The sequence of tenses shows the relationship between the tense of the verb in the independent clause of a sentence and the tense of a verb in a dependent clause or a verbal. In a particular sentence, your choices for the tense of the verb in a dependent clause or a verbal are limited by the meaning and by conventions about particular sequences.

- **By the time he *lent* her the money, she *had declared* bankruptcy.**

## 1 Verb sequence with infinitives

The infinitive of a verb is *to* plus the base form (*to go*, *to be*). Use the present infinitive to indicate actions or desires occurring at the same time as (or later than) the action of the main verb in the clause.

- **The child *waved to greet* the passing trains.**

  The waving and the greeting occurred at the same time in the past.

- **Each couple *hopes to win* the dance contest.**

  The hoping is present; the winning is in the future.

Use the perfect infinitive (*to have* plus the past participle) to indicate that an action occurred before the action of the main verb.

- **He *was reported to have left* his fortune to his cat.**

  The leaving of the fortune took place before the reporting.

## 2 Verb sequence with participles

Use the present participle (base form plus *-ing*) to indicate actions occurring at the same time as the action of the main verb.

- ***Seeking* to relieve unemployment, Roosevelt established several public-works programs.**

Use the past participle or the present perfect participle (*having* plus the past participle) to indicate action occurring before that of the main verb.

- ***Flown* to the front, the troops *joined* their hard-pressed comrades.**
- ***Having changed* his mind, he *voted* against the proposal.**

### 3 Verb sequence and habitual actions

In conversation, people often use *will* or *would* to describe habitual actions. In writing, however, stick to the present and past tenses for this purpose.

- **When I have a deadline, I ~~will~~ work all night.**

- **While we sat on the porch, the children ~~would play~~ played.**

### EXERCISE 32.4

Edit each of the following sentences to create the appropriate sequence of tenses. Example:

He needs to ~~send~~ have sent in his application before today.

1. When she saw *Chicago*, it had made her want to become an actress even more.
2. Leaving England in December, the settlers arrived in Virginia in May.
3. I hoped to finish reading the book before today.
4. Working with great dedication as a summer intern at the magazine, Mohan called his former supervisor in the fall to ask about a permanent position.
5. When we walked home from school, we would often stop for ice cream.

**bedfordstmartins.com/smhandbook** For more exercises on verb tense sequence, go to Exercise Central and click on **Verbs**.

## 32g Voice

Voice tells whether the subject is acting (*he questions us*) or being acted upon (*he is questioned*). When the subject is acting, the verb is in the active voice; when the subject is being acted upon, the verb is in the passive voice (45b).

**ACTIVE VOICE** The storm *uprooted* huge pine trees.

**PASSIVE VOICE** Huge pine trees *were uprooted* by the storm.

The passive voice uses the appropriate form of the auxiliary verb *be* followed by the past participle of the main verb: *he is being questioned, he was questioned, he will be questioned, he has been questioned.*

Most contemporary writers use the active voice as much as possible because it livens up their prose. Passive-voice verbs often make a pas-

### Editing the verbs in your own writing

- Circle all forms of *be*, *do*, and *have* used as main verbs. Try in each case to substitute a stronger, more specific verb. (45a)
- Check verb endings that cause you trouble. (32c)
- Use the appropriate forms of *lay* and *lie*, *sit* and *set*, *raise* and *rise* for your meaning. (32d)
- If you have problems with verb tenses, use the guidelines on p. 606.
- If you are writing about a literary work, refer to the action in the work in the present tense. (32e1)
- Check all uses of the passive voice for appropriateness. (32g)
- Check all verbs used to introduce quotations, paraphrases, and summaries. If you rely on *say*, *write*, and other very general verbs, try substituting more vivid, specific verbs (*claim*, *insist*, *wonder*, for instance). (45a)

sage hard to understand and remember. In addition, writers sometimes use the passive voice to avoid taking responsibility for what they have written. A government official who admits that "mistakes were made" skirts the pressing question: made by whom?

The passive voice can work to good advantage in some situations. Journalists often use the passive voice to protect the confidentiality of their sources, as in the phrase *it is reported that*. The passive voice is also appropriate when the performer of an action is unknown or less important than the recipient:

> **DALLAS, Nov. 22 — President John Fitzgerald Kennedy was shot and killed by an assassin today.** — TOM WICKER, *New York Times*

Wicker uses the passive voice with good reason: to focus on Kennedy, not on who killed him. Much technical and scientific writing uses the passive voice to highlight what is being studied:

> **The volunteers' food intake was closely monitored.**

To shift a sentence from the passive to the active voice (36c), make the performer of the action the subject of the sentence, and make the recipient of the action an object.

- **His ~~acting career was destroyed by his~~ unprofessional behavior** *destroyed his acting career.* **on the set~~.~~**

### EXERCISE 32.5

Convert each sentence from active to passive voice or from passive to active, and note the differences in emphasis these changes make. Example:

*The* ... *is advised by Machiavelli*
~~Machiavelli advises the~~ prince to gain the friendship of the people.

1. The surfers were informed by the lifeguard of a shark sighting.
2. The comic-book artist drew a superhero with amazing crime-fighting powers.
3. For months, the baby kangaroo is protected, fed, and taught how to survive by its mother.
4. The lawns and rooftops were covered with the first snow of winter.
5. A new advertising company was chosen by the board members.

**bedfordstmartins.com/smhandbook** For more exercises on active and passive voice, go to Exercise Central and click on **Verbs**.

## 32h Mood

The mood of a verb indicates the attitude of the writer toward what he or she is saying or writing. The indicative mood states facts and opinions or asks questions. The imperative mood gives commands and instructions. The subjunctive mood (used mainly in clauses beginning with *that* or *if*) expresses wishes or conditions that are contrary to fact.

| | |
|---|---|
| **INDICATIVE** | I *did* the right thing. |
| **IMPERATIVE** | *Do* the right thing. |
| **SUBJUNCTIVE** | If I *had done* the right thing, I would not be in trouble now. |

### 1 Subjunctive mood forms

The present subjunctive uses the base form, no matter what the subject of the verb is.

- **It is important that children *be* psychologically ready for a new sibling.**

The past subjunctive is the same as the simple past except for the verb *be*, which uses *were* for all subjects.

- **He spent money as if he *had* infinite credit.**
- **If the store *were* better located, it would attract more customers.**

### 2 Subjunctive mood in certain dependent clauses

Because the subjunctive can create a rather formal tone, many people today tend to substitute the indicative mood in informal conversation.

- **If I *was* a better swimmer, I would try out for the team.**

Nevertheless, formal writing still requires the use of the subjunctive in the following kinds of dependent clauses:

#### *Clauses expressing a wish*

- **He wished that his mother *were* still living nearby.**

#### As if *and* as though *clauses*

- **He started down the trail as if he *were* walking on ice.**

#### That *clauses expressing a request or demand*

- **The job demands that the employee *be* in good physical condition.**

#### If *clauses expressing a condition that does not exist*

- **If the sale of tobacco *were* banned, tobacco companies *would* suffer a great loss.**

One common error is to use *would* in both clauses. Use the subjunctive in the *if* clause and *would* in the main clause.

- **If I ~~would have~~ had played harder, I would have won.**

### FOR MULTILINGUAL WRITERS: The subjunctive

"If you were to practice writing every day, it would eventually seem much easier to you." For a discussion of this and other uses of the subjunctive, see 57f.

## EXERCISE 32.6

Revise any of the following sentences that do not use the appropriate subjunctive verb forms required in formal writing. Example:

> I saw how carefully he moved, as if he ~~was~~ *were* caring for an infant.

1. Her stepsisters treated Cinderella as though she was a servant.
2. Marvina wished that she was able to take her daughter along on the business trip.
3. Protesters demanded that the senator resign from her post.
4. If more money was available, we would be able to offer more scholarships.
5. It is critical that the liquid remains at room temperature for at least seven hours.

**bedfordstmartins.com/smhandbook** For more exercises on mood, go to Exercise Central and click on **Verbs.**

## THINKING CRITICALLY ABOUT VERBS

**Reading with an Eye for Verbs**

Some years ago a newspaper in San Francisco ran the headline "Giants Crush Cardinals, 3–1," provoking the following friendly advice from John Updike about the art of sports-headline verbs:

> The correct verb, San Francisco, is *whip*. Notice the vigor, force, and scorn obtained. . . . [These examples] may prove helpful: 3–1 — *whip*; 3–2 — *shade*; 2–1 — *edge*. 4–1 gets the coveted verb *vanquish*. Rule: Any three-run margin, *provided the winning total does not exceed ten*, may be described as a vanquishing.

Take the time to study a newspaper with an eye for its verbs. Copy down several examples of strong verbs as well as a few examples of weak or overused verbs. For the weak ones, try to come up with better choices.

**Thinking about Your Own Use of Verbs**

Writing that relies too heavily on the verbs *be*, *do*, and *have* almost always bores readers. Look at something you've written recently to see whether you rely too heavily on these verbs, and revise accordingly.

# Subject-Verb Agreement

# 33

In everyday terms, the word *agreement* refers to an accord of some sort: you reach an agreement with your boss about salary; friends agree to go to a movie; the members of a family agree to share household chores; the United States and Russia negotiate an agreement about reducing nuclear arms. This meaning covers grammatical agreement as well. In academic varieties of English, verbs must agree with their subjects in number (singular or plural) and in person (first, second, or third). In practice, only a very few subject-verb constructions cause confusion.

## 33a Verbs with third-person singular subjects

To make a verb in the present tense agree with a third-person singular subject, add *-s* or *-es* to the base form.

- **A vegetarian diet *lowers* the risk of heart disease.**

To make a verb in the present tense agree with any other subject, use the base form of the verb.

- **I *miss* my family.**
- **They *live* in another state.**

*Have* and *be* do not follow the *-s* or *-es* pattern with third-person singular subjects. *Have* changes to *has*; *be* has irregular forms in both the present and past tenses and in the first person as well as the third person. (See Chapter 32.)

- **War *is* hell.**
- **The soldier *was* brave beyond the call of duty.**

In some varieties of African American or regional English, third-person singular verb forms do not end with *-s* or *-es*.

- **She *go* to work seven days a week.**

In academic English, this sentence would begin *She goes*. You may see verb forms such as this example in literature, especially in dialogue, and you may quote passages using this or other varieties of English in your writing. In most academic writing, however, your audience will expect third-person singular verb forms to end in *-s* or *-es*.

## 33b Subjects and verbs separated by other words

Make sure the verb agrees with the subject and not with another noun that falls in between.

- **A vase of flowers *makes* a room attractive.**

- **Many books on the best-seller list ~~has~~ little literary value.** [have]

  The simple subject is *books*, not *list*.

Be careful when you use phrases beginning with *as well as*, *along with*, *in addition to*, *together with*, or similar prepositions. They do not make a singular subject plural.

- **The president, along with many senators, *opposes* the bill.**

- **A passenger, as well as the driver, ~~were~~ injured in the accident.** [was]

  Though this sentence has a grammatically singular subject, it suggests the idea of a plural subject. The sentence makes better sense with a compound subject: *The driver and a passenger were injured in the accident.*

### EXERCISE 33.1

Underline the appropriate verb form in each of the following sentences. Example:

The benefits of family planning (*is/are*) not apparent to many peasants.

1. Soldiers who are injured while fighting for their country (*deserves/deserve*) complete medical coverage.
2. The dog, along with his owner, (*races/race*) wildly down the street every afternoon.
3. Just when I think I can go home, another pile of invoices (*appears/appear*) on my desk.
4. The system of sororities and fraternities (*supplies/supply*) much of the social life on some college campuses.
5. The buck (*stops/stop*) here.

6. The police officer, in addition to a couple of pedestrians, (*was/were*) pinned to the wall as the crowd rushed by.
7. Garlic's therapeutic value as well as its flavor (*comes/come*) from sulfur compounds.
8. The fiber content of cereal (*contributes/contribute*) to its nutritional value.
9. The graphics on this computer game often (*causes/cause*) my system to crash.
10. Current research on AIDS, in spite of the best efforts of hundreds of scientists, (*leaves/leave*) serious questions unanswered.

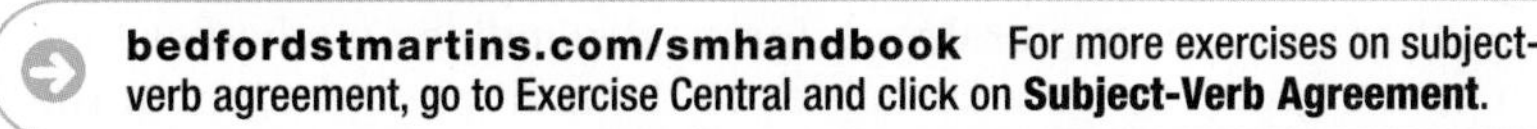

**bedfordstmartins.com/smhandbook** For more exercises on subject-verb agreement, go to Exercise Central and click on **Subject-Verb Agreement.**

## 33c Verbs with compound subjects

Two or more subjects joined by *and* generally require a plural verb form.

- **Tony and his friend *commute* from Louisville.**
- **A backpack, a canteen, and a rifle ~~was~~ were issued to each recruit.**

When subjects joined by *and* are considered a single unit or refer to the same person or thing, they take a singular verb form.

- **George W. Bush's older brother and political ally *is* the governor of Florida.**
- **Drinking and driving ~~remain~~ remains a major cause of highway fatalities.**

  In this sentence, *drinking and driving* is considered a single activity, and a singular verb is used.

If the word *each* or *every* precedes subjects joined by *and*, the verb form is singular.

- **Each boy and girl *chooses* one gift to take home.**

With subjects joined by *or* or *nor*, the verb agrees with the part closest to the verb.

- **Neither my roommate nor my neighbors *like* my loud music.**

▶ **Either the witnesses or the defendant ~~are~~ is lying.**

If you find this sentence awkward, put the plural noun closest to the verb: *Either the defendant or the witnesses are lying.*

## 33d Verbs with collective nouns or fractions

Collective nouns — such as *family, team, audience, group, jury, crowd, band, class,* and *committee* — refer to a group. Collective nouns can take either singular or plural verb forms, depending on whether they refer to the group as a single unit or to the multiple members of the group. The meaning of a sentence as a whole is your guide to whether a collective noun refers to a unit or to the multiple parts of a unit.

▶ **After deliberating, the jury *reports* its verdict.**

The jury acts as a single unit.

▶ **The jury still *disagree* on a number of counts.**

The members of the jury act as multiple individuals.

▶ **The family of ducklings ~~scatters~~ scatter when the cat approaches.**

*Family* here refers to the many ducks; they cannot scatter as one.

Treat fractions that refer to singular nouns as singular and those that refer to plural nouns as plural.

**SINGULAR** Two-thirds of the park *has* burned.

**PLURAL** Two-thirds of the students *were* commuters.

Treat phrases starting with *the number of* as singular and with *a number of* as plural.

**SINGULAR** The number of applicants for the internship *was* unbelievable.

**PLURAL** A number of applicants *were* put on the waiting list.

## 33e Verbs with indefinite-pronoun subjects

Indefinite pronouns do not refer to specific persons or things. Most take singular verb forms.

**SOME COMMON INDEFINITE PRONOUNS**

| | | | |
|---|---|---|---|
| another | each | much | one |
| any | either | neither | other |
| anybody | everybody | nobody | somebody |
| anyone | everyone | no one | someone |
| anything | everything | nothing | something |

- **Of the two jobs, neither *holds* much appeal.**

- **Each of the plays ~~depict~~ depicts a hero undone by a tragic flaw.**

*Both*, *few*, *many*, *others*, and *several* are plural.

- **Though many *apply*, few *are* chosen.**

*All*, *any*, *enough*, *more*, *most*, *none*, and *some* can be singular or plural, depending on the noun they refer to.

- **All of the cake *was* eaten.**

- **All of the candidates *promise* to improve the schools.**

## 33f Verbs with antecedents of *who*, *which*, and *that*

When the relative pronouns *who*, *which*, and *that* are used as a subject, the verb agrees with the antecedent of the pronoun.

- **Fear is an ingredient that *goes* into creating stereotypes.**

- **Guilt and fear are ingredients that *go* into creating stereotypes.**

Problems often occur with the words *one of the*. In general, *one of the* takes a plural verb, while *only one of the* takes a singular verb.

- **Carla is one of the employees who always ~~works~~ work overtime.**

Some employees always work overtime. Carla is among them. Thus *who* refers to *employees*, and the verb is plural.

**Ming is the only one of the employees who always ~~work~~ works overtime.**

Only one employee always works overtime, and that employee is Ming. Thus *one*, and not *employees*, is the antecedent of *who*, and the verb form is singular.

## 33g Linking verbs and their subjects

A linking verb should agree with its subject, which usually precedes the verb, not with the subject complement, which follows it (31c2).

**Three key treaties ~~is~~ are the topic of my talk.**

The subject is *treaties*, not *topic*.

**Nero Wolfe's passion ~~were~~ was orchids.**

The subject is *passion*, not *orchids*.

## 33h Verbs with singular subjects ending in *-s*

Some words that end in *-s* appear plural but are singular and thus take singular verb forms.

**Measles still ~~strike~~ strikes many Americans.**

Some nouns of this kind (such as *statistics* and *politics*) may be either singular or plural, depending on context.

| | |
|---|---|
| **SINGULAR** | Statistics *is* a course I really dread. |
| **PLURAL** | The statistics in that study *are* highly questionable. |

## 33i Verbs with subjects that follow them

In English, verbs usually follow subjects. When this order is reversed, make the verb agree with the subject, not with a noun that happens to precede it.

**Beside the barn ~~stands~~ stand silos filled with grain.**

The subject is *silos*; it is plural, so the verb must be *stand*.

## Editing for subject-verb agreement

- Identify the subject that goes with each verb. Cover up any words between the subject and the verb to identify agreement problems more easily. (33b)
- Check compound subjects. Those joined by *and* usually take a plural verb form. With those subjects joined by *or* or *nor*, however, the verb agrees with the part of the subject closest to the verb. (33c)
- Check collective-noun subjects. These nouns take a singular verb form when they refer to a group as a single unit but a plural form when they refer to the multiple members of a group. (33d)
- Check indefinite-pronoun subjects. Most take a singular verb form. *Both*, *few*, *many*, *others*, and *several* take a plural form; and *all*, *any*, *enough*, *more*, *most*, *none*, and *some* can be either singular or plural, depending on the noun they refer to. (33e)

In sentences beginning with *there is* or *there are* (or *there was* or *there were*), *there* serves only as an introductory word; the subject follows the verb.

**There *are* five basic positions in classical ballet.**

The subject, *positions*, is plural, so the verb must also be plural.

## 33j Verbs with titles and words used as words

When the subject is the title of a book, film, or other work of art, the verb form is singular even if the title is plural in form.

***One Writer's Beginnings* describes Eudora Welty's childhood.**

Similarly, a word referred to as a word requires a singular verb form even if the word itself is plural.

***Steroids* is a little word that packs a big punch in the world of sports.**

### EXERCISE 33.2

Revise any of the following sentences as necessary to establish subject-verb agreement. (Some of the sentences do not require any change.) Example:

Into the shadows ~~dart~~ darts the frightened raccoon.

1. If rhythm and blues is your kind of music, try Mary Lou's.
2. *Green Eggs and Ham* are one of Dr. Suess's best-loved children's books.
3. At the intersection is four gas stations.
4. Most of the students oppose the shortened dining hall hours.
5. Each of the security workers are considered trained after viewing a twenty-minute videotape.
6. Neither his charm nor his expensive wardrobe were enough to get him the job.
7. A jury rarely make a decision based on evidence alone.
8. My grandmother is the only one of my relatives who still goes to church.
9. Sweden was one of the few European countries that was neutral in 1943.
10. Economics involve the study of the distribution of goods and services.

**bedfordstmartins.com/smhandbook** For more exercises on subject-verb agreement, go to Exercise Central and click on **Subject-Verb Agreement**.

## THINKING CRITICALLY ABOUT SUBJECT-VERB AGREEMENT

### Reading with an Eye for Subject-Verb Agreement

The following passage, from a 1990 essay questioning a "traditional" view of marriage, includes several instances of complicated subject-verb agreement. Note the rules governing subject-verb agreement in each case.

> Marriage seems to me more conflict-ridden than ever, and the divorce rate — with or without new babies in the house — remains constant. The fabric of men-and-women-as-they-once-were is so thin in places no amount of patching can weave that cloth together again. The longing for connection may be strong, but even stronger is the growing perception that only people who are real to themselves can connect. Two shall be as one is over, no matter how lonely we get.
>
> — VIVIAN GORNICK, "Who Says We Haven't Made a Revolution?"

### Thinking about Your Own Use of Subject-Verb Agreement

*Visiting relatives is/are treacherous*. Either verb makes a grammatically acceptable sentence, yet the verbs result in two very different statements. Write a brief explanation of the two possible meanings. Then write a paragraph or two about visiting relatives. Using the information in this chapter, examine each subject and its verb. Do you maintain subject-verb agreement throughout? Revise to correct any errors you find. If you find any patterns, make a note to yourself of things to look for routinely as you revise your writing.

# Pronouns

34

Pronouns "are tricky rather than difficult," says H. W. Fowler in *A Dictionary of Modern English Usage.* The trickiness of pronouns results primarily from two potential problems. The first has to do with matching the pronoun with its function in the sentence (choosing "I" rather than "me" for the subject, for example). The second problem comes up when a pronoun stands in for another word — a noun or another pronoun — called the *antecedent.* Choosing the correct pronoun and making sure that the pronoun both agrees with its antecedent and refers clearly to its antecedent can sometimes be tricky tasks.

## 34a Pronoun case

Most speakers of English know intuitively when to use *I*, *me*, or *my*. The choice reflects differences in case, the form a pronoun takes to indicate its function in a sentence. Pronouns functioning as subjects are in the subjective case; those functioning as objects are in the objective case; and those functioning as possessives are in the possessive case.

**SUBJECTIVE PRONOUNS**

I/we you he/she/it they who/whoever

**OBJECTIVE PRONOUNS**

me/us you him/her/it them whom/whomever

**POSSESSIVE PRONOUNS**

my/our your his/hers/its their whose

mine/ours yours his/hers/its theirs

### 1 Subjective case

Use the subjective case when a pronoun is a subject of a clause, a subject complement, or an appositive renaming a subject or subject complement (31c).

**SUBJECT OF A CLAUSE**

*They* could either fight or face certain death with the lions.

*Who* is your closest friend?

Pedro told the story to Carla, *who* told all her friends.

**SUBJECT COMPLEMENT**

The person in charge was *she*.

**APPOSITIVE RENAMING A SUBJECT OR SUBJECT COMPLEMENT**

Three colleagues — Peter, John, and *she* — worked on the program.

Americans often use the objective case for subject complements, especially in conversation: *Who's there? It's me.* Nevertheless, you should use the subjective case in formal writing. If you find the subjective case for a subject complement stilted or awkward, try rewriting the sentence using the pronoun as the subject.

She was the
**~~The~~ first person to see Kishore after the awards. ~~was she.~~**

## 2 Objective case

Use the objective case when a pronoun functions as a direct or indirect object (of a verb or verbal), an object of a preposition, an appositive renaming an object, or a subject of an infinitive (31c2 and c3).

**OBJECT OF A VERB OR VERBAL**

The professor surprised *us* with a quiz. [direct object of *surprised*]

The grateful owner gave *him* a reward. [indirect object of *gave*]

The Parisians were wonderful about helping *me*. [direct object of gerund]

**OBJECT OF A PREPOSITION**

Several friends went with *him*.

**APPOSITIVE RENAMING AN OBJECT**

The committee elected two representatives, Sach and *me*.

**SUBJECT OF AN INFINITIVE**

The students convinced *him* to vote for the school bond.

Use the objective case when the pronoun is preceded by a verb and followed by an infinitive. Though the pronoun in such constructions is called the subject of the infinitive, it is in the objective case because it is the object of the sentence's verb.

## 3 Possessive case

A pronoun should be in the possessive case when it shows possession or ownership. Notice that there are two forms of possessive pronouns: adjective forms, which are used before nouns or gerunds (*my, your, his, her, its, our, their, whose*), and noun forms, which take the place of a noun (*mine, yours, his, hers, its, ours, theirs, whose*).

**ADJECTIVE FORMS**

People were buying *their* tickets weeks in advance of the show.

*Whose* fault was the accident?

**NOUN FORMS**

The responsibility is *hers*.

*Whose* is this blue backpack?

A pronoun that appears before a gerund should be in the possessive case (*my/our*, *your*, *his/her/its*, *their*). Distinguishing gerunds from present participles, which both take *-ing* forms, can be tricky.

- **I remember *his* singing.**

  The gerund *singing* is the object of *remember*.

- **I remember *him* singing.**

  The participle *singing* modifies *him*.

Use the possessive case to emphasize the person; use the objective case if you want to emphasize the action.

## 34b Who, whoever, whom, and whomever

A common problem with pronoun case is deciding whether to use *who* or *whom*. Even when traditional grammar requires *whom*, many Americans use *who* instead, especially in speech. Nevertheless, in formal written English, which includes most college writing, the case of the pronoun should reflect its grammatical function. Use *who* and *whoever*, the subjective-case forms, when the pronoun is a subject or subject complement. Use *whom* and *whomever*, the objective-case forms, when the pronoun is an object.

Two particular situations lead to confusion with *who* and *whom*: when they begin a question and when they introduce a dependent clause.

### 1 Who or whom in a question

You can determine whether to use *who* or *whom* at the beginning of a question by answering the question using a personal pronoun. If the answer is in the subjective case, use *who*; if it is in the objective case, use *whom*.

## TALKING THE TALK: Correctness or stuffiness?

"I think saying *Everyone has their opinion* sounds better than *Everyone has his or her opinion.* And I've never said *whom* in my life. Why should I write that way?" Over time, the conventions governing certain usages — such as *who* versus *whom*, or *their* versus *his or her* when it refers to an indefinite pronoun like *everyone* (34f and g) — have become much more relaxed. To many Americans, *Whom did you talk to?* and *No one finished his or her test* — both of which are technically "correct" — sound unpleasantly fussy. However, other people object to less formal constructions such as *Who did you talk to?* and *No one finished their test*; to them, such usages signal a certain lack of discrimination. How can you please everyone? Unfortunately, you can't. Your best bet is to use whatever you are most comfortable with in speaking but to be more careful in formal writing. If you don't know whether your audience will prefer more or less formality, try recasting your sentence to avoid such constructions.

Who
- **~~Whom~~ do you think wrote the story?**
  ^

I think *she* wrote the story. *She* is subjective; so *who* is correct.

Whom
- **~~Who~~ did you visit?**
  ^

I visited them. *Them* is objective; so *whom* is correct.

### 2 *Who, whoever, whom,* or *whomever* in a dependent clause

The function a pronoun serves in a dependent clause determines whether you should choose *who* or *whom*, *whoever* or *whomever* — no matter how that clause functions in the sentence. If the pronoun acts as a subject or subject complement in the clause, use *who* or *whoever*. If the pronoun acts as an object, use *whom* or *whomever*.

whoever
- **The center is open to ~~whomever~~ wants to use it.**
  ^

*Whoever* is the subject of the clause *whoever wants to use it*. (The clause is the object of the preposition *to*, but the clause's function in the sentence does not affect the case of the pronoun.)

▶ **The new president was not ~~who~~ whom she had expected.**

*Whom* is the object of the verb *had expected* in the clause *whom she had expected.*

If you are not sure which case to use, try separating the dependent clause from the rest of the sentence. Rewrite the clause as a new sentence, and substitute a personal pronoun for *who(ever)* or *whom(ever)*. If the pronoun is in the subjective case, use *who* or *whoever*; if it is in the objective case, use *whom* or *whomever.*

▶ **The minister grimaced at (*whoever/whomever*) made any noise.**

Isolate the clause *whoever/whomever made any noise.* Substituting a personal pronoun gives you *they made any noise. They* is in the subjective case; therefore, *The minister grimaced at whoever made any noise.*

▶ **The minister smiled at (*whoever/whomever*) she greeted.**

Isolate and transpose the clause to get *she greeted whoever/whomever.* Substituting a personal pronoun gives you *she greeted them. Them* is in the objective case; therefore, *The minister smiled at whomever she greeted.*

▶ **The minister grimaced at *whoever* ~~she thought~~ made any noise.**

Ignore such expressions as *he thinks* and *she says* when you isolate the clause.

## EXERCISE 34.1

Insert *who*, *whoever*, *whom*, or *whomever* appropriately in the blank in each of the following sentences. Example:

She is someone __*who*__ will go far.

1. ______ did you say was our most likely suspect?
2. ______ the committee recommends is likely to receive a job offer.
3. The manager promised to reward ______ sold the most cars.
4. Professor Quiñones asked ______ we wanted to collaborate with.
5. ______ received the highest score?

**bedfordstmartins.com/smhandbook** For more exercises on *who* and *whom*, go to Exercise Central and click on **Pronouns.**

## 34c Case in compound structures

When a pronoun is part of a compound subject, complement, object, or appositive, put it in the same case you would use if the pronoun were alone.

- **Come to the park with José and ~~I.~~** me.

  Eliminating the other part of the compound, *José and*, leaves *Come to the park with me.*

- **When ~~him~~** he **and Zelda were first married, they lived in New York.**

- **The next two speakers will be Philip and ~~her.~~** she.

- **The boss invited ~~she~~** her **and her family to dinner.**

- **This morning saw yet another conflict between my sister and ~~I.~~** me.

Pronoun case in a compound appositive is determined by the word the appositive renames. If the word functions as a subject or subject complement, the pronoun should be in the subjective case; if it functions as an object, the pronoun should be in the objective case.

- **Both panelists — Tony and ~~me~~** I **— were stumped.**

  *Panelists* is the subject of the sentence, so the pronoun in the appositive *Tony and I* should be in the subjective case.

## 34d Case in elliptical constructions

In elliptical constructions, some words are left out but understood. When an elliptical construction ends in a pronoun, the pronoun should be in the case it would be in if the construction were complete.

- **His brother has always been more athletic than *he* [is].**

In some elliptical constructions, the case depends on the meaning intended.

- **Willie likes Lily more than *she* [likes Lily].**

  *She* is the subject of the implied clause *she likes Lily.*

- **Willie likes Lily more than [he likes] *her*.**

  *Her* is the object of the verb *likes* in the implied clause *he likes her.*

## 34e *We* and *us* before a noun

If you are unsure about whether to use *we* or *us* before a noun, recast the sentence without the noun. Use whichever pronoun would be correct if the noun were omitted.

- We
  **~~Us~~ fans never give up hope.**
  ^

  *Fans* is the subject, so the pronoun should be subjective.

- us
  **The Rangers depend on ~~we~~ fans.**
  ^

  *Fans* is the object of a preposition, so the pronoun should be objective.

### EXERCISE 34.2

Underline the appropriate pronoun from the pair in parentheses in each of the following sentences. Example:

The possibility of (<u>*their*</u>/*them*) succeeding never occurred to me.

1. Max has had more car accidents than Ruby, but he still insists he is a better driver than (*she*/*her*).

## Editing for case

- Are all pronouns after forms of the verb *be* in the subjective case? (34a1)
- To check for correct use of *who* and *whom* (and *whoever* and *whomever*), try answering the question or rewriting the clause using *he* or *him*. If *he* is correct, use *who* or *whoever*; if *him*, use *whom* or *whomever*. (34b)
- In compound structures, make sure pronouns are in the same case they would be in if used alone (*Jake and she were living in Spain*). (34c)
- When a pronoun follows *than* or *as*, complete the sentence mentally. If the pronoun is the subject of an unstated verb, it should be in the subjective case (*I like her better than he* [*likes her*]). If it is the object of an unstated verb, it should be in the objective case (*I like her better than* [*I like*] *him*). (34d)
- Circle all the pronouns to see if you rely too heavily on any one pronoun or case, especially *I*. If you find that you do, try rewriting some sentences to change *I* to *me*, *she* to *her*, and so on.

2. Going to the ballpark with Uncle Henry and (*they/them*) made everyone feel ten years younger.
3. The coach gave honorable-mention ribbons to the two who didn't win any races — Aiden and (*I/me*).
4. We tried to think of an explanation for (*them/their*) winning the game against all odds.
5. Tomorrow (*we/us*) raw recruits will have our first on-the-job test.

**bedfordstmartins.com/smhandbook** For more exercises on pronoun case, go to Exercise Central and click on **Pronouns**.

## 34f Pronoun-antecedent agreement

The antecedent of the pronoun is the word the pronoun refers to. The antecedent usually appears before the pronoun — earlier in the sentence or in a previous sentence. Pronouns and antecedents are said to agree when they match up in person, number, and gender.

- **The conductor raised *her* baton, and the boys picked up *their* music.**

## 1 Compound antecedents

Compound antecedents joined by *and* require plural pronouns.

- **My parents and I tried to resolve *our* disagreement.**

A compound antecedent preceded by *each* or *every*, however, takes a singular pronoun.

- **Every plant and animal has *its* own ecological niche.**

With a compound antecedent joined by *or* or *nor*, the pronoun agrees with the nearest antecedent. If the parts of the antecedent are of different genders or persons, however, this kind of sentence can be awkward.

**AWKWARD** Neither Annie nor Barry got *his* work done.

**REVISED** Annie didn't get *her* work done, and neither did Barry.

When a compound antecedent contains both singular and plural parts, the sentence may sound awkward unless the plural part comes last.

- **Neither the ~~radio stations~~ newspaper nor the ~~newspaper~~ radio stations would reveal ~~its~~ their sources.**

## 2 Collective-noun antecedents

A collective-noun antecedent (*herd*, *team*, *audience*) that refers to a single unit requires a singular pronoun.

- **The audience fixed *its* attention on center stage.**

When such an antecedent refers to the multiple parts of the unit, however, it requires a plural pronoun.

- **The director chose this cast because *they* had experience in their roles.**

## 3 Indefinite-pronoun antecedents

Indefinite pronouns (33e) do not refer to specific persons or things. A pronoun whose antecedent is an indefinite pronoun should agree with it in number. Many indefinite pronouns are always singular (as with *one*); a few are always plural (as with *many*). Some can be singular or plural depending on the context.

### Editing for pronoun-antecedent agreement

- Check all subjects joined by *and*, *or*, or *nor* to be sure they are treated as singular or plural, as appropriate. Recast any sentence in which agreement creates awkwardness. (34f1)
- Check all uses of *anyone*, *each*, *everybody*, *many*, and other indefinite pronouns (see list in 33e) to be sure they are treated as singular or plural, as appropriate. (34f3 and 34g)
- If you find *he*, *his*, or *him* used to refer to persons of either sex, revise the pronouns, or recast the sentences altogether. (34g)

- **One of the ballerinas lost *her* balance.**
- **Many in the audience jumped to *their* feet.**
- **Some of the furniture was showing *its* age.** [singular meaning for *some*]
- **Some of the farmers abandoned *their* land.** [plural meaning for *some*]

## 34g Sexist pronouns

Indefinite pronouns (33e) often refer to antecedents that may be either male or female. Writers used to use a masculine pronoun, known as the generic *he*, in such cases. However, many people have pointed out that wording that ignores or excludes females should be avoided.

When an antecedent is a singular indefinite pronoun, some people avoid the generic *he* by using a plural pronoun.

- **Everybody had *their* own theories about Jennifer's resignation.**

Although this usage is gaining acceptance, many readers still consider it incorrect. In formal writing, do not use a plural pronoun to refer to a grammatically singular indefinite pronoun.

- **Everybody had a theory about Jennifer's resignation.**

### EXERCISE 34.3

Revise the following sentences as needed to create pronoun-antecedent agreement and to eliminate the generic *he* and any awkward pronoun references. Some can be revised in more than one way. Example:

## Editing out the generic use of *he, his,* or *him*

**Every citizen should know *his* rights under the law.**

Here are three ways to express the same idea without *his*:

1. Revise to make the antecedent plural.

   *All citizens should know* their *legal rights.*

2. Revise the sentence altogether.

   *Every citizen should have some knowledge of basic legal rights.*

3. Use both masculine and feminine pronouns.

   *Every citizen should know* his *or* her *legal rights.*

The last option can be awkward when repeated several times in a passage.

or her
Every graduate submitted his diploma card.
^

All graduates their cards.
~~Every graduate~~ submitted ~~his~~ diploma ~~card.~~
^ ^ ^

1. With tuition on the rise, a student has to save money wherever they can.
2. Congress usually resists a president's attempt to encroach on what they consider their authority.
3. Marco and Ellen were each given a chance to voice their opinion.
4. Although a firefighter spends most of his days reading and watching television, he is ready to answer an urgent call at a moment's notice.
5. Every dog and cat has their own personality.

**bedfordstmartins.com/smhandbook** For more exercises on pronoun-antecedent agreement, go to Exercise Central and click on **Pronouns**.

## 34h Ambiguous pronoun references

If a pronoun can refer to more than one antecedent, revise the sentence to make the meaning clear.

the bridge
▶ **The car went over the bridge just before ~~it~~ fell into the water.**
^

What fell into the water — the car or the bridge? The revision makes the meaning clear by replacing the pronoun *it* with *the bridge.*

"I
▶ **Kerry told Ellen, ~~she~~ should be ready soon."**
^

Reporting Kerry's words directly, in quotation marks, eliminates the ambiguity.

If a pronoun and its antecedent are too far apart, you may need to replace the pronoun with the appropriate noun.

▶ **The right-to-life coalition believes that a *zygote*, an egg at the moment of fertilization, is as deserving of protection as is the born human being and thus that abortion is as much murder as is the killing of a child. The coalition's focus is on what ~~it~~** the zygote **will become as much as on what it is now.**

In the original, the pronoun *it* is too far away from the antecedent *zygote* in the first sentence, thus making the second sentence unclear to readers.

## 34i Vague use of *it, this, that,* and *which*

Writers often use *it*, *this*, *that*, or *which* as a shortcut for referring to something mentioned earlier. But such shortcuts can cause confusion. Make sure that these pronouns refer clearly to a specific antecedent.

▶ **When the senators realized the bill would be defeated, they tried to postpone the vote but failed. ~~It~~** The entire effort **was a fiasco.**

▶ **Nancy just found out that she won the lottery, ~~which~~** and her sudden wealth **explains her resignation.**

If a *that* or *which* clause refers to a specific noun, put the clause directly after the noun, if possible.

- **We worked all night on the float ~~for the Rose Parade~~ that our club was going to sponsor** ^for the Rose Parade.

Does *that* refer to the float or the parade? The editing makes the meaning clear.

## 34j Inappropriate use of *who, which*, and *that*

Be careful to use *who*, *which*, and *that* appropriately. *Who* refers primarily to people or to animals with names. *Which* refers to animals or to things, and *that* refers to animals, things, and occasionally anonymous or collective groups of people.

- **The veterinarian ~~that~~** ^who **operated saved my dog's life.**
- **Cats, ~~who~~** ^which **are my favorite animals, often remain aloof from their owners.**

## 34k Indefinite use of *you, it,* and *they*

In conversation, we frequently use *you*, *it*, and *they* in an indefinite sense in such expressions as *you never know*; *it said in the paper*; and *on television, they said*. In college writing, however, use *you* only to mean "you, the reader," and *they* or *it* only to refer to a clear antecedent.

- **Commercials try to make ~~you~~** ^people **buy without thinking.**
- ^The **~~On the~~ Weather Channel~~, it~~ reported that the earthquake devastated parts of Pakistan.**
- ^Most restaurants in France **~~In France, they~~ allow dogs**^. **~~in most restaurants.~~**

## 34l Implied antecedents

Though an adjective or possessive may imply a noun antecedent, it does not serve as a clear antecedent.

**In** her **~~Alexa's~~ formal complaint,** Alexa **~~she~~ showed why the test question was wrong.**

### EXERCISE 34.4

Revise each of the following items to clarify pronoun reference. Most of the items can be revised in more than one way. If a pronoun refers ambiguously to more than one possible antecedent, revise the sentence to reflect each possible meaning. Example:

> Miranda found Jane's keys after ~~After~~ Jane left~~,~~. ~~Miranda found her keys.~~
>
> Miranda found her own keys after ~~After~~ Jane left~~,~~. ~~Miranda found her keys.~~

1. All scholarship applicants must fill out a financial aid form, meet with the dean, and write a letter to the committee members. The deadline is October 24, so they should start the process as soon as possible.
2. Patients on medication may relate better to their therapists, be less vulnerable to what disturbs them, and be more responsive to them.
3. Sasha hurried to call her sister before she flew to Brazil.
4. In Texas, you often hear about the influence of big oil corporations.
5. Company policy prohibited smoking, which many employees resented.

**bedfordstmartins.com/smhandbook** For more exercises on pronoun reference, go to Exercise Central and click on **Pronouns**.

### Editing for clear pronoun reference

1. Identify a specific antecedent that each pronoun refers to. If you cannot find a specific antecedent, supply one. (34h, i, and k)
2. If the pronoun refers to more than one antecedent, revise the sentence. If the pronoun and its antecedent are so far apart that the reader cannot connect the two, replace the pronoun with the appropriate noun. (34h)
3. Be sure that any use of *you* refers to your specific reader or readers. (34k)

### EXERCISE 34.5

Revise the following paragraph to establish a clear antecedent for every pronoun that needs one.

In the summer of 2005, the NCAA banned the use of mascots that could be considered offensive to American Indians at any of their championship games. In order to understand this, it is important to consider that movies and television programs for years portrayed them as savage warriors that were feared and misunderstood. That is why some schools have chosen to use Indians as their mascot, a role typically played by wild animals or fictional beasts. You would not tolerate derogatory terms for other ethnic groups being used for school mascots. In the NCAA's new ruling, they ask schools to eliminate mascots that may be hurtful or offensive to America's Indian population.

**bedfordstmartins.com/smhandbook** For more exercises on pronoun-antecedent agreement, go to Exercise Central and click on **Pronouns**.

## THINKING CRITICALLY ABOUT PRONOUNS

**Reading with an Eye for Pronouns**

Read the following passage from a brief review of *Harry Potter and the Goblet of Fire*, paying special attention to every pronoun: What antecedent does it refer to, and is the reference clear and direct? Does the use of any one pronoun case seem overused? Then go through and replace every pronoun with what it refers to, and read the two versions side by side to see the efficiency of good pronoun use.

> Sexual attraction has entered the Harry Potter universe. Harry (Daniel Radcliffe) is now 14, and he's one of four contestants competing in the dangerous Tri-Wizard Tournament. The first event requires him to capture a golden egg that's guarded by a ferocious Hungarian flying dragon. Terrifying as this is, it pales in comparison with having to ask the beguiling Cho Chang (Katie Leung) to Hogwarts's Yule Ball. Now, *that* takes courage. . . .
>
> The uncontestable triumph of "Goblet of Fire," however, is Brendan Gleeson's Alastor (Mad-Eye) Moody, the grizzled new Defense Against the Dark Arts professor. With a face like cracked pottery and a manner both menacing and mentoring, he becomes Harry's protector as he faces life-threatening tests. Gleeson, one of the screen's greatest character actors, steals every scene he's in — no small feat when you're up against Maggie Smith and Alan Rickman.
>
> — DAVID ANSEN

**Thinking about Your Own Use of Pronouns**

Turn to a recent piece of your writing (something at least four pages long), and analyze your use of pronouns. Look carefully at the pronoun case you tend to use most; if it is first person, ask whether *I* is used too much. And if you find that you rely heavily on any one case (*you*, for example), decide whether your writing seems monotonous as a result. Take a look as well at whether you tend to use masculine pronouns exclusively to refer to people generally; if so, ask whether you would be more inclusive if you used both masculine and feminine pronouns or if you should revise to use plural pronouns that are not marked as either masculine or feminine (such as *we* or *they*). Finally, check to make sure that your pronouns and their antecedents agree and that the pronouns refer clearly and directly to antecedents.

# Adjectives and Adverbs

# 35

As words that describe other words, adjectives and adverbs add liveliness and color to writing, helping writers show rather than just tell. In addition, adjectives and adverbs often provide indispensable meanings to the words they modify. In basketball, for example, there is an important difference between a *flagrant* foul and a *technical* foul, a layup and a *reverse* layup, or an *angry* coach and an *abusively angry* coach. In each instance, the modifiers are crucial to accurate communication.

## 35a Distinguishing adjectives from adverbs

Adjectives modify nouns and pronouns, answering the question *which? how many?* or *what kind?* Adverbs modify verbs, adjectives, other adverbs, or entire clauses; they answer the question *how? when? where?* or *to what extent?* Many adverbs are formed by adding *-ly* to adjectives (*slight, slightly*), but many are not (*outdoors, very*). And some words that end in *-ly* are adjectives (*lovely, homely*). To tell adjectives and adverbs apart, identify the word's function in the sentence.

## 35b Adjectives after linking verbs

When adjectives come after linking verbs, they usually describe the subject: *I am patient.* Note that in specific sentences, some verbs may or may not act as linking verbs — *look, appear, sound, feel, smell, taste, grow,* and *prove,* for instance. When a word following one of these verbs modifies the subject, use an adjective; when the word modifies the verb, use an adverb.

**ADJECTIVE** Fluffy looked *angry.*

**ADVERB** Fluffy looked *angrily* at the poodle.

Linking verbs suggest a state of being, not an action. In the preceding examples, *looked angry* suggests the state of being angry; *looked angrily* suggests an angry action.

**FOR MULTILINGUAL WRITERS: Adjectives with plural nouns**

In Spanish, Russian, and many other languages, adjectives agree in number with the nouns they modify. In English, however, adjectives do not change number this way: *her kittens are cute* (not *cutes*).

## 35c Adverbs

In everyday conversation, you will often hear (and perhaps use) adjectives in place of adverbs. When you write in standard academic English, however, use adverbs to modify verbs, adjectives, and other adverbs.

- **You can feel the song's meter if you listen ~~careful~~ carefully.**
- **The audience was ~~real~~ really disappointed by the show.**

**FOR MULTILINGUAL WRITERS: Adjective sequence**

Should you write *these beautiful blue kitchen tiles* or *these blue beautiful kitchen tiles*? See 58f for guidelines on adjective sequence.

### Good *and* well, bad *and* badly

The modifiers *good*, *well*, *bad*, and *badly* cause problems for many writers because the distinctions between *good* and *well* and between *bad* and *badly* are often not observed in conversation. Problems also arise because *well* can function as either an adjective or an adverb. *Good* and *bad* are always adjectives, and both can be used after a linking verb. Do not use them to modify a verb, an adjective, or an adverb; use *well* or *badly* instead.

- **The weather looks *good* today.**
- **We had a *bad* night with the new baby.**

**He plays the trumpet ~~good~~** well **and the trombone not ~~bad.~~** badly.

*Badly* is an adverb and can be used to modify a verb, an adjective, or another adverb. Do not use it after a linking verb; use *bad* instead.

**In her first recital, the soprano sang *badly*.**

**I feel ~~badly~~** bad **for the Cubs' fans.**

As an adjective, *well* means "in good health"; as an adverb, it means "in a good manner" or "thoroughly."

| | |
|---|---|
| **ADJECTIVE** | After a week of rest, Julio felt *well* again. |
| **ADVERB** | She plays *well* enough to make the team. |

### Right *smart*, wicked *fun*

Most regions have certain characteristic adjectives and adverbs. Some of the most colorful are intensifiers, adverbs meaning *very* or *absolutely*. In parts of the South, for example, and particularly in Appalachia, you are likely to hear the following: *He paid a right smart price for that car* or *She was plumb tuckered out*. In New England, you might hear *That party was wicked fun*. In each case, the adverb (*right*, *plumb*, *wicked*) acts to intensify the meaning of the adjective (*smart*, *tuckered out*, *fun*).

As with all language, use regional adjectives and adverbs only when they are appropriate (28d). In writing about a family member in Minnesota, for example, you might well quote her, bringing midwestern expressions into your writing. For most academic writing, however, you should use academic English.

### EXERCISE 35.1

Revise each of the following sentences to maintain correct adverb and adjective use. Then identify each adjective or adverb that you have revised, and point out the word each modifies. Example:

The attorney delivered a ~~superb~~ superbly conceived summation.

1. Getting tickets at this late date is near impossible.
2. Derek apologized for behaving so violent and immature on the football field.

3. Nora felt badly that the package would arrive one week later than promised.
4. The summers are real hot and humid here, but in the winter the wind chill is frequent below zero.
5. He talked loud about volunteering, but he was not really interested.
6. Paramedics rushed to help the victim, who was bleeding bad from the head.
7. The skater performed good despite the intense competition.
8. Arjun felt terrifically about his discussion with Professor Greene.
9. After we added cinnamon, the stew tasted really well.
10. Scientists measured the crater as accurate as possible.

**bedfordstmartins.com/smhandbook** For more exercises on adjectives and adverbs, go to Exercise Central and click on **Adjectives and Adverbs**.

## 35d Comparatives and superlatives

Most adjectives and adverbs have three forms: positive, comparative, and superlative.

| POSITIVE | COMPARATIVE | SUPERLATIVE |
|---|---|---|
| large | larger | largest |
| early | earlier | earliest |
| careful | more careful | most careful |
| delicious | more delicious | most delicious |

- **Canada is *larger* than the United States.**
- **My son needs to be *more careful* with his money.**
- **This is the *most delicious* coffee we have tried.**

The comparative and superlative of most short (one-syllable and some two-syllable) adjectives are formed by adding *-er* and *-est*. With some two-syllable adjectives, longer adjectives, and most adverbs, use *more* and *most*: *scientific*, *more scientific*, *most scientific; elegantly*, *more elegantly*, *most elegantly*. If you are not sure whether a word has *-er* and *-est* forms, consult the dictionary entry for the simple form.

### 1 Irregular forms

Some adjectives and adverbs have irregular comparative and superlative forms.

| POSITIVE | COMPARATIVE | SUPERLATIVE |
|---|---|---|
| good, well | better | best |
| bad, badly, ill | worse | worst |
| little (quantity) | less | least |
| many, some, much | more | most |

## 2 Comparatives vs. superlatives

In academic writing, use the comparative to compare two things; use the superlative to compare three or more.

- **Rome is a much *older* city than New York.**

- **Damascus is one of the ~~older~~ oldest cities in the world.**

- **Which of the two candidates is the ~~strongest~~ stronger for the job?**

## 3 Double comparatives and superlatives

Double comparatives and superlatives unnecessarily use both *more* or *most* and the *-er* or *-est* ending. Occasionally they can act to build a special emphasis, as in the title of Spike Lee's movie *Mo' Better Blues*. In college writing, however, make sure not to use *more* or *most* before adjectives or adverbs ending in *-er* or *-est*.

- **Paris is the ~~most~~ loveliest city in the world.**

## 4 Incomplete comparisons

Be sure that comparisons you make in writing are complete and clear (41e).

- **The patients taking the drug appeared healthier~~.~~** than those receiving a placebo.

## 5 Absolute concepts

Some adjectives and adverbs — such as *perfect*, *final*, and *unique* — are absolute concepts, so it is illogical to form comparatives or superlatives of these words.

- **Anne has ~~the most~~ a unique sense of humor.**

### 6 Multiple negatives

Some speakers of English sometimes use more than one negative at a time (*I can't hardly see you*). Emphatic double negatives — and triple, quadruple, and more — appear in African American vernacular English (*Don't none of you know nothing at all*).

Even though double negatives occur in many varieties of English (and in many other languages), in academic or professional writing you will play it safe if you avoid them — unless you are quoting regional dialogue or creating a special effect.

## 35e Nouns as modifiers

Sometimes a noun can function as an adjective by modifying another noun, as in *chicken soup* or *money supply*. If noun modifiers pile up, however, they can obscure meaning.

**AWKWARD** The cold war–era Rosenberg espionage trial and execution continues to arouse controversy.

**REVISED** The Rosenbergs' trial and execution for espionage during the cold war continues to arouse controversy.

### Editing adjectives and adverbs

- Scrutinize each adjective and adverb. Consider synonyms for each one to see whether you have chosen the best word possible.
- See if a more specific noun would eliminate the need for an adjective (*mansion* rather than *enormous house*, for instance); do the same with verbs and adverbs.
- Consider adding an adjective or adverb that might make your writing more vivid or specific.
- Make sure all adjectives modify nouns or pronouns and all adverbs modify verbs, adjectives, or other adverbs. (35a) Check especially for proper use of *good* and *well*, *bad* and *badly*, *real* and *really*. (35c)
- Make sure all comparisons are complete. (35d4)
- If English is not your first language, check that adjectives are in the right order. (58f)

## EXERCISE 35.2

Revise each of the following sentences to use modifiers correctly, clearly, and effectively. Many of the sentences can be revised in more than one way. Example:

> bill to approve a financial plan for the
> He is sponsoring a ^ housing project. ^ ~~finance plan approval bill.~~

1. Alicia speaks both Russian and German, but she speaks Russian best.
2. People in Rome are more friendlier to children than people in Paris are.
3. The crown is set with some of the preciousest gemstones in the world.
4. Most of the elderly are women because women tend to live longer.
5. Minneapolis is the largest of the Twin Cities.
6. She came up with the most perfect plan for revenge.
7. We think you will be pleased with our very unique design proposal.
8. The student cafeteria is operated by a college food service system chain.
9. It is safer to jog in daylight.
10. Evan argued that subtitled films are boringer to watch than films dubbed in English.

**bedfordstmartins.com/smhandbook** For more exercises on comparatives and superlatives, go to Exercise Central and click on **Adjectives and Adverbs**.

## THINKING CRITICALLY ABOUT ADJECTIVES AND ADVERBS

**Reading with an Eye for Adjectives and Adverbs**

> Gwendolyn Brooks "describes the 'graceful life' as one where people glide over floors in softly glowing rooms, smile correctly over trays of silver, cinnamon, and cream, and retire in quiet elegance."
>
> — MARY HELEN WASHINGTON, "Taming All That Anger Down"

Identify the adjectives and adverbs in the preceding passage, and comment on what they add to the writing. What would be lost if they were removed?

**Thinking about Your Own Use of Adjectives and Adverbs**

Take a few minutes to study something you can observe or examine closely. In a paragraph or two, describe your subject for someone who has never seen it. Using the guidelines in this chapter, check your use of adjectives and adverbs, and revise your paragraphs. How would you characterize your use of adjectives and adverbs?

# Part 7

# SENTENCE CLARITY

# 36 Shifts

A shift in writing is an abrupt change of some sort that results in inconsistency. Sometimes writers shift deliberately, as Dave Barry does in noting he "would have to say that the greatest single achievement of the American medical establishment is nasal spray." Barry's shift in tone from the serious (the American medical establishment) to the banal (nasal spray) makes us laugh, as Barry wishes us to. Although writers sometimes deliberately make such shifts for good reasons, unintentional shifts can be jolting and confusing to readers.

## 36a Shifts in tense

If the verbs in a passage refer to actions occurring at different times, they may require different tenses. Be careful, however, not to change tenses for no reason.

- **A few countries produce almost all of the world's illegal drugs, but addiction ~~affected~~ affects many countries.**

## 36b Shifts in mood

Be careful not to shift from one mood to another without good reason. The mood of a verb can be indicative (*he closes the door*), imperative (*close the door*), or subjunctive (*if the door were closed*). (See 32h.)

- **Keep your eye on the ball, and ~~you should~~ bend your knees.**

  The writer's purpose is to give orders, but the original version shifts unnecessarily from the imperative to the indicative; the editing makes both verbs imperative.

## 36c Shifts in voice

Do not shift without reason between the active voice (*she sold it*) and the passive voice (*it was sold*). (See 32g.) Sometimes a shift in voice is justified, but often it only confuses readers.

me
▶ **Two youths approached ~~me,~~ and ~~I was~~ asked ^ for my wallet.**

The original sentence shifts from the active (*youths approached*) to the passive (*I was asked*), so it is unclear who asked for the wallet. Making both verbs active clears up the confusion.

## 36d Shifts in person and number

Unnecessary shifts in point of view between first person (*I*, *we*), second person (*you*), and third person (*he*, *she*, *it*, *one*, or *they*) or between singular and plural subjects can be very confusing to readers.

You
▶ **~~One~~ ^ can do well on this job if you budget your time.**

Is the writer making a general statement or giving advice to someone? Eliminating the shift eliminates this confusion.

nurses have
▶ **Nurses receive much less pay than doctors, even though ~~a nurse has~~ ^ the primary responsibility for daily patient care.**

The writer had no reason to shift from third-person plural (*nurses*) to third-person singular (*a nurse*).

Many shifts in number are actually problems with pronoun-antecedent agreement (34f).

| | |
|---|---|
| **INCONSISTENT** | I have difficulty seeing another *person's* position, especially if *their* opinion contradicts mine. |
| **REVISED** | I have difficulty seeing other *people's* positions, especially if *their* opinions contradict mine. |
| **REVISED** | I have difficulty seeing another *person's* position, especially if *his or her* opinion contradicts mine. |

### FOR MULTILINGUAL WRITERS: Shifts in speech

If Al said to Maria, "I will marry you," why did she then correctly tell her mom, "He said that he *would* marry me"? For guidelines on reporting speech, see 59c.

## 36e Shifts between direct and indirect discourse

When you quote someone's exact words, you are using direct discourse: *She said, "I'm an editor."* When you report what someone says without repeating the exact words, you are using indirect discourse: *She said she was an editor.* (See 59c.) Shifting between direct and indirect discourse in the same sentence can cause problems, especially with questions.

- **Viet asked what ~~could~~ he could ~~he~~ do to help~~?~~.**

The editing eliminates an awkward shift by reporting Viet's question indirectly. The sentence could also be edited to quote Viet directly: *Viet asked, "What can I do to help?"*

### EXERCISE 36.1

Revise the following sentences to eliminate unnecessary shifts in tense, mood, voice, or person and number and between direct and indirect discourse. Most of the items can be revised in more than one way. Examples:

When a person goes to college, you face many new situations.
When a person goes to college, he or she faces many new situations.
When people go to college, they face many new situations.

1. The greed of the 1980s gave way to the occupational insecurity of the 1990s, which in turn gives way to reinforced family ties in the early 2000s.
2. The building inspector suggested that we apply for a construction permit and that we should check with his office again when the plans are complete.
3. She studied the package, wondered what could it be, and tore off the wrapping.
4. Suddenly, we heard an explosion of wings off to our right, and you could see a hundred or more ducks lifting off from the water.
5. In my previous job, I sold the most advertising spots and was given a sales excellence award.
6. A cloud of snow powder rose as skis and poles fly in every direction.
7. The flight attendant said, "Please turn off all electronic devices," but that we could use them again after takeoff.
8. Workers with computer skills were in great demand, and a programmer could almost name their salary.
9. When in Florence, be sure to see the city's famed cathedral, and many tourists also visit Michelangelo's statue *David*.
10. The aroma, which wafts through the house, lured the adults from their beds.

**bedfordstmartins.com/smhandbook** For more exercises on shifts, go to Exercise Central and click on **Shifts**.

## 36f Shifts in tone and diction

Tone, a writer's attitude toward a topic or audience, is related to diction or word choice, and to overall formality or informality. Watch out for tone or diction shifts that could confuse readers and leave them wondering what your real attitude is. (See 7g4.)

**INCONSISTENT TONE**

The question of child care forces a society to make profound decisions about its economic values. Can most families with children actually live adequately on only one salary? If some conservatives had their way, June Cleaver would still be stuck in the kitchen baking cookies for Wally and the Beaver and waiting for Ward to bring home the bacon, except that with only one income, the Cleavers would be lucky to afford hot dogs.

In the preceding version, the first two sentences set a serious, formal tone as they discuss child care in fairly general, abstract terms. But in the third sentence, the writer shifts suddenly to sarcasm, to references

### Editing for confusing shifts

- Make sure you have a reason for shifting from one verb tense to another. (36a)
- Make sure that any shifts in mood — perhaps from an indicative statement to an imperative — are necessary. (36b)
- Check for shifts from active voice (*She asks questions*) to passive voice (*Questions are asked*). Are they intentional — and if so, for what reason? (36c)
- Make sure you have good reasons for any shifts in person or number — from *we* to *you*, for example. (36d)
- Revise sentences that shift incorrectly between direct and indirect discourse. (36e)
- Check your writing for consistency in tone and diction. If your tone is serious, make sure it is consistently so. (36f)

to television characters of an earlier era, and to informal language like *stuck* and *bring home the bacon*. Readers cannot tell whether the writer is presenting a serious analysis or preparing for a humorous satire. The revision makes the tone consistently formal.

**REVISED**

> The question of child care forces a society to make profound decisions about its economic values. Can most families with young children actually live adequately on only one salary? Some conservatives believe that women with young children should not work outside the home, but many mothers are forced to do so for financial reasons.

## THINKING CRITICALLY ABOUT SHIFTS

**Reading with an Eye for Shifts**

The following paragraph includes several necessary shifts in person and number. Read the paragraph carefully, marking all such shifts. Notice how careful the author must be as he shifts back and forth among pronouns.

> It has been one of the great errors of our time to think that by thinking about thinking, and then talking about it, we could possibly straighten out and tidy up our minds. There is no delusion more damaging than to get the idea in your head that you understand the functioning of your own brain. Once you acquire such a notion, you run the danger of moving in to take charge, guiding your thoughts, shepherding your mind from place to place, controlling it, making lists of regulations. The human mind is not meant to be governed, certainly not by any book of rules yet written; it is supposed to run itself, and we are obliged to follow it along, trying to keep up with it as best we can. It is all very well to be aware of your awareness, even proud of it, but never try to operate it. You are not up to the job.
>
> — LEWIS THOMAS, "The Attic of the Brain"

**Thinking about Any Shifts in Your Own Writing**

Find an article about a well-known person you admire. Then write a paragraph or two about him or her, making a point of using both direct and indirect discourse. Using the information in 36e, check your writing for any inappropriate shifts between direct and indirect discourse, and revise as necessary.

# Parallelism

37

## 37a Parallel structures in series, lists, outlines, and headings

All items in a series should be in parallel form — all nouns, all prepositional phrases, all adverb clauses, and so on. Such parallelism makes a series both graceful and easy to follow.

- **The quarter horse skipped, pranced, and ~~was sashaying.~~** sashayed.

- **The children ran down the hill, skipped over the lawn, and** jumped **into the swimming pool.**

- **The duties of the job include baby-sitting, house-cleaning, and ~~preparation of~~** preparing **meals.**

Items in a list should be parallel.

- **Kitchen rules: (1) Coffee to be made only by library staff. (2) Coffee service to be closed at 4:00 PM. (3) Doughnuts to be kept in cabinet. (4) ~~No faculty members should handle coffee materials.~~** Coffee materials not to be handled by faculty.

Items on a formal outline and headings in a paper should be parallel. Section 37b, for example, uses parallel prepositional phrases for each of its two lower-level headings.

Parallel grammatical structures are common not only in everyday expressions — *sink or swim* — but also in elegant prose. See how Jonathan Franzen uses parallelism in talking about a job:

*Since* I was paid better than the minimum wage, and *since* I enjoyed topological packing puzzles, and *since* the Geyers liked me and gave me lots of cake, it was remarkable *how* fiercely I hated the job — *how* I envied even those friends of mine who *manned* the deep-fry station at Long John Silver's or *cleaned* the oil traps at Kentucky Fried Chicken.

The parallelism indicated by the underscores brings a sense of orderliness to a long yet cohesive sentence. Making similar structures parallel will help clarify your writing.

## 37b Parallel structures to pair ideas

Parallel structures can help you pair two ideas effectively. The more nearly parallel the two structures are, the stronger the connection between the ideas will be. Parallel structures are especially appropriate when two ideas are compared or contrasted.

- **History became popular, and historians became alarmed.**
  — WILL DURANT

- **I type in one place, but I write all over the house.** — TONI MORRISON

To create an especially forceful impression, writers may construct a balanced sentence, one with two clauses that mirror each other.

- **Mankind must put an end to war, or war will put an end to mankind.**
  — JOHN F. KENNEDY

### *With coordinating conjunctions*

When you link ideas with a coordinating conjunction — *and, but, or, nor, for, so, yet* — try to make the ideas parallel in structure.

- **We performed *whenever folks would listen* and *wherever they would pay*.**

- **Consult a friend ^who is^ in your class or who is good at math.**

### *With correlative conjunctions*

Use the same structure after both parts of a correlative conjunction — *either . . . or, both . . . and, neither . . . nor, not . . . but, not only . . . but also, just as . . . so, whether . . . or.*

- **The organization provided both *scholarships for young artists* and *grants for established ones*.**

- **I wanted not only to go away to school but also to ^live in^ New England.**

  The edited sentence is more balanced. Both parts of the correlative conjunction (*not only . . . but also*) precede a verb.

### EXERCISE 37.1

Complete the following sentences, using parallel words or phrases in each case. Example:

> The wise politician *promises the possible*, *faces the unavoidable*, and *accepts the inevitable*.

1. Before buying a used car, you should ______, ______, and ______.
2. My favorite pastimes include ______, ______, and ______.
3. Working in a restaurant taught me not only ______ but also ______.
4. We must either ______ or ______.
5. Graduates find that the job market ______, ______, and ______.

### EXERCISE 37.2

Revise the following sentences as necessary to eliminate any errors in parallel structure. Example:

> I enjoy skiing, playing the guitar, and ~~I send~~ sending email to my friends.

1. I remember watching it the first time, realizing I'd never seen anything like it, and immediately vowed never to miss an episode of *The Daily Show*.
2. A crowd stood outside the school and were watching as the graduates paraded by.
3. An effective Web site is well designed, provides useful information, and links are given to other relevant sites.
4. It is impossible to watch *The Simpsons* and not seeing a little of yourself in one of the characters.
5. TV networks now face the question of either coming up with new situations, or they'll have to acknowledge the death of the sitcom.

**bedfordstmartins.com/smhandbook** For more exercises on parallelism, go to Exercise Central and click on **Parallelism**.

## 37c Including all necessary words

In addition to making parallel elements grammatically similar, be careful to include all words — prepositions, articles, verb forms, and so on — that are necessary for clarity or grammar. (See also 41e.)

in
**We'll move to a city in the Southwest or ^ Mexico.**

To a city in Mexico or to Mexico in general? The editing makes the meaning clear.

seen
**I had never before ^ and would never again see such a sight.**

In the unedited version, *had . . . see* is not grammatical.

## 37d Parallelism for emphasis and effect

Parallel structures can help a writer emphasize the most important ideas in a sentence, as Joan Didion does in the following sentence:

> I would like to promise her that she will grow up with a sense of her cousins and of rivers and of her great-grandmother's teacups, would like to pledge her a picnic on a river with fried chicken and her hair uncombed, would like to give her *home* for her birthday, but we live differently now and I can promise her nothing like that.
> — JOAN DIDION, "On Going Home"

The first two parallel phrases — *would like to promise her, would like to pledge her* — introduce a series of specific, concrete details and images that lead up to the general statement in the last phrase, that she

### Editing for parallelism

- Look for any series of three or more items, and make all of the items parallel in structure. If you want to emphasize one particular item, try putting it at the end of the series. (37a and d)
- Be sure items in lists are parallel in form. (37a)
- Be sure headings are parallel in form. (37a)
- Check for sentences that compare, contrast, or otherwise pair two ideas. Often these ideas will appear on either side of *and, but, or, nor, for, so,* or *yet* or after each part of *either . . . or, both . . . and, neither . . . nor, not only . . . but also, just as . . . so,* or *whether . . . or*. Edit to make the two ideas parallel in structure. (37b)
- Check all parallel structures to be sure you have included all necessary words — articles, prepositions, the *to* of the infinitive, and so on. (37c)

*would like to give her* daughter a sense of home. Although Didion could have stated this general point first and then gone on to illustrate it with concrete details, she achieves greater emphasis by making it the last in a series of parallel structures.

## THINKING CRITICALLY ABOUT PARALLELISM

**Reading with an Eye for Parallelism**

Read the following paragraph about a bareback rider practicing her circus act, and identify all the parallel structures. Consider what effect they create on you as a reader, and try to decide why the author chose to put his ideas in such overtly parallel form. Try imitating the next-to-last sentence, the one beginning *In a week or two*.

> The richness of the scene was in its plainness, its natural condition — of horse, of ring, of girl, even to the girl's bare feet that gripped the bare back of her proud and ridiculous mount. The enchantment grew not out of anything that happened or was performed but out of something that seemed to go round and around and around with the girl, attending her, a steady gleam in the shape of a circle — a ring of ambition, of happiness, of youth. (And the positive pleasures of equilibrium under difficulties.) In a week or two, all would be changed, all (or almost all) lost: the girl would wear makeup, the horse would wear gold, the ring would be painted, the bark would be clean for the feet of the horse, the girl's feet would be clean for the slippers that she'd wear. All, all would be lost.
>
> — E. B. WHITE, "The Ring of Time"

**Thinking about Your Own Use of Parallelism**

Read carefully several paragraphs from a draft you have recently written, noting any series of words, phrases, or clauses. Using the guidelines in this chapter, determine whether the series are parallel, and if not, revise them for parallelism. Then reread the paragraphs, looking for places where parallel structures would add emphasis or clarity, and revise accordingly. Can you draw any conclusions about your use of parallelism?

# 38 Comma Splices and Fused Sentences

A comma splice results from placing only a comma between two independent clauses. We sometimes see comma splices used for special effect in fiction or essays and especially in advertising or on bumper stickers, where they can give slogans a catchy rhythm.

Dogs have owners, cats have staff.
— BUMPER STICKER

A related construction is a fused, or run-on, sentence, which results from joining two independent clauses with no punctuation or connecting word between them. The bumper sticker as a fused sentence would be "Dogs have owners cats have staff."

You will seldom profit from using comma splices or fused sentences in academic writing. In fact, doing so will almost always draw an instructor's criticism.

## 38a Separating the clauses into two sentences

The simplest way to revise comma splices or fused sentences is to separate them into two sentences.

| | |
|---|---|
| COMMA SPLICE | **My mother spends long hours every spring tilling the soil and moving manure~~,~~. ~~this~~ This part of gardening is nauseating.** |
| FUSED SENTENCE | **My mother spends long hours every spring tilling the soil and moving manure. ~~this~~ This part of gardening is nauseating.** |

If the two clauses are very short, making them two sentences may sound abrupt and terse, so some other method of revision is probably preferable.

## 38b Linking the clauses with a comma and a coordinating conjunction

If the ideas in the two clauses are closely related and equally important, you can join them with a comma and a coordinating conjunction: *and*, *but*, *or*, *nor*, *for*, *so*, or *yet*. (See Chapter 46.) The conjunction helps indicate what kind of link exists between the two clauses. For instance, *but* and *yet* signal opposition or contrast; *for* and *so* signal cause-effect relationships.

| | |
|---|---|
| **COMMA SPLICE** | **I got up feeling bad, so I took some aspirin.** |
| **FUSED SENTENCE** | **I should pay my tuition, but I need a new car.** |

## 38c Linking the clauses with a semicolon

If the ideas in the two clauses are closely related and you want to give them equal emphasis, you can link them with a semicolon.

| | |
|---|---|
| **COMMA SPLICE** | **This photograph is not at all realistic, ; it uses dreamlike images to convey its message.** |
| **FUSED SENTENCE** | **The practice of journalism is changing dramatically; advances in technology have sped up news cycles.** |

Be careful when you link clauses with a conjunctive adverb or a transitional phrase. You *must* precede such words and phrases with a semicolon (see Chapter 47), with a period, or with a comma combined with a coordinating conjunction (31b7).

| | |
|---|---|
| **COMMA SPLICE** | **Many Third World countries have very high birthrates, ; therefore, most of their citizens are young.** |
| **FUSED SENTENCE** | **Many Third World countries have very high birthrates. Therefore, most of their citizens are young.** |
| **FUSED SENTENCE** | **Many Third World countries have very high birthrates, and therefore, most of their citizens are young.** |

**SOME CONJUNCTIVE ADVERBS AND TRANSITIONAL PHRASES**

| | | |
|---|---|---|
| also | in contrast | next |
| anyway | indeed | now |
| besides | in fact | otherwise |
| certainly | instead | similarly |
| finally | likewise | still |
| furthermore | meanwhile | then |
| however | moreover | therefore |
| in addition | namely | thus |
| incidentally | nevertheless | undoubtedly |

**FOR MULTILINGUAL WRITERS: Sentence length**

In U.S. academic contexts, readers sometimes find a series of short sentences "choppy" and undesirable. If you want to connect two independent clauses into one sentence, be sure to join them with a comma followed by a coordinating conjunction (*and*, *but*, *so*, *nor*, *or*, or *yet*) or with a semicolon. Doing so will help you avoid a comma-splice error. Another useful tip for writing in American English is to avoid writing several very long sentences in a row. If you find this pattern in your writing, try breaking it up by including a shorter sentence occasionally. See the tips in 44a and 44b for altering the sentence lengths and patterns in your writing.

## 38d Recasting two clauses as one independent clause

Sometimes you can reduce two spliced or fused clauses to a single independent clause that is more direct and concise.

COMMA SPLICE **A large part of my mail is advertisements, ~~most of the rest is~~ bills.** [inserted: and]

## 38e Recasting one independent clause as a dependent clause

When one independent clause is more important than the other, try converting the less important one to a dependent clause.

**COMMA SPLICE** which reacted against mass production,
**The arts and crafts movement, called for handmade objects. ~~it reacted against mass production.~~**

In the revision, the writer chooses to emphasize the first clause, the one describing what the movement advocated, and to make the second clause, the one describing what it reacted against, into a dependent clause.

**FUSED SENTENCE** Although
**Zora Neale Hurston is regarded as one of America's major novelists, she died in obscurity.**

In the revision, the writer chooses to emphasize the second clause and to make the first one into a dependent clause by adding the subordinating conjunction *although* (31b7).

## 38f Linking two independent clauses with a dash

In informal writing, you can use a dash to join two independent clauses, especially when the second clause elaborates on the first.

**COMMA SPLICE** **Exercise has become too much like work — it's a bad trend.**

### Editing for comma splices and fused sentences

If you find no punctuation between two of your independent clauses — groups of words that can stand alone as sentences — you have identified a fused sentence. If you find two such clauses joined only by a comma, you have identified a comma splice. Here are six methods of editing comma splices and fused sentences. As you edit, look at the sentences before and after the ones you are revising. Doing so will help you determine how a particular method will affect the rhythm of the passage.

1. Separate the clauses into two sentences. (38a)

It
- ***Education* is an elusive word. ~~it~~ often means different things to different people.**

*(continued on next page)*

*(continued from p. 659)*

2. Link the clauses with a comma and a coordinating conjunction (*and, but, or, nor, for, so,* or *yet*). (38b)

- ***Education* is an elusive word, [for] it often means different things to different people.**

3. Link the clauses with a semicolon. (38c)

- ***Education* is an elusive word~~,~~[;] it often means different things to different people.**

If the clauses are linked with only a comma and a conjunctive adverb — a word like *however, then, therefore* — add a semicolon.

- ***Education* is an elusive word~~,~~[;] indeed, it often means different things to different people.**

4. Recast the two clauses as one independent clause. (38d)

- **[An elusive word, education] ~~*Education* is an elusive word, it~~ often means different things to different people.**

5. Recast one independent clause as a dependent clause. (38e)

- ***Education* is an elusive word~~,~~ [because] it often means different things to different people.**

6. In informal writing, link the clauses with a dash. (38f)

- ***Education* is an elusive word~~,~~ [—] its meaning varies.**

## EXERCISE 38.1

Using two of the methods in this chapter, revise each item to correct its comma splice or fused sentence. Use each of the methods at least once. Example:

I had misgivings about the marriage, [so] I did not attend the ceremony.

[Because] I had misgivings about the marriage, I did not attend the ceremony.

1. Listeners prefer talk shows to classical music, the radio station is changing its programming.
2. The tallest human on record was Robert Wadlow he reached an amazing height of eight feet, eleven inches.
3. Some students read more online than in print, some do the opposite.
4. The number of vaccine manufacturers has plummeted the industry has been hit with a flood of lawsuits.
5. Most crustaceans live in the ocean, some also live on land or in freshwater habitats.
6. She inherited some tribal customs from her grandmother, she knows the sewing technique called Seminole patchwork.
7. Don't throw your soda cans in the trash recycle them.
8. The West Indian woman has lived in New England for years, nevertheless, she always feels betrayed by winter.
9. The Hope diamond in the Smithsonian Institution is impressive in fact, it looks even larger in person than online.
10. You adopted the puppy now you'll have to train him.

## EXERCISE 38.2

Revise the following paragraph, eliminating all comma splices by using a period or a semicolon. Then revise the paragraph again, this time using any of the other methods in this chapter. Comment on the two revisions. What differences in rhythm do you detect? Which version do you prefer, and why?

> My sister Maria decided to paint her house last summer, thus, she had to buy some paint. She wanted inexpensive paint, at the same time, it had to go on easily and cover well, that combination was unrealistic to start with. She was a complete beginner, on the other hand, she was a hard worker and willing to learn. Maria went out and bought "dark green" paint for $6.99 a gallon, it must have been mostly water, in fact, you could almost see through it. She put one coat of this paint on the house, as a result, her white house turned a streaky light green. Maria was forced to buy all new paint, the job ended up costing more than it would have if she had bought good paint at the start.

**bedfordstmartins.com/smhandbook** For more exercises on comma splices and fused sentences, go to Exercise Central and click on **Comma Splices and Fused Sentences**.

## THINKING CRITICALLY ABOUT COMMA SPLICES AND FUSED SENTENCES

**Reading with an Eye for Special Effects**

Roger Angell is known as a careful and correct stylist, yet he often deviates from the "correct" to create special effects, as in this passage about pitcher David Cone:

> And then he won. Next time out, on August 10th, handed a seven-run lead against the A's, he gave up two runs over six innings, with eight strike-outs. He had tempo, he had poise. — ROGER ANGELL, "Before the Fall"

Angell uses a comma splice in the last sentence to emphasize parallel ideas; any conjunction, even *and*, would change the causal relationship he wishes to show. Because the splice is unexpected, it attracts just the attention that Angell wants for his statement.

Look through some stories or essays to find comma splices and fused sentences. Copy down one or two and enough of the surrounding text to show context, and comment in writing on the effects they create.

**Thinking about Any Comma Splices and Fused Sentences in Your Own Writing**

Go through some essays you have written, checking for comma splices and fused sentences. Revise any you find, using one of the methods in this chapter. Comment on your chosen methods.

# Sentence Fragments

# 39

Our Lifetime Guarantee may come as a shock. *Or a strut. Or a muffler.* Because once you pay to replace them, Toyota's Lifetime Guarantee covers parts and labor on any dealer-installed muffler, shock, or strut for as long as you own your Toyota! So if anything should ever go wrong, your Toyota dealer will fix it. *Absolutely free.*

— TOYOTA ADVERTISEMENT

The three fragments (italicized here) grab our attention, the first two by creating a play on words and the third by emphasizing that something is free.

As this ad illustrates, sentence fragments are groups of words that are not sentences but are punctuated as sentences. Although you will often see and hear fragments, you will seldom want to use them in academic writing, where some readers might regard them as errors.

## 39a Phrase fragments

Phrases are groups of words that lack a subject, a verb, or both (31c3). When phrases are punctuated like sentences, they become fragments. To revise these fragments, attach them to an independent clause, or make them a separate sentence.

**NBC is broadcasting the debates~~.~~, ~~With~~ with discussions afterward.**

The word group *with discussions afterward* is a prepositional phrase, not a sentence. The editing combines the phrase with an independent clause.

**The town's growth is controlled by zoning laws~~.~~, ~~A~~ a strict set of regulations for builders and corporations.**

*A strict set of regulations for builders and corporations* is an appositive phrase renaming the noun *zoning laws*. The editing attaches the fragment to the sentence containing that noun.

**Kamika stayed out of school for three months after Linda was born. ~~To~~ She did so to recuperate and to take care of the baby.**

*To recuperate and to take care of the baby* includes verbals, not verbs. The revision — adding a subject (*she*) and a verb (*did*) — turns the fragment into a separate sentence.

### Fragments beginning with transitions

If you introduce an example or explanation with one of the following transitions, be certain you write a sentence, not a fragment.

| again | but | like |
|---|---|---|
| also | finally | or |
| and | for example | specifically |
| as a result | for instance | such as |
| besides | instead | that is |

**Joan Didion has written on many subjects~~.~~, ~~Such~~ such as the Hoover Dam and migraine headaches.**

In the original, the second word group is a phrase, not a sentence. The editing combines it with an independent clause.

## 39b Compound-predicate fragments

A compound predicate consists of two or more verbs, along with their modifiers and objects, that have the same subject. Fragments occur when one part of a compound predicate lacks a subject but is punctuated as a separate sentence. These fragments usually begin with *and*, *but*, or *or*. You can revise them by attaching them to the independent clause that contains the rest of the predicate.

**They sold their house~~.~~ ~~And~~ and moved into an apartment.**

### EXERCISE 39.1

Revise each of the following items to eliminate any sentence fragments, either by combining fragments with independent clauses or by rewriting them as separate sentences. Example:

~~Zoe looked close to tears.~~ Standing with her head bowed~~.~~, Zoe looked close to tears.

Zoe looked close to tears. ~~Standing~~ She was standing with her head bowed.

1. Long stretches of white beaches and shady palm trees. Give tourists the impression of an island paradise.

2. Being a celebrity. That is what many Americans yearn for.
3. Much of New Orleans is below sea level. Which makes it susceptible to flooding.
4. Uncle Ron forgot to bring his clarinet to the party. Fortunately for us.
5. Oscar night is an occasion for celebrating the film industry. And criticizing the fashion industry.
6. Diners in Creole restaurants might try shrimp gumbo. Or order turtle soup.
7. Tupperware parties go back to the late 1940s. Parties where the hosts are salespersons.
8. Attempting to lose ten pounds in less than a week. I ate only cottage cheese and grapefruit.
9. None of the adults realized that we were hiding there. Under the porch.
10. Thomas Edison was famous for his inventions. As well as for his entrepreneurial skills.

**bedfordstmartins.com/smhandbook** For more exercises on sentence fragments, go to Exercise Central and click on **Sentence Fragments**.

## 39c Dependent-clause fragments

Dependent clauses contain both a subject and a verb, but they cannot stand alone as sentences because they depend on an independent clause to complete their meaning. Dependent clauses usually begin with words such as *after*, *because*, *before*, *if*, *since*, *though*, *unless*, *until*, *when*, *where*, *while*, *who*, *which*, and *that* (31b7 and 31b3). You can usually combine dependent-clause fragments with a nearby independent clause.

- **The team had a dismal record~~.~~, ~~Which~~** which **spurred the owner to fire the manager.**

If you cannot smoothly attach a dependent clause to a nearby independent clause, try deleting the opening subordinating word and turning the dependent clause into a sentence.

- **The majority of injuries in automobile accidents occur in two ways. ~~When an~~** An **occupant either is hurt by something inside the car or is thrown from the car.**

## Editing for sentence fragments

A group of words must meet the following three criteria to form a complete sentence. If it does not meet all three, it is a fragment. Revise a fragment by combining it with a nearby sentence or by rewriting it as a complete sentence.

1. A sentence must have a subject. (31a)
2. A sentence must have a verb, not just a verbal. A verbal needs an auxiliary verb in order to function as a sentence's verb. (31c3)

   **VERBAL** The terrier *barking.*

   **VERB** The terrier *is barking.*

3. Unless it is a question, a sentence must have at least one clause that does not begin with a subordinating word (31b7). Following are some common subordinating words:

| | | |
|---|---|---|
| although | if | when |
| as | since | where |
| because | that | whether |
| before | though | who |
| how | unless | why |

### EXERCISE 39.2

Identify all the sentence fragments in the following items, and explain why each is grammatically incomplete. Then revise each one in at least two ways. Example:

Controlling my temper, ~~That~~ has been one of my goals this year.
*One of my goals this year has been controlling*
~~Controlling~~ my temper. ~~That has been one of my goals this year.~~

1. As soon as the seventy-five-year-old cellist walked onstage. The audience burst into applause.
2. The patient has only one goal. To smoke behind the doctor's back.
3. Fishing for Alaskan king crab, one of the most dangerous professions there is.
4. After writing and rewriting for almost three years. She finally felt that her novel was complete.
5. In the wake of the earthquake. Relief workers tried to provide food and shelter to victims.

6. Forster stopped writing novels after *A Passage to India*. Which is one of the greatest novels of the twentieth century.
7. Because the speaker's fee was astronomical. The student organization invited someone else.
8. The jury found the defendant guilty. And recommended the maximum sentence.
9. Production began in late September. Four months ahead of schedule.
10. Her parents simply could not understand. Why she hated her childhood nickname.

**bedfordstmartins.com/smhandbook** For more exercises on sentence fragments, go to Exercise Central and click on **Sentence Fragments**.

## THINKING CRITICALLY ABOUT FRAGMENTS

**Reading with an Eye for Fragments**

Identify the fragments in the following passage. What effect does the writer achieve by using fragments rather than complete sentences?

> On Sundays, for religion, we went up on the hill. Skipping along the hexagon-shaped tile in Colonial Park. Darting up the steps to Edgecomb Avenue. Stopping in the candy store on St. Nicholas to load up. Leaning forward for leverage to finish the climb up to the church. I was always impressed by this particular house of the Lord. — KEITH GILYARD, *Voices of the Self*

**Thinking about Any Fragments in Your Own Writing**

Read through some essays you have written. Using the guidelines on the opposite page, see whether you find any sentence fragments. If so, do you recognize any patterns? Do you write fragments when you're attempting to add emphasis? Are they all dependent clauses? phrases? Note any patterns you discover, and make a point of routinely checking your writing for fragments. Finally, revise any fragments to form complete sentences.

# 40 Modifier Placement

Modifiers enrich writing by making it more concrete or vivid, often adding important or even essential details. To be effective, modifiers should refer clearly to the words they modify and be placed close to those words. Consider, for example, a sign seen recently in a hotel:

DO NOT USE THE ELEVATORS IN CASE OF FIRE.

Should we really avoid the elevators altogether for fear of causing a fire? Repositioning the modifier *in case of fire* eliminates such confusion — and makes clear that we are to avoid the elevators only if there is a fire: *IN CASE OF FIRE, DO NOT USE THE ELEVATORS.*

## 40a Misplaced modifiers

Misplaced modifiers are words, phrases, and clauses that cause confusion because they are not close enough to the words they modify or because they seem to modify more than one word in the sentence.

clearly.

- **~~Clearly~~ I could hear the instructor lecturing.** ^

  The original sentence is ambiguous; the editing repositions the modifier *clearly* next to the word *lecturing*, which the writer wants to describe.

Phrases should usually be placed right before or after the words they modify.

on voodoo

- **She teaches a seminar ^ this term ~~on voodoo~~ at Skyline College.**

  The voodoo is not at the college; the seminar is.

We

- **~~Billowing from every window, we~~ saw clouds of smoke** billowing from every window. ^

  People cannot billow from windows.

Although you have some flexibility in the placement of dependent clauses, try to position them close to what they modify.

that line the walks are
▶ **The shrubs trimmed in the shapes of animals**
and ^
**~~that line the walks~~ delight visitors.**
^

Do animals line the walks?

After he lost the 1962 race,
▶ **Nixon said he would get out of politics. ~~after he lost the 1962 race.~~**
^ ^

The unedited sentence implies that Nixon planned to lose the race.

## EXERCISE 40.1

Revise each of the following sentences by moving any misplaced modifiers so that they clearly modify the words they should. Example:

When they propose sensible plans, politicians
~~Politicians~~ earn support from the people. ~~when they propose sensible plans.~~
^ ^

1. The comedian had the audience doubled over with laughter relating her stories in a deadpan voice.
2. News reports can increase a listener's irrational fears that emphasize random crime or rare diseases.
3. Studying legal documents and court records from hundreds of years ago, ordinary people in the Middle Ages teach us about everyday life at that time.
4. Risking their lives in war zones, civilians learn about the conflict from the first-hand accounts of journalists abroad.
5. We recorded a wolf pack at play with our new digital camera while we were camping last summer.
6. Doctors recommend a new test for cancer, which is painless.
7. Every afternoon I find flyers for free pizza on my windshield.
8. I knew that the investment would pay off in a dramatic way before I decided to buy the stock.
9. The bank offered flood insurance to the homeowners underwritten by the federal government.
10. Revolving out of control, the maintenance worker shut down the turbine.

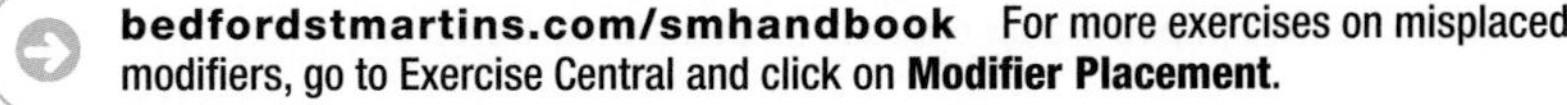

**bedfordstmartins.com/smhandbook** For more exercises on misplaced modifiers, go to Exercise Central and click on **Modifier Placement**.

### Limiting modifiers

Be especially careful with the placement of limiting modifiers such as *almost*, *even*, *hardly*, *just*, *merely*, *nearly*, *only*, *scarcely*, and *simply*. In general, these modifiers should be placed right before or after the words they modify. Putting them in other positions may produce not just ambiguity but a completely different meaning.

| | |
|---|---|
| **AMBIGUOUS** | The court *only* hears civil cases on Tuesdays. |
| **CLEAR** | The court hears *only* civil cases on Tuesdays. |
| **CLEAR** | The court hears civil cases on Tuesdays *only*. |

In the first sentence, placing *only* before *hears* makes the meaning ambiguous. Does the writer mean that civil cases are the only cases heard on Tuesdays or that those are the only days when civil cases are heard?

almost
**The city ~~almost~~ spent ^ $20 million on the new stadium.**

The original sentence suggests the money was almost spent; moving *almost* makes clear that the amount spent was almost $20 million.

### Squinting modifiers

If a modifier can refer to *either* the word before it *or* the word after it, it is a squinting modifier. Put the modifier where it clearly relates to only a single word.

**SQUINTING** Students who practice writing *often* will benefit.

Does the writer mean that students often benefit from practice or that they benefit from practicing often?

| | |
|---|---|
| **REVISED** | Students who *often* practice writing will benefit. |
| **REVISED** | Students who practice writing will *often* benefit. |

### EXERCISE 40.2

Revise each of the following sentences in at least two ways. Move the limiting or squinting modifier so that it unambiguously modifies one word or phrase in the sentence. Example:

completely
The course we hoped would ^ engross us ~~completely~~ bored us.

completely.
The course we hoped would engross us ~~completely~~ bored us~~.~~ ^

1. The candidate promised quickly to reduce class size.
2. The soldier was apparently injured by friendly fire.
3. The collector who owned the painting originally planned to leave it to a museum.
4. Doctors can now restore limbs that have been severed partially to a functioning condition.
5. Ever since I was a child, I have only liked green peas with ham.

**bedfordstmartins.com/smhandbook** For more exercises on misplaced modifiers, go to Exercise Central and click on **Modifier Placement**.

## 40b Disruptive modifiers

Disruptive modifiers interrupt the connections between parts of a sentence, making it hard for readers to follow the progress of the thought. Most disruptive modifiers are adverbial clauses or phrases. In general, do not place such modifiers between the parts of a verb phrase, between a subject and a verb, or between a verb and an object.

If they are cooked too long, vegetables will
- **~~Vegetables will, if they are cooked too long,~~ lose most of their nutritional value.**

Separating the parts of the verb phrase, *will* and *lose*, disrupts the flow of the sentence.

were discarded
- **The books, because the librarians had decided they were no longer useful,. ~~were discarded.~~**

Separating the subject *books* from the verb *were discarded* is awkward.

a secondhand car
- **He bought with his first paycheck. ~~a secondhand car.~~**

Separating the verb *bought* from the object *a secondhand car* makes it hard to follow the thought.

### Modifiers splitting an infinitive

In general, do not place a modifier between the *to* and the verb of an infinitive (*to often complain*). Doing so makes it hard for readers to recognize that the two go together.

surrender
**Hitler expected the British to ^ fairly quickly. ~~surrender.~~**

In some cases, however, a modifier sounds awkward if it does not split the infinitive. In such cases, you may want to reword the sentence to eliminate the infinitive altogether.

**SPLIT** I hope *to* almost *equal* my last year's income.

**REVISED** I hope that I will earn almost as much as I did last year.

### EXERCISE 40.3

Revise each of the following sentences by moving the disruptive modifier so that the sentence reads smoothly. Example:

During the recent economic depression, many
~~Many~~ unemployed college graduates ~~during the recent economic depression~~ ^attended graduate school.

1. Strong economic times have, statistics tell us, led to increases in the college dropout rate.
2. Sometimes in negotiations a radical proposal, due to its shock value, stimulates creative thinking by labor and management.
3. The court's ruling allows cities to lawfully seize private property and sell it to the highest bidder.
4. Michael Jordan earned, at the pinnacle of his career, roughly $40 million a year in endorsements.
5. The stock exchange became, because of the sudden trading, a chaotic circus.

**bedfordstmartins.com/smhandbook** For more exercises on disruptive modifiers, go to Exercise Central and click on **Modifier Placement**.

## 40c Dangling modifiers

Dangling modifiers are words that modify nothing in particular in the rest of a sentence. They often *seem* to modify something that is implied but not actually present in the sentence. Dangling modifiers frequently appear at the beginnings or ends of sentences.

**DANGLING** Driving nonstop, Salishan Lodge is two hours from Portland.

**REVISED** Driving nonstop from Portland, you can reach Salishan Lodge in two hours.

**REVISED** If you drive nonstop, Salishan Lodge is two hours from Portland.

The preceding revised sentences illustrate two ways to fix a dangling modifier. Often you need to add a subject that the modifier clearly refers to. Sometimes, however, you have to turn the dangling modifier itself into a phrase or clause.

our family gave
**Reluctantly, ^ the hound ~~was given away~~ to a neighbor.**

In the original sentence, was the dog reluctant, or was someone else who is not mentioned reluctant?

When he was
**^ ~~As~~ a young boy, his aunt told stories of her years as a country doctor.**

His aunt was never a young boy.

My
**~~Thumbing through the magazine, my~~ ^ eyes automatically noticed the perfume ads ^** as I was thumbing through the magazine.

Eyes cannot thumb through a magazine.

he was
**Although ^ a reserved and private man, everyone enjoyed his company.**

The original clause does not refer to *everyone* or *his company*. It needs its own subject and verb.

## EXERCISE 40.4

Revise each of the following sentences to correct the dangling phrase. Example:

a viewer gets
Watching television news, ^ an impression ~~is given~~ of constant disaster.

1. Determined to increase its audience share, news may become entertainment.
2. Trying to attract younger viewers, news is blended with comedy on late-night talk shows.

## Editing for misplaced or dangling modifiers

1. Identify all the modifiers in each sentence, and draw an arrow from each modifier to the word it modifies.
2. If a modifier is far from the word it modifies, try to move the two closer together. (40a)
3. Does any modifier seem to refer to a word other than the one it is intended to modify? If so, move the modifier so that it refers clearly to only the intended word. (40a and b)
4. If you cannot find the word to which a modifier refers, revise the sentence: supply such a word, or revise the modifier itself so that it clearly refers to a word already in the sentence. (40c)

3. Highlighting local events, important international news stories may get overlooked.
4. Chosen for their looks, the journalistic credentials of newscasters may be weak.
5. As a visual medium, complex issues are hard to present on television.

**bedfordstmartins.com/smhandbook** For more exercises on dangling modifiers, go to Exercise Central and click on **Modifier Placement**.

## THINKING CRITICALLY ABOUT MODIFIERS

**Reading with an Eye for Modifiers**

Look at the limiting modifier italicized in the following passage. Identify which word or words it modifies. Then try moving the modifier to some other spot in the sentence, and consider how the meaning of the sentence changes as a result.

> It was, among other things, the sort of railroad you would occasionally ride *just* for the hell of it, a higher existence into which you would escape unconsciously and without hesitation. — E. B. WHITE, "Progress and Change"

**Thinking about Your Own Use of Modifiers**

As you examine two pages of a draft, check for clear and effective modifiers. Can you identify any misplaced, disruptive, or dangling modifiers? Using the guidelines in this chapter, revise as need be. Then look for patterns — in the kinds of modifiers you use and in any problems you have placing them. Make a note of what you find.

# Consistent and Complete Structures

# 41

You probably hear inconsistent and incomplete structures all the time in conversations. For instance, during an interview, Orlando Bloom was asked whether he had been intimidated when cast in the film version of *The Lord of the Rings*. Bloom's response included this statement:

*Can you imagine for me, coming out of drama school, being thrown into a group of actors like Ian McKellen, Ian Holm, and Christopher Lee — yes, it was incredibly daunting.*

Bloom's sentence begins one way but then takes off in another direction. The mixed structure posed no problem for the interviewer, but a sentence such as this can be confusing to a reader. Recognizing and editing mixed and incomplete structures can help you write more clearly.

## 41a Faulty sentence structure

Faulty sentence structure poses problems for both writers and readers. A mixed structure results from beginning a sentence with one grammatical pattern and then switching to another one:

**MIXED** The fact that I get up at 5:00 AM, a wake-up time that explains why I'm always tired in the evening.

The sentence starts out with a subject (*The fact*) followed by a dependent clause (*that I get up at 5:00 AM*). The sentence needs a predicate to complete the independent clause (31a and c), but instead it moves to another phrase (*a wake-up time*) followed by a dependent clause (*that explains why I'm always tired in the evening*), and what results is a fragment (Chapter 39).

**REVISED** The fact that I get up at 5:00 AM explains why I'm always tired in the evening.

Deleting *a wake-up time that* changes the rest of the sentence into a predicate.

**REVISED** I get up at 5:00 AM, a wake-up time that explains why I'm always tired in the evening.

Deleting *The fact that* turns the beginning of the sentence into an independent clause.

Here is another example of a mixed structure:

▶ **Because hope was the only thing left when Pandora finally closed up the mythical box, ~~explains why~~ even today we never lose hope.**

The dependent clause beginning with *Because* is followed by a predicate (beginning with *explains*) without a subject. Deleting *explains why* changes the predicate into an independent clause to which the dependent clause is attached.

## 41b Consistent subjects and predicates

Another kind of faulty sentence structure, called faulty predication, occurs when a subject and predicate do not fit together grammatically or simply do not make sense together. Many cases of faulty predication result from using forms of *be* when another verb would be stronger.

▶ **~~A characteristic that~~ I admire ~~is~~ a generous person.**

A person is not a characteristic.

▶ **The rules of the corporation ~~expect~~ ^require that^ employees ~~to~~ be on time.**

Rules cannot expect anything.

### *Is when, is where, and the reason . . . is because*

Constructions using *is when*, *is where*, and *the reason . . . is because* are used frequently in informal contexts, but they are inappropriate in academic writing because they use an adverb clause rather than a noun as a subject complement (31c4).

▶ **A stereotype is ~~when someone characterizes~~ ^an unfair characterization of^ a group. ~~unfairly.~~**

▶ **A confluence is ^a place^ where two rivers join to form one.**

▶ **~~The reason~~ I like to play soccer ~~is~~ because it provides aerobic exercise.**

### EXERCISE 41.1

Revise each of the following sentences in two ways to make its structures consistent in grammar and meaning. Example:

Because
~~The fact that~~ our room was cold, we put a heater between our beds.
led us to
The fact that our room was cold, ~~we~~ put a heater between our beds.

1. To enjoy my job, my dream in life, which has kept me in school and working hard.
2. The reason air-pollution standards should not be relaxed is because many people would suffer.
3. By not prosecuting white-collar crime as vigorously as violent crime encourages white-collar criminals to think they can ignore the law.
4. Irony is when you expect one thing and get something else.
5. The best meal I've ever eaten was sitting by a river eating bread and cheese from a farmers' market.

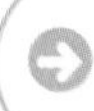

**bedfordstmartins.com/smhandbook** For more exercises on inconsistent structures, go to Exercise Central and click on **Consistent and Complete Structures.**

## 41c Elliptical constructions

Sometimes writers omit a word in a compound structure. They succeed with such an elliptical construction when the word omitted later in the compound is exactly the same as the word earlier in the compound.

- **That bell belonged to the figure of Miss Duling as though it grew directly out of her right arm, as wings grew out of an angel or a tail [grew] out of the devil.** — EUDORA WELTY, *One Writer's Beginnings*

The omitted word, *grew*, is exactly the same verb that follows *it* and *wings* in the earlier parts of the compound. You should not omit a word that does not exactly match the word used in the other part(s) of the compound.

- **His skills are weak, and his performance ^is^ only average.**

The verb *is* does not match the verb in the other part of the compound (*are*), so the writer needs to include it.

## 41d Missing words

The best way to catch inadvertent omissions is to proofread carefully, reading each sentence slowly — and aloud.

**The new Web site makes it easier to look** at **and choose from the company's inventory.**

## FOR MULTILINGUAL WRITERS: Deciding which articles to use

Do you say "I'm working on a paper" or "I'm working on *the* paper"? Deciding when to use the articles *a, an,* and *the* can be challenging for multilingual writers since many languages have nothing directly comparable to them. See 58e for help using articles.

## 41e Complete comparisons

When you compare two or more things, the comparison must be complete, logically consistent, and clear.

**I was embarrassed because my parents were so different** from my friends' parents.

Different from what? Adding *from my friends' parents* completes the comparison.

**Woodberry's biography is better than** the one by **Fields.**

This sentence illogically compares a book with a person.

**UNCLEAR** Aneil always felt more affection for his brother than his sister.

Did Aneil feel more affection for his brother than his sister did — or more affection for his brother than he felt for his sister?

**CLEAR** Aneil always felt more affection for his brother *than his sister did.*

**CLEAR** Aneil felt more affection for his brother *than he did for his sister.*

### EXERCISE 41.2

Revise each of the following sentences to eliminate any inappropriate elliptical constructions; to make comparisons complete, logically consistent, and clear; and to supply any other omitted words that are necessary for meaning. Example:

## Editing for consistency and completeness

- If you find an especially confusing sentence, check to see whether it has a subject and a predicate. If not, revise as necessary. (41a) If you find both a subject and a predicate and you are still confused, see whether the subject and verb make sense together. If not, revise so that they do. (41b)
- Revise any *is when*, *is where*, and *the reason . . . is because* constructions. (41b)

the practice of sending
**Spamming is ~~where companies send~~ electronic junk mail.**

- Check all comparisons for completeness. (41e)

we like
**We like Marian better than Margaret.**

is
Most of the candidates are bright, and one brilliant.

1. Convection ovens cook more quickly and with less power.
2. Argentina and Peru were colonized by Spain, and Brazil by Portugal.
3. She argued that children are even more important for men than women.
4. Were the traffic jams in Texas any worse than many other states?
5. The equipment in our new warehouse is guaranteed to last longer than our current facility.

**bedfordstmartins.com/smhandbook** For more exercises on incomplete structures, go to Exercise Central and click on **Consistent and Complete Structures**.

## THINKING CRITICALLY ABOUT CONSISTENCY AND COMPLETENESS

Read over three or four paragraphs from a draft or completed essay you have written recently. Check for mixed sentences and incomplete or missing structures. Revise the paragraphs to correct any problems you find. If you find any, do you recognize any patterns? If so, make a note of them for future reference.

# Part 8

# SENTENCE STYLE

# 42 Effective Sentences

Effective sentences have two main characteristics: they emphasize ideas clearly, and they do so as concisely as possible. We can see these characteristics in many sets of instructions, such as those found on a prescription drug label:

*Take one tablet daily. Some nonprescription drugs may aggravate your condition, so read all labels carefully. If any include a warning, check with your doctor. Refill prescription only until 12/12/07.*

You probably won't often need to squeeze information onto a three-inch label, but you will want to write as emphatically and concisely as you can in other contexts.

## 42a Emphasis

When we speak, we achieve emphasis by raising our voices or putting extra stress on an important word or phrase. And much of the writing we see — in advertisements, on Web sites, in magazines — gains emphasis in similar fashion, with color or bold type, for instance. Even though most academic writing can't rely on such graphic devices, writers use other techniques to emphasize parts of their sentences.

### 1 Using closing and opening positions for emphasis

When you read a sentence, you usually remember the ending. This part of the sentence moves the writing forward by providing new information, as in the following example:

- **To protect her skin, she took along *plenty of sunblock lotion.***

A less emphatic but still important position in a sentence is the opening, which often connects the new sentence with what has come before.

- **When Rosita went to the beach, she was anxious not to get a sunburn. *So plenty of sunblock lotion* went with her.**

If you place relatively unimportant information in the memorable closing position of a sentence, you may undercut what you want to emphasize or give more emphasis to the closing words than you intend.

Last month, she ... $500,000.
- ~~She~~ gave ~~$500,000 to~~ the school capital campaign ~~last month.~~

Moving *$500,000* to the end of the sentence emphasizes the amount.

## 2 Using climactic order

Presenting ideas in climactic order means arranging them in order of increasing importance or drama so that your writing builds to a climax. By saving its most dramatic item for last, the following sentence makes its point forcefully:

- **After they've finished with the pantry, the medicine cabinet, and the attic, [neat people] will throw out the red geranium (too many leaves), sell the dog (too many fleas), and send the children off to boarding school (too many scuffmarks on the hardwood floors).**

— SUSANNE BRITT, "Neat People vs. Sloppy People"

The original version of the next sentence fails to achieve strong emphasis because its verbs are not sequenced in order of increasing power; the editing provides climactic order.

offend our ears, and
- **Soap operas assault our eyes, damage our brains, ~~and offend our ears.~~**

### EXERCISE 42.1

Revise each of the following sentences to highlight what you take to be the main or most important ideas. Example:

hybrids of cold-blooded capabilities,
Theories about dinosaurs have run the gamut — simple lizards, fully adapted warm-blooded creatures, ~~hybrids of cold-blooded capabilities.~~

1. The president persuaded the American people, his staff, and Congress.
2. We can expect a decade of record-breaking tropical storms and hurricanes, if meteorologists are correct in their predictions.
3. From the sightseeing boat, we saw a whale dive toward us and then, before crashing its tail on the waves, lift itself out of the water.
4. The presence of the Indian in these movies always conjures up destructive stereotypes of scalping, horse theft, and drunkenness.
5. Victorian women were warned that if they smoked, they would become sterile, grow a mustache, die young, or contract tuberculosis.

 **bedfordstmartins.com/smhandbook** For more exercises on emphasis, go to Exercise Central and click on **Effective Sentences**.

## 42b Conciseness

Usually you'll want to be concise — to make your point in the fewest possible words.

- **One thing that her constant and continual use of vulgar expressions or four-letter words indicated to the day-care workers was that she might really have a great deal of trouble in terms of her ability to get along in a successful manner with other four-year-olds in her age group.**

Why write that sentence when you could write this one instead?

- **Her constant use of four-letter words told the day-care workers she might have trouble getting along with other four-year-olds.**

Brevity is particularly important in such online contexts as email messages, forum postings, and home-page content (see Chapter 24).

### 1 Eliminating redundant words

Sometimes writers say that something is large *in size* or red *in color* or that two ingredients should be combined *together*. The italicized words are redundant, or unnecessary for meaning, as are the deleted words in these examples:

Attendance
- **~~Compulsory attendance~~ at assemblies is required.**
^

- **Many different forms of hazing occur, such as physical ~~abuse~~ and mental abuse.**

### 2 Eliminating empty words

Empty words are so general and so overused that they contribute no real meaning to a sentence.

**EMPTY WORDS**

angle, area, aspect, case, element, factor, field, kind, nature, scope, situation, thing, type

Many modifiers are so common that they have become empty words.

**MEANINGLESS MODIFIERS**

absolutely, awesome, awfully, central, definitely, fine, great, literally, quite, really, very

When you cannot simply delete empty words, try to think of a more specific way to say what you mean.

Housing strongly influence social

▶ **~~The housing situation~~ can ~~have a really significant impact on the social aspect of~~ a student's life.**

## 3 Replacing wordy phrases

Wordy phrases are those that can be reduced to a word or two with no loss in meaning.

| WORDY | CONCISE |
|---|---|
| at all times | always |
| at the present time | now/today |
| at that point in time | then |
| due to the fact that | because |
| for the purpose of | for |
| in order to | to |
| in spite of the fact that | although |
| in the event that | if |

## 4 Simplifying sentence structure

Using simple grammatical structures will often strengthen your sentences considerably.

widespread

▶ **Hurricane Katrina, ~~which was certainly~~ one of the most powerful storms ever to hit the Gulf Coast, caused damage ~~to a very wide area.~~**

Reducing a clause to an appositive, deleting unnecessary words, and replacing five words with one tighten the sentence and make it easier to read.

**When ~~she was~~ questioned about her previous job, she seemed nervous, and ~~She also~~ tried to change the subject.**

Combining two sentences produces one concise sentence.

Other ways to simplify grammatical structures include using strong verbs and nouns, avoiding expletive constructions, and using the active rather than the passive voice (see Chapter 45).

## Editing for emphasis and conciseness

### For emphasis

- Identify the words you want to emphasize. If you've buried those words in the middle of a sentence, edit the sentence to change their position. The end and the beginning are generally the most emphatic. (42a1)
- Note any sentences that include a series of words, phrases, or clauses. Arrange the items in the series in climactic order, with the most important item last. (42a2)

### For conciseness

- Look for redundant words. If you are unsure about a word, read the sentence without it; if the meaning is not affected, leave the word out. (42b1)
- Delete empty words such as *aspect* or *factor*, *definitely* or *very*. (42b2)
- Replace wordy phrases with a single word. Instead of *because of the fact that*, try *because*. (42b3)
- Simplify grammatical structures whenever possible. For example, you might reduce an adjective clause to an appositive or combine two sentences that have the same subject or predicate. (42b4)

## THINKING CRITICALLY ABOUT SENTENCES

**Reading with an Eye for Sentence Style**

Read the following sentence from "A Sweet Devouring" by Eudora Welty, and decide how Welty achieves such strong emphasis. Then look for strong, emphatic sentences in a piece by one of your favorite writers. Bring in one or two sentences to compare with those chosen by your classmates.

> The pleasures of reading itself — who doesn't remember? — were like those of a Christmas cake, a sweet devouring.

**Thinking about Your Own Sentences**

Find two or three paragraphs you have written recently, and study them with an eye for empty words. Using 42b2 for guidance, eliminate meaningless words such as *aspect*, *factor*, *quite*, and *very*. Compare notes with one or two classmates to see what empty words, if any, you all tend to use. Finally, make a note of empty words you use, and try to avoid them in the future.

# 43 Coordination and Subordination

In speech, people tend to use *and* and *so* as all-purpose connectors.

*He enjoys psychology, and the course requires a lot of work.*

The meaning of this sentence may be perfectly clear in speech, which provides clues through voice, facial expressions, and gestures. But in writing, the sentence could have more than one meaning.

*Although he enjoys psychology, the course requires a lot of work.*

*He enjoys psychology although the course requires a lot of work.*

As these examples show, coordinating conjunctions like *and* give ideas equal weight, whereas subordinating conjunctions like *although* emphasize one idea over another.

## 43a Coordination to relate equal ideas

When used well, coordination relates separate but equal ideas. The element that links the ideas, usually a coordinating conjunction (*and, but, for, nor, or, so, yet*) or a semicolon, makes the precise relationship clear. The following sentences all use coordination, but the relationship between independent clauses differs in each sentence:

- **They acquired horses, and their ancient nomadic spirit was suddenly free of the ground.**
- **There is perfect freedom in the mountains, but it belongs to the eagle and the elk, the badger and the bear.**
- **No longer were they slaves to the simple necessity of survival; they were a lordly and dangerous society of fighters and thieves, hunters and priests of the sun.**

— N. SCOTT MOMADAY, *The Way to Rainy Mountain*

Coordination can help make explicit the relationship between two ideas.

- **My son watches *The Simpsons* religiously~~.~~; ~~Forced~~ forced to choose, he would probably pick Homer Simpson over his sister.**

Connecting these two sentences with a semicolon strengthens the connection between two closely related ideas.

When you connect ideas within a sentence, make sure the relationship between the ideas is clear.

> **Watching television is a common way to spend leisure time, ~~and~~ but it makes viewers apathetic.**

What does television's being a common form of leisure have to do with viewers' being apathetic? Changing *and* to *but* better relates the two ideas.

### Using coordination for special effect

Coordination can create special effects, as in a passage by Carl Sandburg describing the reaction of the American people to Abraham Lincoln's assassination.

> Men tried to talk about it and the words failed and they came back to silence.
>
> To say nothing was best.
>
> Lincoln was dead.
>
> Was there anything more to say?
>
> Yes, they would go through the motions of grief and they would take part in a national funeral and a ceremony of humiliation and abasement and tears.
>
> But words were no help.
>
> Lincoln was dead. — CARL SANDBURG, *Abraham Lincoln: The War Years*

Together with the other short simple sentences, the coordinate clauses, phrases, and words in the first and fifth sentences create a powerful effect. Everything in the passage is grammatically equal, flattened out by the pain and shock of the death. In this way, the sentence structure and grammar mirror the dazed state of the populace. The short sentences and independent clauses are almost like sobs that illustrate the thought of the first sentence, that "the words failed."

### EXERCISE 43.1

Using coordination to signal equal importance or to create special effects, combine and revise the following twelve short sentences into several longer and more effective ones. Add or delete words as necessary.

> The bull-riding arena was fairly crowded. The crowd made no impression on me. I had made a decision. It was now time to prove myself. I was scared. I walked to the entry window. I laid my money on the counter. The clerk held up a Stetson hat filled with slips of paper. I reached in. I picked one. The slip held the number of the bull I was to ride. I headed toward the stock corral.

**bedfordstmartins.com/smhandbook** For more exercises on coordination, go to Exercise Central and click on **Coordination and Subordination**.

## 43b Subordination to distinguish main ideas

Subordination allows you to distinguish major points from minor points or to bring in supporting details. If, for instance, you put your main idea in an independent clause, you might then put any less significant ideas in dependent clauses, phrases, or even single words. The following sentence shows the subordinated point in italics:

> **Mrs. Viola Cullinan was a plump woman *who lived in a three-bedroom house somewhere behind the post office.***
>
> — MAYA ANGELOU, "My Name Is Margaret"

The dependent clause adds information about Mrs. Cullinan, but it is subordinate to the independent clause.

Notice that the choice of what to subordinate rests with the writer and depends on the intended meaning. Angelou might have given the same basic information differently.

> **Mrs. Viola Cullinan, *a plump woman*, lived in a three-bedroom house somewhere behind the post office.**

Subordinating the information about Mrs. Cullinan's size to that about her house would suggest a slightly different meaning, of course. As a writer, you must think carefully about what you want to emphasize and then subordinate information accordingly.

Subordination also helps establish logical relationships among ideas. These relationships are often specified by subordinating conjunctions — words such as *after*, *because*, and *so that* — and relative pronouns, words such as *which*, *who*, and *that*. Look, for example, at another sentence by Angelou. The subordinate clause is italicized, and the subordinating conjunction is underlined (31b7 and 31c4).

> **She usually rested her smile until late afternoon *when her women friends dropped in and Miss Glory, the cook, served them cold drinks on the closed-in porch.***
>
> — MAYA ANGELOU, "My Name Is Margaret"

Finally, subordination can help readers recognize your most important ideas. By subordinating some of the less important ideas in the following passage, the editing helps highlight the main idea:

- **Many people come home tired in the evening, and so they turn on the television to relax. ~~They~~** Though they **may intend to watch just the news, ~~but then~~ a game show comes on next, ~~and~~** which **they decide to watch ~~it~~ for just a short while, ~~and~~** Eventually, **they get too comfortable to get up, and they end up spending the whole evening in front of the television.**

Like coordination, however, subordination can become excessive. When too many subordinate clauses are strung together, readers may have trouble keeping track of the main idea expressed in the independent clause.

**TOO MUCH SUBORDINATION**

- **Philip II sent the Spanish Armada to conquer England, which was ruled by Elizabeth, who had executed Mary because she was plotting to overthrow Elizabeth, who was a Protestant, whereas Mary and Philip were Roman Catholics.**

**REVISED**

- **Philip II sent the Spanish Armada to conquer England, which was ruled by Elizabeth, a Protestant. She had executed Mary, a Roman Catholic like Philip, because Mary was plotting to overthrow her.**

  Putting the facts about Elizabeth executing Mary into an independent clause makes key information easier to recognize.

You can use a variety of grammatical structures — not only dependent clauses — to subordinate a less important element within a sentence:

- **The parks report was persuasively written. It contained five typed pages.** [no subordination]
- **The parks report, *which contained five typed pages*, was persuasively written.** [dependent clause]
- **The parks report, *containing five typed pages*, was persuasively written.** [participial phrase]
- **The *five-page* parks report was persuasively written.** [adjective]

- **The parks report, *five typed pages*, was persuasively written.** [appositive]
- **The parks report, *its five pages neatly typed*, was persuasively written.** [absolute]

## EXERCISE 43.2

Combine each of the following sets of sentences into one sentence that uses subordination to signal the relationships among ideas. Example:

I was looking over my books.
I noticed that *Paradise* was missing.
This book is a favorite of my roommate.

*While I was looking over my books, I noticed that Paradise, one of my roommate's favorite books, was missing.*

1. The *Hindenburg* was gigantic.
   It was an airship.
   It was destroyed in an explosion.
2. Athena was the goddess of wisdom.
   Ancient Greeks relied on Athena to protect the city of Athens.
   Athens was named in Athena's honor.
3. Stephen King was arrested in 1970.
   He had stolen traffic cones.
   His fine was one hundred dollars.
4. Flappers seemed rebellious to their parents' generation.
   They broke with 1920s social conventions.
   They cut their hair short and smoked in public.
5. Skateboarding originated in Venice, California.
   The time was the mid-seventies.
   There was a drought.
   The swimming pools were empty.

**bedfordstmartins.com/smhandbook** For more exercises on subordination, go to Exercise Central and click on **Coordination and Subordination**.

### *Using subordination for special effect*

Some particularly fine examples of subordination come from Martin Luther King Jr. In the following passage, he piles up dependent clauses beginning with *when* to build up suspense for his main statement, given in the independent clause at the end:

Perhaps it is easy for those who have never felt the stinging darts of segregation to say, "Wait." But *when* you have seen vicious mobs lynch your mothers and fathers at will and drown your sisters and brothers at whim; *when* you have seen hate-filled policemen curse, kick, and even kill your black brothers and sisters; . . . *when* you have to concoct an answer for a five-year-old son who is asking: "Daddy, why do white people treat colored people so mean?"; *when* you take a cross-country drive and find it necessary to sleep night after night in the uncomfortable corners of your automobile because no motel will accept you; . . . *when* your first name becomes "nigger," your middle name becomes "boy" (however old you are) and your last name becomes "John," and your wife and mother are never given the respected title "Mrs."; . . . *when* you are forever fighting a degenerating sense of "nobodiness" — then you will understand why we find it difficult to wait.

— MARTIN LUTHER KING JR., "Letter from Birmingham Jail"

A dependent clause can also create an ironic effect if it somehow undercuts the independent clause. A master of this technique, Mark Twain once opened a paragraph with this sentence:

▶ **Always obey your parents, *when they are present.***

— MARK TWAIN, "Advice to Youth"

## Editing for coordination and subordination

How do your ideas flow from one sentence to another? Do they connect smoothly and clearly? Are the more important ideas given more emphasis than the less important ones? These guidelines will help you edit with such questions in mind.

- Look for strings of short sentences that might be combined to join related ideas. (43a)

▶ **The report was short~~.~~, ~~It was~~ [but] persuasive~~.~~; ~~It~~ [it] changed my mind.**

- If you often link ideas with *and*, are the linked ideas equally important? If they are not, edit to subordinate the less important ones. (43b)
- Are the most important ideas in independent clauses? If not, edit so that they are. (43b)

▶ **~~The~~ [Even though the] report was short, ~~even though~~ it changed my mind.**

## THINKING CRITICALLY ABOUT COORDINATION AND SUBORDINATION

**Reading with an Eye for Coordination and Subordination**

Read over the first draft of "All-Powerful Coke" (see p. 75), paying special attention to the coordination and subordination. Do you notice any patterns — is there some of each? more of one than the other? Identify the coordination and subordination in one paragraph. Are they used appropriately? If not, revise the paragraph by following the guidelines in this chapter.

**Thinking about Your Own Use of Coordination and Subordination**

Analyze two paragraphs from one of your drafts. Do the independent clauses contain the main ideas? How many dependent clauses do you find? Should the ideas in the dependent clauses be subordinate to those in the independent clauses? Revise the paragraphs to use coordination and subordination effectively. What conclusions can you draw about your use of coordination and subordination?

# Sentence Variety

44

Row upon row of trees identical in size and shape may appeal, at some level, to our sense of orderliness, but in spite of that appeal, the rows soon become boring. If variety is the spice of life, it is also the spice of sentence structure, where sameness can result in dull, listless prose.

In one college classroom, a peer-response group worked on an essay for almost an hour, but its overall effect still seemed boring. Finally, one student exclaimed, "These sentences all look the same!"

And they were: every sentence in the essay was about the same length, and every sentence started with the subject. The group went to work again, shortening some sentences and revising others to create new rhythms. With the resulting sentence variety, the essay took on new life; it flowed.

## 44a Sentence length

Deciding how and when to vary sentence length is not always easy. Is there a "just right" length for a particular sentence or idea? The answer depends on, among other things, the writer's purpose, intended audience, and topic. A children's story, for instance, may call for mostly short sentences, whereas an article on nuclear disarmament may call for considerably longer ones.

Although a series of short or long sentences can sometimes be effective, alternating sentence length is usually the best approach. For example, after one or more long sentences with complex ideas or images, the punch of a short sentence can be dramatic:

> **The fire of, I think, five machine-guns was pouring upon us, and there was a series of heavy crashes caused by the Fascists flinging bombs over their own parapet in the most idiotic manner. It was intensely dark.**
>
> — GEORGE ORWELL, *Homage to Catalonia*

Similarly, try using a long sentence after several short ones.

> ***Sith.* What kind of a word is that? It sounds to me like the noise that emerges when you block one nostril and blow through the other, but to George Lucas it is a name that trumpets evil.**
>
> — ANTHONY LANE

### EXERCISE 44.1

The following paragraph can be improved by varying sentence length. Read it aloud to get a sense of how it sounds. Then revise it, creating some short, emphatic sentences and combining other sentences to create more effective long sentences. Add words or change punctuation as you need to.

> Before planting a tree, a gardener needs to choose a good location and dig a deep enough hole. The location should have the right kind of soil, sufficient drainage, and enough light for the type of tree chosen. The hole should be slightly deeper than the root-ball and about twice as wide. The gardener must unwrap the root-ball, for even burlap, which is biodegradable, may be treated with chemicals that will eventually damage the roots. The roots may have grown into a compact ball if the tree has been in a pot for some time, and they should be separated or cut apart in this case. The gardener should set the root-ball into the hole and then begin to fill the hole with loose dirt. After filling the hole completely, he or she should make sure to water the tree thoroughly. New plantings require extra water and extra care for about three years before they are well rooted.

## 44b Sentence openings

If sentence after sentence begins with a subject, a passage may become monotonous or even hard to read.

**The way football and basketball are played is as interesting as the players.** *Because football* **~~Football~~ is a game of precision**, *each* **~~Each~~ play is diagrammed to accomplish a certain goal. Basketball**, *however,* **is a game of endurance.** *In fact, a* **~~A~~ basketball game looks like a track meet**; *the* **~~The~~ team that drops of exhaustion first loses.**

The editing adds variety by using a subordinating word (*Because*) and transitions (*however* and *In fact*) and by linking sentences. Varying sentence openings prevents the passage from seeming to jerk or lurch along.

You can add variety to your sentence openings by using transitions, various kinds of phrases, and introductory dependent clauses.

### 1 Using transitional expressions

See how transitions bring variety and clarity to this passage.

In order to be alert Friday morning in New York, I planned to take the shuttle from Washington Thursday night. *On Thursday morning* it began to

> snow in Washington and to snow even harder in New York. *By mid-afternoon* I decided not to risk the shuttle and caught a train to New York. *Seven hours later* the train completed its three-hour trip. I arrived at Penn Station to find a city shut down by the worst blizzard since 1947.
>
> — LINDA ELLERBEE, "And So It Goes"

Here the transitional words establish chronology and help carry readers smoothly through the paragraph. (For more on transitions, see 7d4.)

### 2 Using phrases

Prepositional, verbal, and absolute phrases can also provide variety in sentence openings.

**PREPOSITIONAL PHRASES**

*Before dawn*, tired commuters drink their first cups of coffee.

*From a few scraps of wood in the Middle Ages to a precisely carved, electrified instrument in our times*, the guitar has gone through uncounted changes.

**VERBAL PHRASES**

*Frustrated by the delays*, the driver shouted at his car radio.

*To qualify for the finals*, a speller must win a regional championship.

*Having jumped the last hurdle*, she sprinted toward the finish line.

**ABSOLUTE PHRASES**

*Our hopes for victory shattered*, we started home.

*His nose against the window*, Rover gazed hopefully at the street.

In general, use a comma after these phrases when they open a sentence (46a).

### 3 Using dependent clauses

Dependent clauses are another way to open a sentence.

*While the boss sat on his tractor*, I was down in a ditch, pounding in stakes.

*What they want* is a place to call home.

In general, use a comma after an adverb clause that opens a sentence (46a).

## 44c Sentence types

In addition to using different lengths and openings, you can use different types of sentences. Sentences can be classified in three different ways: grammatically, functionally, and rhetorically.

### 1 Grammatical types

Grammatically, sentences fall into four categories — simple, compound, complex, and compound-complex — based on the number of independent and dependent clauses they contain (31d1). Varying your sentences among these grammatical types can help you create readable, effective prose.

### 2 Functional types

In terms of function, sentences are declarative (making a statement), interrogative (asking a question), imperative (giving a command), or exclamatory (expressing strong feeling). Most sentences are declarative, but occasionally a command, a question, or an exclamation may be appropriate.

**COMMAND**

Coal-burning plants undoubtedly harm the environment in various ways; for example, they contribute to acid rain. *But consider the alternatives.*

**QUESTION**

*Why would sixteen middle-aged people try to backpack thirty-seven miles?* At this point, I was not at all sure.

**EXCLAMATION**

*Divorcés! They were everywhere!* Sometimes he felt like a new member of an enormous club, the Divorcés of America, that he had never before even heard of.

### 3 Rhetorical types

By highlighting sentence endings and beginnings, periodic and cumulative sentences can create strong effects.

#### *Periodic sentences*

Periodic sentences postpone the main idea (usually in an independent clause) until the very end of the sentence. They are especially useful for creating tension or building toward a climactic, surprise, or inspirational ending.

> **Even though large tracts of Europe and many old and famous states have fallen or may fall into the grasp of the Gestapo and all the odious apparatus of Nazi rule, *we shall not flag or fail.***
>
> — WINSTON CHURCHILL

Look at the following sentence and its revision to see how periodic order can provide emphasis:

**ORIGINAL SENTENCE**

The nations of the world have no alternative but coexistence because another world war would be unwinnable and because total destruction would certainly occur.

**REVISED AS A PERIODIC SENTENCE**

Because another world war would be unwinnable and because total destruction would certainly occur, the nations of the world have no alternative but coexistence.

Nothing is wrong with the first sentence. But to emphasize the idea in the independent clause — *no alternative but coexistence* — the writer chose to revise using the periodic pattern.

### Cumulative sentences

Cumulative sentences, which begin with an independent clause and then add details in phrases and in dependent clauses (as does the preceding sentence labeled *original*), are far more common than periodic sentences. They are useful when you want to provide both immediate understanding of the main idea and a great deal of supporting detail.

> ***I can still see her*, a tiny nun with a sharp pink nose, confidently drawing a dead-straight horizontal line like a highway across the blackboard, flourishing her chalk at the end of it, her veil flapping out behind her as she turned back to class.** — KITTY BURNS FLOREY

> ***Powther threw small secret appraising glances at the coffee cup*, lipstick all around the edges, brown stains on the side where the coffee had dripped and spilled over, the saucer splotched with a whole series of dark brown rings.** — ANN PETRY, *The Narrows*

### EXERCISE 44.2

Revise each of the following sentences twice, once as a periodic sentence and once as a cumulative sentence.

1. Obviously not understanding reporters, the politician did not know their names, did not answer their questions, and did not read their stories.

## Editing for sentence variety

- Check sentence *length* by counting the words in each sentence. If the difference between the longest and the shortest sentences is fairly small — say, five words or fewer — try revising some sentences to create greater variety. Should two or more short sentences be combined because they deal with closely related ideas? Should a long sentence be split up because it contains too many important ideas? (44a)
- Look at sentence *openings*. If most sentences start with a subject, try recasting some to begin with a transition, a phrase, or a dependent clause. (44b)
- Vary *types* of sentences to make your writing more interesting. Do you use simple, compound, complex, and compound-complex sentences — or does one type predominate? Would a particular declarative sentence be more effective as a command or question or exclamation? Could you use a periodic or cumulative sentence for special effect? (44c)

2. With an intense dedication to the sport of cycling, Lance Armstrong trained in grueling conditions, ate a carefully planned diet, and spoke out against the negative effects of doping.

## THINKING CRITICALLY ABOUT SENTENCE VARIETY

**Reading with an Eye for Sentence Variety**

Read something by an author you admire. Analyze two paragraphs for sentence length, opening, and type. Compare the sentence variety in these paragraphs with that in one of your paragraphs. What similarities or differences do you recognize, and what conclusions can you draw about sentence variety?

**Thinking about Your Own Sentence Variety**

Choose a piece of writing you have recently completed, and analyze two or three pages for sentence variety. Note sentence length, opening, and type (grammatical, functional, and rhetorical). Choose a passage you think can be improved for variety, and make those revisions.

# Memorable Prose

45

How many times have you read or heard something so striking that you wanted immediately to share it with a friend? All of us recognize, and can even quote, memorable words that have been written or spoken or sung — the opening of Jane Austen's *Pride and Prejudice*, perhaps, or passages from Martin Luther King's "I Have a Dream" speech, or lyrics to an Eminem song. As writers, we can profit by examining — and using — some of the elements that help make such pieces memorable: strong verbs, active voice, and special effects such as repetition, antithesis, and inversion.

## 45a Strong verbs

The greatest writers have a genius for choosing the exact words that will hold a reader's attention. In your own writing, you can help gain this attention by using strong, precise verbs.

### 1 Using precise verbs

Verbs serve as the real workhorses of our language. Look, for instance, at the strong, precise verbs in the following passage:

> **A fire engine, out for a trial spin, *roared* past Emerson's house, hot with readiness for public duty. Over the barn roofs the martens *dipped* and *chittered*. A swarthy daughter of an asparagus grower, in culottes, shirt, and bandanna, *pedalled* past on her bicycle.**
>
> — E. B. WHITE, "Walden"

If White had used more general verbs — such as *drove*, *flew*, *called*, and *rode* — the passage would be much less effective. With White's verbs, however, readers can hear the roar of the fire engine, see the martens swooping downward and hear them chirping shrilly, and feel the young woman pushing on the pedals of her bicycle.

Some of the most common verbs in English — especially *be*, *do*, and *have* — carry little or no sense of specific action. Try not to overuse them in situations where precise verbs would be more effective. Look at how the following sentences are strengthened when precise verbs are used:

- **Constant playing of video games ~~is harmful to~~ children's development.** [inserted: stunts and distorts]
- **Sidewalk artists offered to ~~do~~ my portrait in ten minutes.** [inserted: sketch]
- **We ~~had~~ basic training at Fort Ord.** [inserted: sweated through]

### *Expletives*

One weak verb construction to use sparingly is the expletive, which begins with *there* or *it* followed by a form of *be* or another linking verb (*there are*, *it seems*, and so on). However, a writer can use an expletive effectively to introduce an idea with extra emphasis:

> ***It is* for us, the living, to ensure that We the People shall become the powerful.** — JUNE JORDAN, "Inside America"

Here the *it is* slows down the opening of the sentence and sets up a formal rhythm that emphasizes what follows. Often, however, writers do not use expletives to add emphasis. Instead, they merely overuse them. Note how the following sentences are strengthened by deleting the expletives:

- **~~There are many~~ people ~~who~~ fear success because they do not believe they deserve it.** [inserted: Many]
- **~~It is necessary for presidential~~ candidates ~~to~~ perform well on television.** [inserted: Presidential; must]

## 2 Changing nouns to verbs

Much modern writing expresses action through nouns formed from verbs, a process called *nominalization*. Although nominalization can help make prose more concise — for example, using *abolition* instead of *the process of abolishing* — it can also produce the opposite effect, making a sentence unnecessarily wordy and hard to read. Nominalization reduces the active quality of a sentence by burying the action and by forcing the writer to use weak verbs and too many prepositional phrases. Too often, writers use nominalization not to simplify a complex explanation but to make an idea sound more complex than it is.

- **The firm is now ~~engaged in an assessment of~~** assessing **its procedures for ~~the development of~~** developing **new products.**

The original sentence sounds pretentious, and the nominalization clouds the message. In contrast, the edited version is clear and forceful.

## 45b Active and passive voice

In addition to choosing strong, precise verbs, you can help make your prose memorable by using those verbs appropriately in active or passive voice (32g). Look at the following passage:

> **[John F. Kennedy] died of a wound in the brain caused by a rifle bullet that was fired at him as he was riding through downtown Dallas in a motorcade.**
>
> **Vice President Lyndon Baines Johnson, who was riding in the third car behind Mr. Kennedy's, was sworn in as the 36th President of the United States 99 minutes after Mr. Kennedy's death.**
>
> — TOM WICKER, *New York Times*

As this passage indicates, the passive voice works effectively in certain situations: when the performer is unknown, unwilling to be identified, or less important than the recipient of the action. In general, however, try to use the active voice whenever possible. Because the passive voice diverts attention from the performer of an action and because it is usually wordier than the active voice, using it excessively makes for dull and difficult reading.

Edit an unnecessary passive construction to make it active.

- **In ~~Gower's~~** his **research, ~~it was~~** Gower **found that pythons often dwell in trees.**

### EXERCISE 45.1

Look at the following sentences, in which some of the verbs are active and some passive. Then rewrite each sentence in the other voice, and decide which version you prefer and why. Example:

~~You are~~ I hereby relieved you of your duties. ~~by me.~~

1. Mistakes were made.
2. Musical legends such as Ray Charles, Billie Holiday, and Johnny Cash have all influenced Norah Jones.
3. The students who made the prank calls were suspended by the school board.
4. The leader of the rebels was assassinated by his longtime enemy.
5. In a patient with celiac disease, intestinal damage can be caused by the body's immunological response to gluten.

**bedfordstmartins.com/smhandbook** For more exercises on active and passive voice, go to Exercise Central and click on **Verbs**.

### EXERCISE 45.2

Revise the following paragraph to eliminate weak verbs, unnecessary nominalizations and expletives, and inappropriate use of the passive voice.

> As dogs became domesticated by humans over many thousands of years, the canine species evolved into hundreds of breeds designed to perform specific tasks such as pulling sleds and guarding sheep. Over time, the need for many breeds decreased. For example, as humans evolved from hunter-gatherers into farmers, it was no longer necessary for them to own hunting dogs. Later, as farming societies became industrialized, shepherds were rarely needed. But by this time humans had grown accustomed to dogs' companionship, and breeding continued. Today, most dogs are kept by their owners simply as companions, but some dogs still do the work they were intentionally bred for, such as following a scent, guarding a home, or leading the blind.

## 45c Special effects

Contemporary movies often succeed on the basis of their special effects. Similarly, special effects like repetition, antithesis, and inversion can animate your prose and help make it memorable.

### 1 Using repetition

Carefully used, repetition of sounds, words, phrases, or other grammatical constructions serves as a powerful stylistic device. Orators have long known its power. Here is a famous use of repetition from one of Winston Churchill's addresses to the British people during World War II:

> **We shall not flag or fail, we shall go on to the end. We shall fight in France, we shall fight on the seas and oceans, we shall fight with growing confidence and growing strength in the air, we shall defend our island, whatever the cost may be; we shall fight on the beaches,**

> **. . . we shall fight in the fields and in the streets, . . . we shall never surrender.**
> — WINSTON CHURCHILL

In this passage, Churchill uses the constant hammering of *we shall* accompanied by the repetition of *f* sounds (*flag, fail, fight, France, confidence, defend, fields*) to strengthen his listeners' resolve.

Though we may not be prime ministers, we can use repetition to equally good effect. Here is another example:

> **So my dream date turned into a nightmare. Where was the quiet, considerate, caring guy I thought I had met? In his place appeared this jerk. He strutted, he postured, he preened — and then he bragged, he bellowed, he practically brayed — just like the donkey he so much reminded me of.**

Be careful, however, to use repetition only for a deliberate purpose.

### *Multiple negatives*

One common type of repetition is to use more than one negative term in a negative statement. In *I can't hardly see you*, for example, both *can't* and *hardly* carry negative meanings. Emphatic double negatives — and triple, quadruple, and more — are especially common in the South and among speakers of some African American varieties of English, who may say, for example, *Don't none of my people come from up North.*

Multiple negatives have a long history in English and can be found in the works of Chaucer and Shakespeare, as well as in other languages. In the eighteenth century, however, in an effort to make English more logical, double negatives came to be labeled as incorrect. In college writing, you may well have reason to quote passages that include them (whether from Shakespeare, Toni Morrison, or your grandmother), but it is safer to avoid other uses of double negatives in academic writing.

### EXERCISE 45.3

Go through the examples in 45c1, identifying the uses of repetition. Using one example as a model, write a passage of your own with effective repetition.

## 2 Using antithesis

Antithesis is the use of parallel structures to highlight contrast or opposition (see Chapter 37). Like other uses of parallelism, antithesis provides a pleasing rhythm that calls readers' attention to the contrast, often in a startling or amusing way.

- **Love is an ideal thing, marriage a real thing.**
- **The congregation didn't think much of the new preacher, and what the new preacher thought of the congregation she didn't wish to say.**
- **It is a sin to believe evil of others — but it is not a mistake.**

— H. L. MENCKEN

## EXERCISE 45.4

Using one of the preceding examples as a guide, create a sentence of your own that uses antithesis. You might begin by thinking of opposites you could build on: hope/despair, good/evil, fire/ice. Or you might begin with a topic you want to write about: success, greed, generosity, and so on.

### 3 Using inverted word order

Writers may use inversion of the usual word order, such as putting the verb before the subject or the object before the subject and verb, to create surprise or to emphasize a particular word or phrase.

Out of the tree ^ two dead birds. ^
- **~~Two dead birds~~ plummeted ~~out of the tree.~~**

The inverted word order creates a more dramatic sentence by putting the emphasis at the end, on *two dead birds*.

As with any unusual sentence pattern, use inverted word order sparingly, only to create occasional special effects.

### Editing verbs and nouns

- Underline all verbs, and look to see whether you rely too much on *be*, *do*, and *have*. If so, try to substitute more specific verbs. (45a1)
- Identify all expletives, and delete any that do not create special emphasis. (45a1)
- Note nouns whose meaning could be expressed by a verb. Try revising using the verbs instead of the nouns. (45a2)
- Look for passive verbs, and decide whether they obscure the performer of the action or dull the sentence. If so, recast the sentence in the active voice. (45b)

- **Into this grey lake plopped the thought, I know this man, don't I?**
  — DORIS LESSING

- **In a hole in the ground there lived a hobbit.** — J. R. R. TOLKIEN

## EXERCISE 45.5

Look at something you have written, and find a sentence that might be more effective with inverted word order. Experiment with the word order. Read the results aloud, and compare the effects.

## THINKING CRITICALLY ABOUT PROSE STYLE

**Reading with an Eye for Prose Style**

Chapters 42–45 present many elements that mark effective prose. One entertaining way to practice these elements is to imitate them. Choose a writer you admire. Reread (or listen to) this writer's work, getting a feel for the rhythms, the structures, the special effects. Make a list of the elements that contribute to the distinctive style. Then choose a well-known story, and retell it in that writer's style. Following is the opening of "The Three Little Pigs" as one student imagined Edgar Allan Poe might have told it.

> It began as a mere infatuation. I admired them from afar, with a longing that only a wolf may know. Soon, these feelings turned to torment. Were I even to set eyes upon their porcine forms, the bowels of my soul raged, as if goaded by some festering poison. As the chilling winds of November howled, my gullet yearned for them. I soon feasted only upon an earnest and consuming desire for the moment of their decease.

**Thinking about Your Own Prose Style**

Read over something you have written, looking for memorable sentences. If few sentences catch your eye, choose some that show promise — ones with strong verbs or a pleasing rhythm, perhaps. Using this chapter for guidance, try revising one or two sentences to make them more effective and memorable. Finally, note some ways in which your writing is effective and some strategies for making it more effective.

# Part 9



# PUNCTUATION

# 46 Commas

It's hard to go through a day without encountering commas. Even the directions for making hot cereal depend on the careful placement of a comma: *Add Cream of Wheat slowly, stirring constantly.* Here the comma tells the cook to *add the cereal slowly.* If the comma came before the word *slowly*, however, the cook might add the cereal all at once and *stir slowly* — perhaps ending up with lumpy cereal.

Because the comma can play many roles in a sentence, comma use often doesn't follow hard and fast rules. Using commas effectively requires you to make decisions that involve audience, purpose, rhythm, and style — not just grammar.

## 46a Commas after introductory elements

A comma usually follows an introductory word, expression, phrase, or clause.

- **Slowly, Drue became conscious of her predicament.**
- **However, health care costs keep rising.**
- **In the end, only you can decide.**
- **Wearing new running shoes, Logan prepared for the race.**
- **To win the contest, Connor needed skill and luck.**
- **Pencil poised in anticipation, Audrey waited for the drawing contest to begin.**
- **While the storm was raging, we tried to read by candlelight.**

Some writers omit the comma if the introductory element is short and does not seem to require a pause after it.

- ***At the racetrack* Henry lost nearly his entire paycheck.**

However, you will seldom be wrong if you use a comma after an introductory element. If the introductory element is followed by inverted word order, with the verb preceding the subject, do not use a comma unless misreading might occur.

- **From directly behind my seat, came huge clouds of cigar smoke.**
- **Before he went, on came the rains.**

EXERCISE 46.1

In the following sentences, add any commas that are needed after the introductory element. Example:

> To find a good day-care provider, parents usually need both time and money.

1. At the worst possible moment a computer crash made me lose my document.
2. To our surprise the charity auction raised enough money to build a new technology center.
3. Unaware that the microphone was on the candidate made an offensive comment.
4. Whenever someone rings the doorbell her dog goes berserk.
5. Therefore answering the seemingly simple question is very difficult.
6. With the fifth century came the fall of the Roman Empire.
7. A tray of shrimp in one hand and a pile of napkins in the other the waiter avoided me.
8. Toward the rapids floated an empty rubber raft.
9. When they woke up the exhausted campers no longer wanted to hike.
10. Covered in glitter the children proudly displayed their art project.

**bedfordstmartins.com/smhandbook** For more exercises on using commas with introductory elements, go to Exercise Central and click on **Commas**.

## 46b Commas in compound sentences

A comma usually precedes a coordinating conjunction (*and*, *but*, *for*, *nor*, *or*, *so*, or *yet*) that joins two independent clauses in a compound sentence.

- **The title sounds impressive, but *administrative clerk* is just another word for *photocopier*.**

- **The show started at last, and the crowd grew quiet.**

With very short clauses, writers sometimes omit the comma before *and* or *or*. You will never be wrong to include it, however.

- **She saw her chance and she took it.**
- **She saw her chance, and she took it.**

Always use the comma if there is any chance of misreading the sentence without it.

- **The game ended in victory, and pandemonium erupted.**

You may want to use a semicolon rather than a comma when the clauses are long and complex or contain their own commas.

- **When these early migrations took place, the ice was still confined to the lands in the far north; but eight hundred thousand years ago, when man was already established in the temperate latitudes, the ice moved southward until it covered large parts of Europe and Asia.**

— ROBERT JASTROW, *Until the Sun Dies*

Be careful not to use *only* a comma between independent clauses. Doing so is a serious error called a comma splice (see Chapter 38). Either use a coordinating conjunction after the comma, or use a semicolon.

| | |
|---|---|
| **COMMA SPLICE** | Do not say luck is responsible for your new job, give yourself the credit you deserve. |
| **REVISED** | Do not say luck is responsible for your new job, *but* give yourself the credit you deserve. |
| **REVISED** | Do not say luck is responsible for your new job; give yourself the credit you deserve. |

## EXERCISE 46.2

Use a comma and a coordinating conjunction (*and*, *but*, *for*, *nor*, *or*, *so*, or *yet*) to combine each of the following pairs of sentences into one sentence. Delete or rearrange words if necessary. Example:

I had finished studying for the test, so I went to bed.

1. The chef did not want to serve a heavy dessert. She was planning to have a rich stew for the main course.
2. My mother rarely allowed us to eat sweets. Halloween was a special exception.
3. Scientists have mapped the human genome. They learn more every day about how genes affect an individual's health.
4. The playwright disliked arguing with directors. She avoided rehearsals.
5. Tropical fish do not bark. They are not cuddly pets.

**bedfordstmartins.com/smhandbook** For more exercises on using commas in compound sentences, go to Exercise Central and click on **Commas**.

## 46c Commas to set off nonrestrictive elements

Nonrestrictive elements are clauses, phrases, and words that do *not* limit, or restrict, the meaning of the words they modify. Since such elements are not essential to the meaning of a sentence, they should be set off from the rest of the sentence with commas. Restrictive elements, on the other hand, *do* limit meaning and should *not* be set off with commas.

**RESTRICTIVE** Drivers *who have been convicted of drunken driving* should lose their licenses.

In the preceding sentence, the clause *who have been convicted of drunken driving* is essential to the meaning because it limits the word it modifies, *Drivers*, to only those drivers who have been convicted of drunken driving. Therefore, it is *not* set off by commas.

**NONRESTRICTIVE** The two drivers involved in the accident, *who have been convicted of drunken driving*, should lose their licenses.

In the second sentence, however, the clause *who have been convicted of drunken driving* is not essential to the meaning because it does not limit what it modifies, *The two drivers involved in the accident*, but merely provides additional information about these drivers. Therefore, the clause is set off with commas.

Notice how using or not using commas to set off such an element can change the meaning of a sentence.

- **The bus drivers rejecting the management offer remained on strike.**
- **The bus drivers, rejecting the management offer, remained on strike.**

The first sentence says that only some bus drivers, the ones who rejected the offer, remained on strike, implying that other drivers went back to work. The second sentence implies that all of the drivers remained on strike.

To decide whether an element is restrictive or nonrestrictive, mentally delete the element. Does the deletion change the meaning of the rest of the sentence or make it unclear? If so, the element is probably restrictive, and you should not set it off with commas. If it does not change the meaning, the element is probably nonrestrictive and requires commas.

### 1 Adjective and adverb clauses

Adjective clauses (31c4) that begin with *that* are always restrictive; do not set them off with commas. Adjective clauses beginning with *which* may be either restrictive or nonrestrictive. (Some writers prefer to use *which* only for nonrestrictive clauses, which they set off with commas.)

**NONRESTRICTIVE CLAUSES**

- **I borrowed books from the rental library of Shakespeare and Company, *which was the library and bookstore of Sylvia Beach at 12 rue de l'Odeon.*** — ERNEST HEMINGWAY, *A Moveable Feast*

The adjective clause describing Shakespeare and Company is not necessary to the meaning of the independent clause and therefore is set off with a comma.

In general, set off an adverb clause (31c4) that follows a main clause only if it begins with *although*, *even though*, *while*, or another subordinating conjunction expressing the idea of contrast. (For a list of subordinating conjunctions, see 31b7.)

- **He uses semicolons frequently, while she prefers periods and short sentences.**

The adverb clause *while she prefers periods and short sentences* expresses the idea of contrast; therefore, it is set off with a comma.

**RESTRICTIVE CLAUSES**

- **The claim *that men like seriously to battle one another to some sort of finish* is a myth.**

  — JOHN MCMURTRY, "Kill 'Em! Crush 'Em! Eat 'Em Raw!"

  The adjective clause is necessary to the meaning of the sentence because it explains which claim is a myth; therefore, the clause is not set off with commas.

- **The man~~,~~ who rescued Jana's puppy~~,~~ won her eternal gratitude.**

  The adjective clause *who rescued Jana's puppy* is necessary to the meaning because only the man who rescued the puppy won the gratitude; the clause is restrictive and so takes no commas.

With the exceptions noted, do *not* set off an adverb clause that follows a main clause.

- **Remember to check your calculations~~,~~ before you submit the form.**

## 2 Participles and phrases

Participles and participial phrases (31c3) may be either restrictive or nonrestrictive. Prepositional phrases are usually restrictive, but sometimes they are not essential to the meaning of a sentence and are set off with commas.

**NONRESTRICTIVE PHRASES**

- **Stephanie, amazed, stared at the strange vehicle.**

  The participle *amazed* does not limit the meaning of *Stephanie*.

- **Many baby boomers, fearing that Social Security funds will be insufficient, are saving for their retirement through company investment plans.**

  The participial phrase beginning with *fearing* does not limit the meaning of *Many baby boomers* or change the central meaning of the sentence.

- **The bodyguards, in dark suits and matching ties, looked quite intimidating.**

The prepositional phrase *in dark suits and matching ties* does not limit the meaning of *The bodyguards*.

**RESTRICTIVE PHRASES**

- **A bird *in the hand* is worth two *in the bush*.**

  The prepositional phrases *in the hand* and *in the bush* are essential to the meaning.

- **Wood *cut from living trees* does not burn as well as dead wood.**

  The participial phrase *cut from living trees* is essential to the meaning.

- **The bodyguards were the men *in dark suits and matching ties*.**

  The prepositional phrase *in dark suits and matching ties* is essential to the meaning.

### 3 Appositives

An appositive is a noun or noun phrase that renames a nearby noun (31c3). When an appositive is not essential to identify what it renames, set it off with commas.

**NONRESTRICTIVE APPOSITIVES**

- **Jon Stewart, the irreverent news commentator, often pokes fun at political leaders.**

  Mr. Stewart's name identifies him; the appositive simply provides extra information.

- **Beethoven's opera, *Fidelio*, includes the "Prisoners' Chorus."**

  Beethoven wrote only one opera, so its name is not essential.

**RESTRICTIVE APPOSITIVES**

- **The news commentator *Jon Stewart* often pokes fun at political leaders.**

  The appositive *Jon Stewart* identifies the specific commentator.

- **Mozart's opera *The Marriage of Figaro* was considered revolutionary.**

  The appositive is restrictive because Mozart wrote more than one opera.

### EXERCISE 46.3

Use commas to set off nonrestrictive clauses, phrases, and appositives in any of the following sentences that contain such elements.

1. Anyone who lived through the Vietnam War remembers it as stressful and heartbreaking.
2. Embalming is a technique that preserves a cadaver.
3. I would feel right at home in the city dump which bears a striking resemblance to my bedroom.
4. The rescue workers exhausted and discouraged stared ahead without speaking.
5. The latest strip mall in our town offers the same useless junk as all the others.
6. Viruses unlike bacteria can reproduce only by infecting live cells.
7. Napoléon was forced into exile after his defeat by the British at Waterloo.
8. Hammurabi an ancient Babylonian king created laws that were carved on a stone for public display.
9. Birds' hearts have four chambers whereas reptiles' have three.
10. My grandfather always picked up pennies if he saw them lying on the sidewalk.

**bedfordstmartins.com/smhandbook** For more exercises on using commas with nonrestrictive elements, go to Exercise Central and click on **Commas**.

## 46d Commas to separate items in a series

Except in journalism writing, use a comma between items in a series of three or more words, phrases, or clauses.

> **I bumped into professors, horizontal bars, agricultural students, and swinging iron rings.** — JAMES THURBER, "University Days"

> **He has plundered our seas, ravaged our coasts, burnt our towns, and destroyed the lives of our people.**
> — THOMAS JEFFERSON, Declaration of Independence

You may see a series with no comma after the next-to-last item, particularly in newspaper writing. Occasionally, however, omitting the comma can cause confusion.

> **All the vegetables the cafeteria offered — broccoli, green beans, peas, and carrots — were cooked to an unrecognizable mush.**

Without the comma after *peas*, you wouldn't know if the cafeteria offered three vegetables (the third being a *mixture* of peas and carrots) or four.

When the items in a series contain commas of their own or other punctuation, separate them with semicolons rather than commas (47b).

Coordinate adjectives, those that relate equally to the noun they modify, should be separated by commas.

- **The *long*, *twisting*, *muddy* road led to a shack in the woods.**

In a sentence like *The cracked bathroom mirror reflected his face*, however, *cracked* and *bathroom* are not coordinate because *bathroom mirror* is the equivalent of a single word, which is modified by *cracked*. Hence, they are *not* separated by commas.

You can usually determine whether adjectives are coordinate by inserting *and* between them. If the sentence makes sense with the *and*, the adjectives are coordinate and should be separated by commas.

- **They are sincere *and* talented *and* inquisitive researchers.**

  The sentence makes sense with the *and*s, so the adjectives should be separated by commas: *They are sincere, talented, inquisitive researchers.*

- **Byron carried an elegant *and* gold *and* pocket watch.**

  The sentence does not make sense with the *and*s, so the adjectives should not be separated by commas: *Byron carried an elegant gold pocket watch.*

### EXERCISE 46.4

Revise any of the following sentences that require commas to set off words, phrases, or clauses in a series.

1. The students donated clothing school supplies and nonperishable food.
2. The tiny brown-eyed Lafayette twins were the only children in the kindergarten class who could already read.
3. Landscape architects need to consider many aspects of a plant: how often it blooms how much sunlight it needs and how tall it will grow.
4. Several art historians inspected the Chinese terra-cotta figures.
5. The young athletes' parents insist on calling every play judging every move and telling everyone within earshot exactly what is wrong with the team.

**bedfordstmartins.com/smhandbook** For more exercises on using commas in a series, go to Exercise Central and click on **Commas**.

## 46e Commas to set off parenthetical and transitional expressions

Parenthetical expressions add comments or information. Because they often interrupt the flow of a sentence or digress, they are usually set off with commas. Transitional expressions (7d and e) are also usually set off with commas. They include conjunctive adverbs (31b7) such as *however* and *furthermore* and other words and phrases used to connect parts of sentences.

- **Brain imaging, *incidentally*, shows that partisan political views, *of all things*, may be more emotional than rational.**
- **Roald Dahl's stories, *it turns out*, were often inspired by his own childhood.**
- **Ceiling fans are, *moreover*, less expensive than air conditioners.**
- **Shark attacks, *for example*, happen extremely rarely.**

## 46f Commas to set off contrasting elements, interjections, direct address, and tag questions

**CONTRASTING ELEMENTS**

- **On official business it was she, *not my father*, one would usually hear on the phone or in stores.**

— RICHARD RODRIGUEZ, "Aria: A Memoir of a Bilingual Childhood"

**INTERJECTIONS**

- ***My God*, who wouldn't want a wife?** — JUDY BRADY, "I Want a Wife"

**DIRECT ADDRESS**

- **Remember, *sir*, that you are under oath.**

**TAG QUESTIONS**

- **The governor did not veto the unemployment bill, *did she*?**

### EXERCISE 46.5

Revise each of the following sentences, using commas to set off parenthetical and transitional expressions, contrasting elements, interjections, words used in direct address, and tag questions.

1. One must consider the society as a whole not just its parts.
2. Many of the parents and students did in fact support the position of the teacher who resigned.
3. You don't expect me to read this speech do you?
4. Coming in ahead of schedule and under budget it appears is the only way to keep this client happy.
5. Ladies and gentlemen I bid you farewell.

**bedfordstmartins.com/smhandbook** For more exercises on using commas with these elements, go to Exercise Central and click on **Commas**.

## 46g Commas with dates, addresses, titles, and numbers

### Dates

Use a comma between the day of the week and the month, between the day of the month and the year, and between the year and the rest of the sentence, if any.

- **The attacks on the morning of *Tuesday*, *September 11*, *2001*, took the United States by surprise.**

Do not use commas with dates in inverted order or with dates consisting of only the month and the year.

- **She dated the letter *18 October 2006*.**
- **Thousands of Germans swarmed over the Berlin Wall in *November 1989*.**

### Addresses and place-names

Use a comma after each part of an address or place-name, including the state if no ZIP code is given. Do not precede a ZIP code with a comma.

- **Forward my mail to the Department of English, The Ohio State University, Columbus, Ohio 43210.**
- **Portland, Oregon, is much larger than Portland, Maine.**

### *Titles*

Use commas to set off a title such as *MD* and *PhD* from the name preceding it and from the rest of the sentence. The titles *Jr.* and *Sr.*, however, often appear without commas.

- **Jaime Mejía, *PhD*, will speak about his anthropological research.**
- **Martin Luther King *Jr.* was one of the twentieth century's greatest orators.**

### *Numbers*

In numerals of five digits or more, use a comma between each group of three digits, starting from the right.

- **The city's population rose to *158,000* in the 2000 census.**

The comma is optional within numerals of four digits but is never used in years with four digits.

- **The college had an enrollment of *1,789* [or *1789*] in the fall of 2006.**

Do not use a comma within house or building numbers, ZIP codes, or page numbers.

- **My parents live at *11311* Wimberly Drive, Richmond, Virginia *23233*.**
- **Turn to page *1566*.**

### EXERCISE 46.6

Revise each of the following sentences, using commas appropriately with dates, addresses, place-names, titles, and numbers.

1. The abridged version of the assigned novel is 1200 pages long.
2. More than 350000 people gathered for the protest on the Washington Mall.
3. New Delhi India and Islamabad Pakistan became the capitals of two independent nations at midnight on August 15 1947.

4. MLA headquarters are at 26 Broadway New York New York 10004.
5. I was convinced that the nameplate I. M. Well MD was one of my sister's pranks.

**bedfordstmartins.com/smhandbook** For more exercises on using commas with these elements, go to Exercise Central and click on **Commas**.

## 46h Commas with quotations

Commas set off a quotation from words used to introduce or identify the source of the quotation. A comma following a quotation goes inside the closing quotation mark.

- **A German proverb warns, "Go to law for a sheep, and lose your cow."**
- **"All I know about grammar," said Joan Didion, "is its infinite power."**

Do not use a comma after a question mark or exclamation point.

- **"What's a thousand dollars?," asks Groucho Marx in *Cocoanuts*. "Mere chicken feed. A poultry matter."**
- **"Out, damned spot!," cries Lady Macbeth.**

Do not use a comma to introduce a quotation with *that*.

- **The writer of Ecclesiastes concludes that, "all is vanity."**

Do not use a comma with a quotation when the rest of the sentence does more than introduce or identify the source of the quotation.

- **People who say, "Have a nice day" irritate me.**
- **He put off military service because he had, "other priorities."**

Do not use a comma before an indirect quotation — one that does not use the speaker's exact words.

- **Patrick Henry declared, that he wanted either liberty or death.**

### EXERCISE 46.7

Insert a comma in any of the following sentences that require one.

1. "The public be damned!" William Henry Vanderbilt was reported to have said. "I'm working for my stockholders."
2. My professor insisted "The cutting edge gets dull very quickly."
3. Who remarked that "youth is wasted on the young"?
4. "Learning without thought is labor lost; thought without learning is perilous" Confucius argued.
5. "Do you have any idea who I am?" the well-dressed man asked belligerently.

**bedfordstmartins.com/smhandbook** For more exercises on using commas with quotations, go to Exercise Central and click on **Commas**.

## 46i Commas for understanding

Sometimes a comma is necessary to make a sentence easier to read or understand.

- **The members of the dance troupe strutted in, in matching tuxedos and top hats.**
- **Before, I had planned to major in biology.**

## 46j Unnecessary commas

Excessive use of commas can spoil an otherwise fine sentence.

### *Around restrictive elements*

Do not use commas to set off restrictive elements — elements that limit, or define, the meaning of the words they modify or refer to (46c).

- **My mother dislikes films, that include foul language.**
- **A law, reforming campaign financing, was passed in 2002.**

- **My only defense~~,~~ against my allergies~~,~~ is to stay indoors.**
- **The actor~~,~~ Philip Seymour Hoffman~~,~~ might win the award.**

### *Between subjects and verbs, verbs and objects or complements, and prepositions and objects*

Do not use a comma between a subject and its verb, a verb and its object or complement, or a preposition and its object. This rule holds true even if the subject, object, or complement is a long phrase or clause.

- **Watching old movies late at night~~,~~ is a way for me to relax.**
- **Parents must decide~~,~~ how much television their children should watch.**
- **The winner of~~,~~ the community-service award stepped forward.**

### *In compound constructions*

In compound constructions (other than compound sentences — see 46b), do not use a comma before or after a coordinating conjunction that joins the two parts.

- **Donald Trump was born rich~~,~~ and has used his money to make money.**

  The *and* here joins parts of a compound predicate, which should not be separated by a comma.

- **Ellen Johnson-Sirleaf~~,~~ and George Weah both claimed to have won the election.**

  The *and* here joins parts of a compound subject, which should not be separated by a comma.

### *In a series*

Do not use a comma before the first or after the last item in a series (46d).

## Editing for commas

Research for this book shows that five of the most common errors in college writing involve commas. Check your writing for these errors:

- Check every sentence that doesn't begin with the subject to see whether it opens with an introductory element (a word, phrase, or clause that tells when, where, how, or why the main action of the sentence occurs). Use a comma to separate the introductory material from the main part of the sentence. (46a)
- Look at every sentence that contains one of the conjunctions *and*, *but*, *for*, *nor*, *or*, *so*, or *yet*. If the groups of words before and after the conjunction both function as complete sentences, you have a compound sentence. Make sure to use a comma before the conjunction. (46b)
- Look at each adjective clause beginning with *which*, *who*, *whom*, *whose*, *when*, or *where*, and at each phrase and appositive. Decide whether the element is essential to the meaning of the sentence. If the rest of the sentence would be unclear without it, you should not set off the element with commas. (46c)
- Identify all adjective clauses beginning with *that*, and make sure they are not set off with commas. (46c1 and 46j)
- Do not use commas to set off restrictive elements; between subjects and verbs, verbs and objects or complements, or prepositions and objects; to separate parts of compound constructions other than compound sentences; or before the first or after the last item in a series. (46j)

**The auction included~~,~~ furniture, paintings, and china.**

**The swimmer took slow, powerful~~,~~ strokes.**

### THINKING CRITICALLY ABOUT COMMAS

**Reading with an Eye for Commas**

The following poem uses commas to create rhythm and guide readers. Read the poem aloud, listening especially to the effect of the commas at the end of the first and fifth lines. Then read it again as if those commas were omitted, noting the difference. What is the effect of the poet's decision not to use a comma at the end of the third line?

Some say the world will end in fire,
Some say in ice.
From what I've tasted of desire
I hold with those who favor fire.
But if it had to perish twice,
I think I know enough of hate
To say that for destruction ice
Is also great
And would suffice.

— ROBERT FROST, "Fire and Ice"

**Thinking about Your Own Use of Commas**

Choose a paragraph that you have written. Remove all of the commas, and read it aloud. What is the effect of leaving out the commas? Now, punctuate the passage with commas, consulting this chapter. Did you replace all of your original commas? Did you add any new ones? Explain why you added the commas you did.

# Semicolons

# 47

If you've ever pored over the fine print at the bottom of an ad for a big sale, looking for the opening hours or the address of the store nearest you, then you've seen plenty of semicolons in action. Here's an example from a Bloomingdale's ad:

*Store Hours—*
*Short Hills:*
*SUN., 12–6;*
*MON., 10–9:30;*
*TUES., 10–5;*
*WED. through*
*FRI., 10–9:30;*
*SAT., 10–8.*

The semicolons separate the information for one day's hours from the next. Semicolons create a pause stronger than that of a comma but not as strong as the full pause of a period.

## 47a Semicolons with independent clauses

You can join independent clauses in several ways: with a comma and a coordinating conjunction (46b), with a colon (51d), with a dash (51c), or with a semicolon. Semicolons provide writers with subtle ways of signaling closely related clauses. The clause following a semicolon often restates an idea expressed in the first clause; it can also expand on or present a contrast to the first.

- **Immigration acts were passed; newcomers had to prove, besides moral correctness and financial solvency, their ability to read.**

  — MARY GORDON, "More Than Just a Shrine"

  Gordon uses a semicolon to lead to a clause that expands on the first one. The semicolon also gives the sentence an abrupt rhythm that suits the topic: laws that imposed strict requirements.

A semicolon should link independent clauses joined by conjunctive adverbs such as *therefore, however*, and *indeed* or transitional expressions such as *in fact, in addition*, and *for example* (38c).

- **The circus comes as close to being the world in microcosm as anything I know; in a way, it puts all the rest of show business in the shade.**

  — E. B. WHITE, "The Ring of Time"

If two independent clauses joined by a coordinating conjunction contain commas, you may use a semicolon instead of a comma before the conjunction to make the sentence easier to read.

- **Every year, whether the Republican or the Democratic Party is in office, more and more power drains away from the individual to feed vast reservoirs in far-off places; and we have less and less say about the shape of events which shape our future.**

— WILLIAM F. BUCKLEY JR., "Why Don't We Complain?"

### EXERCISE 47.1

Combine each of the following pairs of sentences into one sentence by using a semicolon. Example:

Take the bus to Henderson Street~~.~~; ~~Meet~~ meet me under the clock.

1. Joining the chorus was a great experience for Will. It helped him express his musical talent and gave him a social life.
2. City life offers many advantages. In many ways, however, life in a small town is much more pleasant.
3. The door contains an inflatable slide to be used in an emergency. In addition, each seat can become a flotation device.
4. Most car accidents occur within twenty-five miles of the home. Therefore, you should wear a seat belt on every trip.
5. The debate over political correctness affects more than the curriculum. It also affects students' social relationships.

**bedfordstmartins.com/smhandbook** For more exercises on using semicolons, go to Exercise Central and click on **Semicolons**.

## 47b Semicolons to separate items in a series

Ordinarily, commas separate items in a series (46d). But when the items themselves contain commas or other punctuation, using semicolons to separate the items will make the sentence clearer and easier to read.

- **Anthropology encompasses archaeology, the study of ancient civilizations through artifacts; linguistics, the study of the structure and development of language; and cultural anthropology, the study of customs, language, and behavior.**

## 47c Misused or overused semicolons

A comma, not a semicolon, should separate an independent clause from a dependent clause or a phrase.

- **The police found a set of fingerprints~~;~~, which they used to identify the thief.**

A colon, not a semicolon, should introduce a series.

- **The tour includes visits to the following art museums~~;~~: the Prado, in Madrid; the Louvre, in Paris; and the Rijksmuseum, in Amsterdam.**

Be careful not to use semicolons too often. Sentence upon sentence punctuated with semicolons may sound monotonous and jerky.

- **Like many people in public life, he spoke with confidence~~;~~, perhaps ~~he~~ even ~~spoke~~ with arrogance; yet I noted a certain anxiety~~;~~ that ~~it~~ touched and puzzled me~~;~~. He ~~he~~ seemed too eager to demonstrate his control of a situation.**

### EXERCISE 47.2

Revise the following passage, eliminating any misused or overused semicolons and, if necessary, replacing them with other punctuation.

Hosting your first dinner party can be very stressful; but careful planning and preparation can make it a success. The guest list must contain the right mix of people; everyone should feel comfortable; good talkers and good listeners are both important; while they don't need to agree on everything, you don't want them to have fistfights, either. Then you need to plan the menu; which should steer clear of problem areas; for vegans; no pork chops; for guests with shellfish allergies, no lobster; for teetotallers; no tequila. In addition; make sure your home is clean and neat, and check that you have enough chairs; dishes; glasses; napkins; and silverware. Leave enough time to socialize with your guests; and save a little energy to clean up when it's over!

**bedfordstmartins.com/smhandbook** For more exercises on using semicolons, go to Exercise Central and click on **Semicolons**.

## Editing for semicolons

- When you use semicolons, be sure they appear only between independent clauses — groups of words that can stand alone as sentences (47a) — or between items in a series. (47b)
- If you find few or no semicolons in your writing, ask yourself whether you should use some. Would any closely related ideas in two sentences be better expressed in one sentence with a semicolon? (47a)
- If you find too many semicolons in your writing, try deleting some of them. Would making some clauses into separate sentences make your writing smoother or less monotonous? (47c)

## 47d Semicolons with quotation marks

A semicolon goes *outside* closing quotation marks (50e).

- **Shirley Jackson's most famous story is "The Lottery"; its horrifying ending depicts a result of relying too heavily on tradition.**

### THINKING CRITICALLY ABOUT SEMICOLONS

**Reading with an Eye for Semicolons**

Read the following paragraph, which describes a solar eclipse, with attention to the use of semicolons. What different effect would the paragraph have if the author had used periods instead of semicolons? What if she had used commas and coordinating conjunctions? What is the effect of all the semicolons?

> You see the wide world swaddled in darkness; you see a vast breadth of hilly land, and an enormous, distant, blackened valley; you see towns' lights, a river's path, and blurred portions of your hat and scarf; you see your husband's face looking like an early black-and-white film; and you see a sprawl of black sky and blue sky together, with unfamiliar stars in it, some barely visible bands of cloud, and over there, a small white ring. The ring is as small as one goose in a flock of migrating geese — if you happen to notice a flock of migrating geese. It is one 360th part of the visible sky. The sun we see is less than half the diameter of a dime held at arms' length. — **ANNIE DILLARD, "Solar Eclipse"**

**Thinking about Your Own Use of Semicolons**

Think of something you might take five or ten minutes to observe — a football game, a brewing storm, an argument between friends — and write a paragraph describing your observations point by point and using semicolons to separate each point, as Annie Dillard does in the preceding paragraph. Then, look at the way you used semicolons. Are there places where a period or a comma and a coordinating conjunction would better serve your meaning? Revise appropriately. What can you conclude about effective ways of using semicolons?

# 48 End Punctuation

Periods, question marks, and exclamation points often appear in advertising to create special effects.

*You have a choice to make. Where can you turn for advice?*
*Talk to our experts today!*

End punctuation tells us how to read each sentence — as a matter-of-fact statement, a query, or an emphatic request. Making appropriate choices with end punctuation allows your readers to understand exactly what you mean.

## 48a Periods

Use a period to close sentences that make statements or give mild commands.

- **All books are either dreams or swords.**
  — AMY LOWELL
- **Don't use a fancy word if a simpler word will do.**
  — GEORGE ORWELL, "Politics and the English Language"

A period also closes indirect questions, which report rather than ask questions.

- **I asked how old the child was.**
- **We all wonder who will win the election.**

Until recently, periods have been used with most abbreviations (see Chapter 53) in American English. However, more and more abbreviations are appearing without periods.

| | | |
|---|---|---|
| Mr. | MD | BC *or* B.C. |
| Ms. | PhD | BCE *or* B.C.E. |
| Mrs. | MBA | AD *or* A.D. |
| Dr. | RN | AM *or* a.m. |
| Jr. | Sen. | PM *or* p.m. |

Some abbreviations rarely if ever appear with periods. These include the postal abbreviations of state names, such as *FL* and *TN* (though the traditional abbreviations, such as *Fla.* and *Tenn.*, do call for periods), and most groups of initials (*MLA*, *CIA*, *AIDS*, *UNICEF*). If you are not sure whether a particular abbreviation should include periods, check a dictionary or follow the style guidelines (such as those of the Modern Language Association) you are using in a research paper.

## 48b Question marks

Use a question mark to close sentences that ask direct questions.

- **Have you finished the essay, or do you need more time?**

Question marks do not close *indirect* questions, which report rather than ask questions.

- **She asked whether I opposed his nomination?.**

Do not use a comma or a period immediately after a question mark that ends a direct quotation (50e).

- **"Am I my brother's keeper?," Cain asked.**

- **Cain asked, "Am I my brother's keeper?".**

Questions in a series may have question marks even when they are not separate sentences.

- **I often confront a difficult choice: should I go to practice? finish my homework? spend time with my friends?**

A question mark in parentheses can be used to indicate that a writer is unsure of a date, a figure, or a word.

- **Quintilian died in AD 96 (?).**

## 48c Exclamation points

Use an exclamation point to show surprise or strong emotion.

- **In those few moments of geologic time will be the story of all that has happened since we became a nation. And what a story it will be!**

  — JAMES RETTIE, "But a Watch in the Night"

- **Look out!**

Use exclamation points very sparingly because they can distract your readers or suggest that you are exaggerating. In general, try to create emphasis through diction and sentence structure rather than with exclamation points (42a).

- **This university is so large, so varied, that attempting to tell someone everything about it would take three years!.**

Do not use a comma or a period after an exclamation point that ends a direct quotation.

- **On my last visit, I looked out the sliding glass doors and ran breathlessly to Connor in the kitchen: "There's a *huge* black pig in the backyard!",**

  — ELLEN ASHDOWN, "Living by the Dead"

### EXERCISE 48.1

Revise each of the following sentences, adding appropriate punctuation and deleting any unnecessary punctuation you find. Example:

She asked the travel agent, "What is the air fare to Greece,?"

1. Social scientists face difficult questions: should they use their knowledge to shape society, merely describe human behavior, or try to do both.
2. The court denied a New Jersey woman's petition to continue raising tigers in her backyard!
3. I screamed at Jamie, "You rat. You tricked me."
4. The reporter wondered whether anything more could have been done to save lives?
5. Trish asked the receptionist if Dr Margolies had office hours that afternoon
6. "Have you seen the new Spielberg film?," Mia asked casually.

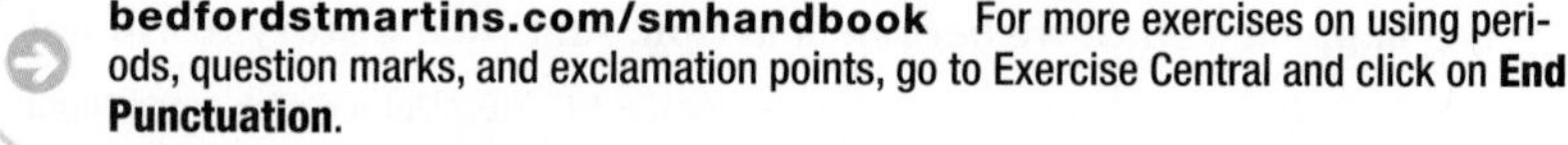

**bedfordstmartins.com/smhandbook** For more exercises on using periods, question marks, and exclamation points, go to Exercise Central and click on **End Punctuation.**

## Editing for end punctuation

- If you find that all or almost all of your sentences end with periods, see if any of them might be phrased more effectively as questions or exclamations. (48a, b, and c)
- Check to be sure you use question marks appropriately. (48b)
- If you use exclamation points, consider carefully whether they are justified. Does the sentence call for extra emphasis? If in doubt, use a period instead. (48c)

## THINKING CRITICALLY ABOUT END PUNCTUATION

**Reading with an Eye for End Punctuation**

Consider the use of end punctuation in the following paragraph. Then experiment with the end punctuation. What would be the effect of deleting the exclamation point from the quotation by Cicero or of changing it to a question mark? What would be the effect of changing Cicero's question to a statement?

> To be admired and praised, especially by the young, is an autumnal pleasure enjoyed by the lucky ones (who are not always the most deserving). "What is more charming," Cicero observes in his famous essay *De Senectute*, "than an old age surrounded by the enthusiasm of youth! . . . Attentions which seem trivial and conventional are marks of honor — the morning call, being sought after, precedence, having people rise for you, being escorted to and from the forum. . . . What pleasures of the body can be compared to the prerogatives of influence?" But there are also pleasures of the body, or the mind, that are enjoyed by a greater number of older persons.
>
> — MALCOLM COWLEY, *The View from 80*

**Thinking about Your Own Use of End Punctuation**

Look through something you have written recently, noting its end punctuation. Using the guidelines in this chapter, see if your use of end punctuation follows any patterns. Try revising the end punctuation in a paragraph or two to emphasize (or deemphasize) some point. What conclusions can you draw about ways of using end punctuation to draw attention to (or away from) a sentence?

# 49 Apostrophes

The little apostrophe can sometimes make a big difference in meaning. One man found that out when he agreed to look after a neighbor's apartment for a few days. "I'll leave instructions on the kitchen counter," the neighbor said as she gave him her key. The instructions he found said, "The cat's food is on the counter. Once a day on the patio. Thanks. I'll see you Friday."

Because the note said *cat's*, he expected one cat — and when he saw one, he put it and the food outside on the patio. When the neighbor returned, she found one healthy cat — and a second, very weak one that had hidden under the bed. The difference between *cat's* and *cats'* in this instance almost cost his neighbor a pet.

## 49a Apostrophes to signal possessive case

The possessive case denotes ownership or possession of one thing by another (34a3).

### Singular nouns and indefinite pronouns

Add an apostrophe and *-s* to form the possessive of most singular nouns, including those that end in *-s*, and of indefinite pronouns (33e).

- **The *bus's* fumes overpowered her.**
- ***Star Wars* made George *Lucas's* fortune.**
- **Anyone's guess is as good as mine.**

Apostrophes are not used with the possessive forms of personal pronouns: *yours*, *his*, *hers*, *its*, *ours*, *theirs*.

- **His favorite movies have nothing in common with ~~her's~~ hers.**

### Plural nouns

For plural nouns that do not end in *-s*, add an apostrophe and *-s*.

- **Most suits in the ~~mens'~~ men's department are appropriate business attire.**

For plural nouns ending in *-s*, add only the apostrophe.

clowns'
- The three ~~clowns's~~ costumes were bright green and orange.
  ^

### Compound words

For compound words, make the last word in the group possessive.

- **The *secretary of state's* speech was televised.**
- **Both her *daughters-in-law's* birthdays fall in July.**
- **My *in-laws'* disapproval dampened our enthusiasm.**

### Two or more nouns

To signal individual possession by two or more owners, make each noun possessive.

- **The differences between Ridley Scott's and Jerry Bruckheimer's films are enormous.**

  Scott and Bruckheimer make different films.

To signal joint possession, make only the last noun possessive.

- **Wallace and Gromit's creator is Nick Park.**

  Wallace and Gromit have the same creator.

### EXERCISE 49.1

Complete each of the following sentences by inserting *'s* or an apostrophe alone to form the possessive case of the italicized words. Example:

*A.J.'s* older *brother's* name is Griffin.
^ ^

1. Grammar is *everybody* favorite subject.
2. An *ibis* wingspan is about half as long as a *flamingo*.
3. *Charles and Camilla* first visit to the United States as a married couple included a stop at the White House.
4. The owners couldn't fulfill all the *general manager* wishes.
5. *Stephen King and Nicholas Sparks* writing styles couldn't be more different.

**bedfordstmartins.com/smhandbook** For more exercises on using apostrophes, go to Exercise Central and click on **Apostrophes**.

## 49b Apostrophes to signal contractions and other omissions

Contractions are two-word combinations formed by leaving out certain letters, which are indicated by an apostrophe.

| | | |
|---|---|---|
| it is, it has/it's | I would, I had/I'd | will not/won't |
| was not/wasn't | he would, he had/he'd | let us/let's |
| I am/I'm | would not/wouldn't | who is, who has/who's |
| he is, he has/he's | do not/don't | cannot/can't |
| you will/you'll | does not/doesn't | |

Contractions are common in conversation and informal writing. Some academic and professional work, however, calls for greater formality.

### *Distinguishing its and it's*

*Its* is the possessive form of *it*. *It's* is a contraction for *it is* or *it has*.

- **This disease is unusual; it's symptoms vary from person to person.**

- **It s a difficult disease to diagnose.**

### *Signaling omissions*

An apostrophe signals omissions in some common phrases:

| | | |
|---|---|---|
| ten of the clock | rock and roll | class of 2003 |
| ten o'clock | rock 'n' roll | class of '03 |

In addition, writers can use an apostrophe to signal omitted letters in approximating the sound of speech or a specific dialect.

- **You should'a seen'em playin' together.**

## 49c Apostrophes to form certain plurals

Many style guides advise against apostrophes for any plurals.

- **The gymnasts need marks of *8*s and *9*s to qualify for the finals.**

Others use an apostrophe and *-s* to form the plural of numbers, letters, symbols, and words referred to as terms.

## Editing for apostrophes

- Check each noun that ends in *-s* and shows ownership or possession. Is the apostrophe in the right place, either before or after the *-s*? (49a)
- Check the possessive form of each indefinite pronoun, such as *someone's*. Be sure an apostrophe comes before the *-s*. (49a)
- Check each *its*. Does it show possession? If not, add an apostrophe before the *-s*. (49b)
- Check each *it's*. Does it mean "it is" or "it has"? If not, remove the apostrophe. (49b)

**The five *Shakespeare*'s in the essay were spelled five different ways.**

Check your instructor's preference. In any case, italicize numbers, letters, symbols, and terms but not the plural ending.

### EXERCISE 49.2

The following sentences, from which all apostrophes have been deleted, appear in Langston Hughes's "Salvation." Insert apostrophes where appropriate. Example:

"Sister Reed, what is this child's name?"

1. There was a big revival at my Auntie Reeds church.
2. I heard the songs and the minister saying: "Why dont you come?"
3. Finally Westley said to me in a whisper: . . . "Im tired o sitting here. Lets get up and be saved."
4. So I decided that maybe to save further trouble, Id better lie. . . .
5. That night . . . I cried, in bed alone, and couldnt stop.

**bedfordstmartins.com/smhandbook** For more exercises on using apostrophes, go to Exercise Central and click on **Apostrophes**.

### THINKING CRITICALLY ABOUT APOSTROPHES

Write a brief paragraph, beginning "I've always been amused by my neighbor's (or roommate's) _______." Then note every use of an apostrophe. Use the guidelines in this chapter to check that you have used apostrophes correctly.

# 50 Quotation Marks

As a way of bringing other people's words into our own, quotation can be a powerful writing tool.

*Mrs. Macken urges parents to get books for their children, to read to them when they are "li'l," and when they start school to make certain they attend regularly. She holds herself up as an example of a "millhand's daughter who wanted to be a schoolteacher and did it through sheer hard work."*

— SHIRLEY BRICE HEATH, *Ways with Words*

The writer could have paraphrased, but by quoting, she lets her subject speak for herself — and lets readers hear that person's voice.

## 50a Quotation marks to signal direct quotations

Use double quotation marks to signal a direct quotation.

- **President Bush referred to an "axis of evil" in his speech.**
- **She smiled and said, "Son, this is one incident I will never forget."**

Single quotation marks enclose a quotation within a quotation. Open and close the quoted passage with double quotation marks, and change any quotation marks that appear *within* the quotation to single quotation marks.

- **James Baldwin says, "The title 'The Uses of the Blues' does not refer to music; I don't know anything about music."**

### FOR MULTILINGUAL WRITERS: Quoting in American English

American English and British English use opposite conventions for double and single quotation marks. Writers of British English use single quotation marks first and, if necessary, double quotation marks for quotations within quotations. If you have studied British English, be careful to follow the U.S. conventions for quotation marks: double quotation marks first and, if necessary, single quotation marks within double.

### 1 Longer passages

If the prose passage you wish to quote exceeds four typed lines, set it off from the rest of the text by starting it on a new line and indenting it one inch (or ten spaces) from the left margin. This format, known as block quotation, does not require quotation marks.

> In Winged Words: American Indian Writers Speak, Leslie Marmon Silko describes her early education:
>
> > I learned to love reading, and love books, and the printed page, and therefore was motivated to learn to write. The best thing . . . you can have in life is to have someone tell you a story . . . but in lieu of that . . . I learned at an early age to find comfort in a book, that a book would talk to me when no one else would. (145)

This block quotation, including the ellipses and the page number in parentheses at the end, follows the style of the Modern Language Association (MLA). Other organizations, such as the American Psychological Association (APA) and the University of Chicago Press, have different guidelines for ellipses and block quotations. (See Chapters 18–21.)

### 2 Poetry

If the quotation is fewer than four lines, include it within your text, enclosed in double quotation marks. Separate the lines of the poem with slashes, each preceded and followed by a space, to tell the reader where one line of the poem ends and the next begins.

> In one of his best-known poems, Robert Frost remarks, “Two roads diverged in a wood, and I — / I took the one less traveled by, / And that has made all the difference.”

To quote four or more lines of poetry, indent the block one inch (or ten spaces) from the left margin, and do not use quotation marks.

> The duke in Robert Browning’s “My Last Duchess” is clearly a jealous, vain person, whose own words illustrate his arrogance:
>
> > She thanked men — good! but thanked
> > Somehow — I know not how — as if she ranked
> > My gift of a nine-hundred-years-old name
> > With anybody’s gift.

When you quote poetry, take care to follow the indention, spacing, capitalization, punctuation, and other features of the original poem.

### FOR MULTILINGUAL WRITERS: Quotation marks

Remember that the way you mark quotations in English (“ ”) may not be the same as in other languages. In French, for example, quotations are marked with *guillemets* (« »), while in German, quotations take split-level marks („ “).

### 3 Dialogue

When you write dialogue or quote a conversation, enclose the words of each speaker in quotation marks, and mark each shift in speaker by beginning a new paragraph.

**“But I can see you’re bound to come,” said the father. “Only we ain’t going to catch us no fish, because there ain’t no water left to catch ’em in.”**

**“The river!”**

**“All but dry.”**

— EUDORA WELTY, “Ladies in Spring”

Because of the paragraph breaks in the preceding example, we know when the father is speaking and when the child is speaking without the author’s having to repeat *said the father*, *the child said*, and so on.

## 50b Quotation marks to signal titles and definitions

Quotation marks are used to enclose the titles of short poems, short stories, articles, essays, songs, sections of books, and episodes of television and radio programs.

- **“Dover Beach” moves from calm to sadness.** [poem]
- **Walker’s “Everyday Use” is not just about quilts.** [short story]
- **Arctic Monkeys’ single “I Bet You Look Good on the Dancefloor” helped fuel sales of their first album.** [song]
- **The *Atlantic* published an article titled “Illiberal Education.”** [article]
- **In the chapter called “Complexion,” Richard Rodriguez describes his sensitivity about his skin color.** [section of book]
- **The *Nature* episode “Echo of the Elephants” denounces ivory hunters.** [television series episode]

Use italics rather than quotation marks for the titles of television series, books, magazines, and other longer works (54a).

Definitions are sometimes set off with quotation marks.

- **The French phrase *idée fixe* means literally "fixed idea."**

## 50c Quotation marks to signal irony and invented words

To show readers that you are using a word or phrase ironically, or that you invented it, enclose it in quotation marks.

- **The "banquet" consisted of dried-out chicken and canned vegetables.**

  The quotation marks suggest that the meal was anything but a banquet.

- **Your whole first paragraph or first page may have to be guillotined in any case after your piece is finished: it is a kind of "forebirth."**

  — JACQUES BARZUN, "A Writer's Discipline"

  The writer made up the term *forebirth.*

### EXERCISE 50.1

Revise each of the following sentences, using quotation marks appropriately to signal titles, definitions, irony, or invented terms.

1. Stephen Colbert introduced Americans to the concept he calls truthiness on the first episode of *The Colbert Report*.
2. In his article Race against Time, Anthony S. Fauci warns of the critical threat posed by the potent avian flu virus.
3. "The little that is known about gorillas certainly makes you want to know more," writes Alan Moorehead in his essay A Most Forgiving Ape.
4. The fun of surgery begins before the operation ever takes place.
5. Should America the Beautiful replace The Star-Spangled Banner as the national anthem?
6. In the chapter called The Last to See Them Alive, Truman Capote shows the utterly ordinary life of the Kansas family.
7. A special *Simpsons* episode called The Treehouse of Horror airs each Halloween.
8. A remix of Elvis Presley's A Little Less Conversation reached number one on the charts twenty-five years after the superstar had died.

9. My dictionary defines *isolation* as the quality or state of being alone.
10. In his poem The Shield of Achilles, W. H. Auden depicts the horror of modern warfare.

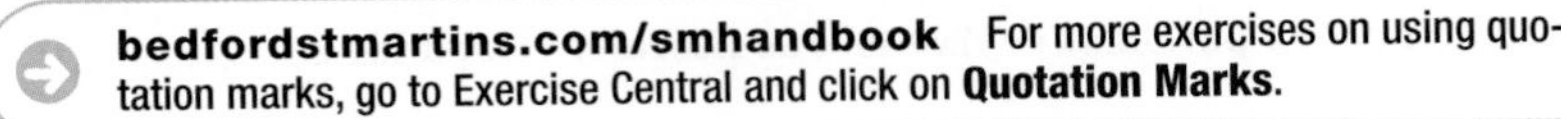

**bedfordstmartins.com/smhandbook** For more exercises on using quotation marks, go to Exercise Central and click on **Quotation Marks**.


## 50d Misused quotation marks

Do not use quotation marks for *indirect* quotations — those that do not use someone's exact words.

- **The teacher warned Dana that ~~"~~she could be expelled.~~"~~**

Do not use quotation marks just to emphasize particular words or phrases.

- **Julia said that her views might not be ~~"~~politically correct~~"~~ but that she wasn't going to change them for anything.**

- **Much time was spent speculating about their ~~"~~relationship.~~"~~**

Do not use quotation marks around slang or colloquial language; they create the impression that you are apologizing for using those words. Instead, try to express the idea in formal language. If you have a good reason to use a slang or colloquial term, use it without quotation marks (29a1).

- **After our twenty-mile hike, we were** completely exhausted. **~~"wiped out".~~**

## 50e Quotation marks with other punctuation

Periods and commas go *inside* closing quotation marks.

- **"Don't compromise yourself," said Janis Joplin. "You are all you've got."**

EXCEPTION When you use parenthetical documentation with a short quotation, place the period after the parentheses with source information (18b, 19b).

- **In places, de Beauvoir “sees Marxists as believing in subjectivity” (Whitmarsh 63).**

Colons, semicolons, and footnote numbers go *outside* closing quotation marks.

- **I felt only one emotion after reading “Eveline”: sorrow.**
- **Everything is dark, and “a visionary light settles in her eyes”; this light is her salvation.**
- ***Tragedy* is defined by Aristotle as “an imitation of an action that is serious and of a certain magnitude.”[1]**

Question marks, exclamation points, and dashes go *inside* closing quotation marks if they are part of the quotation, *outside* if they are not.

PART OF THE QUOTATION

- **The cashier asked, “Would you like to super-size that?”**
- **“Jump!” one of the firefighters shouted.**

NOT PART OF THE QUOTATION

- **What is the theme of “A Good Man Is Hard to Find”?**

## Editing for quotation marks

- Use quotation marks around direct quotations and titles of short works. (50a and b)
- Do not use quotation marks around set-off quotations of more than four lines of prose or three lines of poetry or around titles of long works. (50a and b)
- Use quotation marks to signal irony and invented words, but do so sparingly. (50c)
- Never use quotation marks around indirect quotations. (50d)
- Do not use quotation marks just to add emphasis to words. (50d)
- Check other punctuation used with closing quotation marks. (50e)
  Periods and commas should be *inside* the quotation marks.
  Colons, semicolons, and footnote numbers should be *outside*.
  Question marks, exclamation points, and dashes should be *inside* if they are part of the quoted material, *outside* if they are not.

▶ **“Break a leg” — that phrase is supposed to bring good luck to a performer.**

For help using quotation marks in various documentation styles, see Chapters 18–21.

## THINKING CRITICALLY ABOUT QUOTATION MARKS

**Reading with an Eye for Quotation Marks**

Read the following passage about the painter Georgia O’Keeffe, and pay particular attention to the use of quotation marks. What effect is created by the author’s use of quotation marks with *hardness*, *crustiness*, and *crusty*? How do the quotations by O’Keeffe help support the author’s description of her?

> “Hardness” has not been in our century a quality much admired in women, nor in the past twenty years has it even been in official favor for men. When hardness surfaces in the very old we tend to transform it into “crustiness” or eccentricity, some tonic pepperiness to be indulged at a distance. On the evidence of her work and what she has said about it, Georgia O’Keeffe is neither “crusty” nor eccentric. She is simply hard, a straight shooter, a woman clean of received wisdom and open to what she sees. This is a woman who could early on dismiss most of her contemporaries as “dreamy,” and would later single out one she liked as “a very poor painter.” (And then add, apparently by way of softening the judgment: “I guess he wasn’t a painter at all. He had no courage and I believe that to create one’s own world in any of the arts takes courage.”) This is a woman who in 1939 could advise her admirers that they were missing her point, that their appreciation of her famous flowers was merely sentimental. “When I paint a red hill,” she observed coolly in the catalogue for an exhibition that year, “you say it is too bad that I don’t always paint flowers. A flower touches almost everyone’s heart. A red hill doesn’t touch everyone’s heart.”
>
> — JOAN DIDION, “Georgia O’Keeffe”

**Thinking about Your Own Use of Quotation Marks**

Choose a topic that is of interest on your campus, and interview one of your friends about it. On the basis of your notes from the interview, write two or three paragraphs about your friend’s views, using several direct quotations that support the points you are making. Then see how closely you followed the conventions for quotation marks explained in this chapter. Note any usages that caused you problems.

# Other Punctuation Marks

# 51

Parentheses, brackets, dashes, colons, slashes, and ellipses are all around us. Pick up the television listings, for instance, and you will find these punctuation marks in abundance, helping viewers preview programs in a clear and efficient way.

**❼ ⑧ College Football**
*3:30* 501019/592361 — *Northwestern Wildcats at Ohio State Buckeyes. The Buckeyes are looking for their 20th straight win over Northwestern. (Live) [Time approximate.]*

You can use these marks of punctuation to signal relationships among sentence parts, to create particular rhythms, and to help readers follow your thoughts.

## 51a Parentheses

Parentheses enclose material that is of minor or secondary importance in a sentence — material that supplements, clarifies, comments on, or illustrates what precedes or follows it. Parentheses also enclose numbers or letters that precede items in a list, and sometimes they enclose source citations or publication information.

### *Enclosing less important material*

- **Inventors and men of genius have almost always been regarded as fools at the beginning (and very often at the end) of their careers.**

  — FYODOR DOSTOYEVSKY

- **During my research, I found problems with the flat-rate income tax (a single-rate tax with no deductions).**

A period may be placed either inside or outside a closing parenthesis, depending on whether the parenthetical text is part of a larger sentence. A comma, if needed, is always placed *outside* a closing parenthesis (and never before an opening one).

- **Gene Tunney's single defeat in an eleven-year career was to a flamboyant and dangerous fighter named Harry Greb ("The Human Windmill"), who seems to have been, judging from boxing literature, the dirtiest fighter in history.**

  — JOYCE CAROL OATES, "On Boxing"

If the material in parentheses is a question or an exclamation, use a question mark or exclamation point inside the closing parenthesis.

- **Our laughing (so deep was the pleasure!) became screaming.**

— RICHARD RODRIGUEZ, "Aria: A Memoir of a Bilingual Childhood"

Use parentheses judiciously, for they break up the flow of a sentence or passage, forcing readers to hold the original train of thought in their minds while considering a secondary one.

### *Enclosing numbers or letters in a list*

- **Five distinct styles can be distinguished: (1) Old New England, (2) Deep South, (3) Middle American, (4) Wild West, and (5) Far West or Californian.** — ALISON LURIE, *The Language of Clothes*

### *Enclosing textual citations or publication information*

The first of the following in-text citations shows the style of the American Psychological Association (see Chapter 19); the second shows the style of the Modern Language Association (see Chapter 18).

> A later study resulted in somewhat different conclusions (Murphy & Orkow, 1985).

> Zamora notes that Kahlo referred to her first self-portrait, given to a close friend, as "your Botticelli" (110).

The following note follows the citation style recommended by *The Chicago Manual of Style* (see Chapter 20):

> 1. John A. Garraty, Quarrels That Have Shaped the Constitution (New York: Harper and Row, 1987), 7–14.

## 51b Brackets

Use brackets to enclose parenthetical elements in material that is itself within parentheses and to enclose explanatory words or comments that you are inserting into a quotation.

### *Setting off material within parentheses*

- **Eventually the investigation examined the major agencies (including the National Security Agency [NSA]) that were conducting covert operations.**

### *Inserting material within quotations*

- **Massing notes that "on average, it [Fox News] attracts more than eight million people daily — more than double the number who watch CNN."**

  The bracketed words clarify *it* in the original quotation.

In the quotation in the following sentence, the artist Gauguin's name is misspelled. The bracketed Latin word *sic*, which means "so," tells readers that the person being quoted — not the writer using the quotation — made the mistake.

- **One admirer wrote, "She was the most striking woman I'd ever seen — a sort of wonderful combination of Mia Farrow and one of Gaugin's [*sic*] Polynesian nymphs."**

### EXERCISE 51.1

Revise the following sentences, using parentheses and brackets correctly. Example:

> She was in fourth grade (or was it third?) when she became blind.
> ^ ^

1. The committee was presented with three options to pay for the new park: 1 increase vehicle registration fees, 2 install parking meters downtown, or 3 borrow money from the reserve fund.
2. The FISA statute authorizes government wiretapping only under certain circumstances for instance, the government has to obtain a warrant.
3. The health care expert informed readers that "as we progress through middle age, we experience intimations of our own morality *sic*."
4. Some hospitals train nurses in a pseudoscientific technique called therapeutic touch TT that has been discredited by many rigorous studies.
5. The obnoxious actions of one marcher who, as it turned out, was an undercover police officer marred the otherwise peaceful protest.

**bedfordstmartins.com/smhandbook** For more exercises on using parentheses and brackets, go to Exercise Central and click on **Other Punctuation**.

## 51c Dashes

In contrast to parentheses, dashes give more rather than less emphasis to the material they enclose. With most computer software, a dash is made with two hyphens (- -) with *no* spaces before, between, or after. Many word-processing programs automatically convert two typed hyphens into a solid dash (—).

### *Inserting a comment*

- **Leeches — yuck — turn out to have valuable medical uses.**

### *Emphasizing explanatory material*

- **Indeed, several of modern India's greatest scholars — such as the Mughal historian Muzaffar Alam of the University of Chicago — are madrasa graduates.** — WILLIAM DALRYMPLE

A single dash toward the *end* of a sentence may serve to emphasize the material at the end, to mark a shift in tone or a hesitation in speech, or to summarize or explain what has come before.

### *Emphasizing material at the end of a sentence*

- **In the twentieth century it has become almost impossible to moralize about epidemics — except those which are transmitted sexually.**

  — SUSAN SONTAG, "AIDS and Its Metaphors"

### *Marking a sudden change in tone*

- **New York is a catastrophe — but a magnificent catastrophe.**

  — LE CORBUSIER

### *Indicating a hesitation in speech*

- **As the officer approached his car, the driver stammered, "What — what have I done?"**

### *Introducing a summary or explanation*

- **In walking, the average adult person employs a motor mechanism that weighs about eighty pounds — sixty pounds of muscle and twenty pounds of bone.** — EDWIN WAY TEALE

### EXERCISE 51.2

Punctuate the following sentences with dashes where appropriate. Example:

He is quick, violent, and mean — they don't call him Dirty Harry for nothing — but appealing nonetheless.

1. Many people would have ignored the children's taunts but not Ace.
2. Even if marijuana is dangerous an assertion disputed by many studies it is certainly no more harmful to human health than alcohol and cigarettes, which remain legal.
3. If too much exposure to negative news stories makes you feel depressed or anxious and why wouldn't it? try going on a media fast.
4. Union Carbide's plant in Bhopal, India, sprang a leak a leak that killed more than 2,000 people and injured an additional 200,000.
5. Hybrid vehicles especially those that require no external electric power continue to grow more popular.

**bedfordstmartins.com/smhandbook** For more exercises on using dashes, go to Exercise Central and click on **Other Punctuation**.

## 51d Colons

Use a colon to introduce something (such as an explanation) and to separate some elements (such as titles and subtitles) from one another.

### *Introducing an explanation, an example, or an appositive*

- **The men may also wear the getup known as Sun Belt Cool: a pale beige suit, open-collared shirt (often in a darker shade than the suit), cream-colored loafers and aviator sunglasses.**

— ALISON LURIE, *The Language of Clothes*

### *Introducing a series, a list, or a quotation*

- **At the baby's one-month birthday party, Ah Po gave him the Four Valuable Things: ink, inkslab, paper, and brush.**

— MAXINE HONG KINGSTON, *China Men*

- **The teachers wondered: "Do boys and girls really learn differently? Do behavioral differences reflect socialization or biology?"**

The preceding example could have used a comma instead of a colon before the quotation (46h). Use a colon rather than a comma to introduce a quotation when the lead-in is a complete sentence on its own.

- **The State of the Union address contained one surprising statement: "America is addicted to oil."**

### *Separating elements*

SALUTATIONS IN FORMAL LETTERS

- **Dear Dr. Mahira:**

TITLES AND SUBTITLES

- ***The Joy of Insight: Passions of a Physicist***

HOURS, MINUTES, AND SECONDS

- **4:59 PM**
- **2:15:06**

CITIES AND PUBLISHERS IN BIBLIOGRAPHIC ENTRIES

- **Boston: Bedford, 2006**

RATIOS

- **a ratio of 5:1**

BIBLICAL CHAPTERS AND VERSES

- **I Corinthians 3:3–5**

### *Eliminating misused colons*

Do not put a colon between a verb and its object or complement, unless the object is a quotation.

- **Some natural fibers are~~:~~ cotton, wool, silk, and linen.**

Do not put a colon between a preposition and its object or after such expressions as *such as*, *especially*, or *including*.

- **In poetry, additional power may come from devices such as~~:~~ simile, metaphor, and alliteration.**

### EXERCISE 51.3

In the following items, insert a colon in any sentence that needs one and delete any unnecessary colons. Some sentences may be correct as written. Example:

> *Images: My Life in Film* includes revealing material written by Ingmar Bergman.

1. The article made one point forcefully and repeatedly the United States must end its dependence on foreign oil.
2. Another example is taken from Psalm 139 16.
3. Roberto tried to make healthier choices, such as: eating organic food, walking to work, and getting plenty of rest.
4. A number of quotable movie lines come from *Casablanca*, including "Round up the usual suspects."
5. Sofi rushed to catch the 5 45 express but had to wait for the 6 19.

**bedfordstmartins.com/smhandbook** For more exercises on using colons, go to Exercise Central and click on **Other Punctuation**.

## 51e Slashes

Use slashes to mark line divisions in poetry quoted within running text (50a2), to separate alternative terms, and to separate the parts of fractions and Internet addresses. When a slash separates lines of poetry, it should be preceded and followed by a space.

### *Marking line divisions in poetry*

- **In "Digging," Seamus Heaney observes, "Between my finger and my thumb / The squat pen rests; snug as a gun."**

### *Separating alternatives*

- **Then there was Daryl, the cabdriver/bartender.**

— JOHN L'HEUREUX, *The Handmaid of Desire*

### *Separating parts of fractions and Internet addresses*

- **138 1/2**
- **bedfordstmartins.com/smhandbook**

## 51f Ellipses

Ellipses, or ellipsis points, are three equally spaced dots. Ellipses usually indicate that something has been omitted from a quoted passage, but they can also signal a pause or hesitation in speech in the same way that a dash can.

### *Indicating omissions*

Just as you should carefully use quotation marks around any material that you quote directly from a source, so you should carefully use ellipses to indicate that you have left out part of a quotation that otherwise appears to be a complete sentence.

The ellipses in the following example indicate two omissions — one in the middle of the sentence and one at the end. When you omit the last part of a quoted sentence, add a period after the ellipses, for a total of four dots. Be sure a complete sentence comes before and after the four points. If you are adding your own ellipses to a quotation that already has other ellipses, enclose yours in brackets.

**ORIGINAL TEXT**

- **The quasi-official division of the population into three economic classes called high-, middle-, and low-income groups rather misses the point, because as a class indicator the amount of money is not as important as the source.** — PAUL FUSSELL, "Notes on Class"

**WITH ELLIPSES**

- **As Paul Fussell argues, "The quasi-official division of the population into three economic classes . . . rather misses the point. . . ."**

If your shortened quotation ends with a source (such as a page number, a name, or a title), follow these steps:

1. Use three ellipsis points but no period after the quotation.
2. Add the closing quotation mark, closed up to the third ellipsis point.
3. Add the source documentation in parentheses.
4. Use a period to indicate the end of the sentence.

- **Packer argues, "The Administration is right to reconsider its strategy . . ." (34).**

## Editing for effective use of punctuation

- Be sure that any material enclosed in parentheses or set off with dashes requires special treatment — and that the punctuation doesn't make the sentence difficult to follow. Use parentheses to de-emphasize the material they enclose and dashes to add emphasis. (51a and c)
- Use brackets to enclose parenthetical elements in material that is already within parentheses and to enclose words or comments inserted into a quotation. (51b)
- Be sure that you have *not* used a colon between a verb and its object or complement, between a preposition and its object, or after such expressions as *such as*, *especially*, or *including*. (51d)
- Use slashes to mark line divisions in poetry you are quoting in running text. (51e)
- Use ellipses (three equally spaced dots) to indicate omissions from quoted passages. (51f)

### *Indicating a pause or a hesitation*

**Then the voice, husky and familiar, came to wash over us — "The winnah, and still heavyweight champeen of the world . . . Joe Louis."**

— MAYA ANGELOU, *I Know Why the Caged Bird Sings*

### EXERCISE 51.4

The following sentences use the punctuation marks presented in this chapter very effectively. Read the sentences carefully; then choose one, and use it as a model for writing a sentence of your own, making sure to use the punctuation marks in the same way in your sentence.

1. The dad was — how can you put this gracefully? — a real blimp, a wide load, and the white polyester stretch-pants only emphasized the cargo.

   — GARRISON KEILLOR, "Happy to Be Here"

2. Not only are the distinctions we draw between male nature and female nature largely arbitrary and often pure superstition: they are completely beside the point.

   — BRIGID BROPHY, "Women"

3. If no one, including you, liked the soup the first time round (and that's why you've got so much left over), there is no point in freezing it for some hopeful future

date when, miraculously, it will taste delicious. But bagging leftovers — say, stews — in single portions can be useful for those evenings when you're eating alone.
— NIGELLA LAWSON, *How to Eat*

## THINKING CRITICALLY ABOUT PUNCTUATION

**Reading with an Eye for Punctuation**

In the following passage, Tom Wolfe uses dashes, parentheses, ellipses, and a colon to create rhythm and build momentum in a very long (178-word) sentence. The editorial comment inserted in brackets calls attention to the fact that the "right stuff" was, in the world Wolfe describes here, always male. Look carefully at how Wolfe and the editors use these punctuation marks, and then try writing a description of something that effectively uses as many of them as possible. Your description should be about the same length as Wolfe's passage, but it need not be all one sentence.

> Likewise, "hassling" — mock dogfighting — was strictly forbidden, and so naturally young fighter jocks could hardly wait to go up in, say, a pair of F-100s and start the duel by making a pass at each other at 800 miles an hour, the winner being the pilot who could slip in behind the other one and get locked in on his [never *her* or *his or her!*] tail ("wax his tail"), and it was not uncommon for some eager jock to try too tight an outside turn and have his engine flame out, whereupon, unable to restart it, he has to eject . . . and he shakes his fist at the victor as he floats down by parachute and his million-dollar aircraft goes *kaboom!* on the palmetto grass or the desert floor, and he starts thinking about how he can get together with the other guy back at the base in time for the two of them to get their stories straight before the investigation: "I don't know what happened, sir. I was pulling up after a target run, and it just flamed out on me."
>
> — TOM WOLFE, *The Right Stuff*

**Thinking about Your Own Use of Punctuation**

Look through a draft you have recently written or are working on, and check your use of parentheses, brackets, dashes, colons, slashes, and ellipses. Do you follow the conventions presented in this chapter? If not, revise accordingly. Check the material in parentheses to see if it could use more emphasis and thus be set off instead with dashes. Then check any material in dashes to see if it could do with less emphasis and thus be punctuated with commas or parentheses.

# Part 10



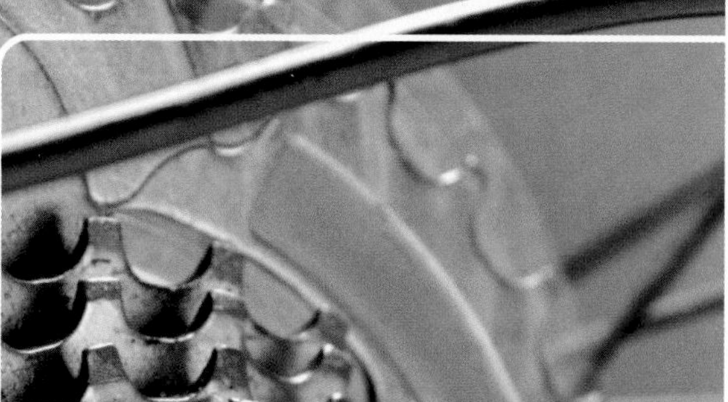

# MECHANICS

# 52 Capital Letters

Capital letters are a key signal in everyday life. Look around any store to see their importance: you can shop for Coca-Cola or *any* cola, for Levi's or *any* blue jeans, for Kleenex or *any* tissues. In each of these instances, the capital letter indicates a particular brand.

Sometimes, however, writers use too many capitals, asking readers TO READ TEXT THAT LOOKS LIKE THIS. With capitalization, as with other "mechanical" aspects of writing, it is usually best to follow established conventions.

## 52a The first word of a sentence or a line of poetry

Capitalize the first word of a sentence.

- **Posing relatives for photographs is a challenge.**
- **Could you move a little to the left?**

If you are quoting a full sentence, capitalize its first word.

- **Everyone was asking, "Is there any more of that pie?"**

Capitalizing a sentence following a colon is optional.

- **Gould cites the work of Darwin: The [*or* the] theory of natural selection incorporates the principle of evolutionary ties between all animals.**

Capitalize a sentence within parentheses unless the parenthetical sentence is inserted into another sentence.

- **Gould cites the work of Darwin. (Other researchers cite more recent evolutionary theorists.)**
- **Gould cites the work of Darwin (see page 150).**

When citing poetry, follow the capitalization of the original poem. Though most poets capitalize the first word of each line in a poem, some poets do not.

> **Morning sun heats up the young beech tree**
> **leaves and almost lights them into fireflies**
>
> — JUNE JORDAN, "Aftermath"

## 52b Proper nouns and proper adjectives

Capitalize proper nouns (those naming specific persons, places, and things) and most proper adjectives (those formed from proper nouns). All other nouns are common nouns and are not capitalized unless they begin a sentence or are used as part of a proper noun: *a street* or *the street where you live*, but *Elm Street*. The following list shows proper nouns and adjectives on the left and related common nouns and adjectives on the right.

**PEOPLE**

| | |
|---|---|
| Ang Lee | the film's director |
| Nixonian | political |

**NATIONS, NATIONALITIES, ETHNIC GROUPS, AND LANGUAGES**

| | |
|---|---|
| Brazil, Brazilian | their native country, his citizenship |
| Italian American | an ethnic group |
| Cantonese | one of the nation's languages |

**PLACES**

| | |
|---|---|
| Pacific Ocean | an ocean |
| Hawaiian Islands | tropical islands |

**STRUCTURES AND MONUMENTS**

| | |
|---|---|
| the Lincoln Memorial | a monument |
| the Eiffel Tower | a landmark |

**SHIPS, TRAINS, AIRCRAFT, AND SPACECRAFT**

| | |
|---|---|
| the *Queen Mary* | a cruise ship |
| the *City of New Orleans* | the 6:00 train |

**ORGANIZATIONS, BUSINESSES, AND GOVERNMENT INSTITUTIONS**

| | |
|---|---|
| United Auto Workers | a trade union |
| Library of Congress | certain federal agencies |
| Desmond-Fish Library | the local library |
| General Motors Corporation | a blue-chip company |

| **ACADEMIC INSTITUTIONS AND COURSES** | |
|---|---|
| University of Maryland | a state university |
| Political Science 102 | my political science course |
| **HISTORICAL EVENTS AND ERAS** | |
| the Easter Uprising | a rebellion |
| the Renaissance | the fifteenth century |
| **RELIGIONS AND RELIGIOUS TERMS** | |
| God | a deity |
| the Qur'an | a holy book |
| Catholicism, Catholic | a religion, their religious affiliation |
| **TRADE NAMES** | |
| Nike | running shoes |
| Cheerios | cereal |

Some contemporary companies use capitals called *InterCaps* in the middle of their own or their product's names. Follow the style you see in company advertising or on the product itself — *eBay*, *FedEx*, *iPod*.

### *Titles of individuals*

Capitalize titles used before a proper name. When used alone or following a proper name, most titles are not capitalized. One common exception is the word *president*, which many writers capitalize whenever it refers to the President of the United States.

| | |
|---|---|
| Chief Justice Roberts | John Roberts, the chief justice |
| Professor Lisa Ede | my English professor |
| Dr. Edward A. Davies | Edward A. Davies, our doctor |

## 52c Titles of works

Capitalize most words in titles of books, articles, stories, speeches, essays, plays, poems, documents, films, paintings, and musical compositions. Do not capitalize an article (*a*, *an*, *the*), a preposition, a conjunction, or the *to* in an infinitive unless it is the first or last word in a title or subtitle.

| | |
|---|---|
| *Walt Whitman: A Life* | "Where I'm Calling From" |
| "As Time Goes By" | Declaration of Independence |
| "Shooting an Elephant" | *Charlie and the Chocolate Factory* |
| *The Producers* | *Rebel without a Cause* |

## 52d The pronoun *I*

Always capitalize the pronoun *I*.

- **I'm afraid I don't know the answer.**

## 52e Unnecessary capitalization

Do not capitalize a compass direction unless the word designates a specific geographic region.

- **Voters in the South and much of the West tend to favor socially conservative candidates.**

- **John Muir headed ~~West,~~ west, motivated by the need to explore.**

Do not capitalize a word indicating a family relationship unless the word is used as part of the name or as a substitute for the name.

- **I could always tell when Mother was annoyed with Aunt Rose.**

- **When she was a child, my ~~Mother~~ mother shared a room with my ~~Aunt.~~ aunt.**

Do not capitalize seasons of the year and parts of the academic or financial year.

| | |
|---|---|
| spring | fall semester |
| winter | winter term |
| autumn | third-quarter earnings |

## 52f Capitalizing in email

In general, capitalize online as you would in print. (For more on writing online, see 24c.) Using few (or no) capital letters in email can be hard on readers and result in text that looks unprofessional.

## FOR MULTILINGUAL WRITERS: English capitalization

Capitalization systems vary considerably among languages, and some languages (Arabic, Chinese, Hindi, and Hebrew, for example) do not use capital letters at all. English may be the only language to capitalize the first-person singular pronoun (*I*), but Dutch and German capitalize some forms of the second-person pronoun (*you*). German capitalizes all nouns; English used to capitalize more nouns than it does now (see, for instance, the Declaration of Independence).

Capitalizing whole words or phrases for emphasis comes across to readers as SHOUTING. So instead of uppercase letters, use italics, underlining, or asterisks to add emphasis.

- **Sorry for the abrupt response, but I am *very* busy.**

### EXERCISE 52.1

Capitalize words as needed in the following sentences. Example:

T. S. Eliot, The Waste Land, Faber Faber.
~~t.s. eliot,~~ who wrote ~~*the waste land,*~~ was an editor at ~~faber~~ and ~~faber.~~

1. the town in the south where i was raised had a statue of a civil war soldier in the center of main street.
2. reporters speculated about the secret location where vice president cheney had remained for several weeks.
3. the corporation for public broadcasting relies on donations as well as on grants from the national endowment for the arts.
4. every artist on a major label seems to want a lexus or a lincoln navigator and a chauffeur to drive it.
5. most americans remember where they were when they heard about the *columbia* disaster.
6. accepting an award for his score for the john wayne film *the high and the mighty,* dmitri tiomkin thanked beethoven, brahms, wagner, and strauss.

**bedfordstmartins.com/smhandbook** For more exercises on using capitalization, go to Exercise Central and click on **Capitalization**.

## Editing for capitalization

- Capitalize the first word of each sentence. If you quote a poem, follow its original capitalization. (52a)
- Check to make sure you have appropriately capitalized proper nouns and proper adjectives. (52b)
- Review where you have used titles of people or of works to be sure you have capitalized them correctly. (52b and c)
- Double-check the capitalization of geographic directions (*north* or *North*?), family relationships (*dad* or *Dad*?), and seasons of the year (*winter*, not *Winter*). (52e)
- In email, check to see that you have capitalized words as you would in print and have followed other email conventions. (52f)

## THINKING CRITICALLY ABOUT CAPITALIZATION

The following poem uses unconventional capitalization. Read it over a few times, at least once aloud. What effect does the capitalization have? Why do you think the poet chose to use capitals as she did?

A little Madness in the Spring
Is wholesome even for the King,
But God be with the Clown —
Who ponders this tremendous scene —
This whole Experiment of Green —
As if it were his own!

— EMILY DICKINSON

# 53 Abbreviations and Numbers

Anytime you open up a telephone book, you see an abundance of abbreviations and numbers, as in the following movie theater listing from the Berkeley, California, telephone book:

*Oaks Theater 1875 Solano Av Brk*

Abbreviations and numbers allow writers to present detailed information in a small amount of space. In academic writing, abbreviations and numbers follow conventions that vary from field to field.

## 53a Abbreviating titles and academic degrees

When used before or after a name, some personal and professional titles and academic degrees are abbreviated, even in academic writing.

| | |
|---|---|
| Ms. Susanna Moller | Henry Louis Gates Jr. |
| Mr. Aaron Oforlea | Gina Tartaglia, MD |
| Dr. Edward Davies | Jamie Barlow Kayes, PhD |

Other titles — including religious, military, academic, and government titles — should be spelled out in academic writing. In other writing, they may be abbreviated when they appear before a full name but should be spelled out when used with only a last name.

| | |
|---|---|
| Rev. Franklin Graham | Reverend Graham |
| Prof. Beverly Moss | Professor Moss |
| Sen. Barack Obama | Senator Obama |

Academic degrees may be abbreviated when used alone, but other titles used alone are never abbreviated.

- **She received her *PhD* this year.**
- **He was a demanding ~~prof.,~~ and we worked hard.** [professor,]

Use either a title or an academic degree, but not both, with a person's name.

| | |
|---|---|
| **INAPPROPRIATE** | Dr. James Dillon, PhD |
| **REVISED** | Dr. James Dillon |
| **REVISED** | James Dillon, PhD |

Note that academic degrees such as *PhD* and *RN* often appear without periods (48a).

## 53b Abbreviations with years and hours

You can use the following abbreviations with numerals. Notice that AD precedes the numeral; all other abbreviations follow the numeral. Today, BCE and CE are generally preferred over BC and AD, and periods in all four of these abbreviations are optional.

399 BCE ("before the common era") or 399 BC ("before Christ")

49 CE ("common era") or AD 49 (*anno Domini*, Latin for "year of our Lord")

11:15 AM (*or* a.m.)

9:00 PM (*or* p.m.)

For abbreviations, you may use full-size capital letters or small caps, a typographical option in word-processing programs.

## 53c Acronyms and initial abbreviations

Acronyms are abbreviations that can be pronounced as words: OPEC, for example, is the acronym for the Organization of Petroleum Exporting Countries. Initial abbreviations, on the other hand, are pronounced as separate initials: NRA for National Rifle Association, for instance. Many of these abbreviations come from business, government, and science: NASA, PBS, DNA, GE, UNICEF, AIDS, SAT.

As long as you are sure your readers will understand them, use such abbreviations in your college writing. If the abbreviation may be unfamiliar to your readers, however, spell out the term the first time you use it, and give the abbreviation in parentheses. After that, you can use the abbreviation by itself.

- **The International Atomic Energy Agency (IAEA) is the central intergovernmental forum for cooperation in the nuclear arena.**

## 53d Abbreviations in company names

Use such abbreviations as *Co.*, *Inc.*, *Corp.*, and *&* if they are part of a company's official name. Do not, however, use these abbreviations in most other contexts.

▶ **Sears, Roebuck & Co. was the only large ~~corp.~~ [corporation] in town.**

## 53e Latin abbreviations

In general, avoid these Latin abbreviations except when citing sources:

| | |
|---|---|
| cf. | compare (*confer*) |
| e.g. | for example (*exempli gratia*) |
| et al. | and others (*et alia*) |
| etc. | and so forth (*et cetera*) |
| i.e. | that is (*id est*) |
| N.B. | note well (*nota bene*) |

▶ **Many firms have policies to help working parents — ~~e.g.,~~ [for example,] flexible hours, parental leave, and day care.**

▶ **Before the conference began, Haivan unpacked the name tags, programs, pens, ~~etc.~~ [and so forth.]**

## 53f Abbreviating reference information, geographic terms, and months

Though abbreviations for such words as *chapter* (ch.), *edition* (ed.), *page* (p.), or *pages* (pp.) are common in source citations, they are not appropriate in the body of your text.

▶ **The 1851 ~~ed.~~ [edition] of *Twice-Told Tales* is now a valuable collectible.**

Place-names and months of the year are often abbreviated in source citations, but they should almost always be written out within sentences.

▶ **In ~~Aug.,~~ [August,] I moved from Lodi, ~~Calif.,~~ [California,] to ~~L.A.~~ [Los Angeles.]**

Common exceptions are *Washington*, *DC*, and *U.S.* The latter is acceptable as an adjective but not as a noun.

- **The *U.S. delegation* negotiated the treaty.**

- **The exchange student enjoyed the ~~U.S.~~** United States.

## 53g Symbols and units of measurement

In English and the other humanities, symbols such as *%*, *+*, *$*, and *=* are acceptable in charts and graphs. Dollar signs are acceptable with figures: *$11* (but not with words: *eleven dollars*). Units of measurement can be abbreviated in charts and graphs (*4 in.*) but not in the body of a paper (*four inches*). Check with your instructor about using a word or a figure with the word *percent*: some documentation styles, such as MLA, require a word (*ten percent*), while others, such as *Chicago*, require a figure whether the word (*10 percent*) or the symbol (*10%*) is used.

- **The ball sailed 425 ~~ft.~~** feet **over the fence.**

### EXERCISE 53.1

Revise each of the following sentences to eliminate any abbreviations that would be inappropriate in most academic writing. Example:

> The population of the ~~U.S.~~ United States grew considerably in the 1980s.

1. Every Fri., my grandmother would walk a mi. to the P.O. and send a care package to her brother in Tenn.
2. An MX missile, which is 71 ft. long and 92 in. around, weighs 190,000 lbs.
3. Enron officials met with the V.P. of the U.S. to discuss the admin.'s energy policy, but soon afterward the Tex. co. declared bankruptcy.
4. A large corp. like AT&T may help finance an employee's M.B.A.
5. Rosie always began by saying, "If you want my two ¢," but she never waited to see if I wanted it or not.

**bedfordstmartins.com/smhandbook** For more exercises on using abbreviations, go to Exercise Central and click on **Abbreviations**.

## Abbreviations and numbers in different fields

Use of abbreviations and numbers varies in different fields. See a typical example from a biochemistry textbook:

> The energy of a green photon . . . is 57 kilocalories per mole (kcal/mol). An alternative unit of energy is the joule (J), which is equal to 0.239 calorie; 1 kcal/mol is equal to 4.184 kJ/mol.
>
> — LUBERT STRYER, *Biochemistry*

These two sentences demonstrate how useful figures and abbreviations can be; reading the same sentences would be very difficult if the numbers and units of measurement had to be written out.

Be sure to use the appropriate system of measurement for the field you are discussing and for the audience you are addressing. Scientific fields generally use metric measurements, which are the standard in most nations other than the United States.

Become familiar with the conventions governing abbreviations and numbers in your field. The following reference books provide guidelines:

*MLA Handbook for Writers of Research Papers* for literature and the humanities

*Publication Manual of the American Psychological Association* for the social sciences

*Scientific Style and Format: The CSE Manual for Authors, Editors, and Publishers* for the natural sciences

*The Chicago Manual of Style* for the humanities

*AIP Style Manual* for physics and the applied sciences

## 53h Numbers within sentences

If you can write out the number in one or two words, do so. Use figures for longer numbers.

- **Her screams were heard by ~~38~~ thirty-eight people, none of whom called the police.**
- **A baseball is held together by ~~two hundred sixteen~~ 216 red stitches.**

If one of several numbers *of the same kind* in the same sentence requires a figure, use figures for all the numbers in that sentence.

$100
- **Our audio systems range in cost from ~~one hundred~~ dollars to $2,599.**

## 53i Numbers that begin sentences

When a sentence begins with a number, either spell out the number or rewrite the sentence.

One hundred nineteen
- **~~119~~ years of CIA labor cost taxpayers sixteen million dollars.**

Most readers find it easier to read figures than three-word numbers; thus the best solution may be to rewrite this sentence: *Taxpayers spent sixteen million dollars for 119 years of CIA labor.*

## 53j Conventions with figures

| | |
|---|---|
| **ADDRESSES** | 23 Main Street; 175 Fifth Avenue |
| **DATES** | September 17, 1951; 6 June 1983; 4 BCE; the 1860s |
| **DECIMALS AND FRACTIONS** | 65.34; 8½ |
| **PERCENTAGES** | 77 percent (*or* 77%) |
| **EXACT AMOUNTS OF MONEY** | $7,348; $1.46 trillion; $2.50; thirty-five (*or* 35) cents |
| **SCORES AND STATISTICS** | an 8–3 Red Sox victory; a verbal score of 600; an average age of 22; a mean of 53 |
| **TIME OF DAY** | 6:00 AM (*or* a.m.) |

### FOR MULTILINGUAL WRITERS: The term *hundred*

The term *hundred* is used idiomatically in English. When it is linked with numbers like two, eight, and so on, the word *hundred* remains singular: *Eight hundred years have passed, and still old animosities run deep.* Add the plural *-s* to *hundred* only when no number precedes the term: *Hundreds of priceless books were lost in the fire.*

## Editing abbreviations and numbers

- Use abbreviations and numbers according to the conventions of a specific field (see p. 768): for example, *57%* might be acceptable in a math paper, but *57 percent* may be more appropriate in a sociology essay. (53g)
- If you use an abbreviation readers might not understand, spell out the term the first time you use it, and give the abbreviation in parentheses. (53c)
- If you use an abbreviation more than once, make sure you use it consistently.

### EXERCISE 53.2

Revise the numbers in the following sentences as necessary for correctness and consistency. Some sentences may be correct as written. Example:

> twenty-first
> Did the ~~21st~~ century begin in 2000 or 2001?

1. Al Gore won the popular vote with 50,996,116 votes, but he was still short by 5 electoral votes.
2. 2500 people wanted tickets, but the arena held only 1800.
3. The senator who voted against the measure received 6817 angry emails and only twelve in support of her decision.
4. Walker signed a three-year, $4.5-million contract.
5. In that age group, the risk is estimated to be about one in 2,500.

**bedfordstmartins.com/smhandbook** For additional exercises on numbers, go to Exercise Central and click on **Numbers**.

## THINKING CRITICALLY ABOUT ABBREVIATIONS AND NUMBERS

**Reading with an Eye for Abbreviations and Numbers**

The paragraph by Roger Angell at the end of Chapter 55 follows the style of the *New Yorker* magazine, which often spells out numbers in situations where this chapter recommends using figures. Read the paragraph carefully, and then consider whether it would have been easier to read if figures had been used for some of the numbers. If so, which ones? Then consider how the paragraph would have been different if Angell had used *semi-professional* instead of *semi-pro*. What effect does the abbreviated form create?

**Thinking about Your Own Use of Abbreviations and Numbers**

Look over an essay that you have written, noting all abbreviations and numbers. Check your usage for correctness, consistency, and appropriateness. If you discover a problem with abbreviations or numbers, make a note of it so that you can avoid the error in the future.

# 54 Italics

The slanted type known as *italics* is more than just a pretty typeface. Indeed, italics give words special meaning or emphasis. In the sentence "Many people read *People* on the subway every day," the italics (and the capital letter) tell us that *People* is a publication.

You may use a computer to produce italic type; if not, underline words that you would otherwise italicize. But remember not to overuse italics to emphasize important words: doing so will get *very boring* to readers *very quickly*.

## 54a Italics for titles

In general, use italics for titles of long works; use quotation marks for shorter works (50b and 52c).

| | |
|---|---|
| **BOOKS** | *The Da Vinci Code* |
| **CHOREOGRAPHIC WORKS** | Agnes de Mille's *Rodeo* |
| **FILMS AND VIDEOS** | *Brokeback Mountain* |
| **LONG MUSICAL WORKS** | *Brandenburg Concertos* |
| **LONG POEMS** | *Bhagavad Gita* |
| **MAGAZINES AND JOURNALS** | *Ebony*, the *New England Journal of Medicine* |
| **NEWSPAPERS** | the *Cleveland Plain Dealer* |
| **PAINTINGS AND SCULPTURE** | Georgia O'Keeffe's *Black Iris* |
| **PAMPHLETS** | Thomas Paine's *Common Sense* |
| **PLAYS** | *Sweeney Todd* |
| **RADIO SERIES** | *All Things Considered* |
| **RECORDINGS** | *Slade Alive!* |
| **SOFTWARE** | *Dreamweaver* |
| **TELEVISION SERIES** | *The Sopranos* |
| **WEB SITES** | *Voice of the Shuttle* |

Do not use italics for sacred books, such as the Bible and the Qur'an; for public documents, such as the Constitution and the Magna Carta; or for the titles of your own papers. With magazines and newspapers, do not italicize or capitalize an initial *the*, even if part of the official name.

## 54b Italics for words, letters, and numbers referred to as terms

Italicize words, letters, and numbers referred to as terms.

- **One characteristic of some New York speech is the absence of postvocalic *r*, with some New Yorkers, for example, pronouncing *four* as "fouh."**
- **The first four orbitals are represented by the letters *s*, *p*, *d*, and *f*.**
- **On the back of his jersey was the famous *24*.**

## 54c Italics for non-English words and phrases

Italicize words and phrases from other languages unless they have become part of English, such as the French word "bourgeois" and the Italian "pasta." If a word is in an English dictionary, it does not need italics.

- **At last one of the phantom sleighs gliding along the street would come to a stop, and with gawky haste Mr. Burness in his fox-furred *shapka* would make for our door.**

— VLADIMIR NABOKOV, *Speak, Memory*

Always italicize Latin genus and species names.

- **The caterpillars of *Hapalia*, when attacked by the wasp *Apanteles machaeralis*, drop suddenly from their leaves and suspend themselves in air by a silken thread.**

— STEPHEN JAY GOULD, "Nonmoral Nature"

## 54d Italics for names of vehicles

Italicize names of specific aircraft, spacecraft, ships, and trains. Do not italicize types and classes, such as Learjet and space shuttle.

| | |
|---|---|
| **AIRCRAFT AND SPACECRAFT** | the *Spirit of St. Louis*, the *Discovery* |
| **SHIPS** | the *Santa Maria*, the USS *Iowa* |
| **TRAINS** | the *Orient Express*, Amtrak's *Lakeshore Limited* |

## 54e Italics for special emphasis

Italics can help create emphasis in writing, but use them sparingly for this purpose. It is usually better to create emphasis with sentence structure and word choice.

> **Great literature and a class of literate readers are nothing new in India. What is new is the emergence of a gifted generation of Indian writers *working in English*.** — SALMAN RUSHDIE

### EXERCISE 54.1

In each of the following sentences, underline any words that should be italicized, and circle any italicized words that should not be. Example:

The film Good Night, and Good Luck tells the story of a CBS newsman who helped to end the career of Senator Joseph McCarthy.

1. One critic claimed that few people listened to *The Velvet Underground and Nico* when the record was issued but that everyone who did formed a band.
2. Homemade *sushi* can be dangerous, but so can deviled eggs kept too long in a picnic basket.

### Editing for italics

- Check that all titles of long works are italicized. (54a)
- If you use any words, letters, or numbers as terms, make sure they are in italics. (54b)
- Italicize any non-English words or phrases that are not in an English dictionary. (54c)
- If you use italics to emphasize words, be sure you use the italics sparingly. (54e)

3. The Web site Poisonous Plants and Animals lists tobacco (Nicotiana tobacum) as one of the most popular poisons in the world.
4. The monster in the Old English epic Beowulf got to tell his own side of the story in John Gardner's novel Grendel.
5. In Ray, Jamie Foxx looks as if he is actually singing Ray Charles's songs.

**bedfordstmartins.com/smhandbook** For more exercises on using italics, go to Exercise Central and click on **Italics**.

## THINKING CRITICALLY ABOUT ITALICS

**Reading with an Eye for Italics**

Read the following passage about a graduate English seminar carefully, particularly noting the effects created by the italics. How would it differ without any italic emphasis? What other words or phrases might the author have italicized?

> There were four big tables arranged in a square, with everyone's feet sticking out into the open middle of the square. You could tell who was nervous, and how much, by watching the pairs of feet twist around each other. The Great Man presided awesomely from the high bar of the square. His head was a majestic granite-gray, like a centurion in command; he *looked* famous. His clean shoes twitched only slightly, and only when he was angry.
>
> It turned out he was angry at me a lot of the time. He was angry because he thought me a disrupter, a rioter, a provocateur, and a fool; also crazy. And this was twenty years ago, before these things were *de rigueur* in the universities. Everything was very quiet in those days: there were only the Cold War and Korea and Joe McCarthy and the Old Old Nixon, and the only revolutionaries around were in Henry James's *The Princess Casamassima*.
>
> — CYNTHIA OZICK, "We Are the Crazy Lady"

**Thinking about Your Own Use of Italics**

Write a paragraph or two describing the most eccentric person you know, italicizing some words for special emphasis. Read your passage aloud to hear the effect of the italics. Now explain each use of italics. If you find yourself unable to give a reason, ask yourself whether the word should be italicized at all.

Then revise the passage to eliminate *all but one* use of italics. Try revising sentences and choosing more precise words to convey emphasis. Decide which version is more effective. Can you reach any conclusions about using italics for emphasis?

# 55 Hyphens

As Hall of Fame pitcher Jim Palmer once said, "The difference between *re-sign* and *resign* is a hyphen." This statement shows how important a hyphen can be.

Hyphens are undoubtedly confusing to many people — hyphen problems are now one of the twenty most common surface errors in student writing. The confusion is understandable. Over time, the conventions for hyphen use in a given word can change (*tomorrow* was once spelled *to-morrow*). New words, even compounds such as *firewall*, generally don't use hyphens, but controversy continues to rage over whether to hyphenate *email* (or is it *e-mail*?). And some words are hyphenated when they serve one kind of purpose in a sentence and not when they serve another.

## 55a Hyphens with compound words

Some compounds are one word (*rowboat*), some are separate words (*hard drive*), and some require hyphens (*sister-in-law*). You should consult a dictionary to be sure. However, the following conventions can help you decide when to use hyphens with compound words.

### Compound adjectives

Hyphenate most compound adjectives that precede a noun but not those that follow a noun.

| | |
|---|---|
| a *well-liked* boss | My boss is *well liked.* |
| a *six-foot* plank | The plank is *six feet long.* |

In general, the reason for hyphenating compound adjectives is to facilitate reading.

- **Designers often use potted plants as living-room dividers.**

  Without the hyphen, *living* may seem to modify *room dividers.*

Commonly used compound adjectives do not usually need to be hyphenated for clarity — *income tax reform* or *first class mail* would seldom if ever be misunderstood.

Never hyphenate an *-ly* adverb and an adjective.

- **They used a widely-distributed mailing list.**

Compound adjectives formed from compound proper nouns are hyphenated if the noun is hyphenated: *Austro-Hungarian history* but *Latin American literature.*

### Coined compounds

You may sometimes need hyphens to link coined compounds, combinations of words that you are using in an unexpected way, especially as an adjective.

- **She gave me her *I-told-you-so* look before leaving the party.**

### Fractions and compound numbers

Use a hyphen to write out fractions and to spell out compound numbers from twenty-one to ninety-nine, both when they stand alone and when they are part of larger numbers. (Usually such larger numbers should be written as numerals. See Chapter 53.)

| | |
|---|---|
| one-seventh | thirty-seven |
| two and seven-sixteenths | three hundred fifty-four thousand |

### Suspended hyphens

A series of compound words that share the same base word can be shortened by the use of suspended hyphens.

- **Each student should do the work *him-* or *herself.***

## 55b Hyphens with prefixes and suffixes

Most words containing prefixes or suffixes are written without hyphens: *antiwar, gorillalike.* Here are some exceptions:

| | |
|---|---|
| **BEFORE CAPITALIZED BASE WORDS** | un-American, non-Catholic |
| **WITH FIGURES** | pre-1960, post-1945 |
| **WITH CERTAIN PREFIXES AND SUFFIXES** | all-state, ex-partner, self-possessed, quasi-legislative, mayor-elect, fifty-odd |
| **WITH COMPOUND BASE WORDS** | pre-high school, post-cold war |

| | |
|---|---|
| **FOR CLARITY OR EASE OF READING** | re-cover, anti-inflation, troll-like |

*Re-cover* means "cover again"; the hyphen distinguishes it from *recover*, meaning "get well." In *anti-inflation* and *troll-like*, the hyphens separate confusing clusters of vowels and consonants.

## 55c Hyphens to divide words at the end of a line

Word-processing programs generally wrap a word to the next line instead of breaking it with a hyphen. If you wish to divide a word at the end of a line, however, follow certain conventions.

- Break words between syllables only. All dictionaries show syllable breaks, so to divide words correctly, simply look them up.
- Never divide one-syllable words or abbreviations, contractions, or figures.
- Leave at least two letters on each line when dividing a word. Do not divide words such as *acorn* (*a-corn*) and *scratchy* (*scratch-y*) at all, and break a word such as *Americana* (*A-mer-i-can-a*) only after the *r* or the *i*.
- Divide compound words, such as *anklebone* and *mother-in-law*, only between their parts (*ankle-bone*) or after their hyphens.
- Divide words with prefixes or suffixes after the prefix (*dis-appearance*) or before the suffix (*disappear-ance*). Divide prefixed words that include a hyphen, such as *self-righteous*, after the hyphen.

## 55d Unnecessary hyphens

Unnecessary hyphens are at least as common a problem as omitted ones. Do not hyphenate the parts of a two-word verb such as *depend on*, *turn off*, or *tune out* (60b).

- **Players must pick-up a medical form before football tryouts.**

  The words *pick up* act as a verb and should not be hyphenated.

However, be careful to check that the two words do indeed function as a verb in the sentence; if they function as an adjective, a hyphen may be needed (31b1, b4).

- **Let's sign up for the early class.**

  The verb *sign up* should not have a hyphen.

- **Where is the sign-up sheet?**

  The compound adjective *sign-up*, which modifies the noun *sheet*, needs a hyphen.

Do not hyphenate a subject complement — a word group that follows a linking verb (such as a form of *be* or *seem*) and describes the subject (31c).

- **Audrey is almost three~~-~~years~~-~~old.**

### EXERCISE 55.1

Insert or delete hyphens as necessary in the following sentences. Use your dictionary if you are not sure whether or where to hyphenate a word. Example:

The governor-elect joked about the polls.

1. She insisted that the line workers pick-up the pace.
2. Line-up quietly and wait for my signal.
3. Her ability to convey her ideas clearly has made her well-respected in the office.
4. After he spent four weeks in an alcohol re-habilitation program, he apologized to his wife for twenty two years of heavy drinking.

### Editing for hyphens

- Double-check compound words to be sure they are properly closed up, separated, or hyphenated. If in doubt, consult a dictionary. (55a)
- Check all terms that have prefixes or suffixes to see whether you need hyphens. (55b)
- If you break words at the end of a line, make sure they are divided at an appropriate point. (55c)
- Do not hyphenate two-word verbs or word groups that serve as subject complements. (55d)

5. Having an ignore the customer attitude may actually make a service-industry job less pleasant.
6. Both pro and antiState Department groups registered complaints.
7. At a yard sale, I found a 1964 pre CBS Fender Stratocaster in mint condition.
8. Applicants who are over fifty-years-old may face age discrimination.
9. Neil Armstrong, a selfproclaimed "nerdy engineer," was the first person to set foot on the moon.
10. Carefully-marketed children's safety products suggest to new parents that the more they spend, the safer their kids will be.

**bedfordstmartins.com/smhandbook** For more exercises on using hyphens, go to Exercise Central and click on **Hyphens**.

## THINKING CRITICALLY ABOUT HYPHENATION

The following paragraph uses many hyphens. Read it carefully, and note how the hyphens make the paragraph easier to read. Why do you think *semi-pro* is hyphenated? Why is *junior-college* hyphenated in the last sentence?

> All semi-pro leagues, it should be understood, are self-sustaining, and have no farm affiliation or other connection with the twenty-six major-league clubs, or with the seventeen leagues and hundred and fifty-two teams . . . that make up the National Association — the minors, that is. There is no central body of semi-pro teams, and semi-pro players are not included among the six hundred and fifty major-leaguers, the twenty-five-hundred-odd minor-leaguers, plus all the managers, coaches, presidents, commissioners, front-office people, and scouts, who, taken together, constitute the great tent called organized ball. (A much diminished tent, at that; back in 1949, the minors included fifty-nine leagues, about four hundred and forty-eight teams, and perhaps ten thousand players.) Also outside the tent, but perhaps within its shade, are five college leagues, ranging across the country from Cape Cod to Alaska, where the most promising freshman, sophomore, and junior-college ballplayers . . . compete against each other. . . .
>
> — ROGER ANGELL, "In the Country"

# Part 11

# FOR MULTILINGUAL WRITERS

# 56 Writing in U.S. Academic Contexts

You already know that writing differs from one context to another. Right now, learning what counts as effective writing in the context of college is a major goal. Of course, writing for college presents many challenges; such writing differs in many ways from high school writing as well as from personal writing like email. If you grew up speaking and writing in other languages, however, the transition to producing effective college writing can be even more complicated. Not only will you have to learn new information and new ways of thinking and arguing, but you also have to do it in a language that may not come naturally to you — especially in unfamiliar rhetorical situations.

## 56a U.S. academic writing

Xiaoming Li, now a college English teacher, says that before she came to the United States as a graduate student, she had been a "good writer" in China — in both English and Chinese. Once in the United States, however, she struggled to grasp what her teachers expected of her college writing. While she could easily use grammar books and dictionaries, her instructors' unstated expectations seemed to call for her to write in a way that was new to her.

The expectations for college writing are often taken for granted by instructors. To complicate the matter further, there is no single "correct" style of communication in any country, including the United States. Effective oral styles differ from effective written styles, and what is considered good writing in one field of study is not necessarily appropriate in another. Within a field, different rhetorical situations and genres may require different ways of writing. In business, for example, memos are usually short and simple, while a market analysis report may require complex paragraphs with tables, graphs, and diagrams. Even the variety of English often referred to as "standard" covers a wide range of styles (see Chapter 28). In spite of this wide variation, several features are often associated with U.S. academic English in general:

- conventional grammar, spelling, punctuation, and mechanics
- organization that links ideas explicitly (Chapter 6)

- an easy-to-read typesize and typeface, conventional margins, and double spacing
- explicitly stated claims supported by evidence (Chapter 11)
- careful documentation of all sources (Chapters 18–21)
- consistent use of an appropriate level of formality (26g and 29a)
- conventional use of idioms (Chapter 60)
- the use of conventional academic formats, such as literature reviews, research essays, lab reports, and research proposals

This brief list suggests features of the genre often described as U.S. academic writing. Yet these characteristics can lead to even more questions: What does *conventional* mean? How can a writer determine what is appropriate in any given rhetorical situation? Most students can benefit from some instruction in how new contexts require the use of different sets of conventions, strategies, and resources. This is especially the case for multilingual writers.

## 56b Genre conventions

Those who read your college writing — your teachers and peers — will hold some expectations about the texts you produce and about the features of those texts. Many writers learn these expectations through practice rather than through instruction. But if you have had limited exposure to various types, or *genres*, of academic writing in English, it may be helpful to think about these conventions explicitly.

### Genres of texts

At some point in your writing process, you should consider the genre or kind of text the instructor expects you to write. The expectation may be clear from the assignment, especially when the instructor is explicit about the purpose, audience, possible methods of organization, and criteria for assessment. In many cases, however, the assignment is not explicit about what the text should look like or accomplish. For example, if the instructor asks for a five-page essay about efforts to conserve the environment, can the essay take the form of a personal narrative or reflection on your frustrating experience with recycling? Is it supposed to examine a problem related to conservation and pose a solution? Or does it need to be an academic essay that presents new knowledge or insight about a specific aspect of conservation efforts supported by original data, secondary sources, or both?

If you are not sure what kind of text you are supposed to write, ask your instructor for clarification and examples. (Some examples may also be available at your school's writing center.) You may want to find multiple examples so that you can develop a sense of how different writers approach the same writing task. Another strategy is to discuss the assignment with a few classmates or a writing center tutor. You may find the help you need, or you may be surprised to see that you are not the only one struggling to understand the assignment.

## Strategies for analyzing genre features

Find some examples of the kind of text the assignment requires, and study them carefully for various features. Here are some questions to consider:

- What does the genre look like? How is the text laid out on the page? How are any visual features — such as headings, bylines, sidebars, and footnotes — incorporated into the main text? (23d)
- How long is the whole text, each section, each paragraph, and each sentence?
- How does the text introduce the topic? How and where does it present the main point? Is the main point stated explicitly or implicitly?
- What are the major divisions of the text? Are they marked with transitions or headings? (7d and 23c)
- How does each section contribute to the main point? How is the main point of each section supported?
- How are the key terms defined? How much and what kind of background information is provided?
- What is the level of formality? Does the text use technical terms, contractions (such as *I'm* and *isn't* instead of *I am* and *is not*), or many dependent or subordinate clauses? (43b)
- Does the text take a personal stance (*I*, *we*), address the audience directly (*you*), or talk about the subject without explicitly referring to the writer or the reader?
- How many sources are used in the text? How are they introduced? Are sources mentioned in the text, cited in parentheses, or both? Which documentation style — such as MLA or APA — is followed? (Chapters 18–21)
- How are the characteristics of the text similar to or different from similar genres in your native language?

Although the genres of writing required in college vary among fields of study and even among courses, research shows that the most common out-of-class writing assignments in college include the following: research-based papers that draw on sources from your library and online searches (Chapters 12–21); reports that include some interpretation (19e); summaries, which may or may not call for analysis (14f4); proposals (21d); reviews or critiques (62d); and close readings or explications of a text (62c). This handbook provides basic information on all these kinds of writing.

One of the most common writing tasks for college students happens in class, in the form of short-answer questions and very brief essays on exams (Chapter 66). For this kind of writing, you will almost always be expected to display knowledge you have learned in the course. In this setting, demonstrating that you know the material may be more important than developing new or original ideas about the topic — unless the assignment specifically asks you to synthesize or present your own perspective.

## Strategies for in-class writing tasks

For many multilingual students, the major problem presented by in-class writing is running out of time. You can overcome this problem by preparing carefully in advance.

- Review all the material carefully.
- Create a list of key terms and their definitions.
- Anticipate the questions, and write practice answers to them. (Do not, however, memorize answers to questions you think might be on the exam, since doing so might lead you to rely on answers that don't fit the questions on the actual test.)
- Explain the material you will be tested on — either orally or in writing — to someone unfamiliar with it.
- Do some timed writing right before class to get your writing muscles warmed up.

Here are some strategies you can use during the exam to minimize the risk of running out of time:

- Create a brief outline at the beginning of the exam to organize your thoughts and to keep you on track.
- State your answer or main point at the beginning before providing the background information or explanation.

### Strategies for borrowing without plagiarizing

To avoid plagiarism:

- Try not to reproduce the whole sentence; instead, borrow phrases that are not central to the author's idea.
- Find sample pieces of sentence structure from similar genres but on different topics so that you will be borrowing a typical structure (which does not belong to anyone), not the idea or the particular way the idea is phrased.
- Write your own sentence first, and look at other people's sentences to guide your revision.

## 56c Adapting structures and phrases from a genre

If English is not your strongest language, you may find it useful to borrow and adapt transitional devices and pieces of sentence structure from other people's writing in the genre you are working in. You should not

| Original Abstract from a Social Science Paper | Effective Borrowing of Structures from a Genre |
|---|---|
| Using the interpersonal communications research of J. K. Brilhart and G. J. Galanes, and W. Wilmot and J. Hocker, along with T. Hartman's personality assessment, I observed and analyzed the leadership roles and group dynamics of my project collaborators in a communications course. Based on results of the Hartman personality assessment, I predicted that a single leader would emerge. However, complementary individual strengths and gender differences encouraged a distributed leadership style, in which the group experienced little confrontation and conflict. Conflict, because it was handled positively, was crucial to the group's progress. | Drawing on the research of Deborah Tannen on men's and women's conversational styles, I analyzed the conversational styles of six first-year students at DePaul University. Based on Tannen's research, I expected that the three men I observed would use features typical of male conversational style and the three women would use features typical of female conversational style. In general, these predictions were accurate; however, some exceptions were also apparent. |

| Original Abstract from a Social Science Paper | Inappropriate Borrowing of Ideas and Sentences |
| --- | --- |
| Using the interpersonal communications research of J. K. Brilhart and G. J. Galanes, and W. Wilmot and J. Hocker, along with T. Hartman's personality assessment, I observed and analyzed the leadership roles and group dynamics of my project collaborators in a communications course. Based on results of the Hartman personality assessment, I predicted that a single leader would emerge. However, complementary individual strengths and gender differences encouraged a distributed leadership style, in which the group experienced little confrontation and conflict. Conflict, because it was handled positively, was crucial to the group's progress. | Using the interpersonal communications research of J. K. Brilhart and G. J. Galanes, and W. Wilmot and J. Hocker, along with T. Hartman's personality assessment, I observed and analyzed the leadership roles and group dynamics of my peers in a communications course. Based on findings of the Hartman personality assessment, I predicted that one leader of the group would appear. However, complementary individual strengths and differences in gender resulted in a distributed leadership style, in which there was little confrontation and conflict. Because it was handled positively, conflict was crucial to the group's progress. |

copy the whole sentence or sentence structure verbatim, however, or your borrowed sentences may seem plagiarized (Chapter 16 and 18c).

The first example on the previous page illustrates effective borrowing. The student writer borrows phrases that are commonly used in academic writing in the social sciences to perform particular functions. Notice how the student also modifies these phrases to suit his or her needs.

The next example above illustrates poor borrowing practices. The student plagiarizes both ideas and whole sentences from the original text.

## 56d Strategies for learning from search engines

To multilingual writers, Internet search engines such as Google offer more than a tool for finding information. They also provide a useful way of developing vocabulary or checking sentence structure and word usage. A number of common strategies can help. For example, you can include a wildcard in a keyword search to find all the forms of a word; a wildcard search using *reciproc** will yield *reciprocate*, *reciprocating*, *reciprocated*, *reciprocal*, and *reciprocity*. Most search engines use an asterisk (*) as a wildcard, though some use a question mark or other wildcard symbol. You can use *define:* to look up the definition of a word or a phrase (such as *define:social science*) or enclose a phrase in quotation marks to find Web pages that include it (such as "*language in society*").

In addition, you can use search engines to check your use of common expressions. For example, if you are not sure whether you should use an infinitive form (*to* + verb) or a gerund (*-ing*) for the verb *confirm* after the main verb *expect* (57d), you can search for both "*expected confirming*" and "*expected to confirm*" in quotation marks to see which search term yields more results. A Google search for "*expected confirming*" yields many entries with a comma between the two words, indicating that one phrase ends with *expected* and another begins with *confirming*.

Google

**Web** Images Groups News Froogle Maps **more »**

"expected confirming" [Search] Advanced Search Preferences

Number of hits

**Web** Results **1** - **10** of about **543** for **"expected confirming"**. (**0.23** seconds)

PC Review - Re: Astonshing interpretation of tab delimited input ...
Again choose Format > Cells , I see the "Text " type highlighted as **expected confirming** it really did change to text format . 4. From the menu , choose Edit ...
www.pcreview.co.uk/forums/thread-990055.php - 54k - Supplemental Result - Cached - Similar pages

Phys. Rev. A 69, 063402 (2004): Shuman et al. - I dependence of ...
... as **expected, confirming** that the field dependence of DR can be used to extract information about the contributions of energetically unresolved I states ...
dx.doi.org/10.1103/PhysRevA.69.063402 - Similar pages

Staff/Student Roles & Responsibilities - City University London
The supervisor should ensure that the student is made aware of any inadequacy of progress or standards of work below that generally **expected, confirming** ...
www.city.ac.uk/researchstudies/rr_student.html - 48k - Cached - Similar pages

[DOC] Draft Supervisor/Supervisee Agreement
File Format: Microsoft Word - View as HTML
The supervisor will ensure that the supervisee is made aware of any inadequacy of progress or standards of work below that generally **expected, confirming** ...
www.city.ac.uk/researchstudies/ dps/draft_learning_contract.doc - Similar pages

IDC - Press Release
The IT investment index has flattened, as **expected, confirming** that IT investment growth this year is not likely to exceed that of 2004. ...
www.idc.com/getdoc.jsp?containerId=pr2005_06_20_151638 - 23k - Cached - Similar pages

*Search results for* "expected confirming."

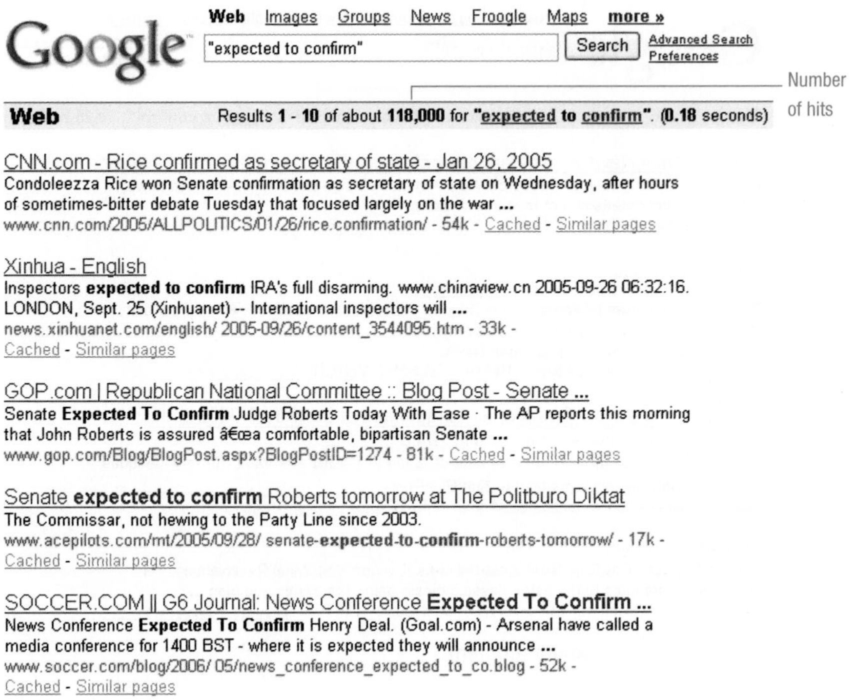

Google

Web Images Groups News Froogle Maps more »

"expected to confirm" Search Advanced Search Preferences

Number of hits

**Web** Results **1** - **10** of about **118,000** for **"expected to confirm"**. (**0.18** seconds)

CNN.com - Rice confirmed as secretary of state - Jan 26, 2005
Condoleezza Rice won Senate confirmation as secretary of state on Wednesday, after hours of sometimes-bitter debate Tuesday that focused largely on the war ...
www.cnn.com/2005/ALLPOLITICS/01/26/rice.confirmation/ - 54k - Cached - Similar pages

Xinhua - English
Inspectors **expected to confirm** IRA's full disarming. www.chinaview.cn 2005-09-26 06:32:16. LONDON, Sept. 25 (Xinhuanet) -- International inspectors will ...
news.xinhuanet.com/english/ 2005-09/26/content_3544095.htm - 33k -
Cached - Similar pages

GOP.com | Republican National Committee :: Blog Post - Senate ...
Senate **Expected To Confirm** Judge Roberts Today With Ease · The AP reports this morning that John Roberts is assured â€œa comfortable, bipartisan Senate ...
www.gop.com/Blog/BlogPost.aspx?BlogPostID=1274 - 81k - Cached - Similar pages

Senate **expected to confirm** Roberts tomorrow at The Politburo Diktat
The Commissar, not hewing to the Party Line since 2003.
www.acepilots.com/mt/2005/09/28/ senate-**expected-to-confirm**-roberts-tomorrow/ - 17k -
Cached - Similar pages

SOCCER.COM || G6 Journal: News Conference **Expected To Confirm ...**
News Conference **Expected To Confirm** Henry Deal. (Goal.com) - Arsenal have called a media conference for 1400 BST - where it is expected they will announce ...
www.soccer.com/blog/2006/ 05/news_conference_expected_to_co.blog - 52k -
Cached - Similar pages

*Search results for* "expected to confirm."

On the other hand, a search for "*expected to confirm*" yields many more hits than a search for "*expected confirming*" — 118,000 instead of 543, for example, in the searches shown on these pages. These results indicate that *expected to confirm* is the more commonly used expression.

But you should also note that in the search above, some of the entries shown are news headlines, which means that they may not use the same construction used in ordinary English sentences (newspaper headlines, for example, often omit *be* verbs). To check whether ordinary sentences also use *expected to confirm* rather than *expected confirming*, you would want to click through a few more pages of search results, seeking out examples that do not come from headlines.

An alternative option is to use an asterisk as a wildcard in the Google search box ("*expect* confirm**"). An example of such a wildcard search is shown on the following page.

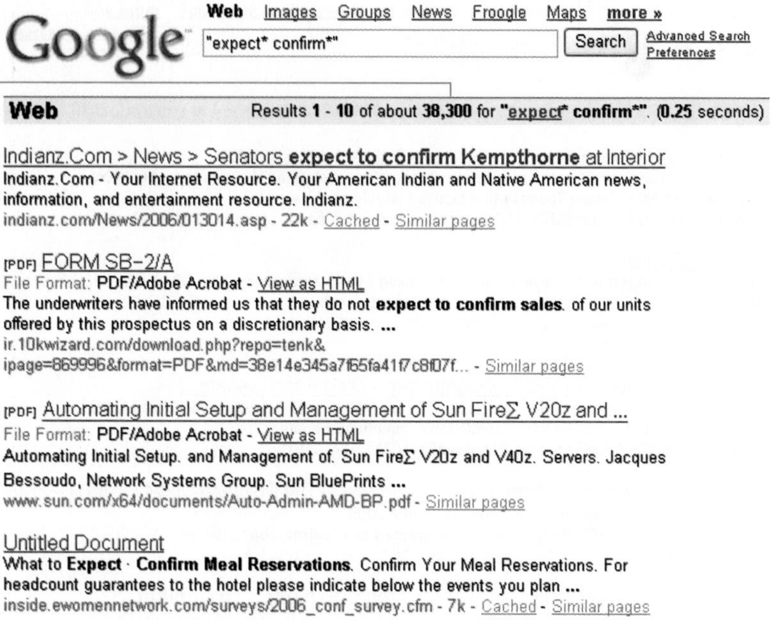

Google Web Images Groups News Froogle Maps more »
"expect* confirm*" Search Advanced Search Preferences

Number of hits

**Web** Results **1** - **10** of about **38,300** for **"expect* confirm*"**. (**0.25** seconds)

Indianz.Com > News > Senators **expect to confirm Kempthorne** at Interior
Indianz.Com - Your Internet Resource. Your American Indian and Native American news, information, and entertainment resource. Indianz.
indianz.com/News/2006/013014.asp - 22k - Cached - Similar pages

[PDF] FORM SB-2/A
File Format: PDF/Adobe Acrobat - View as HTML
The underwriters have informed us that they do not **expect to confirm sales**. of our units offered by this prospectus on a discretionary basis. ...
ir.10kwizard.com/download.php?repo=tenk&ipage=869996&format=PDF&md=38e14e345a7f65fa41f7c8f07f... - Similar pages

[PDF] Automating Initial Setup and Management of Sun FireΣ V20z and ...
File Format: PDF/Adobe Acrobat - View as HTML
Automating Initial Setup. and Management of. Sun FireΣ V20z and V40z. Servers. Jacques Bessoudo, Network Systems Group. Sun BluePrints ...
www.sun.com/x64/documents/Auto-Admin-AMD-BP.pdf - Similar pages

Untitled Document
What to **Expect** · **Confirm Meal Reservations**. Confirm Your Meal Reservations. For headcount guarantees to the hotel please indicate below the events you plan ...
inside.ewomennetwork.com/surveys/2006_conf_survey.cfm - 7k - Cached - Similar pages

*Search results for* "expect* confirm*."

This search yields results that also suggest "*expect to confirm*" is the more commonly used expression. To check this, however, you will need to look closely at the search results. The second result above uses *expect to confirm* in an ordinary English sentence, but you should examine results on a few additional pages to be sure that this usage is a typical one.

# Clauses and Sentences

# 57

Short phrases, or sound bites, surround us — from Taco Bell's "Think Outside the Bun" to Volkswagen's "Drivers Wanted." These short, simple slogans may be memorable, but they don't tell us very much. Particularly in writing, we usually need more complex sentences to convey meaning. The requirements for forming sentences can differ across languages, and English has its own sets of rules. Among the more difficult features of English sentence formation are explicit subjects and objects, word order, noun clauses, infinitives and gerunds, adjective clauses, and conditional sentences.

## 57a Explicit subjects and objects

English sentences consist of a subject and a predicate. While many languages can omit a sentence subject, English very rarely allows this. Though you might write *Responsible for analyzing data* on a résumé, in most varieties of spoken and written English, it is necessary to explicitly state the subject. In fact, with only a few exceptions, all clauses in English must have an explicit subject.

- **They took the Acela Express to Boston because** it **was fast.**

English even requires a kind of "dummy" subject to fill the subject position in certain kinds of sentences.

- ***It* is raining.**
- ***There* is a strong wind.**

Transitive verbs typically require that objects — and sometimes other information — also be explicitly stated (31c2). For example, it is not enough to tell someone *Give!* even if it is clear what is to be given to whom. You must say *Give it to me* or *Give her the passport* or some other such sentence. Similarly, saying *Put!* or *Put it!* is insufficient when you mean *Put it on the table*; however, *Put it down!* is fine because it includes the required destination.

Many dictionaries identify whether a verb is transitive (requiring an object) or intransitive (not followed by an object).

## 57b Word order

In general, subjects, verbs, and objects must be placed in specific positions within a sentence (31c).

SUBJECT VERB OBJECT ADVERB
**Mario left Venice reluctantly.**

The only word in this sentence that can be moved to different locations is the adverb *reluctantly* (*Mario reluctantly left Venice* or *Reluctantly, Mario left Venice*). The three key elements of subject, verb, and object are moved out of their normal order only to create special stylistic effects (45c3).

## 57c Noun clauses

Examine the following sentence:

> In my last year in high school, my adviser urged that I apply to several colleges.

This complex sentence is built out of two sentences, one of them (B) embedded in the other (A):

> A. In my last year in high school, my adviser urged B.
> B. I (should) apply to several colleges.

When these are combined as in the original sentence, sentence B becomes a noun clause introduced by *that* and takes on the role of object of the verb *urged* in sentence A. Now look at the following sentence:

> It made a big difference that she wrote a strong letter of recommendation.

Here the two component sentences are C and D:

> C. D made a big difference.
> D. She wrote a strong letter of recommendation.

In this case, the noun clause formed from sentence D functions as the subject of sentence C so that the combination reads as follows:

> That she wrote a strong letter of recommendation made a big difference.

This sentence is gramatically acceptable but not typical. When a lengthy noun clause is the subject, it is usually moved to the end of the sentence. The result is *It made a big difference that she wrote a strong letter of recommendation*, which inserts the dummy subject *It* to fill the slot of the subject.

## 57d Infinitives and gerunds

Infinitives are verbs in the *to* + verb form (*to write*, *to read*, *to go*); gerunds are verbs that end in *-ing* and are situated in subject or object positions within a sentence. In general, infinitives tend to represent intentions, desires, or expectations, and gerunds tend to represent facts. Knowing whether to use an infinitive or a gerund in a particular sentence can be a challenge. Though no simple explanation will make it an easy task, some hints might be helpful (see 56d for another strategy).

- **My adviser urged me *to apply* to several colleges.**
- ***Applying* took a great deal of time.**

In the first sentence, the infinitive conveys the message that the act of applying was something desired, not an accomplished fact. In the second sentence, the gerund calls attention to the fact that the application process was actually carried out.

### *Using infinitives to state intentions*

- **Kumar *expected to get* a good job after graduation.**
- **Last year, Fatima *decided to become* a math major.**
- **The strikers have *agreed to go* back to work.**

Here it is irrelevant whether the actions or events referred to by the infinitives did or did not occur; at the moment indicated by the verbs *expect*, *decide*, and *agree*, those actions or events were merely intentions. These three verbs, as well as many others that specify intentions (or negative intentions, such as *refuse*), must always be followed by an infinitive, never by a gerund. Many learner dictionaries provide information about verbs that must be followed by an infinitive instead of a gerund.

### *Using gerunds to state facts*

- **Jerzy enjoys *going* to the theater.**
- **We resumed *working* after our coffee break.**
- **Kim appreciated *getting* candy from Sean.**

In all of these cases, the gerund indicates that the action or event that it expresses has actually occurred. Verbs like *enjoy*, *resume*, and *appreciate* can be followed only by gerunds, not by infinitives. In fact, even when these verbs do not convey clear facts, the verb form that follows must still be a gerund. Again, many dictionaries provide this information.

- **Kim would appreciate *getting* candy from Sean, but he hardly knows her.**

### *Understanding other rules and guidelines*

A few verbs can be followed by either an infinitive or a gerund. With some, such as *begin* and *continue*, the choice makes little difference in meaning. With others, however, the difference in meaning is striking.

- **Carlos was working as a medical technician, but he *stopped to study* English.**

  The infinitive indicates that Carlos intended to study English when he left his job. We are not told whether he actually did study English.

- **Carlos *stopped studying* English when he left the United States.**

  The gerund indicates that Carlos actually did study English but then stopped doing so when he left.

The distinction between fact and intention is not a rule but only a tendency, and it can be outweighed by other rules. For example, use a gerund — never an infinitive — directly following a preposition.

- **This fruit is safe for ~~to eat.~~** eating.

- **This fruit is safe ~~for~~ to eat.**

- **This fruit is safe for** us **to eat.**

For a full list of verbs that can be followed by an infinitive and verbs that can be followed by a gerund, see *Grammar Troublespots*, Third Edition, by Ann Raimes (Cambridge UP, 2004), or *Cambridge International Dictionary of English* (Cambridge UP, 1999).

## 57e Adjective clauses

An adjective clause provides more information about a preceding noun.

- **The company *Yossi's uncle invested in* went bankrupt.**

The subject is a noun phrase in which the noun *company* is modified by the article *the* and the adjective clause *Yossi's uncle invested in*. The sentence as a whole says that a certain company went bankrupt, and the adjective clause identifies the company more specifically by saying that Yossi's uncle had invested in it.

One way of seeing how the adjective clause fits into the sentence is to rewrite it like this: *The company* (*Yossi's uncle had invested in it*) *went bankrupt*. This is not a normal English sentence, but it helps demonstrate a process that leads to the sentence we started with. Note the following steps:

1. Change the personal pronoun *it* to the relative pronoun *which*: *The company* (*Yossi's uncle had invested in which*) *went bankrupt*.
2. Move either the whole prepositional phrase *in which* to the beginning of the adjective clause, or move just the relative pronoun: *The company in which Yossi's uncle had invested went bankrupt* or *The company which Yossi's uncle had invested in went bankrupt*. While both of these are correct English sentences, the first version is somewhat more formal than the second.
3. If no preposition precedes the relative pronoun, substitute *that* for *which*, or omit the relative pronoun entirely: *The company that Yossi's uncle had invested in went bankrupt* or *The company Yossi's uncle had invested in went bankrupt*. Both of these are correct English sentences. While they are less formal than the forms in step 2, they are still acceptable in much formal writing.

## 57f Conditional sentences

English pays special attention to the degree of confidence we have in the truth or likelihood of an assertion. Therefore, English distinguishes among many different types of conditional sentences — that is, sentences that focus on questions of truth and that are introduced by *if* or its equivalent. The following examples illustrate a range of different conditional sentences. Each of these sentences makes different assumptions about the likelihood that what is stated in the *if* clause is true.

- **If you *practice* (or *have practiced*) writing frequently, you *know* (or *have learned*) what your chief problems are.**

This sentence assumes that what is stated in the *if* clause may very well be true; the alternatives in parentheses indicate that any tense that is appropriate in a simple sentence may be used in both the *if* clause and the main clause.

- **If you *practice* writing for the rest of this term, you *will* (or *may*) *understand* the process better.**

This sentence makes a prediction about the future and again assumes that what is stated may very well turn out to be true. Only the main clause uses the future tense (*will understand*) or some other modal that can indicate future time (*may understand*). The *if* clause must use the present tense, even though it, too, refers to the future.

- **If you *practiced* (or *were to practice*) writing every single day, it *would* eventually *seem* much easier to you.**

This sentence casts some doubt on the likelihood that what is stated will be put into effect. In the *if* clause, the verb is either past tense —actually, past subjunctive (32h) — or *were to* + the base form, even though it refers to future time. The main clause contains *would* + the base form of the main verb.

- **If you *practiced* writing on Mars, you *would find* no one to read your work.**

This sentence contemplates an impossibility at present or in the foreseeable future. As with the preceding sentence, the past subjunctive is used in the *if* clause, although past time is not being referred to, and *would* + the base form is used in the main clause.

- **If you *had practiced* writing in ancient Egypt, you *would have used* hieroglyphics.**

This sentence shifts the impossibility back to the past; obviously, you are not going to find yourself in ancient Egypt. But since past forms have already been used in the preceding two sentences, this one demands a form that is "more past": the past perfect in the *if* clause and *would* + the perfect form of the main verb in the main clause.

## EXERCISE 57.1

Revise the following sentences as necessary. Not all sentences contain an error.

1. The scholar who deciphered finally hieroglyphics was Jean François Champollion.
2. Champollion enjoyed to study the languages of the Middle East.
3. By comparing the Greek and Egyptian inscriptions on the Rosetta Stone, he made progress in understanding hieroglyphics.
4. Was of great importance that he knew Coptic, a later form of the Egyptian language.
5. In 1822 Champollion wrote a paper which he presented his solution to the puzzle of hieroglyphics in it.
6. If the Rosetta Stone was not discovered, it would have been much more difficult to decipher hieroglyphics.

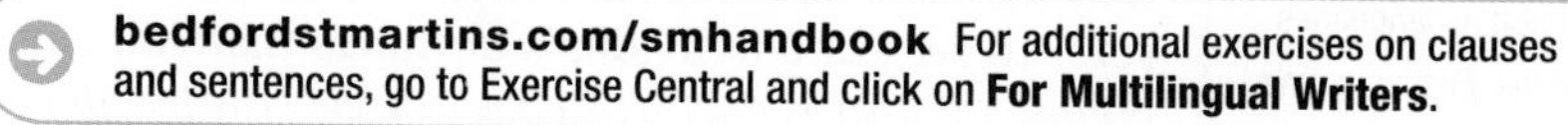

**bedfordstmartins.com/smhandbook** For additional exercises on clauses and sentences, go to Exercise Central and click on **For Multilingual Writers**.

# 58 Nouns and Noun Phrases

Since all human languages are built on the same foundation, there are similarities between English and other languages. For example, in all languages, sentences are built out of two primary components—nouns and verbs.

Although all languages have nouns, English nouns differ from those in some other languages in various ways, such as their division into count and noncount nouns and the use of plural forms, articles, and other modifiers.

## 58a Count and noncount nouns

Look at the following sentences:

- ***Research* shows that this chemical can be dangerous.**
- ***Studies* show that this chemical can be dangerous.**

*Studies* is a count noun, and *research* is a noncount noun. Count nouns (also called countable nouns) refer to separate individuals or things that you can count: *a study, a doctor, a book, a tree*; *studies, doctors*, three *books*, ten *trees*. Noncount nouns (also called mass nouns or uncountable nouns) refer to masses or collections without distinctly separate parts: *research, milk, ice, blood, grass*. You cannot count noncount nouns unless you use a quantifier: *one blade of grass, two glasses of milk, three pints of blood.*

Count and noncount nouns also differ in their use of plural forms. Count nouns generally have singular and plural forms: *study, studies*. Noncount nouns generally have only a singular form: *research*.

| COUNT | NONCOUNT |
|---|---|
| facts | information |
| suggestions | advice |
| people (plural of *person*) | humanity |
| tables, chairs, beds | furniture |
| letters | mail |
| pebbles | gravel |
| beans | rice |

Some nouns can be either count or noncount, depending on the meaning.

**COUNT** Before there were video games, children played with *marbles.*

**NONCOUNT** The floor of the palace was made of *marble.*

When you learn a noun in English, it is useful to know whether it is count, noncount, or both. Many dictionaries provide this information — two examples include *Oxford Advanced Learner's Dictionary of Current English* and *Longman Dictionary of American English.*

## 58b Plural forms

Look at these sentences from a traffic report:

- **All four *bridges* into the *city* are jammed with *cars* right now. The *traffic* is terrible.**

The first sentence has three count nouns: *bridges*, *city*, and *cars*. *Bridges* is plural because there are four bridges. *City* is singular because the sentence is referring to only one city. *Cars* is plural because multiple cars crowd the bridges. The second sentence has one noncount noun, *traffic*. Although this noun means "vehicles moving along a route," it is singular. Since noncount nouns generally have no plural forms, they can be counted or quantified only with a preceding phrase: *one quart of milk, three pounds of rice, several pieces of information.* In these cases, the noncount nouns remain singular.

## 58c Proper nouns

In addition to count and noncount nouns, English has proper nouns. These nouns include names of people, places, objects, and institutions — for example, *California*, *Yolanda*, *IBM*, and *First National Bank*. Proper nouns are always capitalized and generally cannot vary in number, so they are either singular (*John*, *the* New York Times) or plural (*the Netherlands*, *the Rocky Mountains*).

## 58d Determiners

Determiners are words that identify or quantify a noun, such as <u>*this*</u> *study*, <u>*all*</u> *people*, <u>*his*</u> *suggestions*.

**COMMON DETERMINERS**

- the articles *a/an*, *the*
- *this*, *these*, *that*, *those*
- *my*, *our*, *your*, *his*, *her*, *its*, *their*
- possessive nouns and noun phrases (*Sheila's* paper, *my friend's* book)
- *whose*, *which*, *what*
- *all*, *both*, *each*, *every*, *some*, *any*, *either*, *no*, *neither*, *many*, *much*, *(a) few*, *(a) little*, *several*, *enough*
- the numerals *one*, *two*, etc.

Some determiners, such as *a*, *an*, *this*, *that*, *one*, and *each*, can only be used with singular nouns; others, such as *these*, *those*, *all*, *both*, *many*, *several*, and *two*, can only be used with plural nouns. Still other determiners — *my*, *the*, and *which*, for example — can be used with singular or plural nouns. See the chart on the next page for additional examples.

### Determiners with singular count nouns

Every singular count noun must be preceded by a determiner. Place any adjectives between the determiner and the noun.

my
- **sister**
^

the
- **growing population**
^

that
- **old neighborhood**
^

### Determiners with plural count nouns or with noncount nouns

Noncount and plural count nouns sometimes have determiners and sometimes do not. For example, *This research is important* and *Research is important* are both acceptable but have different meanings.

### Remembering which determiners go with which types of noun

The chart following describes which determiners can be used with which types of nouns.

| These determiners . . . | . . . can precede these noun types | Examples |
|---|---|---|
| *a, an, every, each* | singular count nouns<br>some proper nouns | *a* book, *an* American<br>*each* word<br>*every* Buddhist |
| *this, that* | singular count nouns<br>noncount nouns | *this* book<br>*that* milk |
| *(a)little, much* | noncount nouns | *a little* milk<br>*much* affection |
| *some, enough* | noncount nouns<br>plural count nouns | *some* milk, *enough* trouble<br>*some* books<br>*enough* problems |
| *the* | singular count nouns<br>plural count nouns<br>noncount nouns | *the* doctor<br>*the* doctors<br>*the* information |
| *these, those, (a)few, many, both, several* | plural count nouns | *these* books, *those* plans<br>*a few* ideas<br>*many* students<br>*both* hands, *several* trees |

## 58e Articles

Articles (*a*, *an*, and *the*) are a type of determiner. In English, choosing which article to use — or whether to use an article at all — can be challenging. Although there are exceptions, the following general guidelines can help.

### *Using* a *or* an

Use *a* and *an*, indefinite articles, with singular count nouns. Use *a* before a consonant sound (*a car*) and *an* before a vowel sound (*an uncle*). Consider sound rather than spelling: *a house, an hour*. Do not use indefinite articles with plural count nouns or with noncount nouns.

*A* or *an* tells readers they do not have enough information to identify specifically what the noun refers to (in other words, it's an unspecified, or indefinite, noun). The writer may or may not have a particular thing in mind but in either case will use *a* or *an* if the reader lacks the information necessary for identification. Compare these sentences:

- **I need *a* new coat for the winter.**
- **I saw *a coat* that I liked at Dayton's, but it wasn't heavy enough.**

The coat in the first sentence is hypothetical rather than actual. Since it is indefinite to the writer and the reader, it is used with *a*, not *the*. The second sentence refers to an actual coat, but since the writer cannot expect the reader to know which one, it is used with *a* rather than *the*.

If you want to speak of an indefinite quantity rather than just one indefinite thing, use *some* or *any* with a noncount noun or a plural count noun. Note that *any* is used in negative sentences.

- **This stew needs *some* more *salt*.**
- **I saw *some plates* that I liked at Gump's.**
- **This stew doesn't need *any* more salt.**
- **I didn't see *any* plates that I liked at Gump's.**

### *Using* the

The definite article *the* is used with both count and noncount nouns whose identity is already known or is about to be made known to readers. The necessary information for identification can come from the noun phrase itself, from elsewhere in the text, from context, from general knowledge, or from a superlative.

- **Let's meet at ^the fountain in front of Dwinelle Hall.**

  The phrase *in front of Dwinelle Hall* identifies the specific fountain. We know from the use of *the* that there is only one fountain in front of Dwinelle Hall.

- **Last Saturday, a fire that started in a restaurant spread to a neighboring clothing store. ~~Store~~ ^The store was saved, although it suffered water damage.**

  The word *store* is preceded by *the*, which directs our attention to the information in the previous sentence, where the store is first identified.

- **She asked him to shut ^the door when he left her office.**

  She expects him to understand that she is referring to the door in her office.

- ~~Pope~~ The Pope **is expected to visit Africa in October.**

  There is only one living pope, and *the* before *pope* signals that this sentence refers to him. Similar examples include *the president* (*of the United States*), *the earth*, and *the moon*.

- **Bill is now** the **best singer in the choir.**

  The superlative *best* identifies the noun *singer*.

### Using the zero article

If a noun appears without *the*, *a* or *an*, or any other determiner (even if it is preceded by other adjectives), it is said to have a zero article. The zero article can be used with plural count nouns (*plans*, *assignments*), noncount nouns (*homework*, *information*), and proper nouns (*Carmen*, *New York*). With plural count nouns and noncount nouns, the zero article is used to make generalizations.

- **In this world nothing is certain but death and taxes.**

  — BENJAMIN FRANKLIN

  The zero article indicates that Franklin refers not to a particular death or specific taxes but to death and taxes in general.

Here English differs from many other languages that would use the definite article to make generalizations. In English, a sentence like *The snakes are dangerous* can refer only to particular, identifiable snakes, not to snakes in general.

It is sometimes possible to make general statements with *the* or *a/an* and singular count nouns.

- ***First-year college students* are confronted with many new experiences.**
- ***A first-year student* is confronted with many new experiences.**
- ***The first-year student* is confronted with many new experiences.**

These sentences all make the same general statement, but the emphasis of each sentence is different. The first sentence refers to first-year college students as a group, the second focuses on a hypothetical student taken at random, and the third sentence, which is characteristic of formal written style, projects the image of a typical student as representative of the whole class.

## 58f Modifiers

Modifiers are words that give more information about a noun; that is, they *modify* the meaning of the noun in some way. Some modifiers precede the noun, and others follow it, as indicated in the chart below.

If there are two or more adjectives, their order is variable, but English has strong preferences, described below.

- Subjective adjectives (those that show the writer's opinion) go before objective adjectives (those that merely describe): *these beautiful old-fashioned kitchen tiles.*
- Adjectives of size generally come early: *these beautiful large old-fashioned kitchen tiles.*
- Adjectives of color generally come late: *these beautiful large old-fashioned blue kitchen tiles.*
- Adjectives derived from proper nouns or from nouns that refer to materials generally come after color terms and right before noun modifiers: *these beautiful large old-fashioned blue Portuguese ceramic kitchen tiles.*

| Modifier Type | Arrangement | Example |
|---|---|---|
| determiners | at the beginning of the noun phrase | *these old-fashioned tiles* |
| *all* or *both* | before any other determiners | *all these tiles* |
| numbers | after any other determiners | *these six tiles* |
| noun modifiers | directly before the noun | *these kitchen tiles* |
| adjectives | between determiners and noun modifiers | *these old-fashioned kitchen tiles* |
| phrases or clauses | after the noun | *the tiles on the wall*<br>*the tiles that we bought* |

- All other objective adjectives go in the middle, and adjectives for which no order is preferred are separated by commas: *these beautiful large decorative, heat-resistant, old-fashioned blue Portuguese ceramic kitchen tiles.*

Of course, the very long noun phrases presented as illustrations on p. 804 would be out of place in most kinds of writing. Academic and professional types of writing tend to avoid long strings of adjectives.

### EXERCISE 58.1

Each of the following sentences contains an error. Rewrite each sentence correctly.

1. Before a middle of the nineteenth century, surgery was usually a terrifying, painful ordeal.
2. Because anesthesia did not exist yet, only painkiller available for surgical patients was whiskey.
3. The pain of surgical procedures could be so severe that much people were willing to die rather than have surgery.
4. In 1846, one of the hospital in Boston gave ether to a patient before he had surgery.
5. The patient, who had a large on his neck tumor, slept peacefully as doctors removed it.

### EXERCISE 58.2

Insert articles as necessary in the following passage from *The Silent Language*, by Edward T. Hall. Some blanks may not need an article.

Hollywood is famous for hiring ______ various experts to teach ______ people technically what most of us learn informally. ______ case in point is ______ story about ______ children of one movie couple who noticed ______ new child in ______ neighborhood climbing ______ tree. ______ children immediately wanted to be given ______ name of his instructor in ______ tree climbing.

**bedfordstmartins.com/smhandbook** For additional exercises on nouns and noun phrases, go to Exercise Central and click on **For Multilingual Writers**.

# 59 Verbs and Verb Phrases

Verbs can be called the heartbeat of every language, but in English the metaphor is especially meaningful. With a few stylistic exceptions, all written English sentences must include a verb. Some of the distinctive features of English verbs include modals, perfect tenses, and progressive forms.

## 59a Forming verb phrases

Verb phrases can be built up out of a main verb and one or more auxiliaries (32b).

- **Immigration figures *rise* every year.**
- **Immigration figures *are rising* every year.**
- **Immigration figures *have risen* every year.**
- **Immigration figures *have been rising* every year.**

Verb phrases have strict rules of order. If you try to rearrange the words in any of these sentences, you will find that most alternatives are impossible. You cannot say *Immigration figures rising are every year* or *Immigration figures been have rising every year*. The only permissible change to word order is to form a question, moving the first auxiliary to the beginning of the sentence: *Have immigration figures been rising every year?*

### 1 Putting auxiliary verbs in order

In the sentence *Immigration figures may have been rising*, the main verb *rising* follows three auxiliaries: *may*, *have*, and *been*. Together these auxiliaries and main verb make up a verb phrase.

- *May* is a modal (59b) that indicates possibility; it is followed by the base form of a verb.
- *Have* is an auxiliary verb (32b) that in this case indicates the perfect tense (32e); it must be followed by a past participle (*been*).

- Any form of *be*, when it is followed by a present participle ending in *-ing* (such as *rising*), indicates the progressive tense (32a and e).
- *Be* followed by a past participle, as in *New immigration policies have been passed in recent years*, indicates the passive voice (45b).

As shown in the following chart, when two or more auxiliaries appear in a verb phrase, they must follow a particular order based on the type of auxiliary: (1) modal, (2) a form of *have* used to indicate a perfect tense, (3) a form of *be* used to indicate a progressive tense, and (4) a form of *be* used to indicate the passive voice. (Very few sentences include all four kinds of auxiliaries.)

Only one modal is permitted in a verb phrase.

be able to
**She will ~~can~~ speak Czech much better soon.**

| | Modal | Perfect *Have* | Progressive *Be* | Passive *Be* | Main Verb | |
|---|---|---|---|---|---|---|
| Sonia | — | has | — | been | invited | to visit a family in Prague. |
| She | should | — | — | be | finished | with school soon. |
| The invitation | must | have | — | been | sent | in the spring. |
| She | — | has | been | — | studying | Czech. |
| She | may | — | be | — | feeling | nervous. |
| She | might | have | been | — | expecting | to travel else-where. |
| The trip | will | have | been | being | planned | for a month by the time she leaves. |

### 2 Forming auxiliary verbs

Whenever you use an auxiliary, check the form of the word that follows. The guidelines that follow describe the appropriate forms.

#### *Modal + base form*

Use the base form of a verb after *can*, *could*, *will*, *would*, *shall*, *should*, *may*, *might*, and *must*.

- **Alice *can read* Latin.**
- **Sanjay *should have* studied for the test.**
- **They *must be* going to a fine school.**

In many other languages, modals such as *can* and *must* are followed by an infinitive (*to* + base form). In English, only the base form follows a modal.

- **Alice can ~~to~~ read Latin.**

Notice that a modal auxiliary can express tense (for example, *can* or *could*), but it never changes form to agree with the subject.

#### *Perfect* have *+ past participle*

To form the perfect tenses, use *have*, *has*, or *had* with a past participle.

- **Everyone *has gone* home.**
- **They *have been* working all day.**

#### *Progressive* be *+ present participle*

A progressive form of a verb is signaled by two elements, a form of the auxiliary *be* (*am*, *is*, *are*, *was*, *were*, *be*, or *been*) and the *-ing* form of the next word: *The children are studying*.

- **The children ^are studying in school.**
- **The children are ~~study~~ ^studying in school.**

Some verbs are rarely used in progressive forms. These verbs express unchanging conditions or mental states rather than deliberate actions: *believe, belong, hate, know, like, love, need, own, resemble, understand.*

### *Passive be + past participle*

Use *am, is, are, was, were, being, be,* or *been* with a past participle to form the passive voice.

- **Tagalog *is spoken* in the Philippines.**

Notice that with the progressive *be* the following word (the present participle) ends in *-ing*, but with the passive *be* the following word (the past participle) never ends in *-ing*.

- **Meredith *is studying* music.**
- **Natasha *was taught* by a famous violinist.**

If the first auxiliary in a verb phrase is *be* or *have*, it must show either present or past tense, and it must agree with the subject: *Meredith has played in an orchestra* or *Meredith had played in an orchestra before she joined the band.*

## 59b Modals

The nine basic modal auxiliaries are *can, could, will, would, shall, should, may, might,* and *must.* There are a few others as well, in particular *ought to*, which is close in meaning to *should.* Occasionally *need* can be a modal rather than a main verb.

The nine basic modals fall into the pairs *can/could, will/would, shall/should, may/might,* and the loner *must.* In earlier English, the second member of each pair was the past tense of the first. To a limited degree, the second form still functions as a past tense, especially in the case of *could.*

- **Ingrid *can* ski.**
- **Ingrid *could* ski when she was five.**

But, for the most part, in present-day English, all nine modals typically refer to present or future time. When you want to use a modal to refer to the past, you follow the modal with a perfect auxiliary.

- **If you have a fever, you *should see* a doctor.**
- **If you had a fever, you *should have seen* a doctor.**

In the case of *must*, refer to the past by using *had to*.

- **You *must* renew your visa by the end of this week.**
- **You *had to* renew your visa by the end of last week.**

### Using modals to make requests or to give instructions

Modals are often used in requests and instructions. Imagine making the following request of a flight attendant:

- ***Will* you bring me a pillow?**

This request may appear demanding or rude. Using a modal makes the request more polite by acknowledging that fulfilling the request may not be possible.

- ***Can* you bring me a pillow?**

Another way of softening the request is to use the past form of *will*, and the most discreet choice is the past form of *can*.

- ***Would* you bring me a pillow?**
- ***Could* you bring me a pillow?**

Using the past tense of modals is considered more polite than using their present forms because it makes any statement or question less assertive.

Consider the meanings of each of the following instructions:

1. You *can* submit your report electronically.
2. You *may* submit your report electronically.
3. You *should* submit your report electronically.
4. You *must* submit your report electronically.
5. You *will* submit your report electronically.

Instructions 1 and 2 give permission to submit the report electronically but do not require it; of these, 2 is more formal. Instruction 3 adds a strong recommendation; 4 allows no alternative; and 5 implies, "Don't even think of doing otherwise."

### *Using modals to indicate doubt or certainty*

Modals can also indicate how confident the writer is about his or her claims. Look at the following set of examples, which starts with a tentative suggestion and ends with an indication of complete confidence:

- **The study *might* help explain the findings of previous research.**
- **The study *may* help explain the findings of previous research.**
- **The study *will* help explain the findings of previous research.**

## 59c Present and past tenses

Every English sentence must have at least one verb or verb phrase that is not an infinitive (*to write*), a gerund (*writing*), or a participle (*written*) without any auxiliaries. Furthermore, every such verb or verb phrase must have a tense (32e).

In some languages, such as Chinese and Vietnamese, the verb form never changes regardless of when the action takes place. In English, the time of the action must be clearly indicated by the tense form of every verb, even if the time is obvious or it is indicated elsewhere in the sentence.

- **During the Cultural Revolution, millions of young people ~~cannot~~ [could not] go to school and ~~are~~ [were] sent to the countryside.**
- **Last night I ~~call~~ [called] my aunt who ~~live~~ [lives] in Santo Domingo.**

### *Direct and indirect quotations*

Changing direct quotations to indirect quotations can sometimes lead to tense shifts.

| | |
|---|---|
| **DIRECT** | She said, "My work *is* now complete." |
| **INDIRECT** | She *told* me that her work *was* now complete. |
| **INDIRECT** | She *tells* me that her work *is* now complete. |

In general, the verb introducing the indirect quotation (sometimes called the reporting verb) will agree in tense with the verb in the indirect quotation; there are, however, some exceptions. For example, if the reporting verb is in the past tense but the information that follows holds true in the present, shifting to a present-tense verb is acceptable.

- **She *told* me that her work *is* as exciting as ever.**

In academic writing, reporting verbs are used regularly to refer to ideas from other texts or authors. Depending on the documentation style you use, you will probably use the present tense, the present perfect tense, or the simple past for these verbs.

Lee *claims* that . . .
Lee *writes* . . .
Lee *has argued* that . . .
Lee *found* that . . .

## 59d Perfect and progressive verb phrases

The perfect and progressive auxiliaries combine with the present or past tense, or with modals, to form complex verb phrases with special meanings (32f).

### *Distinguishing the simple present and the present perfect*

- **My sister *drives* a bus.**

The simple present (*drives*) merely tells us about the sister's current occupation. But if you were to add the phrase *for three years*, it would be incorrect to say *My sister drives a bus for three years*. Instead, you need a time frame that goes from the past up to the present. The present perfect or present perfect progressive expresses this time frame.

- **My sister *has driven* a bus for three years.**
- **My sister *has been driving* a bus for three years.**

### *Distinguishing the simple past and the present perfect*

- **Since she started working, she *has bought* a new car and a VCR.**

The clause introduced by *since* sets up a time frame that runs from past to present and requires the present perfect (*has bought*) in the subsequent clause. Furthermore, the sentence does not say exactly when she bought the car or the VCR, and that indefiniteness also calls for the perfect. It would be less correct to say *Since she started working, she bought a new car and a VCR.* But if you say when she bought the car, you should use the simple past tense.

- **She *bought* the car two years ago.**

It would be incorrect to say *She has bought the car two years ago* because the perfect cannot be used with definite expressions of time. In this case, use the simple past (*bought*).

### Distinguishing the simple present and the present progressive

Use the present progressive tense when an action is in progress at the present moment. In contrast, use the simple present for actions that frequently occur during a period of time that might include the present moment (though the simple present does not necessarily indicate that the action is taking place now).

- **My sister *drives* a bus, but she *is taking* a vacation now.**
- **My sister *drives* a bus, but she *takes* a vacation every year.**

Many languages use the simple present (*drives, takes*) for both types of sentences. In English, however, the first sentence would be incorrect if it said *but she takes a vacation now.*

### Distinguishing the simple past and the past progressive

- **Sally *spent* the summer in Italy.**

The simple past tense is used in this case because the action occurred in the past and is now finished.

The past progressive tense is used relatively infrequently in English. It is used to focus on duration or continuousness and especially to call attention to past action that went on at the same time as something else.

- **Sally *was spending* the summer in Italy when she *met* her future husband.**

## 59e Participial adjectives

Many verbs refer to feelings—for example, *bore, confuse, excite, fascinate, frighten, interest*. The present and past participles of such verbs can be used as ordinary adjectives (see 31c3). Use the past participle to describe a person having the feeling.

- **The *frightened* boy started to cry.**

Use the present participle to describe the thing (or person) causing the feeling.

- **The *frightening* dinosaur display gave him nightmares.**

Be careful not to confuse the two types of adjectives.

- **I am ~~interesting~~ interested in African literature.**

- **African literature seems ~~interested.~~ interesting.**

### EXERCISE 59.1

Each of the following sentences contains an error. Rewrite each sentence correctly.

1. Over the past forty years, average temperatures in the Arctic increase by several degrees.
2. A few years ago, a robin was observe in Inuit territory in northern Canada.
3. Inuit people in previous generations will never have seen a robin near their homes.
4. The Inuit language, which called *Inuktitut*, has no word for *robin*.
5. Many Inuits are concerning that warmer temperatures may change their way of life.

### EXERCISE 59.2

Rewrite the following passage, adapted from "Cold Comfort" by Atul Gawande (*New Yorker*, March 11, 2002), adding appropriate auxiliaries and verb endings where necessary. The total number of words required in each case is indicated in parentheses.

The notion that a chill ____(put—1)____ you at risk of catching a cold is nearly universal. Yet science ____(find—2)____ no evidence for it. One of the first studies on the matter ____(lead—2)____ by Sir Christopher Andrewes. He ___(take—1)___ a group of volunteers and ___(inoculate—1)___ them with a cold virus; previously, half of the group ___(keep—3)___ warm, and the other half ___(make—3)___ to take a bath and then to stand for half an hour without a towel while the wind ___(blow—2)___ on them. The chilled group ___(get—1)___ no more colds than the warm group.

**bedfordstmartins.com/smhandbook** For additional exercises on verbs and verb phrases, go to Exercise Central and click on **For Multilingual Writers.**

# 60 Prepositions and Prepositional Phrases

Words such as *to*, *from*, *over*, and *under* show the relations between other words; these words are prepositions, and they are one of the more challenging elements of English writing. You will need to decide which preposition to use for your intended meaning and understand how to use verbs that include prepositions, such as *take off*, *pick up*, and *put up with*.

## 60a Using prepositions idiomatically

Even if you know where to use a preposition, it can be difficult to determine which preposition to use. Each of the most common prepositions has a wide range of applications, and this range never coincides exactly from one language to another. See, for example, how *in* and *on* are used in English.

- **The peaches are *in* the refrigerator.**
- **The peaches are *on* the table.**
- **Is that a diamond ring *on* your finger?**

### *If you speak Spanish*

The Spanish translations of these sentences all use the same preposition (*en*), a fact that might lead you astray in English.

- **Is that a ruby ring ~~in~~ *on* your finger?**

There is no easy solution to the challenge of using English prepositions idiomatically, but the following strategies can make it less troublesome.

### EXERCISE 60.1

Insert prepositions as necessary in the following paragraph.

Haivan skated _______ the pond, looking _______ her new engagement ring. As she skated, she thought about the plans for her wedding. Should it be _______ September or October? Could the caterer _______ her neighborhood do a good job? Would her sister manage to be _______ time?

## Strategies for using prepositions idiomatically

1. **Keep in mind typical examples of each preposition.**

   **IN** The peaches are *in* the refrigerator.
   There are still some pickles *in* the jar.
   The book you are looking for is *in* the bookcase.

   Here the object of the preposition *in* is a container that encloses something.

   **ON** The peaches are *on* the table.
   There are still some pickles *on* the plate.
   The book you are looking for is *on* the top shelf.

   Here the object of the preposition *on* is a horizontal surface that supports something with which it is in direct contact.

2. **Learn other examples that show some similarities and some differences in meaning.**

   **IN** You shouldn't drive *in* a snowstorm.

   Here there is no container, but like a container, the falling snow surrounds the driver. The preposition *in* is used for other weather-related expressions as well: *in a tornado, in the sun, in the rain.*

   **ON** Is that a diamond ring *on* your finger?

   The preposition *on* is used to describe things we wear: *the hat on his head, the shoes on her feet, the tattoo on his back.*

3. **Use your imagination to create mental images that can help you remember figurative uses of prepositions.**

   **IN** Michael is *in* love.

   The preposition *in* is often used to describe a state of being: *in love, in pain, in a panic.* As a way to remember this, you might imagine the person immersed *in* this state of being.

4. **Try to learn prepositions not in isolation but as part of a system.** For example, in identifying the location of a place or an event, you can use the three prepositions *at, in,* and *on.*

   *At* specifies the exact point in space or time.

   **AT** There will be a meeting tomorrow *at* 9:30 AM *at* 160 Main Street.

*(continued on p. 818)*

*(continued from p. 817)*

Expanses of space or time within which a place is located or an event takes place might be seen as containers and so require *in*.

**IN** I arrived *in* the United States *in* January.

*On* must be used in two cases: with the names of streets (but not the exact address) and with days of the week or month.

**ON** The airline's office is *on* Fifth Avenue.
I'll be moving to my new apartment *on* September 30.

## 60b Using two-word verbs idiomatically

Some words that look like prepositions do not always function as prepositions. Consider the following two sentences:

- **The balloon rose *off* the ground.**
- **The plane took *off* without difficulty.**

In the first sentence, *off* is a preposition that introduces the prepositional phrase *off the ground*. In the second sentence, *off* does not function as a preposition. Instead, it combines with *took* to form a two-word verb with its own meaning. Such a verb is called a phrasal verb, and the word *off*, when used in this way, is called an adverbial particle. Many prepositions can function as particles to form phrasal verbs.

The verb + particle combination that makes up a phrasal verb is a single entity that usually cannot be torn apart.

- **The plane took** ^off **without difficulty**. ~~**off.**~~

The exceptions are the many phrasal verbs that are transitive, meaning that they take a direct object (31c2). Some transitive phrasal verbs have particles that may be separated from the verb by the object.

- **I *picked up my baggage* at the terminal.**
- **I *picked my baggage up* at the terminal.**

If a personal pronoun (such as *it*, *her*, or *him*) is used as the direct object, it must separate the verb from its particle.

- **I *picked it up* at the terminal.**

Some idiomatic two-word verbs, however, are not phrasal verbs.

▶ **We *ran into* our neighbor on the train.**

In such verbs, the second word is a preposition, which cannot be separated from the verb. For example, it is not correct to say *We ran our neighbor into on the train.* Verbs like *run into* are called prepositional verbs, which are another kind of two-word verb.

In the sample sentence above, *ran into* consists of the verb *ran* followed by the preposition *into*, which introduces the prepositional phrase *into our neighbor*. Yet *to run into our neighbor* is different from a normal verb + prepositional phrase, such as *to run into the room.* If you know the typical meanings of *run* and *into*, you can interpret *to run into the room.* Not so with *to run into our neighbor*; the combination *run* + *into* has a special meaning ("find by chance") that could not be determined from the typical meanings of *run* and *into*.

Prepositional verbs include such idiomatic two-word verbs as *take after*, meaning "resemble" (usually a parent or other older relative); *get over*, meaning "recover from"; and *count on*, meaning "trust." They also include verb + preposition combinations in which the meaning is predictable, but the specific preposition that is required is less predictable and must be learned together with the verb (for example, *depend on, look at, listen to, approve of*). There are also phrasal-prepositional verbs, which are verb + adverbial particle + preposition sequences (for example, *put up with, look forward to, give up on, get away with*).

## EXERCISE 60.2

Each of the following sentences contains a two-word verb. In some sentences, the verb is used correctly; in others, it is used incorrectly. Identify each two-word verb, indicate whether it is a phrasal or prepositional verb, and rewrite any incorrect sentences correctly.

1. Soon after I was hired for my last job, I learned that the company might lay off me.
2. I was counting on the job to pay my way through school, so I was upset.
3. I decided to pick up a newspaper and see what other jobs were available.
4. As I looked the newspaper at, I was surprised to see that I was qualified for a job that paid much better than mine.
5. I gave my old job up and took the new one, which made attending school much easier.

**bedfordstmartins.com/smhandbook** For more exercises on prepositions and prepositional phrases, go to Exercise Central and click on **For Multilingual Writers.**

Part 12

# ACADEMIC AND PROFESSIONAL WRITING

# 61 Academic Work in Any Discipline

A recent survey confirmed that good writing plays an important role in almost every profession. As one MBA wrote, "Those who advance quickly in my company are those who write and speak well — it's as simple as that." But we all know that writing works in different ways in different disciplines. As you prepare essays or other written assignments for various courses, then, you will need to become familiar with the discourse — the expectations, vocabularies, styles, methods of proof, and conventional formats — used in each field.

## 61a Writing for every discipline

Students in the humanities tend to expect that writing will play a central role in their education; students in other areas sometimes imagine that writing will be of secondary importance to them. Yet faculty working in engineering, the sciences, social sciences, business, and other areas have a different understanding. Here, for example, is what some faculty members in chemistry have to say:

> Is writing important in chemistry? Don't chemists spend their time turning knobs, mixing reagents, and collecting data? They still get to do those things, but professional scientists also make presentations, prepare reports, publish results, and submit proposals. Each of these activities involves writing. If you remain skeptical about the need for writing skills, then ask your favorite professor, or any other scientist, to track the fraction of one workday spent using a word-processing program. You (and they) may be surprised at the answer.
>
> — OREGON STATE UNIVERSITY, *Writing Guide for Chemistry*

A student pursuing an education major agrees: "Writing is the key to just about everything I do, from constructing lesson plans to writing reviews of literature to learning to respond — in writing — to the students I will eventually teach."

As these statements suggest, writing is central to learning regardless of the discipline; in fact, writing plays a major role in the life of any working professional. So whether you are explaining the results of a telephone survey you conducted for a psychology class, preparing a lab report for biology, conducting a case study for anthropology, or working on a proposal for material sciences and engineering, writing helps you get the job done.

## 61b Reading for every discipline

As you move through your college years, you will have a chance to read texts in fields from anthropology to zoology — and everything in between. In fact, your ability to read and comprehend texts will be central to your success. As you already know, reading isn't a "one size fits all" activity: you will need to adjust your reading strategies to fit the task at hand. Most of the time, your instructors probably won't give you specific instruction in how to read these texts; they will simply assume that you know how.

The more you read in a discipline, the easier you will find it to understand. So read a lot, and pay attention to the texts you are reading. To get started, choose an article in an important journal in the field you plan to major in and then answer the following questions:

- How does a journal article in this discipline begin?
- How is the article organized? Does it have specific sections with subheads?
- What sources are cited, and how are they used — as backup support, as counter-examples, or as an argument to refute?
- What audience does the text seem to address? Is it a narrow technical or disciplinary audience, or is it aimed at a broader reading public? Is it addressed to readers of a specific journal? Is it published electronically and intended for an international readership?

Finally, make sure you know whether articles you are reading are from juried or nonjuried journals (13a2). Juried journals use panels of expert readers to analyze proposed articles and recommend publication (or not) to the journal editor, so articles in juried journals have been examined and accepted by experts in the field. Nonjuried journals can also offer valuable information, but they may bear the stamp of the editor and that person's biases more strongly than a juried journal would.

For additional guidelines on reading critically, see 1c and 2c.

## 61c Academic assignments

Since academic assignments vary widely from course to course and even from professor to professor, the tips this section offers can only be general. For any discipline, make sure you are in control of the assignment rather than letting the assignment be in control of you. To take control, you need to understand the assignment fully and to understand what professors in the particular discipline expect in response.

When you receive an assignment, make sure you understand what that assignment is asking you to do. Some assignments may be as vague as "Write a five-page essay on one aspect of the Civil War" or "Write an analysis of the group dynamics at play in your recent collaborative project for this course." (See 19e for one student's essay in response to this last assignment.) Others may be fairly specific: "Collect, summarize, and interpret data drawn from a sample of letters to the editor published in two newspapers, one in a small rural community and one in an urban community, over a period of three months. Organize your research report according to APA requirements." Whatever the assignment, you must take charge of analyzing it. Answering the questions in the accompanying box can help you do so.

### Analyzing an assignment

- *What is the purpose of the assignment?*
- *Who is the audience?* The instructor will be one audience, but are there others? If so, who are they?
- *What does the assignment ask of you?* Look for key terms such as *summarize, explain, evaluate, interpret, illustrate,* and *define.*
- *Do you need clarification of any terms?* If so, ask your instructor.
- *What do you need to know or find out to complete the assignment?* You may need to do background reading, develop a procedure for analyzing or categorizing information, or carry out some other kind of preparation.
- *What does the instructor expect in a written response?* How will you use sources (both written and visual)? How should you organize and develop the assignment? What is the expected format and length?
- *Can you find a model of an effective response to a similar assignment?*
- *What do other students think the assignment requires?* Talking over an assignment with classmates is one good way to test your understanding.

### EXERCISE 61.1

Analyze the following assignment from a communications course using the questions in 61c.

Assignment: Distribute a questionnaire to twenty people (ten male, ten female) asking these four questions: (1) What do you expect to say and do when you meet a stranger? (2) What don't you expect to say and do when you meet a stranger? (3) What do you expect to say and do when you meet a very close friend? (4) What don't you expect to say and do when you meet a very close friend?

When you have collected your twenty questionnaires, read them over and answer the following questions:

- What, if any, descriptions were common to all respondents' answers?
- How do male and female responses compare?
- What similarities and differences did you find between the responses to the stranger and to the very close friend?
- What factors (environment, time, status, gender, and so on) do you think had an impact on these responses?

Discuss your findings, using concepts and theories explained in your text.

## 61d Specialized vocabulary

Entering into an academic discipline or a profession is like going to a party where you do not know anyone. At first you feel like an outsider, and you may not understand much of what you hear or see. Before you enter the conversation, you have to listen and observe carefully. Eventually, however, you will be able to join in — and if you stay long enough, participating in the conversation becomes easy and natural.

To learn the routines, practices, and ways of knowing in a new field, you must also make an effort to enter into the conversation, and that means taking action. One good way to get started is to study the vocabulary of the field you are most interested in.

Highlight the key terms in your reading or notes to learn how much specialized or technical vocabulary you will be expected to know. If you find only a small amount of specialized vocabulary, try to master the new terms quickly by reading your textbook carefully, looking up key words or phrases, and asking questions. If you find a great deal of specialized vocabulary, however, you may want to familiarize yourself with it methodically. Any of the following procedures may help:

- Keep a log of unfamiliar or confusing words *in context.* Check definitions in your textbook's glossary or index, or consult a specialized dictionary.

- Review your class notes each day. Underline important terms, review definitions, and identify anything that is unclear. Use your textbook or ask questions to clarify anything confusing before the class moves on to a new topic.
- See if your textbook has a glossary of terms or sets off definitions. Study pertinent sections to master the terms.
- Try to use and work with key concepts. Even if they are not yet entirely clear to you, working with them will help you understand them. For example, in a statistics class, try to work out (in words) how to do an analysis of *covariance*, step by step, even if you are not sure of the precise definition of the term. Or try to plot the narrative progression in a story even if you are still not entirely sure of the definition of *narrative progression.*
- Find the standard dictionaries or handbooks of terms for your field. Ask your instructor or a librarian for help finding the standard references.
- Take special note of the ways technical language or disciplinary vocabulary are used in online information related to a particular field. Sometimes, you can find definitions of terms on a Web site's FAQ page, if one exists.

Whatever your techniques for learning a specialized vocabulary, begin to use the new terms whenever you can — in class, in discussions with instructors and other students, and in your assignments. This ability to use what you learn in speaking and writing is crucial to your full understanding of and participation in the discipline.

## 61e Disciplinary style

Another important way to initiate yourself into a discipline or field of study is to identify stylistic features of the writing in that field. You will begin to assimilate these features automatically if you immerse yourself in reading and thinking about the field. To get started, study some representative pieces of writing in the field with the following questions in mind:

- How would you describe the overall tone of the writing? Is it very formal, somewhat formal, or informal? (See 4c and 6g4.)

- Would you describe the titles in this field as basically descriptive ("Findings from a Double Blind Study of the Effect of Antioxidants"), persuasive ("Antioxidants Proven Effective"), or something else? How does the title shape your expectations?
- To what extent do writers in the field strive for a distanced, objective stance? What strategies help them to achieve this stance? (See 3g.)
- In general, how long are the sentences? How long are the paragraphs?
- Are verbs generally active or passive? Why? (See 45b.)
- Do writers in the field prefer the first-person *I* or third-person terms such as *the investigator*? What is the effect of this choice?
- Do writers typically use visual elements — graphs, tables, charts, computer graphics, or maps? How are visuals integrated into the text? How are they documented? (See 23d and Chapters 18–21.)
- What role, if any, do headings and other formatting elements play in the writing? (See 23b and c.)
- What documentation style (such as MLA, APA, *Chicago*, or CSE) is used? (See Chapters 18–21.)

Of course, writings within a single discipline may have different purposes and different styles. Although a research report probably follows a conventional form, a speech greeting specialists at a convention may well be less formal and more personal no matter what the field. Furthermore, answering questions like these will not guarantee that you can immediately produce a piece of writing similar to the ones you are analyzing. Nevertheless, looking carefully at writing in the field brings you one step closer to writing effectively in that discipline.

### TALKING THE TALK: The first person

"Is it true that I should never use *I* in college writing?" In much writing in college, using the first-person *I* is perfectly acceptable to most instructors. As always, think about the context — if your own experience is relevant to the topic, you are better off saying *I* than trying too hard not to. But don't overdo it, especially if the writing isn't just autobiographical. And check with your instructor if you aren't sure: in certain academic disciplines, such as the natural sciences, using *I* may be seen as inappropriate.

## 61f Use of evidence

What is acceptable and persuasive evidence in one discipline may be less so in another. Observable, quantifiable data may constitute the best evidence in experimental psychology, but the same kind of data may be less appropriate — or impossible to come by — in a historical study. An engineering proposal will be backed up with drawings, maps, and detailed calculations. A case study in cultural anthropology, on the other hand, may depend almost entirely on interview data. As you grow familiar with an area of study, you will develop a sense of what it takes to prove a point in that field. You can speed up this process, however, by investigating and questioning. The following questions will help you think about the use of evidence in materials you read:

- How do writers in the field use precedent and authority? What or who counts as an authority in this field? How are the credentials of an authority established? (See 11e.)
- What kinds of quantitative data (countable or measurable items) are used, and for what purposes? How are the data gathered and presented?
- How are qualitative data (systematically observed items) used?
- How are statistics used and presented? Are tables, charts, graphs, or other visuals important, and why?
- How is logical reasoning used? How are definition, cause and effect, analogy, and example used?
- How does the field use primary and secondary sources? (See 13a1.) What are the primary and secondary materials? How is each type of source presented?
- What kinds of textual evidence are cited?
- How are quotations and other references to sources used and integrated into the text? (See Chapter 15.)

In addition to carrying out your own investigation, ask your instructor how you can best go about making a case in this field.

### EXERCISE 61.2

Read a few journals associated with your prospective major or a discipline of particular interest to you, using the preceding questions to study the use of evidence in that discipline. If you are keeping a writing log, make an entry summarizing what you have learned.

## 61g Conventional patterns and formats

To produce effective writing in a discipline, you need to know the field's generally accepted formats for organizing and presenting evidence. A typical laboratory report, for instance, follows a fairly standard organizational framework (see 64c for an example). A case study in sociology or education or anthropology likewise follows a typical organizational plan.

Your job in any discipline is to discover its conventional formats and organizing principles (those used widely in the field) so that you can practice using them. Ask your instructor to recommend some excellent examples of the kind of writing you will do in the course. Then analyze these examples in terms of format and organization. You might also look at major scholarly journals in the field to see what types of formats seem most common and how each is organized. Study these examples, and keep in mind the following questions about organization and format:

- What types of articles, reports, or documents are common in this field? What is the purpose of each?
- What can a reader expect to find in each type of writing? What does each type assume about its readers?
- Do articles or other documents typically begin with an abstract? If so, does the abstract describe the parts of the article to come, or does it provide substantive information such as findings or conclusions? (For an example of an abstract from a professional journal, see p. 830; for a student's abstract, see 19e.)
- How is each type of text organized? What are its main parts? How are they labeled?
- How does a particular type of essay, report, or document show the connections among ideas? What assumptions does it take for granted? What points does it emphasize?

Remember that there is a close connection between the writing patterns and formats a particular area of study uses and the work that scholars in that field undertake. Here are statements from two writing guides developed by faculty members in philosophy and microbiology. What do these comments suggest about disciplinary patterns and formats?

**PHILOSOPHY**

Like baking a pie, planning a vacation, or raising a child, good writing in philosophy requires creativity, thought, and a set of [eight] basic skills. . . . These include (1) identifying a philosophical problem; (2) organizing ideas;

(3) defining concepts; (4) analyzing arguments; (5) comparing and contrasting; (6) giving examples; (7) applying theory to practice; and (8) testing hypotheses.

— OREGON STATE UNIVERSITY, *Writing Philosophy Papers: A Student Guide*

**MICROBIOLOGY**

The main purpose of most scientific writing is to inform and educate other people about research that has been performed. A scientific report should explain clearly how the research was performed and what results were observed. "Good science" must be repeatable — other scientists should be able to repeat the experiment in order to see if they come up with the same results or not. And, lastly, an argument or opinion might be proposed based on the results obtained.

— OREGON STATE UNIVERSITY, *Writing for Microbiology Majors*

## THINKING CRITICALLY ABOUT READING AND WRITING IN A DISCIPLINE

### Reading with an Eye for Disciplinary Discourse

The following abstract introduces an article titled "Development of the Appearance-Reality Distinction." This article appeared in *Cognitive Psychology*, a specialized academic journal for researchers in the subfield of psychology that focuses on human cognition. Read this abstract carefully to see what you can infer about the discourse of cognitive psychology — about its characteristic vocabulary, style, use of evidence, and so on.

Young children can express conceptual difficulties with the appearance-reality distinction in two different ways: (1) by incorrectly reporting appearance when asked to report reality ("phenomenism"); (2) by incorrectly reporting reality when asked to report appearance ("intellectual realism"). Although both phenomenism errors and intellectual realism errors have been observed in previous studies of young children's cognition, the two have not been seen as conceptually related and only the former errors have been taken as a symptom of difficulties with the appearance-reality distinction. Three experiments investigated 3- to 5-year-old children's ability to distinguish between and correctly identify real versus apparent object properties (color, size, and shape), object identities, object presence-absence, and action identities. Even the 3-year-olds appeared to have some ability to make correct appearance-reality discriminations and this ability increased with age. Errors were frequent, however, and almost all children who erred made both kinds. Phenomenism errors predominated on tasks where the appearance versus reality of the three object properties was in question; intellectual realism errors predominated on the other three types of tasks. Possible reasons for this curious error pattern were advanced. It was also suggested that young children's problems with the appearance-reality distinction

> may be partly due to a specific metacognitive limitation, namely, a difficulty in analyzing the nature and source of their own mental representations.
>
> — JOHN H. FLAVELL, ELEANOR R. FLAVELL, AND FRANCES L. GREEN, *Cognitive Psychology*

**Thinking about Your Own Writing in a Discipline**

Choose a piece of writing you have produced for a particular discipline — a hypertext essay, a laboratory report, a review of the literature, or any other written assignment. Examine your writing closely for its use of that discipline's vocabulary, style, methods of proof, and conventional formats. How comfortable are you writing a piece of this kind? In what ways are you using the conventions of the discipline easily and well? What conventions give you difficulty, and why? You might talk to an instructor in this field about the conventions and requirements for writing in the discipline. Make notes about what you learn about being a better writer in the field.

# 62 Writing for the Humanities

Disciplines in the humanities are concerned with what it means to be *human.* Historians study and reconstruct the past. Literary critics analyze and interpret texts, often to help others explore a text's meaning. Philosophers raise questions about truth, knowledge, beauty, and justice. Scholars of other languages learn not just to speak but to inhabit other cultures. In these and other ways, those in the humanities strive to explore, interpret, and reconstruct the human experience.

## 62a Reading texts in the humanities

In humanities disciplines, the interpretation and creation of texts are central. The nature of texts can vary widely, from poems and plays to novels, articles, philosophical treatises, films, advertisements, paintings, and so on. But whether the text being studied is ancient or modern, literary or historical, verbal or visual, textual analysis plays a critical role in the reading and writing that people in the humanities undertake. How, then, can you become a strong reader of the humanities so that you can join in creating and interpreting texts?

To read critically in the humanities (1c and 9b), you will need to pose questions and construct hypotheses as you read. You may ask, for instance, why a writer might be making some points or developing some examples but omitting others. Rather than finding meaning only in the surface information that texts or artifacts convey, you should use your own questions and hypotheses to create fuller meanings — to construct the significance of what you read.

### *Critical reading and interpretation*

The ability to interpret and analyze fiction, poetry, essays, and other kinds of writing is a key skill not just in English literature but in all the humanities as well. To successfully engage texts, you must recognize that you are not a neutral observer, not an empty cup into which the meaning of a work is poured. If such were the case, writing would have exactly the same meanings for all of us, and reading would be a fairly boring affair. If you have ever gone to a movie with a friend and each come away with a completely different understanding or response, you already have ample evidence that a text never has just one meaning. (For a student analysis of film, see 62d.)

Nevertheless, you may in the past have been willing to accept the first meaning to occur to you — to take a text at face value. Most humanities courses, however, will expect you to exercise your interpretive powers. The following guidelines can help you build your strengths as a close reader of humanities texts.

### Guidelines for close reading

1. *Get an overall impression.* After reading (or viewing) straight through, jot down first impressions. What does the work make you think about — and why? What is most remarkable or memorable? What confuses you?
2. *Reread the work and annotate it.* Be prepared to "talk back," ask questions, note emerging patterns or themes, and point out anything out of place or ineffective.
3. *Pay attention to genre.* What category does the work fall into (graphic novel, lyric poetry, creative nonfiction, Hollywood western)? What is noteworthy about the form of the work? How does it conform to your expectations about the genre or subvert them?
4. *What is the point of view? Who is narrating?* How does the point of view affect your response? How reliable and convincing does the narrator seem? Does the text's creator intend to give this effect?
5. *What major themes does the work discuss?* What evidence in the text supports these themes?
6. *Look at the context.* Consider the time and place represented in the work as well as when and where the writer lived. You may also consider social, political, or personal forces that may have affected the writer.
7. *Think about the audience.* Who are the readers or viewers the writer seems to address? Do they include you?
8. *Review your notes.* Highlight the ideas that most interest you. Freewrite about your overall response to this work and the key point(s) you would like to make.

### A student's annotation of an essay

Interesting title

Yorick is mentioned in *Hamlet*. How does that relate to the grandmother?

Where is Dorset? And is "stewed pork" significant? Does it relate to the "grave" in the next sentence?

Buttons disappear — no match is ever found. Why keep the tin of single buttons?

*"Yorick: Uncovering the Bones of a Grandmother's Past" (Opening Paragraph)*

On the windowsill of my childhood stood a dust-colored round tin with black letters printed on it: "Dorset. Stewed Pork." The tin served as a communal grave for all single buttons. Every now and then, a button would fall off a cuff, roll under the bed — and that was it. Grope as you might or run the broom under the bed, it was gone forever. Then the contents of "Dorset" would be shaken out on the table and picked over with one finger, like grains of buckwheat, in search of a pair, but of course nothing matching could ever be found. After a bit of hesitation, the other button would be snipped off — what can you do? — the orphan would be thrown into the pile, and a half-dozen new buttons wrapped in muddy, tea-colored waxed paper would be purchased at the variety store.

— TATYANA TOLSTAYA, *New Yorker*

Why does the author start with the windowsill? What could she see from that window?

The opening still hasn't introduced the grandmother, but it makes me expect that these buttons were important to her. Buttons were made out of bone once, weren't they? Could the buttons be the "bones" in the title?

## 62b Writing texts in the humanities

Strong writers in the humanities take what they have gleaned from their close reading of a text or artifact and use those findings to develop an argument or to construct an analysis.

### Assignments

Common assignments that make use of these skills of close reading, analysis, and argument include summaries, response pieces, position papers, critical analyses, and research-based projects. Some of the assignments, such as summaries and analytic essays, encourage looking very closely at a particular text, while others, such as research projects and case studies, call for going well beyond a primary text.

Many humanities assignments — in disciplines such as the modern languages, literature, and philosophy — will ask you to format your documents according to the style of the Modern Language Association (MLA style). Other disciplines, such as history, use formats prescribed by the University of Chicago Press (*Chicago* style). If you have questions about which formats to use, consult your instructor. (For MLA style, see Chapter 18; for *Chicago* style, see Chapter 20.)

### Analysis and critical stance

To analyze a text, you need to develop a *critical stance* — the approach you will take to the work — that can help you develop a thesis or major claim (see 5c, 6c, and 11c). In general, student writers tend to adopt one of three primary stances: a *text-based stance* that builds an argument through close reading — by focusing on specific features of the text in question and reading the text very closely for those features; a *context-based stance* that builds an argument by focusing on the context in which a text was written or now exists and exploring how that context informs the text; a *reader-based stance* that focuses on the personal response of a reader to the text and the interpretation that grows out of that response; or a combination of these approaches.

Whatever stance you take, be sure to ground your analysis in one or more important questions that you have about the work. For example, a student writing about Shakespeare's *Macbeth* might find her curiosity piqued by the many comic moments that appear in this tragedy. She could eventually build on her curiosity by turning the question of why Shakespeare uses so much comedy in *Macbeth* into the following thesis statement, which proposes an answer to the question: "The many unexpected comic moments in *Macbeth* emphasize how disordered the world becomes for murderers like Macbeth and his wife."

## 62c A student's close reading of poetry

Student Writer

Bonnie Sillay

The following paper, a text-based close reading of two poems by E. E. Cummings, was written by Bonnie Sillay, a student at the University of Georgia. This essay follows MLA style (see Chapter 18). However, because Bonnie is creating her own interpretation, the only works she cites are the poems she analyzes (reprinted following her paper). Note that this essay has been reproduced in a narrow format to allow for annotation. (For sample research papers in MLA style, see 18e and 62d.)

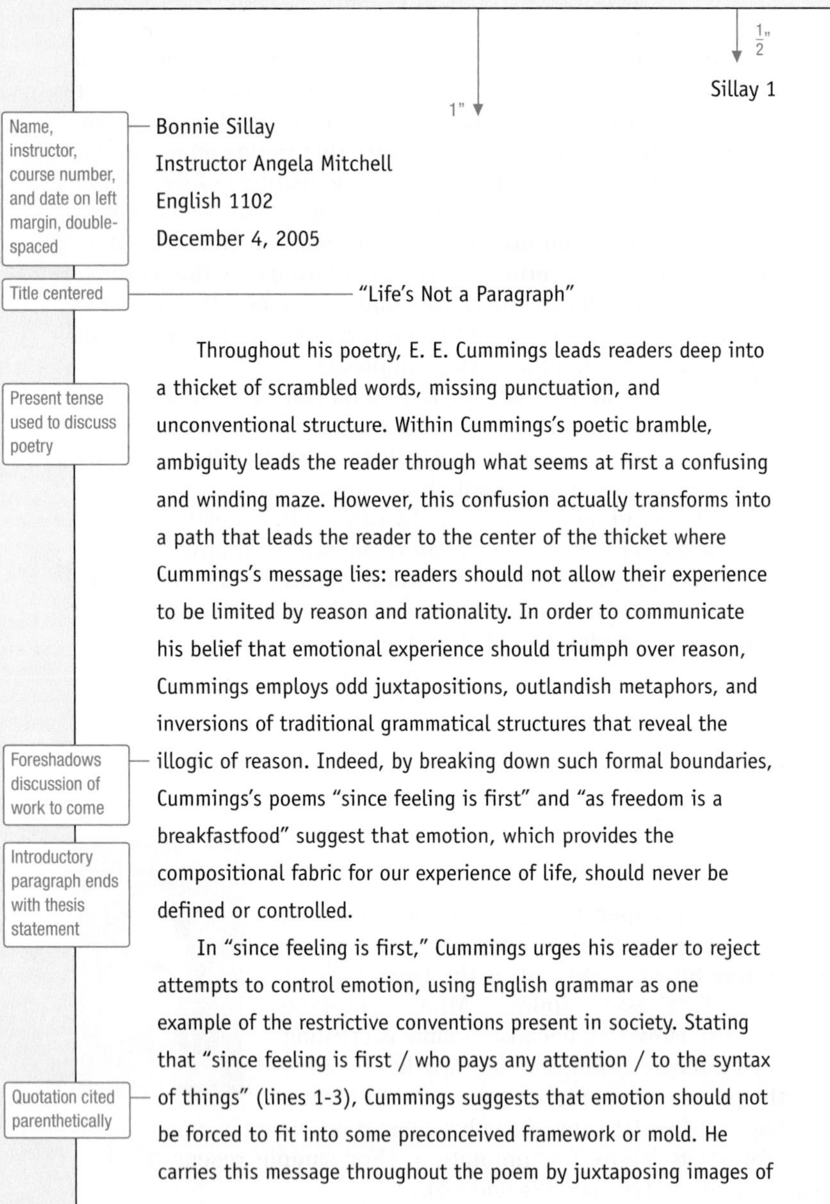


Sillay 1

Bonnie Sillay

Instructor Angela Mitchell

English 1102

December 4, 2005

"Life's Not a Paragraph"

Throughout his poetry, E. E. Cummings leads readers deep into a thicket of scrambled words, missing punctuation, and unconventional structure. Within Cummings's poetic bramble, ambiguity leads the reader through what seems at first a confusing and winding maze. However, this confusion actually transforms into a path that leads the reader to the center of the thicket where Cummings's message lies: readers should not allow their experience to be limited by reason and rationality. In order to communicate his belief that emotional experience should triumph over reason, Cummings employs odd juxtapositions, outlandish metaphors, and inversions of traditional grammatical structures that reveal the illogic of reason. Indeed, by breaking down such formal boundaries, Cummings's poems "since feeling is first" and "as freedom is a breakfastfood" suggest that emotion, which provides the compositional fabric for our experience of life, should never be defined or controlled.

In "since feeling is first," Cummings urges his reader to reject attempts to control emotion, using English grammar as one example of the restrictive conventions present in society. Stating that "since feeling is first / who pays any attention / to the syntax of things" (lines 1-3), Cummings suggests that emotion should not be forced to fit into some preconceived framework or mold. He carries this message throughout the poem by juxtaposing images of

1"

Sillay 2

Paper header on each page includes last name and page number

the abstract and the concrete--images of emotion and of English grammar. Cummings's word choice enhances his intentionally strange juxtapositions, with the poet using grammatical terms that suggest regulation or confinement. For example, in the line "And death i think is no parenthesis" (16), Cummings uses the idea that parentheses confine the words they surround in order to warn the reader not to let death confine life or emotions.

The structure of the poem also rejects traditional conventions. Instead of the final stanzas making the main point, Cummings opens his poem with his primary message, that "feeling is first" (1). Again, Cummings shows that emotion rejects order and structure. How can emotion be bottled in sentences and interrupted by commas, colons, and spaces? To Cummings, emotion is a never-ending run-on sentence that should not be diagramed or dissected.

Transition sentence connects the previous paragraph to this one

Quotation introduced effectively

Writer uses a metaphor that captures the spirit of Cummings's point

In the third stanza of "since feeling is first," Cummings states his point outright, noting "my blood approves, / and kisses are a better fate / than wisdom" (7-9). Here, Cummings argues for reveling in the feeling during a fleeting moment such as a kiss. He continues, "the best gesture of my brain is less than / your eyelids' flutter" (11-12). Cummings wants the reader to focus on a pure emotive response (the flutter of an eyelash)--on the emotional, not the logical--on the meanings of words instead of punctuation and grammar.

Quotation integrated into writer's sentence

Cummings's use of words such as *kisses* and *blood* (8, 7) adds to the focus on the emotional. The ideas behind these words are difficult to confine or restrict to a single definition: kisses mean different things to different people, blood flows through the body freely and continually. The words are not expansive or free enough to encompass all that they suggest. Cummings ultimately paints

Sillay 3

language as more restrictive than the flowing, powerful force of emotion.

Paragraph reiterates Cummings's claim and sums up his argument

The poet's use of two grammatical terms in the last lines, "for life's not a paragraph / And death i think is no parenthesis," warns against attempts to format lives and feelings into conventional and rule-bound segments (15-16). Attempts to control, rather than feel, are rejected throughout "since feeling is first." Emotion should be limitless, free from any restrictions or rules.

Clear and explicit transition from discussion of first poem

While "since feeling is first" argues that emotions should not be controlled, ordered, or analyzed, "as freedom is a breakfastfood" suggests the difficulty of defining emotion. In this poem, Cummings uses deliberately far-fetched metaphors such as "freedom is a breakfastfood" and "time is a tree" (1, 26). These metaphors seem arbitrary: Cummings is not attempting to make profound statements on time or freedom. Instead, he suggests that freedom and time are subjective, and attempts at narrow definition are ridiculous. Inversions of nature, such as "robins never welcome spring" and "water most encourage flame" (16, 7), underscore emotion's ability to defy reason. These inversions suggest the arbitrariness of what "since feeling is first" calls "the syntax of things" (3).

Although most of "as freedom is a breakfastfood" defies logic, Cummings shifts the tone at the end to deliver one last metaphor: "but love is the sky" (27). The word *but* separates this definition from the rest of the poem and subtly implies that, unlike the metaphors that have come before it, "love is the sky" is an accurate comparison. In order to reach this final conclusion, however, Cummings has taken his readers on a long and often ambiguous journey.

Sillay 4

Nevertheless, the confusion has been deliberate. Cummings wants his readers to follow him through the winding thicket because he believes the path of the straight and narrow limits the possibilities of experience. Through the unconventionality of his poetic structures, Cummings urges his readers to question order and tradition. He wants his readers to realize that reason and rationality are always secondary to emotion and that emotional experience is a free-flowing force that should not be constrained. Cummings's poetry suggests that in order to get at the true essence of something, one must look past the commonsensical definition and not be limited by "the syntax of things."

Writer returns to the image of the thicket from the introduction to create a closing that resonates with the opening

Sillay 5

Works Cited

Cummings, E. E. "as freedom is a breakfastfood." *E. E. Cummings: Complete Poems 1904-1962*. Ed. George J. Firmage. New York: Liveright, 1991. 511. Print.

Second work by same author uses three hyphens in place of name

---. "since feeling is first." *E. E. Cummings: Complete Poems 1904-1962*. Ed. George J. Firmage. New York: Liveright, 1991. 291. Print.

**since feeling is first**

since feeling is first
who pays any attention
to the syntax of things
will never wholly kiss you;

wholly to be a fool
while Spring is in the world

my blood approves,
and kisses are a better fate
than wisdom
lady i swear by all flowers. Don't cry
— the best gesture of my brain is less than
your eyelids' flutter which says

we are for each other: then
laugh, leaning back in my arms
for life's not a paragraph

And death i think is no parenthesis

**as freedom is a breakfastfood**

as freedom is a breakfastfood
or truth can live with right and wrong
or molehills are from mountains made
— long enough and just so long
will being pay the rent of seem
and genius please the talentgang
and water most encourage flame

as hatracks into peachtrees grow
or hopes dance best on bald men's hair
and every finger is a toe
and any courage is a fear
— long enough and just so long
will the impure think all things pure
and hornets wail by children stung

or as the seeing are the blind
and robins never welcome spring
nor flatfolk prove their world is round
nor dingsters die at break of dong
and common's rare and millstones float
— long enough and just so long
tomorrow will not be too late

worms are the words but joy's the voice
down shall go which and up come who
breasts will be breasts and thighs will be thighs
deeds cannot dream what dreams can do
— time is a tree (this life one leaf)
but love is the sky and i am for you
just so long and long enough

## 62d A student's essay on film

Amrit Rao wrote this essay for his first-year writing class at Stanford University. The essay, which combines elements of text-based, context-based, and reader-based stances, follows the MLA guidelines presented in Chapter 18. Note that this essay is reproduced in a narrow format to allow for annotation.

**bedfordstmartins.com/smhandbook** For more student writing samples in the humanities, click on **Student Writing**.

1"

Rao 1

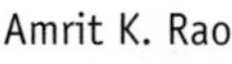

Amrit K. Rao

Mr. Daniel Contreras

FMS 201: Film and Society

January 27, 2004

Name, instructor, course number and title, and date on left margin, double-spaced

The Indian Diaspora in Hindi Cinema

Title centered

My parents are a testament to the fact that America is the land of opportunity. As schoolchildren in India, my mother and father worked hard on their assignments. My father was admitted to the elite Indian Institute of Technology, where the acceptance rate was less than two percent, while my mother, who had moved to the United States, won a full scholarship to her college. After graduation, my father left India to earn his PhD in America. Within ten years, my parents had bought their first house, and by age fifty my father had been named "Engineer of the Year" by a trade magazine.

Introductory paragraph provides background and context for the discussion

My parents, like many Indians, have earned success in the West. Although India's competitive environment gave them their work ethic, the United States and other Western countries continue to reap the benefits of this homegrown diligence. American graduate schools and corporations take many of India's most educated citizens. During the high-tech boom, for example, more U.S. H1B visas were issued to people from India than from any other country in the world (Conway and Stone 36).

Reader-based stance connects the story of the writer's parents to the Indian diaspora and "brain drain" of the next paragraph

In recent years, the "brain drain" of educated workers from India has grown. But the phenomenon has been taking place for decades. In 1980, more than ninety percent of the Indian Institute of Technology (IIT) graduates left India for the West (Swani 72). And many Indians who amass wealth abroad fail to give back to their motherland. For example, Kanwal Rekhi, an Indian-born

1/2"

Header on each page includes last name and page number

Rao 2

multimillionaire now living in the United States, has denounced what he calls "handouts to India" and argued that India must help itself. His way of giving back to the country of his birth has been to contribute to IIT--whose graduates overwhelmingly move abroad--and to a group of Indo-American engineers (Rekhi). Successful Indians like Rekhi thus actively encourage the "brain drain" rather than invest in India's future.

Supports "brain drain" claim

Not surprisingly, many Indians resent the achievements of their country's citizens who live abroad. They see the mass emigration of India's most educated workers as a stain on their country's reputation and a threat to its future. Many Indians who remain in their homeland feel increasingly suspicious of nonresident Indians, known as NRIs, perhaps because NRIs tend to be far wealthier than Indians at home. Whatever the causes of these suspicions, however, the Indian-NRI divide has percolated up through popular culture, where it is now playing out in Bollywood films.

Narrows focus to the debate represented in Indian popular culture

Bollywood, as the Indian film industry is known, produces "the most-seen movies in the world" and dominates Indian popular culture (Kabir 1). Therefore, the industry's take on the status of NRIs is significant. One recent Bollywood blockbuster that addresses the NRI question uses Indian-born and American-born characters to suggest that a Western lifestyle will lead to weakened family ties and disgraceful behavior; the filmmakers appear to be trying either to discourage resident Indians from moving to the West or encourage those abroad to return home.

Leads into discussion of hit film that deals with the issue

In Subhash Ghai's film *Pardes* ("Foreign Land"), an NRI named Kishorilal (Amrish Puri) travels to India for the first time in ten years. Penniless when he emigrated to the West, Kishorilal is returning a very rich man. While visiting a childhood friend, he

Provides overview of the film's plot

1"

Rao 3

arranges a marriage between his own son, born and raised in the United States, and his friend's daughter, a sweet and traditionally dressed girl living with her large extended family on a rural Indian estate. "What we NRIs need are girls like yours,"[1] he explains, implying that those who have left India need the stabilizing influence of a resident Indian's morals and traditions--and making an implicit comparison with the immoral women of the West.

While Kishorilal wants to bring Indian values to his Westernized son, the local children beg Kishorilal to take them to America. Concerned, the millionaire changes his Western clothing for a traditional *kurtha* and sings, "I have seen London, Paris, and Japan. . . . After all of this, I still know that India is the best." The verses are in Hindi, but when he reaches the chorus, Kishorilal sings in English, "I love India. I love my India."

Includes quotations from the film (which cannot include parenthetical page numbers)

The nationalistic overtones of this scene are obvious: many resident Indians dream of going to America and getting rich, and here is a millionaire NRI confessing (in both Hindi and English) that India will always be closest to his heart. Indian landmarks like the Red Fort (see Fig. 1 on p. 4) are shown during the song, adding to the hard-sell atmosphere. The song, which appears as a motif throughout the film, may aim to inspire longing--or guilt--in NRIs as well as patriotism in resident Indians. During *Pardes*'s smash theatrical release, this song in particular "had the audience on its feet," notes Madhu Jain (307).

Uses text-based stance to analyze the film's images and symbols of nationalism

Figure introduced before its placement in the text

As soon as Kishorilal persuades his friend to consent to an arranged marriage between their children, he calls his American-

[1] Translations are taken from subtitles throughout unless otherwise noted.

Footnote offers additional information

Rao 4

Fig. 1. *Delhi Gate in the Red Fort.*

born son, Rajiv. Here the filmmakers contrast Western rebelliousness with Indian filial piety, a concept repeated throughout *Pardes*. While the daughter, Ganga (Mahima Chaudhary), accepts her father's choice, the arrogant Rajiv (Apoorva Agnihotri) does all he can to prevent age-old Indian tradition from hindering his bachelor lifestyle. In order to persuade Rajiv to marry Ganga, Kishorilal must enlist the help of his "Little Master," his foster son Arjun.

Contrast between the two young men elaborated

Unlike Rajiv, Arjun was born and raised in India. Brought to America by Kishorilal five years earlier, after the death of his parents, he has proven an able manager of Kishorilal's affairs. Arjun (Shahrukh Khan, one of Bollywood's biggest stars) is also a successful musician and the author of the "I Love India" song. He demonstrates the Indian ideal of filial piety and respect, putting his foster father's interests before his own. In one scene, for example, he walks out on a journalist interviewing him about his musical career simply because Kishorilal pages him. He also plans to return to India after making his fortune so that he can dedicate his life to

Rao 5

helping the poor, a stark contrast with those successful NRIs who rarely give back to India.

Arjun takes Rajiv to India to help fulfill Kishorilal's wishes that Rajiv marry Ganga. Arjun recognizes the value of a beautiful girl from an Indian village who trusts her parents and her traditions, and he and Ganga become fast friends. He acts as a translator of Indian culture for Rajiv, who is annoyed and mystified by Ganga's ways. In one scene, he explains to his foster brother that young Indian women do not go out in the fields alone with men for private conversations. Then he translates Western culture for Ganga's parents, telling them (by reciting poetry) that they should allow Rajiv and Ganga enough privacy to allow them to get to know each other. With Arjun as dedicated go-between, the marriage plans move forward. In fact, in spite of Rajiv's poor showing when he meets Ganga--his allergies act up, and he insults the bride at their first meeting--Arjun does such a good job of portraying Rajiv as an ideal groom that Ganga is still willing to marry him. Later, when Ganga finds Rajiv's stash of cigarettes and confronts Arjun, asking what else Rajiv may be hiding from her, Arjun admits that Rajiv smokes but insists that his foster brother has no other vices.

Rajiv then insists that Ganga accompany him to America before the wedding, and her family agrees to let her see the country she will be adopting as her own. When she arrives in California, however, the NRI women in Kishorilal's household sneer at her clothing and provincial ways. Rajiv takes his fiancée to rowdy nightclubs and dance parties--and then ignores her in order to concentrate on his ex-girlfriend. Rajiv, the kind of NRI who makes fun of traditional morals and attitudes, seems to expect Ganga to do the same, or at least not to object to his behavior.

Rao 6

Good-natured, India-loving Arjun, by contrast, tries his best to help Ganga enjoy her new land. He sticks by her side and consoles her when Rajiv is mean. Arjun's loyal devotion to Kishorilal, however, means that Arjun's role as Rajiv's advocate must take precedence over his growing friendship with Ganga. Unfortunately, this means that Arjun must conceal Rajiv's drinking and continued relationship with his Westernized lover. Despite Arjun's efforts, though, Ganga discovers Rajiv's dark side.

The relationship between Ganga and Rajiv finally crashes to a halt during a trip to Las Vegas, where Rajiv attends a friend's kitschy, meaningless wedding. Then, drunk, Rajiv tries to get the chaste Ganga to sleep with him. When she refuses, reminding him that he only has to wait a few more days for the wedding, he rants, "You bloody Indians start whining and crying when someone mentions the word *sex*, yet you manage to have the world's largest population! Such hypocrisy!" He compares India to a toilet, and Ganga responds that America is "drug-infested." Rajiv then tries to rape Ganga, the representative of her country's virtue, but she fights back physically (knocking him unconscious with a liquor bottle) and escapes his lustful wrath.

The conflict between values reaches its climax

Introduces various ways of reading or interpreting the film's key scene

This scene can be interpreted in multiple ways. On the surface it is simply about two characters, a repulsive NRI and a virginal Indian heroine, but the scene--and the characters in general--can also be read allegorically. Rajiv goes out of his way to insult his future bride, with whom he has no real connection and for whom he has no respect; he has little interest in her if she is unwilling to throw her traditional ways aside. If Rajiv is a representation of the corrupt West (or of corrupt NRIs), and Ganga represents pure and traditional India, then their struggle suggests that the West is

Rao 7

taking advantage of India's values (a respect for education and hard work) and resources (its workers) for selfish reasons, a situation the film sees as reprehensible.

Protagonists in Hindi films typically have luck on their side, and Arjun is no different. Miraculously, he finds Ganga at a train station. Although he wants her to see Kishorilal and explain, she insists that she has taken a vow never to go back. Arjun sees that his duty is to take her back to India to her family. Rajiv pursues his unwanted bride and his foster brother because he is unwilling to let anyone else have Ganga and, as he starkly tells a friend, "because I'm bad." Kishorilal, enraged at Arjun's apparent treachery, also travels to India to settle the score.

Eventually, the hero Arjun (after suffering a terrible beating and confessing that he loves Ganga but will not pursue her out of respect for his foster father and Ganga's parents) delivers a moving oration in which he denounces the acts of Indo-Americans like his foster brother Rajiv. "These sons of India are sons, yes--Indians, no!" he exclaims. His speech and Ganga's convincing demonstration that Rajiv has treated her shabbily convince Kishorilal that Rajiv has been too tainted by Western values to deserve such a gem. Instead, he decides that Arjun, the "good son" who loves India and respects traditions and parents, should marry the pure Ganga.

Arjun's speech practically strips away the cultural citizenship of first-generation NRIs, and the screenplay of *Pardes* implies that they deserve nothing less. The characterization of the American-born Indian throughout the film is that of a spoiled and sinful brat who deserves Arjun's reprimand. The filmmakers, it seems, can imagine no worse insult than to insist that Rajiv is not really Indian. Arjun, on the other hand, has managed to live in the West

Rao 8

The conflict is resolved in favor of homegrown Indian values

without being polluted by Western values. His triumph is a victory for India, which wins the metaphorical onscreen battle to demonstrate that its values are purer and finer than those of the West.

Presents an alternate view of the film

While *Pardes* brought Indian audiences to their feet, many NRI teenagers see such characterizations of NRIs as a form of defamation. We all know that India, as seen in *Pardes* and countless other films, is the most spiritual of lands, and when Western children are shown as preoccupied with external sources of pleasure, it reflects badly on our mini-community. It is as if Bollywood writers want to warn resident Indians that their children will end up selfish and "bad" if they leave the moral security of India.

Conclusion focuses on how the film relates to India's attempts to reach out to NRIs and reverse the "Indian diaspora" of the title

In the end, of course, the deserving Arjun gets his Ganga, and the families--including the NRI Kishorilal and his American-dwelling foster son--are reconciled. The audience understands that Arjun and Ganga plan to remain in India, their true homeland. In light of Bollywood's stress on NRI-India relations, this ending can be viewed as a conciliatory gesture on behalf of India to NRIs who felt that they had to leave for economic reasons. The filmmakers appear to suggest that India will welcome its NRIs back with open arms. This, after all, is the ultimate situation India is working toward--having successful NRIs move back home.

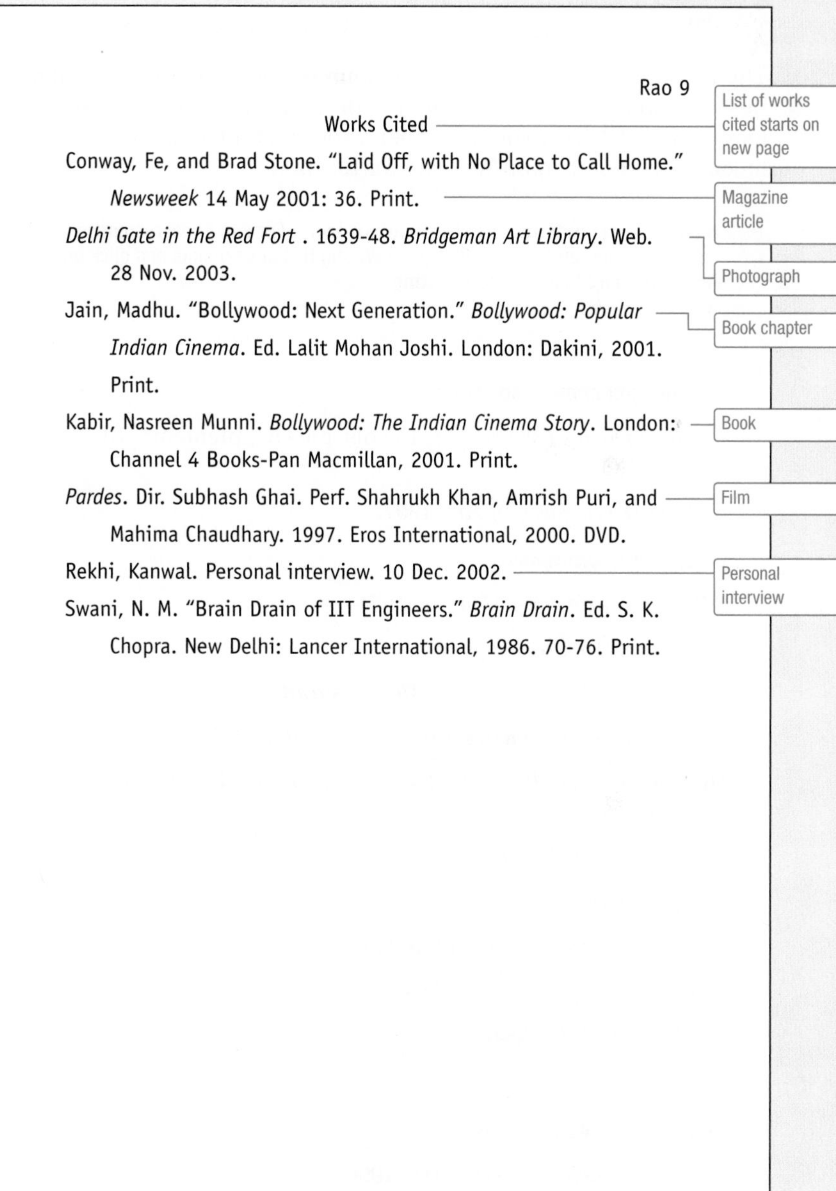
Rao 9

Works Cited

Conway, Fe, and Brad Stone. "Laid Off, with No Place to Call Home." *Newsweek* 14 May 2001: 36. Print.

*Delhi Gate in the Red Fort* . 1639-48. *Bridgeman Art Library*. Web. 28 Nov. 2003.

Jain, Madhu. "Bollywood: Next Generation." *Bollywood: Popular Indian Cinema*. Ed. Lalit Mohan Joshi. London: Dakini, 2001. Print.

Kabir, Nasreen Munni. *Bollywood: The Indian Cinema Story*. London: Channel 4 Books-Pan Macmillan, 2001. Print.

*Pardes*. Dir. Subhash Ghai. Perf. Shahrukh Khan, Amrish Puri, and Mahima Chaudhary. 1997. Eros International, 2000. DVD.

Rekhi, Kanwal. Personal interview. 10 Dec. 2002.

Swani, N. M. "Brain Drain of IIT Engineers." *Brain Drain*. Ed. S. K. Chopra. New Delhi: Lancer International, 1986. 70-76. Print.

## 62e Research sources for the humanities

The following lists contain print resources for students of the humanities and names of resources online. Because an online resource's URL may change, URLs are not listed here; you can find them, with up-to-date links, on the companion Web site for this book.

**bedfordstmartins.com/smhandbook** For additional resources in the humanities and up-to-date URLs, go to Writing Resources/Links and click on **Academic and Professional Writing.**

### *Art*

#### GENERAL REFERENCE SOURCES

*Encyclopedia of World Art.* 15 vols. plus supplements. 1959–68; 1983; 1987.

*Oxford Dictionary of Art.* 1997.

#### INDEXES AND DATABASES

*ARTBibliographies Modern.* 1974–.

*Art Index.* 1929–.

*Art Information: Research Methods and Resources.* 1990.

*Avery Index to Architectural Periodicals.* 1965–.

*BHA: Bibliography of the History of Art.* 1991–. (Online as *Art Literature International*)

*Fine Arts: A Bibliographic Guide to Basic Reference Books.* 1990.

#### WEB RESOURCES

Art History Resources on the Web

Virtual Library Museums Pages

World Wide Arts Resources

### *Classics*

#### GENERAL REFERENCE SOURCES

*Oxford Classical Dictionary.* 1996.

*Oxford Companion to Classical Civilization.* 1998.

**DATABASE**

*L'Année Philologique.* 1928–.

**WEB RESOURCES**

Classics Web

Internet Ancient History Sourcebook

Perseus Project

## History

**GENERAL REFERENCE SOURCES**

*Cambridge Ancient History.* 12 vols. 1939–82, with later revisions.

*Cambridge Encyclopedia of Latin America and the Caribbean.* 1992.

*Cambridge History of Africa.* 8 vols. 1975–86.

*Cambridge Medieval History.* 9 vols. 1911–75.

*Dictionary of Concepts in History.* 1986.

*Dictionary of the Middle Ages.* 13 vols. 1982–89.

*Encyclopedia of American Social History.* 3 vols. 1993.

*Encyclopedia of Asian History.* 4 vols. 1988.

*Encyclopedia of the Renaissance.* 1987.

*Timeless Atlas of World History.* 1993.

**INDEXES AND DATABASES**

*America: History and Life.* 1964–.

*Historical Abstracts.* 1955–.

*Reference Sources in History: An Introductory Guide.* 1990.

**WEB RESOURCES**

Bedford/St. Martin's: Make History

The Library of Congress: American Memory

World History Archives

The WWW Virtual Library: History Central Catalogue

## *Literature and linguistics*

**GENERAL REFERENCE SOURCES**

*Contemporary Authors*. 1998.

*Contemporary Literary Criticism*. 2001.

*Dictionary of Literary Biography*. 1978–.

*Encyclopedia of World Literature in the Twentieth Century*. 5 vols. 1981–93.

*A Handbook to Literature*. 9th ed., 2002.

*International Encyclopedia of Linguistics*. 4 vols. 1991.

*Oxford Companion to American Literature*. 1995.

*Oxford Companion to English Literature*. 2000.

**INDEXES AND DATABASES**

*Annual Bibliography of English Language and Literature* (ABELL). 1920–.

*Contemporary Literary Criticism*. 2001.

*Dictionary of Literary Biography*. 1978–.

*MLA International Bibliography of Books and Articles on the Modern Languages and Literature*. 1921–.

*Reference Works in British and American Literature*. 2 vols. 1990–91.

**WEB RESOURCES**

Linguistic Society of America

Literary Resources on the Net

The Voice of the Shuttle

## *Music*

**GENERAL REFERENCE SOURCES**

*New Grove Dictionary of Music and Musicians*. 20 vols. 2001.

*New Oxford Companion to Music*. 2 vols. 1983.

*New Oxford History of Music*. 9 vols. 1986–90.

#### INDEXES AND DATABASES

*Music: A Guide to the Reference Literature.* 1987.

*Music Index: A Subject-Author Guide to Current Music Periodical Literature.* 1949–.

*Music Reference and Research Materials: An Annotated Bibliography.* 1993.

*RILM Abstracts of Music Literature.* 1966–. (CD-ROM as *Muse*)

#### WEB RESOURCES

Music Libraries

Worldwide Internet Music Resources

The WWW Virtual Library: Music

### *Philosophy, religion, and ethics*

#### GENERAL REFERENCE SOURCES

*Dictionary of Philosophy.* 1984.

*Encyclopedia of Philosophy.* 4 vols. 1973.

*Encyclopedia of Religion.* 16 vols. 1987.

#### INDEXES AND DATABASES

*Philosopher's Index.* 1967–.

*Philosophy: A Guide to the Reference Literature.* 1986.

*Religion Index.* 1975–.

*Religious and Theological Abstracts.* 1958–.

#### WEB RESOURCES

Internet Resources: Religion and Philosophy

The WWW Virtual Library: Philosophy

(The sacred texts of most religions are also available online.)

### *Theater and film*

**GENERAL REFERENCE SOURCES**

*American Film Institute Desk Reference.* 2002.

*Film Encyclopedia.* 2005.

*McGraw-Hill Encyclopedia of World Drama.* 5 vols. 1984.

**INDEXES AND DATABASES**

*Film Literature Index.* 1973–.

*International Index to Film Periodicals.* 1972–.

**WEB RESOURCES**

The Internet Movie Database

The Internet Theatre Database

McCoy's Brief Guide to Internet Resources in Theatre and Performance Studies

Movie Review Query Engine

The WWW Virtual Library: Theatre and Drama

## THINKING CRITICALLY ABOUT WRITING IN THE HUMANITIES

Choose at least two projects or assignments you have written for different disciplines in the humanities — say, history and film. Reread these papers with an eye to their similarities. What features do they have in common? Do they use similar methods of analysis and value similar kinds of evidence, for instance? In what ways do they differ? Based on your analysis, what conclusions can you draw about these two disciplines?

# Writing for the Social Sciences

# 63

When do most workers begin to save toward retirement? What role do television ads play in the decision-making process of potential voters? How do children learn to read?

The social sciences — which include psychology, anthropology, political science, speech, communication, sociology, economics, and education — try to answer such questions by looking both to the humanities and to the sciences. The social sciences share with the humanities an interest in what it means to be human. But the social sciences also share with the sciences the goal of engaging in a systematic, observable study of human behavior. Whatever their focus, all the social sciences attempt to identify, understand, and explain patterns of human behavior.

## 63a Reading texts in the social sciences

Strong readers in the social sciences — as in any subject — ask questions, analyze, and interpret as they read, whether they are reading an academic paper that sets forth a theoretical premise or overall theory and defends it, a case study that describes a particular case and draws out inferences and implications from it, or a research report that presents the results of an investigation into an important question in the field. They realize, as well, that social-science disciplines often use special terms for basic concepts. In the abstract to the article titled "Development of the Appearance-Reality Distinction" on p. 830, for example, the author uses the terms *phenomenism* and *intellectual realism* as shorthand for complex ideas that otherwise would take paragraphs to explain.

### *Qualitative and quantitative studies*

Different texts in the social sciences may call for different reading strategies. Texts that report the results of *quantitative* studies emphasize statistical evidence based on surveys, polls, experiments, and tests. For example, a study of voting patterns in southern states might rely on quantitative data such as statistics. Texts that report the results of *qualitative* studies are more subjective: they do not aim for scientific objectivity but rather rely on interviews and observations to reveal social patterns. A study of the way children in one kindergarten class develop rules of play, for instance, would draw on qualitative data — observations of social interaction, interviews with students and teachers, and so on. Of course, some work in the social sciences combines quantitative and qualitative data and methods: an educational report might begin with statistical data related to a problem and then move to a qualitative case study to exemplify what the statistics show.

Readers of both quantitative and qualitative studies need to interpret and analyze what they read, but they may use these reading skills somewhat differently. Someone reading a quantitative study, for instance, might carefully analyze the information presented in graphs and charts, since these often summarize a quantitative study's findings. A qualitative study makes different demands on readers because its findings are usually not so easily recognizable. Moreover, because researchers undertaking qualitative studies base their analyses on interpretations of what they have studied, it is important to pay close attention to the kind of data the writer is using and what those data can — and cannot — prove. Readers of qualitative studies must assess the soundness and consistency of interpretations as well as the appropriateness of the theories that guide them.

### *Conventional formats*

Make use of conventional disciplinary formats to help guide your reading in the social sciences. Many such texts conform to the format and documentation style of the American Psychological Association (APA). In addition, articles often include standard features — an abstract that gives an overview of the findings, followed by an introduction, review of literature, methods, results, discussion, and references. Readers who become familiar with such a format and others advocated by the APA can easily find the information they need. (For more on APA style, see Chapter 19.)

## 63b Writing texts in the social sciences

Perhaps because the social sciences share concerns with both the humanities and the sciences, the forms of writing within the social sciences are particularly varied, including summaries, abstracts, literature reviews, reaction pieces, position papers, radio scripts, briefing notes, book reviews, briefs, research papers, quantitative research reports, case studies, and ethnographic analyses. Such an array of writing assignments could seem overwhelming, but in fact these assignments can be organized under five main categories:

*Writing that encourages student learning* (reaction pieces, position papers)

*Writing that demonstrates student learning* (summaries, abstracts, research papers)

*Writing that reflects common on-the-job communication tasks undertaken by members of a discipline* (radio scripts, briefing notes, brief informational reports)

*Writing that requires students to analyze and evaluate the writings of others* (literature reviews, book reviews, briefs)

*Writing that asks students to replicate the work of others or to engage in original research* (quantitative research reports, case studies, ethnographic analyses)

Many forms of writing in the social sciences call either explicitly or implicitly for argument (see Chapter 11). If you write an essay reporting on the results of a survey you developed about attitudes toward physician-assisted suicide among students on your campus, you will make an explicit argument about the significance of your data. But even in other forms of writing, such as summaries and book reports, you will implicitly argue that your description and analysis provide a clear, thorough overview of the text(s) you have read.

### The literature review

Students of the social sciences carry out literature reviews to find out the most current thinking about a topic, to learn what research has already been carried out on that topic, to evaluate the work that has been done, and to set any research they will do in context. The following guidelines are designed to help you explore and question sources, looking for flaws or gaps. Such a critical review could then lead to a discussion of how your own research will avoid such flaws and advance knowledge.

- What is your topic of interest or dependent variable (the item or characteristic being studied)?
- What is already known about this topic? What characteristics does the topic or dependent variable have? What other factors are involved, and how are they related to each other and to your topic or variable? What theories are used to explain the way things are now?

- How has research been done so far? Who or what has been studied? How have measurements been taken?
- Has there been change over time? What has caused any changes?
- What problems do you identify in the current research? What questions have not been answered yet? What conclusions have researchers drawn that might not be warranted?
- What gaps will your research fill? How is it new? What problems do you want to correct?

### *Style in the social sciences*

Students sometimes assume that the writing they do in the social sciences should be dry and jargon-ridden. This is hardly the case. While you need to understand the conventions, concepts, and habits of mind typical of a particular discipline, you can still write clear prose that engages readers. Here, for instance, is an introduction to a literature review written by sociologist Mark Edwards. Note that he is reviewing quantitative research that relates to his own paper on the employment of parents with children. Also note the stylistic strategies he uses to engage readers: parallel sentence structures (sentences 1 and 2), everyday language (*kids*, *missing out*), active verbs, a clear statement of purpose, and so on. The verb tenses he uses also conform to APA style (see Chapter 19): when discussing research sources, he uses the past or present perfect tense.

> Nearly 60% of mothers of preschoolers are in the labor force. Over 90% of fathers of preschoolers are in the labor force. While many families appear to be juggling the work/family conflict adequately, others claim to feel guilty about leaving their kids in the care of other adults and perhaps missing out on important events in the young child's life. Meanwhile, the potential setbacks in their careers make it difficult for young parents to consider taking time out of the labor force. Employers are also concerned about this issue as the state continues to pass and consider new laws providing family leave and as they seek to retain skilled workers. . . .
>
> This paper identifies the characteristics of families and young mothers and fathers which are associated with full- and part-time employment while the first child is still an infant. Unlike earlier studies that rely on cross-sectional data, this analysis follows the early life histories of young families to locate not only how demographic characteristics but also how the timing and order of events influence the likelihood of a new mother or father returning quickly to paid work.
>
> —MARK EDWARDS, *Writing within Sociology: A Guide for Undergraduates*

### EXERCISE 63.1

Identify a literature review in a social-science field you are interested in (ask your instructor or a librarian for help in finding one), and read it carefully, noting how it addresses the questions on pp. 859–60. Bring your notes to class for discussion.

## 63c A student's brief psychology report

Following is an example of effective writing in the social sciences, a brief report by Katie Paarlberg requiring a series of short responses to questions about a telephone survey that she and her classmates at Hope College conducted among fellow students. (For a sample research paper in APA style, see 19e.)

**bedfordstmartins.com/smhandbook** For more student writing samples in the social sciences, click on **Student Writing**.

K. Paarlberg
Psych 100-01
February 24, 2006

Centered title identifies the assignment clearly

Report #2 — Response to Questions about Attitude Survey

**1. How could the construction of the survey and the ways in which the questions were phrased have influenced the students' responses?**

Passive voice (*were asked*) used appropriately to put the emphasis on the respondent rather than the person conducting the survey

Cautious tone and qualifiers such as *may* and *could have* used for reporting more tentative results

One way in which the construction of the survey could have influenced the results is that many of the statements that respondents were asked to agree or disagree with centered not just on *gender* issues but on *women's* issues as well. For example, one statement read, "Women are just as capable as men when it comes to holding positions of responsibility and authority" instead of "Women and men are *equally* capable. . . ." Spotlighting women as the gender in question may have suggested to certain respondents that a particular answer was expected. This may well have been the point of the survey, but the wording of certain statements could have influenced the results.

Another factor that may have had an effect on people's answers was the fact that demographic questions appeared in the survey. For example, students were asked whether they were male or female and whether their mothers worked while they were growing up. Some may have felt that they were in some way expected to represent their groups. For example, a survey responder who felt that his answers had to represent the "male/mother did not work" column might alter responses to fit this perception.

The topic of the survey was somewhat controversial; this also may have influenced students' responses. If the survey had asked about favorite colors instead of about gender attitudes, the

Attitude Survey 2

Shortened title and page number on every page after the first

respondents might not have felt the need to avoid offending the surveyor. If students had been asked to give their names on this survey, which they were not asked to do, their answers might have been even less truthful.

**2. What effect could the identity of the surveyor have had on the students' responses? Would the survey results have been different if the surveyor had been a faculty member?**

The results of the survey were most likely somewhat influenced by the fact that students were reporting their attitudes to their peers and classmates, not to their instructors. If they had been surveyed by the faculty, respondents might have been more likely to search their minds for the "right" answers on which they were being "tested" rather than expressing genuine opinions.

Writer acknowledges effect of her participation on the responses elicited

**3. How did you select the respondents for your survey? Was your sample population representative of the larger college community? Why or why not? What about the national population of college students? Was your sample population representative of that larger group?**

In order to obtain a representative sample of Hope students, we selected numbers at random from the Hope telephone directory. We used a random number chart to choose page and listing numbers, and then switched numbers with others in order to avoid knowing subjects' names.

Explains methods clearly

Our sample might not be representative of the Hope community because many Hope students do not have on-campus numbers in the directory. Many commute from surrounding areas, and we did not ask those students to participate. Juniors and seniors are also more likely to live off-campus; their views as a group on this topic might differ from those of freshmen and sophomores.

These survey results probably do not represent the views of the American college population as a whole. Attitudes of students vary widely. Students from a school in western Michigan, the majority of whose students come from western Michigan, cannot be used as a representative sample of all American college students.

**4. Did anything about the results of your survey surprise you? Why?**

The results I found most unexpected were that 64% of all students, and 58% of men, said that they would sacrifice their careers to raise a family. I was surprised that so many students — who are presumably preparing for a career — were willing to put family obligations first. The fact that men and women were closely aligned on this issue was also surprising; men are traditionally less likely to devote time to family over careers. Perhaps students felt obligated to give politically correct responses, or perhaps attitudes really are changing more than I had known.

Avoids making sweeping or unjustified claims

**5. What about the results did you find most interesting? Why do you think students responded the way they did?**

I was interested to see that the population was split almost evenly among students whose mothers did not work when they were growing up, students whose mothers worked part-time, and students whose mothers worked full-time. Many students grew up during the 1980s, a time of developing economic freedom for women, when more mothers were entering the workforce. It was also interesting to note that while no women disagreed with the statement that women are as capable as men when it comes to holding positions of authority and responsibility, 13% of the men did disagree. Women are more likely to defend the ability of their sex and take such a statement personally, while men need not defend personal ability by agreeing with this statement. The men who disagreed may also have taken the fact that women do hold fewer powerful positions in the United States than men as evidence that women are less capable.

Maintains a neutral, objective tone throughout

## 63d Research sources for the social sciences

The following lists contain print resources for students of the social sciences and names of resources online. Because an online resource's URL may change, URLs are not listed here; you can find them, with up-to-date links, on the companion Web site for this book.

**bedfordstmartins.com/smhandbook** For additional resources in the social sciences and up-to-date URLs, go to Writing Resources/Links and click on **Academic and Professional Writing.**

### *Anthropology*

#### GENERAL REFERENCE SOURCE

*Encyclopedia of Anthropology.* 1976.

#### INDEXES AND DATABASES

*Abstracts in Anthropology.* 1970–.

*Anthropological Literature.* 1979–.

#### WEB RESOURCES

Anthro.Net

The WWW Virtual Library: Anthropology

### *Communication and journalism*

#### GENERAL REFERENCE SOURCES

*Communication Yearbook.* 1977–.

*International Encyclopedia of Communication.* 4 vols. 1989.

*International Encyclopedia of Linguistics.* 4 vols. 1991.

*Webster's New World Dictionary of Media and Communications.* 1990.

#### INDEXES AND DATABASES

*Communication Abstracts.* 1978–.

*Vanderbilt Television News Archive.* 1968–.

#### WEB RESOURCES

Online Communication Studies Resources

The WWW Virtual Library: Communications and Media

### Education

#### GENERAL REFERENCE SOURCES

*Encyclopedia of Education.* 10 vols. 1971.

*Encyclopedia of Educational Research.* 4 vols. 1992.

*International Encyclopedia of Education: Research and Studies.* 10 vols. 1992.

#### INDEXES AND DATABASES

*Current Index to Journals in Education* (CIJE). 1969–.

*Education: A Guide to Reference and Information Sources.* 1989.

*Educational Resources Information Center* (ERIC). 1966–.

*Education Index.* 1929–. (Online, CD-ROM)

#### WEB RESOURCES

The Educator's Reference Desk

U.S. Department of Education

The World Lecture Hall

The WWW Virtual Library: Education

### Ethnic studies

#### GENERAL REFERENCE SOURCES

*The American Indian: A Multimedia Encyclopedia.* 1993.

*Blackwell Companion to Jewish Culture: From the Eighteenth Century to the Present.* 1989.

*Dictionary of Asian American History.* 1986.

*Dictionary of Mexican American History.* 1981.

*Encyclopedia of Native American Tribes.* 1988.

*Encyclopedia of World Cultures*. 10 vols. 1990–1995.

*Harvard Encyclopedia of American Ethnic Groups*. 1980–.

*The Hispanic-American Almanac*. 1993.

*The Negro Almanac: A Reference Work on the African American*. 1990.

*Sourcebook of Hispanic Culture in the United States*. 1982.

*The State of Black America*. 1976–.

#### INDEXES AND DATABASES

*Afro-American Reference: An Annotated Bibliography of Selected Sources*. 1985.

*Asian American Studies: An Annotated Bibliography and Research Guide*. 1989.

*Chicano Index*. 1989–.

*Ethnic News Watch*. 1995–.

*Guide to Research on North American Indians*. 1983.

*Hispanic American Periodicals Index* (HAPI). 1970–.

*Index to Black Periodicals*. 1984–.

*Native Americans: An Annotated Bibliography*. 1991.

*Women of Color in the United States: A Guide to the Literature*. 1989.

#### WEB RESOURCES

Africa Web Links: An Annotated Resource List

Columbia University: Latino Studies Links

NativeWeb

The WWW Virtual Library: Asian Studies

The WWW Virtual Library: Migration and Ethnic Relations

### Political science

#### GENERAL REFERENCE SOURCES

*Almanac of American Politics: The President, the Senators, the Representatives, the Governors: Their Records and Election Results, Their States and Districts*. 1972–. Biennial.

*Congressional Quarterly Almanac*. 1945–.

*Political Handbook of the World*. 1927–.

*State Legislative Sourcebook: A Resource Guide to Legislative Information in the Fifty States*. Annual.

**INDEXES AND DATABASES**

*A Bibliography of Current Contents: Political Science and Government* (ABC Pol Sci). 1969–.

*Political Science: A Guide to Reference and Information Sources*. 1990.

*Population Index*. 1935–.

*United States Political Science Documents*. 1975–.

**WEB RESOURCES**

Fedworld

The Gallup Organization

Legal Information Institute

Political Resources on the Net

Political Science Resources on the Web

Thomas: Legislative Information on the Internet

United Nations

World Wide Political Science Archives

## Psychology

**GENERAL REFERENCE SOURCES**

*Encyclopedia of Psychology*. 8 vols. 2000.

*Oxford Companion to the Mind*. 1987.

**INDEXES AND DATABASES**

*Bibliographic Guide to Psychology*. 1974–.

*Mental Health Abstracts*. 1969–.

*Psychological Abstracts*. 1927–. (Online as PsycINFO, CD-ROM as PsycLIT)

**WEB RESOURCES**

American Psychological Association

American Psychological Society

Internet Mental Health

PsychWeb

The WWW Virtual Library: Psychology

### Sociology

**GENERAL REFERENCE SOURCE**

*Encyclopedia of Social Work*. 3 vols. 1990.

**INDEXES AND DATABASES**

*Social Work Research and Abstracts*. 1977–.

*Sociological Abstracts*. 1952–. (CD-ROM as SocioFile)

**WEB RESOURCES**

A Sociological Tour through Cyberspace

Sociology Links

SocioSite

The Socioweb

U.S. Census Bureau

The WWW Virtual Library: Sociology

## THINKING CRITICALLY ABOUT WRITING IN THE SOCIAL SCIENCES

**Reading with an Eye for Writing in the Social Sciences**

Using the preceding list of sources to help you, choose two readings from a social-science discipline, and read them with an eye toward issues of style. Does the use of disciplinary terms and concepts seem appropriate? In what ways do the texts attempt to engage readers? If the texts are not clear and understandable, how might they be improved?

**Thinking about Your Own Writing in the Social Sciences**

Choose a text you like that you have written for a social-science discipline. Then examine your style in this paper to see how well you have engaged your readers. Note variation in sentence length and type (do you, for example, use any questions?), number of active and passive verbs, use of concrete examples and everyday language, and so on. How would you rate your writing as a social scientist?

# 64 Writing for the Natural and Applied Sciences

Whether they are studying geological faults or developing a stronger support structure for suspension bridges, scientists in the natural and applied sciences want to understand how the physical and natural worlds work. Natural sciences such as biology, chemistry, and physics study the natural world and its phenomena; applied sciences such as nanotechnology and the various fields of engineering apply knowledge from the natural sciences to practical problems. More than many other scholars, scientists are likely to leave the privacy of their office or lab to engage in fieldwork and experimentation. Whether done in the lab or the field, however, writing — from the first grant proposal to the final report or scientific paper — plays a key role in the natural and applied sciences.

## 64a Reading texts in the natural and applied sciences

Scientists work with evidence that can be observed, verified, and controlled. Though scientists cannot avoid interpretation, they strive for objectivity by using the scientific method — observing or studying phenomena, formulating a hypothesis about the phenomena, and testing that hypothesis through controlled experiments. Scientists aim to generate precise, replicable data; they develop experiments to account for extraneous factors. In this careful, precise way, scientists test and write about particular theories relating to the world.

### *Identifying argument*

As you read in the sciences, try to become familiar with disciplinary terms, concepts, and formats as soon as possible, and practice reading for detail. If you are reading a first-year biology textbook, you can draw upon general critical-reading strategies (1c). In addition, charts, graphs, illustrations, models, and other visuals often play an important role in scientific writing, so your ability to read and comprehend these visual displays of knowledge is particularly important.

When you read a science textbook, you can assume that the information presented there is authoritative and as objective as possible. When you read specialized materials, however, recognize that although scholarly reports undergo significant peer review, they nevertheless represent arguments (see Chapter 9). The connection between facts and claims in the sciences, as in all subject areas, is created by the author rather than simply revealed by the data. So read both facts and claims with a questioning eye: Did the scientist choose the best method to test the hypothesis? Are there other reasonable interpretations of the experiment's results? Do other studies contradict the conclusions of this experiment? When you read specialized texts in the sciences with questions like these in mind, you are reading — and thinking — like a scientist.

### *Conventional formats*

As you advance in your course work, you will need to develop reading strategies for increasingly specialized texts. Most scientific texts conform to the format and documentation style of the Council of Science Editors (CSE). In addition, articles often include standard features — an abstract that gives an overview of the findings, followed by an introduction, literature review, materials and methods, results, discussion, and references. (For more on CSE style, see Chapter 21.)

You might expect to read a journal article for a science course from start to finish, giving equal weight to each section. However, an experienced scientist might skim an abstract to see if an article warrants further reading. If it does — and this judgment is based on the reader's own research interest — the scientist might then read the introduction to understand the rationale for the experiment and then skip to the results. A scientist with a specific interest in the methods will read that section with particular care.

### EXERCISE 64.1

Choose a respected journal in a discipline in the natural or applied sciences that interests you. (Ask your instructor or a reference librarian if you need help identifying a journal.) Then read quickly through two articles, taking notes on the author's use of any headings and subheadings, specialized vocabulary, visuals, and evidence. Bring the results of your investigation to class for discussion.

## 64b Writing texts in the natural and applied sciences

It's no surprise that scientists particularly value clarity in written prose, as noted in the following statement by chemistry professors:

> Although the exchange of information in science usually focuses on content rather than writing style, it is important that work be presented using accepted conventions and in an appropriate style. Whether your audience consists of readers, reviewers, seminar attendees, or the boss, a clear, concise writing style can help gain their confidence, maintain their interest, and convince them of your work's value.
>
> — OREGON STATE UNIVERSITY DEPARTMENT OF CHEMISTRY, *A Writing Guide for Chemistry*

### *Types of writing in the sciences*

Students in the sciences must be able to respond to a diverse range of writing tasks. Often, they must maintain lab notebooks that include careful records of experiments. They also write papers, literature reviews, and progress reports; in addition, they may develop print and Web-based presentations for both technical and lay audiences. Particularly common writing assignments in the sciences are the literature review, research proposal, and research report.

Scientists undertake literature reviews to keep up with and evaluate developments in their field. Literature reviews are an essential first step in any research effort, for they enable scientists to discover what research has already been completed and how they might build on earlier efforts. Successful literature reviews demonstrate a student's ability to identify relevant research on a topic and to summarize and in some instances evaluate that research.

Most scientists spend a great deal of time writing research or grant proposals aimed at securing funds to support their research. Undergraduate writers often have an opportunity to make similar proposals — to an office of undergraduate research or to a science-based firm that supports student research, for instance. (See 21d for an example.) Funding agencies often have guidelines for preparing a proposal. Proposals for research funding generally include the following sections: title page, introduction, purpose(s) and significance of the study, methods, timeline, budget, and references. You may also need to submit an abstract.

Research reports, another common writing form in the sciences, may include both literature reviews and discussions of primary research, most often experiments. Like journal articles, research reports generally follow this form: title, author(s), abstract, introduction, literature review, materials and methods, results, discussion, and references. Many instructors ask students to write lab reports (64c), which are briefer versions of research reports and may not include a literature review.

Today, a great deal of scientific writing is collaborative. As students move from introductory to advanced courses and then to the workplace, they increasingly find themselves working as part of teams or groups. Indeed, in such areas as engineering, collaborative projects are often the norm. (For more on collaboration, see Chapter 8.)

### *Style in the natural and applied sciences*

In general, use the present tense for most writing you do in the natural and applied sciences. Use the past tense, however, when you are describing research already carried out (by you or others) or published in the past.

Writers in the sciences need to produce complex figures, tables, images, and models and use software designed to analyze data or run computer simulations. In addition, they need to present data carefully. If you create a graph, you should provide headings for columns, label axes with numbers or units, and identify data points. Caption figures and tables with a number and descriptive title. And avoid *orphan data* — data that you present in a figure or table but don't comment on in your text. (For more information on CSE manuscript style, see 21a.)

## 64c A student's chemistry lab report

The following piece of student writing is a lab report on a chemistry experiment by Allyson Goldberg, a student at Yale University. Note that this report has been reproduced in a narrow format to allow for annotation. (For a sample research proposal in CSE style, see 21d.)

Student Writer

Allyson Goldberg

**bedfordstmartins.com/smhandbook** For more student writing samples in the natural and applied sciences, click on **Student Writing**.

Title page includes relevant information about lab

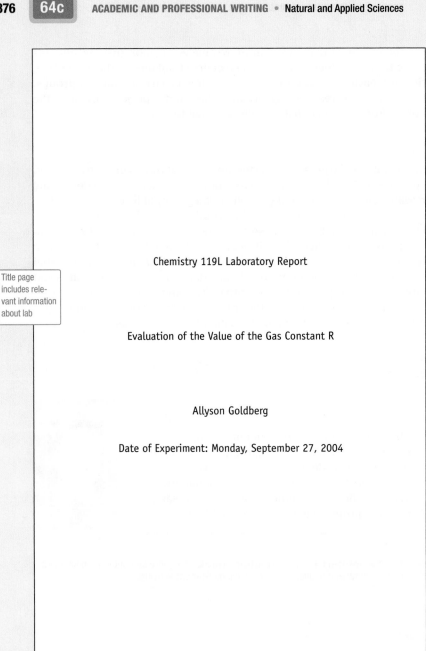

Chemistry 119L Laboratory Report

Evaluation of the Value of the Gas Constant R

Allyson Goldberg

Date of Experiment: Monday, September 27, 2004

Goldberg 2

Introduction

Introduction explains purpose of lab and gives overview of results

The purpose of this investigation was to experimentally determine the value of the universal gas constant, R. To accomplish this goal, a measured sample of magnesium (Mg) was allowed to react with an excess of hydrochloric acid (HCl) at room temperature and pressure so that the precise amount and volume of the product hydrogen gas ($H_2$) could be determined and the value of R could be calculated using the ideal gas equation, PV=nRT.

Materials & Methods

Materials and methods section explains lab setup and procedure

Two samples of room temperature water, one about 250mL and the other about 400mL, were measured into a smaller and larger beaker respectively. 15.0mL of HCl was then transferred into a side arm flask that was connected to the top of a buret (clamped to a ringstand) through a 5/16″ diameter flexible tube. (This "gas buret" was connected to an adjacent "open buret," clamped to the other side of the ringstand and left open to the atmosphere of the laboratory at its wide end, by a 1/4″ diameter flexible tube. These two burets were adjusted on the ringstand so that they were vertically parallel and close together.) The HCl sample was transferred to the flask such that none came in contact with the inner surface of the neck of the flask. The flask was then allowed to rest, in an almost horizontal position, in the smaller beaker.

The open buret was adjusted on the ringstand such that its 20mL mark was horizontally aligned with the 35mL mark on the gas buret. Room temperature water was added to the open buret until the water level of the gas buret was at about 34.00mL.

Goldberg 3

Passive voice throughout typical of writing in natural sciences

A piece of magnesium ribbon was obtained, weighed on an analytical balance, and placed in the neck of the horizontal side arm flask. Next, a screw cap was used to cap the flask and form an airtight seal. This setup was then allowed to sit for 5 minutes in order to reach thermal equilibrium.

After 5 minutes, the open buret was adjusted so that the menisci on both burets were level with each other; the side arm flask was then tilted vertically to let the magnesium ribbon react with the HCl. After the brisk reaction, the flask was placed into the larger beaker and allowed to sit for another 5 minutes.

Next, the flask was placed back into the smaller beaker, and the open buret was adjusted on the ringstand such that its meniscus was level with that of the gas buret. After the system sat for an additional 30 minutes, the open buret was again adjusted so that the menisci on both burets were level.

This procedure was repeated two more times, with the exception that HCl was not again added to the side arm flask, as it was already present in enough excess for all reactions from the first trial.

Results and calculations show measurements and calculations of final value of R

Results and Calculations

| Trial # | Lab Temp. (°C) | Lab Pressure (mbar) | Mass of Mg Ribbon Used (g) | Initial Buret Reading (mL) | Final Buret Reading (mL) |
|---|---|---|---|---|---|
| 1 | 24.4 | 1013 | 0.0147 | 32.66 | 19.60 |
| 2 | 24.3 | 1013 | 0.0155 | 33.59 | N/A* |
| 3 | 25.0 | 1013 | 0.0153 | 34.35 | 19.80 |

*See note in Discussion section.

Goldberg 4

| Trial # | Volume of $H_2$ (L) | Moles of $H_2$ Gas Produced | Lab Temp. (K) | Partial Pressure of $H_2$ (atm) | Value of R (L atm/ mol K) | Mean Value of R (L atm/ mol K) |
|---|---|---|---|---|---|---|
| 1 | .01306 | $6.05 \times 10^{-4}$ | 298 | 0.970 | 0.0704 | 0.0728 |
| 2 | N/A | N/A | N/A | N/A | N/A | |
| 3 | 0.01455 | $6.30 \times 10^{-4}$ | 298 | .968 | 0.0751 | |

Table 1 Experimental results

(Sample Calculations—see Table 1)

Volume of $H_2$ gas = final buret reading – initial buret reading

Volume of $H_2$ gas = 32.66mL – 19.60mL = 13.06mL = 0.01306 L

Moles of $H_2$ gas produced = mass of Mg used/molar mass of Mg

Moles of $H_2$ gas produced = 0.0147g/24.305g $mol^{-1}$ = $6.05 \times 10^{-4}$ mol

Kelvin temperature = Celsius temperature + 273.15 = 24.3°C + 273.15
= 298 K

Partial Pressure of $H_2$ gas in the gas buret = $P_{atmosphere}$ – pressure due to water vapor at the temperature of interest

$P_{atmosphere}$ = 1013 mbar

(unit conversion of $P_{atmosphere}$) $\frac{1013.25 \text{ mbar}}{1 \text{ atm}} = \frac{1013 \text{ mbar}}{x \text{ atm}}$ (conversion value taken from Ganapathi [2004])

x = 0.9998 atm

(unit conversion of pressure due to water vapor) $\frac{22.4 \text{ mm Hg}}{x \text{ atm}} = \frac{760 \text{ mm}}{1 \text{ atm}}$ (values taken from Ganapathi [2004])

x = 0.0295 atm

Partial Pressure of $H_2$ gas in the gas buret = 0.9998 atm – 0.0295 atm = 0.9703 atm

Value of R:

$R = PV/nT$

$R = [(0.9703 \text{ atm}) (0.01306 \text{ L})]/[(6.05 \times 10^{-4} \text{ mol}) (297.5 \text{ K})]$

$R = 0.01267 \text{ L atm}/0.180 \text{ mol K}$

$R = 0.0704 \text{ L atm/mol K}$

Mean Value of $R = (\text{R-value}_1 + \text{R-value}_3)/2$

Mean Value of $R = (0.0704 \text{ L atm/mol K} + 0.0751 \text{ L atm/mol K})/2$

Mean Value of $R = 0.0728 \text{ L atm/mol K}$

Percent Error = [(measured value − accepted value)/accepted value] × 100

Percent Error = absolute value of [(0.0728 L atm/mol K − 0.08206 L atm/mol K)/0.08206 L atm/mol K] × 100

Percent Error = 11.3%

Discussion section analyzes results and possible sources of inaccuracy

## Discussion

Despite the adherence to the experimental procedure, the mean value of R determined in this investigation deviated slightly from the accepted value, 0.08206 L atm/mol K. This deviation was most likely due to the leakage of some $H_2$ gas through the screw cap of the side arm flask during the reaction. Though this could have been better avoided, the tightening of the screw cap onto the side arm flask was necessarily a compromise between an extremely tight seal and a seal too strong to be later removed; thus, any error during experimentation was difficult both to judge and to avoid. In this way, the buret reading after the reaction in Trial 2 was read at 30.80mL. With only a 2.79mL change in the volume of the gas in the buret, it was evident (from comparison with the previous trial) that not all of the hydrogen gas produced in the reaction was captured in the gas buret. Thus, upon recognition of this error, the experimental procedure for that trial was suspended, and data from Trial 2 was disregarded in analyses.

However, detailed attention to pressure was paid during the experiment, such that the position of the open buret was adjusted several times in order to equilibrate its water level with that of the gas buret. This was done to equalize the pressure of the hydrogen gas with that of the atmospheric pressure in the laboratory, as the pressure of the hydrogen gas itself was impossible to measure inside the gas buret. Subsequently, because the atmospheric pressure in the laboratory remained constant throughout the procedure, it was differences in other components of the ideal gas equation (volume, number of moles, and temperature) that made for the varying R-values calculated.

Additionally regarding pressure was the need to account for the contribution of the partial pressure of water vapor when determining the pressure of the $H_2$ gas produced. Because the ideal gas equation was used to calculate R-values, it was necessary to use the purest values possible relating to the hydrogen gas when substituting values into the equation. Though the hydrogen gas produced was not quite an ideal gas, the light weight of and weak attractive forces between its molecules rendered it close enough to one that it was suitable for this experiment. The water vapor molecules, on the other hand, had much larger masses, and the electronegativity of the oxygen atoms added an attractive force that would have added more deviation from the accepted value for R.

Accuracy in this experiment could have been compromised by a number of factors. Regarding pressure, more accurate values could have been obtained if the digital barometer used was allowed to

Goldberg 7

have been taken to each workstation, rather than remaining in the front desk; atmospheric pressure likely varied a little bit around the room. Regarding volume, the ruler technique used to confirm that the water level in each buret was horizontally equivalent was helpful, but could have been more effective had the tool used been a level. (Additionally, it was important to note at the beginning of the experiment that both burets were not only close enough together to judge equivalent water levels, but that the two were vertically parallel as well.) Further, the accuracy of temperature measurements could have been improved had there been an apparatus to hold the bulb of the thermometer in midair; resting the thermometer on, or even too near to, the surface of the lab table gave temperature readings that were lower than that of the air surrounding the experimental system.

Conclusions section analyzes purpose of experiment: to teach concept and lab technique

## Conclusions

Conceptually, this experiment was fairly simple to grasp. Experimentally, however, it provided the opportunity to become more intimate with common laboratory equipment, as well as provided a hands-on explanation of the ideal gas equation. For example, the previously learned technique of using a glass stirring rod to channel a liquid into a narrow opening proved to be useful in this procedure when it was necessary to pour HCl into the side arm flask without getting any of the acid inside the neck of the flask. Additionally, the need to account for the partial pressure of water vapor provided a tangible example of what it means to be an ideal gas versus a real gas, and how the concept of the ideal gas equation applies in the real world.

Goldberg 8

References

References section follows CSE style for citing books

Ganapathi N. Chemistry 119L laboratory manual. New Haven (CT): Yale University Press; 2004.

Oxtoby DW, Gillis HP, Nachtrieb NH. Principles of modern chemistry. 5th ed. Farmington Hills (MI): Thompson Learning; 2002.

## 64d Research sources for the natural and applied sciences

The following lists contain print resources for students of the natural and applied sciences and names of resources online. Because an online resource's URL may change, URLs are not listed here; you can find them, with up-to-date links, on the companion Web site for this book.

**bedfordstmartins.com/smhandbook** For additional resources in the natural and applied sciences and up-to-date URLs, go to Writing Resources/Links and click on **Academic and Professional Writing**.

### General science sources

*Boston University Libraries Research Guides*

*General Science Full Text.* 1984–.

### Astronomy

#### GENERAL REFERENCE SOURCE

*Encyclopedia of Astronomy and Astrophysics.* 2001.

#### INDEXES AND DATABASES

*Astronomy and Astrophysics Abstracts.* 1969–.

#### WEB RESOURCES

Astronomy Café

Astronomy Net

AstroWeb: Astronomy/Astrophysics on the Internet

NASA

### Biology and biosciences

#### GENERAL REFERENCE SOURCES

*Encyclopedia of Bioethics.* 2 vols. 1982.

*Encyclopedia of Human Biology.* 8 vols. 1997.

*Encyclopedia of Microbiology.* 4 vols. 1992.

*Grzimek's Animal Life Encyclopedia.* 13 vols. 1972–74.

*Mammals: A Multimedia Encyclopedia.* 1996.

#### INDEXES AND DATABASES

*Biological Abstracts*. 1926–.

*Biological and Agricultural Index*. 1964–.

#### WEB RESOURCES

Biosciences Index

Links to the Genetic World

Scott's Botanical Links

The WWW Virtual Library: Biosciences

### Chemistry

#### GENERAL REFERENCE SOURCE

*Kirk-Othmer Encyclopedia of Chemical Technology*. 27 vols. 1991–.

#### INDEXES AND DATABASES

*Chemical Abstracts*. 1907–.

#### WEB RESOURCES

Chemistry.org

CHEMINFO

The WWW Virtual Library: Chemistry

### Computer science

#### GENERAL REFERENCE SOURCES

*Encyclopedia of Computer Science*. 1993.

*Encyclopedia of Computer Science and Technology*. 2003.

*McGraw-Hill Multimedia Encyclopedia of Science and Technology*. 1997.

#### INDEXES AND DATABASES

*ACM Guide to Computing Literature*. 1980–. (Online as ACM Portal)

#### WEB RESOURCES

MIT Laboratory for Computer Science

Webopedia

The WWW Virtual Library: Computing and Computer Science

## Earth science

GENERAL REFERENCE SOURCES

*Encyclopedia of Earth Sciences*. 24 vols. 1966–.

*Encyclopedia of Earth System Science*. 4 vols. 1992.

*Encyclopedia of Minerals*. 1974–.

*McGraw-Hill Dictionary of Earth Sciences*. 1997.

INDEXES AND DATABASES

*Bibliography and Index of Geology*. 1969–.

WEB RESOURCES

Internet Resources in the Earth Sciences

NASA's Global Change Master Directory (GCMD)

The WWW Virtual Library: Earth Science

## Engineering

GENERAL REFERENCE SOURCES

*Annual Book of ASTM Standards*. 1990–.

*CRC Handbook of Tables for Applied Engineering Science*. 1973.

*Encyclopedia of Materials Science and Engineering*. 8 vols. 1986.

*Handbook of Engineering Fundamentals*. 1990.

*Handbook of Industrial Engineering*. 2001.

*Marks' Standard Handbook for Mechanical Engineers*. 1987–.

*McGraw-Hill Encyclopedia of Engineering*. 1993.

*Perry's Chemical Engineer's Handbook*. 1997.

*Standard Handbook for Civil Engineers*. 1996.

*Standard Handbook for Electrical Engineers*. 1986.

*Standard Handbook of Environmental Engineering*. 1990.

INDEXES AND DATABASES

Engineering Index Monthly. 1884–.

Inspec. 1969–.

#### WEB RESOURCES

IEEE Spectrum Online

The WWW Virtual Library: Engineering

## Environmental studies

#### GENERAL REFERENCE SOURCES

*Dictionary of Energy*. 1988.

*Encyclopedia of Environmental Science and Technology*. 2000.

*Facts on File Dictionary of Environmental Science*. 1991.

*Grzimek's Encyclopedia of Ecology*. 1976–.

*McGraw-Hill Encyclopedia of Environmental Science and Engineering*. 1993.

*United States Energy Atlas*. 1986.

#### INDEXES AND DATABASES

*Ecological Abstracts*. 1980–.

*Environment Abstracts*. 1971–.

*Environmental Periodicals Bibliography*. 1972–.

*Pollution Abstracts*. 1970–.

#### WEB RESOURCES

EnviroLink

The WWW Virtual Library: Public Health: Environmental Health

## Mathematics

#### GENERAL REFERENCE SOURCES

*CRC Handbook of Mathematical Sciences*. 1987.

*Encyclopedic Dictionary of Mathematics*. 4 vols. 1987.

#### INDEXES AND DATABASES

*Mathematical Reviews*. 1940–. (Online as Math on the Web, CD-ROM as MathSciDisc)

#### WEB RESOURCES

American Mathematical Society's Math on the Web

Math Archives Undergrads' Page

Math Forum Internet Mathematics Library

NIST (National Institute of Standards and Technology) Virtual Library

### Medicine/nursing

#### GENERAL REFERENCE SOURCES

*Cecil Textbook of Medicine*. 2000.

*Conn's Current Therapy 2006*. 2006.

*Gale Encyclopedia of Medicine*. 5 vols. 1999.

*Handbook of Clinical Nursing Research*. 1999.

#### INDEXES AND DATABASES

*The CINAHL Database*. 1977–.

*Cumulative Index to Nursing and Allied Health Literature*. 1961–.

*Index Medicus*. 1899–1926; 1960–.

*Public Health Databases*

#### WEB RESOURCES

HealthWorld Online

National Institutes of Health

National Science Foundation: Biology

Nursing Net

Weill Cornell Medical Library

### Physics

#### GENERAL REFERENCE SOURCES

*American Institute of Physics Handbook*. 1972.

*Encyclopedia of Physics*. 1991.

*McGraw-Hill Dictionary of Physics*. 1997.

**INDEXES AND DATABASES**

*Information Sources in Physics*. 1985.

*Physics Abstracts*. 1898–.

**WEB RESOURCES**

AIP Physics Information

Contemporary Physics Education Project

PhysLink.com

The WWW Virtual Library: Physics

## FOR COLLABORATION

Team up with a classmate who is interested in the same scientific field or major. Find an article in that field that is clearly argued and well written. Read the article individually, and then go through it again together, taking notes on how it is organized, on its tone and style, and on its use of evidence and sources. Determine how effective this article is in presenting its information, and bring the results of your analysis to class for discussion.

## THINKING CRITICALLY ABOUT WRITING FOR THE SCIENCES

**Reading with an Eye for Writing in the Sciences**

Identify one or more features of scientific texts, and consider their usefulness. Why, for instance, does an abstract precede the actual article? How do scientific nomenclatures, classification systems, and other features of scientific writing aid the work of scientists? Try to identify the functions that textual elements such as these play in the ongoing work of science. Finally, research the scientific method to see how it is served by the features of scientific writing discussed in this chapter.

**Thinking about Your Own Writing in the Sciences**

Choose a piece of writing you did for a natural or applied science class — a lab report, a research report, a proposal — and read it carefully. Note the format and headings you used, how you presented visual data, what kinds of evidence you used, and what citation system you used. Compare your piece of writing with a similar piece of writing published in a journal in the field. How well does your writing compare? What differences are most noticeable between your writing and that of the published piece?

# 65 Writing for Business

In today's wired business world, the global economy is now a commonplace concept, and both corporate giants and home-office eBay operations conduct business worldwide. Yet in the midst of these changes one constant remains: written communication is essential in identifying and solving the complex problems of today's companies. To succeed in business, you need to know how to manage many kinds of writing — from negotiating an ever-increasing number of email messages to communicating effectively with readers from Manhattan, Montgomery, Mexico City, and Mumbai.

## 65a Reading texts for business

Readers in business face a dizzying array of demands. A team of businesspeople today has almost unlimited access to information and to people, such as economists and scientists, whose expertise can be of use in the business world. Somehow, the members of this team need to negotiate a huge stream of information and to evaluate that information.

To meet these demands, you can draw on general strategies for effective reading (1c). One such strategy — keeping a clear purpose in mind when you read — is particularly important when you are engaged in work-related reading. Are you reading to solve a problem? to gather and synthesize information? to make a recommendation? Knowing why you are reading will increase your productivity. Time constraints and deadline pressures will also affect your decisions about what and how to read; the ability to identify important information quickly is a skill you will cultivate as a business reader.

## 65b Writing texts for business

Writing assignments in business classes serve two related functions. While their immediate goal is to help you master the theory and practice of business, these assignments also prepare you for the kinds of writing you will face in the world of work. For this reason, students in *every* discipline need to know how to write effective business memos, emails, letters, résumés, and reports.

## 1 Memo

Memos are a common form of print or electronic correspondence sent within and between organizations. Memos tend to be brief, internal documents, often dealing with only one subject.

### Guidelines for writing effective memos

- Write the name of the recipient, your name, the subject, and the date on separate lines at the top.
- Begin with the most important information: depending on the memo's purpose, you may have to provide background information, define the task or problem, or clarify the memo's goal.
- Use your opening paragraph to focus on how the information you convey affects your readers.
- Focus each subsequent paragraph on one idea pertaining to the subject.
- Present information concisely and from the readers' perspective.
- Emphasize specific action — exactly what you want readers to do and when.
- Use attachments for detailed supporting information.
- For print memos, initial your memo next to your name.
- Adjust your style and tone to fit your audience: use a more formal tone in a memo to a supervisor or someone in another company than in a memo to a co-worker.
- Attempt to build goodwill in your conclusion.

Following is a memo, written by two student writers, Michelle Abbott and Carina Abernathy, that presents an analysis and recommendation to help an employer make a decision.

Student Writer

Michelle Abbott

Student Writer

Carina Abernathy

**bedfordstmartins.com/smhandbook** For more student samples of business writing, click on **Student Writing**.

MEMO

Initials of senders added in ink

Paragraphs not indented

Opening paragraph provides background and states purpose

Most important information emphasized

Double-space between paragraphs

Options presented

Relevant factors explained

Final recommendation

Closing builds goodwill by offering further help

❖ *Jenco* ❖

**INTEROFFICE MEMORANDUM**

**TO:** ROSA DONAHUE, SALES MANAGER

**FROM:** MICHELLE ABBOTT & CARINA ABERNATHY MA CA

**SUBJECT:** TAYLOR NURSERY BID

**DATE:** 1/30/2007

**CC:**

As you know, Taylor Nursery has requested bids on a 25,000-pound order of private-label fertilizer. Taylor Nursery is one of the largest distributors of our Fertikil product. The following is our analysis of Jenco's costs to fill this special order and a recommendation for the bidding price.

**The total cost for manufacturing 25,000 pounds of the private-label brand for Taylor Nursery is $44,075**. This cost includes direct material, direct labor, and variable manufacturing overhead. Although our current equipment and facilities provide adequate capacity for processing this special order, the job will involve an excess in labor hours. The overtime labor rate has been factored into our costs.

The absolute minimum price that Jenco could bid for this product without losing money is $44,075 (our cost). Applying our standard markup of 40% results in a price of $61,705. Thus, you could reasonably establish a price anywhere within that range.

In making the final assessment, we advise you to consider factors relevant to this decision. Taylor Nursery has stated that this is a one-time order. Therefore, the effort to fill this special order will not bring long-term benefits.

Finally, Taylor Nursery has requested bids from several competitors. One rival, Eclipse Fertilizers, is submitting a bid of $60,000 on this order. Therefore, our recommendation is to slightly underbid Eclipse with a price of $58,000, representing a markup of approximately 32%.

Please let us know if we can be of further assistance in your decision on the Taylor Nursery bid.

## 2 Email

Email is used continually in business, industry, and the professions. Business email can be formatted much like a print memo but is easier to create and store and faster to distribute. Remember, however, that email is essentially public and that employers have easy access to email written by employees. As always, it's best to use discretion and caution in email, especially on the job. (For guidelines for and an example of effective email, see 22b1.)

## 3 Letter

Despite the popularity of email, letters remain an important form of communication. When you send a business or professional letter, you are writing either as an individual or as a representative of an organization. In either case, and regardless of your purpose, a business letter should follow certain conventions.

One particular type of letter, the letter of application or cover letter (p. 894), often accompanies a résumé. The purpose of a letter of application is to demonstrate how the experiences and skills you outline in your résumé have prepared you for a particular job. In a letter of application, then, it is important to focus on how you can benefit the company, not how the company can help you. If you are responding to a particular advertisement, mention it in the opening paragraph. Finally, be sure to indicate how you can be reached for an interview.

The following application letter for a summer internship was written by Nastassia Lopez, a student at Stanford University. Note that the letter has been reproduced in a narrow format to allow for annotation.

Student Writer

Nastassia Lopez

bedfordstmartins.com/smhandbook For more student samples of business writing, click on **Student Writing**.

LETTER OF APPLICATION

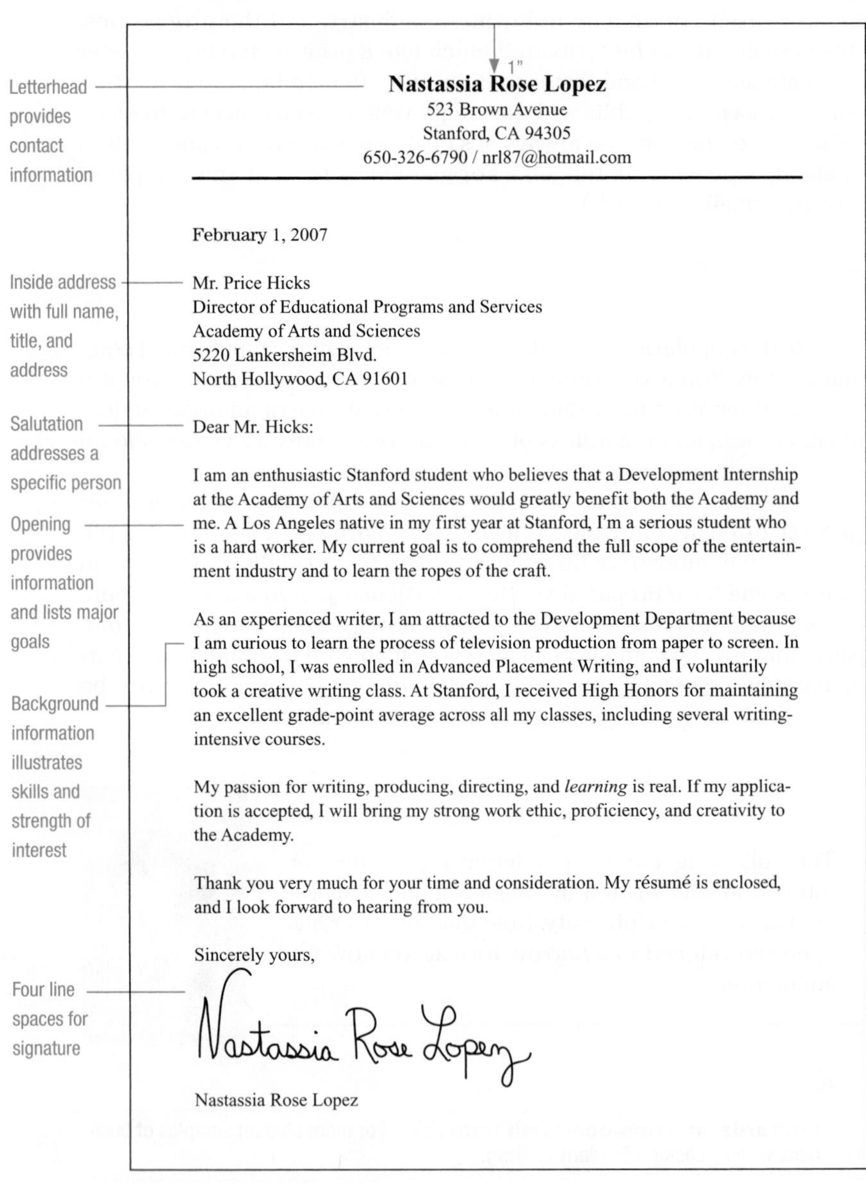


**Nastassia Rose Lopez**
523 Brown Avenue
Stanford, CA 94305
650-326-6790 / nrl87@hotmail.com

February 1, 2007

Mr. Price Hicks
Director of Educational Programs and Services
Academy of Arts and Sciences
5220 Lankersheim Blvd.
North Hollywood, CA 91601

Dear Mr. Hicks:

I am an enthusiastic Stanford student who believes that a Development Internship at the Academy of Arts and Sciences would greatly benefit both the Academy and me. A Los Angeles native in my first year at Stanford, I'm a serious student who is a hard worker. My current goal is to comprehend the full scope of the entertainment industry and to learn the ropes of the craft.

As an experienced writer, I am attracted to the Development Department because I am curious to learn the process of television production from paper to screen. In high school, I was enrolled in Advanced Placement Writing, and I voluntarily took a creative writing class. At Stanford, I received High Honors for maintaining an excellent grade-point average across all my classes, including several writing-intensive courses.

My passion for writing, producing, directing, and *learning* is real. If my application is accepted, I will bring my strong work ethic, proficiency, and creativity to the Academy.

Thank you very much for your time and consideration. My résumé is enclosed, and I look forward to hearing from you.

Sincerely yours,

Nastassia Rose Lopez

Nastassia Rose Lopez

### Guidelines for writing effective letters

- Use a conventional format. Many letters use the block format, in which all text aligns at the left margin. Some writers prefer a modified block format, aligning the return address, date, close, and signature on the right. When using a letterhead, you may center the return address (see p. 894).
- Whenever possible, write to a specific person (*Dear Tom Robinson* or *Dear Ms. Otuteye*) rather than to a general *Dear Sir or Madam*.
- Open cordially and be polite — even if you have a complaint.
- State the reason for your letter clearly. Include whatever details will help your reader see your point and respond.
- If appropriate, make clear what you hope your reader will do.
- Express appreciation for your reader's attention.
- Make it easy for your reader to respond by including your telephone or fax number, your email address, and, if appropriate, a self-addressed, stamped envelope.

### 4 Résumé

As noted previously, a letter of application and a résumé often travel together. While a letter of application usually emphasizes specific parts of the résumé, telling how your background is suited to a particular job, a résumé summarizes your experience and qualifications and provides support for your letter. An effective résumé is brief, usually one or two pages.

Research shows that employers generally spend less than a minute reading a résumé. Remember that they are interested not in what they can do for you but what you can do for them. They expect a résumé to be printed neatly on high-quality paper or formatted neatly on a Web page or in an electronic file. In all cases, your aim is to use clear headings, adequate spacing, and conventional formats that will make your résumé easy to read. Although you may be tempted to use colored paper or unusual type styles because you want your résumé to stand out, avoid such temptations. A well-written résumé with a standard format and typeface is the best way to distinguish yourself.

Your résumé may be arranged chronologically (from most to least recent) or functionally (based on skills or expertise). Either way, you will probably include the following information:

1. *Name, address, phone and fax numbers, and email address*, often centered at the top.
2. *Career objective(s)*. List immediate or short-term goals and specific jobs for which you realistically qualify.
3. *Educational background*. Include degrees, diplomas, majors, and special programs or courses that pertain to your field of interest. List honors and scholarships and your grade-point average if it is high.
4. *Work experience*. Identify each job — whether a paying job, an internship, or military experience — with dates and names of organizations. Describe your duties by carefully selecting strong action verbs. Highlight any of your activities that improved business in any way.
5. *Skills, personal interests, activities, awards, and honors*. Identify your technology skills. List hobbies, offices held, volunteer work, and awards.
6. *References*. List two or three people who know your work well, first asking their permission. Give their titles, addresses, and phone or fax numbers. Or simply say that your references are available on request.
7. *Keywords* (for a scannable résumé). In general, nouns function as keywords for résumés that are scanned by Web search engines and organized in databases. For this reason, look for places where you can convert verbs (*performed laboratory tests*) to nouns (*laboratory technologist*). Place the most important keywords toward the beginning of the résumé: many programs start scanning at the top of the document.

The conventions for scannable résumés are in flux. In recent years, it has been common to develop a scannable résumé for both online and electronic databases. Increasingly, though, job seekers who want to target the Internet are composing online résumés as hypertext screen documents, which make keywords more visible to search engines and thus tend to produce more hits. In addition, some businesses ask applicants to fill out résumé forms on company Web sites. In such cases, take special care to make sure that you have caught any error or typo before submitting the form.

EXERCISE 65.1

Take a close look at the two versions of Dennis Tyler's résumé on pp. 898–99, and note the differences in presentation and content. What purposes might these differences serve? Can you identify differences in the audience — and audience expectations — for these résumés?

## 65c Special considerations in business writing

In the contemporary work environment, collaboration, or the ability to work with team members, is a highly valued skill. Thanks to electronic networks, email, and so on, much business writing is easily undertaken collaboratively. Such collaboration happens when a salesperson drafts a letter to a potential client and emails it to a manager, asking her for editorial advice. It happens when an important document such as a company brochure is reviewed online for its accuracy and effectiveness. And it happens when members of a team handle different responsibilities for a document and communicate with each other via email to complete the work. (For more on collaboration, see Chapter 8.)

The following pages show student Dennis Tyler's résumé in two formats, one in conventional print style, the other formatted for scanning.

Student Writer

Dennis Tyler Jr.

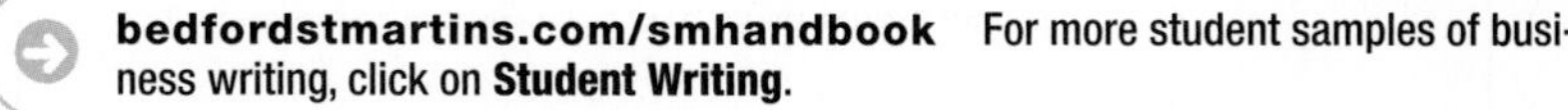

**bedfordstmartins.com/smhandbook** For more student samples of business writing, click on **Student Writing**.

## RÉSUMÉ

Name in boldface and larger type size

**DENNIS TYLER JR.**

| CURRENT ADDRESS | PERMANENT ADDRESS |
|---|---|
| P.O. Box 12345 | 506 Chanelle Court |
| Stanford, CA 94309 | Baton Rouge, LA 70128 |
| Phone: (650) 498-4731 | Phone: (504) 246-9847 |
| Email: dtyler@yahoo.com | |

Position being sought

CAREER OBJECTIVE Position on editorial staff of a major newspaper

EDUCATION

Educational background

9/00 – 6/04 **Stanford University**, Stanford, CA
BA, ENGLISH AND AMERICAN STUDIES, June 2004

9/02 – 12/02 **Morehouse College**, Atlanta, GA
STANFORD STUDY EXCHANGE PROGRAM

Work experience relevant to position being sought

EXPERIENCE

6/03 – 9/03 **Business Scholar Intern**, Finance, AOL Time Warner, New York, NY
Responsible for analyzing data for strategic marketing plans. Researched the mergers and acquisitions of companies to which Time Inc. sells advertising space.

1/02 – 6/03 **Editor-in-Chief**, *Enigma* (a literary journal), Stanford University, CA
Oversaw the entire process of *Enigma*. Edited numerous creative works: short stories, poems, essays, and interviews. Selected appropriate material for the journal. Responsible for designing cover and for publicity to the greater community.

8/02 – 12/02 **Community Development Intern**, University Center Development Corporation (UCDC), Atlanta, GA
Facilitated workshops and meetings on the importance of home buying and neighborhood preservation. Created UCDC brochure and assisted in the publication of the center's newsletter.

6/02 – 8/02 **News Editor**, *Stanford Daily*, Stanford University, CA
Responsible for editing stories and creating story ideas for the newspaper. Assisted with the layout for the newspaper and designs for the cover.

Talents and honors not listed above

SKILLS AND HONORS

- Computer Skills: MS Word, Excel, PageMaker, Microsoft Publisher; Internet research
- Language: Proficient in Spanish
- Trained in making presentations, conducting research, acting, and singing
- Mellon Fellow, Gates Millennium Scholar, Public Service Scholar, National Collegiate Scholar
- Black Community Service Arts Award, 2003 – 2004

REFERENCES Available upon request

## SCANNABLE RÉSUMÉ

Dennis Tyler Jr.

Current Address
P.O. Box 12345
Stanford, CA 94309
Phone: (650) 498-4731
Email: dtyler@yahoo.com

Permanent Address
506 Chanelle Court
Baton Rouge, LA 70128
Phone: (504) 246-9847

Keywords: journalist; journal editor; literary publishing; finance; community development; design; leadership; newspaper writer; PageMaker; Spanish; editor-in-chief

Education
BA in English and American Studies, June 2004, Stanford University, Stanford, CA
Morehouse College Study Exchange, fall 2002, Atlanta, GA

Experience
Business Scholar Intern, fall 2003
Finance, AOL Time Warner, New York, NY
Data analyst for strategic marketing plans. Researcher for the mergers and acquisitions of companies to which Time Inc. sells advertising.

Editor-in-Chief, 2002–2003, Enigma (a literary journal), Stanford University, CA
Oversaw the entire process of Enigma. Editor for numerous works: short stories, poems, essays, and interviews. Content selection for the journal. Cover design and publicity to the greater community.

Community Development Intern, fall 2002
University Center Development Corporation (UCDC), Atlanta, GA
Workshops on the importance of home buying and neighborhood preservation. Publication responsibility for UCDC brochure and the center's newsletter.

News Editor, summer 2002, Stanford Daily, Stanford University, CA
Story editor for the newspaper. Layout and cover design for the newspaper.

Skills and Honors
Computer skills: MS Word, Excel, PageMaker, Microsoft Publisher; Internet research
Language: Proficient in Spanish
Trained presenter, researcher, actor, singer
Mellon Fellow, Gates Millennium Scholar, Public Service Scholar, National Collegiate Scholar
Black Community Service Arts Award, 2003–2004

References
Available upon request

Each phone number or email address on a separate line

Standard typeface (Times Roman) and type size

Keywords to aid in computer searches

No underlining, italics, boxes, borders, or columns

White space separates sections

Verbs converted to nouns wherever possible

Keywords used in body of résumé wherever possible

### Cross-cultural communication

Precisely because people throughout the world now have the ability to work and write together, people in business must be able to communicate effectively within and across cultures. Even email conventions can vary from culture to culture or from one form of English to another. What is considered polite in one culture may be considered rude in another, so those who communicate globally must take care to avoid giving — and taking — offense where none was intended. The more knowledge you have about different cultural norms, the more effectively you can communicate with someone from a culture other than your own, whether that person is in another part of the United States or another part of the world. (For more on writing across cultures, see Chapter 26.)

### Business ethics

Business writers face a number of complex ethical questions. Imagine, for instance, that you are part of a team of writers responsible for a newsletter for company employees. How do you determine the priorities for your newsletter? To what extent should these priorities reflect the party line of top officials in the company? To what extent should they reflect the concerns of the majority of its workers? Or imagine that you work in a consumer-relations department. Clearly, the texts you write must serve the interests and goals of the business for which you work. But what about the needs of the consumer and of the general public? Or suppose you hold a low-level management position in a multinational corporation and you receive internal memos that lead you to suspect that the company is reporting false earnings: what is your responsibility, and to whom do you turn to investigate your suspicions? These and many other ethical issues can arise in business writing. What if your supervisor encourages you to manipulate data to enhance the desirability of your product or to make a problematic situation look more positive? What if an advertising team presents you with an ad that uses distorted or slanted visuals to enhance the visual appeal of a product?

Fortunately, some guidelines for ethics in business already exist. If local, state, or federal regulations apply to the work you do, you have an ethical obligation to follow them. Many professions and companies also have their own codes or standards of ethics. These guidelines can help you make decisions about day-to-day writing. Even so, you will undoubtedly encounter situations where the “right” decision is rather murky. Someone who regularly responds to complaints, for instance, may have to decide whether to reply with a form letter or an original letter — and this decision could have serious consequences for the person who initiated the complaint. On a more global level, the language that companies use in annual reports and other public documents can have significant consequences not only for investors and workers but also for the country at large, as the Enron case demonstrated.

## 65d Research sources for business

The following lists contain print resources for students in business and names of resources online. Because an online resource's URL may change, URLs are not listed here; you can find them, with up-to-date links, on the companion Web site for this book.

**bedfordstmartins.com/smhandbook** For additional resources for business writers and up-to-date URLs, go to Writing Resources/Links and click on **Academic and Professional Writing**.

#### GENERAL REFERENCE SOURCES

*Encyclopedia of Banking and Finance*. 1991.

*McGraw-Hill Dictionary of Modern Economics*. 1994.

*The New Palgrave: A Dictionary of Economics*. 1987.

*Occupational Outlook Handbook*. 1949–.

#### INDEXES AND DATABASES

*Business Index*. 1979–.

*Business Periodicals Index*. 1958–. (CD-ROM as Wilson Business Abstracts)

*Encyclopedia of Business Information Sources*. 1988.

*International Bibliography of Economics*. 1955–.

*Predicasts F&S Index: United States*. 1972–.

**WEB RESOURCES**

Federal Reserve Board

Internet Public Library: Business and Economics

Rutgers Accounting Web

SEC's EDGAR database

WebEc — World Wide Web Resources in Economics

World Trade Organization

## THINKING CRITICALLY ABOUT BUSINESS WRITING

**Reading with an Eye for Writing in Business**

Monitor your mail and email for a few days, saving everything that tries to sell a product, provide a service, or solicit information or money. Then go through these pieces of business writing and advertising, and choose the one you find most effective. What about the writing appeals to you or gets and holds your attention? What might lead you to buy the product, choose the service, or make a contribution? What might make the piece of writing even more effective? Bring the results of your investigation to class for discussion.

**Thinking about Your Own Business Writing**

Chances are, you have written a letter of application for a job, completed a résumé, or sent some business-related letters or email messages. Choose a piece of business-related writing that is important to you or that represents your best work, and then analyze it carefully. How clear is the writing? How well do you represent yourself in the writing? Do you follow the conventions for business letters, résumés, memos, and so on? Make notes on what you could do to improve this piece of writing.

# Essay Examinations and Portfolios

# 66

Essay examinations and portfolios are two tools commonly used to assess progress in an academic course. However, the skills you need to perform well on a written exam or to present a collection of your work to good advantage are skills that can serve you in your nonacademic life. Being prepared to present information effectively is always useful — for example, when you are asked to submit a personal statement to accompany an application for insurance, an internship, or a loan or when you are choosing samples of your best work in the hope of landing your dream job.

## 66a Preparing for essay examinations

### 1 Taking notes and practicing

Nothing can take the place of knowing the subject well, so you can start preparing for an essay examination by taking careful notes on lectures and readings. You may want to outline a reading assignment, list its main points, list and define its key terms, or briefly summarize its argument. A particularly effective method is to divide your notes into two categories, labeling the left-hand side *Summaries and Quotations* and the right-hand side *Questions and Comments*. Then, as you read, use the left side to record summaries of major points and note worthy quotations. On the right, record questions that your reading has not answered, puzzling ideas, and your own comments. This note-taking encourages active, critical reading and, combined with careful class notes, will do much to prepare you. Here are one student's notes:

| SUMMARIES AND QUOTATIONS | QUESTIONS AND COMMENTS |
|---|---|
| Rhetoric — "the art of discovering, in any particular case, all available means of persuasion." (Aristotle, on p. 3) | Maybe all language is persuasive, but if I greet people warmly, I don't *consciously* try to persuade them that I'm glad to see them. I just respond naturally. |
| All language is argumentative — purpose is to persuade | |

In addition to taking careful, detailed notes, you can prepare by writing out essay answers to questions you think are likely to appear on the exam. Practicing ahead of time is much more effective than last-minute cramming. On the day of the exam, do ten to fifteen minutes of writing just before you go into the examination to warm up your thinking muscles.

### EXERCISE 66.1

Create a question you think you might be likely to encounter on an essay examination in a class you are currently taking. Then write a paragraph or two about what you would need to know in order to write an A+ answer.

### 2 Analyzing essay questions

Before you begin writing, read the question carefully several times, and analyze what it asks you to do. Most essay examination questions contain two kinds of terms, strategy terms that describe your task in writing the essay and content terms that define the scope and limits of the topic.

| **STRATEGY** | **CONTENT** |
|---|---|
| Analyze | Jesus's Sermon on the Mount. |
| **STRATEGY** | **CONTENT** |
| Describe | the major effects of Reconstruction. |
| **STRATEGY** | **CONTENT** |
| Explain | the advantages of investing in government securities. |

Words like *analyze*, *describe*, and *explain* tell what logical strategy to use and often set the form your answer takes. Since not all terms mean the same thing in every discipline, be sure you understand exactly what the term means in context of the material covered on the examination. In general, however, the most commonly used strategy terms have standard meanings, as shown on p. 905. Do not hesitate to ask your instructor to clarify terms you're unsure of.

If strategy terms are not explicitly stated in an essay question, you need to infer a strategy from the content terms. For example, a question that mentions two groups working toward the same goal may imply comparison and contrast, and a question referring to events in a given time period may imply summary.

### Common strategy terms

*Analyze*: Divide an event, idea, or theory into its component elements, and examine each one in turn.

Analyze Milton Friedman's theory of permanent income.

*Compare and/or contrast*: Demonstrate similarities or dissimilarities between two or more events or topics.

Compare the portrayal of women in *Beloved* with that in *Their Eyes Were Watching God.*

*Define*: Identify and state the essential traits or characteristics of something, differentiating it clearly from other things.

Define *osmosis*.

*Describe*: Tell about an event, person, or process in detail, creating a clear and vivid image of it.

Describe the dress of a medieval knight.

*Evaluate*: Assess the value or significance of the topic.

Evaluate the contributions of jazz musicians to American music.

*Explain*: Make a topic as clear and understandable as possible by offering reasons, examples, and so on.

Explain the functioning of the circulatory system.

*Summarize*: State the major points concisely and comprehensively (14f3).

Summarize the major arguments against using animals in laboratory research.

## 3 Thinking through your answer

You may be tempted to begin writing an essay examination at once. Time is precious — but so, too, are organizing and planning. So spend some time (about 10 percent of the allotted time is a good rule of thumb) thinking through your answer.

Begin by deciding which major points you need to make and in what order to present them. Jot down support for each point. Craft a clear, succinct thesis that satisfies the strategy term of the exam question. In most writing situations, you start from a working thesis, but when writing under pressure you will probably find it more efficient to outline (or simply jot down) your ideas and craft your thesis from your outline. For example, if you were asked to define the three major components of personality according to Freud, you could write a brief informal outline as a framework for your answer.

Id
basic definition — what it is and is not
major characteristics
functions

Ego
basic definition — what it is and is not
major characteristics
functions

Superego
basic definition — what it is and is not
major characteristics
functions

From this outline, you can develop a thesis: *According to Freud, the human personality consists of three major and interlocking elements: the id, the ego, and the superego.*

**FOR MULTILINGUAL WRITERS: Writing notes in your own language**

Before writing an essay answer in English, consider making some notes in whatever language you are most comfortable writing in. Writing down key words and main points in your native language may help you organize your answer more quickly and ensure that you don't leave out something important.

## 66b Writing an essay examination response

Your goal in producing an essay examination answer is twofold: to demonstrate that you have mastered the course material and to communicate your ideas and information clearly, directly, and logically.

### 1 Drafting

During the drafting stage, follow your outline as closely as you can. If you depart from it, you will lose time and perhaps have trouble returning to the main discussion. As a general rule, develop each major point into at least one paragraph. Be sure to make clear the connections among your main points by using transitions. *The last element of the human personality, according to Freud, is the superego.*

Besides referring to your outline for guidance, pause and read what you have written before going on to a new point. Rereading may remind you of other ideas while you still have time to include them and should also help you establish a clear connection with whatever follows. If you are writing on paper, write neatly, skip lines, and leave ample margins so that you have space for changes or additions when you revise. If you are writing your essay exam on a computer, use double spacing and paragraph indentations.

### 2 Revising and editing

Leave enough time (at least five to ten minutes) to read through your essay answer carefully. Consider the following questions:

- Is the thesis clearly stated? Does it answer the question?
- Are all the major points covered?
- Are the major points adequately developed and supported?
- Is each sentence complete?
- Are spelling, punctuation, and syntax as correct as you can make them?
- Is the handwriting legible? If you are using a computer, take time to run your spell checker.

## 66c Take-home exams

You may sometimes be asked to do your essay exam at home. If so, make sure to clarify any guidelines about how much time you should spend working on the exam, how long your answer should be, and how you should submit the exam (for example, through email or to the instructor's campus mailbox).

In general, remember that you will not have as much time on a take-home essay exam as you would for a regular academic essay, so follow the same procedures you would for an in-class exam. In addition, be direct in your response, starting right in with your thesis, and use a straightforward beginning-middle-conclusion organizational sequence. Most important, as you plan for your take-home exam, bring in ways to show that you know the subject matter of the course and that you can provide concrete, detailed examples to support the main points you are making. As with any essay exam, look closely at the question itself and make sure that you are responding to the question in appropriate ways.

## 66d A student essay exam response

See how one student handled an essay and short-answer examination in a first-year American history course. She had fifty-five minutes to answer two of three essay questions and three of five short-answer questions. She chose to answer the following question first.

> Between 1870 and 1920, African Americans and women both struggled to establish certain rights. What did each group want? Briefly analyze the strategies each group used, and indicate how successful they were.

This student began her exam with this question because she knew the most about this topic. With another essay and three short answers to write, she decided to devote no more than twenty minutes to this essay.

First, she analyzed what the question asked her to do, noting the strategy terms. She decided that the first sentence of the question strongly implied comparison and contrast of the two struggles. The second sentence asked for an explanation of the goals of each group, and in the third sentence, she took *analyze* and *indicate* to mean "explain what each group did and how well it succeeded." (As it turned out, this was a very shrewd reading of the question; the instructor later remarked that those who had included a comparison and contrast produced better answers than those who did not.) Note that, in this instance, the strategy the instructor expected is not stated explicitly in the question. Instead, class members were expected to read between the lines to infer the strategy.

The student then identified content terms around which to develop her answer: the groups — African Americans and women — and their actions, goals, strategies, and degrees of success. Using these terms, she spent about three minutes producing the following informal outline:

Introduction
goals, strategies, degree of success

African Americans
want equality
two opposing strategies: DuBois and Washington
even with vote, great opposition

Women
many goals (economic, political, educational), but focus on vote
use man's rhetoric against them
use vote to achieve other goals

Conclusion
educational and economic differences between groups

From this outline, the student crafted the following thesis: *In the years between 1870 and 1920, African Americans and women were both fighting for equal rights but in significantly different ways.* She then wrote the following answer:

Thesis

The years between 1870 and 1920 saw two major groups--African Americans and women--demanding more rights, but the two groups approached the problem of inequality in different ways. Initially, women wanted the vote, equality within the family, and equal job and education opportunities. Their attempts to achieve all these goals at once were unsuccessful, as men countered by accusing them of attacking the sanctity of the family institution.

Section on women and their goals

(Demanding equality in the family meant confronting Christianity, which subordinated women to men.) With the lead of Carrie Chapman Catt, women narrowed their goal to a focus on the vote. They emphasized that they would vote to benefit middle-class Americans (like themselves), reduced the stridency of their rhetoric, and said that they would clean up an often corrupt government (they turned the men's strategy against them here by emphasizing their own purity and virtue). They also invited Wilson to talk at their conventions and won him to their side. Because of their specific focus and reorganization, women did finally receive the vote, which then gave them the power to work toward their other reform goals.

Strategy used to achieve goal

Degree of success

Less well organized and less formally educated than middle-class white women, African Americans often were unable to dedicate their full effort to the cause of equality because of severe economic problems. In addition, their leaders disagreed over strategy. Washington told them to work hard and earn the vote and equality, while DuBois maintained that they, like all other Americans, deserved it already. African Americans also had to overcome fierce racial prejudice. Even after they finally won the vote, whites passed laws (literacy tests and grandfather clauses) and used force (particularly through the Ku Klux Klan) to keep African Americans from voting. Therefore, even after African Americans got the vote in name, they had to fight to keep and use it.

Section on African Americans and their goals

Dual strategy used to achieve goals

Degree of success

Thus both women and African Americans fought for (and are still fighting for) equal rights, but women were more successful than African Americans in late nineteenth-century America. Educated, organized, and financially secure, they concentrated their efforts on getting the vote as a means to higher political objectives, and they got it. African Americans, on the other hand, had to overcome great financial barriers that reduced access to education and worked against strong organization. Even after they received the vote, these Americans were kept subjugated by prejudicial laws and practices.

Two groups contrasted

## 66e Portfolio planning

Depending on your purpose, audience, and the type of work you plan to include, you may want to create a traditional paper portfolio in a folder or binder, an electronic portfolio online, or some other kind of portfolio. Your concept of what the portfolio should accomplish will affect the form it takes.

### 1 Purpose

Some possible purposes for a writing portfolio include fulfilling course requirements, showing work to a prospective employer, entering a competition, and keeping a record of your college (or artistic) work. Each of these purposes will lead to different decisions about what to include, how to arrange the material, and whether to make work available online, in print, or in some other format.

### 2 Audience

Your audience will also affect what materials you include. If, for example, your audience is a writing instructor, you will need to demonstrate what you've learned; if it is a prospective employer, you may need to focus on what you can do. In some cases, the primary audience for a portfolio may be yourself.

### 3 Organization

Your audience and purpose should guide you in deciding how to organize the material. If you are presenting a portfolio as the final component of a course, your instructor may designate an organizational arrangement. If not, you may decide to arrange the portfolio in chronological order and comment on your progress throughout the course. Other methods of organization include arranging material by theme, by importance, or by some other category that makes sense for your work.

### 4 Selection

How many entries should you include in a portfolio? The answer depends on your purpose. If you are developing an electronic portfolio, you may include a variety of materials — essays, problem sets, photos,

Web texts, multimedia presentations, a résumé, or anything else that seems relevant — because those reviewing your portfolio will click on only those items that interest them. If you are developing a print portfolio for a writing class, however, you should probably limit yourself to five to seven examples of your writing. Here are some kinds of writing you might include in a portfolio:

- an academic essay demonstrating your ability to argue a claim
- a personal essay that shows self-insight and demonstrates your ability to paint vivid pictures with words
- a brief report for a class or community project
- a writing project showing your ability to analyze and solve a problem
- your favorite piece of writing
- writing based on field and/or library research
- a piece of writing for a group, club, or campus publication
- an example of a collaboratively written document, accompanied by a description of how the team worked and what you contributed
- an example of your best writing on an essay examination
- correspondence, such as a letter of inquiry, an email, or a job application

You should also include the assignments for your work, whenever applicable. If your portfolio is for a writing course, you may be expected to include examples of your notes and early drafts as well as any responses you got from other readers.

One student who had done spoken-word performances throughout his college years decided to assemble a portfolio of those performances. To do so, he digitized the videotapes he had of his work and compiled a DVD that he could distribute when applying for scholarships and for admission to graduate school — and that he could keep as a record of his writing and performing. Given his purpose and potential audiences, he organized the portfolio chronologically and made each piece easily accessible for future use.

EXERCISE 66.2

Make a list of the times you have organized some of your work — to apply for a job, to create a record of your writing from middle through high school, or for some other reason. What spurred you on to carry out these tasks? Did you have an audience other than yourself in mind? What criteria did you use in choosing pieces? Bring your list to class to compare with those of other students.

## 66f Completing a portfolio

To complete a portfolio, you will need to prepare a written statement, assemble your material, obtain feedback from others, and prepare the final revised copy.

### 1 Written statement

You should introduce a portfolio with a written statement that explains and reflects on your work. This statement might be in the form of a memo, cover letter, personal essay, or home page, depending on the format your portfolio takes. Think carefully about the overall impression you want the portfolio to create, and make sure that the tone and style of your statement set the stage for the entire portfolio. The statement should include the following:

- *a description of what is in the portfolio*: what was the purpose of each work (or of the portfolio as a whole)?
- *an explanation of your choices*: how did you decide that these pieces represent your best work?
- *a reflection on your strengths and abilities*: What have you learned by completing the work for the portfolio? What problems have you encountered, and how have you solved them?

### 2 Final assembly

For a print portfolio, number all pages in consecutive order, and prepare a table of contents. Label and date each piece of writing if you haven't done so previously. Put a cover sheet on top with your name and the date; if the portfolio is for a class, include the course title and number (see the sample cover in 23e). Assemble everything in a folder.

For an electronic portfolio, prepare navigation that identifies your work to its best advantage, and check the links to each piece. (For more on creating an effective online document, see Chapter 24.)

### 3 Responses

Once you have assembled your portfolio, seek responses to it from several classmates or friends and, if possible, from at least one instructor. (You may want to refer your reviewers to the guidelines on reviewing a draft in 6b.) Revise accordingly.

If this portfolio is part of your work in a course, ask your instructor whether a few handwritten corrections are acceptable. If you intend to use it as part of a job search, however, you will want to print out clean copies. Either way, the time and effort you spend revising and editing the contents of your portfolio will be time well spent.

## 66g A student's portfolio cover letter

Here is the cover letter that James Kung wrote to introduce the portfolio he submitted at the conclusion of his first-year writing course at Stanford University. His instructor had asked for print documents only. Note that in his cover letter James does not simply describe the portfolio but also analyzes each work included — and his strengths, weaknesses, and development as a writer — in some detail.

December 6, 2005

Dear Professor Ashdown:

Addresses audience directly

"Writing is difficult and takes a long time." This simple yet powerful statement has been uttered so many times in our class that it has essentially become our motto. In just ten weeks, my persuasive writing skills have improved dramatically, thanks to many hours spent writing, revising, polishing, and (when I wasn't writing) thinking about my topic. These improvements are clearly illustrated by the various drafts, revisions, and other materials included in my course portfolio.

Reflects on improvement

I entered this first-quarter Writing and Rhetoric class with both strengths and weaknesses. I was strong in the fundamentals of writing: logic and grammar. I have always written fairly well-organized essays. However, despite this strength, I struggled throughout the term to narrow and define the various aspects of my research-based argument.

Analyzes overall strengths and weaknesses

The first aspect of my essay that I had trouble narrowing and defining was my major claim, or my thesis statement. In my first writing assignment for the class, the "Proposal for Research-Based Argument" (1A), I proposed to argue about the case of Wen Ho Lee, the Los Alamos scientist accused of copying restricted government documents, but most of the major claims I made were too broad. For example, I stated, "The Wen Ho Lee incident deals with the persecution of not only one man, but of a whole ethnic group." You commented that the statement was a "sweeping claim" that would be "hard to support."

Analyzes first piece included

Explains revision process

After seeing the weaknesses in my claims, I spent weeks trying to rework them to make them more specific and debatable. I came up with so many claims that I almost lost interest in the Wen Ho Lee trial. Finally, as seen in my "Writer's Notebook 10/16/05" (5A), I analyzed my argument and decided that I had chosen the Lee case as my topic in the first place because of my belief that the political inactivity of Asian Americans contributed to the case against Wen Ho Lee. Therefore, I decided to focus on this issue in my thesis.

While my new major claim was more debatable than previous claims, it was still problematic because I had established a cause-effect claim, one of the most difficult types of claims to argue. Therefore, I once again revised my claim, stating that the political inactivity did not cause but rather contributed to racial profiling in the Wen Ho Lee case. In 6C, 6D, and the final draft, I tempered the claim to make it more feasible: "Although we can't possibly prove that the political inactivity of Asian Americans was the sole cause of the racial profiling of Wen Ho Lee, we can safely say that it contributed to the whole fiasco."

I also had trouble defining my audience. When I first wrote my "Analysis of Audience and Sources," I barely touched on issues of audience. I briefly alluded to the fact that my audience was a "typical American reader." However, I later decided to address my paper to an Asian American audience for two reasons. First, it would establish a greater ethos for myself as a Chinese American. Second, it would enable me to target the people the Wen Ho Lee case most directly affects: Asian Americans. As a result, in my final research-based argument, I was much more sensitive to the needs and concerns of my audience, and my audience trusted me more.

The actual process of writing the essay was also important. For instance, when I wrote my first informal outline for the "Structure and Appeals" assignment, I had not yet put much of the research-based argument down on paper. Although the informal outline made perfect sense on paper, as I began actually to write my research paper, I found that many of the ideas that were stressed heavily in the informal outline had little relevance to my thesis and that issues I had not included in the informal outline suddenly seemed important.

Analyzes benefits of writing process

I hope to continue to improve my writing of research-based arguments. The topic that I am currently most interested in researching is Eastern medicine--a controversial topic, and one that interests a diverse audience. I will probably apply for undergraduate research funds to work on this project, and I will be able to use all of the argumentative firepower that I have learned in this class.

Concludes with future plans

Sincerely,

James Kung

Signature

James Kung

## 66h A student's portfolio home page

Jenny Ming composed the following home page for her electronic portfolio in her senior year at Rensselaer Polytechnic Institute, as she was preparing to look for a job. She wanted to get her work out for others to see, and so she created an eye-catching graphic as background for her name along with a menu of her work on the left side of the page. Her welcoming text introduces herself clearly and simply and invites viewers to take a look at her work and to contact her with comments or questions. Note that she includes a link to her résumé (as a PDF file) at the bottom of the page.

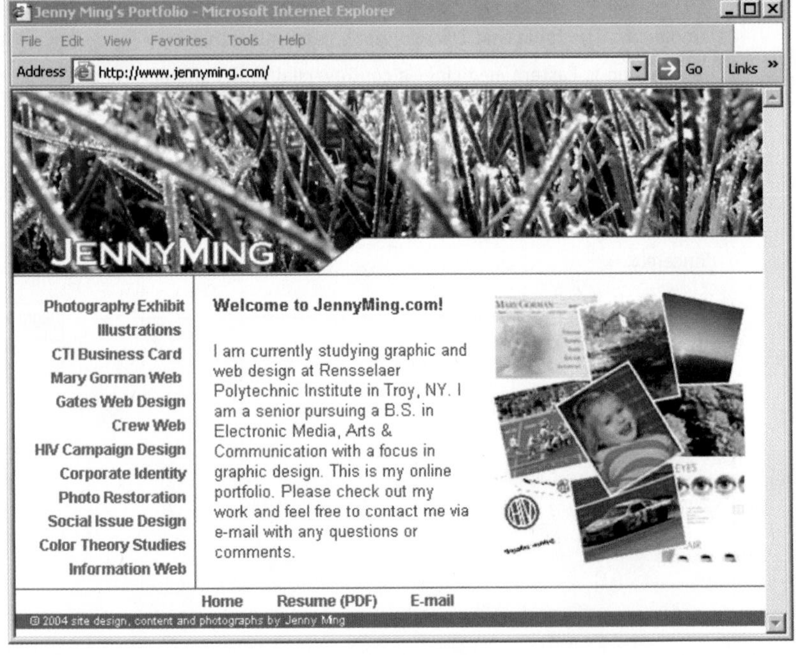

## THINKING CRITICALLY ABOUT ESSAY EXAMINATIONS AND PORTFOLIOS

Choose either an essay exam or a portfolio cover letter or home page that you have recently created.

For an essay exam, use the guidelines in 66a to analyze what the exam question asked you to do. Then reread your answer carefully. Did you do what the question asked — and if not, how should you have responded? Then, referring to 66b, reconstruct how you went about answering the question. How could you improve the content and presentation of your answer? Note any new strategies you could use for improving your success in taking essay exams.

For a portfolio cover letter or home page, ask first how your portfolio introduces your work to readers. How does the cover letter or home page represent your strengths as a communicator? How well do you present the portfolio physically? What could you change, add, or delete to make your portfolio more effective?

# Glossary of Terms

**absolute phrase** See *phrase.*

**active voice** The form of a verb when the subject performs the action: *Lata sang the chorus again.* See also *voice.*

**adjective** A word that modifies, quantifies, identifies, or describes a noun or a word or words acting as a noun. Most adjectives precede the noun or other word(s) they modify (*a good book*), but a **predicate adjective** follows the noun or pronoun it modifies (*the book is good*). A **proper adjective** is formed from a proper noun (*Egyptian*) and is capitalized.

**adjective clause** See *clause.*

**adjective forms** Changes in an adjective from the **positive** degree (*tall, good*) to the **comparative** (comparing two — *taller, better*) or the **superlative** (comparing more than two — *tallest, best*). Short regular adjectives (*tall*) add *-er* and *-est*, but most adjectives of two syllables or more form the comparative by adding *more* (*more beautiful*) and the superlative by adding *most* (*most beautiful*). A few adjectives have irregular forms (*good, better, best*), and some (*only, forty*) do not change form.

**adverb** A word that qualifies, modifies, limits, or defines a verb, an adjective, another adverb, or a clause, frequently answering the questions *where? when? how? why? to what extent?* or *under what conditions?* Adverbs derived from adjectives and nouns commonly end in the suffix *-ly. She will soon travel south and will probably visit her very favorite sister.* See also *conjunction.*

**adverb clause** See *clause.*

**adverb forms** Changes in an adverb from the **positive** degree (*eagerly*) to the **comparative** (comparing two — *more eagerly*) or the **superlative** (comparing more than two — *most eagerly*). Most adverbs add *more* to form the comparative and *most* to form the superlative, but a few add *-er* and *-est* or have irregular forms (*fast, faster, fastest; little, less, least*).

**adverbial particle** A preposition combined with a verb to create a phrasal verb.

**agreement** The correspondence of a pronoun with the word it refers to (its antecedent) in person, number, and gender or of a verb with its subject in person and number. See also *antecedent, gender, number, person.*

**antecedent** The specific noun that a pronoun replaces and to which it refers. A pronoun and its antecedent must agree in person, number, and gender. *Ginger Rogers moved her feet as no one else has.*

**antithesis** The use of parallel structures to highlight contrast or opposition.

**appositive** A noun or noun phrase that identifies or adds identifying information to a preceding noun phrase. *Zimbardo, an innovative researcher, designed the Stanford Prison Experiment. My sister Janet has twin boys.*

**appositive phrase** See *appositive.*

**argument** A text that makes and supports a **claim**. See also *evidence, warrant.*

**article** *A, an,* or *the.* Articles are the most common adjectives. *A* and *an* are **indefinite**;

they do not specifically identify the nouns they modify. *I bought an apple and a peach. The* is **definite**, or specific. *The peach was not ripe.*

**auxiliary verb** A verb that combines with the base form or with the present or past participle of a main verb to form a verb phrase. The primary auxiliaries are forms of *do, have,* and *be. Did he arrive? We have eaten. She is writing.* **Modal** auxiliaries such as *can, may, shall, will, could, might, should, would,* and *ought* [*to*] have only one form and show possibility, necessity, obligation, and so on.

**base form** The form of a verb that is listed in dictionaries, such as *go* or *listen.* For all verbs except *be,* it is the same as the first-person singular form in the present tense.

**Boolean operator** The word AND, OR, or NOT that allows for computer database searches using multiple words. Example: *Kahlo, Frida* AND *American literature.*

**case** The form of a noun or pronoun that reflects its grammatical role in a sentence. Nouns and indefinite pronouns can be **subjective**, **possessive**, or **objective**, but they change form only in the possessive case. *The dog* (subjective) *barked. The dog's* (possessive) *tail wagged. The mail carrier called the dog* (objective). The personal pronouns *I, he, she, we,* and *they,* as well as the relative or interrogative pronoun *who,* have different forms for all three cases. *We* (subjective) *took the train to Chicago. Our* (possessive) *trip lasted a week. Maria met us* (objective) *at the station.* See also *person, pronoun.*

**claim** An arguable statement.

**clause** A group of words containing a subject and a predicate. An **independent clause** can stand alone as a sentence. *The car hit the tree.* A **dependent clause**, as the name suggests, is grammatically subordinate to an independent clause, linked to it by a subordinating conjunction or a relative pronoun. A dependent clause can function as an adjective, an adverb, or a noun. *The car hit the tree that stood at the edge of the road* (**adjective clause**). *The car hit the tree when it went out of control* (**adverb clause**). *The car hit whatever grew at the side of the road* (**noun clause**). See also *nonrestrictive element, restrictive element.*

**climactic order** Arranging ideas in order of increasing importance or power.

**collective noun** A noun that refers to a group or collection (*herd, mob*).

**comma splice** An error resulting from joining two independent clauses with only a comma.

**common noun** See *noun.*

**comparative** or **comparative degree** The form of an adjective or adverb used to compare two things (*happier, more quickly*). See also *adjective forms, adverb forms.*

**complement** A word or group of words completing the predicate in a sentence. A **subject complement** follows a linking verb and renames or describes the subject. It can be a **predicate noun** (*Anorexia is an illness*) or a **predicate adjective** (*Karen Carpenter was anorexic*). An **object complement** renames or describes a direct object (*We considered her a prodigy and her behavior extraordinary*).

**complete predicate** See *predicate.*

**complete subject** See *subject.*

**complex sentence** See *sentence.*

**compound adjective** A combination of words that functions as a single adjective (*blue-green sea, ten-story building, get-tough policy, high school outing, north-by-northwest journey*). Most, but not all, compound adjectives need hyphens to separate their individual elements.

**compound-complex sentence** See *sentence.*

**compound noun** A combination of words that functions as a single noun (*go-getter, in-law, Johnny-on-the-spot, oil well, southeast*).

**compound predicate** See *predicate.*

**compound sentence** See *sentence.*

**compound subject** See *subject.*

**conciseness** Using the fewest possible words to make a point effectively.

**conditional sentence** A sentence that focuses on a question of truth or fact, introduced by *if* or its equivalent. *If we married, our parents would be happy.*

**conjunction** A word or words that join words, phrases, clauses, or sentences. **Coordinating conjunctions** (*and, but, for, nor, or, so,* or *yet*) join grammatically equivalent elements (*Marx and Engels* [two nouns]; *Marx wrote one essay, but Engels wrote the other* [two independent clauses]). **Correlative conjunctions** (such as *both . . . and, either . . . or,* or *not only . . . but also*) are used in pairs to connect grammatically equivalent elements (*neither Marx nor Engels; Marx not only studied the world but also changed it*). A **subordinating conjunction** (such as *although, because, if, that,* or *when*) introduces a dependent clause and connects it to an independent clause. *Marx moved to London, where he did most of his work. Marx argued that religion was an "opiate."* A **conjunctive adverb** (such as *consequently, moreover,* or *nevertheless*) modifies an independent clause following another independent clause. A conjunctive adverb generally follows a semicolon and is followed by a comma. *Thoreau lived simply at Walden; however, he regularly joined his aunt for tea in Concord.*

**conjunctive adverb** See *conjunction.*

**coordinate adjective** Adjectives in a sequence that relate equally to the noun they modify and are separated by commas: *the long, twisting, muddy road.*

**coordinating conjunction** See *conjunction.*

**coordination** Relating separate but equal ideas or clauses in a sentence and clarifying the emphasis given to each, usually using a coordinating conjunction or semicolon. *The report was short, but it was persuasive.*

**correlative conjunction** See *conjunction.*

**count noun** See *noun.*

**cumulative sentence** A sentence that adds details, in phrases and dependent clauses, to an independent clause. *Sarah waited, anxious and concerned that the class had been canceled.*

**dangling modifier** A word, phrase, or clause that does not logically modify any element in the sentence to which it is attached. *Studying Freud, the meaning of my dream became clear* is incorrect because *the meaning* could not have been studying Freud. *Studying Freud, I began to understand the meaning of my dream* is correct because *I* was studying.

**database** A collection of information, organized for ease of searching for and retrieving information.

**declarative sentence** See *sentence.*

**definite article** The word *the.* See also *article.*

**degree** See *adjective forms, adverb forms.*

**demonstrative pronoun** See *pronoun.*

**dependent clause** A word group containing a subject and a predicate but unable to stand alone as a sentence; usually beginning with a subordinating conjunction (*because, although*) or a relative pronoun (*that, which*). See also *clause.*

**determiner** In a noun phrase, a word used to identify or quantify the noun, including articles (*a, an, the*), possessive nouns (*Bob's*), numbers, and pronouns such as *my, our,* and *this.*

**direct address** Using a noun or pronoun to name the person or thing spoken to. *Hey, Jack. You, get moving.*

**direct discourse** A quotation reproducing a speaker's exact words, marked with quotation marks.

**direct object** A noun or pronoun receiving the action of a transitive verb. *We mixed paints.* See also *indirect object.*

**elliptical construction** or **elliptical structure** A construction in which some words are left out but understood. *Josh is more aggressive than Jake* [*is*]. *The service was good, but the food* [*was*] *average.*

**evidence** Support for an argument's claim.

**exclamatory sentence** See *sentence.*

**expletive** A construction that introduces a sentence with *there* or *it*, usually followed by a form of *be. There are four candidates in the race. It was a dark and stormy night.*

**faulty predication** A mixed structure in which a subject and predicate do not fit together grammatically or logically.

**faulty sentence structure** An error in which a sentence begins with one grammatical pattern and switches to another.

**first person** See *person.*

**font** The typeface or style and size of text characters.

**fragment** A group of words that is not a grammatically complete sentence but is punctuated as one. See also *sentence fragment.*

**fused sentence** A sentence in which two independent clauses are run together without a conjunction or punctuation between them. Also known as a **run-on sentence**.

**future tense** See *simple tense.*

**gender** The classification of a noun or pronoun as masculine (*god, he*), feminine (*goddess, she*), or neuter (*godliness, it*).

**gerund** A verbal form ending in *-ing* and functioning as a noun. *Sleeping is a bore.*

**helping verb** See *auxiliary verb.*

**imperative mood** The form of a verb used to express a command or a request. An imperative uses the base form of the verb and may or may not have a stated subject. *Leave. You be quiet. Let's go.* See also *mood.*

**imperative sentence** See *sentence.*

**indefinite article** The words *a* and *an*. See also *article.*

**indefinite pronoun** A word such as *each, everyone,* or *nobody* that does not refer to a specific person or thing. See also *pronoun.*

**independent clause** A word group containing a subject and a predicate that can stand alone as a sentence. See also *clause.*

**indicative mood** The form of a verb used to state a fact or an opinion or to ask a question. *Washington crossed the Delaware. Did he defeat the Hessians?* See also *mood.*

**indirect discourse** A paraphrased quotation that does not repeat another's exact words and hence is not enclosed in quotation marks. *Coolidge said that if nominated he would not run.*

**indirect object** A noun or pronoun identifying to whom or to what or for whom or for what a transitive verb's action is performed. The indirect object almost always precedes the direct object. *I handed the dean my application and told her that I needed financial aid.* See also *direct object.*

**indirect question** A sentence pattern in which a question is the basis of a subordinate clause. An indirect question should end with a period, not a question mark. *Everyone wonders why young people start smoking.* (The question, phrased directly, is "Why do young people start smoking?")

**indirect quotation** See *indirect discourse.*

**infinitive** The base form of a verb, preceded by *to* (*to go, to run, to hit*). An infinitive can serve as a noun, an adverb, or an adjective. *To go would be unthinkable* (noun). *We stopped to rest* (adverb). *The company needs space to grow* (adjective). An infinitive can be in either the active (*to hit*) or passive (*to be hit*) voice and in either the present (*to* [*be*] *hit*) or perfect (*to have* [*been*] *hit*) tense. An **infinitive phrase** consists of an infinitive together with its modifiers, objects, or complements. See *phrase.*

**intensifier** A modifier that increases the emphasis of the word or words it modifies. *I would very much like to go. I'm so happy.* Despite their name, intensifiers are stylistically weak; they are best avoided in academic and professional writing.

**intensive pronoun** See *pronoun.*

**interjection** A grammatically independent word or group of words that is usually an exclamation of surprise, shock, dismay, or the like. *Ouch! For heaven's sake, what do you think you're doing?*

**interrogative pronoun** See *pronoun.*

**interrogative sentence** See *sentence.*

**intransitive verb** A verb that does not need a direct object to complete its meaning. *The children laughed.*

**inversion** Changing the usual order of a sentence to create surprise or emphasis.

**irregular verb** A verb whose past tense and past participle are not formed by adding *-ed* or *-d* to the base form, such as *see, saw, seen.*

**keyword** A word or phrase used to search a computer database.

**linking verb** A verb that joins a subject with a subject complement or complements. Common linking verbs are *appear, be, become, feel,* and *seem. The argument appeared sound. It was actually a trick.* See also *verb.*

**main clause** An independent clause. See *clause.*

**main verb** The verb that carries the central meaning in a verb phrase, such as *given* in the phrase *could be given.*

**mechanical error** An error in the use of capitalization, italics, or punctuation.

**misplaced modifier** A word, phrase, or clause positioned so that it appears to modify a word other than the one the writer intended. *With a credit card, the traveler paid for the motel room and opened the door.* Unless the writer intended to indicate that the traveler used the credit card to open the door, *with a credit card* should follow *paid* or *room.*

**mixed structure** A sentence that begins with one grammatical pattern and switches to another.

**modal** See *auxiliary verb.*

**modifier** A word, phrase, or clause that acts as an adjective or an adverb and qualifies the meaning of another word, phrase, or clause. See also *adjective, adverb, clause, phrase.*

**mood** The form of a verb that indicates the writer's or speaker's attitude toward the idea expressed by the verb. Different moods are used to state a fact or an opinion or to ask a question (**indicative**); to give a command or request (**imperative**); and to express a wish, a suggestion, a request or requirement, or a condition that does not exist (**subjunctive**). *The sea is turbulent* (indicative). *Stay out of the water* (imperative). *I wish the water were calm enough for swimming* (subjunctive). See also *imperative mood, indicative mood, subjunctive mood.*

**noncount noun** See *noun.*

**nonrestrictive element** A word, phrase, or clause that modifies but does not change the essential meaning of a sentence element. A nonrestrictive element is set off from the rest of the sentence with commas, dashes, or parentheses. *Quantum physics, which is a difficult subject, is fascinating.* See also *restrictive element.*

**noun** A word that names a person, place, object, concept, action, or the like. Nouns serve as subjects, objects, complements, and appositives. Most nouns form the plural with the addition of *-s* or *-es* and the possessive with the addition of *'s* (see *number, case*). **Common nouns** (*president, state, month*) name classes or general groups. **Proper**

**nouns** (*Bill Clinton, Florida, July*) name particular persons or things and are capitalized. **Collective nouns** (*family, committee, jury*) refer to a group of related elements. **Count nouns** (*women, trees*) refer to things that can be directly counted. **Noncount nouns** (*sand, rain, violence*) refer to collections of things or to ideas that cannot be directly counted.

**noun clause** See *clause*.

**noun phrase** See *phrase*.

**number** The form of a noun or pronoun that indicates whether it is singular (*book, I, he, her, it*) or plural (*books, we, they, them, their*).

**object** A word or words, usually a noun or pronoun, influenced by a transitive verb, a verbal, or a preposition. See also *direct object, indirect object, object of a preposition*.

**object complement** See *complement*.

**objective case** See *case*.

**object of a preposition** A noun or pronoun connected to a sentence by a preposition. The preposition, the object, and any modifiers make up a **prepositional phrase**. *I went to the party without her*.

**participial phrase** A phrase consisting of a participle and any modifiers, objects, and complements and acting as an adjective. See also *participle, phrase*.

**participle** A verbal with properties of both an adjective and a verb. Like an adjective, a participle can modify a noun or pronoun; like a verb, it has present and past forms and can take an object. The **present participle** of a verb always ends in *-ing* (*going, being*). The **past participle** usually ends in *-ed* (*ruined, injured*), but many verbs have irregular forms (*gone, been, brought*). Present participles are used with the auxiliary verb *be* to form the **progressive tenses** (*I am making, I will be making, I have been making*). Past participles are used with the auxiliary verb *have* to form the **perfect tenses** (*I have made, I had made, I will have made*) and with *be* to form the passive voice (*I am seen, I was seen*). These combinations of auxiliary verbs and participles are known as **verb phrases**. See also *adjective, phrase, tense, verbal, voice*.

**particle** A preposition or adverb that combines with a verb in a two-part verb: *the plane took off*.

**parts of speech** The eight grammatical categories into which words can be grouped depending on how they function in a sentence. Many words act as different parts of speech in different sentences. The parts of speech are *adjectives, adverbs, conjunctions, interjections, nouns, prepositions, pronouns*, and *verbs*.

**passive voice** The form of a verb when the subject is being acted on rather than performing the action. *The batter was hit by a pitch*. See also *voice*.

**past participle** See *participle*.

**past perfect** or **past perfect tense** The form a verb takes to show that an action or a condition was completed before another event in the past (*The virus had killed six people before investigators learned of its existence*). See also *tense*.

**past subjunctive** See *subjunctive mood*.

**past tense** See *simple tense*.

**perfect progressive** or **perfect progressive tense** The form a verb takes to show an action or a condition that continues up to some point in the past, present, or future (*The workers had been striking for a month before they signed the contract; She has been complaining for days; The experiment will have been continuing for a year next May*). See also *tense*.

**perfect tense** The form a verb takes to show a completed action in the past, present, or future (*They had hoped to see the parade but ended up stuck in traffic; I have never understood this equation; By tomorrow, the *governor will have vetoed the bill*). See also *tense*.

**periodic sentence** A sentence that builds to a climactic ending by postponing the main idea until the very end.

**person** The relation between a subject and its verb, indicating whether the subject is speaking about itself (**first person** — *I* or *we*), being spoken to (**second person** — *you*), or being spoken about (**third person** — *he, she, it*, or *they*). *Be* has several forms depending on the person (*am, is*, and *are* in the present tense and *was* and *were* in the past tense). Other verbs change form only in the present tense with a third-person singular subject (*I fall, you fall, she falls, we fall, they fall*).

**personal pronoun** See *pronoun*.

**phrasal-prepositional verb** A verb phrase made up of a verb, particle, and preposition: *put up with, made up of*.

**phrasal verb** A verb that combines with a preposition. *The plane took off*.

**phrase** A group of words that functions as a single unit but lacks a subject, verb, or both. An **absolute phrase** modifies an entire sentence. It usually includes a noun or pronoun followed by a participle (sometimes implied) or participial phrase. *The party having ended, everyone left*. A **gerund phrase** includes a gerund and its objects, complements, and modifiers. It functions as a noun, acting as a subject, a complement, or an object. *Exercising regularly and sensibly is a key to good health* (subject). An **infinitive phrase** includes an infinitive and its objects, complements, and modifiers. It functions as an adjective, an adverb, or a noun. *The Pacific Coast is the place to be* (adjective). *She went to pay her taxes* (adverb). *To be young again is all I want* (noun). A **noun phrase** includes a noun and its modifiers. *A long, rough road crossed the barren desert*. A **participial phrase** includes a present or past participle and its objects, complements, and modifiers. It functions as an adjective. *Absentmindedly climbing the stairs, he stumbled. They bought a house built in 1895*. A **prepositional phrase** is introduced by a preposition and ends with a noun or pronoun, called the object of the preposition. It functions as an adjective, an adverb, or a noun. *The gas in the laboratory was leaking* (adjective). *The firefighters went to the lab to check* (adverb). *The smell came from inside a wall* (noun). A **verb phrase** is composed of a main verb and one or more auxiliaries, acting as a single verb in the sentence predicate. *I should have come to the review session*.

**plural** The form of a noun, pronoun, or adjective that refers to more than one person or thing, such as *books, we*, or *those*.

**positive** or **positive degree** The basic form of an adjective or adverb (*cold, quick*). See also *adjective forms, adverb forms*.

**possessive** or **possessive case** The form of a noun or pronoun that shows possession. Nouns and indefinite pronouns in the possessive case use apostrophes (*Harold's, the children's, everyone's, your parents'*), while personal pronouns in the possessive case do not (*my, mine, its, yours, hers*). See also *case*.

**possessive pronoun** A word used in place of a noun that shows possession. See also *possessive, pronoun*.

**predicate** The verb and related words in a clause or sentence. The predicate expresses what the subject does, experiences, or is. The **simple predicate** is the verb or verb phrase. *For years the YMHA has been a cultural center in New York City*. The **complete predicate** includes the simple predicate and any modifiers, objects, or complements. *John gave Sarah an engagement ring*. A **compound predicate** has more than one simple predicate. *The athletes swam in a relay and ran in a marathon*.

**predicate adjective** See *complement*.

**predicate noun** See *complement*.

**prefix** An addition to the beginning of a word that alters its meaning (*anti-French*, *suburban*).

**preposition** A word or group of words that indicates the relationship of a noun or pronoun, called the object of the preposition, to another part of the sentence. *He was at the top of the ladder before the others had climbed to the fourth rung.* See also *phrase*.

**prepositional phrase** A group of words beginning with a preposition and ending with its object. A prepositional phrase can function as an adjective, an adverb, or a noun. See also *phrase*.

**present participle** See *participle*.

**present perfect** or **present perfect tense** The form a verb takes to show that an action or a condition has been completed before the present (*The team has worked together well*). See also *tense*.

**present progressive** The form a verb takes to show an action or a condition that is ongoing in the present (*He is planning a sales presentation*). See also *tense*.

**present tense** See *simple tense*.

**primary source** A research source that offers firsthand knowledge of its subject.

**progressive tense** The form a verb takes to show an action or a condition that is continuing in the past, present, or future (*He was singing too loudly to hear the telephone; The economy is surging; Business schools will be competing for this student*). See also *tense*.

**pronoun** A word used in place of a noun, called the antecedent of the pronoun. **Demonstrative pronouns** (*this, that, these, those*) identify or point to specific nouns. *These are Peter's books.* **Indefinite pronouns** (*any, each, everybody, some,* and similar words) do not refer to specific nouns. *Many are called, but few are chosen.* **Intensive pronouns** (such as *myself* and *themselves*) emphasize their antecedents and have the same form as reflexive pronouns. *She wanted to make dinner herself.* **Interrogative pronouns** (*who, which, that*) ask questions. *Who will attend?* **Personal pronouns** (*I, you, he, she, it, we,* and *they*) refer to particular people or things. They have different forms (*I, me, my, mine*) depending on their case. **Possessive pronouns** (*my, your, her, hers,* and similar words) show ownership. **Reciprocal pronouns** (*each other, one another*) refer to individual parts of a plural antecedent. *The partners helped each other.* **Reflexive pronouns** (such as *yourselves* and *himself*) end in *-self* or *-selves* and refer to the subject of the clause in which they appear. *We taught ourselves to type.* **Relative pronouns** (*who, whose, that, whatever,* and similar words) connect a dependent clause to a sentence. *I don't care what happens.*

**proper adjective** See *adjective*.

**proper noun** See *noun*.

**reciprocal pronoun** See *pronoun*.

**reflexive pronoun** See *pronoun*.

**regular verb** A verb whose past tense and past participle are formed by adding *-d* or *-ed* to the base form (*care, cared, cared; look, looked, looked*). See also *irregular verb*.

**relative pronoun** See *pronoun*.

**restrictive element** A word, phrase, or clause that limits the essential meaning of the sentence element it modifies or provides necessary identifying information about it. A restrictive element is not set off from the rest of the sentence with commas, dashes, or parentheses. *The tree that I hit was an oak.* See also *nonrestrictive element*.

**root** A word from which other words grow, usually through the addition of prefixes or suffixes.

**run-on sentence** See *fused sentence*.

**secondary source** A research source that reports information from research done by others. See also *primary source.*

**second person** See *person.*

**sentence** A group of words containing a subject and a predicate and expressing a complete thought. In writing, a sentence begins with a capital letter and ends with a period, a question mark, or an exclamation point. A sentence may be **declarative**, making a statement (*The sun rose*); **interrogative**, asking a question (*Did the sun rise?*); **exclamatory**, indicating surprise or other strong emotion (*The earth moved!*); or **imperative**, expressing a command (*Get here at six*). Sentences are also classified grammatically. A **simple sentence** consists of a single independent clause without dependent clauses. *I left the house.* Its subject, predicate, or both may be compound. *Jorge and Tim designed and programmed the site.* A **compound sentence** contains two or more independent clauses linked with a coordinating conjunction, a correlative conjunction, or a semicolon. *I did not go, but she did.* A **complex sentence** contains an independent clause and one or more dependent clauses. *After he cleaned the kitchen, he went to bed.* A **compound-complex sentence** contains at least two independent clauses and at least one dependent clause. *We had planned to hike, but we did not go because it rained all day.* See also *clause.*

**sentence fragment** A group of words that is not a grammatically complete sentence but is punctuated as one. Usually a fragment lacks a subject, a verb, or both or is a dependent clause that is not attached to an independent clause. In academic and professional writing, fragments should be revised to be complete sentences.

**sequence of tenses** See *tense.*

**simple past tense** See *tense.*

**simple predicate** See *predicate.*

**simple subject** See *subject.*

**simple tense** Past (*It happened*), present (*Things fall apart*), or future (*You will succeed*) forms of verbs. See also *tense.*

**singular** The form of a noun, a pronoun, or an adjective that refers to one person or thing, such as *book, it,* or *this.*

**split infinitive** The often awkward intrusion of an adverb between *to* and the base form of the verb in an infinitive (*to better serve* rather than *to serve better*).

**squinting modifier** A misplaced word, phrase, or clause that could refer equally, but with different meanings, to words either preceding or following it. For example, in *Playing poker often is dangerous*, the position of *often* fails to indicate whether the writer meant that frequent poker playing is dangerous or that poker playing is often dangerous.

**subject** The noun or pronoun and related words that indicate who or what a sentence is about. The **simple subject** is the noun or pronoun. The **complete subject** is the simple subject and its modifiers. In *The timid gray mouse fled from the owl, mouse* is the simple subject; *The timid gray mouse* is the complete subject. A **compound subject** includes two or more simple subjects. *The mouse and the owl* heard the fox.

**subject complement** See *complement.*

**subjective case** See *case.*

**subjunctive mood** The form of a verb used to express a wish, a suggestion, a request or requirement, or a condition that does not exist. The present subjunctive uses the base form of the verb. *I asked that he be present. Long live the Queen!* The past subjunctive uses the same verb form as the past tense except for the verb *be*, which uses *were* for all subjects. *If I were president, I would change things.* See also *mood.*

**subordinate clause** A dependent clause. See *clause.*

**subordinating conjunction** A word or phrase such as *although, because,* or *even though* that introduces a dependent clause and joins it to an independent clause. See also *conjunction.*

**subordination** A way of distinguishing major points from minor ones. Minor points are often placed in dependent clauses.

**suffix** An addition to the end of a word that alters the word's meaning or part of speech, as in *migrate* (verb) and *migration* (noun) or *late* (adjective or adverb) and *lateness* (noun).

**superlative** The form of an adjective or adverb used in a comparison of three or more items (*happiest, most gladly*). See also *adjective forms, adverb forms.*

**syntax** The arrangement of words in a sentence in order to reveal the relation of each to the whole sentence and to one another.

**tense** The form of a verb that indicates the time at which an action takes place or a condition exists. The times expressed by tense are basically **present**, **past**, and **future**. Each tense has **simple** (*I enjoy*), **perfect** (*I have enjoyed*), **progressive** (*I am enjoying*), and **perfect progressive** (*I have been enjoying*) forms. The relationship of a verb with other verbs in the same sentence or surrounding sentences is called the **sequence of tenses**.

**third person** See *person.*

**transition** A word or phrase that signals a progression from one sentence or part of a sentence to another.

**transitive verb** A verb that takes a direct object, which receives the action expressed by the verb. A transitive verb may be in the active or passive voice. *The artist drew the sketch. The sketch was drawn by the artist.* See also *verb.*

**verb** A word or group of words, essential to a sentence, that expresses what action a subject takes or receives or what the subject's state of being is. *Edison invented the incandescent bulb. Gas lighting was becoming obsolete.* Verbs change form to show tense, number, voice, and mood. See also *auxiliary verb, intransitive verb, irregular verb, linking verb, mood, person, regular verb, tense, transitive verb, verbal, voice.*

**verbal** A verb form that functions as a noun, an adjective, or an adverb. The three kinds of verbals are gerunds, infinitives, and participles. See also *gerund, infinitive, participle.*

**verbal phrase** A phrase using a gerund, a participle, or an infinitive. See *phrase.*

**verb phrase** See *phrase.*

**verb tense** See *tense.*

**voice** The form of a verb that indicates whether the subject is acting or being acted on. When a verb is in the **active voice**, the subject performs the action. *Parker played the saxophone fantastically.* When a verb is in the **passive voice**, the subject receives the action. *The saxophone was played by Parker.* The passive voice is formed with the appropriate tense of the verb *be* and the past participle of the transitive verb. See also *verb.*

**warrant** Assumptions, sometimes unstated, that connect an argument's claims to the reasons for making the claims.

# Glossary of Usage

Conventions of usage might be called the "good manners" of discourse. And just as manners vary from culture to culture and time to time, so do conventions of usage. Matters of usage, like other language choices you must make, depend on what your purpose is and on what is appropriate for a particular audience at a particular time.

**a, an** Use *a* with a word that begins with a consonant (*a book*), a consonant sound such as "y" or "w" (*a euphoric moment, a one-sided match*), or a sounded *h* (*a hemisphere*). Use *an* with a word that begins with a vowel (*an umbrella*), a vowel sound (*an X-ray*), or a silent *h* (*an honor*).

**accept, except** The verb *accept* means "receive" or "agree to." *Except* is usually a preposition that means "aside from" or "excluding." *All the plaintiffs except Mr. Kim decided to accept the settlement.*

**advice, advise** The noun *advice* means "opinion" or "suggestion"; the verb *advise* means "offer advice." *Charlotte's mother advised her to dress warmly, but Charlotte ignored the advice.*

**affect, effect** As a verb, *affect* means "influence" or "move the emotions of"; as a noun, it means "emotions" or "feelings." *Effect* is a noun meaning "result"; less commonly, it is a verb meaning "bring about." *The storm affected a large area. Its effects included widespread power failures. The drug effected a major change in the patient's affect.*

**aggravate** The formal meaning is "make worse." *Having another mouth to feed aggravated their poverty.* In academic and professional writing, avoid using *aggravate* to mean "irritate" or "annoy."

**all ready, already** *All ready* means "fully prepared." *Already* means "previously." *We were all ready for Lucy's party when we learned that she had already left.*

**all right, alright** Avoid the spelling *alright.*

**all together, altogether** *All together* means "all in a group" or "gathered in one place." *Altogether* means "completely" or "everything considered." *When the board members were all together, their mutual distrust was altogether obvious.*

**allude, elude** *Allude* means "refer indirectly." *Elude* means "avoid" or "escape from." *The candidate did not even allude to her opponent. The suspect eluded the police for several days.*

**allusion, illusion** An *allusion* is an indirect reference. An *illusion* is a false or misleading appearance. *The speaker's allusion to the Bible created an illusion of piety.*

**a lot** Avoid the spelling *alot.*

**already** See *all ready, already.*

**alright** See *all right, alright.*

**altogether** See *all together, altogether.*

**among, between** In referring to two things or people, use *between.* In referring to three or more, use *among. The relationship between the twins is different from that among the other three children.*

**amount, number** Use *amount* with quantities you cannot count; use *number* for quantities you can count. *A small number of volunteers cleared a large amount of brush.*

**an** See *a, an.*

**and/or** Avoid this term except in business or legal writing. Instead of *fat and/or protein,* write *fat, protein, or both.*

**any body, anybody, any one, anyone** *Anybody* and *anyone* are pronouns meaning "any person." *Anyone* [or *anybody*] *would enjoy this film. Any body* is an adjective modifying a noun. *Any body of water has its own ecology. Any one* is two adjectives or a pronoun modified by an adjective. *Customers could buy only two sale items at any one time. The winner could choose any one of the prizes.*

**anyplace** In academic and professional discourse, use *anywhere* instead.

**anyway, anyways** In writing, use *anyway*, not *anyways*.

**apt, liable, likely** *Likely to* means "probably will," and *apt to* means "inclines or tends to." In many instances, they are interchangeable. *Liable* often carries a more negative sense and is also a legal term meaning "obligated" or "responsible."

**as** Avoid sentences in which it is not clear if *as* means "when" or "because." For example, does *Carl left town as his father was arriving* mean "at the same time as his father was arriving" or "because his father was arriving"?

**as, as if, like** In academic and professional writing, use *as* or *as if* instead of *like* to introduce a clause. *The dog howled as if* [not *like*] *it were in pain. She did as* [not *like*] *I suggested.*

**assure, ensure, insure** *Assure* means "convince" or "promise"; its direct object is usually a person or persons. *She assured voters she would not raise taxes. Ensure* and *insure* both mean "make certain," but *insure* usually refers specifically to protection against financial loss. *When the city rationed water to ensure that the supply would last, the Browns could no longer afford to insure their car-wash business.*

**as to** Do not use *as to* as a substitute for *about. Karen was unsure about* [not *as to*] *Bruce's intentions.*

**at, where** See *where*.

**awful, awfully** *Awful* and *awfully* mean "awe-inspiring" and "in an awe-inspiring way." In academic and professional writing, avoid using *awful* to mean "bad" (*I had an awful day*) and *awfully* to mean "very" (*It was awfully cold*).

**awhile, a while** Always use *a while* after a preposition such as *for, in*, or *after. We drove awhile and then stopped for a while.*

**bad, badly** Use *bad* after a linking verb such as *be, feel*, or *seem*. Use *badly* to modify an action verb, an adjective, or another verb. *The hostess felt bad because the dinner was badly prepared.*

**because of, due to** Use *due to* when the effect, stated as a noun, appears before the verb *be. His illness was due to malnutrition.* (*Illness*, a noun, is the effect.) Use *because of* when the effect is stated as a clause. *He was sick because of malnutrition.* (*He was sick*, a clause, is the effect.)

**being as, being that** In academic or professional writing, use *because* or *since* instead of these expressions. *Because* [not *being as*] *Romeo killed Tybalt, he was banished to Padua.*

**beside, besides** *Beside* is a preposition meaning "next to." *Besides* can be a preposition meaning "other than" or an adverb meaning "in addition." *No one besides Francesca would sit beside him.*

**between** See *among, between*.

**breath, breathe** *Breath* is a noun; *breathe*, a verb. *"Breathe," said the nurse, so June took a deep breath.*

**bring, take** Use *bring* when an object is moved from a farther to a nearer place; use *take* when the opposite is true. *Take the box to the post office; bring back my mail.*

**but, yet** Do not use these words together. *He is strong but* [not *but yet*] *gentle.*

**but that, but what** Avoid using these as substitutes for *that* in expressions of doubt.

*Hercule Poirot never doubted that* [not *but that*] *he would solve the case.*

**can, may** *Can* refers to ability and *may* to possibility or permission. *Since I can ski the slalom well, I may win the race.*

**can't hardly** *Hardly* has a negative meaning; therefore, *can't hardly* is a double negative. This expression is commonly used in some varieties of English but is not used in academic English. *Tim can* [not *can't*] *hardly wait.*

**can't help but** This expression is redundant. Use the more formal *I cannot but go* or less formal *I can't help going* rather than *I can't help but go.*

**censor, censure** *Censor* means "remove that which is considered offensive." *Censure* means "formally reprimand." *The newspaper censored stories that offended advertisers. The legislature censured the official for misconduct.*

**compare to, compare with** *Compare to* means "regard as similar." *Jamie compared the loss to a kick in the head. Compare with* means "examine to find differences or similarities." *Compare Tim Burton's films with David Lynch's.*

**complement, compliment** *Complement* means "go well with." *Compliment* means "praise." *Guests complimented her on how her earrings complemented her gown.*

**comprise, compose** *Comprise* means "contain." *Compose* means "make up." *The class comprises twenty students. Twenty students compose the class.*

**conscience, conscious** *Conscience* means "a sense of right and wrong." *Conscious* means "awake" or "aware." *Lisa was conscious of a guilty conscience.*

**consensus of opinion** Use *consensus* instead of this redundant phrase. *The family consensus was to sell the old house.*

**consequently, subsequently** *Consequently* means "as a result"; *subsequently* means "then." *He quit, and subsequently his wife lost her job; consequently, they had to sell their house.*

**continual, continuous** *Continual* means "repeated at regular or frequent intervals." *Continuous* means "continuing or connected without a break." *The damage done by continuous erosion was increased by the continual storms.*

**could of** *Have*, not *of*, should follow *could, would, should*, or *might. We could have* [not *of*] *invited them.*

**criteria, criterion** *Criterion* means "standard of judgment" or "necessary qualification." *Criteria* is the plural form. *Image is the wrong criterion for choosing a president.*

**data** *Data* is the plural form of the Latin word *datum*, meaning "fact." Although *data* is used informally as either singular or plural, in academic or professional writing, treat *data* as plural. *These data indicate that fewer people are smoking.*

**different from, different than** *Different from* is generally preferred in academic and professional writing, although both phrases are widely used. *Her lab results were no different from* [not *than*] *his.*

**discreet, discrete** *Discreet* means "tactful" or "prudent." *Discrete* means "separate" or "distinct." *The leader's discreet efforts kept all the discrete factions unified.*

**disinterested, uninterested** *Disinterested* means "unbiased." *Uninterested* means "indifferent." *Finding disinterested jurors was difficult. She was uninterested in the verdict.*

**distinct, distinctive** *Distinct* means "separate" or "well defined." *Distinctive* means "characteristic." *Germany includes many distinct regions, each with a distinctive accent.*

**doesn't, don't** *Doesn't* is the contraction for *does not*. Use it with *he, she, it,* and singular nouns. *Don't* stands for *do not*; use it with *I, you, we, they,* and plural nouns.

**due to** See *because of, due to*.

**each other, one another** Use *each other* in sentences involving two subjects and *one another* in sentences involving more than two.

**effect** See *affect, effect*.

**elicit, illicit** The verb *elicit* means "draw out." The adjective *illicit* means "illegal." *The police elicited from the criminal the names of others involved in illicit activities.*

**elude** See *allude, elude*.

**emigrate from, immigrate to** *Emigrate from* means "move away from one's country." *Immigrate to* means "move to another country." *We emigrated from Norway in 1999. We immigrated to the United States.*

**ensure** See *assure, ensure, insure*.

**enthused, enthusiastic** Use *enthusiastic* rather than *enthused* in academic and professional writing.

**equally as good** Replace this redundant phrase with *equally good* or *as good*.

**every day, everyday** *Everyday* is an adjective meaning "ordinary." *Every day* is an adjective and a noun, meaning "each day." *I wore everyday clothes almost every day.*

**every one, everyone** *Everyone* is a pronoun. *Every one* is an adjective and a pronoun, referring to each member of a group. *Because he began after everyone else, David could not finish every one of the problems.*

**except** See *accept, except*.

**explicit, implicit** *Explicit* means "directly or openly expressed." *Implicit* means "indirectly expressed or implied." *The explicit message of the ad urged consumers to buy the product, while the implicit message promised popularity if they did so.*

**farther, further** *Farther* refers to physical distance. *How much farther is it to Munich? Further* refers to time or degree. *I want to avoid further delays.*

**fewer, less** Use *fewer* with nouns that can be counted. Use *less* with general amounts that you cannot count. *The world needs fewer bombs and less hostility.*

**finalize** *Finalize* is a pretentious way of saying "end" or "make final." *We closed* [not *finalized*] *the deal.*

**firstly, secondly, etc.** *First, second,* etc., are more common in U.S. English.

**flaunt, flout** *Flaunt* means to "show off." *Flout* means to "mock" or "scorn." *The drug dealers flouted authority by flaunting their wealth.*

**former, latter** *Former* refers to the first and *latter* to the second of two things previously mentioned. *Kathy and Anna are athletes; the former plays tennis, and the latter runs.*

**further** See *farther, further*.

**good, well** *Good* is an adjective and should not be used as a substitute for the adverb *well*. *Gabriel is a good host who cooks well.*

**good and** *Good and* is colloquial for "very"; avoid it in academic and professional writing.

**hanged, hung** *Hanged* refers to executions; *hung* is used for all other meanings.

**hardly** See *can't hardly*.

**herself, himself, myself, yourself** Do not use these reflexive pronouns as subjects or as objects unless they are necessary. *Jane and I* [not *myself*] *agree. They invited John and me* [not *myself*].

**he/she, his/her** Better solutions for avoiding sexist language are to write out *he or she*, to eliminate pronouns entirely, or to make the subject plural. Instead of writing *Everyone should carry his/her driver's license*, try *Drivers should carry their licenses* or *People should carry their driver's licenses.*

**himself** See *herself, himself, myself, yourself.*

**hisself** Use *himself* instead in academic or professional writing.

**hopefully** *Hopefully* is often misused to mean "it is hoped," but its correct meaning is "with hope." *Sam watched the roulette wheel hopefully* [not *Hopefully, Sam will win*].

**hung** See *hanged, hung.*

**illicit** See *elicit, illicit.*

**illusion** See *allusion, illusion.*

**immigrate to** See *emigrate from, immigrate to.*

**impact** Avoid the colloquial use of *impact* or *impact on* as a verb meaning "affect." *Population control may reduce* [not *impact*] *world hunger.*

**implicit** See *explicit, implicit.*

**imply, infer** To *imply* is to suggest indirectly. To *infer* is to guess or conclude on the basis of an indirect suggestion. *The note implied they were planning a small wedding; we inferred we would not be invited.*

**inside of, outside of** Use *inside* and *outside* instead. *The class regularly met outside* [not *outside of*] *the building.*

**insure** See *assure, ensure, insure.*

**interact, interface** *Interact* is a vague word meaning "do something that somehow involves another person." *Interface* is computer jargon; when used as a verb, it means "discuss" or "communicate." Avoid both verbs in academic and professional writing.

**irregardless, regardless** *Irregardless* is a double negative. Use *regardless.*

**is when, is where** These vague expressions are often incorrectly used in definitions. *Schizophrenia is a psychotic condition in which* [not *is when* or *is where*] *a person withdraws from reality.*

**its, it's** *Its* is the possessive form of *it. It's* is a contraction for *it is* or *it has. It's important to observe the rat before it eats its meal.*

**kind, sort, type** These singular nouns should be modified with *this* or *that*, not *these* or *those*, and followed by other singular nouns, not plural nouns. *Wear this kind of dress* [not *those kind of dresses*].

**kind of, sort of** Avoid these colloquialisms. *Amy was somewhat* [not *kind of*] *tired.*

**later, latter** *Later* means "after some time." *Latter* refers to the second of two items named. *Juan and Chad won all their early matches, but the latter was injured later in the season.*

**latter** See *former, latter* and *later, latter.*

**lay, lie** *Lay* means "place" or "put." Its main forms are *lay, laid, laid.* It generally has a direct object, specifying what has been placed. *She laid her books on the desk. Lie* means "recline" or "be positioned" and does not take a direct object. Its main forms are *lie, lay, lain. She lay awake until two.*

**leave, let** *Leave* means "go away." *Let* means "allow." *Leave alone* and *let alone* are interchangeable. *Let me leave now, and leave* [or *let*] *me alone from now on!*

**lend, loan** In academic and professional writing, do not use *loan* as a verb; use *lend* instead. *Please lend me your pen so that I may fill out this application for a loan.*

**less** See *fewer, less.*

**let** See *leave, let.*

**liable** See *apt, liable, likely.*

**lie** See *lay, lie.*

**like** See *as, as if, like.*

**likely** See *apt, liable, likely.*

**literally** *Literally* means "actually" or "exactly as stated." Use it to stress the truth of a statement that might otherwise be understood as figurative. Do not use *literally* as an intensifier in a figurative statement. *Mirna was literally at the edge of her seat* may be accurate, but *Mirna is so hungry that she could literally eat a horse* is not.

**loan** See *lend, loan.*

**loose, lose** *Lose* is a verb meaning "misplace." *Loose* is an adjective that means "not securely attached." *Sew on that loose button before you lose it.*

**lots, lots of** Avoid these informal expressions meaning "much" or "many" in academic or professional discourse.

**man, mankind** Replace these terms with *people, humans, humankind, men and women*, or similar wording.

**may** See *can, may.*

**may be, maybe** *May be* is a verb phrase. *Maybe* is an adverb that means "perhaps." *He may be the head of the organization, but maybe someone else would handle a crisis better.*

**media** *Media* is the plural form of the noun *medium* and takes a plural verb. *The media are* [not *is*] *obsessed with scandals.*

**might of** See *could of.*

**moral, morale** A *moral* is a succinct lesson. *The moral of the story is that generosity is rewarded. Morale* means "spirit" or "mood." *Office morale was low.*

**myself** See *herself, himself, myself, yourself.*

**nor, or** Use *either* with *or* and *neither* with *nor.*

**number** See *amount, number.*

**off of** Use *off* without *of. The spaghetti slipped off* [not *off of*] *the plate.*

**OK, O.K., okay** All are acceptable spellings, but avoid the term in academic and professional discourse.

**on account of** Use this substitute for *because of* sparingly or not at all.

**one another** See *each other, one another.*

**or** See *nor, or.*

**outside of** See *inside of, outside of.*

**owing to the fact that** Avoid this and other wordy expressions for *because.*

**per** Use the Latin *per* only in standard technical phrases such as *miles per hour.* Otherwise, find English equivalents. *As mentioned in* [not *As per*] *the latest report, the country's average food consumption each day* [not *per day*] *is only 2,000 calories.*

**percent, percentage** Use *percent* with a specific number; use *percentage* with an adjective such as *large* or *small. Last year, 80 percent of the members were female. A large percentage of the members are women.*

**plenty** *Plenty* means "enough" or "a great abundance." *They told us America was a land of plenty.* Colloquially, it is used to mean "very," a usage you should avoid in academic and professional writing. *He was very* [not *plenty*] *tired.*

**plus** *Plus* means "in addition to." *Your salary plus mine will cover our expenses.* Do not use *plus* to mean "besides" or "moreover." *That dress does not fit me. Besides* [not *Plus*], *it is the wrong color.*

**precede, proceed** *Precede* means "come before"; *proceed* means "go forward." *Despite the storm that preceded the ceremony, the wedding proceeded on schedule.*

**pretty** Avoid using *pretty* as a substitute for "rather," "somewhat," or "quite." *Bill was quite* [not *pretty*] *disagreeable.*

**principal, principle** When used as a noun, *principal* refers to a head official or an amount of money; when used as an adjective, it means "most significant." *Principle* means "fundamental law or belief." *Albert went to the principal and defended himself with the principle of free speech.*

**proceed** See *precede, proceed.*

**quotation, quote** *Quote* is a verb, and *quotation* is a noun. *He quoted the president, and the quotation* [not *quote*] *was preserved in history books.*

**raise, rise** *Raise* means "lift" or "move upward." (Referring to children, it means "bring up.") It takes a direct object; someone raises something. *The guests raised their glasses to toast. Rise* means "go upward." It does not take a direct object; something rises by itself. *She saw the steam rise from the pan.*

**rarely ever** Use *rarely* by itself, or use *hardly ever. When we were poor, we rarely went to the movies.*

**real, really** *Real* is an adjective, and *really* is an adverb. Do not substitute *real* for *really*. In academic and professional writing, do not use *real* or *really* to mean "very." *The old man walked very* [not *real* or *really*] *slowly.*

**reason is because** Use either *the reason is that* or *because* — not both. *The reason the copier stopped is that* [not *is because* ] *the paper jammed.*

**reason why** This expression is redundant. *The reason* [not *reason why*] *this book is short is market demand.*

**regardless** See *irregardless, regardless.*

**respectfully, respectively** *Respectfully* means "with respect." *Respectively* means "in the order given." *Karen and David are, respectively, a juggler and an acrobat. The children treated their grandparents respectfully.*

**rise** See *raise, rise.*

**set, sit** *Set* usually means "put" or "place" and takes a direct object. *Sit* refers to taking a seat and does not take an object. *Set your cup on the table, and sit down.*

**should of** See *could of.*

**since** Be careful not to use *since* ambiguously. In *Since I broke my leg, I've stayed home,* the word *since* might be understood to mean either "because" or "ever since."

**sit** See *set, sit.*

**so** In academic and professional writing, avoid using *so* alone to mean "very." Instead, follow *so* with *that* to show how the intensified condition leads to a result. *Aaron was so tired that he fell asleep at the wheel.*

**someplace** Use *somewhere* instead in academic and professional writing.

**some time, sometime, sometimes** *Some time* refers to a length of time. *Please leave me some time to dress. Sometime* means "at some indefinite later time." *Sometime I will take you to London. Sometimes* means "occasionally." *Sometimes I eat sushi.*

**sort** See *kind, sort, type.*

**sort of** See *kind of, sort of.*

**stationary, stationery** *Stationary* means "standing still"; *stationery* means "writing paper." *When the bus was stationary, Pat took out stationery and wrote a note.*

**subsequently** See *consequently, subsequently.*

**supposed to, used to** Be careful to include the final *-d* in these expressions. *He is supposed to attend.*

**sure, surely** Avoid using *sure* as an intensifier. Instead, use *surely* (or *certainly* or *without a doubt*). *I was surely glad to see you.*

**take** See *bring, take.*

**than, then** Use *than* in comparative statements. *The cat was bigger than the dog.* Use *then* when referring to a sequence of events. *I won, and then I cried.*

**that, which** A clause beginning with *that* singles out the item being described. *The book that is on the table is a good one* specifies the book on the table as opposed to some other book. A clause beginning with *which* may or may not single out the item, although some writers use *which* clauses only to add more information about an item being described. *The book, which is on the table, is a good one* contains a *which* clause between the commas. The clause simply adds extra, nonessential information about the book; it does not specify which book.

**theirselves** Use *themselves* instead in academic and professional writing.

**then** See *than, then.*

**to, too, two** *To* generally shows direction. *Too* means "also." *Two* is the number. *We, too, are going to the meeting in two hours.* Avoid using *to* after *where. Where are you flying* [not *flying to*]?

**two** See *to, too, two.*

**type** See *kind, sort, type.*

**uninterested** See *disinterested, uninterested.*

**unique** *Unique* means "the one and only." Do not use it with adverbs that suggest degree, such as *very* or *most. Adora's paintings are unique* [not *very unique*].

**used to** See *supposed to, used to.*

**very** Avoid using *very* to intensify a weak adjective or adverb; instead, replace the adjective or adverb with a stronger, more precise, or more colorful word. Instead of *very nice,* for example, use *kind, warm, sensitive, endearing,* or *friendly.*

**way, ways** When referring to distance, use *way. Graduation was a long way* [not *ways*] *off.*

**well** See *good, well.*

**where** Use *where* alone, not with words such as *at* and *to. Where are you going* [not *going to*]?

**which** See *that, which.*

**who, whom** Use *who* if the word is the subject of the clause and *whom* if the word is the object of the clause. *Monica, who smokes incessantly, is my godmother.* (*Who* is the subject of the clause; the verb is *smokes.*) *Monica, whom I saw last winter, lives in Tucson.* (*Whom* is the object of the verb *saw.*)

**who's, whose** *Who's* is a contraction for *who is* or *who has. Who's on the patio? Whose* is a possessive form. *Whose sculpture is in the garden? Whose is on the patio?*

**would of** See *could of.*

**yet** See *but, yet.*

**your, you're** *Your* shows possession. *Bring your sleeping bag along. You're* is the contraction for *you are. You're in the wrong sleeping bag.*

**yourself** See *herself, himself, myself, yourself.*

**Bruce Catton.** "Grant and Lee: A Study in Contrasts." Excerpted from *The American Story* edited by Earl Schenck Miers. Copyright © Earl Schenck Miers. Reprinted with permission from the United States Capitol Historical Society. www.uschs.org.

**Rebecca M. Chory-Assad and Ron Tamborini.** Excerpted text, posted on EBSCOhost Research Databases, from "Television Sitcom Exposure and Aggressive Communication: A Priming Perspective." From *North American Journal of Psychology*, vol. 6, Issue 3. Copyright © 2006. Reprinted by permission.

**Aaron Copland.** Excerpt from *What to Listen for in Music* by Aaron Copland. Copyright © 1939 by Aaron Copland. Reprinted by permission.

**e.e. cummings.** One line from "as freedom is a breakfastfood." *From Complete Poems: 1904–1962* by E.E. Cummings, edited by George J. Firmage. Copyright © 1940, © 1968, 1991 by the Trustees for the E.E. Cummings Trust. Used by permission of Liveright Publishing Corporation. One line from poem on p. 35 in *100 Selected Poems by e.e. cummings*. Copyright © 1923, 1925, 1931, 1935, 1938, 1939, 1940, 1944, 1945, 1946, 1947, 1948, 1950, 1954 by e.e. cummings. Published by Grove Weidenfeld, a division of Grove, Press, Inc. Reprinted by permission of Grove/Atlantic, Inc. All rights reserved.

**Emily Dickinson.** "A little madness in the Spring." From *The Poems of Emily Dickinson*, Thomas H. Johnson, ed. The Belknap Press of Harvard University Press. Copyright © 1951, 1955, 1979, 1983 by the President and Fellows of Harvard College. Reprinted by permission of the publishers and the Trustees of Amherst College.

**Joan Didion.** Excerpt from "On Going Home." From *Slouching Towards Bethlehem* by Joan Didion. Copyright © 1965, 1866, 1968 by Joan Didion. "Georgia O'Keeffe." From *The White Album* by Joan Didion. Copyright © 1979 by Joan Didion. Reprinted for permission of Farrar, Straus and Giroux, LLC.

**EBSCO Information Services.** "Research Databases." 2 EBSCOhost screen dumps. Copyright © 2006 EBSCO Publishing. Courtesy of EBSCO.

**Robert Frost.** "The Road Not Taken." Excerpt from *The Poetry of Robert Frost* edited by Edward Connery Lathem. Copyright © 1916, 1969 by Henry Holt and Company. Copyright © 1944 by Robert Frost. Reprinted by permission of Henry Holt and Company, LLC.

**Atul Gawande.** Excerpted text from "Cold Comfort." Published in *The New Yorker*, March 11, 2002. Copyright © 2002 by Atul Gawnade. Reprinted by permission of the author.

**Chester Himes.** Excerpted text from *Hot Day, Hot Night*. Original title, "Blind Man with a Pistol." Copyright © 1969 by the Estate of Chester Himes. In print with Vintage Books. Permission granted by Roselyn Tart Literary Agency, Inc.

**John Hockenberry.** "The Blogs of War." Framed text from story in *Wired*, August 2005, p. 10. Copyright © 2005 by John Hockenberry. Reprinted by permission of John Hockenberry and the Watkins/Loomis Agency.

**Langston Hughes.** "A Dream Deferred — Harlem [2]." From *The Collected Poems of Langston Hughes* by Langston Hughes. Copyright © 1994 by The Estate of Langston Hughes. Used by permission of Alfred A. Knopf, a division of Random House, Inc. and Harold Ober Associates Incorporated.

**James Hunter.** "Outlaw Classics." Excerpted from album review entitled "Outlaw Classics" in *Rolling Stone* issue dated March 9, 2006. Copyright © Rolling Stone LLC 2006. All Rights Reserved. Reprinted by permission.

**June M. Jordan.** "Aftermath." Two lines from *Aftermath*. Copyright © June Jordan. Reprinted by permission of the June M. Jordan Literary Estate Trust. www.JuneJordan.com.

**Martin Luther King, Jr.** "Our God Is Marching On" and "Letter from Birmingham Jail." Copyright © 1963 Martin Luther King Jr., copyright renewed 1991 Coretta Scott King. Copyright © 1965 Martin Luther King Jr. Copyright renewed 1993 Coretta Scott King. Reprinted by arrangement with the Estate of Martin Luther King Jr., c/o Writers House as agent for the proprietor New York, NY.

**Professor Douglas O. Linder.** "The Scopes Trial: An Introduction." Posted on the Scopes Trial Home Page website. www.umkc.edu. Famous Trials in American History: Tennessee vs. John Scopes, The "Monkey Trial" (1925). Reprinted by permission of Professor Douglas O. Linder.

**Alan L. Miller.** Excerpt from "Epidemiology, etiology, and natural treatment of seasonal affective disorder." From *Alternative Medicine Review*, March 2005, v. 10 il. p. 5 (9). Abstract text & 2 lines from the Introduction. Copyright © 2005 by Thorne Research, Inc. Used with permission. All rights reserved.

**Gary Monroe.** "The Highwaymen, Florida's African-American Landscape Painters. Book jacket and copyright page. Copyright © 2001 by Gary Monroe. Reprinted by permission of The University Press of Florida. All rights reserved.

**Rodney Morales.** "When the Shark Bites." Excerpt from *When the Shark Bites* by Rodney

Morales. Copyright © Rodney Morales. Reprinted by permission of the University of Hawaii Press.

**Apurva Narechania.** "Hearing Is Believing." Masthead page from *The American Scholar*, Volume 74, No. 3, Summer 2005. Copyright © 2005 by the author and the Phi Beta Kappa Society. Reprinted by permission of *The American Scholar*.

**Barack Obama.** "The Audacity of Hope." Excerpt from the keynote address delivered at the 2004 Democratic National Convention. Reprinted by permission of the University of Texas @ Tyler, Dept. of Communication.

**George Orwell.** Excerpt from "Shooting an Elephant." From *Shooting an Elephant and Other Essays* by George Orwell. Copyright © 1950 by Sonia Brownell Orwell. Renewed 1978 by Sonia Pitt-Rivers. Reprinted by permission of Harcourt, Inc. Excerpt from "Homage to Catalonia." Copyright © 1952 and renewed 1980 by Sonia Brownell Orwell. Reprinted by permission of Harcourt, Inc. Copyright © George Orwell, 1945 by permission of Bill Hamilton as the Literary Executor of the Estate of the Late Sonia Brownell Orwell and Seeker & Warburg Ltd.

**Richard Rodriguez.** Postscript to "Aria: A Memoir of a Bilingual Childhood." Copyright © 1980 by Richard Rodriguez. First published in *The American Scholar*. Reprinted by permission.

**Howard Schuman, Barry Schwartz, and Hannah D'Arcy.** "Elite Revisionists and Popular Beliefs: Christopher Columbus, Hero or Villain?" From *Public Opinion Quarterly*, volume 69, #1, April 2005 issue, page 2. Copyright © 2005 by Howard Schuman, Barry Schwartz, and Hannah D'Arcy. Reprinted by permission of Oxford University Press via Copyright Clearance Center.

**Alex Shoumatoff.** "The Navajo Way." By Alex Shoumatoff. From *Rolling Stone*, November 1998. © Rolling Stone LLC 1998. All rights reserved. Reprinted by permission. Full text available at www.dispatchesfromthevanishingworld.com.

**Louise Story.** "Many Women at Elite Colleges Set Career Path to Motherhood." From *The New York Times*, September 20, 2005, 24A, B. Copyright © 2005 The New York Times Company. Reprinted with permission.

**Tatyana Tolstaya.** "Yorick, Uncovering the Bones of a Grandmother." First published in *The New Yorker*, December 19, 2005 and January 2, 2006. © 2005 and 2006 by Tatyana Tolstaya. Reprinted by permission of The Wylie Agency.

**William Tsutsui.** *Godzilla on My Mind* cover and copyright page. Copyright © William Tsutsui 2004. Reprinted with permission of Palgrave macmillan.

**James B. Twitchell.** *Living It Up — America's Love Affair with Luxury*. Cover and copyright page. Copyright © 2002 by Columbia University Press. Reprinted by permission of the publisher.

**Peg Tyre and Sarah Staveley-O'Carroll.** "How to Fix School Lunch." From *Newsweek*, August 8, 2005, pp. 50–51. Copyright © 2005 Newsweek, Inc. Reprinted by permission of Newsweek, Inc.

**Mark Unger.** "Prisons and Politics in Contemporary Latin America." From *Human Rights Quarterly* 25 (2003) 909–914. © The Johns Hopkins University Press. Reprinted with permission of The Johns Hopkins University Press.

**Maurice Wallace.** Excerpt from "Richard Wright's 'Black Medusa.'" Copyright © 2003 for the Study of Afro-American Life and History, Inc. Reprinted with permission.

**Eudora Welty.** Excerpt from "A Sweet Devouring" in *The Eye of the Story* by Eudora Welty. Copyright 1978 by Eudora Welty. Used by permission of Random House, Inc. Copyright © 1957 by Eudora Welty, renewed in 1985 by Eudora Welty. Reprinted by the permission of Russell & Volkening as agents for the author. Short passage from "Ladies in Spring" published in *Revelation and Other Fiction from the Sewanee Review: A Centennial Anthology*. Copyright © 1992 Harmony House Publishers. Edited by George Core. Reprinted with permission of the publisher. One paragraph from *One Writer's Beginnings* by Eudora Welty. Copyright © 1983, 1984 by Eudora Welty. Reprinted by permission of the publisher, Harvard University Press.

**Abe Whaley.** "Once Unique, Soon a Place Like Any Other." From *Newsweek*, November 14, 2005. Copyright © 2005 Newsweek, Inc. Reprinted by permission. All rights reserved.

**E. B. White.** "Walden" (4 lines). From *One Man's Meat* by E. B. White. Copyright © 1937, 1939, 1940, 1941, 1942, 1943, 1944 by E. B. White. Two quotations (11 lines) from "The Ring of Time" in *The Points of My Compass* by E. B. White. Copyright © 1956 by E. B. White. Originally appeared in the *New Yorker*. Reprinted by permission of HarperCollins Publishers and Allene White.

**Tom Wicker.** "Governor Connally Shot, Mrs. Kennedy Safe, President Is Shot." From *The New York Times*, November 23, 1963. Copyright © 1963. The New York Times Company. Reprinted with permission.

**Walter C. Willett, M.D., Dr. P.H.** *Eat, Drink and Be Healthy*. Cover and copyright page. Copyright © 2001, 2005 by the President and Fellows of Harvard College. Reprinted with the permission of Simon & Schuster Adult Publishing Group.

**Richard Wright.** Eight lines from *Black Boy*. Copyright © 1937, 1942, 1944, 1945 by Richard Wright. Copyright renewed 1973 by Ellen Wright. Reprinted by permission of HarperCollins Publishers and Random House (UK).

## ART

**Part-opening illustrations: Part 1, p. 13,** © PhotoDisc/Getty Images; **Part 2, p. 145,** © Comstock/Picture Quest/Jupiter Images; **Part 3, p. 211,** © ThinkStock/Index Stock Imagery; **Part 4, p. 433,** © Science Museum/SSPL/ The Image Works; **Part 5, p. 503,** © Steve Dunwell/Index Stock Imagery; **Part 6, p. 565,** © Brian Yarvin/Photo Researchers, Inc.; **Part 7, p. 645** , © Image Source Photography/Veer, Inc.; **Part 8, p. 681,** © Corbis Photography/Veer, Inc. **Part 9, p. 709,** © Chris Minerva/Index Stock Imagery; **Part 10, p. 757,** © Thinkstock/Picture Quest/Jupiter Images; **Part 11, p. 781,** © Charles Walker/Topfoto/The Image Works; **Part 12, p. 821,** © Tony Freeman/PhotoEdit.

**Other illustrations: p. 50,** courtesy www.adbusters.org; **p. 51,** (top left) Bettmann/ Corbis; (top center) John S. Pritchett; (top right) Bettmann/Corbis; **p. 52,** www.ready.gov; **p. 65,** (top) Royalty-Free/Corbis; (bottom left) Image Source/Corbis; (bottom center) Image Source/ Corbis; (bottom right) Image Source/Corbis; **p. 66,** Lippincott Williams and Wilson, 2004; **p. 69,** Bettmann/Corbis; **p. 85,** Microsoft; **p. 93,** Microsoft; **p. 116,** Royalty-Free/Corbis; **p. 117,** Corbis; **p. 119,** Royalty-Free/Corbis; **p. 120,** Bettmann/Corbis; **p. 123,** U.S. Dept. of Energy Joint Genome Institute; **p. 146,** Katje Heinemann/ Aurora Photos; **p. 150,** Carmelo's Restaurant; **p. 159,** AP-WideWorld Photos; **p. 161,** (left) © Thierry Roge/Reuters/Corbis; (right) AP-Wide World Photos; **p. 167,** Michael Ochs Archive; **p. 171,** poster design by Spur Artwork, copyright © 2003 Spur Design; **p. 172,** by permission of the Mike Luckovich and Creators Syndicate, Inc.; **p. 175,** (center) © Benetton Group S.P.A. 2004, photo: James Mollison; (bottom) courtesy www.adbusters.org; **p. 176,** Khalib Bendib; **p. 184,** Environmental Protection Agency; **p. 185,** Ogilvy & Mather; **p. 193,** (top) U.S. Census Bureau; (bottom) General Accounting Office; **p. 197,** photo by Thememoryhole.org via Getty Images; **p. 201,** Bonnie Kamin/PhotoEdit; **p. 223,** (upper left) Michigan Quarterly Review; (lower left) reprinted with permission from the publisher, The Berkeley Electronic Press, © 2006. Originally published in Business and Politics, available at http://www.bepress.com/bap/; (upper right) Scientific American, Inc.; (lower right) Salon.com; **p. 228,** University of Wyoming Libraries, Dean of Libraries; **p. 230,** (top) used with permission of The University of North Carolina at Chapel Hill Libraries; (bottom) used with permission of The University of North Carolina at Chapel Hill Libraries; **p. 231,** used with permission of The University of North Carolina at Chapel Hill Libraries; **p. 233,** Copyright 2006 LexisNexis, a division of Reed Elsevier Inc. All rights reserved. LexisNexis and the Knowledge Burst logo are registered trademarks of Reed Elsevier Properties Inc. and are used with the permission of LexisNexis; **p. 234,** copyright 2006 LexisNexis, a division of Reed Elsevier Inc. All rights reserved. LexisNexis and the Knowledge Burst logo are registered trademarks of Reed Elsevier Properties Inc. and are used with the permission of LexisNexis; **p. 236,** (top) EBSCOhost; (bottom) **p. 236,** EBSCOhost; **p. 239,** Google.com; **p. 240,** Google.com; **p. 241,** Google.com; **p. 255,** WebMD; **p. 317,** illustration by Bryon Thompson; **p. 323,** from *InfoTrac* by Thomson Gale. Reprinted by permission of The Gale Group; **p. 327,** The Nobel Foundation/(stamp) Topham/The Image Works; **p. 363,** (article) from *Newsweek* August 8, 2005, © 2005 Newsweek, Inc. All rights reserved. Reprinted by permission; (Jaime Oliver) Julian Makey/Rex USA; (vegetables) Lauren Fleishman; **p. 367,** EBSCOhost; **p. 369,** © 2005 African Economic Research Consortium; **p. 387,** (book pages) reprinted with permission of the University Press of Florida. Permission is granted for this edition and format only; (painting) reprinted with permission of Mrs. Dorethea Hair Truesdell; **p. 391,** courtesy of Wired Magazine; **p. 391,** (top) courtesy of Wired Magazine; (bottom) Douglas O. Linder, *Tennessee v John Scopes* ("The Monkey Trial"), *Famous Trials* (a site maintained at the UMKC School of Law) http://www.law.umkc.edu/ faculty/projects/ftrials/scopes/scopes.htm; **p. 399,** Chicago Aerial Survey Co.; **p. 401,** Art Institute of Chicago; **p. 404,** photograph by H. Frederick Koeper. Courtesy College of Architecture and the Arts, University of Illinois at Chicago; **p. 425,** from *InfoTrac* by Thomson Gale. Reprinted with permission of the Gale Group; **p. 445,** site designed by Jonathan Fast. PhD, MSW; **p. 448,** Brian J. Skerry/National Geographic Image Collection; Greg Marshall/National Geographic; **p. 449,** (top) Centers for Disease Control and Prevention; (bottom) Bartleby.com; **p. 450,** United States Postal Service; **p. 456,** (bottom center) Charles Maxwell/Underwater Video Services; (bottom right) U.S. Air Force photo by Tech. Sgt. Lance Cheung; **p. 458**, (cartoon) Ares/www.caglecartoons.com/espanol; (photo) Brand X Pictures/fotosearch; **p. 460**, West Coast Environmental Law, **p. 461**, screen shot courtesy of Environmental Working Group; **p. 462**, courtesy of the American Veterinary Medical Association; **p. 463**, Justin Wind; **p. 464**, www.teachingcenter@stanford.edu; **p. 467**, Stanford University; **p. 468**, Justin Kitzes; **p. 469**, Google Maps; **p. 477**, The DePaul University Writing Centers Home Page screen shot.www.depaul.edu/~writing. Copyright 2006. Reprinted with permission of the DePaul University Writing Centers; **p. 481**, Diana Dopfel; **pp. 494–97**, From *Persepolis: the Story of a Childhood* by Marjane Satrapi, translated by Mattias Ripa & Blake Ferris, copyright © 2003 by L'Association, Paris, France. Used by permission of Pantheon Books, a division of Random House, Inc.; **p. 499**, (top left) photograph H. Frederick Koeper. Courtesy College of Architecture and the Arts, University of Illinois at Chicago; (top center) Yanul/Chicago; (top right) rendering by Solomon Cordwell Buenz, Chicago, IL; **p. 512**, Getty Images; **p. 518**, Josh Anderson; **p. 520**, Alexis Rosenfeld/Photo Researchers, Inc.; **p. 523**, Karl Switak/Photo Researchers, Inc.; **p. 547**, The Bridgeman Art Library/Getty Images; **p. 625**, Peanuts: © United Feature Syndicate, Inc.; **p. 788**, Google.com; **p. 789**, Google.com; **p. 790**, Google.com; **p. 846**, The Bridgeman Art Library.

# Notes

# Notes

# Notes

# Notes

# Index

Definitions from Glossary of Terms are indicated in **boldface**.

## S

# Directory of Student Writing

## In the Book



## On the Web Site

### *Researched Writing*

MLA: Montgomery, "Do College and Religion Mix?"

MLA: Ricker, "Video Games: Buyers Beware!"

APA: Clendening, "A Content Analysis of Letters to the Editor"

MLA: Palma, "Hollywood and the Hero: Solving a Case of Mistaken Identity"

### *Writing in the Disciplines*

BIOLOGY: Rao, "3D Photography for Calculating Pre- and Post-Operative Volume in Breast Surgery" (CSE)

ECONOMICS: Adamson, "Malleability, Misrepresentation, Manipulation: The Rhetoric of Images in Economic Forecasting" (APA)

HISTORY: MacKintosh-Sims, "Reflections of an Empire: The British Celts as Indicators of Roman Seld-Perception" (*Chicago*)

HISTORY: Baird, "A Love 'Too Thick': Slave Mothers and Infanticide" (*Chicago*)

LITERATURE: Schraeder, "'He Wants to Put His Story Next to Hers': Gender in Toni Morrison's *Beloved*" (MLA)

PSYCHOLOGY: Bredin and Rodney, "Birth Order: A Factor in Determining Parental Attention and Academic Achievement" (APA)

### *Business Writing*

ESSAY: Abbott, "McKinsey and Company: Managing Knowledge and Learning"

PROPOSAL: Kea

### *Oral and Multimedia Presentations*

POWERPOINT SLIDES: Hornbeak, "Human Genome Project"

POWERPOINT SLIDES AND SCRIPT: Cabello, "Art for Your Kids"

POWERPOINT PRESENTATION: Husbands and Brown, "Project W.R.I.T.E."

POWERPOINT PRESENTATION VIDEO: Canning, "Health Is Golden"

RADIO ESSAY: Thrower, "Dr. Seuss and the Path to Advocating Human Equality"

# Advice for Multilingual Writers

## Chapters of Advice for Multilingual Writers



## Boxed Tips for Multilingual Writers



## If You Speak . . .

## Advice for "Talking the Talk" in College



## Advice for Considering Disabilities

# Revision Symbols

Some instructors use these symbols as a kind of shorthand to guide you in revision. The numbers refer to a chapter number or a section of a chapter.

| | |
|---|---|
| *abb* | abbreviation 53 |
| *ad* | adjective/adverb 35 |
| *agr* | agreement 33, 34 |
| *awk* | awkward |
| *cap* | capitalization 52 |
| *case* | case 34 |
| *cliché* | cliché 29d |
| *coord* | coordination 43a |
| *cohere* | coherence 7d |
| *com* | incomplete comparison 35d4 |
| *concl* | weak conclusion 6f3, 7d, 17c2 |
| *cs* | comma splice 38 |
| *d* | diction 29 |
| *def* | define 7c |
| *dev* | development needed 7c |
| *dm* | dangling modifier 40c |
| *doc* | documentation 18–21 |
| *emph* | emphasis unclear 42a |
| *ex* | example needed 7c |
| *frag* | sentence fragment 39 |
| *fs* | fused sentence 38 |
| *hyph* | hyphen 55 |
| *inc* | incomplete construction 41 |
| *intro* | weak introduction 6f2, 7f |
| *ital* | italics (or underlining) 54 |
| *jarg* | jargon 29a2 |
| *lc* | lowercase letter 52e |
| *log* | logic 9f, 11f |
| *lv* | language variety 28 |
| *mix* | mixed construction 41a |
| *mm* | misplaced modifier 40a |
| *ms* | manuscript form 23 |
| *no ,* | no comma 46j |
| *num* | number 53 |
| *org* | organization 5e, 11j |
| ¶ | paragraph 7 |
| *//* | faulty parallelism 7d, 37 |
| *paraph* | paraphrase 15a and c |
| *pass* | inappropriate passive 32, 45b |
| *ref* | unclear pronoun reference 34h |
| *run-on* | run-on (fused) sentence 38 |
| *sexist* | sexist language 27b, 34g |
| *shift* | shift 36 |
| *slang* | slang 29al |
| *sp* | spelling 30e and f |
| *subord* | subordination 43b |
| *sum* | summarize 15a and d |
| *t* | tone 6g4, 29a and d |
| *trans* | transition 7d4, 7e, 7f3, and 44b |
| *u* | unity 7b, 42a |
| *verb* | verb form 232a–d |
| *vs* | verb sequence 32f |
| *vt* | verb tense 32e, f, and h |
| *wrdy* | wordy 42b |
| *wv* | weak verb 45a |
| *ww* | wrong word 29a and b |
| , | comma 46 |
| ; | semicolon 47 |
| . ? ! | period, question mark, exclamation point 48 |
| ' | apostrophe 49 |
| " " | quotation marks 50 |
| ( ) [ ] — | parentheses, brackets, dash 51 |
| : / . . . | colon, slash, ellipses 51 |
| ^ | insert |
| ∾ | transpose |
| ⁀ | close up |
| x | obvious error |